The Adams Papers

L. H. BUTTERFIELD, EDITOR IN CHIEF

SERIES II

Adams Family Correspondence

Adams Family Correspondence

L. H. BUTTERFIELD and MARC FRIEDLAENDER

EDITORS

———————— ☆ ————————

Volume 4 · October 1780–September 1782
Index

THE BELKNAP PRESS
OF HARVARD UNIVERSITY PRESS
CAMBRIDGE, MASSACHUSETTS

1973

Funds for editing *The Adams Papers* were originally furnished by Time, Inc., on behalf of *Life*, to the Massachusetts Historical Society, under whose supervision the editorial work is being done. Further funds have been provided by a grant from the Ford Foundation to the National Archives Trust Fund Board in support of this and four other major documentary publications. In common with these and many other enterprises like them, *The Adams Papers* benefits from the continuing and indispensable cooperation and aid of the National Historical Publications Commission, whose chairman is the Archivist of the United States.

Library of Congress Catalog Card Number 63-14964
SBN 674-00405-1
Printed in the United States of America

Contents

Descriptive List of Illustrations

vii

addressed to her son John Quincy Adams in the Netherlands. Having received no letters from either of her sons since they had left Paris for Amsterdam the previous summer, and only meager news of them through their father's short and infrequent letters, Mrs. Adams could deal with little but generalities in writing her sons, but her letter is nevertheless extremely characteristic and a model of maternal advice for the time. She hoped the well-known proclivity of the Dutch for cleanliness, industry, and other admired personal and domestic habits would have its due effect on John Quincy's own habits, and she urged him to study Dutch history because—as her husband was pointing out in his propaganda for a rapprochement between the Dutch and American republics—there were striking parallels between the revolution of the United Provinces against Spain two hundred years earlier and that of the United States against Great Britain currently.

For reasons the reader may judge for himself, the family editor, Charles Francis Adams, omitted two passages from the manuscript text of this letter on the two occasions he printed it, in 1848 and 1876. He omitted the entire fourth paragraph, in which occurs a phrase possibly offensive to Victorian gentility; and all but the first and last sentences of the last paragraph, perhaps merely to save space.

From the original in the Adams Papers.

Two efforts to decode James Lovell's cipher, a task often resisted and that seemed to Abigail and to John Adams sometimes beyond accomplishment. The cipher was built upon an acceptance by those who would use the cipher that encoding a passage involved substituting numbers (1–27) for equivalent letters, alternately from alphabets (the ampersand was included) in which the initial letters, being agreed upon, provided a key. The letters *c* and *r* constituted the key to the cipher Lovell used in correspondence with the Adamses and others, and were thus the equivalents of the number *1* in the two alphabets. Decoding should have been a simple matter in which letters from the two alphabets were substituted alternately for numbers in the coded text. The Appendix to this volume undertakes a full account of ciphers of this type and of the difficulties Lovell's cipher presented to the Adamses.

The first effort is an undated fragmentary sheet, in the hand of Richard Cranch, on both sides of which he has attempted to record horizontally, according to the key provided by Lovell, letter equivalents to the numbers constituting four ciphered passages in Lovell's letter to Abigail Adams of 26 June 1781, below. Cranch has labeled these passages A to D, and having managed the decoding after a fashion, has then written out the transliteration satisfactorily. Although success did crown his efforts, his successive rows of substituted letters reveal one of the sources of the difficulty Lovell's correspondents experienced in reading his cipher. Here the difficulty arose from in-exact alternation between the two alphabets. As an example: what Cranch calls passage B appears in Lovell's letter as 1-25-10-22-3-11-5-4-3; Cranch's top horizontal row of letters substituted for these numbers reads r-&-&-l-t-a-v-u-t. This substitution, inaccurate as it is, is achieved by beginning from the alphabet in which *r* is the equiv-alent of *1* and continuing in alternating sequence from the alphabet in which *c* is the equivalent of *1*. Even with an exact observance of sequence, the result, r-&-&-x-t-m-v-f-t, would have been gibberish, and hence to be discarded. In Cranch's next row the substitution be-gan, properly as it turned out, from the alphabet in which *c* is the equivalent of *1*. His reading appears as c-o-l-x-e-m-g-f-e. When he broke the scheme of strict rotation at the fourth character, he was prevented, except by further tinkering, from arriving at the correct reading, c-o-l-l-e-a-g-u-e. Similar carelessness impeded his efforts to decode each of the other passages for Abigail, but it is evident from the fragment that he understood the elements of the cipher. If she shared that understanding, Abigail was perhaps justified in her later statement to her husband: "I have always been fortunate enough to succeed with it" (17 June 1782, below).

The second effort shown is again an undated sheet, this in John Adams' hand. Across the top is an alphabet and at the left is a column of numbers from *1* to *30*. From the letters *a*, *c*, and *r* of the horizontal alphabet are hung three vertical alphabets in which those letters are the initial letters. A second column of numbers is hung to parallel the *r* alphabet. The whole arrangement is one that should have proved helpful in encoding or decoding the cipher. Any success in its use, however, was prevented by a basic flaw stemming from Lovell's failure to explain or John Adams' failure to grasp that the numbers 28, 29, and 30, often appearing in ciphered passages, were baulks or blinds. This misunderstanding is displayed in assigning to numbers 28, 29, and 30, as well as to numbers *1*, *2*, and *3*, the letters *c*, *d*, and *e* in the *c* alphabet, and the letters *r*, *s*, and *t* in the *r* alphabet. At any use of one of the baulks, the transliteration would then be fouled beyond correction. Both the frustration felt by John Adams with the cipher from having been able "upon the whole" to make nothing of it, but "able sometimes to decypher Words enough to show, that I have the Letters right," and his firm conviction after all attempts that "The Cypher is certainly not taken regularly under the two first Letters of that Name [Cranch]" become understand-able (John Adams to R. R. Livingston, 21 February 1782, LbC, Adams Papers; printed in *The Works of John Adams*, ed. Charles Francis Adams, Boston, 1850–1856, 7:521–530; *The Revolution-ary Diplomatic Correspondence of the United States*, ed. Francis Wharton, Washington, 1889, 5:192–199).

From the originals in the Adams Papers.

The early 19th-century watercolor now in the Milton Historical So-ciety of the house on the brow of Milton (or Neponset) Hill over-looking Quincy Bay and Boston harbor probably represents the

house as it was during the years following 1771 when Gov. Thomas
Hutchinson had added the impressive portico to the house he had
built in 1743. Governor Hutchinson's occupancy ended with his
departure for England in 1774, his ownership upon confiscation by
Massachusetts in 1779 and subsequent sale of the house at auction.
In early 1781 it was sold again by Samuel Broom to Gen. James
Warren for £3,000. The Warrens occupied it from the time of
purchase until they returned to their earlier seat at Plymouth in
1788. (Malcolm Freiberg, *Thomas Hutchinson of Milton*, Milton
Historical Society, 1971.)

To Abigail Adams having her long-time friend, Mercy Otis Warren, and John Adams' old friend, James Warren, as near neighbors
was a bright promise in a generally gloomy and lonely time. She included news of the purchase of the farm in her first letter written to
the Netherlands after word of it reached her (to John Quincy and
Charles Adams, 8 February 1781, below; see note there). She expressed her anticipation with warmth and directness: "I hope [Mrs.
Warren] has not a doubt of the particular satisfaction and pleasure
her Friend takes in the Idea of soon having her for her Neighbour"
(to Mercy Otis Warren, 5 March 1781, below). A visit to Mrs.
Adams by the Warrens upon taking possession of their house was thus
deeply satisfying: "Our Friends from P[lymout]h have made me a
visit upon their remove to *Neponset Hill*. . . . You will congratulate
me I know upon my acquisition in the Neighbourhood, it is a very
agreable circumstance" (to John Adams, 28 May – 1 June 1781,
below). Visits between the ladies seem to have followed thereafter
with some frequency, and young Abigail, as she had earlier at Plymouth, paid more extended visits to the Warren household at Milton
(Abigail Adams 2d to Elizabeth Cranch, April 1782, below).

General Warren, for whom acquisition of the Milton seat seemed
to symbolize retirement from active participation in the political
sphere, looked forward on his side to a time, as each of the Adamses
often did, when a return to Penn's Hill could replace for John Adams
the more distant attractions that they both expressed eagerness to
forgo: "I wish to see you return to our Hills. I shall certainly take
pleasure in roving with you among the Partridges, Squirrels, &c., and
will even venture upon an Emulation with you which shall make his
Hill shine the brightest" (James Warren to John Adams, 7 October
1782, *Warren-Adams Letters*, Massachusetts Historical Society,
Collections, 72–73 [1917–1925], 2:178).

Courtesy of the Milton Historical Society, Milton, Massachusetts.

6. "VIEW TOWARD THE BAR OF BILBAO," 1781, BY JOHN TRUM-
BULL   189
The seascape near Bilbao in ink and wash by John Trumbull, and
titled by him, belongs with a number of drawings in the same medium
which Trumbull completed on shipboard in August and September
1781 during the protracted and circuitous voyage of the *South
Carolina*, Commodore Gillon, from the Texel to the North Sea and
around the British Isles before finding harbor at La Coruña in Spain.
Most of these drawings, like the present one, are deposited by the

Yale University Art Gallery with the Franklin Collection in Sterling Memorial Library. They are listed at pages 114, 116–117 in *The Works of Colonel John Trumbull*, ed. Theodore Sizer, revised edn., New Haven, 1967.

Trumbull drew the "View toward the Bar of Bilbao" after he and Maj. William Jackson, having determined to bear no more of Gillon, had, with Jackson's young charge Charles Adams, embarked on another vessel for Bilbao preparatory to sailing from that port for America on the *Cicero* of Beverly, commanded by Hugh Hill. The normally short run from La Coruña to Bilbao was extended by foul weather and misadventure to a passage of twenty-one days. The little party arrived in Bilbao not much before 26 October and remained there until about 10 December.

The circumstances which led John Adams in July 1781 to permit his son to return home in Major Jackson's custody, the successive mischances which attended the voyage both on the *South Carolina* and after, and the long-delayed arrival at Cape Ann on 21 January 1782 are recounted below in a sequence of letters and their notes beginning in July 1781 and extending through January 1782. Much of the detail provided in those notes is from the colorful narrative of the whole experience in Trumbull's *Autobiography*, ed. Theodore Sizer, New Haven, 1953, p. 74–81.

Trumbull and his companions had good reason to be interested in the bar in the river of Bilbao, aside from the pictorial possibilities it presented. Their ship, after entering the river in late October, ran up to Porto Galette at Bilbao where the process of loading was carried forward and arrangements for clearance finally completed. On 10 December, when they proceeded down river, they "found the wind at the mouth of the river, blowing fresh from the north-ward, which caused such a heavy surf upon the bar that it was impossible to take the ship over," the water there being "so shallow, that a ship of the *Cicero*'s size can pass over, only at spring tides." For the sequel, in which Trumbull and others nearly missed the *Cicero* when it at length did sail, see Trumbull's *Autobiography* as quoted below, p. 280–281.

Courtesy of the Yale University Art Gallery.

7. PIETERSKERK, THE CATHEDRAL CHURCH, LEYDEN   380

This "Gezigt van de St. Pieters Kerk," reproduced from a colored engraving in a series of Dutch views apparently dating from the late 18th century, shows the shops and houses then abutting the Gothic structure. The church, built 1294–1339 and the largest in the city, is in the oldest part of Leyden, had a number of American associations, and was geographically central to the Adamses' activities while they were in Leyden. John Robinson, pastor of the English Separatist congregation that settled in Leyden in 1608, lived in a house on the Kloksteeg (Bell Lane) facing the Pieterskerk, and he was buried within the church in 1625, five years after a substantial part of his congregation sailed to America and founded Plymouth Colony. The names of Robinson and his Pilgrim followers evoked feelings of piety among all the Adamses, although their historical and topographical information about the Pilgrims' sojourn in Leyden was, like that of many Americans who have visited there since, faulty. See below, John Quincy Adams to John Adams, 21, 22 December 1780, and notes there. Most helpful for topographical orientation is the diagram in Henry Martyn Dexter and Morton Dexter, *The England and Holland of the Pilgrims*, Boston and New York, 1905, p. 531.

The Adams boys while in Leyden, December 1780 – June 1781, lived on a narrow curving street called the Lange Brug (Long Bridge) behind the great church and must therefore have often passed through the Pieterskerkhof and by the former Pilgrim colony back of Robinson's house (where the exiles' worship was conducted) on their way to and from the University, which was just across the Rapenburg [canal] from these sites. See No. 9 below.

Courtesy of L. H. Butterfield.

8. THE FRENCH EMBASSY ON THE PRINSESSEGRACHT, THE HAGUE, 1764   380

Painted and engraved by P. C. La Fargue and dated 1764, this view shows the Nieuwen-Uitleg (New Extension) into a wooded area of a residential street on which the façade of the French Embassy on the Prinsessegracht (Princess' Canal) appears prominently. In a letter of 1 April 1782 (below), John Adams wrote his wife from Amsterdam that "The French Ambassadors House . . . has been burnt, which I regret very much, more on Account of the Interruption of his Thoughts and Exertions in these critical Moments, than for the Value of the Loss which is however considerable. The Duc de la Vauguion is an able Minister and my very good Friend."

A year earlier La Vauguyon, who served as French ambassador at The Hague from 1776 to 1784, had, as instructed from Versailles, taken a decided stand against Adams' making overtures to the States General for recognition. Adams' account of his protracted tussle with the ambassador, an influential figure in the Netherlands, occupies several pages in *The Correspondence of the Late President Adams . . . in the Boston Patriot*, Boston, 1809[–1810]. Following the American military successes later in 1781, La Vauguyon gave Adams good advice and strong backing in his successful negotiations with the Dutch in 1782.

Courtesy of the Gemeente-Archief, The Hague.

9. VIEW ACROSS THE RAPENBURG TO THE UNIVERSITY, LEYDEN, 1763.   380

From a colored engraving, probably a modern restrike, after a painting by Abraham Delfos dated 1763 and a drawing by Joannes Jacobus Bylaerd (or Bylaert), entitled "Gezigt op de Academie, te Leyden," which is to say the University of Leyden as seen from across the Rapenburg, and showing the bridge which continued the Kloksteeg, spoken of under No. 7, above. A version of this engraving appears in Frans van Miers, *Beschryving der Stad Leyden*, Leyden, 1770, of which the Widow of A. Honkoop and A. Kallewier were apparently both engravers and publishers.

The University (long commonly called the Academy), dating from 1575, is the oldest in the Netherlands and remains a major center of learning in Europe. In its early centuries it was preeminent in law and medicine and attracted many students in both these fields from England, Scotland, and England's overseas colonies. As an international center of medical education it yielded to Edinburgh only after the death of the illustrious Dr. Hermann Boerhaave in 1738. John Adams was little less than ecstatic when he learned from Benjamin Waterhouse (who had just taken his medical degree at Leyden and was attending lectures on international law) that arrangements could be made for John Quincy and Charles Adams to be privately tutored in Leyden and perhaps attend lectures by some of the distinguished professors. See Waterhouse to John Adams, 13, 21, and 26 December 1780; John Adams to Abigail Adams, 18 December 1780; all below. John Quincy matriculated on the following 10 January, and Charles, by special dispensation on account of his age, matriculated on 29 January. Many letters among the Adams circle in the Netherlands deal with the boys' studies and diversions at Leyden. Their father never tired of asking questions about their reading and their professors, and he visited them as often as he could in order to observe their progress. It was in the boys' lodgings at Leyden that he composed his epochal *Memorial to the States-General* in the spring of 1781 and whence he set out for The Hague to deliver it; see Waterhouse's account of this incident, under John Adams to Abigail Adams, 28 April 1781, below.

Courtesy of L. H. Butterfield.

10. BENJAMIN WATERHOUSE IN 1776, BY GILBERT STUART   380

Benjamin Waterhouse (1754-1846), who became one of America's best-known but perennially controversial physicians, and Gilbert Stuart, the greatest American portrait painter of his generation, were schoolmates in Newport, Rhode Island, in the 1760's. In 1776, though they had traveled different routes, they found themselves together again in London, where Stuart painted this highly attractive portrait of his friend. Whether it is the same as that which, according to Waterhouse's rambling memories furnished years later to William Dunlap, was commissioned by Dr. John Fothergill "as a delicate mode of giving the young American artist ten guineas," is not clear, because Waterhouse said he had no idea what happened to that portrait (William Dunlap, *A History of the Rise and Progress of the Arts of Design in the United States*, ed. Frank W. Bayley and Charles E. Goodspeed, Boston, 1918, 1:204). See also Lawrence Park, comp., *Gilbert Stuart: An Illustrated Descriptive List of His Works*, New York, 1926, 2:790-791.

The relations between Waterhouse and the Adams family, beginning in the Netherlands in 1780, were close and enduring. A summary account of them has been given in a note on Waterhouse's letter from Leyden to John Adams, 13 December 1780, q.v. below, with references there. Other Waterhouse letters also appear here, and hundreds more survive that were exchanged, respectively, with John Adams and John Quincy Adams for sixty years thereafter. Still

others were evidently destroyed by Waterhouse heirs. The selection in Worthington C. Ford, ed., *Statesman and Friend: Correspondence of John Adams and Benjamin Waterhouse, 1784–1822*, Boston, 1927, though valuable, is the merest sampling.
Courtesy of the Redwood Library and Athenaeum, Newport, Rhode Island.

11. JEAN LUZAC, "THE TERROR OF THE OPPRESSORS, THE COMFORT OF THE OPPRESSED," BY LUDWIG GOTTLIEB PORTMAN   380
From an engraving on copper, published in *Leidens Ramp* (*The Disaster of Leyden*) by Willem Bilderdijk and Matthijs Siegenbeek, Amsterdam, 1808.

Dutch patriot, legal, classical, and historical scholar, sometime Rector Magnificus of the University of Leyden, and publisher of *Nouvelles extraordinaires de divers endroits* (more commonly known as the *Gazette de Leyde* and one of the most influential European newspapers of its time), Jean Luzac (1746–1807) became an early, warm, and extremely helpful friend to John Adams during the latter's Dutch mission. He kept a kindly eye on the Adams boys while they studied at Leyden in 1781, printed in generous measure documents and news furnished him by Minister Adams to the advantage of the American cause, and instigated petitions among merchants and others favoring the recognition of American independence.

The ties of the Adams family with Luzac were renewed when John Quincy Adams returned to the Netherlands as American minister in the 1790's, and a substantial correspondence between them ensued. "Last week at Leyden," John Quincy wrote his father from The Hague, 3 December 1794, "I saw our old friend professor Luzac, who is at this time Rector Magnificus of the University. He received us with great cordiality, and I found him in his political sentiments moderate and rational. The instance is rare, and accordingly he suits neither of the parties in this Country. The 'Tories call him Whig, and Whigs a Tory,' because he neither wishes to be the slave of the ruling power, nor to see his Country liberated by means of being conquered" (Adams Papers). As a result of his outspokenness during the French regime Luzac had to give up all his university connections, and shortly thereafter the *Gazette de Leyde* was suppressed. In retirement he continued his scholarly and literary labors, but in January 1807 he and other members of his family were killed by the devastating explosion of a powder ship stationed in the Rapenburg near his house.

Upon resigning his rectorship in 1795 Luzac pronounced a Latin *Oration on Socrates as a Citizen*, which was published the following year and dedicated to John Adams with a warm tribute to Adams' political and intellectual services to his country. A copy of the pamphlet is in the Adams Papers, together with a manuscript English translation in an unidentified hand (Microfilms, Reel No. 226), probably as prepared for publication in the *Port Folio*, the Philadelphia journal in which a translation appeared serially in April–May 1803. "He is one of the sound hearts and choice Spirits, that I most loved and esteemed in this World," John Adams told his friend Van der Kemp, who had also known Luzac before emigrating to America.

To this, Adams added a little later: "My Wife, My Daughter and my two Sons all knew him and revered him. He is a large Portion of the Salt of the Earth, and if it were not for a few such Lotts, it seems to me, the whole Sodom [of Europe] must soon be burn'd up." (Letters of 30 April 1806, 29 January 1807, both in Historical Society of Pennsylvania.)

The quotation characterizing Luzac in the caption of the present entry is a translation of the inscription on a small but impressive memorial in the Pieterskerk (see No. 7 above) erected by friends to Luzac's memory in 1809. The University of Leyden and the Gemeente-Archief (Municipal Archives) of that city have for some time been engaged in searching out fugitive Luzac documents to add to or record in the large collection of the papers of this famous scholar and editor now in the University Library.

Courtesy of the Prenten-Kabinet, Leyden (University of Leyden Art History Center).

12. PASSPORT FORM BEARING BOYLSTON ARMS ISSUED BY JOHN
    ADAMS FOLLOWING DUTCH RECOGNITION, APRIL 1782   381

The satisfaction with which John Adams could order inscribed: "Nous John Adams, Ecuyer, Ministre Plénipotentiaire des Etats Unis de l'Amérique, auprès de leurs Hautes Puissances, les Etats Généraux des Provinces Unies des Pays-Bas," was to be measured by the difficulties that had beset him as he pursued his long and lonely campaign for recognition that had ended in triumph in April 1782.

The prerogative of a minister from the American states to a nation of Europe to issue passports of his own devising to American citizens traveling in the country to which he was accredited was exercised as early as 1780 by Benjamin Franklin in Paris. The form Franklin devised and several times issued bore a coat of arms in the lower left-hand corner (Randolph G. Adams, *The Passports Printed by Benjamin Franklin at his Passy Press*, Ann Arbor, 1925). The form which John Adams had occasion to devise at The Hague, modeled on that of Franklin, survives among the family's papers in a unique example that for a time was used as a wrapper for insurance policies. The coat of arms it bears is that of John Adams' mother's family, the Boylstons. The woodblock apparently used in the printing of the coat of arms is in the Massachusetts Historical Society and is illustrated in *A Catalogue of the Books of John Quincy Adams Deposited in the Boston Athenæum*, ed. Worthington C. Ford, Boston, 1938, facing p. 136.

The circumstances which determined John Adams' choice of the Boylston arms for passports issued by him, as well as his subsequent use of the Boylston seal in affixing his signature to the Preliminary Treaty with Great Britain are not entirely clear. Perhaps no further explanation need be sought than that he had *that* seal with him in Europe. Whether in setting out for Europe he had taken the seal which family tradition has him inheriting from his mother, or whether the Boylston "arms" he had received while in Europe from his cousin John Boylston was in the form of a seal, cannot be determined. However, the possession of the seal permitted the cutting of the woodblock.

For a description of the Boylston arms, the uses to which John

Adams put the arms for passport and treaty-signing, the later adaptations effected in the arms by John Adams and his descendants to commemorate its use in the Treaty, and what can be known of the origin of the seal he used, see below, John Boylston to John Adams, 31 August 1781, note 5; also Henry Adams 2d's note on "The Treaty Seal," in the *Catalogue of the Books of John Quincy Adams*, p. 136 ff.

From the original in the Adams Papers.

13. JOHN QUINCY ADAMS' FIRST BOOKPLATE, 1781, HAND-LETTERED AND ENGRAVED   381

The simple bookplate which John Quincy Adams, not yet fourteen, designed and executed by hand is the first of the many that members of the Adams family used to identify as theirs the multitude of volumes that were the fruits of their avid book-collecting. In Henry Adams 2d's note on "The Seals and Book-Plates of the Adams Family" it bears the designation "Book-Plate A" (*A Catalogue of the Books of John Quincy Adams Deposited in the Boston Athenæum*, Boston, 1938, p. 135–136; another specimen of the plate is illustrated there, facing p. 45). The slips themselves were printed from a wood engraving made from John Quincy's drawing. They served his needs, apparently, until 1783, when, in London with his father, he caused a second bookplate to be made, this one bearing the Boylston seal (see No. 12, above).

In the Adams Papers are two examples of Bookplate A, each affixed to a bound manuscript in the hand of John Quincy Adams and dating from the first half of 1781. The first of these is a treatise on the Greek language in 104 folios which John Quincy, in writing of it to his father (3 February 1781, below), credited to Professor Hemsterhuis of the University of Leyden but which is attributed to his disciple and successor Valckenaer in its title: *Dictata Celeberrimi Valckenarii ad Analogiam Linguæ Graecae* (Adams Papers, Microfilms, Reel 217). The dates in the manuscript indicate that the copy was begun on the 21st and concluded on the 31st of January 1781. The second is of 100 folios containing a translation into French of five books of Phædrus' *Fables*, dated at its beginning 10 February, and at its end 11 May 1781 (Adams Papers, Microfilms, Reel 218; facing the Prologue to Book 1 and Fable 1 are verse translations in English in John Quincy Adams' mature hand, dated 12 and 17 May 1831). When, a week after completing it, John Quincy offered to send it to his father to read he wrote of it as "a fair copy of Phaedrus bound," and as "My Master's Translation," by which he apparently referred to his language master, Wensing or Wenshing (19 May 1781, below, and note there).

From the original in the Adams Papers.

14. CARD OF INVITATION TO THE "CELEBRATION OF THE ANNIVERSARY OF INDEPENDENCE" IN AMSTERDAM, 4 JULY 1782   381

The invitation to supper on "Thursdag next the 4th of July" issued to John Thaxter by the American Society in Amsterdam was to its celebration of the 4th in 1782 (a Thursday). Thaxter was prevented by illness from attending that observance, and we know nothing of it beyond the information contained on the card of invitation. However, it may be, though their High Mightinesses had recognized the United States during the intervening year, that the occasion differed but little from the celebration held the year before. Of that observance, we have a detailed account. In 1781 Thaxter did attend the supper at the Nieuwe Stads Herberg hotel, as did Francis Dana before his departure on the 7th with John Quincy Adams for St. Petersburg, Maj. William Jackson, Col. James Searle, Edmund Jenings, Messrs. Sigourney, Ingraham, and Bromfield, and others of the American community in the Netherlands who appear in the pages of the present volumes. Minister Adams did not attend, having left on 2 July for Paris.

Thaxter, writing to Abigail Adams a little later (21 July, below), noted of the "Celebration of the Anniversary of Independence" that "Every thing was conducted with the utmost order and decency— in one word, We were merry and wise." With his letter he enclosed an account of the observance that had appeared in the local press (not now in the Adams Papers). It may be that that account was the same as that which was printed in the *Boston Gazette*, 24 September 1781, p. 3, cols. 1–2, as from "foreign papers" and datelined "Amsterdam, July 5":

"At the rising of the sun, the American ship Apollo hoisted Continental colours, and saluted the day with 13 Cannon, and at Two o'clock she fired 13 more, when the flags of the United States of America, and the Seven United Provinces, were displayed from the top of the house where the . . . gentlemen assembled. . . .

"At six o'clock the two flags were struck, 13 cannon fired, and the company repaired to the . . . luxurious supper . . . given by those gentlemen in a large and magnificent hall, decorated with the following emblematical devices:

"1. The genius's of the two Republics, in characters of women reciprocally tendering each other their trade and commerce.

"2. A ship crossing the western ocean from America to Holland.

"3. America and her inhabitants represented in their different branches of commerce, offering their staple commodities to the subjects of the Seven United Provinces.

"4. The Seven United Provinces accepting the products of America in exchange for their principal manufactures.

"5. The colours of the two Republics, with the motto LIBERTY.

"The evening insensibly passed in social mirth and gaiety—Joy and satisfaction appeared in every countenance. Thirteen patriotic toasts were drank, and at twelve o'clock the company peaceably retired, much satisfied with their festival meeting."

Courtesy of the Massachusetts Historical Society.

VOLUME 4

Family Correspondence

1780–1782

Adams Family Correspondence

Fleury to Abigail Adams

Madame   Newport 6th. 8[bre]. 1780

I had the honor of forwarding to you two months ago, some Letters of your husband, deliver'd to me at Paris; and two small pack's that I suppose to be silk handkerchiefs, or some goods of the same kind. I do not know if you have Receiv'd them. I beg you would inform me of it, that I could inquire after, if they are not in your hands.

There is I believe a french fregate, going soon for France; if you will send me, your and Mrs. Dana Letters, I shall take care of them. I have the honor to be with great Respect your most obedient servant,

Fleury,[1] Regt. of Saintonge

RC (Adams Papers); endorsed in Richard Cranch's hand: "Coll. Fleury's Lett[er] to Mrs. Adams."

[1] François Louis Teissèdre de Fleury, a French volunteer officer, on whom see JA to AA, 24 March, vol. 3, above, and references in note there.

Abigail Adams to John Adams

My Dearest Friend   October 8 1780

My unkle who is very attentive to acquaint me with every opportunity of conveyance, last Evening let me know of a vessel going to Spain, and tho my Letters cost you much more than they are worth; I am bound as well by inclination, as your repeated injunctions to omit no opportunity of writeing.

My last to you was by way of Bilboa. A vessel will soon sail for Amsterdam, by which I shall write largely to you, to my dear Boys, and to my agreable correspondent.

I am not without some prospect that the Letters may find you at that very port. I not long ago learnt that a commission for Holland was forwarded to you.

I was much surprized to find that you had not heard from C[on-gre]ss by the date of your last, the 17 of June. The communication from that Quarter is worse than it is from here, bad enough from both, for an anxious wife and an affectionate Mother.

I know not how to enter into a detail of our publick affairs—they are not what I wish them to be. The successes of the Enemy at Charlestown are mortifying. General Gates misfortune [1] will be anounced to you before this reaches you, and the enclosed Gazet will give you all the information of the treachery of Arnold which has yet come to hand.

How ineffectual is the tye of Honour to bind the Humane Mind, unless accompanied by more permanent and Efficacious principals? Will he who laughs at a future state of Retribution, and holds himself accountable only to his fellow Mortals disdain the venal Bribe, or spurn the Ignoble hand that proffers it.

Yet such is the unhappy lot of our native land, too, too many of our chief Actors *have been and are unprincipled wretches*, or we could not have sufferd as we have done. It is Righteousness, not Iniquity, that exalteth a Nation. There are so many and so loud complaints against some persons in office that I am apt to think neither *age* nor *Fame* will screen them. All hopes that I had entertained of a vigorous campaign, have been obstructed by a superiour British naval force, and the daily Rumours of a reinforcement from France, rise and vanish with the day. The season is now so far advanced, that little or no benifit would accrue from their arrival, yet with all the force of Graves and Rodny nothing has yet been attempted, they content themselves with the conquests of Clinton, and give out that the Northern States are not worth possessing.

Peace, Peace my beloved object is farther and farther from my Embraces I fear, yet I have never asked you a Question which from the Nature of your Embassy I knew you could not determine. It is however an object so near my Heart, that it lies down and rises with me. Yet could you bring the olive Branch, even at the expiration of an *other year*, my present sacrifices should be my future triumph, and I would then try if the Honour, as I am sometimes told, could then compensate for the substantial Blessings I resign. But my dear Friend well knows that the Honour does not consist so much in the Trust reposed, as in the able, the Honest, the upright and faithfull discharge of it. From these sources I can derive a pleasure, which neither accumulated Honours, wealth, or power, could bestow without them.

But whether does my pen lead me? I meant only to write you a

2

short Letter, if writing to you I could do so. Some months ago I wrote you an account of the death of sister A[dam]s and of her leaving a poor Babe, only 3 days old.[2] The death of Mr. H[al]l, who full of years, was last week gatherd to the great congregation, will be no matter of surprize to you.[3] Your M[othe]r is gone to your B[rothe]r, till a change in his condition may render her services unnecessary, which with a young family of 5 children, is not likely to be very soon. Whatever she call[s] upon me for shall endeavour to supply her with. She would have been more comfortable with me, but her compassion lead her to him. She desires me to remember, ever her tenderest affection to you. I always make her a sharer with me in whatever I receive from you, but some small present from your own Hand to her, would I know be particularly gratefull to her, half a dozen yards of dark chints, if you are at a loss to know what, or any thing—it is not the value but the notice which would be pleasing. Excuse my mentioning it, I know you burdend with matters of more importance, yet these attentions are the more gratefull on that very account.

Pray make my Respectfull complements to Mr. D[an]a and tell him that his Lady made me a Friendly visit last week, and we talked as much as we pleased of our dear *Absents*, compared Notes, Sympathized, Responded to each other, and mingled with our sacrifices some *little pride* that no Country could boast two worthyer Hearts than *we* had *permitted* to go abroad—and then they were such honest souls too, and so intirely satisfied with their American dames, that we had not an apprehension of their roveing. We mean not however to defy the Charmes of the Parissian Ladies, but to admire the constancy and fidelity with which they are resisted—but enough of Romance.

Be so good as to let Mr. T[haxte]r know that his Friends are all well, and will write by the Amsterdam vessel. This will be so expensive a conveyance that I send only a single Letter.

I have been very sick for a month past with a slow fever, but hope it is leaving me. For many years I have not escaped a sickness in the Fall.—I hope you enjoy Health, Dr. L[e]e says you grow very fat. My poor unfortunate trunk has not yet reachd America, that was forced to share the Fate of party and caballs, was detaind by Dr. W[indshi]p. I wish it in other Hands, do not let it go for Philadelphia if you can prevent it. Mr. L[ovel]l has sent me a set of Bills, which I enclose, but is much short of the balance reported in your favour. I take the remainder to be included with the other gentlemens accounts. After having stated the balance they say thus—"we beg leave to remark, that the examination of the coppy of an account marked A, which they received with Mr. A's other accounts and is for joint expences of himself Doctr. F[rankli]n and Mr. D[ean]e, cannot be gone into at present, the monies credited therein having been received, and the vouchers to said account remaining with them." [4]

Our dear daughter is in B[osto]n but would send her duty and Love by all opportunities tho I cannot prevail with her to write so often as I wish.

Little Tom sends his Duty, learns fast now he has got a school master. My tenderest regard to my two dear Sons. The account of their good conduct is a gratefull Balm to the Heart of their & your ever affectionate   A A

PS   Stevens Friends are all well. You will hear a strange story about the Alliance—the officers of the Ship ran away with her to Boston. Barre has got the command of her now.[5] Pray write me by way of Bilboa. Holland is a fine place for Buisness—there is much trade from here there, many vessels go and come from thence, as well as to Spain. I am quite impatient to hear from you again, 4 months since the last date.

RC (Adams Papers); docketed in John Thaxter's hand: "October 8th. 1780." Enclosed "Gazet" and "set of Bills" not found; the former was probably the *Boston Gazette* of 9 Oct. (added before the letter was sent), which reported the first news of the Arnold-André plot.

[1] Gates was defeated and put to flight by Cornwallis at Camden, S.C., on 16 August.

[2] Mary (Crosby) Adams, wife of JA's brother Peter Boylston Adams, and their daughter Elizabeth; see AA to JA, 15 April, vol. 3, above, and references in note 5 there.

[3] Lieut. John Hall, JA's stepfather, died on 27 Sept. at the age of 83 (Quincy, First Church, MS Records; see also Adams Genealogy).

[4] Extracted from the Treasury Board's report to Congress on JA's accounts, 25 Oct. 1779, printed as an enclosure in Lovell to AA, 14 May, vol. 3, above. For the real explanation of the discrepancy that perplexed AA, see note 7 on that letter.

[5] Capt. John Barry (1745–1803); see James Warren to JA, 12 Oct. (Adams Papers; *Warren-Adams Letters*, 2:141–142); *DAB*.

Edward Wigglesworth to Abigail Adams

Madam   Harvard College Octo. 13. 1780

I am directed by the Corporation to advise you, that the Hon. Mr. Adams, in his Letter favoured by the Hon. A. Lee, informed them, "that you would deliver five Volumes of M. Court de Gebelin's Monde Primitif with the L'Histoire natural de la Parole for our Library."

M. Gebelin has been pleased to enrich our public Library with that very learned Work. And as Mr. Adams had the five first Volumes of it in his own Library here, to avoid the Risque of the Sea, he has retained those Volumes of M. Gebelin's with him, and been so kind as to direct that his own Set should be placed in our Library in their Stead.

If you should have an Opportunity of sending the Books, either to the Care of Ebenezer Storer Esqr.[1] at Boston, or to mine here, it will be gratefully acknowledged by the Gentlemen of the Corporation.

I am, Madam, with Respect and Esteem, your most obedient humble servant,
Edward Wigglesworth[2]

RC (Adams Papers); at foot of text: "Hon. Mrs. Adams."

[1] Treasurer of Harvard College and, through his second marriage, to the former Hannah (Quincy) Lincoln, connected with AA's family. There is a brief identifying note on Storer at vol. 2:48, but see also Sibley-Shipton, *Harvard Graduates*, 12:208–214, and Adams Genealogy.

[2] The work in question was Antoine Court de Gébelin's huge and ongoing compilation of data and speculation on the origins of religion and language, which had a comparably lengthy title but is usually called for convenience *Monde primitif*. See notes on both the book and its author at vol. 3:106–107, above, and in JA, *Diary and Autobiography*, 2:323.

On 3 March JA had written to "The Reverend the President and Corporation of Harvard Colledge" as follows:
"I have the Honour to transmit you a Letter from Monsieur Court de Gebelin, who has sent me Six Volumes of his learned Work, intituled Monde Primitif to be sent by me, as a Present from him to Harvard Colledge. I shall discharge this Trust with great Pleasure as soon as I can find a good Opportunity: but it will be somewhat difficult to find a Friend who can take so large a Bundle to a Seaport, and from thence to America: the first however that I can find, will have the Honour to convey it" (LbC, Adams Papers).

The present letter, from Edward Wigglesworth, professor of divinity and a member of the Corporation, shows that JA later hit on a different mode of proceeding: by the hand of Arthur Lee he

sent another letter (so far not found), in which he proposed to hold back the volumes just presented him by the author for Harvard, and instructed the Corporation to apply to AA for the corresponding volumes that were already in his own library at Braintree.

The second plan did not work out, and the earlier one did. The Harvard College Library has a complete set of the *Monde primitif*, of which volumes 1–6 and 8 contain early bookplates bearing the notation "The Gift of the Author, M. Court de Gebelin of Paris   Recorded 27 Nov. 1780." (Volumes 7 and 9 were not acquired until 1900 and 1923 respectively.) And in the University Archives is Court de Gébelin's letter of presentation, dated "Paris 2e. Mars 1780" and addressed to the President and Corporation, which must have been enclosed in JA's letter of 3 March, quoted above in this note. It is a long and effusive one:
"Habitans d'un Monde nouveau, Membres d'une Societé qui prend une forme nouvelle et qui s'elevant sur des bases pleines de sagesse, annonce l'avenir le plus flatteur, Vous jetterez sans doute avec plaisir un coup d'oeil sur un Ouvrage qui retrace les tems anciens: qui montre comment se formerent et s'eleverent ces Societés primitives et respectables que l'Antiquité celebra, dont le souvenir c'est transmis jusqu'à nous, et dignes de n'etre pas oubliées par les heureux habitans du Nouveau Monde."
There is much more in this vein, including an appeal to the scholars at Har-

vard to aid the author in bringing his work "à une plus grande perfection" by their criticisms and by furnishing information concerning "les Langues de ces vastes Contrées, leurs usages, leurs traditions, leur culte, leurs mots sacrés: ces vieilles Chansons conservées parmi eux et qu'ils n'entendent qu'à peine."

The arrival of the volumes presented by the author, to whom the Corporation voted on 27 Nov. to send its thanks, precluded the need to send the same volumes from Braintree. JA's set in nine volumes (with an extra copy of vol. 7), Paris, 1775–1782, is now among his books in the Boston Public Library. In his old age, when reading widely in the field of comparative religion, he annotated most of the volumes, and although he found much to correct, he declared that Court de Gébelin's work as a whole "does honor to human Nature and has been useful to Mankind. No Man can read it without being richly rewarded for his Time and pains" (Frank E. Manuel, *The Eighteenth Century Confronts the Gods*, Cambridge, 1959, p. 274).

Abigail Adams to John Adams

My Dearest Friend   October 15 1780

I closed a long Letter to you only two days ago and sent it to Cales,[1] but as no opportunity is omitted by me, I embrace this, as Col. Flury was kind enough to write me on purpose from Newport to inform me of it, and to promise a carefull attention to it. Yet I feel doubtfull of its safety, the Enemy seem to be collecting a prodigious force into these seas, and are bent upon the destruction of our Allies. We are not a little anxious for them, and cannot but wonder that they are not yet reinforced. Graves Fleet, Arbuthnots and Rodneys, all here. With such a superiority, can it be matter of surprize, if Mr. de Ternay should fall a sacrifice? My own Mind I own is full of apprehension, yet I trust we shall not be deliverd over to the vengance of a Nation more wicked and perverse than our own. We daily experience the correcting and the defending Arm. The enclosed paper will give you the particulars of an infernal plot, and the providential discovery of it—for however the Belief of a particular Providence may be exploded by the Modern Wits, and the Infidelity of too many of the rising generation deride the Idea, yet the virtuous Mind will look up and acknowledge the great first cause, without whose notice not even a sparrow falls to the ground.

I am anxious to hear from you. Your last Letter which I have received was dated in June the 17. I have wrote you repeatedly that my Trunk was not put on Board the Alliance. That poor vessel was the sport of more than winds and waves, the conduct with regard to her is considerd as very extrodanary. She came to Boston as you have no doubt heard. Landay is suspended—the Man must be new made before he can be entitled to command. I hope Capt. Sampson arrived safe, he carried the resolve of Congress which you wanted.

As to our domestick affairs Mr. H[al]l is dead, and your M[othe]r went to your B[rothe]r he having lost his wife in the Spring, and was there taken Ill. I sent for her home, and have nursed the old Lady through a severe turn of a fever in which I feard for her life. She is however upon the recovery and desires her tenderest regards to you, tho she fears she shall not live to see your return. I am myself just recovering from a slow fever, weak and feeble yet. If you have an opportunity by way of Holland by Mr. Austin to send me some paint and oil, stone coulour, I wish you would. You tell me to send you price current. I will aim at it.[2] Corn is now 30 pound, Rye 27 per Bushel, flower from a hundred and 40 to a hundred and 30 per hundred, Beaf 8 dollors per pound, Mutton 9, Lamb 6, 7 and 8, Butter 12 dollors per pound, cheese 10, Sheeps Wool 30 dollors per pound, flax 20. West India articles Sugar from a hundred and 70 to 2 hundred pounds per hundred, Molasses 48 dollors per Gal., Tea 90, Coffe 12, cotton Wool 30 per pound. Exchange from 70 up to 75 for hard Money. Bills at 50—Money scarce, plenty of Goods, *enormous* Taxes. —Our State affairs are thus. H[ancoc]k will be Governour by a *very great* Majority—the Senate will have to choose the Leiut. Governour —our constitution is read with great admiration in New York and pronounced by the royall Governour to be the best Republican form he ever saw, but with sincere hopes that it might not be accepted. How will it be administered is now the important Question?

I request you would write to me by the way of Bilboa and Holland. I have sent you a set of Bill[s] for 4 hundred dollors. I have one more for a hundred which I have not yet enclosed. I did not know but I had best send it to Holland or Bilboa, but am not determined. Enclose a Letter for Mr. T[haxte]r. Shall write again to Amsterdam a vessel will soon sail. Let Mr. D[an]a know that I heard last Night from Mrs. D—a that she, the judge and family were all well.—The Report of the day is that 3 thousand troops are arrived at New York from England.

Adieu most affectionately *yours.*

RC (Adams Papers); endorsed by Thaxter: "Portia Octr. 15. 1780." Enclosures not found.

[1] Thus in MS, but AA unquestionably meant Cadiz since the long letter she had "closed" two days before must have been that dated 8 Oct., above, sent by "a vessel going to Spain."

[2] The following list has been repunctuated for clarity.

John Bishop to Abigail Adams

Mrs. Adams   Medford 16th. Octr. 1780

I received yours of the 14th. ultmo.,[1] should not have defer'd answering it so long had I been able to have wrote you, but have had a lame hand, and was unable to put Pen to Paper when I receiv'd it.

I sent you a b[arre]l of Flower which you acknowledge the Rec[eip]t off in your Letter. I hope it will prove good. I got Mr. Hall (Baker of this place) to exammine all the Flower we then had in Store which was very considerable, and to chuse out One bl. of it for you, which he should think to be the best; accordingly he did, and inform'd me, that he tho't it equal, if, not superior, to any he had seen since the War, and hope it will prove as good as he tho't it to be. The Current Price then for Flower was 8 Hard Dollars or, the exchange.

You mention'd in your Letter that you had some Silk Handkerchiefs which you would prefer making Payment for the Flower, rather than the Money; I have Handkerchiefs by me which at present have no demand for. With Respect to the ballance due on the Flower, you need not trouble yourself about, but when it's convenient you may send it. The trouble you was kind enough to take in getting my Stockings Wove, join'd with the other favors receiv'd lays me under infinite Obligations, and have the Honr. to be, Madam, Your mo. Humble St.,   John Bishop[2]

RC (Adams Papers).

[1] Not found.
[2] Presumably John Bishop (1722–1791), a miller of Medford, who had married Abigail Tufts, sister of Dr. Cotton Tufts and cousin of AA (Brooks, *Medford*, p. 394, 501, 545).

Abigail Adams to John Adams

My Dearest Friend   October 18 1780

The vessel by which I mean to send this is bound for Amsterdam and had very nigh given me the slip.

I have been writing to you when ever I was able by other opportunities, and should have compleated several Letters for this conveyance, but I have been very sick with a slow fever, and your Mother has been sick here of a fever, occasiond by great fatigue, the old gentleman dyeing about 3 weeks ago of a fever. Both of us are much better.

I have got out, tho she has not yet left her chamber. The rest of our Friends are well.

I wish this Letter might find you in Holland. I think it not improbable if you have received a Commission forwarded to you some months ago.

My Trunk about which you have been so anxious, and so often wished me safe, is not on board the Alliance to my no small mortification. You have found out the cause I dare say before this time. Party and cabal ran so high that the person to whose care it was intrusted, did not chuse to come in the ship—so that it may possibly lay in France till Sampson arrives. If it should I wish it may be put on Board of him and be so good as to get an invoice of Mr. Moylan and send the first opportunity. This I wish you to do. If it should come by the Dr., it will be no damage to compare them.

Holland is so much improved in the way of Trade, that ten nay twenty opportunities offer for sending from there, to one from France.

Enclosed I send a set of Bills received from Mr. L[ovel]l. They do not amount to near the Balance reported in your favour, but I suppose the rest to be connected with the other Gentlemens accounts, which they say can not be gone into at present for want of a state of theirs. I have however written to Mr. L——l to know if it is really so.[1]

As to politicks if I begin I shall not know where to end, yet I must tell you of a horrid plot, just ready to have been sprung, which would have given us a shock indeed. Arnold, you know him unprincipald as the ——. He missirable wretch had concerted a plan to give up West point where he commanded with its dependancies, into the hands of the Enemy. He had made returns of every important matter to them; with a plan (but a little before concerted, between the General officers) and State of the Army. Major Andry was the person upon whom these papers were found. An officer in the British Army, sensible, bold and enterprizing, universally beloved by them, and regreated with many tears—he was young and very accomplished, but taken in our Camp as a Spy, he was tried, comdemned and Executed. Arnold upon the first allarm that Andry was taken, conveyd himself on Board a ship of war and deserted to the Enemy. I have by two late papers sent you enclosed to you the whole of this Black transaction, so providentially discoverd which must excite gratitude in every Breast not wholy devoid of principal.[2]—It is now a long time since I heard from you, the 17 of June was the last date.

I have just sent Letters for Mr. T[haxte]r to Newport to go in a French Frigate. I shall write to him by a vessel soon to sail for France and to my dear Boys. Remember me tenderly to them. Ah! when shall I see them again, or their dear parent?—I must bid you good Night, tis late and I am yet feable and weak. Believe me with sentiments of tenderness & affection *ever yours.*

RC (Adams Papers); endorsed: "Portia," to which CFA added later: "October 18th 1780." Enclosures not found.

¹ See Lovell to AA, 14 May, vol. 3, above, with enclosure, and references in note 3 there.

² The classic modern account of Benedict Arnold's treason and Major John André's capture, trial, and execution as a spy is in Carl Van Doren's *Secret His-* *tory of the American Revolution,* N.Y., 1941, p. 143–388, to which are appended full texts of the Arnold-André correspondence and Sir Henry Clinton's narrative of the plot and its outcome, p. 437–495.

John Adams to the Rector and Preceptor of the Latin School at Amsterdam

18th October 1780

Mr. Adams presents his Compliments to the Rector and the Preceptor, and acquaints them that his eldest Son is thirteen Years of Age: that he has made considerable progress already in Greek and Latin: that he has been long in Virgil and Cicero, and that he has read a great deal for his Age, both in French and English; and therefore Mr. Adams thinks it would discourage him to be placed and kept in the lower Forms or Classes of the School; and that it would be a damage to interrupt him in Greek, which he might go on to learn without understanding Dutch. Mr. Adams therefore requests that he may be put into the higher Forms, and put upon the Study of Greek.¹

LbC (Adams Papers); in John Thaxter's hand; at foot of text: "not sent."

¹ On the placement of JQA and CA as boarding students in the Latin School on the Singel in Amsterdam at the end of August, with JQA's diary entries about their life there, see JA to AA, 25 Sept., vol. 3 above. The present letter, which on second thought JA did not send, indicates that the school authorities had held JQA back from his proper scholastic level because of his deficiency in the Dutch language—a decision that JA thought unwise and that soon proved so in its effect on JQA. For the upshot see the exchange of notes between Rector Verheyk and JA under 10 Nov., below.

Mercy Otis Warren to Abigail Adams

My Dear Friend   Plimouth 20th October 1780

A Promiss made to my son to spend a week with our Friends at Braintree is readily Caught at nor Can I Receed had I inclination. I hope his Behaviour is such as no one will think it too Long Except his mamah who is very Choice of the Precious Moments of Youth. But you will put into his hand such Books as will both instruct and Entertain.[1]

I am sorry Naby is not at home. Why will my Friend be so Ceremonious. Why not sometimes a Letter Gratis. You have a Great deal of Leasure when Compared with me, who Constantly am preparing a Large Family to Go from home. Half a Dozen agreable young are now a going from me among whom I sat down to write. Judge what sort of Letter you are Like to have. How ever tis no matter. Inteligence I Can Give You none. Sentiment you dont Need. Therefore an Expression or two off Friendship is all I shall aim at, in which your sister will Ever have a share Though have Niether Letter or Message from her, but suppose she is all the Mother. Tell her to Gaurd her heart. These little Encroachers soon Get full Possession. The Entrenchments are made strong about them, and when Time, Curiousity or Bussiness Calls them to a distant World, or Death Calls them out of it: what a shock. How shatered the Citadel, how weakned the whole Fabrick. But I can Neither speculate, Morallize or Anticipate. The Room is a Meer Wind Mill. One says Mamah your Letter Cant be very Elegant, another is still more saucy. But I aim at Nothing of the kind, and must spite of my inclination Abruptly bid you Adieu. Though not without assuring you of the affection of your Friend,

M. Warren

Let me hear from you.

RC (Adams Papers).

[1] The Warrens had five sons, of whom two were away and the others were still in their teens: Charles, Henry, and George (Mrs. Washington A. Roebling, *Richard Warren of the Mayflower* . . . , Boston, 1901, p. 28). Which of the three younger sons was to visit Braintree does not appear.

Rector Verheyk to John Adams

Monsieur   [*Amsterdam, 10 November 1780*]

La Desobeissance et L'impertinence de Monsieur votre Fils ainé, qui fait de son mieux pour corrompre son aimable Frere, n'etant plus a soufrir, puis qu'il cherche lui même par sa brutalité, a s'attirer le chatiment qu'il merite, dans l'Esperance de quitter les Ecoles, sous ce pretexte.

Je vous prie donc Monsieur d'avoir la bonté de le retirer d'ici,

plutot que de voir la Discipline publique rendue risible, puisque je
serai a la fin obligé de le traiter selon les Loix de notre Ecole.

J'ai L'honneur d'être Monsieur Votre Tres Humble Serviteur,

H. Verheyk   Rector Gymn. Publ.

RC (Adams Papers); in a clerical hand, signed by Verheyk. JA's reply,
q.v. following, is on the verso of Verheyk's note and furnishes the date here
assigned.

John Adams to Rector Verheyk

Sir   Nov. 10. 1780

I have this moment received, with Surprise and Grief, your Billet.
I pray you Sir, to send my Children to me this Evening and your
Account, together with their Chests and Effects tomorrow. I have
the Honour to be, with great Respect, Sir, your humble servant,

John Adams[1]

FC (Adams Papers); in JA's hand, written on verso of Verheyk's note,
q.v. preceding; at foot of text: "M. H. Verheyk, Rector Gymn. Publ."

[1] For the background of this exchange with Verheyk, see JA to AA, 25 Sept. and note (vol. 3, above), and JA's letter, "not sent," to the Rector and Preceptor of the Latin School, 18 Oct., above.

From surviving correspondence it does not appear that JA explicitly told AA of this incident, but a few weeks later, in reporting to her that he was sending the two boys with Thaxter to continue their studies at Leyden, he spoke bitterly of the mean-spiritedness of Dutch schoolmasters (to AA, 18 Dec., below).

Abigail Adams to John Adams, with a List of Articles wanted from Holland

My dearest Friend   November 13th 1780

How long is the space since I heard from my dear absent Friends?
Most feelingly do I experience that sentiment of Rousseaus' "that one
of the greatest evils of absence, and the only one which reason cannot
alleviate, is the inquietude we are under concerning the actual state
of those we love, their health, their life, their repose, their affections.
Nothing escapes the apprehension of those who have every thing to
lose." Nor are we more certain of the present condition than of the
future. How tormenting is absence! How fatally capricious is that
Situation in which we can only enjoy the past Moment, for the present
is not yet arrived. Stern Winter is making hasty Strides towards me,
and chills the warm fountain of my Blood by the Gloomy prospect of
passing it *alone*, for what is the rest of the World to me?

"Its pomp, its pleasures and its nonesence all?"[1]

The fond endearments of social and domestick life, is the happiness I sigh for, of that I am in a great measure deprived by a seperation from my dear partner and children, at the only season in life when it is probable we might have enjoyed them all together. In a year or two, the sons will be so far advanced in life, as to make it necessary for their Benifit, to place them at the Seats of Learning and Science, indeed the period has already arrived, and whilst I still fondle over one, it is no small relief to my anxious mind, that those, who are seperated from me, are under your care and inspection. They have arrived at an age, when a Mothers care becomes less necessary and a Fathers more important. I long to embrace them. The Tears my dear Charles shed at parting, have melted my Heart a thousand times. Why does the mind Love to turn to those painfull scenes and to re-collect them with pleasure?

I last week only received a Letter written last March, and sent by Monseiur John Baptiste Petry.[2] Where he is I know not. After name-ing a Number of persons of whom I might apply for conveyance of Letters, you were pleased to add, they were your great delight when they did not censure, or complain, when they did they were your greatest punishment.

I am wholy unconscious of giving you pain in this way since your late absence. If any thing of the kind formerly escaped my pen, had I not ample retaliation, and did we not Balance accounts tho the sum was rather in your favour even after having distroyed some of the proof. In the most Intimate of Friendships, there must not be any recrimination. If I complaind, it was from the ardour of affection which could not endure the least apprehension of neglect, and you who was conscious that I had no cause would not endure the supposi-tion. We however wanted no mediating power to adjust the difference, we no sooner understood each other properly, but as the poet says, "The falling out of Lovers is the renewal of Love."

> Be to my faults a little Blind
> Be to my virtues ever kind

and you are sure of a Heart all your own, which no other Earthly object ever possessd. Sure I am that not a syllable of complaint has ever stained my paper, in any Letter I have ever written since you left me. I should have been ungratefull indeed, when I have not had the shadow of a cause; but on the contrary, continual proofs of your attention to me. You well know I never doubted your Honour. Virtue and principal confirm the indissoluable Bond which affection first began and my security depends not upon your passion, which other

13

objects might more easily excite, but upon the sober and setled dictates of Religion and Honour. It is these that cement, at the same time that they ensure the affections.

"Here Love his golden shafts employs; here lights
His *constant* Lamp, and waves his purple wings."

November 24.

I had written thus far when Capt. Davis arrived. The News of your being in Amsterdam soon reachd me, but judge of my dissapointment when I learnt that he had thrown over all his Letters, being chased by an American privateer, who foolishly kept up British coulours till she came along side of him. One only was saved by some accident and reachd me after hearing that the whole were lost. This tho short was a cordial to my Heart, not having received a line of a later date than 15 [*i.e.* 17] of June. This was the fourth of Sepbr., and just informd me of your Health and that you had been in Amsterdam a few weeks. My dear sons were not mentiond, and it was only by a *very* polite Letter from Mr. de Neufville that I learnt they were with you, and well. He is pleased to speak in high terms of them, I hope they deserve it.[3]

A week after a Brig arrived at Providence and brought me your favour of Sepbr. 15 and Mr. Thaxters of August and Sepbr. from Paris.[4] You do not mention in either of your Letters which were saved, how long you expect to reside in Holland. I fancy longer than you then Imagined, as Capt. Davis informs that you had not heard of the Capture of Mr. Lawrence.[5] This event will make your stay there necessary. I fear for your Health in a Country so damp, abounding in stagnant water, the air of which is said to be very unfriendly to Foreigners. Otherways if I was to consult my own feelings I should wish your continuance there, as I could hear more frequently from you. If it is not really nearer, its being a sea port, gives me that Idea, and I fancy the pains of absence increase in proportion to distance, as the power of attraction encreases as the distance diminishes. Magnets are said to have the same motion tho in different places. Why may not we have the same sensations tho the wide Atlantick roll between us? I recollect your story to Madam Le Texel upon the Nature and power of Attraction and think it much more probable to unite Souls than Bodies.[6]

You write me in yours of Sepbr. 15 that you sent my things in the Alliance. This I was sorry to see, as I hoped Mr. Moylan had informd you before that time, that Dr. Winship to whom he deliverd them

14

neither came in the vessel or sent the things. I am not without fears that they will be embezzled. I have taken every opportunity to let you know of it, but whether you have got my Letters is uncertain.[7] The cabals on Board the Ship threw the officers into parties, and Winship chose to involve my trunk in them. He certainly sent goods by the same vessel to other persons. General W[arre]n, my unkle and others examined and went on Board, but could find no Trunk for me. The Articles sent by private hands I believe I have got, except you sent more than one packet by Col. Flury who arrived at Newport [and] sent forward a package containing a few yards of Black Silk. A month afterwards, received a Letter from him desireing to know if I received two packages and some Letters which he brought.[8] I received no Letter, and but one package by him. I have been endeavouring to find out the mistery, but have not yet develloped it.—The Articles you sent me from Bilboa have been of vast service to me, and greatly assisted me in dischargeing the load of Taxes which it would have otherways been impossible for me to have paid; I will enclose you a list of what I have paid, and yet remains due from july to this day. The Season has been so unfortunate in this state, that our produce is greatly diminished. There never was known so severe and so long a drought, the crops of corn and grass were cut of. Each Town in this State is called upon to furnish a suffering Army with provision. This Towns supply is 40 thousand weight of Beaf or money to purchase it. This has already been collected. Our next tax is for Grain to pay our six months and our 3 Months militia, to whom we wisely voted half a Bushel per day, the state pay, and a Bounty of a Thousand dollors each or money Equivalent to purchase the Grain. This is now collecting and our Town tax only is four times larger than our continential.[9] You hear no such sound now, as that money is good for nothing. Hard money from 70 to 75 is made the standard, that or exchange is the way of dealing, everything is high, but more steady than for two years before. My Tenants say they must leave the Farm, that they cannot live. I am sure I cannot pay more than my proportion yet I am loth they should quit. They say two Cows would formerly pay the taxes upon this place, and that it would now take ten. They are not alone in their complaints. The burden is greater I fear than the people will bear—and whilst the New England states are crushed by this weight, others are lagging behind, without any exertions, which has produced a convention from the New England States. A motion has been made, but which I sincerely hope will not be adopted by our Goverment, I mean to vest General Washington

15

with the power of marching his Army into the state that refuses supplies and exacting it by Martial Law. Is not this a most dangerous step, fraught with Evils of many kinds. I tremble at the Idea. I hope Congress will never adopt such a measure, tho our delegates should receive such Instructions.[10]

Our publick affair[s] wear a more pleasing aspect, as you will see by the inclosed Gazet yet are we very far from extirpating the British force. If we are not to look for peace till that event takes place, I fear it is very far distant. Small as our Navy is, it has captured near all the Quebeck Fleet, 19 have arrived safe in port, and fill'd Salem and Cape Ann with Goods of all kinds. Besides not a week passes but gives us a prize from some Quarter.

As to the affairs of our common wealth, you will see who is Govenour. Two good Men have been chosen as Leiut. Governour, both of whom have refused. The late judge of probate is now Elected, and tis thought will accept.[11] Last week his Excellency gave a very Grand Ball, to introduce our Republican form of Goverment properly upon the Stage.[12]

It was a maxim of Edward king of Portugal, that what ever was amiss in the manners of a people, either proceeds from the bad example of the Great, or may be cured by the Good. He is the patriot who when his Country is overwhelmed by Luxery, by his example stems the Torrent and delivers it from that which threatens its ruin. A writer observes with Regard to the Romans, that there must have been a considerable falling off, when Sylla won that popular favour by a shew of Lions, which in better times he could only have obtained by substantial services.

I have twice before enclosed a set of Bills, received from Mr. Lovell for you. I ventured to detain one hopeing for an opportunity to send to Holland. I enclose it now together with a list of the Articles if you think you can afford them to me. If not I shall be better satisfied in a refusal than in a compliance. The Articles you were so kind as to send me were not all to my mind. The Led coulourd Silk was clay coulour, not proper for the use I wanted it for, it was good however. A large Quantity of ordinary black ribbon, which may possibly sell for double what it cost, if it had been coulourd there would have been no difficulty with it. The tape is of the coarsest kind, I shall not lose by it, but as I wanted it for family use, it was not the thing. The Tea was Excellent, the very best I ever had and not so high priced as from other places. All the rest of the articles were agreable.—I have written to Mr. de Neufville encloseing a duplicate Bill, and a list of the same articles, but directed him to take your orders and govern himself by them.[13] When ever you send me any thing for sale, Linnens especially Irish, are always saleable. Common calico, that comes cheep from Holland, any thing of the wollen kind such as Tamies, Durants or caliminco[14] with ordinary linnen hankerchiefs answer well.

I have written a very long letter. To what port it will go first [I] know not; it is too late for any vessel to go to Holland this winter from hence.—Our Friends all well. Your Brother has lost his youngest daughter.[15] I will write to my dear John and Charles and hope [my?][16] Letters will not meet the fate of theirs.

Ever & at all time yours,   Portia

ENCLOSURE

26 yards of Dutch bed tick
2 Gray muffs and tippets
2 Bundles of english pins
2 sets of House Brushes
1 doz. of blew and white china tea cups and sausers
half a doz. pint china Bowls
half a doz. diaper table cloths   2, 5 Ells wide   2 four   2 three.
one Scotch carpet 4 yards square or 6 Ells.
half a doz. white gauze handerchifs the same size that the black were
NB   an Ell in Holland is but 3 quarters of our yard.

You will be so good as to find out where that young gentleman is and forward the Letter.[17]

RC (Adams Papers); endorsed in Thaxter's hand: "Portia 18th.–24th. Novr. 1780." Only one of the numerous enclosures mentioned in the text has been found; it is printed herewith; see further, Neufville & Son to AA, 25 May 1781 and enclosure.

[1] Closing quotation mark supplied. Throughout this letter AA's very indifferent punctuation has been minimally regularized.

[2] JA to AA, 18 March 1780, in Adams Papers but omitted here, a brief note in which the only significant passage (beyond introducing Petry) is paraphrased by AA at the end of the present paragraph.

JA's note was one of nine he wrote on the same date to friends in Boston and Philadelphia introducing in complimentary terms "Monsieur John Baptiste Petry, Secretary of the Comte de Chate-

let [elsewhere "Chatelux," i.e. Chastellux] a Marshall of the Camps and Armies of the King of France." It is somewhat doubtful, however, whether Petry came to America at this time, or at any rate to Boston. He is not mentioned in Chastellux' *Travels*, and in a letter to JA of 22 Nov., James Warren said he had neither seen nor heard from "the Gentleman . . . recommended" (*Warren-Adams Letters*, 2:150–151). But a Jean Baptiste Petry served as vice consul of France at Wilmington, N.C., and Charleston, S.C., 1783–1792, and appears as consul in Pennsylvania in 1793 or 1794 and evidently stayed until 1798. There have been doubts whether this was the same J. B. Petry who came to America in 1815, upon the restoration of the French monarchy, as consul at New Orleans and who became consul general of France at Washington in 1819. From allusions in JQA's diary entries in Paris during "the hundred days," when Petry and JQA exchanged visits, it seems clear that it was the same Petry who served in America at such long intervals. See JQA, Diary, 14 Feb., 7, 27 April, 12 May 1815. During JQA's secretaryship of state he and Petry became good friends, and CFA recorded on 24 Dec. 1823 Petry's keen regret upon leaving the United States to take a post in Spain o which he had been ordered (CFA, Diary, 1:20; see also JQA, Diary, Dec. 1823 – Jan. 1824, *passim*). Information on Petry's tours of duty in America has been furnished to the editors by Howard C. Rice Jr., Princeton University Library, who has long collected biographical data on French consular agents in the United States. See also A. P. Nasatir and G. E. Monell, comps., *French Consuls in the United States: A Calendar of Their Correspondence in the Archives Nationales*, Washington, 1967, p. 553, 567.

³ The letter from Jean de Neufville, Amsterdam, 2 Sept. 1780, is printed in vol. 3, above.

⁴ These letters will also be found in vol. 3.

⁵ Henry Laurens had sailed from Philadelphia on 13 Aug. in the brigantine *Mercury*, which was captured off Newfoundland on 3 Sept. by the British frigate *Vestal*. Laurens was taken into St. John's and then to England in the sloop *Fairy* in a somewhat ambiguous status. Arriving in London on 5 Oct., he was promptly committed to the Tower under "suspicion of high treason." See Laurens' "Narrative," S.C. Hist. Soc., *Colls.*, 1 (1857):18–25. JA's secret informant in England, Thomas Digges, who wrote over a great variety of signatures, reported with remarkable promptness, accuracy, and indignation what happened with respect to Laurens in the ensuing weeks. His first letter on the subject was dated 3 Oct., even before Laurens reached London. Although this

letter was delayed in transit, JA had word of Laurens' capture by the 11th and of his incarceration by the 14th. See "W.S.C." [Thomas Digges] to "Ferdinando Ramon San" [JA], 3, 6, 10, 17, 20, 24 Oct. (Adams Papers); JA to Huntington, 11 Oct. (PCC, No. 84, II, printed in Wharton, ed., *Dipl. Corr. Amer. Rev.*, 4:95); "F.R.S." to "W.S.C.," 14 Oct. (LbC, Adams Papers, printed in JA, *Works*, 7:315). JA furnished extracts from some of Digges' letters to Dumas at The Hague for publication in Dutch papers (JA to Dumas, 3 Nov., LbC, Adams Papers); the extracts will be found in Wharton, 4:84–85.

⁶ This alludes to one of the racier anecdotes in JA's Autobiography, recorded by him to illustrate the (to him) shocking freedom of conversation between the sexes in France. The incident had occurred at a dinner party in Bordeaux in April 1778, when JA had just arrived in France for the first time. In his Autobiography he did not name his dinner companion who asked him an embarrassing question that he handled with great finesse, identifying her only as "One of the most elegant Ladies at Table, young and handsome" (*Diary and Autobiography*, 4:36–37).

⁷ JA had already made inquiries about the missing trunk of goods intended for AA; see his letter to James Moylan at Lorient, 28 Oct. (LbC, Adams Papers).

⁸ Fleury to AA, 6 Oct., above.

⁹ On these matters, indicative of the burdens borne by ordinary citizens in the fifth year of the war, see the votes of the town meetings of 17 July, 28 Sept., and 23 Oct. in *Braintree Town Records*, p. 513, 515–516.

¹⁰ The convention to which AA alludes was held at Hartford, Conn., in mid-November. The four New England states and New York sent delegates; copies of the proceedings were transmitted to the governors of all the states, to General Washington, and to Congress. The ten resolutions adopted by the Convention were designed to guarantee—by "Coertion" if necessary, since some states were seriously delinquent—the filling up of state quotas of "Men Money Provisions or other Supplies" levied by Congress. The premise on which the Convention acted in this the bleakest year

of the Revolution was that "Our present Embarrassments ... arise in a great Measure from a Defect in the present Governments of the United States," which meant to those who held this view that Congress lacked effective power over the state governments. As E. James Ferguson and others have pointed out, the Hartford Convention of 1780 betokened a shift in American leadership from those who had begun and hitherto largely conducted the struggle for independence to a more conservative class of merchants and propertied men who thought the cause was faltering through want of vigorous, efficient, centralized authority. The leaders now coming forward were "nationalists," whose thinking anticipated that of the majority of members of the Federal Convention of 1787 and of the Federalist party of the 1790's. See E. James Ferguson, *The Power of the Purse: A History of American Public Finance, 1776–1790*, Chapel Hill, 1961, ch. 6; also the older account of the Hartford Convention of 1780 in George Bancroft, *History of the Formation of the Constitution of the United States of America*, N.Y., 1882, 1:12–16. The letters and proceedings of the Convention as laid before Congress and committed on 12 Dec. (JCC, 18:1141) are in PCC, No. 33:391–418. Texts of these, contributed by Bancroft and apparently not available in print elsewhere, are in *Magazine of Amer. Hist.*, 8 (1882):688–698.

As soon as the recommendations of the Convention became known they excited strong feelings among those less "nationalist" in their outlook–the "old revolutionaries," so to speak. One clause in the fourth resolution, to which AA is alluding here, proved particularly offensive because it proposed to elevate military over civil power in a way painfully suggestive of Roman precedents familiar to all literate Americans. The original reads:

"That it be earnestly recommended to the several States represented in this Convention to Instruct their respective Delegates to use their Influence in Congress. That the Commander in Chief of the Army of the United States be Authorized and Impowered to take such Measures as he may deem proper and

the publick Service may render necessary to induce the several States to a punctual Compliance with the Requisitions which have been or may be made by Congress for Supplies for the Years 1780 and 1781."

James Warren interpreted this passage in the same manner and with the same alarm as AA did. Writing Samuel Adams on 4 Dec., he said:

"I suppose you have before this seen the doings and Resolutions of the Hartford Convention. If one of them does not astonish you I have forgot my political Catechism. Surely History will not be Credited when it shall record that a Convention of Delegates from the four New England States and from the next to them met at Hartford in the Year 1780, and in the heigth of our Contest for public Liberty and Security solemnly Resolved to recommend it to their several States to Vest the Military with Civil Powers of an Extraordinary kind and, where their own Interest is Concerned, no less than a Compulsive power over deficient States to oblige them by the point of the Bayonet to furnish money and supplies for their own pay and support. This must have been done without recollecting political Maxims, without attending to Historical Admonitions and warnings, or the Principles upon which our Opposition to Britain rests. General Washington is a Good and a Great Man. I love and Reverence him. But he is only a Man and therefore should not be vested with such powers, and besides we do not know that his successor will be either Great or Good. Much less can we tell what Influence this precedent may have half a Century since." (*Warren-Adams Letters*, 2:151–152.)

When the Convention's proposals came before Congress in December, the fourth resolution appeared to be essentially a renewal of a motion made in that body early in September by John Mathews of South Carolina and then defeated. Its substance is known only through a passage in a letter from James Lovell to Elbridge Gerry (both "old revolutionaries"), written on 20 November. Under its terms Washington was to be "fully authorized and empowered to carry into Execut'n in the most compleat and ample manner such measures as shall appear to him best calculated for raising and bringing into the field on or before the 1st day of Jan'ry next, an army of 25000 men to continue in the service of these United States during the present war with Great Britain," together with the arms, ammunition, and stores required by them. "And the Congress of these United States do in the most solemn manner pledge themselves to the said Gen. W fully and vigorously to support him and to ratify whatever shall be by him done in the premises." A second resolve declared these virtually unlimited "powers and authorities . . . to be in full force" until 1 Dec. 1781. (Burnett, ed., *Letters of Members,* 5:542). We know something of the circumstances that led to the defeat of this motion from a letter that Mathews, its mover, addressed to Washington on 15 Sept.; it was thought, he said, to be "too strongly tinctured with . . . *Army principles*" (same, p. 374). And so was the Hartford Convention's fourth resolution, on which John Witherspoon (a member of the committee to which the resolutions were referred) commented as follows in a letter of 16 Dec. to Governor William Livingston of New Jersey:

"Though it is well known to you that few persons have a higher opinion of or confidence in Gen. Washington than myself or a greater desire of having vigorous executive powers put into the hands of persons at the head of affairs either in the military or civil department, yet that resolution is of such a nature that I should never give my voice for it unless you or my constituents should specifically direct it, perhaps *even not then,* and I have that opinion of Gen. Washington that I do not think he would accept or act in consequence of such powers. What could induce that Convention to recommend such a measure is a mystery to me, but I believe it will have few advocates" (same, p. 487–488).

For the subsequent history of Congress' action, or inaction, on the Convention's proposals, which, minus the more offensive ones, became embodied in administrative reforms carried out after the adoption of the Articles of Confederation in March 1781, see Madison, *Papers,* ed. Hutchinson, 2:318–319.

[11] On the election of John Hancock over James Bowdoin as first governor under the new constitution, see AA to JA, 5 July (vol. 3, above), and note 7, with references there. On 31 Oct., Bowdoin addressed a letter to the General Court declining, "by reason of a continued ill-state of health," his election both as a member of the Senate and as lieutenant governor (*Boston Gazette,* 6 Nov. 1780, p. 2, col. 1–2). On 7 Nov., James Warren was elected lieutenant governor, but he too declined (same, 13 Nov., p. 4, col. 1; his letter of declination, dated 10 Nov. and citing the distance of his residence from Boston and prior obligations, is in same, 20 Nov., p. 4, col. 2). Shortly thereafter, Thomas Cushing, a supporter of Hancock and Suffolk judge of probate, was chosen; after some deliberation he accepted. See Cotton Tufts to JA, 27 Nov., below.

[12] "Thursday evening last [23 Nov.] a ball and entertainment was given by His Excellency the Governor to the officers of the army and navy, and principal ladies and gentlemen of this city" (*Continental Journal,* 30 Nov. 1780, p. 3, col. 1).

[13] This letter and its enclosure have not been found.

[14] Tamis (variously spelled), a cloth made for straining or bolting; durant, a woolen stuff, sometimes called "everlasting"; calamanco, a Flemish woolen cloth with a glossy surface (*OED*).

[15] Elizabeth, daughter of Peter and Mary (Crosby) Adams, born just before her mother's death; see AA to JA, 15 April, vol. 3, above.

[16] One or two words having been rubbed out, the text is obscure.

[17] Perhaps a letter intended for Winslow Warren; see Winslow Warren to AA, 26 May (vol. 3, above), and note 2 there.

William Smith to Abigail Adams

Mrs. Adams   Boston 20 Novr. 1780

Cap. Davis arrived here last Thursday, by him Mr. Adams had sent a number of Letters, and was order'd to throw them over in case he was chased. He was chas'd on his passage and threw them over. Messrs. De Neufville wrote a Letter to my father inclosing one for you which was saved and have sent it by the Bearer. The packet for you will be taken care of as soon as it is out of the Vessell. A Sloop that saild in company with Davis has arrived at Providence, shou'd there be any Letters come to hand I will forward them by the first oppertunity.

Yours Affectionately,   W. Smith

RC (Adams Papers); addressed: "Mrs. Adams   Braintree." Enclosure: Jean de Neufville & Son to AA, 2 Sept., vol. 3, above.

James Lovell to Abigail Adams

Novr. 27th. [1780]

The enclosed is from no *new* Admirer. But it will not be less well-come on that Score to a Female devoid of Coquetry. It came under Cover to the hon. Mr. Bee from Commodore Gillon, who has been so kind as to aid Mr. A—— by interpreting, in Holland.[1] Mr. A—— is authorized to negociate the money matters that were entrusted to Mr. Laurens and had actually received his Powers by the happy Arrival of the hon. Mr. Searle who sailed from hence in the Jay on some Affairs for the State of Pensylvania.[2]

Mr. A was well Sepr. 25. I wish I may be able to say Something to him of the same kind about you before Col. Palfrey sails;[3] it may serve as a Douceur. He writes not to me. He is as captious as P— I will not say who, because the eastern Post has failed Today, and *possibly* there may be in the Office at Fish Kill a "Thank you for forwarding the Bills of Exchange" and an "I wish you happy" with a P at the Bottom of it.[4]

I have not yet seen the Carolina Mr. Brown[5] to prove to him of what worth is a good Word from you. It shall wellcome to me even the "Countenance" of a Saracen.

I hear nothing yet of Capt. P. Jones. I have 3 Commissions respecting Goods to come by him. They are from 3 much esteemed Friends. I will not say of which of the Commissions I am most proud, for I wish to avoid even the *Appearance* of being a Flatterer in these Days of Slander when even Portia has "been left" to miscall *my* Honesty.

Now, Daughter of Eve, for a few Dashes in the News-way. Russia, Sweeden and Denmark are jointly doing Right to their mutual Commerces. Holland is all tameness, pretending to expect that the northern confederating Powers shall guarantee her east india Interests as a preliminary to her joining the Confederation. England releases Captures made upon the 3 first mentioned Nations, but condemns the Hollanders. Minheer I should think will not much longer hold out under such evident Indignity.

The british Force has suddenly left Portsmouth in Virginia without destroying their Works or taking the collected negroes with them. There is a Report that they relanded higher up the Bay and have cooped in our Friends on the Neck to the amount of 5000. I suspect this to be the Fabric of a Speculator. There is more than a single Account that French Ships were off Charlestown Bar.

I forgot to tell you that Mr. A is turned a french Surgeon and is *anatomizing* Govr. Hutchinson. I will give you a Sketch of the Skeleton if I can find Time by next post day.[6]

A Foreigner who has travailed much and knows several Languages told me last Evening that he knew of Nothing that pleased him so much for the Occasion as the Quaker's Farewell.[7]   JL

RC (Adams Papers); addressed: "Mrs. A Adams   Braintree   Care of Isaac Smith Esqr. Mercht. Boston   Philada. Jas. Lovell." Enclosure not found, but see note 1.

[1] Thomas Bee was at this time a South Carolina delegate to the Continental Congress (*Biog. Dir. Cong.*). Alexander Gillon, a naval adventurer from South Carolina, was in Europe attempting to raise funds and buy vessels for his state's war effort; see a note on him in JA, *Diary and Autobiography*, 2:447; also under Benjamin Waterhouse to JA, 26 Dec., below. At Paris early in July, JA had entrusted Gillon with several consignments of letters to America to find conveyance for at Amsterdam; see Thaxter's note following entries for 6 and 8 July 1780 in Lb/JA/12 (Adams Papers, Microfilms, Reel No. 100). But since no letters to AA are specified in these lists, it is not clear, though it is quite possible, that Lovell is here forwarding a letter to her from JA.

[2] On James Searle and his European mission, see Lovell to AA, 14 July, vol. 3 above, and note 4 there.

[3] Col. William Palfrey, of Boston, who had been serving as paymaster general of the Continental Army, was on 4 Nov. elected by Congress the first American consul to reside in France; he sailed in December from Philadelphia in a vessel that was never heard from again (JCC, 18:1018; John Gorham Palfrey, "Life of William Palfrey," in Jared Sparks, ed., *The Library of American Biography*, 2d ser., Boston, 1844–1848, vol. 7:335–448).

[4] By "P" Lovell certainly means "Portia," whom he characterizes as "captious" because in her letter of 3 Sept. she had chided him for his silence, and in her letter of 17 Sept. had called his

letter of the 3d "very Laconick." All three of these letters are in vol. 3 above.

[5] Joseph Brown Jr. of Charleston, S.C.; see JA to AA, 15 March, and AA to Lovell, 3 Sept., both in vol. 3 above.

[6] JA's "anatomizing" of the late Governor Thomas Hutchinson was in his dispatch to President Huntington from Paris, 17 June. AA was shortly furnished

with a copy, which she permitted to be published, anonymously, in the Boston *Independent Chronicle*, 4 Jan. 1781. See JA to AA, 17 June 1780, vol. 3 above, and AA to Nathaniel Willis?, ante 4 Jan. 1781, below.

[7] Lovell evidently means that the best mode of leave-taking is silence.

Cotton Tufts to John Adams, with a Copy of a Letter from Daniel Little

Dear Sir   Weymouth Nov. 27. 1780

I wrote to You last March also in June, the former by Capt. McNeil who had the Misfortune to be taken, the Latter by the Ship Mars Capt. Sampson bound to France, which must have reached You before this Time if no Misfortune has befallen the Ship. By Capt. Sampson I sent You Allens Narrative, a Journal of the Weather from November last with a general Account of Vegetation also a particular Account of a remarkable Darkness that happened here on the 19th. of May last and the Evening of the same Day with some Observations, and Attempts to account for it.[1]—In my several Letters the Proceedings of the Convention were mentioned &c. The Government is now formed —Hon. J. Hancock Esq. Governor—Hon. J. Bowdoin Esq. was chosen by the Senate and House of Rep[resentatives] Lt. Governor—refused on Account of his Health—next Hon. J. Warren—refused on Account of his Office in the Naval Board—next Hon. Thos. Cushing Esq. who is now absent at Hartford and has not given an Answer.

The House and Senate are fully convinced of the Necessity of establishing a standing Army and are taking Measures for that Purpose, as they seem to be determined to carry this Matter into Execution. In the Operation of it I imagine, the Paper Currency will die away and solid Money spring up in its Room, indeed it already circulates and the Value of the former being pretty well known, it has become indifferent to the Buyer and Seller which he pays or receives. The Exchange for several Months has been from 65 to 75, but is generally thought to be falling. Our Markets are stocked with Provisions, the Price dayly falling. Should one Helmsman steer with a steady Hand, a brighter Scene must e'er long open, notwithstanding the Misfortunes of the present Year.

An Academy of Arts and Sciences is now established in this State

President of which is the Hon. James Bowdoin Esq.—Vice President Dr. Cooper—Corresponding Secretary Rev. Jos. Willard—Recording Secretary Revd. Caleb Gannett. At the last Meeting, it was voted to transmit to the Learned Societies in France and in Europe the incorporating Act and invite their Correspondence &c.

Revd. Mr. Little of Wells a Fellow of the Academy has been engaged for some Time past in the Manufacture of Steel, which he has brought to considerable Perfection. In a Conversation with him upon the Subject he expressed a strong Inclination to become acquainted with the Methods practised in Europe more especially the Construction of the Furnaces. It occurd to my Mind sometime after, that Your opportunities of gaining Intelligence would enable You to gratify his Wishes, and not having the least doubt of your Inclination I took the Liberty to inform him that any Questions relative thereto, that he would propose, I would transmit to you by the first Opportunity.— A Copy of his Letter follows.

Wells Octob. 16. 1780

I received Yours of the 17 Augt. a few days since and thank You for so favourable an Opening to further Improvements in the Art of manufacturing Steel. I wish, as You suppose, to be acquainted with the various Methods practised in Europe.

My own Experiments fully evince to me that America affords the best Iron for manufacturing Steel of the first Quality for edge Tools, but I wish to be informed *with what Substance* that best endures the Fire, *and in what Mode* their Furnaces are constructed. Indeed as full an Information as can be obtained of all the different Processes in the Art of making Steel in other Countries I apprehend may hasten the Perfection of the Art in the united States to the great Benefit of the present and succeeding Generations.

Natural History and Botany have engaged my Leisure Hours for some Time past—and since some worthy Gentlemen in France have requested a Minute History of the vegetable Kingdom in America, I wish to be informed of the best Method of preserving the Flowers of Plants in their natural Form and beautiful Colourings to be transported to different Countries, and the rather because the best System of Botany is founded on the Knowledge of the Sexes of Plants, the distinguishing Characters of which are obtained by a minute Knowledge of their Flowers.

I have no Correspondent beyond America. If an Answer to the above Request may be obtained through Your Hand, it will doubtless invite further Inquiries, that will benefit the Public, gratify the Curious, particularly, Yr. obligd Fd. &c. D.L.[2]

Mr. Little is a Gentleman of much Ingenuity, fond of natural History, vastly inquisitive and industrious. I sincerely wish him all possible Encouragement and every Advantage thrown in his Way that may contribute to facilitate his Experiments and make his Researches useful to his Country and to the World in general.—Permit me to engage Your Attention to his Letter, and in due Time to favour Him through my Hands or otherwise with an Answer.

The Treachery of Genl. Arnold—His Flight to the Enemy at New York—The Execution of Major Andre (Aid D.C. to G. Clinton and Adjutt. Gen. of the British Army,) as a Spy—the severe Check the Enemy have met with at the Southward &c.—and many other Articles of Intelligence, You will receive from other Quarters, a minute Detail of which, from an Apprehension of burdening My Friend, with unnecessary Repetitions, have not inserted.

Our Connections are all well. Present my Love and Regards to Your Family and accept the same From Your Affectionate Friend & H. St., C. T.

RC (Adams Papers); endorsed in Thaxter's hand: "Dr. C. Tufts 27. Novr. 1780."

[1] Tufts' letter of "June ... by the Ship Mars Capt. Sampson" was actually dated 25 July 1780 and is printed in vol. 3 above, with two of its several enclosures. Another enclosure was evidently a copy of Ethan Allen, *A Narrative of Colonel Ethen Allen's Captivity*, first published in Philadelphia, 1779, with other editions following in that year and the next (Evans 16180–16182, 16692–16693); JA's copy has not been located.

[2] Daniel Little (1726–1801), for half a century Congregational minister at Kennebunk and a noted missionary to the Maine Indians, had been self-educated but was awarded an honorary A.M. by Harvard in 1766. Like Tufts, he had diversified interests, among which were Indian languages, mountaineering, and natural history as well as the manufacture of steel. His efforts in this last enterprise won him financial support from the Massachusetts General Court in 1778, and in 1785 he published "Observations upon the Art of Making Steel" in the first volume of the American Academy of Arts and Sciences' *Memoirs*, p. 525–528. "But alas," wrote the sympathetic chronicler of the annals of Kennebunk in a charming sketch of Little, "for all his calculations, and the hopes of the public! The laws of nature were against him; his philosophy was not sufficiently extensive. There was a stubborn disposition in some of the materials, which all his wisdom could not subdue, and his fond anticipations were blasted. Reluctantly, and much to his mortification, he was compelled to abandon his enterprise." See Weis, *Colonial Clergy of N.E.*; Edward E. Bourne, *The History of Wells and Kennebunk*, Portland, 1875, p. 708–723, esp. 716–718.

John Adams to Isaac Smith Sr.

Sir   Amsterdam Decr. 6. 1780

Your Favours of August 21. and Sept. 9. I have received and am much obliged to you for them.[1] I hope you will be so good as to write me, by every Vessell.

From the great Number of American Vessells which have arrived, in Europe in the Course of the past summer, I think our Commerce as well as Privateering is on the rising hand, and I hope that next year, it will increase considerably, and that We shall hear oftener from home.

I shall probably reside hereabouts for sometime, nevertheless I hope my friends will not fail to write me by the Way of France and Spain.

Mr. Laurens is in Strict Confinement, and so are Mr. Trumbull and Mr. Tyler, who imprudently went over to England.[2] I believe, that in Time Americans will realize that the English are their Ennemies.

Nobody need be afraid of Privateering, from Apprehensions of Peace. There is no Peace to be had. My affectionate Respects to all the Family.   John Adams

LbC (Adams Papers).

[1] That of 21 Aug. is printed in vol. 3 above; that of 9 Sept. has not been found.
[2] "Govr. Trumbulls Son and Mr. Tyler, are taken up in England and committed for high Treason.—This will cure the Silly Itch of running over to England" (JA to Arthur Lee, 6 Dec., LbC, Adams Papers). On the recent adventures of John Steele Tyler and his companion, John Trumbull the painter, in London, see note on Richard Cranch to JA, 26 April, vol. 3 above, and references there.

Abigail Adams to John Thaxter

My dear Sir   December 8 1780

I have been all impatience for several Months looking and longing to hear from abroad. From june to december would be many Eternitys in the warm imagination of a Lover. Such extravagancys are at no time admissible in a Female Breast, but the anxiety of a wife and the affection of a parent, may be productive of sensations known only to those who feel them, and which language would poorly represent.

You who have a Heart open to Friendship (if not to the softer passions) can commisirate my situation upon the late arrival of Capt. Davis from Amsterdam who being chased threw over all his Letters. I scarcely knew how to endure so cruel a misfortune. A few days however in some measure relieved me; by the arrival of a Brig from the same port, which brought me one Letter from Amsterdam and 3 from France, Bearing date August 21, 27 and Sepbr. 3 [1] for which I most sincerely thank you. You have afforded me much entertainment by your discriptive pen. I felt a degree of pitty mingle with my Indignation at an Institution equally incompatible with publick Good, and private happiness, an Institution which cruelly devotes Beauty and Innocence to slavery, regret and wretchedness, and is contrary to the dictates of that Being who pronounced it not good for Man to be alone and who created Eve, not for a secluded Bower, or a Grated Part[it]ion, but for the associate, the companion, the sharer of the Labours and pleasures of our Ancient Parent, united in them the best affections of the Humane Heart, the tender social ties from whence have flowed all the fond endearing Relatives of Parent, Son, Brother, Husband, Friend; thus a favorite Author discribes the Universal Cause, not "acting by partial, but by general Laws" and making what happiness we justly call, subsist not in the good of *one*, but *all.*

We were formed for a scene of active virtue. He is the Hero who conquers, not he who cowardly flees from the Enemy. Take care my dear Sir that you do not make the fair *Maroni* repent her vows and convert, instead of being converted. She would then bathe with the bitter tears of repentance and remorse, those altars to which she is consecrated. At so early an age can her passions be all sublimated? and the Love of God substituted to the Love of Man? is each prayer accepted and each wish resignd?

> Desires composed, affections ever even?
> Tears that delight, and Sighs that waft to heaven.

Dissapointed Love and the enthusiasm of Religion only can receive consolation in such a seclusion from the world,

> "Where stern Religion quench'es the unwilling flame
> Where dies the best of passions, Love and Fame."

I was sorry to find that any of your Friends had given you uneasiness in the Way you mentiond.[2] You well know that the Love of Slander is the prevailing passion of many in this place, and the spirit of levelling all characters has prompted them to strike at the best, and the most unexceptionable, but I trust their malice left not a Spot behind, since the parties have so lived that no one dared to believe the slander. Others since your absence with Hearts as pure, and with conduct as irreproachable have equally suffered, even the tender and Gentle Eliza[3]

"Whose mind is virtue by the Graces dresst"

from a disorder to which you know she has been long subject, and which will I fear put a period to her days, even in the Bloom of life, has sufferd reproach for no other cause. Let this be your consolation that you have sufferd with good company, and that

"True conscious Honour, is to know no Sin
He's arm'd without that is Innocent within."

You know I ever valued you for a purity of Morals which every young Gentleman would retain, if he knew the Evils ariseing from dissolute connexions, before experience taught them. It is an old observation that a Man is known by his company. You were Intimate with a youth, who I fear is much changed in his manners and principals from Evil communications. You have often lamented his contracted Education, that I fear has led him into company you would Blush to have your name mentiond among. Yet the Sanction of former Intimacy with him prompted a Dissolute Imp of Satan, to Name you as one of those whom she could call hers when she plased. I ventured to send her word by this very person, that she had better take care how she mentioned your Name again. I could assure her you had Friends here who would not suffer your character to be abused with Impunity. This together with a publick exorciseing from the pulpit laid the devil, and I have never heard a syllable of slander since.[4] That you may retain every virtue you exported from America, pure and unsullied, and return with them brightned and improved, is the sincere and ardent wish of your ever affectionate Friend,   Portia

N[a]b desires her Regards to you. I cannot persuade her to write, not even to enquire who the *fair* American is, tho she has great curiosity to know.

RC (MB); addressed: "To Mr. John Thaxter Paris"; endorsed: "Mrs. Adams. 8th. Decr. 1780. R. 19 March 1781." Dft (Adams Papers); without date or name of recipient, but CFA wrote at head of text: "Jany. 1781. Mr. Thaxter." Some passages in Dft were rewritten in more guarded language in RC, but only one of these is editorially noted below.

[1] That of 21 Aug. will be found in vol. 3 above; that of 27 Aug. is in Adams Papers but omitted here except for the paragraph quoted in the following note; that of 3 Sept. has not been found; nor has another, dated 1 Sept., which AA acknowledged in Dft of present letter but apparently by oversight omitted mention of in RC.

[2] "I understand my Character has

been slandered and defamed since my Absence from B[raintree] but I know not in what respects. I charge this to the Score of Misfortune and not to that of Fault. I am as conscious that I have given no occasion for it as I am of my Innocence. I therefore despise the utmost Extremes of the Malice of my Enemies, whoever they may be. I have some to be sure rather bitter and spiteful. I am not indifferent as to my Reputation—my Ambition while there was to deserve and maintain a good one. My Friends (and I flatter myself I have some there) will judge between me and my Calumniators" (Thaxter to AA, 27 Aug. 1780, Adams Papers).

³ Probably Elizabeth Palmer, referred to several times in vol. 3 above.

⁴ In Dft the preceding passage (beginning "Yet the Sanction . . .") reads: "Vanity and impudence prompted the infamous trolope to say, she would not marry a young fellow who was fool enough to be fond of her, because she could have Mr. A—n, Mr. Joh T , Mr. T—r or Mr. V—y when she pleased. I believe only one can be exempted from the Number as Innocent. Evil communications corrupt good manners, and it has been the misfortune of a youth whom you once loved to suffer in that way." The names may be filled out with more or less confidence as follows: Allen or Austin, John Thaxter, Thayer, Veasey.

John Adams to Cotton Tufts

Dear Sir   Amsterdam Decr. 9. 1780

Your Favour of July 25th was received in Paris in my Absence, and I have never had opportunity, to acknowledge it, till now.

You are now I hope happy, both in the Constitution and Administration of Government. It cannot be long before We shall see the Lists.

I am obliged to you for the Journal of the Weather, but cannot admit your Excuse for not writing me Politicks. Every one says you will have publick Affairs from others. So I get them from none.

The Institution of an Accademy of Arts and Sciences, does you much honour in Europe, and it will after a little Time be incouraged, many Ways. But dont set your Hearts upon Benefactions from abroad. It is a shame that We should beg for Benefactions. There have been but two Hollis's—there will perhaps be no more.¹

Indeed America will never derive any good from Europe of any Kind. I wish We were wise enough to depend upon ourselves for every Thing, and upon them for nothing. Ours is the richest and most independent Country under Heaven, and We are continually looking up to Europe for Help! Our Riches and Independance grow annually out of the Ground.

The English are hiring ships here to carry Troops and Provisions to America—they have hired about a Dozen and there are Orders to hire as many as they can.

The Dutch are waiting for the English stocks to fall below Sixty and then every body will put their Money into them. These Gudgeons are deceived. The English Emmissaries give out that there will be Peace, and the credulous Dutch believe it, and they think that after a Peace the English stocks will rise, as they did after 1763. So they hope to get 15 or 20 Per Cent clear Profit. But there is not the least Probability of Peace: nor will the English stocks rise after it, when it comes.

The Dutch have acceeded to the neutral Confederation, but this I suspect, will be brutum Fulmen.

I inclose you a Pamphlet or two[2] and am, with affectionate Respects to the Family &c.

LbC (Adams Papers). The "Pamphlet or two" enclosed in missing RC have not been found, but one has been identified; see note 2.

[1] Thomas Hollis and his adopted heir, Thomas Brand Hollis, were British "republicans" who had been generous benefactors of Harvard College and other American institutions of learning. See *DAB* under Thomas Hollis, and references to both men in JA, *Diary and Autobiography*.

[2] Undoubtedly one of these was a literary effort that had cost JA much time and trouble during the preceding months. Entitled *Pensées sur la révolution de l'Amérique-unie, extraites de l'ouvrage anglois, intitulé Mémoire, adressé aux souverains de l'Europe, sur l'état présent des affaires de l'ancien & du nouveau-monde*, Amsterdam [&c.], n.d. (Sabin 64829), it had a long and complex history which can be given in only summary form here. It was a translation of what JA called an "Abridgment," from his own hand, of an influential pamphlet by Thomas Pownall, *A Memorial Most Humbly Addressed to the Sovereigns of Europe . . .*, London, 1780 (Sabin 64826). JA had prepared his version of this tract in the spring of 1780 and furnished a copy to Congress in the form of a letter to Pres. Samuel Huntington, 19 April (PCC, No. 84, I; LbC, Adams Papers). What appears to be JA's draft or working copy, a holograph MS in nineteen folio pages much corrected in his own and another hand (probably Edmund Jenings'), is in the Adams Papers under the assigned date of 5 Sept. 1780; it bears the title "A Translation of the 'Memorial to the Sovereigns of Europe,' into common Sense and intelligible English." This or another English text was made available in June or early July 1780 to a Parisian named Addenet for translation into French. The translation followed JA to Amsterdam and was sent by him on 5 Sept. to the Leyden scholar-journalist Jean Luzac, who wrote a lengthy and valuable preface and caused the whole to be published anonymously under the title *Pensées, &c.* (as given above in this note). Copies reached JA in mid-November, and he at once began to circulate them diligently. Early in 1781, as a result of efforts by Edmund Jenings, JA's friend in Brussels (on whom see JA, *Diary and Autobiography*, 2:355–356 and *passim*), the London publisher John Stockdale brought out an English edition under the by now sufficiently confusing title *A Translation of the Memorial . . . into Common Sense and Intelligible English* (Sabin 35987). No subsequent edition has ever been issued, since CFA did not include it in JA's *Works,* and Wharton unaccountably omitted from the *Diplomatic Correspondence* JA's letter to Huntington of 19 April 1780 embodying JA's revision of Pownall's observations. This is the more regrettable because Pownall, who posited that the Americans had already won their independence, broke new ground in setting forth the future political and commercial relations between the Americas and Europe. JA's redaction is significant both for what it includes and what it omits.

The foregoing summary is based on extensive correspondence during 1780 and early 1781 between JA and Ad- denet, Jenings, Luzac, and J. D. van der Capellen surviving in the Adams Papers.

Benjamin Waterhouse to John Adams

Respected Sir   Leyden 13th. Decembr. 1780

It so happened that I could not see the persons of whom I wished to enquire concerning the Schools, mode of education &c. untill yesterday, otherwise I should have written before.—The Gentlemen from whom I have my information have each of them a young person under their care about the age of your eldest, and are well acquainted with every thing appertaining to education in this City, from conversing with them I am able to inform you that besides the publick-school which is a good one, there are private masters in the latin and greek, who at the same time they teach these languages, teach the greek and roman History. With boys who are far advanced in greek they read and explain Euripides, Sophocles and others. The same person will if required repeat *any* of the Law-lectures to the pupil, and that indeed is what they are principally employed for, by those whose wives are to be *Mevrouws.*—There is a teacher of this kind in Leyden who is both an elegant schollar and a gentleman, such a one asks 20 ducats a year. There are besides two Professors of the greek languague, the one gives lectures on the new Testament, his hearers are generally students of Theology, the other on Euripides, Sophocles and such like, and are attended by young Gentlemen whose pursuits are similar to what I imagine your sons to be. To reap advantage from these classes it is necessary they should understand the latin pretty well because the explanations of the greek passages are given in that languague.

In regard to living I am persuaded they can live here for much less than at Amsterdam. Three furnished rooms would probably cost 20 guilders a month. We find our own tea, sugar, wine, light and fire, and give one ducat a week for dinner, it is always the same price whether we go to the public-house, or have it brought from thence to our own rooms, and it makes no difference with the people where we live, who never refuse to prepare our tables for us. In respect to their being Americans or Sons of Mr. Adams they will never meet with any thing disagreeable on that head, where any profit is like to accrue little do the Dutchmen care for their political, or even religious principles—Turk, Jew, or Christian make no difference with them. I beleive we may say of them as they said of themselves at Japan when the Japonese enquired if they were christians—they answered, they were Dutchmen. If the Gentlemen should come, I can insure them an agreeable Society and a genteel circle of acquaintance. If they should not, I hope at least they will come and pay us a visit, and I think I need not add how ready I should be to render them any service in my power.

With my compliments to Comdr. Gillon and Mr Searl I remain with much respect your friend & Countryman,

Benjn. Waterhouse[1]

RC (Adams Papers); addressed: "To the Honbe. John Adams Esqr. Amsterdam; endorsed: "Dr. Waterhouse   Decr. 16 ansd." (no answer has been found), to which CFA later added "1780."

[1] Benjamin Waterhouse (1754–1846). This is the first known letter in a correspondence between Waterhouse and successive generations of Adamses which continued with no real intermissions for sixty years and documents a relationship, at all times warm and sometimes peculiarly intimate, between this gifted, eccentric, and controversial physician and the two Adamses who became Presidents of the United States.

Benjamin Waterhouse, born at Newport, R.I., had been apprenticed to a physician there, and then sailed to England from Newport in March 1775 in what is said to have been "the last ship to have left the blockaded port of Boston" (Trent, "London Years," as cited below). His object was to obtain a truly professional medical education and training, and he succeeded in doing so by spending some seven years in Edinburgh, London, and Leyden, three of the chief centers of medical science in Europe.

Of great benefit to him during most of these years were the active patronage and advice of Dr. John Fothergill, a prominent London physician and philanthropist, who was first cousin to Waterhouse's Yorkshire-born mother; see Waterhouse to JA, 26 Dec. 1780, below. At Fothergill's suggestion, Waterhouse enrolled as a student with the medical faculty at Leyden in the fall of 1778, adding to his name in the matriculation register the words "Liberæ Reipublicæ Americanæ Federatæ Civis." This gesture may have demonstrated that

there was no tincture of toryism in Waterhouse's makeup, but since the Dutch had not yet recognized the new United States of America it caused some "uneasiness" among the authorities of the University (Anonymous "Sketch" in *Polyanthos*, as cited below; JA, *Corr. in the Boston Patriot*, p. 572). Waterhouse took his medical degree in April 1780 with a dissertation *De sympathia partium corporis humani*, Leyden, 1780, spent the summer again in Fothergill's London home, and returned to attend lectures in history and the law of nations at Leyden, where JA found him extremely helpful in the critical matter of his sons' education. He was, JA later wrote, "though a sprightly genius, very studious and inquisitive, as well as sociable. . . . As to his morals, I could hear of no reproach or suspicion; as to his politics, though he came from England, he came under the guardianship and pupilage of Dr. Fothergill, who was as good a friend to America, as any Englishman could be. . . . I did not, therefore, hesitate to consider him, in some respects, as one of my family" (*Corr. in the Boston Patriot*, p. 572). Later letters in the present volume show the progress of Waterhouse's friendship with the Adamses. His observation at close range of JA's campaign in the spring of 1781 to win Dutch recognition of American independence filled him with an admiration for JA that increased with the years. "I shall never forget some of his paroxysms of patriotic rage," Waterhouse later wrote of JA's negotiations with the French minister at The Hague, who, under Vergennes' orders, tried to block JA's efforts (Waterhouse to Levi Woodbury, 20 Feb. 1835, DLC:Woodbury Papers, vol. 16. This letter contains a number of details not elsewhere available; among other things it corrects JA's account of his first meeting with Waterhouse, which actually took place "at the table of Dr. Franklin in Paris," and furnishes a vivid description of JA's composition and delivery of his Memorial to the States General of 19 April 1781).

When, in the summer of 1781, JA determined to send CA home, CA sailed with Capt. Alexander Gillon in the *South Carolina* from the Texel. A fellow passenger was Waterhouse, who, unlike CA, continued with Gillon to Havana and in consequence did not reach home until June 1782. In the following year he was appointed first professor of the theory and practice of physic in the Harvard Medical School, then just being organized; before long, he established himself and his (first) wife, the former Elizabeth Oliver, whom he married in 1788, in "a small but handsome seat with ten acres of land, on the Cambridge common, about 200 paces in front of the colleges" (Waterhouse to Dr. James Tilton, 24 March 1815, MHS, *Procs.*, 54 [1920–1921]:163). The house still stands at 7 Waterhouse Street facing the Common on the northwest; see Hannah Winthrop Chapter, National Society, Daughters of the American Revolution, *An Historic Guide to Cambridge*, Cambridge, 1907, p. 142 and facing illustration. When JA sent JQA home from Paris to prepare for admission to Harvard College, he placed him as "your old Acquaintance" under Waterhouse's special care, writing him a remarkable letter detailing JQA's studies to this point (JA to Waterhouse, 23 April 1785, MHi:Adams-Waterhouse Corr.; printed in Ford, ed., *Statesman and Friend*, p. 5–8); and in 1806 JQA lived in the conveniently located Waterhouse home when he gave his first Boylston lectures on rhetoric and oratory at Harvard.

This is not the place to try even to summarize Waterhouse's long and versatile career as a physician, popularizer of natural history studies, promoter of vaccination for smallpox, health crusader, polemicist, journalist, and, during his later years, inveterate beggar of government appointments. It is enough to say, for one thing, as Dr. Trent has very well said, that, although Waterhouse returned from Europe "without doubt one of the best educated men in America," America itself was at the time "not ready for so ambitious a young physician" and promoter of scientific causes. "[H]is experiences abroad," in the company of leaders in medicine, science, and politics, "incapacitated him, in a sense, for the life he had to live at home" as a physician practicing in a provincial town. (See Trent's two articles cited below; also the two studies by Blake, also cited below, which reach similar conclusions from additional evidence, especially in relation to Waterhouse's campaign introducing Jennerian vaccination to the United States, a campaign that was successful but marred by Waterhouse's pervasive egotism and his hankering for "excessive personal pecuniary profit.") Irked by the humdrum of ordinary practice and meeting repeated disappointments in what he considered purely philanthropic projects, he grew embittered and quarrelsome. These traits did not, however, impair his powers as a letter-writer. On the contrary, his habit of telling his troubles in circumstantial detail, mixed with engaging reminiscences, sarcastic wit, and the unfailing inquisitiveness JA had observed in him as a student at Leyden—all these enlivened his correspondence with JA and JQA to the end, and in turn evoked some of their best letters in reply. "[A]s you are among the most pleasant of my Correspondents," JQA wrote Waterhouse as late as 1833, "as well as among the choicest of my friends, I cannot leave home without ... craving the continuance of your kind communications during the ensuing Winter" (21 Oct. 1833, MHi:Adams-Waterhouse Corr.). The truth was—and this is the second telling point to be put on record here—that both of the Adamses shared a fellow feeling with Waterhouse not simply because of their early intimacy with him but because they believed he was to some extent the victim of the same forces in Federalist New England with which the Adamses were increasingly embattled after 1800, "the Junto-men" (as Waterhouse denominated them) who, at least in the eyes of these correspondents, dominated business and politics in Boston and academic affairs at Harvard. Over three hundred letters exchanged by Waterhouse with JA and JQA are known to survive, but this is by no means all that once existed, for Waterhouse's widow (the former Louisa Lee, his second wife, whom he had married in 1819) requested the return of his letters after his death, and her request was complied with, though fortunately only in part. (See correspondence of Mrs. Waterhouse with JQA and CFA in 1847-1848, in the Adams Papers.) It would appear that Mrs. Waterhouse destroyed most if not all of the letters then returned but preserved a substantial number of JA's and JQA's letters to her husband, now comprising the Adams-Waterhouse Correspondence in the MHS. Of these materials Worthington C. Ford edited a portion, chiefly JA's letters, with a few of Waterhouse's replies from the Adams Papers, in the pleasant volume he entitled *Statesman and Friend* (1927); and Donald M. Goodfellow printed one complete letter from JQA and extracts from others in his article, "Your Old Friend, J. Q. Adams," *NEQ*, 21:217-231 (June 1948).

On Waterhouse's career and his relations with the Adams family, see—besides the Ford and Goodfellow collections just mentioned, the specific letters cited above, and Waterhouse's published writings, often autobiographical in character —the following: Anonymous, "Sketch of the Life of Benjamin Waterhouse, M.D.," *The Polyanthos*, 2:74–86 (May 1806); John B. Blake, *Benjamin Waterhouse and the Introduction of Vaccination: A*

Reappraisal, Phila., 1957; John B. Blake, "Benjamin Waterhouse, Harvard's First Professor of Physic," *Jour. of Medical Education*, 33 (1958), unpaged offprint; Robert H. Halsey, *How the President, Thomas Jefferson, and Doctor Benjamin Waterhouse Established Vaccination as a Public Health Procedure* (N.Y. Acad. of Medicine, *Hist. of Medicine Ser.*, No. 5), N.Y., 1936; William Coolidge Lane, "Dr. Benjamin Waterhouse and Harvard University," Cambridge Hist. Soc., *Pubns.*, 4 (1909):5-22; William Roscoe Thayer, ed., "Extracts from the Journal [1836-1844] of Benjamin Waterhouse," same, p. 22-37; Josiah C. Trent, "Benjamin Waterhouse (1754-1846)," *Jour. of the Hist. of Medicine*, 1 (1946):357-364; Josiah C. Trent, "The London Years of Benjamin Waterhouse," same, p. 25-40; Henry R. Viets, article on Waterhouse in *DAB*.

It is certain that Waterhouse kept a journal while in Europe, for references in later letters and writings allude to or imply the existence of such a journal, and a letter from JA, 10 Jan. 1810, cautions Waterhouse: "The Extracts from your Journal I should think, those Parts I mean which relate to [James] Searle and another [Major William Jackson?], I should advise to be reserved from the Publick for the present" (MHi: Adams-Waterhouse Corr., printed in Ford, ed., *Statesman and Friend*). This suggests that Waterhouse was preparing his early journal, at least that part relating to his voyage home with CA and Gillon in 1781-1782, for publication at this time, but perhaps thanks to JA's advice his European journal seems never to have been published, and recent efforts to locate the original have been unsuccessful. It would doubtless shed desired light on the Adamses sojourn in the Netherlands if it could be found.

John Adams to Abigail Adams

My dearest Portia   Amsterdam Decr. 18. 1780

I have this morning sent Mr. Thaxter, with my two Sons to Leyden, there to take up their Residence for some time, and there to pursue their Studies of Latin and Greek under the excellent Masters, and there to attend Lectures of the celebrated Professors in that University. It is much cheaper there than here: the Air is infinitely purer; and the Company and Conversation is better.

It is perhaps as learned an University as any in Europe.

I should not wish to have Children, educated in the common Schools in this Country, where a littleness of Soul is notorious. The Masters are mean Spirited Writches, pinching, kicking, and boxing the Children, upon every Turn.[1]

Their is besides a general Littleness arising from the incessant Contemplation of Stivers and Doits, which pervades the whole People.

Frugality and Industry are virtues every where, but Avarice, and Stingyness are not Frugality.

The Dutch say that without an habit of thinking of every doit, before you spend it, no Man can be a good Merchant, or conduct Trade with Success. This I believe is a just Maxim in general. But I would never wish to see a Son of Mine govern himself by it. It is the sure and certain Way for an industrious Man to be rich. It is the only possible Way for a Merchant to become the first Merchant, or the richest Man in the Place. But this is an Object that I hope none of my Children will ever aim at.

It is indeed true, every where, that those who attend to small Expences are always rich.

I would have my Children attend to Doits and Farthings as devoutly as the meerest Dutchman upon Earth, if such Attention was necessary to support their Independence.

A Man who discovers a Disposition and a design to be independent seldom succeeds—a Jealousy arises against him. The Tyrants are alarmed on one side least he should oppose them. The slaves are allarmed on the other least he should expose their Servility. The Cry from all Quarters is, "He is the proudest Man in the World. He cant bear to be under Obligation."

I never in my Life observed any one endeavouring to lay me under particular Obligations to him, but I suspected he had a design to make me his dependant, and to have claims upon my Gratitude. This I should have no objection to—Because Gratitude is always in ones Power. But the Danger is that Men will expect and require more of Us, than Honour and Innocence and Rectitude will permit Us to perform.

In our Country however any Man with common Industry and Prudence may be independant.

But to put an End to this stuff Adieu, most affectionately Adieu.

RC (Adams Papers).

[1] This is apparently as close as JA came to informing AA at this time of the circumstances attending the withdrawal of JQA and CA from the Latin School in Amsterdam. See JA to the Rector and Preceptor, 18 Oct., "not sent," and the exchange between Rector Verheyk and JA, 10 Nov., all above.

James Lovell to Abigail Adams

Decr. 19th 1780

As you are entitled to a Wife's Portion of Mr. A's Honors and Satisfactions I inclose for your Reading some Papers to be afterwards forwarded to Holland.[1] I do not intend to have any of my future Letters to Mr. A. thrown overboard unless they are specially so directed on the Cover. I chalenge any body to tell the Contents truly. The Letters of Mr. Luzerne are never sunk.—I am told the Enemy have another Mail of ours or yours, this prevents my giving you such Explanations of my private Letter to Mr. A as I at first intended. I will only say that he has most ably and with *becoming Dignity* supported our Plan of March 18. without *much* piquing any great Minister. If you had not bantered me so more than once about my generally-enigmatic manner, and appeared so averse to cyphers I would have long ago enabled you to tell Mr. A some Things which you have most probably omitted, as well as to satisfy your Eve on the present Occasion. I will a little enlarge by *Mr. Penny* in a few days and send you a Key to use upon such Occasions as you may have from Mr. A or to him.—I am told Letters from Holland have been thrown from Vessels now arrived at Boston when only chased. Those losses at least might be avoided.

It is positively said to be a Post *from hence* Novr. 21 that has been robbed. In that Case *I suppose* you have lost a Letter from Mr. Adams covered by a few Lines from me.[2] We did on the 20th receive a Packet from Mr. A. and I see by my Almanack that on the 20th. and 21st. I wrote to many.

20th. Clarke & Nightingale, *Isaac Smith*, Mrs. L[ovell], Jemmy Jnr., Jos. Tho[ma]s, Doctr. Holten, Mr. Gerry.

21. Mrs. L[ovell], Doctr. Whitwell, *Mrs. Adams*, Govr. Hancock, Mr. S. Gridley.

I *hope* I gave the Letter for you to the Gentleman who must have carried those for Clarke & Nightingale and Mr. Smith but I really cannot recollect. I forwarded another to you on the 30th.[3]

The long Letter in the Advertizer is one of Mr. A's among the many that do him great honor.[4] But I really think the Essence would have been the printing of it in a London Paper at the Time it was written. I am my dear Madam yours respectfully,   JL

RC (Adams Papers). For the enclosures see notes 1 and 4.

[1] Presumably these included the following, all in Adams Papers: (1) a "public" letter to JA from Lovell, "for the Committee of foreign Affairs," 12 Dec., covering (2) Congress' resolution of the same date (printed in *JCC*, 18: 1147), acknowledging JA's letter of 26 June, and expressing "the Satisfaction which Congress receives from his Industrious Attentions to the Interest and honor of these United States, abroad, especially in the Transactions communicated to them by that Letter," which related to JA's correspondence with Vergennes on Congress' currency measures (see note 5 on Thaxter to JA, 7 Aug., vol. 3, above), and (3) a "private" letter from Lovell to JA, 14 Dec., which is partly in cipher and which among other things tells how this commendatory resolution came to be passed; also, possibly, (4) Samuel Huntington to JA, 18 Dec., expressing his pleasure and satisfaction in the dispatches received from JA during the past year and announcing that a secretary for foreign affairs is soon to be designated to conduct business with American representatives abroad (Adams Papers; JA, *Works*, 7:343).

[2] No letter from Lovell to AA of 21 Nov. 1780 has been found, and the letter from JA, to whomever addressed, has not been identified.

[3] Lovell to AA, 30 Nov., in Adams Papers but omitted here; it commends JA for the "very *masterly* and *independent* manner" in which he defended Congress' financial policy "against the Sentiments of the Ct. de Vergennes."

[4] Which "Advertizer" this was is not certain, but it was evidently a Philadelphia newspaper. "The long Letter" from JA was that of 2 June to Huntington commenting on Germain's speech of 6 May in Parliament (PCC, No. 84, II, printed in Wharton, ed., *Dipl. Corr. Amer. Rev.*, 3:752–758; LbC, Adams Papers, printed in JA, *Works*, 7:180–186). AA promptly caused it to be reprinted in the Boston papers; see her letter to Nathaniel Willis?, ante 4 Jan. 1781, below.

John Thaxter to John Adams

Sir   Leyden 19th. Decr. 1780

We arrived here last Evening at six oClock. This Morning We have a Sky and Air truly in the American Style. We have been to a Lecture, where many curious Experiments were made by the Professor of Medicine Mr. Horne.[1] At four Clock We go to a Law Lecture.

I have engaged two Rooms at fifteen Guilders per Month, in the same Lodgings with Mr. Waterhouse, whom I find very polite and attentive. On Thursday We take possession of them—I am very sorry We cannot be accommodated sooner.[2]

The Master for the Greek and Latin Languages will be engaged as soon as possible.

I hope soon to learn that your Eyes are much better.

I have the Honour to be, with perfect Respect, Sir, your most obedient Servt.,   J Thaxter Junr.

RC (Adams Papers).

[1] Johann David Hahn; see note 7 on (second) letter of JA to JQA, 23 Dec., below.

[2] For details on the lodgings see JQA to JA, 21 Dec., below.

John Adams to John Quincy Adams

My Son   Amsterdam Decr. 20. 1780

You are now at an University, where many of the greatest Men have received their Education.

Many of the most famous Characters, which England has produced, have pursued their Studies for some time at Leyden. Some, tho not many of the Sons of America, have studied there.

I would have you attend all the Lectures in which Experiments are made whether in Philosophy, Medicine or Chimistry, because these will open your mind for Inquiries into Nature: but by no means neglect the Languages.

I wish you to write me, an Account of all the Professorships, and the names of the Professors.[1] I should also be obliged to you for as good an Account of the Constitution of the University as you can obtain. Let me know what degrees are conferred there; by whom; and what Examination the Candidates undergo, in order to be admitted to them.

I am your affectionate Father,   John Adams[2]

RC (Adams Papers).

[1] JA himself shortly supplied these to JQA, in his (second) letter of 23 Dec., below.

[2] The order in which JA wrote his two letters to JQA of this date has been established only by guesswork. The beginning of the letter here placed second suggests that JA had been expecting a letter from JQA by the post of this day and was disappointed not to receive one. Besides writing twice to JQA, JA wrote twice this day to Thaxter at Leyden (see Thaxter to JA, 22 Dec., below), but these letters have not been found.

John Adams to John Quincy Adams

My dear John   Amsterdam Decr. 20. 1780

I have just received a Letter from Mr. Thaxter and another from your Brother,[1] and should have been equally pleased with one from you.

Write me as often as you can, and let me know what Professors you Attend and what Instructors attend you, whether you understand the Lectures &c.

The Lectures upon the Greek of the New Testament, I would have you all attend, and those upon Euripides, Sophocles, &c. too if you have Time, and it is thought proper.

You have now a Prize in your Hands indeed. Such as if you do not improve to the best Advantage, you will be without Excuse. But as I know you have an Ardent Thirst for Knowledge and a good Capacity to acquire it, I depend upon it, you will do no Dishonour to yourself nor to the University of Leyden.

Your affectionate Father, John Adams

RC (Adams Papers).

[1] Their letters were dated on the 19th, as stated in the following letter. That of Thaxter is printed above, but CA's has not been found.

John Quincy Adams to John Adams

Honoured Sir   Leyden December 21st 1780

Mr. Thaxter and brother Charles wrote both to you the day before yesterday and as I had no subject to write upon, I did not write But I can now give you an account of our journey.

We dined on Monday at Haerlem and arrived at Leyden at Six oclock. We lodged at the Cour de Hollande and saw Mr. Waterhouse that evening. The next day we went to hear a Medicinal lecture by Professor *Horn*, we saw several experiments there. In the afternoon we went to Hear a Law lecture by Professor *Pessel*.[1] Each lecture lasts an hour.

Yesterday Afternoon we moved from the Cour de Hollande to private lodgings in the same house in which Mr. Waterhouse boards our address is Mr. &c. by de Heer Welters, op de lange Burg, tegen over t Mantel Huis. Leyden.[2]

I was to day in company with the parson of the brownist Church Who seems to be a clever man, he is a scotch-man but does not pray for the king of England.[3]

I should be glad to have a pair of Scates they are of various prices from 3 Guilders to 3 Ducats those of a Ducat are as good as need to be but I should like to know whether you would chuse to have me give so much.

Mr. Waterhouse says that for riding I must have a pair leather breeches and a pair of boots. I should be glad if you would answer me upon that as soon as you receive this for there is a vacancy here

39

which begins to morrow and in the vacancy is the best time to begin to learn to ride.

In the vacancy there will be no lectures at all but our Master will attend us all the while as much as when there is no vacancy.

I continue writing in Homer, the Greek Grammar and Greek testament every day.

I am your most dutiful Son,   John Quincy Adams

RC (Adams Papers); addressed: "a Monsieur. Monsieur Adams. Chez Monsieur. Henry Schorn. Amsterdam"; endorsed: "John. Decr. 21," to which CFA added "1780."

¹ Frederik Willem Pestel; see note 4 on (second) letter of JA to JQA, 23 Dec., below.

² That is, at Mr. Welter's (more fully and correctly, F. Weller's or Willer's) in the street called Langebrug (Long Bridge) near the Mantle House. Recent efforts to identify the house have not succeeded, but it was not far from the main University building on the other side of the Rapenburg canal and still closer to the cathedral called the Pieterskerk (views of both buildings are reproduced in this volume) and to the Kloksteeg (Bell Lane), where Pastor John Robinson had ministered to his company of self-exiled English Separatists from 1609 to 1620 (and for some years afterward to those who did not leave for America); see the following note.

³ This passage shows JQA involved in at least a double confusion; and since JA and AA also, like many other Americans—historians and tourists alike—have been similarly confused, JQA's allusion to "the brownist Church" at Leyden requires clarification. By the term "brownist" JQA unquestionably meant the English Separatists, later commonly known as the Pilgrim Fathers; see the preceding note. But to call John Robinson's company Brownists was not accurate, for although the eccentric Robert Browne (1550?–1633?) is regarded as a precursor of New England Congregationalism, those Englishmen who followed Robinson first to Amsterdam in 1608 and in the following May to Leyden rejected much of Browne's teaching, and Robinson expressly rejected the term "Brownist" as applicable to his views. It was hardly to be expected, however,

that 18th-century Americans, great as their reverence was for the Pilgrim Fathers, would be aware of such theological niceties.

A worse confusion, and one that still troubles modern American pilgrims to Leyden, concerns the place where Robinson's company worshiped. JQA implies that it was in a building then still standing. A year and a half later JA was to write: "I have been to that Church in Leyden where the Planters of Plymouth worshiped so many Years, and felt a kind of Veneration for the Bricks and Timbers" (to Samuel Adams, 15 June 1782, NN:Bancroft Coll.). During her only visit to the Netherlands, AA also, of course, paid her respects to the founders of Plymouth Colony: "I would not omit to mention that I visited the Church at Leyden in which our forefathers worshipd when they fled from hierarchical tyranny and persecution. I felt a respect and veneration upon entering the Doors, like what the ancients paid to their Druids" (to Mary Smith Cranch, 12 Sept. 1786, MWA, printed repeatedly in CFA's editions of AA, *Letters*, 1840 *et seq.*). But the fact is, and was, that Robinson's company of Separatists had neither their own church building nor the use of any other in Leyden. If they had, it would have been a matter of public record, and no such record has been found by successive generations of diligent investigators. One of the first and most competent of these, the British scholar George Sumner, writing in 1842, concluded "that their religious assemblies were held in some hired hall, or in the house of Robinson, their pastor," which was in 1611 described as "large"

(George Sumner, "Memoirs of the Pilgrims at Leyden," MHS, *Colls.*, 3d ser., 9 [1846]:51–52). Sumner also identified the source of the Adamses' and others' confusion as Rev. Thomas Prince's famous *Annals*, first published in Boston, 1736, which in a footnote related that "when I was at Leyden in 1714, the most ancient people from their parents, told me, that the city had such a value for them [the English Separatists], as to let them have one of their churches, in the Chancel whereof he [Robinson] lies buried, which the English still enjoy" (Thomas Prince, *A Chronological History of New-England, in the Form of Annals . . .*, Boston, 1826, p. 238). *This* would make the cathedral church of St. Peter's (the great Pieterskerk, 1593) the Pilgrims' church, for here, as Sumner found from its records, Robinson was buried (although not in the chancel). What must have been pointed out by the Leydeners to Prince and later American visitors as the Pilgrim Church was the English (often and perhaps more correctly called the Scotch) Presbyterian or Reformed Church, which by coincidence had been founded at the same time that Robinson's congregation came to Leyden. With state approval and support, this church conducted public worship for almost two hundred years in a chapel allotted to it in a church on the grounds of the Cloister of the Veiled Nuns or Beguines (the Falyde Beguynhof). This church, as the Dutch scholar Plooij has pointed out, was "a part of the Dutch Reformed Church, organized as a separate congregation merely on account of the language used in its meetings." It was "Presbyterian, non-episcopal, and Non-conformist," but was "a State Church" (D. Plooij, *The Pilgrim Fathers from a Dutch Point of View*, N.Y., 1932, p. 47). The building the city provided backed up on the garden plot of Robinson's house on the Kloksteeg and in modern times has been used as part of the University's library; eventually most of the Leyden Pilgrims who stayed behind, including Robinson's widow and children, joined this congregation (same, p. 48, 90–91, 103). Sumner, who located the records of this church in Leyden for the period 1609–1807, concluded that "it is this chapel which, from being shown to American travellers as the old church of the English, has, I believe, been sometimes supposed by them to have been the church of the Pilgrims" (MHS, *Colls.*, 3d ser., 9 [1846]:49; see also p. 63–69).

Clearly this is what happened in the case of the Adamses, and it is confirmed by the extensive researches of the Dexters; a diagram in their monograph, though it is in part conjectural, shows the close physical relationships among the Pieterskerk, John Robinson's house (long since gone) where the Pilgrims conducted their private religious meetings without state support or interference, the large lot behind it on which small houses for some of Robinson's people were built, and the Beguine Cloister abutting that lot (Henry Martyn Dexter and Morton Dexter, *The England and Holland of the Pilgrims*, Boston and N.Y., 1905, p. 500 ff.).

JA eventually corrected himself (and Benjamin Waterhouse) on the distinction between the followers of Browne and those of Robinson, in a letter to Waterhouse of 8 Jan. 1807 (MHi: Adams-Waterhouse Coll.; Ford, ed., *Statesman and Friend*, p. 39–40), but he persisted in believing that the church he had attended in Leyden was the church of the Pilgrims.

The Scottish "parson of the brownist Church" whom JQA met was named William Mitchell, according to the records printed by Sumner (MHS, *Colls.*, 3d ser., 9 [1846]:66).

Mercy Otis Warren to Abigail Adams

My Dear Mrs. Adams   Plimouth Dec. 21 1780

I should have wrote before according to promiss, but have been prevented the use of my Eyes by a Cold fixing there and Even now believe I had better not write, but unless I do your *Excelency* may think it too Great Condesention to inquire after the Cottagers, at Plimouth.

You have spent a week at Boston, and what think you of affairs now. I dare say you have Collected many Curious annecdotes, and have had opportunities of observing much on the Manners, [...]etition,[1] inclinations and Adulation of the times.

We have scarcly heard from the Capital since we left it, and so totally secluded is this place from any thing that passes in the rest of the World, that only one Common News paper has found Its way hither since we were at your house. Yet I have more than a Ballance for all the Amusements the City or the *Court* can give, when my best Friend is my Companion, my Children are well, and Domestic peace reigns under my Roof.

Have you found an opportunity to forward my letter to my son, and do you hear any thing to be Communicated from yours or their Good father.

I forgot to ask when at Braintree why you was so solicitous when at Plimouth for the Copy of a letter to my son on his reading of Chesterfeild. Whither Mrs. Adams had made any use of it, and what, and if she had done with it to return the Manuscript.[2]

Tomorrow is a sort of Festival in this town.[3] I Wish you and yours and some other Choice Friends were hear to make it truly so.

A thousand Reflections might occupy the Mind on this occasion, and then I beleive I must keep them and hasten to shut my Eyes, least I should not be able to read your Epistles which I soon Expect.

Love to My Dear Naby from your assured & affectionate friend,

M Warren

A Word or two on Trade and Commerce. Have not sold a single Article nor Can. The town is full of Hank a[chiefs.][4] Your price is too high. They are dull at a Doller. But shall not sell so without your order. I will send the Apron by Mr. Warren. You need not send the silk till I Call for it. Perhaps I may prefer the taking some other article in Lieu therof.

What did my Freind do with a billet Left to her care for my sister. She never Recevd it.

RC (Adams Papers); addressed: "Mrs. Abigail Adams   Foot of Pens hill Braintree   Favd. by Mr. Green."

[1] Word partly covered by seal.

[2] Mercy Warren's epistolary essay on Lord Chesterfield's letters to his natural son, 24 Dec. 1779, a copy of which remains among the Adams Papers. See AA to Mrs. Warren, 28 Feb. and 1 Sept.,

both in vol. 3 above, and, for the publication of the essay in a Boston newspaper, AA to Nathaniel Willis?, ante 4 Jan. 1781, below.

[3] The earliest American annual patriotic "Festival," Forefathers' Day was celebrated at Plymouth on 22 Dec., beginning in 1769 under the convivial sponsorship of the Old Colony Club. (The Club had a short life, but its role as sponsor was later taken over by the Pilgrim Society.) The date chosen was supposed to be the anniversary of the landing of the Pilgrims at "Forefathers' Rock" (later called Plymouth Rock), given by William Bradford in his *History*

as 11 Dec. 1620. Forgetting, or not knowing, that the difference between the Julian and Gregorian calendars in the 17th century was ten rather than eleven days as in the 18th century, the promoters of the celebration made an error of a day (it should have been the 21st), which later occasioned a warm dispute among antiquarians. The records of the Old Colony Club, 1769–1773, are printed in MHS, *Procs.*, 2d ser., 3 [1886–1887]:382–444. For the dispute over the date, in which JQA found himself somewhat ludicrously involved, see same, vol. 20 [1906–1907]:237–238.

[4] MS torn.

Benjamin Waterhouse to John Adams

Respected Sir   Leyden 21st. Decemr. 1780

I have the satisfaction of informing you that Mr. Thaxter and your Sons are now settled in their lodgings in the same house with me. I could wish the rooms were better as well as larger, but they think the[y] answer very well, and seem well pleased with their situation. Tomorrow we are to converse with the teacher of Latin and Greek, and to make our terms &c. with him, this person teaches the Sons of the *Griffier Fagell*[1] and gives great satisfaction. I imagine your eldest must attend him a while before he attends the public lectures on the greek, the master however can judge of that when he examines him. The christmas vacancy commences this day, but that makes no difference with these private-teachers. I think with Mr. Thaxter and several others that Charles is too young to attend any of the publick lectures yet. The Lectures on Grotius and the Law of nature are what I imagine you wish them to attend, one is given in the forenoon, the other in the afternoon by the same Professor. I am in hopes by Monday next we shall get fairly *under:way*. The gentlemen came into their lodgings but last night, and to day have been visited by all those gentlemen who call themselves the english-Society only because they speak our languague. The English-clergyman[2] came to see us this morning and to tell us how glad he was to have this addition to his little flock. Tomorrow we are invited to Mr. Luzac's,[3] and that finishes our visits. I had sent me a day or two since a number of questions concerning this University, they were written at Boston, or Jamaica-plains by I guess Mr. G.[4] I have answered them as well as I could and sent them to the gentleman who transmitted them to me, they were dated November 4th 1780. The history of this University is I find almost too intricate for a stranger to unravell.

I believe Mr. John reather wishes me to propose to you his learning to ride. I can only say I would not have missed those few lessons I have had for ten times the sum they cost me besides the advantages resulting from the exercise, and the company we generally find there; Mr. Luzac and his brother ride twice a week with us, more for exercise than instruction. We pay, for the first 16. Lessons 30. guilders: for every 16. after 20 Guilders; and generally take three lessons a week. I imagine Mr. Thaxter from what he already sees thinks they three can live here for the sum, that it would cost for *one* at Amsterdam, that may however not be, yet I am confident a person can live here for half the sum he pays at Amsterdam provided he lives and takes his rooms as a student.

Mr. Luzac desires his compliments to you. I am with great respect your friend & Countryman,   Benjn. Waterhouse

RC (Adams Papers); addressed: "Son Excellence Monsieur Adams Ministre Plenipotentiare des Etats Unis de l'Amerique Chez Monsieur Henry Schorn a Amsterdam"; postal marking, stamped(?) in script characters: "Leyden"; endorsed: "Dr. Waterhouse Decr. 21. Leyden," to which CFA added "1780."

[1] Hendrik Fagel (1706–1790), *griffier* (secretary or "graphiary") of the States General, a leading figure in the Dutch government and at the court of the Stadholder (*Nieuw Ned. Biog. Woordenboek*, 3:390–391). JA was to have important relations with him, not always of the pleasantest sort because Fagel was a strong adherent of the House of Orange and hence of the pro-English party in the Netherlands; see JA, *Diary and Autobiography*, 3:1, 5, and *passim*.

[2] William Mitchell; see note 3 on JQA to JA, this date, above.

[3] Jean Luzac (1746–1807), legal and classical scholar, later *rector magnificus* of the University of Leyden, and for many years editor of *Nouvelles extraordi-naires de divers endroits*, better known as the *Gazette de Leyde*, a Dutch newspaper with an international circulation. An apostle of the Enlightenment and a deeply interested observer of events in America, Luzac was one of JA's first and firmest friends in the Netherlands, and their friendship long survived JA's mission there. See *Nieuw Ned. Biog. Woordenboek*, 1:1290–1294; JA, *Diary and Autobiography*, vols. 2–3 *passim*. There is extensive correspondence of both JA and JQA with Luzac in the Adams Papers.

[4] Presumably Rev. William Gordon of Jamaica Plain near Boston, on whom see the editorial note and references at 1:229–230.

John Quincy Adams to John Adams

Honoured Sir   Leyden December 22d 1780

I have this day received two letters from you of the 20th. in one of which you say you would have me attend all the lectures in which Experiments are made, but I shall have to attend two lectures upon law, and therefore shall have no time. As to the lecture upon Greek; there is but one, and the Gentlemen with whom Mr. Thaxter has consulted, think that it is necessary, to have made some proficiency in the Greek Language, to be able to attend it.

I have this day seen the master who is to teach us greek and Latin.[1] He is to come to us twice a day; from twelve to one oclock and from five to six in the afternoon, so that I shall be two hours occupied with our master an hour at each lecture is two more and the rest of my time I shall be writing from Homer, the Greek testament, of Grammar, and learning lessons for our Master.[2]

This is a famous day in new England. The anniversary of the landing of our forefathers at Plimouth.[3]

Our master is to begin with us to morrow.

We are all invited to drink tea with Mr. Luzac to day.

The scene in which Shakespear speaks of Brownist is in the third volume page 121. in Twelfth night or what you will, Act 3 Scene 4th. If you borrow Mr. Searle's Shakespear you will see it there.[4]

I am your Dutiful Son,   John Quincy Adams

RC (Adams Papers); addressed: "A Monsieur Monsieur Adams. Chez Monsieur Henry Schorn. a Amsterdam"; endorsed: "Mr. John Decr. 22. ansd. 23," to which CFA added "1780." This letter was originally enclosed in Thaxter's to JA of this date, following.

[1] JA on 11 Jan. 1781 "Was present [in Leyden] from 12. to one O Clock, when the Præceptor gave his Lessons in Latin and Greek to my Sons. His Name is Wenshing. He is apparently a great Master of the two Languages, besides which he speaks French and Dutch very well. . . . He is pleased with [his pupils] and they with him" (*Diary and Autobiography*, 2:451). John Thaxter in his letter of this date, following, gives the tutor's name as "Wensing."
[2] Punctuation as in MS.

[3] See note 3 on Mrs. Warren's letter to AA of 21 Dec., above.
[4] Sir Andrew Aguecheek: "An't be any way, it must be with valour; for policy I hate. I had as lief be a Brownist as a politician" (*Twelfth Night*, Act III, scene ii, in modern editions). The volume- and page-reference furnished by JQA is to an edition of *The Works of Shakespeare* published at Edinburgh in 8 vols., 1769–1771, Alexander Donaldson printer.

John Thaxter to John Adams

Sir   Leyden 22d. Decr. 1780

I had the Honour of your favour of the 20th[1] this Morning. I am happy to hear that your Eyes are better.

Altho' I have not as yet been able to obtain a Master for the Children, yet they are pursuing their Studies. The Master that is recommended is said to be the best in the place, and has a happy Faculty in teaching the Languages. The Vacancy begins to day and lasts for three Weeks. The Lectures of a Public kind finish to day also, for the same Term as the Vacancy. This is a great Misfortune, but nevertheless the Time may be profitably spent in the Languages with the Master, who will have perhaps the more Leisure.

There are public Lectures here of various Denominations—namely, upon the Law of Nature, upon Grotius, Natural Philosophy, Theology, Medicine, Chymistry, Anatomy, and one upon Greek. Besides these there are private Lectures upon the History and Constitutions of particular Countries and Nations; but these are given to young Gentlemen of those Countries and Nations for their own Information and Instruction. The Professor of Law is a celebrated Character—his Name is ⟨Pestle⟩ Pestel—a German. He gives the private Lectures above-mentioned.

Since writing the above, I have recieved your other Letter of the 20th and the Inclosure.[2] I have engaged the Master this Moment, at the rate of thirty Guilders per month—his Name is Wensing—he is an Usher of the high School here. Mr. Gunter who has resided here for seven Years, and is a Governor to a German Baron, has been very polite in this Business. The Master will attend the Children two Hours every day, and I am informed his Price is modest. He comes tomorrow to give Lessons, and I hope things will go on smoothly.

When I am more informed of the Constitution, Laws and Arrangements of this University, I shall be particularly happy in communicating them to You. As to my Situation, it is agreable as any European Spot of Earth can be. You have desired to know all my Wants and Wishes. I esteem it a fresh Instance of your Kindness to me, Sir: but few fall to my Share at present. Some You know, Sir, every one has, that there is an Impropriety in revealing.

I have the Honour to congratulate [you][3] on the day, and to be with perfect Respect, Sir, your Excellency's most obedient Servant,

J. Thaxter Junr.

RC (Adams Papers); endorsed: "M. Thaxter Decr. 22. ansd. 24. 1780." Enclosure: JQA to JA, 22 Dec., preceding.

[1] Not found.
[2] Neither letter nor enclosure has been found.
[3] Word editorially supplied.

John Adams to John Quincy Adams

My dear Son   Amsterdam Decr. 23. 1780

I last night received yours of 21st. I have written twice to Mr. Thaxter and inclosed in each Letter, one for you and another for Charles.[1] I directed the Letters to Mr. Thaxter a la Cour D'Hollande. Enquire for them at that House.

You tell me you attended a Lecture on Medicine, but you have mistaken the Name of the Professor. It is not Horn, but Hahn. Is not the Professor of Law named Pestel?

Mr. Thaxter may purchase each of you a Pair of Scates. He may go to what Price he thinks proper—but be careful and moderate in the Use of them.

You may get the Leather Breeches and Boots, but have them made large, otherwise, you grow so fast, that you will not be able to wear them many months. I would have you all take some Lessons at the Riding school.

I am pleased to hear that you continue writing in the Greek Testament, &c.

Your Letter is well written, but I think that in order to improve your Hand you should write Copies every day. Write to me, as often as you can, and let me know every Thing concerning that famous University, where you are.—I am your affectionate Father,

John Adams

I have received Lillys Grammar and Clarks Exercises for you.[2] Perhaps you can get them at Leyden. If you can I will keep these. I have this Moment received Mr. Thaxters, inclosing yours and your Brothers of the 22d[3]—shall answer in due time.

RC (Adams Papers); addressed: "Mynheer John"; endorsed: "Pappa's letter of December 23d Answer'd December 24th 1780   No. 3"; docketed by JQA in a later hand: "J. Adams 23 Decr: 1780." (JQA's answer of 24 Dec. has not been found.)

[1] JQA to JA, 21 Dec., is above. JA's two letters to Thaxter have not been found; his letters to JQA, enclosed therein, must be those of 20 Dec., both above; his letters to CA, also enclosed, have not been found.

[2] Both these books survive in the Boston Athenæum, probably in the very copies sent by JA for JQA's use. They are William Lily, *A Short Introduction of Grammar ... of the Latin Tongue,* London, 1742, which bears the inscrip- tion "John Quincy Adams, his Book"; and John Clark, *Introduction à la syntaxe latine,* two copies, both Paris, 1773, but with different publishers' names, one bearing JQA's signature and the date 1778, and the other with his signature, a handwritten jingle, and the date 1779. See *Catalogue of JQA's Books,* p. 107, 91.

[3] Thaxter's and JQA's letters of the 22d are above; no letter from CA of that date has been found.

John Adams to John Quincy Adams

My dear Son   Amsterdam Decr. 23. 1780

Yours of the 22d came to hand this Morning. I shall leave it wholly to Mr. Thaxters Judgment, what Lectures you are to attend, as at this distance I cannot form any opinion.

You will apply the most of your Attention, I hope, to your Latin and Greek Master, for the present.

I am pleased to see that you recollect the 22 of December, the day on which, those Patriots and Heroes landed at Plymouth, who emigrated immediately from the Town where you now are. It is impossible, but you must ever entertain a Veneration for the Memory of those great and good Men, to whose adventurous Spirit and inflexible Virtue you certainly, as well as I owe our Existence.

I wish you, in your next Letter, to transcribe me the Passage of Shakespear, in which the Brownists are mentioned.

You should treat the Minister of that Society, in Leyden with the greatest Respect, and attend his Meeting, every Sunday both in the forenoon and Afternoon.

You will also behave with the Utmost Respect to Mr. Luzacs Family who are worthy People and very good Friends to your Country.

I have heard a very great Character of Mr. Hemsterhuis, formerly Professor of Greek, in the University of Leyden,[1] and that the present Professor of that Language is a Disciple of his Mr. Valkennaar.[2]

And that another Disciple of his Mr. Rhunkenius, is Professor of History and Eloquence. This Mr. Rhunkenius has published an Edition of an Hymn to Ceres, (found in Russia, and supposed to have been composed by Homer) with a Latin Translation and Notes. I would have you purchase that Hymn.[3]

Mr. Pestel is Professor of the Law of nations and of the publick Law.[4]

Mr. Voorda is Professor of the civil Law, that is to say as I understand it, of the Roman Imperial Law, as the Institutes of Justinian &c.[5] Pray enquire whether he reads Lectures upon the whole Corpus Juris, the Digest, the Code, the Novells &c., whether he takes any Notice of the Feudal Law, that is of the Consuetudines Feudorum, and whether any Mention is made of the Cannon Law.

Mr. Vanderkesel is another Professor of the civil Law, but what is his Department?[6]

Mr. Dehahn is Professor of Medicine and Chymistry.[7]

Mr. Allemand is Professor of Experimental Philosophy.[8]

I wish you to make all the Enquiries possible concerning these learned Professors, and let me know whether I have their Names and Departments right.

Let me know also whether you are matriculated into the University. If not, I wish you to procure the Priviledge and Honour, provided you can by the Rules of the University be admitted to it. The Expence is not to be regarded.

I hope in short that you will inform yourself as perfectly as possible concerning, the Origin, the Progress, the Institutions, Regulations, Revenues &c. of that celebrated University, and especially to remark every Thing in it, that may be imitated, in the Universities of your own Country.

Let me know whether there is any Professor of Mathematicks and in what manner they are taught.—Here are Enquiries enough for you, a long time.—Dont neglect to write me often.

Your affectionate Father,   John Adams

RC (Adams Papers); endorsed: "Pappa's letter of Decr: 23   Answer'd Decr: 26–1780   No. 4"; docketed by JQA in a later hand: "J. Adams 23 Decr: 1780." (JQA's answer of 26 Dec. has not been found.)

Also Tr in hand of CFA, numbered by him "No. 275." This is one of the large number of transcripts of family letters, 1780–1843, mentioned in the Introduction to Series II of *The Adams Papers* (vol. 1:xxxiii, above). These were evidently prepared in and about 1843, some doubtless earlier and others quite possibly after JQA's death in 1848, with a view to publishing a more comprehensive collection of family letters than, in the end, CFA issued. The numbering of the earliest letters among the transcripts suggests that CFA proposed to include these in his edition of the JA–AA *Familiar Letters* of 1876, because numbers he assigned them correspond closely with the numbers of adjacently dated letters printed in that volume (see note on JA to JQA, 17 March 1780, vol. 3:309, above); but he finally excluded them and never carried out his earlier plan for a collection of family letters in which JQA was to be the central figure and his parents, wife, brother TBA, and son CFA the other correspondents. It should be stated here that, except for special circumstances, the existence of a CFA transcript alongside the original in the Adams Papers will not hereafter be recorded in descriptive notes on letters in the *Adams Family Correspondence*.

[1] Tiberius Hemsterhuis (1685–1766), professor of Greek and of national (i.e. Dutch or "vaderlandsche") history, 1740–1765 (*Nieuw Ned. Biog. Woordenboek*, 1:1068–1072; *Album studiosorum Academiae Lugduno Batavae, MDLXXV–MDCCCLXXV . . .*, The Hague, 1875). The register of the Leyden faculties in the compilation called the *Album studiosorum* has also been used in the biographical notes below

to confirm dates of appointment, &c.

[2] Lodowijk Caspar Valckenaer (1715–1785), professor of Greek from 1766, and of native history from 1768 (*Nieuw Ned. Biog. Woordenboek*, 1:1514–1516).

[3] David Ruhnken (1723–1798), reader in Greek from 1757, and professor of history and oratory from 1761 (*Nieuw Ned. Biog. Woordenboek*, 10:851–854). His edition of the Hymn

to Ceres, from a codex recently found in Moscow and attributed to Homer, was published this year: *Hymnus in Cererem, nunc primus editus a Davide Ruhnkenio,* Leyden, 1780; a copy was sent by Thaxter to JA under cover of a letter dated 25 Jan. 1781, below, and remains among JA's books in the Boston Public Library (*Catalogue of JA's Library,* p. 122).

[4] Frederik Willem Pestel (1724–1805), professor of jurisprudence from 1763 (*Nieuw Ned. Biog. Woordenboek,* 3:968–969). Pestel was one of the great figures in Dutch legal scholarship, and JA acquired both his *Commentarii de Republica Batava,* Leyden, 1782, and *Fundamenta jurisprudentiae naturalis,* Leyden, 1777 (*Catalogue of JA's Library,* p. 191; see also Thaxter to JA, 1, 23 Jan. 1781, below).

[5] Bavius Voorda (1729–1799), professor of Roman law from 1765; in 1781 he served as *rector magnificus* of the University; because of his prominence in the Dutch Patriotic (anti-Orangist) party he was dismissed from the University in 1788, but was restored in 1795 during the French regime (*Nieuw Ned. Biog. Woordenboek,* 3: 1336–1338).

[6] Dionysius Godefridus van der Keesel (1738–1816), professor of Roman law from 1770 (*Nieuw Ned. Biog. Woordenboek,* 3:674–675).

[7] Johann David Hahn (1729–1784), professor of medical practice and of chemistry from 1775 (*Nieuw Ned. Biog. Woordenboek,* 8:666; mention only).

[8] Jean Nicolas Sébastien Allamand (1713–1787), professor of philosophy and mathematics from 1749, and of experimental physics from 1761 (*Nieuw Ned. Biog. Woordenboek,* 1:75–77).

Abigail Adams to John Adams

My Dearest Friend   December 25 1780

How much is comprised in that short sentance? How fondly can I call you mine, bound by every tie, which consecrates the most inviolable Friendship, yet seperated by a cruel destiny, I feel the pangs of absence sometimes too sensibly for my own repose.

There are times when the heart is peculiarly awake to tender impressions, when philosophy slumbers, or is overpowerd by sentiments more conformable to Nature. It is then that I feel myself alone in the wide world, without any one to tenderly care for me, or lend me an assisting hand through the difficulties that surround me, yet my cooler reason dissaproofs the repineing thought, and bids me bless the hand from whence my comforts flow.

> "Man active resolute and bold
> is fashioned in a different mould."

More independant by Nature, he can scarcly realize all those ties which bind our sex to his. Is it not natural to suppose that as our dependance is greater, our attachment is stronger?—I find in my own breast a sympathetic power always operating upon the near approach of Letters from my dear absent Friend. I cannot determine the exact distance when this secret charm begins to operate. The time is sometimes longer and sometimes shorter, the Busy Sylphs are ever at my ear, no sooner does Morpheus close my Eyes, than "my whole Soul, unbounded flies to thee." Am I superstitious enough for a good Catholick?

A Mr. Ross arrived lately at Philadelphia and punctually deliverd your Letter's.[1] At the same time a vessel arrived from Holland, and brought me yours from Amsterdam of the 25 of Sepbr. which Mr. Lovell was kind enough to forward to me. I have written you largely since Davis arrived here, tho not in reply to Letters brought by him, for old Neptune alone had the handling of them. He was chased and foolishly threw over all his Letters into the sea, to my no small mortification. A Brig which came out with him arrived at Providence and brought me yours of Sepbr. 15th together with some from Mr. Thaxter. —The things you sent came safe to hand. Jones not yet arrived. I suppose he may have the much wanted trunk on Board, which you suppose came in the Alliance. You call upon me to write, by every opportunity. I do not omit any, yet my Letters many of them must take so circuitous a Route, that they must cost you much more than they are worth.

This I hope will go direct to France by Col. Pallfry, if he does not sail before it reaches Philadelphia.—The Enemy have met with many disastrous events in Charlestown. As much as they Boast, they have more occasion to mourn. We have had several successes there which do honour to American Arms.

If the people can strugle through the demands this year made upon them, and accomplish what they are striving after, the filling their Army for 3 years or the War, they will do great things towards a negotiation for peace.

The present demand for supplies for the Army, the payment of our 3 and 6 months Men, together with our continental taxes, and govermental expences, oblige every person to look about them, to retrench every Luxery and economize with the utmost frugality. The remittances you have been so kind as to make me, have enabled me hitherto to answer all demands made upon me. I have still much more to pay before the close of the year. I have been trying to collect a list of the Taxes for the present year but have not yet been able. My Tenants groan and say they cannot live, that the whole stock of the place would not pay the yearly tax. Every body groans, yet every body sees the necessity of complying with the requisition. We have in this Town allready collected money to purchase 22 thousand weight of Beaf. We had just accomplished it when out comes an other tax for 46 thousand weight more to be paid by the first of Jan'ry. We have just paid our 3 months men, and our six are returning with loud calls upon us, 46 men are calld to fill our continental Army for 3 years or the war, which are to be procured at any rate. Can you judge of our present Burden? I hope we shall surmount all and yet see happy and peacefull days.

I told you in a former letter that our Season was embitterd by a most distressing drought, yet the year is crowned with universal Health. We have reason to sing of Mercy and judgment.

Admiral de Ternay died last week with a Fever at Road Island. Our Friends are all well, so is your ever affectionate   Portia

Complements to Mr. Dana. Love to my dear John and Charles. I mourn the loss of their Letters by Davis.

Stevens'ens [2] Brother has received a Letter from him dated in Amsterdam in August, in which he tells him that he had sent a Number of hankerchifs, some for Mr. Bracket and some for Mr. Bass and a Letter with them directing him what to do with the remainder, but is so stupid as not to say, by whom he sent them nor from whence, neither the vessels Name nor captains—they are not come to hand. The owners come to me to inquire. I cannot give them the least direction, know not a word about them. In future if he does Buisness, he had better be more correct—he must write to them about them. [3]

RC (Adams Papers); docketed by CFA: "Portia. Decr. 25th. 1780." As stated in the text, this letter was sent to Philadelphia to be carried to France by William Palfrey, who however sailed before it arrived. James Lovell forwarded it to JA in a letter of 8 Jan. 1781 (Adams Papers); see Lovell to AA, 8 Jan. 1781, below. Concerning the second postscript see note 3.

[1] These letters, clearly not addressed to AA, are not precisely identifiable.
[2] Joseph Stephens (or Stevens), JA's servant, who accompanied JA abroad, has been earlier identified (vol. 3:33).

[3] It is not certain that this second postscript belongs with the foregoing letter. It is on a detached fragment of paper, and though filed with this letter may have been sent at another time.

John Thaxter to John Adams

Sir   Leyden 26th. Decr. 1780

I had the Honour of your favour of the 24th. instant [1] this morning.

The Master has been here twice this day and given for the first time Lessons in Greek and Latin to the Young Gentlemen. I am happy that they have begun. Their Instructor appears to be well acquainted with his Business, and to proceed with great Judgment. The Greek Grammar is one of his own Composition, and at present in Manuscript. It appears an Analysis of the Principles of Grammar. Master John transcribes his Lessons from it, which will be useful to him; for he forms a Grammar as he advances, becomes acquainted by Consequence with its principles, and establishes them firmly in his Mind. One would think this foundation good and sure.

Master Charles transcribes his Lessons in Latin also. In this Language his Exercises are equally good with Master John's in Greek. He has the principles before him, and his Instructor to explain them. The Exercises in the Articles, Nouns, Verbs &c. in both Languages cannot fail to be beneficial. In my humble Opinion they are fundamentally right, and will go on in the Languages with great Satisfaction to You and themselves. They both desire their Duty to You, and desire me to acquaint You that their Instructor has prevented them from acknowledging the Receipt of their Papa's Letter.[2] They have been busy indeed.

As to News, Sir, was I mured in a Cloister I should not hear less. I hear no Politicks at all—every thing is Peace here.

Your Question I will answer in a few days. I hope to have some Conversation on that Subject with a Gentleman, who was about writing an Account of this University.

I have the Honor to be, Sir, your most obedient Servt.,

J. Thaxter

RC (Adams Papers); endorsed: "Mr. Thaxter, Ans. 27. Decr. 1780."

[1] Not found.
[2] JA had written two letters to JQA on the 23d, which are above; no letter to CA of that date or immediately thereafter has been found.

Benjamin Waterhouse to John Adams

Respected Sir   Leyden 26th. Decembr. 1780

I was glad to find by your letter of the 23d. inst.[1] that what we have hitherto done meets with your approbation, and it is with no small satisfaction that I see all three of my countrymen pleased and contented with their situation.

In regard to Mr Charles's attending the lectures there is no rule or custom that forbids him. As there are none so young who attend the public-lectures, we only thought the students would consider him as a little boy brought by his governor to keep him out of harms way and treat him accordingly, but nothing hinders him from frequenting them if you desire it. They began with their language master this day. I stood by this afternoon while he taught them, and I am sure you would be highly pleased both with his method and his pains. He uses no printed grammar, but the boys form one from his dictating, so that I tell Mr. John that he can send his father a greek grammar in his own hand writing, and Charles a latin one. The Master spends an hour with them in the forenoon and an hour in the afternoon leaving them full two hours writing a peice every day. This with two Lectures is I am sure as much as they possibly can do at this season. Mr. Thaxter, Mr Gunther (preceptor of the german Noble) and myself have considered the point with attention and we are convinced they cannot go to three lectures a day and perform the task set them by the Master.

I am not a little afflicted at hearing by the last Mail that Dr. Fothergill was suddenly seized with a very dangerous disorder in the bladder, insomuch that I dread to hear the next news from London. If he dies he will not leave a better man behind him, nor has America a warmer or more constant friend in that country than he. We owe him much, his friendship for our country will be better known and felt in a future day, his partiality for us and our cause have drawn upon him more than once the calumny and hatred of a set of men who are prone to speak evil of *the things they know not.*[2]

I never knew till you mentioned it that the church where we now meet is the same where our venerable forefathers worshiped for a few years before they went to the Land of promise; had I known it, I should like you have venerated the very stones.[3] With no less veneration and wonder will the transactions even of these our days be read and contemplated in future times. I often amuse myself by looking thro', as it were, the mental-telescope to distant times to see if I can discover their opinions concerning us, I mean so far distant when some of our countrymen go over to England in the character of Antiquarians to search into a heap of rubish, where they can scarce believe once stood the capital of a mighty kingdom. I hear them disputing which side of the river St. Paul's stood, and see them struck with astonishment when they are assured that the city which once stood there or thereabouts, was as large as Philadelphia is now! I say when I look thus into future times I am in hopes they will not at least curse their active forefathers of the present day, on the contrary I trust they will venerate some now living with a veneration equal to that of any men of any country that ever was. But I think of these things as I do of our own happy fire:sides in America without remembering the immense tract of rough, rude sea, that lies between us, so am I apt to forget the wars, bloodshed, horrors, and confusion, that will in all probability intervene between this and the time I speak of.

I imagine this frost will impede Comdr. Gillons preparations.[4] If he is bound to Boston I should be very sorry to miss such a favourable oppetunity, but if [he does not][5] go to any port in New England I had pe[rhaps] better wait untill the next Ship.

I am with great respect your friend & Countryman,

Benjn: Waterhouse

RC (Adams Papers); addressed: "Son Excellence Monsieur Adams"; docketed in John Thaxter's hand: "Dr. Waterhouse 26th. Decr. 1780."

[1] Not found.

[2] John Fothergill (1712–1780), of London, Quaker physician, botanist, philanthropist, and friend of Americans and the American cause; he died on the day this letter was written (*DNB*; Betsy Copping Corner and Christopher C. Booth, eds., *Chain of Friendship: Selected Letters of Dr. John Fothergill of London, 1735–1780*, Cambridge, 1971). Waterhouse's close relationship with Fothergill has been noted in the sketch of the former under Waterhouse to JA, 13 Dec., above.

[3] See note 3 on JQA to JA, 21 Dec., above.

[4] Alexander Gillon (1741–1794), said to have been born in Rotterdam but long established in Charleston as a merchant and shipowner, had introduced himself to JA on the road between Paris and Nantes in the spring of 1779. He held the title of commodore of the South Carolina navy and had come to Europe to obtain ships, stores, and funds to launch this navy. When JA arrived in Amsterdam in Aug. 1780, Gillon was readying a vessel, renamed the *South Carolina*, and supplies he had obtained on credit, and he proved helpful as an interpreter and in finding lodgings for JA and his family at the Widow Schorn's. In Aug. 1781, when Gillon finally sailed with great secrecy from the Texel in order to escape his creditors, two of the passengers on board the *South Carolina* were CA and Benjamin Waterhouse. Gillon's route was highly circuitous, quarrels broke out between him and some of his passengers, and in the end CA crossed the Atlantic in another vessel, from La Coruña in Spain. See *Biog. Dir. Cong.*, under Gillon; JA, *Diary and Autobiography*, 2:446–447; JA, *Corr. in the Boston Patriot*, p. 178, 267–268, 345–346, 572; JQA, *Diary*, 11–12 Aug. 1780; Gillon to JA, 12 Nov. 1780 (Adams Papers); John Trumbull, *Autobiography*, ed. Theodore Sizer, New Haven, 1953, p. 75–77; D. E. Huger Smith, "Commodore Alexander Gillon and the Frigate South Carolina," *So. Car. Hist. & Geneal. Mag.*, 9 (1908): 189–219; Madison, *Papers*, ed. Hutchinson, 4:111–113; also letters later in the present volume touching on CA's voyage, especially AA to JA, 29 Sept. 1781, and Waterhouse to JA, 30 Sept. 1781.

[5] Here and below, MS is torn by seal.

John Adams to John Quincy Adams

My Son   Amsterdam Dec. 28. 1780

The Ice is so universal now that I suppose you spend some Time in Skaiting every day. It is a fine Exercise for young Persons, and therefore I am willing to indulge you in it, provided you confine yourself to proper Hours, and to strict Moderation. Skaiting is a fine Art. It is not Simple Velocity[1] or Agility that constitutes the Perfection of it but Grace. There is an Elegance of Motion, which is charming to the sight, and is useful to acquire, because it obliges you to restrain that impetuous Ardour and violent Activity, into which the Agitation of Spirits occasioned by this Exercise is apt to hurry you, and which is inconsistent both with your Health and Pleasure.

At Leyden, I suppose you may see many Gentlemen, who are perfect in the Art.—I have walked, several Times round this City from the Gate of Utrecht to that of Harlem, and seen some thousands Skaiting upon the Cingel, since the Frost set in. I have seen many skait with great Spirit, some with prodigious Swiftness, a few with a tolerably genteel Air, but none with that inimitable Grace and Beauty which I have seen some Examples of, in other Countries, even in our own.

I have seen some Officers of the British Army, at Boston, and some of our Army at Cambridge, skait with as perfect Elegance, as if they had spent their whole Lives in the study of Hogarths Principles of Beauty, and in reducing them to Practice.

I would advise you, my Son, in Skaiting, Dancing and Riding, to be always attentive to this Grace, which is founded in natural Principles, and is therefore as much for your Ease and Use, as for your Pleasure.

Do not conclude from this, that I advise you to spend much of your Time or Thoughts upon these Exercises and Diversions. In Truth I care very little about any of them. They should never be taken but as Exercise and Relaxation of Business and study. But as your Constitution requires vigorous Exercise, it will not be amiss, to spend some of your Time, in swimming, Riding, Dancing, Fencing and Skaiting, which are all manly Amusements, and it is as easy to learn by a little Attention, to perform them all with Taste, as it is to execute them in a slovenly, Awkward and ridiculous Manner.

Every Thing in Life should be done with Reflection, and Judgment, even the most insignificant Amusements. They should all be arranged in subordination, to the great Plan of Happiness, and Utility. That you may attend early to this Maxim is the Wish of your affectionate Father,   John Adams

RC (Adams Papers); endorsed: "Pappa's letter of Dec'r 28th 1780. N. 5"; docketed by JQA in a later hand.

[1] JA wrote "Oelocity," an obvious slip of the pen.

John Thaxter to John Adams

Sir   Leyden, 1st. Jany. 1781

I have the Honour to inclose You "Les fondemons de la Jurisprudence Naturelle" by Professor Pestel. It was originally wrote in Latin; but the french Translation is allowed even by the Professor himself to be well executed.[1]

If You prefer the Original, I will purchase and forward it to You.

The Young Gentlemen have been very steadily employed since they have had an Instructor, and their Improvement is in proportion. The Master seems very desirous to advance them, and their Zeal is equal to his in the Business.

I have the Honour to wish You a happy New Year, and to be with perfect Respect, Sir, your very humble Servant,   J. Thaxter Junr.

RC (Adams Papers).

[1] See JA to JQA, 23 Dec. 1780 (2d letter), above, and note 4 there; also Thaxter to JA, 23 Jan. 1781, below.

Abigail Adams to James Lovell

My dear sir   [*Braintree, 3 January 1781*][1]

Your favour of december 19 was deliverd me this day. I would not omit by this post to thank you for it, and for your confidential communications. I cannot however comprehend your Letter to my best Friend for want of the promised key. I am more reconciled to ambiguity and ciphers, than formerly, and not a little thankfull, that the Robberies have been committed now rather than *twelve Months* ago.[2]

You judged rightly when you thought you should communicate happiness by the Honorable testimony of Congress in favour of my absent Friend. My little Barke attendant sails, persues the triumph and partakes the Gale.

Nor will it be considerd presumtious if I Graft my Love, immortal on his fame. The first of Gratifications arise from his deserving and the next in the approving voice of his country.

If you wrote me the 20 of November the Letter was among those which went to the Enemy.[3] You will see by a Letter written you last post,[4] that I had not received a Letter from you for a *very* long time, but having renewed all your former kindness every dissagreable Idea vanishes. I wish you not to mention the Supposition of my having lost a Letter by the robbery of the Mail to Mr. A[dams]. It will make him still more reserved and cautious, he is enough so now to freze one.

You will greatly oblige me by a continuation of your favours to your—I will not Scruple to say—*affectionate*   Portia

Dft (Adams Papers); without date or indication of addressee; at head of text in CFA's hand: "Mr. Lovell   1781."

[1] Dated from Lovell's acknowledgment on 30 Jan. (in Adams Papers but omitted here).

[2] Among the "confidential communications" enclosed by Lovell in his letter of 19 Dec. was a letter to JA (14 Dec., Adams Papers) which included passages in cipher without reference to a key. In his acknowledgment, Lovell welcomed AA's indication here that she had modified an earlier hostility "to ambiguity and ciphers," and he enclosed an "Alphabet" [i.e. key] for her use. The problem of Lovell's cipher in his letters to the Adamses is recurrent in the years 1780–1782 and has been fully dealt with, in relation to other uses of the cipher, in an appendix to this volume: The Lovell Cipher and Its Derivatives.

[3] Lovell's letter to AA of 21 (*not* 20) Nov. 1780 had indeed been intercepted by the British somewhere above New York City, and was to occasion AA much anguish. See Lovell to AA, 19 Dec. 1780, above, and 8 Jan. 1781, below; also AA to Lovell, 17 March, below, esp. note 4 there.

[4] Letter not found.

Abigail Adams to Nathaniel Willis?

Dear Sir   [*Braintree, ante 4 January 1781*]

Your favour of december 21 [1] was deliverd me enclosing the extract relative to Mr. Hutchinson. As you were pleased to express an approbation of it, and to suggest a publication of it, I have returnd it, that you may make that use of it if you think proper.[2] In a Letter from Mr. Adams dated the 25 of Sepbr. he writes me that the late orders he had received from Congress would oblige him to a continuance in Holland till countermanded. Britain thought not of peace. She forgot the State of Ireland, France, Spain, West Indies, N. America, the Armed Neutrality of the Maritime powers and their own distracted state in their joy for the News of Charlstown. That the Ways of Heaven were dark and intricate. It seems as if they were permitted to have Success enough to lead them on, untill they become the most striking Spectacle of Horrour that ever was seen. That they were revenging the loss of their power upon those who had uniformly endeavourd to save it. Burk, Kepple, Sawbridge, Hartly, all thrown out.

Ought not this to convince every American of the importance of Independance and the wretched State of Slavery and Subjugation they must submit to by a reunion with her.

I take this opportunity Sir to enclose to you a coppy of a Letter which I wish to see published. The writer is well known to you and the Letter stands not in need of any enconium of mine. I requested that it might be given to the publick, and obtain permission.[3] I thought it might serve in some measure as an Antidote to the poison so profusely administered by this celebrated Letter Writer. His Lordship has most certainly laid himself open to the utmost severity of Female pens—but you will find in this Letter Elegance of Stile, Solidity of Judgement, discernment and penetration which would do honour to either Sex but which peculiarly distinguish this Lady. You will be so good Sir as to introduce it in the publick paper secreting the Ladys name and place of abode.

I have the Honour to be with a respectfull esteem your Friend and Humble Servant,   A A

Dft (Adams Papers); without date or indication of addressee (but see note 2 below); docketed by CFA: "1781." Enclosures in (missing) RC are identified in notes 2 and 3 below. Text has been minimally repunctuated for clarity.

[1] Not found.

[2] The "extract relative to Mr. Hutchinson" was originally drawn from JA's letter to President Huntington of Congress, 17 June 1780, commenting on Hutchinson's death in London and his (as JA believed) malign role in the Revolutionary struggle (PCC, No. 84, II; printed in Wharton, ed., *Dipl. Corr. Amer. Rev.*, 3:794–798). The text of these comments had been promised to AA by Lovell in his letter to her of 27 Nov. 1780 (q.v. above), and was forwarded to her a few days later via Rev. Samuel Cooper (Lovell to AA, 30 Nov. 1780, Adams Papers). Cooper may have first suggested that JA's remarks be published in Boston; at any rate they were printed in Nathaniel Willis' *Independent Chronicle*, 4 Jan. 1781, p. 3, col. 2. From these circumstances the editors deduce that the intended recipient of the letter here drafted was Willis and that the letter was written shortly before 4 Jan. 1781. Another possibility, quite as likely, is that this letter was sent to Samuel Cooper for *him* to forward the enclosed "extract" to Willis.

At about this time AA must have furnished another such communication to Willis and also to John Gill, publisher of the Boston *Continental Journal*. This was a longer passage, from JA's letter to Huntington of 2 June 1780 (PCC, No. 84, II; printed in Wharton, 3:752–758), containing strictures on Lord George Germain's speech of 6 May in Parliament. Both papers printed the passage in their issues of 11 Jan. 1781 (*Independent Chronicle*, p. 1–2; *Continental Journal*, p. 1, 4). AA had evidently received it as an enclosure in a letter from Lovell. It had already been printed in a Philadelphia paper of unspecified date and earlier, apparently, in Europe from a text JA must have furnished directly or indirectly; see above, Lovell to AA, 19 Dec. 1780, and note 4 there; also a note by CFA in JA, *Works*, 7:179. AA refers to its publication in Boston in her letter to Mrs. Warren, following, and again in a letter to JA, 15 Jan., below.

[3] AA was now submitting for publication a text of Mercy Warren's letter to her son denouncing the immoral teachings of Lord Chesterfield's letters to his natural son. A copy of this letter, dated 24 Dec. 1779, is in the Adams Papers and has been mentioned several times in this correspondence; see AA to Mrs. Warren, 28 Feb. and 1 Sept. 1780, in vol. 3; Mrs. Warren to AA, 21 Dec. 1780, above; AA to JA, 21 Jan. 1781, below. Willis printed it in his *Independent Chronicle* for 18 Jan. 1781, p. 2, col. 1–3, as "by a Lady, born and edu-

cated in this State, whose friends have repeatedly ventured offending her delicacy by obliging the public with some of her ingenious and elegant productions." The editorial introduction went on to quote most of the present paragraph from AA's letter. Thus the members of the Adams-Warren circle continued their efforts to furnish antidotes to the "poison" of Chesterfield's "libertine Morals and base Principles," as JA had long since characterized them (1:376, above).

Abigail Adams to Mercy Otis Warren

Janry. 8th 1781

No, my dear Madam, not affronted I hope; you did not say so with a good grace, the only time I ever knew you miss it in my life.[1]

Yet by recalling your son so soon, I believe you a little out of the Way. I thought you would have spaird him longer, and given me a little time to have wrote you a Letter. Now I shall only scribble you a line, not worth your worrying your Eyes to read. You have calld upon me too, to tell you a great many things, some I am inclined to, and some Not. The Letter which you wrote me about and which was left to my care I sent with my own by way of Bilboa some time ago; an other which you inquired about, was not in my power to return. I had several uses to appropriate it to, most, if not all of which I have answerd.—As to News from abroad, I have had but one Letter since I saw you of a late date; I meant to give you an extract, but have mislaid it. It however speaks not of peace. Mr. A[dam]s instructions, received by Mr. Searl, will oblige him to continue in Holland this winter. A letter arrived for me at the southward. Mr. L[ovel]l coverd it with a letter of his own, and the Enemy kid Napt them both, when they stole the last Mail.[2] Possibly Mr. Rivington may give it me by and by. I question it however. My absent Friend made wise by experience is so warry that I dare say, they will get no Booty in politicks from him. I saw by the last Pensilvana paper under York News, that they had got a Letter of Dr. Rushs which they have promised to print in the next paper, in which say they, he treats the Rebel Senate with great freedom. That both you and I can believe, from former Specimens. Rush will care as little as any body.[3]—I wait for a key to a letter which I have now in my possession to give you something, I fancy which will be entertaining. I mean to write you soon and send to Boston for conveyance. My hands freaze by the fire.—I return the Muslin having been supplied. The black hankerchiefs Mr. Gorge may sell at 75, but I had rather the coulourd should be returnd if they will not fetch 80. I can part with them so here.

Regards to the young Gentleman. Enclose a Letter and peice of

News paper. Have you seen Hutchinsons character, and an other peice in the paper, remarks upon Gorge Germains spea[c]h in the house of commons? You will know the writer.[4]—Pitty my fingers now, and I will tire you out an other time. Nabby sends Duty, longs to come to Plimouth, but I am jealous of trusting her there again least she should love it better than home. I wish you would not live there. Come to Boston, to Braintre I had rather. I fancy the place will be to be sold again.—Yours most affectionately when you are not affronted. When you are—sorrowfull very sorryfull, &c.

RC (MHi:Warren-Adams Collection); addressed: "To Mrs. Mercy Warren Plymouth"; docketed in an unidentified hand: "Mrs. Abigail Adams Jany. 8th. 1781," to which has been added in another unidentified hand: "No. 13." Enclosed "Letter and peice of News paper" not found.

[1] A recent letter from Mrs. Warren is obviously missing; hence some of the allusions here to inquiries by Mrs. Warren cannot be explained with certainty. Nor can the several other letters AA mentions be identified, though see the following notes.

[2] The post robbed was that of 21 Nov. from Philadelphia; see Lovell to AA, 19 Dec. 1780, above.

[3] The letter in question was presumably Benjamin Rush to Dr. William Shippen, 18 Nov. 1780, a contribution to their bitter dispute over the administration of the medical department of the army. It is printed in Benjamin Rush, *Letters*, 1:256–260, and does indeed treat the Continental Congress "with great freedom."

[4] See the preceding letter and note 2 there.

James Lovell to Abigail Adams

Philada. Jan. 8th. 1781

Yes I will try it. To one of the most sensible, virtuous and consequently most lovely of the Loveliest Sex, it will drop its Ink in Paragraphs of calmer Stile than for the last fifteen minutes. My Penknife formed it at first for the Purposes of Friendship; whence then such a Flow of Bitterness and Execration? All this too to the Husband of Portia! Will he become a Distributor of such Evil? No. He is more philosophic, more benevolent and wise. He can exquisitely feel an Injustice done to his Country, but he will not suffer himself to be transported beyond the Language of *grave* Censure. It must however, be acknowledged that the Provocation was great. Let an Appeal be made to the Throne of Complacency.—Listen then, Portia. I had according to your Wish superscribed your Letter to Mr. Adams[1] to go by the Brig Duke of Leinster that will sail for Europe probably Tomorrow. To wish him every Happiness myself while I conveyed a real Portion of it from you was the main Intent of my adding a new

Cover.[2] Fresh Ideas sprang. Facts came forward on my memory. The Pensylvania Line are mutinous; yet, have they given up two Spies of Clinton's who were tempting them with most seductive Promises. Should such virtuous Soldiers be barebacked and barefooted Subjects of Temptation? By a Vessel which left France late in November I yesterday received Copies of Letters dated in March and April last year, telling of Cloathes going from Nantes to Brest, to Rochelle, here there, to and fro to be shipped for America, Satan knows when. Tis plain not before January 1781. This Thought was too much for my Pen; away it flew over the Paper Gall here, Gall there, Gall and Bitterness every where. I doubted whether it would again ever become fit for civil Purposes. I took it therefore a second Time in Hand just now, with Hesitancy, to acknowledge the Receipt of your Favor of Decr. 25th.[3]

Why did you strive to make me vile in my own Eyes? I "renounce all Connexion with your Sex"!!! Then should I be vile indeed. I entreat you, charming Lady, to consider that the Letter of *Recommendation* which you say I had not noticed is the very one in which you ask "Can he suffer Letters repeatedly to reach him and not deign a Line in Reply"? And was also the identical one of September 3d. to which I had Reference in mine of November 27th, and which I had also acknowledged on the 21st. as Jemmy Rivington well knows, tho he does not tell it in print. I cannot say when I inclosed the Bills of Exchange but I do not find my memoranda in my Almanack cancelled by the mark of your Acknowledgement, June 13, July 17 and 21 and Sept. 26.[4] Perhaps those were only a few Lines of Cover to news papers.

It was only last Week that I had the Pleasure of seeing Mr. Brown whom I acquainted with your kind Mention of his name and Person to me, as I had before done in regard to Doctor Lee. I am out with both those Gentlemen, for tho they expressed their Admiration of you yet they did it not with that extraordinary fervor which accords with my own Sentiments, and which I think an Hour's Conversation with you demands.

Col. Palfrey sailed some time ago. J. P. Jones was at L'Orient Novr. 17th. Should he arrive here, depend upon my Attention to what he may bring for you.—Mr. Dana is appointed to proceed as Minister to Russia; but I am almost decided in Mind that he will not incline to accept the Mission.[5] Col. J. Laurens will be in Boston by the Time this reaches you,[6] and, if he does not ride to Braintree, you can not fail to hear of him by Gen. Warren.

This Evening four Years I passed with you at your Brother Cranche's.[7] Did I imagine on the Noon of that day I was thus long to be seperated from a most amiable Wife? No indeed; nor can I boast of the Patriotism that would have mounted me then on Horseback under such Ideas, with a chearful Resolution. Yrs. affectly.,

JL

RC (Adams Papers).

[1] AA to JA, 25 Dec. 1780, above; see descriptive note there.

[2] Lovell to JA, 8 Jan. 1781 (Adams Papers).

[3] In Adams Papers but mistakenly filed and microfilmed under 25 Dec. [1781]; omitted here.

[4] Lovell's letter of 13 June 1780 is printed in vol. 3 above; that of 21 July is in the Adams Papers but not printed here. That of 27 Nov. is above in the present volume. No letters from Lovell to AA dated 17 July, 26 Sept., or 21 Nov. 1780 have been found; the last is known to have been intercepted by the British; see AA to Lovell, 17 March 1781, below. Her letter to Lovell of 3 Sept. 1780 is in vol. 3 above.

[5] Congress elected Francis Dana minister to Russia on 19 Dec. 1780 and issued his commission and instructions on the same day (JCC, 18:1166–1173). A recent and very illuminating study of the Dana mission to Russia, which was to involve both JA and JQA in vital ways, is by David M. Griffiths, "American Commercial Diplomacy in Russia, 1780 to 1783," *WMQ*, 3d ser., 27:379–410 (July 1970).

[6] John Laurens (1754–1782), son of Henry Laurens, lieutenant colonel in the Continental Army, was elected by Congress on 11 Dec. 1780 a special envoy to the French court to obtain further funds and stores and to plead in particular for increased French naval assistance so that a "superiority" over the British could be maintained along the coast. Laurens sailed from Boston in the *Alliance* early in February, carrying, among other things, a long letter from AA to JA (28 Jan., below). He arrived in France in March and embarked to return at the end of May. Correspondence and other documents relative to this mission, which under the circumstances was remarkably successful, have been printed in "The Mission of Col. John Laurens to Europe in 1781," *So. Car. Hist. & Geneal. Mag.*, 1(1900)–2(1901), running through six consecutive issues. These must be supplemented with his instructions of 23 Dec. 1780 and his final report of 2 Sept. 1781, printed in Wharton, ed., *Dipl. Corr. Amer. Rev.*, 4:205–206, 685–692.

[7] This paragraph may have been added by Lovell to enable AA to read the occasional ciphered passages in his letters. As he kept hinting, without ever actually saying, in *other* letters to AA and JA, the key to his cipher was the name of the family where he and the Adamses had spent their last evening together in Braintree (i.e. *Cranch*). *Here* he mentions the name of the family but *not* the cipher. She was expected by this hint to make the connection. See Appendix to this volume.

Abigail Adams to John Adams

My dearest Friend   Janry. 15 1781

Capt. Caznew is now just about to sail. I wrote large packets to go by him a month ago, but hearing Capt. Trash was going from Newbury to Bilboa I sent them by him. It was thought that Caznew would not sail till Febry.

But all of a suden I am calld upon unprepaird having but an hours warning—he shall not however go without a line or two. Your last which I have received was by way of Philadelphia dated in Sepbr. 15.

I see by last weeks paper that a Capt. Updike is arrived at Providence. I fear he has no Letters for me, as he brings word that the Fame saild the day before him, but has not yet been heard of. We are Fearfull that she is lost, or taken.—I have written to you twice since Davis arrived, and told you that he threw over all his dispatches, being chased, to my great sorrow and mortification. The things however which you were so kind as to order for me, came safe to hand. I shall be obliged for ought I know to part with them, to pay taxes, which are beyond account. 20 thousand dollors are already assessed upon this place for the last year.

I have written to the House of de Neufville for a few articles, which I wrote to you about by way of Bilboa. I have inclosed them a Bill, and at the same time directed them to take your orders with regard to them.[1]

Neither Jones or Sampson have yet reachd America. We have had a moderate winter and a general Health throughout the State. We are making *every* Effort to fill up the continental Army, and hope to succeed. Our paper Credit has kept a steady value for more than 3 months. 75 for one is the rate of exchange. Our hard Money tax is punctually paid for the redemption of it. I cannot say that the Money appreciates yet, but it certainly must from the great taxes which are daily collecting. We now see where our errors lay, but a people must feel to be convinced.

I enclose to you a Letter and resolve of Congress forwarded to me by Mr. L[ovel]l.[2] It contains an approbation of more value to you, than a Lucrative reward and it communicates pleasure to me, in proportion as it is valuable to you, and as it is a testimony, that your assiduity and attention to the publick Interest is gratefully noticed by your Country. To Merrit and receive it, is the only compensation I can receive for the loss I sustain of your society.

The Letter containing remarks upon Lord Gorge Germains Speach, was first published in Philadelphia and sent me by Mr. L——l. I had it republished here—it is much approved of. The Enemy lose ground every day in Carolina. The infamous Arnold is gone with a Number of Troops to Virgina—he was too knowing to come out, as was first talkd of against New england who to a Man would have risen to have crushd the monster. Whilst Andry has been lamented by a Generous Enemy Arnold has been execrated by all ranks.

My Love to my dear Sons, there Letters by Davis I mourn the loss of. I designd to have written to them by this vessel but fear I shall not have time. I wrote by Trash to Mr. Thaxter. Our Friends are all well—excuse haste, from your ever affectionate   Portia

RC (Adams Papers); addressed: "Honble. John Adams   Amsterdam"; endorsed in John Thaxter's hand: "Portia 15th. Jany. 1781." For the enclosures see note 2 below.

[1] AA's letter to Neufville & Son in Amsterdam was dated this day but has not been found. It is acknowledged in their reply of 25 May, below.

[2] The enclosures were doubtless those transmitted by James Lovell in his letter to AA of 19 Dec. 1780, above; see note 1 there.

Richard Cranch to John Adams

My dear Friend and Bror.   Boston Jany: 18th: 1781

As there is a Vessell now here bound for Holland by which (if not sooner) you will doubtless hear various accounts of the Affair that has lately happen'd in the Pensilvania Line of the Army, I embrace the Oportunity to let you know the true state of that affair as far as the Genl. Court has been inform'd of it, to prevent your being misled by false Reports.[1] Genl. Knox who left Head Quarters the 5th. Instant arriv'd here Express last Sunday with Dispatches from Genl. Washington respecting the affairs of the Army, to be laid before the Genl. Court which is now sitting. He was heard before the two Houses.— His account of the Matter, as near as I can collect it, was as follows.— The Soldiers of the Pensilvania Line complained that they were unjustly held to serve during the War, when they inlisted, as they say, conditionally for three Years *or during the War*; supposing it left at their Option to leave the Service at the end of three Years if they pleas'd. They complain'd also that their Wages was near twelve Months behind-hand. That they were unprovided with sufficient Clothing, and short of Provision. All these Grievances seem'd to be agravated in their Minds, on seeing the new Recruits, for filling up the Army, come to Camp with good Clothes and Money in their Pockets (having received a Bounty of twenty four hard Dollars each) while they themselves, who had born the Burden and heat of the Day, were neglected. These Discontents were carried to such a Hight that on the Evening of the first of Jany. Instt. and the Day following, the greatest part of the non-Commission Officers and Soldiers of the Pensilvania Line, amounting to about two Thousand, refused to serve any longer in the Army unless their Grievances were redress'd; and

65

seizing six Field Pieces, stood on the Defensive. The Commission Officers and some of the Men who endeavour'd to quell them, were fir'd upon; one Officer (a Capt.) was kill'd, and several wounded. Some also of the Insurgents were kill'd. After this they march'd to Prince-Town where they determined to make a Stand; for the Purpose, as I conceive, of treating with the Government of Pensilvania about the Redress of their Grievances.—I cannot find from the best Enquiery that I can make, that the Insurgents were moved by any Disaffection to the American Cause, or from any formal design of helping the Enemy, but merely for the Purpose of getting their Grievances removed.

The Genl. Court of this Commonwealth is taking Measures for retrieving the sunk Credit of this Government; for which purpose we are repeling all Laws making Paper-Money a Tender at any other Rate than the current Exchange. We are making a Law that all Debts due from Government shall be liquidated to their just Value, and then to have Interest allow'd annually in hard Money or Paper equivalent. This, it is expected, will induce the loaning of Money freely to Government. Besides this we have in contemplation Imposts and Excises. Without Loans we fear the Taxes will be too heavy to be born, (without murmuring), by the People at large.

We have received Letters from Mr. Austin informing the Court of the large Advances made for this Government by Messrs. Deneufville & Sons, and the Court has given Direction for the immediate purchasing of Bills of Exchange equall to three Thousand Pounds, to be remitted with a Letter of Thanks to that worthy House for their generous Exertions in our favour.

I am so hurried with publick Business that I cannot be so particular on our publick Affairs as I could wish. I must therefore leave some room to tell you that your Hond. Mother and your Brother are well; Your Dear Lady and Children were well last Sunday when I pass'd the Evening at your House. Father Smith, Uncles Quincy, Thaxter, Tufts and Smith are well with their Families.

Please to give my kindest regards to your dear little Boys and to Mr. Thaxter. Mrs. Cranch and our Children join me in wishing you all the success and Happiness that the warmest affection can dictate. A Line from you would greatly oblige your Bror.,   R: Cranch

P.S. Should Messrs: Deneufville & Sons think of making a tryal here in the Commission way I should be glad to serve them. I find the general advance on European Goods is three Pounds Sterling here, for what cost one Pound sterling there. Such Articles as suit the Ladies would be very saleable, also Linnens.

RC (Adams Papers); endorsed in John Thaxter's hand: "Mr. Cranch 18. Jany. 1781." Dft (MHi: Cranch Family Collection).

[1] On this incident, which occurred in the first days of January, see Carl Van Doren, *Mutiny in January*, N.Y., 1943.

Abigail Adams to John Adams

My dearest Friend   Janry. 21 1781

The vessel is not yet gone, and I find I have a towns man going in her. He came this evening to let me know it, and to take Letters from me. What has taken place in the last week Mr. C[ranc]h has informd you of, so that I shall not write politicks. I inclose a paper or two, and a journal or two of congress. In one of the papers you will see an Excellent Letter from a Friend of yours, and a comment by an other who sent it to a Gentleman requesting his care of the publication and with his usual complasance, he has published all, together.[1]— Many of your Friends will write you by this vessel. I hope it will not be long before some one will arrive with Letters from you. I feel impatient.

The Bandano hankerchiefs you was so kind as to send me, are as good an article as has ever come. I can scarcly keep one of them. Tho they are double the price of a Barcelona, they sell much better. Holland is a good place for crockery ware, I should be glad of some for family use from thence.—I wish you to write by every vessel bound to America. Updike arrived at Providence, but we fear the Fame is lost or taken. Friends all well. Adieu *yours* ever *yours.*

RC (Adams Papers); addressed: "To Honbll. John Adams Esqr Minister Plenipotentiary from the United States of America at Paris or Amsterdam"; endorsed in John Thaxter's hand: "Portia 21st Jany. 1781." For the single identifiable enclosure see note 1.

[1] AA was sending JA a copy of Willis' (Boston) *Independent Chronicle* for 18 Jan., containing Mercy Warren's letter to her son on Chesterfield's letters; see note 3 on AA to Nathaniel Willis?, ante 4 Jan., above.

Abigail Adams to John Quincy Adams

My dear Son   Braintree Janry. 21 1781

Tis a long time since I had the pleasure of a Letter from you. If you wrote to me by Capt. Davis as I suppose you did, your Letters were all thrown over Board.

If you have since written by a Brig call'd the *Fame*, I fear it will never reach me. She is still missing and must be taken or lost. The *Mars* from France we daily expect. The last Letters which I received from you came by the Alliance, and were dated in April so that tis Nine Months since a single line from your own hand reachd me.

I expect your observations upon your New Situation, an account of Holland, and what you find there, worthy of remark, what improvements you have made in the languages, in the Sciences, and the fine Arts.

You are now become resident in a Country famous for its industery and frugality, and which has given Birth to many Learned and great Men. Erasmus, Grotius and Boerhaave, so well known in the Literary world, stand foremost in the List of Fame.

You must not be a superficial observer, but study Men and Manners that you may be Skilfull in both. Tis said of Socrates, that the oracle pronounced him the wisest of all Men living because he judiciously made choice of Humane Nature for the object of his Thoughts. Youth is the proper season for observation and attention—a mind unincumberd with cares may seek instruction and draw improvement from all the objects which surround it. The earlier in life you accustome yourself to consider objects with attention, the easier will your progress be, and more sure and successfull your enterprizes. What a Harvest of true knowledge and learning may you gather from the numberless varied Scenes through which you pass if you are not wanting in your own assiduity and endeavours. Let your ambition be engaged to become eminent, but above all things support a virtuous character, and remember that "an Honest Man is the Noblest work of God."

I hope you will not let any opportunity slip or any vessel sail, which is bound for America without Letters from you. Your Friends here all desire to be rememberd to you. Your cousin Billy has written to you several times, and is quite impatient to hear from you. Your sister—not a word in excuse will I say for her. She ought to write to you and I call upon her too, but she is very neglegent.

I am my dear Son with sincere wishes for your Health and happiness affectionately yours, A A

RC (Adams Papers). Dft (Adams Papers); at head of text in CFA's hand: "Draught of the preceding."

John Thaxter to John Adams

Sir   Leyden Jany. 23d 1781

I had the Honour of your Note and the inclosed Extracts yesterday Morning; I waited on Mr. Luzac immediately with the Paper and shewed him the Extracts, with which he was highly gratified.[1] He sent them so late last Evening that I had only time to inclose them to You. The News cannot but be agreable to every one who loves his Country, and feels interested in every Event that affects it: but the Quantity of it is too great to claim an immediate Credit. Altho' the whole and much more may be within the Compass of one's Wishes, and however fashionable it may be to shape one's language to his Wishes, yet after the confident Reports from that quarter of the Continent in the Summer of 1779, and their palpable falsity, one will be moderate in wishing; and modest in speaking, 'till there is an ample Confirmation.

Master John and I attend Professor Pestel's Lectures sur les fondemens de Jurisprudence naturelle. They are very ingenious and learned. His Lectures upon Grotius We do not attend—he has not time. I have thought it most adviseable for him to attend the former of the two. I wish however for your direction. He and his Brother are extremely diligent, and I presume their progress will be satisfactory to You.

The Rector Magnificus has consented to matriculate Master Charles. If it is agreable to You, I will wait upon him for that purpose.[2]

I have the honor to inclose You Mr. Pestel's Latin Edition, and Homer's Hymn to Ceres, and to be with perfect Respect, Sir, your most humble Servt.,   J. Thaxter

RC (Adams Papers); endorsed: "Mr. Thaxter recd. & ansd. 24 Jan. 1781." (This answer has not been found.) For the enclosed or accompanying books written or edited by two professors at Leyden, see notes 3 and 4 under JA to JQA of 23 Dec. 1780 (2d letter), above.

[1] JA's "Note" has not been found. The "Extracts" it covered were acknowledged with touching gratitude by Jean Luzac in a letter to JA of 22 Jan. (Adams Papers); they probably form part of the news and comment on the war in America, especially in the South, printed in the *Gazette de Leyde* and its supplements for 23 and 26 January.

[2] See Thaxter to JA, 1 and 11 Feb., below.

John Thaxter to John Adams

Sir   Leyden 25th. Jany. 1781

Your favour of yesterday[1] was recieved this morning. I suspect it was opened before it came to my hands. The Seal appeared to have been good at first, but when delivered to me, it the Impression was very faint in many places—perhaps it may be accidental.

The Hymn to Ceres was forgotten at the time that I inclosed the fundamenta Jurisprudentiæ Nat:—I shall send it by this Opportunity.

I shall wait on the Rector tomorrow with Master Charles, and procure a Writing Master as soon as possible.

I have recieved Mr. Dana's Letter that You was so good as to inclose. He mentions that two Letters were inclosed in it to You, which I hope You have recieved, as well as the other Letters. You will oblige me, Sir, if You will be kind enough to acquaint me with his Address. His Letter came open to me, or rather without Cover. I presume that it was opened by You, Sir. I am not sorry for it for my part, but You will confer a particular favour upon me, if You will open no more.

The Young Gentlemen are well and desire their Duty to You.

I have the Honour to be, with perfect Respect, Sir, your very humble Servant,   J. Thaxter

RC (Adams Papers); docketed by CFA. Concerning the "Hymn to Ceres," which accompanied this letter, see above, JA to JQA, 23 Dec. 1780 (2d letter), note 3.

[1] Not found.

Abigail Adams to John Adams

My dearest Friend   Janry. 28 1781

Last Evening General Lincoln call'd here introducing to me a Gentleman by the Name of Col. Laurence[1] the Son as I suppose, of your much esteemed Friend, the late president of congress who informed me that he expected to sail for France in a few days, and would take dispatches from me. Altho I closed Letters to you by way of Holland a few days ago, I would not omit so good an opportunity as the present. Tis a long time since the date of your Last Letters, the 25 of Sepbr. I wait with much anxiety, listning to the sound of every Gun, but none anounce the arrival of the Fame from Holland, which we greatly fear is lost, or taken, nor the Mars from France. I wish you had been fortunate enough to have sent Letters by Updike to Providence, who saild the day after the Fame, but suppose you wrote by her, and sailing so near together, did not think it worth your while to write by him.

Col. Laurence is enabled I suppose to give you, every kind of intelligence respecting the Army which you may wish to learn. Mr. Cranch has written you upon the same Subject by way of Holland.[2] Your Friends here complain that you do not write to them. I suppose Davis threw over half a hundred Letters. If you are unfortunate in that way tis not to be helped.

I have the pleasure to inform you that a repeal of the obnoxious Tender act has past the House and Senate.[3] The G[overno]r as has been heretofore predicted, when any thing not quite popular is in agitation, has the Gout and is confined to his Bed.

A false weight and a false ballance are an abomination, and in that light this tender act must be viewed by every impartial person. Who but an Ideot would believe that 40 was equal to 75. But the repeal gives us reason to hope that justice and righteousness will again exalt our Nation, that publick Faith will be restored, that individuals will lend to the publick, and that the heavy taxes which now distress all orders, will be lessned.

A late committe who have been setting upon ways and means for raising money, tell us that a tax for two years more equal to what we have paid in the last would clear this State of debt. You may judge of the weight of them, yet our State taxes are but as a Grain of Mustard Seed, when compared with our Town taxes.

Clinton I hear, has sent out a proclamation upon Germains plan, inviting the people to make a seperate peace, which will only be a new proof of the Ignorance and folly of our Enemies without making a single prosilite—even the revolted Pensilvany Troops gave up to justice the Spys which Clinton sent to them, offering them, cloathing and pay, letting him know that it was justice from their State, not favours from their Enemies that they wanted.

It is reported that Arnold with a Body of troops is gone to Virginia, where it is hoped he and his Myrmidons will meet their fate. Had Clinton been a generous Enemy, or known humane Nature, he would like Aurelian upon a like occasion, have given up the traitor to the hands of justice, knowing that it was in vain to expect fidelity in a man who had betrayed his own Country, which from his defection may learn to place a higher value upon integrity, and virtue, than upon a savage ferocity so often mistaken for courage. He who as an individual is cruel, unjust and immoral, will not be likely to possess those virtues necessary in a General or Statesman. Yet in our Infant Country, Infidelity and debauchery are so fashionably prevalent that less attention is paid to the characters of those who fill important offices, than a Love of virtue, and zeal for publick Liberty, can warrant, which we are told by wise Legislators of old, are the surest preservatives of publick happiness.

You observe in a late Letter[4] that your absence from your Native State will deprive you of an opportunity of being a man of importance in it. I hope you are doing your country more extensive Service abroad than you could have done, had you been confined to one State only, and whilst you continue in the same Estimation amongst your fellow citizens, which you now hold, you will not fail of being of importance to them: at home or abroad.

Heaven preserve the life and Health of my dear absent Friend and in its own time return him to his country, and to the Arms of his ever affectionate   Portia

PS   Love to my Dear Boys. I have sent you a present by Col. Laurence.

RC (Adams Papers); addressed: "To the Honbll. John Adams Esqr Minister Plenipotentiary from the United States of America att Paris or Amsterdam"; endorsed: "Portia. Jan. 28. 1781."

[1] John Laurens. On his mission to Europe see above, James Lovell to AA, 8 Jan., and note 6 there.

[2] Richard Cranch to JA, 18 Jan., above.

[3] An Act for Repealing Certain Parts of an Act Postponing Payment of Government Securities to a Distant Period, &c., passed on 25 Jan. 1781 (Mass., *Acts and Laws*, Acts of Jan. sess., ch. 2).

[4] JA to AA, 25 Sept. 1780, in vol. 3, above, mentioned earlier in the present letter as the latest AA had received from JA.

John Adams to John Quincy Adams

My dear Boy   Amsterdam Jan. 31. 1781

I have received, by the Way of Bilboa, a Letter from your Mamma, of the 8th of October, in which She presents her tender Affection to you and your Brother, as well as her Respects to her agreable Correspondent Mr. Thaxter. Your Sister was at Boston, your youngest Brother at School learning fast.

You should write me a few Lines, now and then, to inform me of your Health and of your Progress in Literature. I have a Set of Popes Works but I am so glad to see an old Acquaintance that I cannot part with him yet.

I hope We shall now, soon have some further News from our dear native Country.

By the Accounts hitherto received, Things are in a good Way, and I have strong Hopes, that We shall not experience so many Mortifications, the ensuing Summer as the last. Our Ennemies will have their Hands too full to do Us much Mischief.

My Love to Mr. Thaxter and your Brother. Your affectionate Father,   John Adams

RC (Adams Papers); at foot of text: "Mr. J. Q. Adams."

John Thaxter to John Adams

Sir   Leyden 1st. Feby. 1781

I have waited on Mr. Luzac with the Crisis, who is much obliged to You for it, and will either translate it into Dutch or French, as shall be most agreable to You, and as soon as possible. You will be so good as to acquaint me, which of the two Languages is your Choice.[1]

I waited a few days agone on the Rector Magnificus with Charley, and was informed by him, that his Matriculation was consented to by the Curators.[2]

The Letter You was so kind to forward me, was from America, dated the 1st. and 16th. of September. I am at a loss how it came, as I hear of no Arrival.

It seems rather difficult to determine upon the various News from the Southward. The American Papers and Accounts differ exceedingly from the English. One knows not what to make of such Contradictions. If it [is] News fabricated by any of our Countrymen, I am very sorry —they are Spots and Blemishes in a good Cause, and such a Species of Aid as our Cause does not require.

The young Gentlemen are well and desire their Duty to You.

I have the Honour to be, with the greatest Respect, Sir, your most humble Servant,   J. Thaxter

RC (Adams Papers).

[1] In a letter from Brussels, 28 Jan. (Adams Papers), William Lee wrote JA: "I send you a Crisis which perhaps you may think worth being translated and publish'd in Holland." This was quite possibly Thomas Paine's *The Crisis Extraordinary*, published in Philadelphia in Oct. 1780 (Evans 16918), but no Dutch or French translation published in the Netherlands has been found.

[2] During a visit to his sons in Leyden early in January, JA recorded that JQA was approved for matriculation (he and John Thaxter were formally admitted on 10 Jan.), but that "Charles was found to be too young, none under twelve Years of Age being admitted" (*Diary and Autobiography*, 2:452). In his letter

to JA of 23 Jan. (above), Thaxter reported that he would wait again upon the Rector to obtain special consent, and on 11 Feb. he wrote JA (letter below) that this had been done and CA had matriculated on 29 January.

John Quincy Adams to John Adams

Hond. Sir   Leyden Feby. the 3d. 1780 [*i.e.* 1781]

I yesterday received your's of the 31st of Jany. in whic you desir'd me to write you a few lines now and then to inform you of my progress in Literature. I have just finish'd Copying a Treatise upon Greek by Mr. Hemsterhuis which our master has been so good as to lend me. It is very rare and there are but very few exemples of it here, and I believe that you would be very much pleas'd with it.[1]

I should be very much obliged to you if you would send me The Vocabulary of Words of the same terminations in French, English, and dutch, which Mr. Searle had.

I am very impatient to see Pope's works. I should be very glad also to see my old acquaintance.

Our master desires me to send his respects to you.

I am your most dutiful Son,   John Quincy Adams

RC (Adams Papers); addressed in an unidentified hand: "A Monsieur Monsieur Adams: chez Monsieur Hendrik Schorn Sur l'agter burgwal by de hoogestraat a Amsterdam"; docketed in John Thaxter's hand: "Johnny 3d. Feby. 1781."

[1] This, though attributed to Professor Hemsterhuis, may in fact be a MS in 104 folios that remains among JQA's papers entitled "Dictata Celeberrimi Valckenarii ad Analogiam Linguæ Graecae" (Adams Papers, Microfilms, Reel 217). JQA dated his copy at the head "January 21st. 81," and at the end "January 31st. 81." It seems doubtful that he was copying still another treatise on Greek at the very same time.

Abigail Adams to John Thaxter

My dear Sir   Febry. 5 1781

I have not had the pleasure of a line from you since your arrival in Holland. I fear I have lost Letters by a missing vessel call'd the Fame, if so I regret the loss of much pleasure and entertainment, which your pen always affords me. I flatter myself you will continue to pay a particular regard to my amusement, by a recital of whatever you meet with worthy of communication.

Rousseau some where observes, "that Science in general may be considerd as a coin of great value, but of use to the possessor only in as much as it is communicated." His maxim is founded upon a liberal and social plan, which might be improved to the advantage of the

Fair Sex to whom little indulgence is shewn in this way. Possess'd at least with an equal share of curiosity with the other sex, little or no care is taken to turn it into a channel of usefull knowledge, or literary endowments.

In America we have heretofore had so little connextion with other countries, and so few Ladies have a taste for Historick knowledge, that even their own Country was not much known to them untill the present revolution, which [is][1] become so interesting, that few I hope remain Ignorant of the principals which led our Ancestors to seek an asylum in the uncultivated wilds of America, nor the dangers which they encounterd in rearing the wilderness into a fruitfull Feild, that they might transmit to us their posterity those treasures, which we find worth our contending for in Blood, against that very Nation whose former userpations peopled America. From this contention we are become connected with other climes, who have discoverd themselves as Friendly, as Britain was Hostile. We therefore feel ourselves Interested in a knowledge of their customs, Manners, Laws, and Goverments. It is not very probable that many of our American Ladies will ever become travellers, yet judgeing of others by myself, we could wish to obtain from those Gentlemen who have that priviledge, and who are capable of observation, a recital of them.

Tho it is a path which has been repeatedly trod, it ought not to discourage a Gentleman of penetration through apprehension that he can observe nothing New. Sir William Temple observes *"that Mankind* are a *various creature,"* that at different periods they differ, from themselves, as much as they do from other Nations.

This you may easily see, by turning your Eye towards a Nation which not half a century ago was famed for her justice, Humanity, Bravery, and her Equitable Goverment—but now! how Arbitary, How cruel, how venal, how prostitute! Other Nations who have not experienced a like misirable change may not furnish so horrid a tale to the Historick page, yet they are ever changeing for the better or worse, and will supply something new in Science, Arts, or Arm's to a critical observer.

I do not remember to have read any History of the united provinces, except Sir William Temples, and that written a Century ago.[2] From his account of the Genious and Manners of the people at that period, I should suppose they had made great improvements of every kind. A writer observes that

> "Their much Loved wealth imparts
> convenience, plenty, Elegance and Arts."

Sir William observes in his day and a more modern writer confirms the observation upon the manners of the people, that they are not airy enough for joy, nor warm enough for Love—a fine climate for a young fellow to repair to after having been an Inhabitant of *Paris* for twelve months.

But as an Inhabitant of a climate where all the softer passions dwell, where they are born of Honour, nursed by virtue, and united by Liberty, I would not wish to exchange it for a Mexico or Peru, if they possesssd the temperature of the united provinces. For Sir William observes that he never knew a man amongst them, that he thought at *Heart* in *Love*, or susceptible of the passion—and what is still more incredible—a woman that seem'd at all to care, whether they were so, or not.

Horrid Horrid place! What defy the power of the sex at this rate? Rob us of more than half our talents. Never never will we become inhabitants of such a frigid country, where Mercury the patron of Merchandize and the God of Gain, by inventing Contracts, weights and measures, and teaching the Arts of Buying and Selling and Trafficking, has formed a League against Cupid and the Graces.

I hope to forward this to you by the Alliance, in which Col. Laurence has taken passage. I knew not that she was designed for Europe till a few days ago, and she is now expected to sail the first fair wind.

Present my complements to Mr. Dana. How will he relish the cold Regions of the North? If he goes[3] to Russia, tell him I shall ask permission to become one of his correspondents. I have not heard from Mrs. Dana, since his appointment, but fear she will be in affliction about it. Every body seems to think that they have a better right to our Husbands, than their partners, and monopolize them accordingly without asking our consent.—This too in a land of Liberty.—O! for absolute power. I would soon be the mistress of mine.[4] I am apprehensive for his Health in Holland. Those sudden changes to which the climate is subject will not suit his constitution. I hope their will be no necessity of his resideing there longer than the winter. If you should find his Health impaired I beg of you to urge his return to Paris.

As to politics, they are a subject that I am not in a humour to write about at present, so refer you to other correspondents. Not that they are less interesting—they are too much so to be lightly considerd. If I had reflected upon them when I first began my Letter, it would have imbibed a tincture of Depression from them.

The young Ladies of your acquaintance remember you with affection, especially the *Fair American* who is much gratified at your *residence* in *Holland*, where she is not like (from the character of the Ladies) to meet a Rival. She is not quite so secure at Paris, tho she builds some security upon the difficulty of forming an acquaintance with unmarried Females, and she has too much reliance upon your honour, to suppose you would form any other.

I hope you received a large packet sent by Capt. Trash to Bilboa, from your affectionate Friend, Portia

RC (MB); addressed: "To Mr. John Thaxter Amsterdam"; endorsed: "Mrs. Adams 5th. Feby. 1781 Recd. 7th. April." Dft (Adams Papers); without date; text incomplete; docketed on face by JA in old age: "A A. to J Thaxter." LbC (Adams Papers); dated "december 1780"; text incomplete. The date of Dec. 1780 at head of LbC is questionable. Although Dft could have been begun in that month and some part of LbC entered, AA's allusions to the respective missions of John Laurens and Francis Dana strongly suggest that she was writing in the middle of or late in Jan. 1781. The order of composing the three versions seems to have been: (1) Dft, which may at one time have been more complete (see note 4 below); (2) LbC, which elaborates in substance and improves in phrasing on Dft; and (3) RC, which on the whole continues the elaboration and improvement.

[1] Supplied from LbC.
[2] Temple's *Observations upon the United Provinces of the Netherlands,* London, 1672, a work which JA characterized as "elegant and entertaining, but very brief and general" (to AA, 21 July 1777; vol. 2:286, above).
[3] LbC ends abruptly here, although the next-to-last paragraph below, on

"The young Ladies of your acquaintance," had been incorporated in LbC text following the paragraph above that ends "against Cupid and the Graces."
[4] Dft ends here, at the foot of a single sheet folded into four pages; a further page or two of Dft may therefore have been written but later have become separated and lost.

Abigail Adams to John Quincy Adams and Charles Adams

My dear sons Febry. 8 1781

I fear you will think Mamma is unmindfull of you if she does not write you a few lines by so good an opportunity. I wrote to both of you by Mr. Beals of this Town about a week ago,[1] and my notice by this vessel is very short. I can only find time to tell you that tis a very long time since I heard from your Pappa, and much longer since I had a Letter from either of you. I think Dr. Lee brought the last.

I hope you are both well and very good children which is the best News I can possibly hear from you. I cannot prevail with your Sister to write—I believe she is affraid you will shew her Letters and she is so proud that she thinks she cannot write well enough. I do not like it that she is not more socible with her Brothers. Thommy would write if he could. He sends Love, is a very good Boy, and wants to know if you cannot send him some present from Holland.

Is my Charles grown as fat as his Brother? Can he talk French, Dutch, &c.

Ask Mr. Thaxter to write me word whether he bought Mr. Trottes and Mrs. Welchs things. I know nothing about them. Tell Pappa I am like to have a fine Neighbour. General W[arre]n has bought the Farm at Milton, that formerly belonged to G[overno]r Hutchinson and moves in April.[2]

We have had a fine pleasent winter, as mild as the last was severe. How has it been in Holland, have you learned to skate finely?

Master Samll['s] Pappa is a going to France. I send this Letter by him.[3] Col. Lawrence has got some for Pappa and Mr. Thaxter.— Your Grandpappa sends his Love to you, talks about you with much pleasure, so does your Grandmamma, who is so very infirm I fear you will never see her again. I do not see any prospect of your speedy return. It wants but a few days of 15 months since you left home. Do you not want to see the rugged rocks of Braintree again?

Some day or other, I wish it may not be far distant when I shall embrace my dear Sons in their Native land. Till that period arrives I would have them ever mindfull of writeing to their affectionate Mother,   A A

Dft or RC (Adams Papers); from the irregularity of the paper, this has more the appearance of a retained draft than of a recipient's copy, but this question is not now answerable.

[1] Letter, or letters, missing.

[2] Former Governor Thomas Hutchinson built his countryseat on Milton Hill, often called Neponset Hill, overlooking Boston Harbor, in 1743. He regularly occupied it during summers from 1754, and occasionally during winters after his Boston house was sacked in 1765, until June 1774, when he abandoned it to sail for England. Seized and sold at auction as tory property in 1779, this fine estate was purchased by James Warren in Jan. 1781 for £3,000. The Warrens lived there from May 1781 until sometime in 1788, when they returned to their Plymouth home. The house survived in radically altered form into the present century but was torn down in 1946. The most detailed and authoritative account of this once celebrated countryseat is in Malcolm Freiberg's *Thomas Hutchinson of Milton* (Milton Hist. Soc., 1971). A water color of the house is reproduced in this volume. For the Warrens' occupancy, see Alice Brown, *Mercy Warren*, N.Y., 1896, ch. 12; *Warren-Adams Letters*, vol. 2: *passim*.

[3] Gabriel Johonnot (d. 1820), son-in-law of Rev. Samuel Cooper and father of JQA's companion and schoolmate in France, Samuel Cooper Johonnot, was a Boston merchant. See above, vol. 2:202–203, and JA, *Diary and Autobiography*, 2:417–418. In a letter to JA of 9 Feb. 1780 [i.e. 1781], Samuel Cooper explained: "Colonel Johonnot who sails in the Frigate Alliance, I expected would have tarried with us a day or two longer. His sudden and unexpected Call to go on Board this Ship which now lies at some Distance from the Town allows me

but a Moment to write you.... [He] goes to France upon a Plan of Business; your Friendship to him in this will oblige us both. He will see you upon the Affairs of his Son" (Adams Papers).

John Quincy Adams to John Adams

Honoured Sir   Leyden Feby. the 11. 1781

I received a day or two agone the vocabulary which I desir'd you to send, for which I am much obliged to you. Last Thursday I went to hear the Rector Magnificus for last year speak an oration. The Rector for this year is professor Voorda. All the Professors of the university, the Burgomasters and the Schepens of the city were there. Professor Hollebeek (the last years rector) is Profesor in theology.[1] He treated upon the advantages of the Christian religion.

Perhaps you may remember when you was here you was speaking of the rules of the drama. There is a book here entitled l'art Dramatique by Mercier with his Dramatick works in 6 Volumes in Octavo which cost 18g. 14 st. but I can buy l'art Dramatique alone for 1. 16. If you please I will buy it.[2]

I am your most dutiful Son,   John Quincy Adams

RC (Adams Papers); addressed: "A Monsieur Monsieur Adams chez Monsieur Henry Schorn a Amsterdam"; endorsed: "John   ansd. 12 Feb. 1781." JQA's punctuation has been slightly rectified for clarity.

[1] Ewald Hollebeek (1719–1796), who at the end of his incumbency as rector gave special permission for CA to be admitted to the University, had been professor of theology since 1762. See *Nieuw Ned. Biog. Woordenboek,* 1:1140–1141; *Album studiosorum Academiae Lugduno Batavae,* The Hague, 1875, p. xii and col. 1136.

[2] In his reply of 12 Feb., below, JA consented to the purchase of the treatise but not the plays. In all likelihood the copy of [Louis Sébastien Mercier,] *Du théâtre, ou nouvel essai sur l'art dramatique,* Amsterdam, 1773, listed in *Catalogue of JA's Library,* now in MB, was bought by JQA at this time.

John Thaxter to John Adams

Sir   Leyden 11th. Feby. 1781

I have the Honour to inform You that Charles was matriculated the 29th. of last Month, by the Consent of the Curators, to whom the Matter was proposed.

The Letter, that You was so good as to inclose, was from Mr. Williams of Nantes, who informs me that the Aurora Captain Porter had arrived at L'Orient to his Address. She mounts eighteen six pounders, and is to be dispatched as soon as possible for Boston, taking any Freight that offers, without being detained however for want of any: that he hopes to get the Marquiss de la Fayette, of twenty four eighteen pounders ready to go out in Company with the Aurora.

If You should incline, Sir, to send any thing to your Family, the Opportunity seems good.

He desires his best Respects to You, and tells me to shew his Letter to You. He says that his Commercial and Family Occupations have a little got the better of his political and friendly Attentions, and desires me to acquaint You, that if You will have patience with him, he will pay You all. The Letter is dated the 30th. Jany., and after taking the Substance from it, it will not be necessary to send the Letter to You.

My Respects and Compliments, where due, Sir, if You please.

I have the Honour to be, with perfect Respect, Sir, your very humble Servt., J. Thaxter

RC (Adams Papers).

John Adams to John Quincy Adams

My dear Son Feb 12. 1781

I received to day, your Favour of 11.

You may purchase L'Art Dramatique, alone if you please. But I know nothing of the Dramatick Character of Mercier. He is not very famous, as I remember, and therefore, I think it is Scarcely worth while to go to the Expence of all his Works.

I shall make you a present of Some Volumes of Pope soon.—I have seen a Terence, in three Volumes, with the Latin on one Side, and a French Translation on the other. Should you be fond of having it?

Terence is remarkable, for good Morals, good Taste and good Latin —his Language has a Simplicity and an elegance, that makes him proper to be accurately studied, as A Model. But perhaps your Master would not choose you should have a Translation.

These great Masters of Antiquity, you must sooner or later, be able to judge of critically. But you must never imitate them. Study nature, and write accordingly, and you will resemble them. But it is nature not the Ancients that you are to imitate and Copy. But I must stop. I wish I had nothing to interrupt me, from indulging this familiar Way of Writing to you.

Your affectionate Father, John Adams

RC (Adams Papers); at foot of text: "John Quincy Adams."

John Quincy Adams to John Adams

Honoured Sir   Leyden Feby. 18th. 1781

The other day I received your letter, of the 12th of this month, in which you ask me whether my Master would choose that I should have Terence with a translation? I believe that he had rather I should not; because when I shall translate him he would desire that I might do it without help.

I should be glad if you would bring me Mr. Cerisier's history of this Country, if you can spare it.[1] There is a gentleman in this city whose name is Keroux who has also wrote a history of this Country in four volumes in octavo. Perhaps you have heard of it.[2]

I should be much obliged to you if you would be so good as to desire Stephens to buy me a penknife, I want one very much, and can't get one here.

I am your most dutiful Son,   John Quincy Adams

RC (Adams Papers); addressed: "A. Monsieur Monsieur Adams. chez Madame la veuve Hendrik Schorn a Amsterdam"; docketed in Thaxter's hand: "Johnny 18th. Feby. 1781."

[1] This work, issued anonymously, was currently in progress: *Tableau de l'histoire générale des Provinces-unies*, 10 vols., Utrecht, 1777–1784. Two sets remain among JA's books in MB. Antoine Marie Cerisier (1749–1828), a journalist of French birth who had long resided in the Netherlands, was a leading propagandist for the Patriot or anti-Orangist party and became an enthusiastic supporter of JA's efforts to win recognition for the United States. See a documented sketch of Cerisier in JA's *Diary and Autobiography*, 2:454.

[2] Louis Gabriel Florence Kerroux, *Abrégé de l'histoire de la Hollande et des Provinces-unies* . . . , 4 vols., Leyden, 1778. The copy at MQA contains JQA's bookplate.

James Lovell to Abigail Adams

Feb. 27. 1781

Your Effects, expected in the Alliance, came in the Ariel. Yesterday two Cases were brought to my Chamber, the Size of which I give on the other Side to govern your future Directions as to Transportation.[1]

Inches { 54 long / 18 high / 16 broad }   { 27 long / 17 broad / 14 high }

I received at the same Time a Box for my Friend Gerry and another for Col. Peabody. Having deliver'd the former agreable to his order, I was told in the Evening that the Articles were in Part rotten. This made me immediately open Col. P's. I found them not much injured. I thoroughly examined, wiped and dried them properly for second Package. The Appearance of his Box indicated his medium Luck: Not so yours, my dear Lady. The large Case was shattered; and, thro' the Cracks appeared neither full nor regularly packt; and it smoaked so in the Sun in my Chamber as to warrant the further Search of my Eye even if I had been warned of its containing only Secrets.

I was agreably disappointed in finding that the Damage was not equal to my Fears. It was such however as to oblige me to pass over every Article seperately; for those which are not really injured were in a warm fermenting moisture. *Your* Diaper, very pretty, was among the worst. Mr. *Shutes* Linnen the next, *your* No. 7507 next, Mr. Wibert's No. 19 next, Brother Cranche's Cambrick No. 1216 next.[2] The other Linnens and Cambricks do not properly fall under the Head of Damage, nor any of the other Articles, except *your* Gloves which are useless in their present *party-colored* State; and They had nearly ruined those of your Articles among which they were wron[g]-fully inserted: They should be wrapped in wollen. There was a good Fire in my Room and a *pretty-handy* Watchman till 5 this morning; in Consequence, all of the smaller Parcels have had due Airing, Wiping and Repacking. I must particularly acquaint *Miss* that, tho the Fans stuck much together, they are now in no Measure defaced. They would have been lost if they had dried in that Posture. One of them is the prettiest of the *shining* Kind that I have yet seen; and a Lady who lately lodged here was supposed to have them the prettyest. I like those better which I used to see 19 years ago. The green Mould is next-to-intirely taken from the Gauzes, among which the Gloves were placed for their Security.—Tell the Men their Cloths are become quite dry without any Change of Colour.—I should have named Miss P. B. A's Linnen Handkerchiefs as damaged, but I suppose within the Power of some of her Arts to recover: Her Chintz was not injured tho' in the same wet Paper; it is almost a Beauty.[3] It has a large Flower too much. Your striped Persian is spotted but I believe the Wind will recover it. Your nice quaker Broad Cloth escaped, tho the wrapper was very wet. You had better keep to your Cardinal and not run into the *Pride* of the female Lucifers of this City with their *uncouloured* Long Cloaks. The Linnens and Diapers are still at the Fire. The best shall be done for them that can be. I hope your Fears will magnify the Damage that you may have more Satisfaction in the End.

The large Case is larger than was necessary, by many Inches. And I suspect will not easily find Transportation when perhaps I shall be able to send the whole Articles in two or three Parcels more readily.

But, now Madam the worst of the Future is to be mentioned: how is the smaller Box to reach you. For the Past, it has escaped well, but I fear the long, rough Waggonnage: Perhaps shortly there will be a most decided Superiority in our favor by Sea so as to make the Winds the only Risque to be run. Capt. Penny sold his China here some time ago, because of the great Risque to Jamaica Plains. But I cannot advise you to part with yours. Nevertheless, I will in my next send you the current Price that if you wish to *chip and change* you may do it with your Eyes open.

The fate of the South is balancing between Cornwallis and Green; and of the Middle States—War between the Commanders near Gardner's Island. I never have yet been so agitated by present Moments since the War began. God be better to us than our Deserts!

Your very humb. Servt.,   JL

RC (Adams Papers); addressed: "Mrs. A. Adams."

[1] The dimensions of the "Cases" are inserted here from the third page of Lovell's letter. These cases contained the goods JA had ordered a year earlier from James Moylan, merchant at Lorient, to be sent as gifts to AA and various relatives and friends; see JA to Moylan, 22 Feb. 1780 (LbC, Adams Papers), the relevant portion of which is quoted in a note on JA's letter to AA, 12 Feb. 1780, vol. 3:273, above. As numerous allusions in the correspondence that followed make clear, the goods were to have been shipped to Boston in the *Alliance* in care of Dr. Amos Windship. But they became the victims of the quarrels that beset that unfortunate vessel and all who had anything to do with it, and were left behind when the *Alliance* finally sailed in the summer. See AA to JA, 3 Sept. (vol. 3:406), 18 Oct., 13–24 Nov. 1780, both above. JA repeatedly inquired what had happened to the goods, and Moylan at length replied on 29 Dec. 1780 that John Paul Jones had "encharged himself" with them and had sailed in the *Ariel* on the 18th of that month (Adams Papers). In a letter to AA of 1 March 1781, below, Lovell furnished an itemized list, and he soon forwarded some of the less bulky articles (see his letter of 5 March, below), but late in April AA was still awaiting most of the shipment and gave vent to her feelings about Moylan's negligence from start to finish (to JA, 23 April, below).

[2] The numbers in this sentence, which are clearly not ciphered forms of words, may possibly be entries in a missing invoice, though it is hard to account for the numbers running so high, and Lovell used *no* numbers in his itemized list at 1 March below.

[3] Lovell's reference to "Miss P.B.A" is characteristically ambiguous. "Miss" is a shortened form of "Mistress," and though it usually designated an unmarried woman, it could still be used for a married one; see entry of 2 Dec. 1760 (and note) in JA, *Diary and Autobiography*, 1:176–177. JA was far more likely to have sent gifts from France to his sister-in-law, Mrs. Peter Boylston Adams (the former Mary Crosby), than to his niece, Mary (1769–1830), later Mrs. Elisha Turner. Mrs. P. B. Adams had, however, died in June 1780; see vol. 3:323, above. On Mary (Adams) Turner see Adams Genealogy.

Isaac Smith Sr. to John Adams

Boston Feby. 27th. 1781

I wrote you a few days since[1] by a ship which goes in Company with this of the success under Genl. Morgan in the Caralinions Over the famous Tarleton. Since which we have the Agreeable Advize of an Expedition of a 64 ship and ⟨2 *frigates*⟩ part of the french fleet att Rd. Island, haveing been to Virginia in order to ketch Genl. ⟨Phillips and⟩ Arnold, which business they have compleated haveing saild from Rd. Island the 9th and returned the 24th with the Romulous a 44 gun and 2 sloops of Warr, of the british with 500 seamen prisoners. They distroyed the most of the transport, and brought of there stores. The Enemy got ashore, but as the Virginians had been under Arms before itts most likely they will be Obliged to surrender As they are deprived of every thing. Itts said to be a plan concerted by Congress and Genl. Washington and has Answered the happy effect. We cant but with gratfully[2] Acknowledgments, Acknowledge the particular kind hand of heaven in the late successes Over the Enemy in the southern goverments. We have not got all the particulars as itt came but last Evening.—We hope in a post or two to have Advize from Virginia. The dispute between Virginia and Maryland About the land Affair is settled and Maryland delegates have signed the Confederacy.[3]

Itt is thought best that Vermont should be a seperate state and will or is Allready.[4]—Mrs. Adams is well. Mrs. Smith has been confined to her Chamber a Month with a fever but through the goodness of god, is geting better.

I am, Sr. Your Most hum. Servt.,   Isaac Smith

PS   A french frigate is just arrived from france with a large sum of Money and the Marrs from Nantes, with a prize, something Valuable.—Do let my friend M. Hadshon[5] know I received his of the 8th Novr. Yours by said Conveyance is forwarded to Mrs. Adams.

[Insted?] of 2 sloops [of] War, some Armed Transports with stores.[6]

The famous Capt. Paul Jones is Arrived att Phila.

RC (Adams Papers).

[1] A very brief note dated at Boston, 24 Feb. 1781, in Adams Papers but omitted here.

[2] Thus in MS.

[3] This was substantially true but in part premature news. The long delay in completing the ratification of the Articles of Confederation, originally submitted to the states in 1777, was owing in good part to differences between states (such

as Virginia) with large claims to western lands and those (such as Maryland) with none. Virginia at last ceded her claims to Congress on 2 Jan. of the present year; in February the Maryland delegates were instructed to ratify; and on 1 March they signed the Articles, the last of the thirteen state delegations to do so. Appropriate acts of celebration followed. See *JCC,* 19:138–140, 208–223; Julian P. Boyd, ed., *The Articles of Confederation and Perpetual Union* (Old South Leaflets, Nos. 228–229), Boston, 1960; Burnett, ed., *Letters of Members,* 6:1–4; Merrill Jensen, *The Articles of Confederation,* Madison, 1959, ch. 12.

⁴ Vermont had assumed the status of an independent republic in 1777–1778; despite efforts of some Vermonters and of some groups in Congress to bring it into the Union, it was not admitted as a state, the fourteenth, until 1791 (Burnett, *Continental Congress,* p. 540–546; *DAH*). See also AA to JA, 23 April, below.

⁵ John Hodshon, head of a mercantile firm in Amsterdam well disposed toward America (*JA, Diary and Autobiography,* 2:444).

⁶ This may refer back to the end of the second sentence in the first paragraph of this letter.

James Lovell to Abigail Adams

March 1st. 1781

[In my last I told] you that the Case [which was brought] to my Lodgings for your Benefit did not appear full according to the common Mode of Packing for a Voyage. I ought to have endeavored to give you a Kind of Invoice of its Contents. I had not Time. It will now perhaps enable you to decide whether there have been Filchings if I give you only the following Sketch.

For Mrs. Adams

18 Ells of Diaper at 10^{tt}
some Persian & Gauze
Gloves & a Band Box with a number of small Articles Fans Ribbons Lace Ferrets
Threads of difft. Colrs. and Cotton for Tambour
3 p[iece]s Linnen
White Broad Cloth & some Yards of blue Silk
a Box of Tea

For Mr. Wibert

Black broad Cloth
2 ps. Linnen
1 ps. Cambrick
Silk Hose. Gloves. Hankerchifs. sewing silk

For Mr. Cranch

Broad [Cloth] & Serge
1 ps. Linnen

1 ps. Cambrick
Silk Hose

For Mr. Shute

6 Ells Linnen

For Mr. Tuffts

1 ps. Cambrick
some Gauze & Fans

Mr. P. B. Adams

1 ps. Linnen
1 ps. Chintz
12 Handkerchfs.
some black Parisnett & Lace

What made me most apprehend Roguery is finding no Cambrick for yourself. However, there was such a general Slovenlyness in the Packing, that there is Room to hope the Vacancy is no Proof of Loss.

[The Articles of Confederation] have been signed by [the delegates of Maryland] this day, which will have a good Effect in Europe if not in America.[1]—But it is needless to enlarge on this or any other Topic of Intelligence as the Opportunity by Doctr. Winship will be slower than the Post. Perhaps I shall send you some little Articles, at least the Band Box, or the Tea Box.

RC (Adams Papers); addressed: "Mrs. A Adams   Braintree near Boston"; endorsed: "March 1. 81." MS has a large hole near the top of all four pages. Conjectural readings have been supplied for the resulting gaps in the text.

[1] See note 3 on the preceding letter.

Abigail Adams to Mercy Otis Warren

My dear Madam   Braintree March 5 1781

Your two sons did me the favour of calling upon me yesterday morning and Breakfasting with me.[1] The bad roads prevented their lodgeing here the Night before as they kindly intended. I was very glad to see them, and would have had them remain[2] with me till the Storm was over, but they were apprehensive of worse weather, and chose to go on.

I feel for these young Gentlemen a particular affection, not only from their own amiable dispositions and agreable Manners, which alone would entitle them to a large share, but from the sincere regard and affection which I bear to their most Excellent Mamma, who

I hope has not a doubt of the particular satisfaction and pleasure her Friend takes in the Idea of soon having her for her Neighbour.

I most sincerely regret the misfortune, both you and your Friends suffer from the disorder of your Eyes, but having a fund of usefull knowledge laid up in store, like the immortal Milton, you may better afford to be deprived of them than others.

I hoped before this time to have given you some intelligence from abroad—but the Mars brings me only two letters from Mr. Thaxter, written before he left Paris. I find by a few lines of Mr. Dana, that Mr. Guile had many Letters, he sailed in October and has not since been heard of. The best that can be hoped of him, is that he may be taken, and even that is a situation to be deprecated considering the inhumane policy which the New Parliment and the Successes of the Britains at Charlestown have induced them to adopt as you will see from extracts from Mr. A[dam]s Letters to Congress, which I enclose to you, but should be glad may be returnd to me as soon as a safe conveyance offers.

Retaliation is a painfull task to the Humane Breasts of Americans, yet is certainly due in justice to the worthy suffering citizens and especially to so aged and so respectable a personage as the late President Laurence, and more particularly so on account of the publick character with which he was invested.[3]

O! My Dear Madam when I reflect upon this worthy Mans situation, I cannot feel sufficient Gratitude to Heaven for preserving my dearest Friend from a similar Situation, and thereby trying me with a calamity which would have "harrowd up my Soul."

I congratulate you Madam upon the rising Hero in the South. General Morgan by his repeated Successes has brightned the page of our History, and immortalized his own Name, whilst the opportunely[4] expedition of our Allies checkd the treacherous Arnold in his cruel ravages, and opens a prospect for his speedy destruction. May the ancient Spirit of America rise with her Successes, and crush the venal passion for Gain, may every virtuous citizen cooperate with the Martial Spirit, and drive from these Distressed States the Mercenary invaders since that and that alone is like to give us peace.

With regard to our commercial affairs, you must have misunderstood me with regard to Tea, because I never had any but what I purchased by the pound for my family. The hankerchiefs sent the other day were a mistake, the flowerd papers had always contain the coulourd hankerchiefs and I did not think to open them.

Nabby desires to be affectionately rememberd to you and rejoices in the prospect of your removeing, sends her Love to Miss Betsy and Master Gorge as there is no other young Gentlemen at home to share it.

Believe me my dear Madam at all times most affectionately Yours,

A A[5]

RC (MHi:Warren-Adams Collection); slightly mutilated; addressed: "To Mrs. Mercy Warre[n] Pli[mouth]"; docketed in two later unidentified hands: "Mrs. Abigail Adams March 5th. 1781 No. 14." Dft (Adams Papers). Enclosed "extracts" not found.

[1] Probably Charles and Henry, third and fourth of the Warren sons, both identified in vol. 3 above.

[2] RC and Dft both read: "remained."

[3] Dft reads: "President Laurence whom they wish to Distroy, (and I fear from the extracts,) either have or will effect their purpose."

[4] Thus in both RC and Dft.

[5] Initialed signature from Dft; lower part of second leaf of RC torn away.

James Lovell to Abigail Adams

Dr. Madam   March 5th. 1781 Midnight

Doctr. Winship left this City Today and has been so kind as to take into his Care two small Packages. I could not impose more on his Goodness. I hope they will escape Thieves and all Injury from Wet or Rubbing. I have cautioned and he has promised. You will find at Mrs. Lovell's or Mr. Smith's after the Doctr. reaches Boston, a Package in a very coarse Wrapper. It contains your Band Box, your Gauzes, your striped Persian and your Gloves, Your Threads and your Tambours Cotton. Mrs. L will find in a small Bag a few Articles for Mr. *Wibert* with some for Mr. Gerry. My Daughter's straw Trunks have also a little parcel for Mr. Wibert with something for Col. Peabody. It would have afforded me much Pleasure to have been able to send *all* the small Articles for my Friend Cranch, Mr. P. B. Adams, Mr. Tuffts and Mr. Wibert. If I do not soon find a Chest Conveyance I shall as the Weather mends the Roads find frequent private Opportunities for small Parcells.

I am not very well; and it is too late to detail News, and the opportunity of Carriage is not that by which I chuse to say the great Deal I have to say about our Friends in Holland. He is doing well I am persuaded.

Yr. respectfully affectte.   JL

RC (Adams Papers).

Elizabeth Ellery Dana to Abigail Adams

My dear Madam   Cambridge March 6 1781

Your favor of the 5th gave me sensible pain. Had I had the least doubt that you was not so happy as to have heard from Mr. Adams by the Mars, I should before this communicated part of the contents of mine from Mr. D[ana] dated Amsterdam Nov. 7th when all friends were well. Mr. D was to leave Holland for Paris the next week but whither in company with Mr. Adams he did not write. He writes that Mr. A—s had recieved a letter from Mr. Smith Boston in which he tells him he forwards letter[s] from you and me. Mr. A—s was fortunate enough to recieve yours some time After—as for mine it had not got to Mr. Dana when he wrote. I cannot but flatter myself that you have a letter. I went into Boston the day after I recieved mine and enquired particularly whither there was letters for you. Mr. Austin told me that you had letters and some things come. I will send to him to Morrow and know what has become of them, and if any forward them immediately. Could persons have but a faint Idea of what we suffer through their inattention they would never neglect our letters as they do, but be as impatient to convey them as we are to recieve. It was above 6 months from the date of my last from Mr. D when I recieved this last welcome one. He mentions writing me in that time. But they are gone. I wish from my heart there was soon to be an end of this intercours by letters—and we in exchange might be happily seated down with the objects of our affections. But to wish and hope is all we can do—and at times I am almost afraid to wish their return without there should be Peace, for should they fall into the hands of the cruel Britain—I will not dwell upon the thought it is too, too, painful. Must hope that before you recieve this that you have been made as happy by letters from Mr. A—s as I was the last week by mine.

The ladies desire their best regards to you Madam and family in which joins them your affectionate and sympathizing Friend,

Eliza Dana

RC (Adams Papers).

John Adams to Abigail Adams

My dear Portia   Leyden March 11. 1781

My Letters by Davis, Mr. Guild[1] &c. are lost.—Pray did you get the Goods by Davis?

This goes by Mr. De L'Etombe Consul of France, a worthy Man. He will do honour to his Country and good to ours.

My Boys are both Students in the University of Leyden.—All well. —Write me by the Way of Spain, France, Holland, Sweeden and every other. Jones carried your Chest, Samson carried another.—Yours with more Tenderness than it would be wise, if it were possible to express.

J.A.[2]

RC (Adams Papers).

[1] Benjamin Guild (on whom see sketch at vol. 3:322–323, above) was captured off Newfoundland on his return voyage in the *Fame*, which was carried to Ireland (AA to James Lovell, 13 May, below). In a manner unknown, Guild soon made his way back to the Netherlands; see JQA to JA, 17 May, below.

[2] It will be noted that this laconic note is the first surviving communication from JA to AA since his letter of 18 Dec. 1780, above. Presumably he had written others, as he implies in his first sentence here, but he did not keep copies of them, and it seems likely that he had not written often or at length. One reason was his fear of enemy interception at sea, but this did not cut off the flow of his dispatches to Congress on European affairs, especially in regard to the Anglo-Dutch war crisis. It may be suggested that, as sometimes before when JA was deeply troubled, he simply did not record his inmost thoughts, either in correspondence or diary entries. (His diary contains essentially no entries between the end of Aug. 1780 and the brief and scattering entries in Jan.–Feb. 1781, and a very long gap ensues.)

A more obvious, yet in some degree superficial, explanation for the lack of personal records by JA at this time would be his quite literal "busyness" on the Dutch scene. During his early months in the Netherlands he was cultivating friends among journalists, moneyed men, and political functionaries; writing and circulating pro-American propaganda; and studying Dutch life, literature, and institutions. The most detailed and thoroughly documented account of these activities yet available is by Sister Mary Briant Foley, The Triumph of Militia Diplomacy: John Adams in the Netherlands, 1780–1782, Loyola Univ. doctoral dissertation, 1968, chs. 2–3.

During the weeks immediately before he wrote the present letter JA had been much on the move between Amsterdam, Leyden, and The Hague. On 25 Feb. he received dispatches from Congress which commissioned and instructed him as minister plenipotentiary to the States General of the United Provinces of the Netherlands, in succession to the captured Henry Laurens, to negotiate a treaty of amity and commerce as voted by Congress on 29 Dec. 1780, and also to adhere on the part of the United States to the Armed Neutrality among the northern maritime powers, according to a resolve of Congress voted on 5 Oct. 1780. See Samuel Huntington to JA, 1 Jan., with duplicate of 9 Jan. 1781, and enclosures (Adams Papers; printed in JA, *Works*, 7:349, letter only; printed from PCC, with letter of credence, in Wharton, ed., *Dipl. Corr. Amer. Rev.*, 4:224–225; for the respective resolves of Congress, including JA's instructions, see JCC, 18:905–906, 1204–1217; 19:17–19). At The Hague on 8 March JA submitted a brief memorial to the States General regarding the Armed Neutrality (Adams Papers; JA, *Works*, 7:373; see the related correspondence which follows in *Works* and also in *Corr. in the Boston Patriot*, p. 392–395).

For JA's strategy and efforts to obtain recognition of American independence by the Dutch as that nation drifted into a full-scale war with Great Britain, see the notes under his next and only slightly less laconic letter to AA, 28 April, below.

John Adams to Isaac Smith Sr.

Sir   Leyden March 11th. 1781

Your favour of the 18th. of Decr.[1] reached me to day. I lament the Loss of my Letters by Davis, but I hope Mrs. Adams did not lose her Present, which I hear nothing of. I thank You, Sir, for the kind News of my Family. Mr. Guild is taken and all my Letters and other things sent by him lost.

I wish I could give You any good News, especially of Peace, but alass there is no hopes of it. The English are labouring with all their Art and Might to spread the Flames of War thro' all Europe. I don't know that they would get or We lose any Advantage by that: but such is their incendiary Temper at present.

I am glad to learn that the Army is to be placed on a more permanent footing. I wish to know the State of Commerce and Privateering. Your Letters Via Spain always reach me.

This will go by Mr. De L'Etombe; the new Consul, a valuable Man —so thinks your's respectfully &c.

LbC in John Thaxter's hand (Adams Papers).

[1] Not found.

Abigail Adams to James Lovell

My dear Sir   March 17 1781

It was not till the last week in Febry. that your favour of Janry. 8th reachd me. I had waited the arrival of each post with impatience but was so repeatedly dissapointed that I almost gave up my correspondent even in the way of Friendship. I struck up of[1] the list of Galantry some time ago. It is a character in my mind very unbefitting a senator notwithstanding the Authority of Chesterfeild against me, yet the Stile of some Letters obliged me to balance a long time and study by detail the character I was scrutinizing. I wished to divest myself for the time of a partiality which I found predominant in my Heart, yet give to every virtue its due weight. I wished for once, for a few moments and 3 hundred miles distance observe, to consider myself in the nearest connexion possible, and then try the force of certain Epethets addressed to a Lady—we will suppose her for Arguments sake amiable, agreable and his Friend. I found from trial that those Epethets only would bear [*i.e.* be bearable]. If they were carried

91

a Syllable beyond, to *Lovely,* to *charming,* they touchd too too sensibly the fine tuned instrument and produced a discord where Harmony alone should subsist. What right has she who is appropriated to appear Lovely or charming in any Eyes but his whose property she is?[2] I am pursuaded says a Lady who had seen much of the world, that a woman who is determined to place her happiness in her Husbands affections should abandon the extravagant desire of engageing pub-lick adoration, and that a *Husband* who tenderly loves his wife should in his turn give up the reputation of being a Gallant. However an-tiquated and unpolite these Ideas may appear to our Modern refiners, I can join with Juba in the play "by Heavens I had rather have that best of Friends approve my deeds than Worlds for my admirers."[3]

A particular reason has led me to wish the Man whose Soul is Benevolence itself flowing out in these exuberances would more cir-cumspectly guard a pen.—A Captured Letter, not to Portia thank for-tune, but to his Friend G[err]y published by the Enemy, has made some talk. I have tried to obtain it that I might judge whether what was said of it was true. Have not yet been able to, but his own con-science must tell him whether any thing written to a confidiential Friend should give just occasion of pain to an affectionate wife. That it has done so I know not, but ought there to be room for the world to suppose it capable of it? I will not judge unheard and unseen, only repeate an observation which I once before made to you, that no situation was more delicate, more critical or more liable to censure than that of a Lady whose Husband has been long seperated from her. The world will judge from selfish motives nor will they consider of any obligation prior to that which binds a man to his family or that the demands of his country must silence the voice of pleading Nature. A similarity of circumstances leads me to sympathize with every sufferer. I own I am exceedingly tenacious of my prerogative and it would wound me to the Soul even to have it suspected.

I had many things in mind to say to you in the political way when I took up my pen, but will defer them for the subject of an other Letter or untill you tell me that you have received this in that Spirit of Friendship with which it flowed from the pen of   Portia[4]

Dft (Adams Papers); without indication of addressee, but this letter set off a long train of exchanges between Lovell and AA, running all the way to the following August; see note 4 below. The (missing) RC was not received by Lovell until late in May, and then in the form of a duplicate RC (also missing) enclosed in hers to him of 10 May (below), the original having either strayed in the mail or actually been captured by the enemy. See Lovell to AA, 14, 29 May, and 16 June, all below.

[1] Thus in MS. AA probably meant to write: "struck him off."

[2] The reasons impelling AA at this juncture "to balance a long time and study by detail" the propriety of the language Lovell had employed in his letter of 8 Jan. (above) and, generally, in other letters he had written her, are discussed in note 4 below. In the present passage, written in some agitation, she is saying that "Epethets" like *amiable* and *agreeable* addressed to a [married] Lady" by a male friend are perfectly acceptable, but *lovely* and *charming* are not. They smack too much of the Chesterfieldian code of "Galantry," which she rejects.

[3] Initial quotation mark supplied. AA is quoting, a little inaccurately, from Addison's *Cato* (1713), Act II, scene v, lines 144–145.

[4] AA's concern and admonitions as expressed in this letter sprang from two different but related causes. Lovell in his correspondence with her habitually indulged in a queer sort of gallantry, imitative of Laurence Sterne's writings, which she in turn indulged him in without protest and thus apparently found acceptable. However, in his letter of 8 Jan., which she found indiscreet (see note 2 above), he spoke of her as one of the "most lovely of the Loveliest Sex," and at the same time blandly mentioned that recent letters of his, including one to her (dated 21 Nov. 1780, not found), had fallen into the hands of "Jemmy Rivington," the tory newspaper printer in New York. This naturally suggested to her that the combination of what she here calls Lovell's "exuberances" and the increasingly frequent British interception of American mails made her reputation more vulnerable than was pleasant to contemplate. Six weeks or so elapsed between Lovell's writing his letter of 8 Jan. and her receipt of it in late February, and meanwhile AA learned that Rivington and other loyalist printers *had* published one or more of Lovell's private letters, specifically one to Elbridge Gerry, 20 Nov. 1780, containing enough indiscretions to excite talk in Boston. Though she had not seen the paper or papers in question, she was bound to wonder what further epistolary indiscretions her correspondent might have committed and she was still to hear about. Waiting for several weeks, and still without sight of what Rivington had printed, AA here phrased her multiple rebukes to Lovell with care and tact. In a letter of 10 May, below (and perhaps in others intervening but not found), and *still* not having seen the offending letter to Gerry, AA renewed her "Strictures" on Lovell's conduct in severe terms; see the notes and references there.

Abigail Adams to John Adams

My dearest Friend   March 19 1781

It was only an hour ago that I was informd of a vessel just ready to sail for Amsterdam; by forgetfullness in the Messenger I have so short warning as to be able to write you only a few lines, yet a few is more than have come to my hand for six months, in all which space only a few lines written last May have reachd me. The Mars arrived the beginning of this Month after a very long passage, but brought me only Letters from Mr. Thaxter written before he left Paris. By a Letter from Mr. Dana to his Lady I find you were all well in November, yet wonder I should not hear so from your own hand.

Jones too has arrived at Phili—pia but brought no Letters for me. I have just heard of the loss [of a][1] vessel belonging to my unkle bound to Cales, by which [I w]rote largely to you in Sepbr.[2]—Such is the Luck of absent Friends. Suppose I have shared the same fate by the loss or Capture of the Fame which has not been heard of since she left Amsterdam. I have written to you by the Captains Hayden and Cuznew who both sailed for Amsterdam and by the Alliance which is once more gone to France, by Trash to Bilboa. I received by Capt. Sampson a very acceptable present 11 peices of Calico. They were as Good and as pretty as I could have wished for, but to my great misfortune so damaged by the long passage as some of them to be nearly ruined.

When I received them, which was as soon as possible after his arrival, they were the cheif of them so wet and mildewed as I never saw any Goods before and this was the fate of his cargo except what was in his own Cabin. I am almost affraid to tell you, least you should be discouraged from trying again, that my Trunk at Philadelphia was in as bad or worse State, by Mr. L[ovel]l['s] account whose care I had requested, if it should arrive there. It was well I did, for it was oweing to his immediate attention, that every thing was not rotten which it contained. He was obliged to unpack and dry by the fire in his chamber every article which were many of them much damaged, the diaper and linnens the worst. I have otherways been fortunate, from Bilboa and from Holland every thing was in good order. My Box of china is safe at Philidelphia where I believe it must remain for the present.

The Fate of the Southern States is balanceing between Green and Cornwallis. The late Successes of General Morgan in Carolina and at Gorgia have occasioned the British Army to collect all t[heir] force to that Quarter, we Dayly expect some important Ev[ent.]

By the loss of one British ship from New York of 74 Guns and the damage of two others, the Capture of the Romulus by the French, the British were so weakned as to induce the Fleet of our Allies to plan an expedition to the Southward in order to give assistance to the American Arms in that Quarter. Two days after they sailed, all the British ships followed, even the disabled one with jury Masts, which shews their weakness. The French took their troops with them and Road Island is now guarded by American millitia. The infamous Arnold by the last accounts was like to fall into the Hands of the justly incensed Americans. Such is our present anxious state.

We have recent accounts of an attack upon Eustatia by the Mad Britains and of a Declaration of war by the united provinces. The Insolence of Sir Joseph York was an abusive declaration of the British.

Excuse haste written late in the Evening. I long to hear from you.

When O! when will the time come. God Grant me happy tidings. My Love to my dear Sons, from whom I have not received a line for nine months.

Yours with sincere affection, Portia

RC (Adams Papers); addressed: "To the Honble john Adams Esqr Amsterdam"; endorsed: "Portia March 19. 1781."

[1] Here and below, MS is torn by seal.
[2] A mistake for October; see AA to JA, 8, 15 Oct. 1780, above.

John Thaxter to Abigail Adams

Madam Leyden 1st. April 1781

I have been duly honoured with your two favours of the 18th. of Novr. and 8th. of December.[1] I am much obliged by the particular Account You have given of the Rise, Progress and fatal Issue of the fond Attachment of Mr. C. to Miss P.[2] I confess with great Candour it contains many Circumstances hitherto unknown to me. I have indeed, Madam, an unavoidable and involuntary Share in the dreadful Catastrophe of this unhappy Man. The Story in itself is affecting— but the polish and Ornaments of your Pen together with those Observations which your nice Sensibility has suggested and which are so judiciously interspersed have rendered it peculiarly interesting. I have weeped his Fate as a Brother—nor is the unhappy Lady less an Object of my tenderest Commiseration. Would to God I had never seen the unfortunate Pair! It has been a Source of constant Misery to me, but this last and fatal Event has been painful and afflicting to an extreme degree. I do not however reproach myself. I have felt Stings and Arrows, but not those of Guilt or Remorse, tho' equally poignant. I am fully confident that I stand justified and acquitted of the least Shadow or particle of Criminality—I may have been innocently accessary.——There are undoubtedly bounds set to the Sacrifices which one may and ought to make to promote the Happiness of another—how far the Obligation may extend in a Circumstance similar to her's or mine, is a Question that involves so many Considerations and interests so much the Passion of Self Love and the social feelings, that it is of difficult Determination. Philosophy has very little to do in general in governing the decision. It is a most unhappy Dilemma— so strong is the desire of promoting our personal Felicity, so essential a Spring is it of our Actions, so fixed are we in deriving it from Objects where our Hopes centre, that, however disposed We may be to advance each other's Happiness, yet in Cases of Competition between personal and relative, the former turns the Scale but too commonly. In an Object so essential as the Choice of a Companion for life, it is proper that it should.——You observe I may be disappointed in my *fair American*—it is very possible and I think upon the whole very probable. I wish her to observe in that Case the same degree of Generosity, which I hope I may say without Vanity I have shewn in a similar one, and that the Issue of my Affection may not be so melancholy as that of the Gentleman who makes the Subject of your excellent Letter. I am as little capable as ambitious of female Conquests. I wish to merit the Esteem of all the fair, and boast the particular Affection of but one. I may be unhappy—may I be innocently so.

As to the fair Maroni, the Vestal Nun, it is long since I have seen or heard from her. The best Answer I can give is in adopting the Words of Your Quotation, stripping it of its Interrogations and substituting an Affirmation, viz. that her "Passions are all sublimated, and the Love of God substituted to that of Man," &c. &c. I am not sufficiently acquainted with her history to determine absolutely her Motives for entering that gloomy Abode. If I was to hazard a Conjecture, I should attribute her Motive to an enthusiastic Zeal rather than to "disappointed Love." It is a silent Retreat for "hopeless Passion," where Sighs, Tears and Woes to the unfeeling speechless Walls are rais'd and shed, but rais'd and shed in vain.

Accept, Madam, my most grateful Acknowledgments for your kind Attention to what is most dear to me, that is my Reputation, which those have attempted to asperse, whose Approbation would be its greatest Blot. There are some Persons in that Town, whose Element is Malice and Envy, who cannot bear to see a Character contrasted with their own. I despise their Calumny—I have little merited it. I feel the most sovereign Contempt for her who has said She could call me her own, or any other of the same Stamp there or in this Country.—God forbid that I should become a Slave to Wretches of that Cast.

The English are in open War with this Republick—have taken Statia, St. Martins and Saba,[3] but yet the Dutch have not a Ship of War or even a Privateer as yet gone out to revenge these Insults. This Irresolution and Inactivity is unaccountable—But my Pen must stop.

My Duty, Respects, and Compliments, if you please, where they are respectively due. My Love to your amiable Daughter, am very sorry She is not to be persuaded to favour me with some of her ingenious epistolary Productions. As to my *fair American* She is so curious about, I must refer her with the other curious young Ladies to her Aunt Cranch to whom I have written. I am with every Sentiment of Respect & Esteem Madam your most obliged & obedient Servt.,

J.T.

RC (Adams Papers).

[1] That of 18 Nov. has not been found; that of 8 Dec. is printed above.

[2] Nathaniel Cranch and Elizabeth Palmer; see Richard Cranch to JA, 26 April 1780, in vol. 3 above, and note 5 there.

[3] Three small and more or less adjacent islands in the Lesser Antilles, St. Eustatius, St. Martin, and Saba, all Dutch possessions except St. Martin, which was divided with France. St. Eustatius, a free port, had served as an important depot for the transshipment of supplies from Europe to America throughout the war. In the winter of 1780–1781 its harbor and warehouses were crammed with ships and goods vital to the American war effort and to the welfare of Dutch merchants and capitalists. Even before the British declaration of war on the Dutch in December 1780, secret orders had been prepared for Admiral Rodney and his fleet in the West Indies to attack St. Eustatius in case of war, and on 3 Feb. 1781 Rodney fell upon the virtually unfortified island and received its absolute surrender. When the news of this devastating loss reached the Netherlands in March, it had a profound effect, dampening what little popular enthusiasm remained for war with England and cutting off all prospects of a loan to the United States. See the classic study by J. Franklin Jameson, "St. Eustatius in the American Revolution," *AHR*, 8:683–708 (July 1903); and, for the calamitous effect of the loss on the Dutch business community, see the letters of Jean de Neufville & Son to JA in March and April, esp. 21, 27 March (Adams Papers).

Much of the enormous booty which was taken and which Rodney had counted on to make himself rich, was before long retaken by a French fleet that intercepted a British convoy off the Scilly Islands; see JA to AA, 16 May, below. Nor was this the final irony that sprang from the capture of St. Eustatius. Jameson pointed out, as did contemporary critics and later naval historians, that Rodney's lingering for more than three months at St. Eustatius had disastrous consequences for Great Britain in the war. While Rodney gathered his treasure, "De Grasse, watched only by Hood, had slipped around the shoulder of Martinique and joined the other French ships in the roadstead of Fort Royal. Yorktown itself might never have happened if this juncture of the French had not been effected, and in all probability it would not have been effected if Rodney, with his whole fleet, had been where Hood wished him to be, to windward of Martinique" (Jameson, p 706–707).

John Thaxter to John Adams

Sir   Leyden April 5th. 1781. 9 o Clock P.M.

Knowing that the Fever of your dear Charles is a Source of continual Anxiety to You, any thing tending to decrease or remove it cannot fail to be agreable. The Fit of this day was mild and only of an hour and an half or two hours duration. It came on at ten—he laid upon his Bed during the Fit, and rose up after it very gay and merry, dined with Us and has been in good Spirits all the Afternoon, and is now reading Gil Blas very devoutly—he will have an easy Night of it. The Professor[1] has been here and says every thing goes on agreably to his Wishes.

I have recieved the English Papers that Mr. De Neufville forwarded.

I have the Honour to be, with the most perfect Respect, Sir, your most obedient & most humble Servant,   J. Thaxter

RC (Adams Papers).

[1] Not identifiable with certainty.

Elizabeth Smith Shaw to Mary Smith Cranch

My dear Sister   Haverhill April 6th. 1781

When I received your last kind, and daily Remembrance of me,[1] I felt doubly obliged, for I knew I was in the arrears, and had not deserved it, and my gratitude rose in proportion. You have greatly the advantage of me in the enjoyment of quiet Life, in thinking over Letters while you [...] at work, and in the possession of your own thoughts. For if Ideas present themselves to my Mind, it is too much like the good seed sown among Thorns, they are soon erased, and swallowed up by the Cares of the World, the wants, and noise of my Family, and Children.

My little Creatures are well now, though they have been often indisposed this winter. Betcy Quincy[2] sleeps but little, wants to be waited upon every moment, and if she can have present necessities supplied, cares nothing about the future, or whether her mamma works, thinks, or plays. I have no patience with the saucy Girl.

I have been uneasy that I could not send my Letter, but I find by yours that Brothers Conduct with regard to the Rates has determined my Father not to let him take the Farm into his own hands.[3] I am sorry for the misfortune and loss, but believe it may be a means of preventing much greater evils.—I shall long to hear how things are. I hope you will continue your kind Informations.

What is the matter that I cannot be favoured with some of my dear Sister Adams's Letters. Does publick speculations, and an absent Husband and Children engross all her attention, and leave not one crevice for a sister who tenderly loves her.

We had a report here that Brother Adams was returned last week with proffers of Peace &c., but I did not believe he had stolen a march again.

I wish I knew what our situation was, with foreign Powers. Can Holland, and the States of Germany see the mart of the world destroyed, and preserve their Neutrality? It has greivously affected our merchants, Capt. Cordis particularly—he is a very great sufferer.

I am very sorry for your loss and dissappointment in Your Goods. I hope you have got them and find them not so bad as you feared. For it costs almost an estate to procure any article either foreign or domestic.—I have been trying to get some spining done, and have hired a Girl into the house for that purpose, but it keeps the house in confusion. I hate it.

I am sorry to hear my Aunt Thaxter has been so unwell.[4] Are any more of my Cousins married. Is my Aunt a Grandmama? Give my Love to them all. I wish they were useful heads of Families in this town. If it was not so great a distance, and such chargeble travelling, I flatter myself I should see them scattered here and there. I want to see them.

I think it strange you cannot any of you find out who Mr. Thaxters favorite is. I think if I had seen him as often as you I should have known who the happy Girl was, for I suppose she will think herself so, when he returns with so much good-sense embelished by the advantages of travelling, and the Graces of the polite World.

I am glad to hear you are like to have such an agreeable addition to your neighbourhood, as Col. Warren's Family. Family Friendships are often-times exceedingly beneficial. They have Sons and you have Daughters.

I should be glad if sister Smith would see about the making Betcy Smith[5] a pair of black draw-boy Shoes.[6] I sent a piece by Sister Adams last Summer—the measure of her foot I send—she wants them directly. She is well and send duty, and Love.

Mr. Shaw presents his regards—he is sick with a Cold. I hope it will be nothing worse. He says you must be very ignorant of his Disposition if you fear he's making any unkind criticisms upon so good a Sister.

Billy is come. Mamma—Mamma.

Bea wants a peice of breaden—peas—mamm—hold your tongue Child—till I subscribe myself your dear Aunt Cranch's most affectionate Sister, Eliza. Shaw

I received the handkercheif.

RC (DLC:Shaw Family Papers); docketed on face in Richard Cranch's hand: "Letter from Mrs. E. Shaw Apl. 6th. 1781."

[1] Letter not found.
[2] Elizabeth Quincy Shaw (1780–1798), on whom see Adams Genealogy.
[3] Presumably the farm in Lincoln where the numerous family of William Smith Jr. (1746–1787) lived. This property was left in trust by Rev. William Smith in 1783 for the support of his errant son's family. See Rev. William Smith's will, Sept. 1783 (attested copy in MHi:Cranch Papers). On William Jr., frequently mentioned in vols. 1–2 above, see also Adams Genealogy.
[4] Anna (Quincy) Thaxter (1719–1799), wife of John Thaxter Sr.; see Adams Genealogy.
[5] "[S]ister Smith" must be the former Catharine Louisa Salmon (1749–1824), wife of William Smith Jr., mentioned above (see note 3). "Betcy" is presumably another niece of the writer, Elizabeth (1770–1849), daughter of Isaac Smith Sr., the Boston merchant; she married John Patton Hall in 1813. See Adams Genealogy under both names.
[6] Shoes made of figure-woven material; see OED under draw-boy.

John Quincy Adams to Abigail Adams

Honour'd Mamma   Leyden April the 8th 1781

I have been wanting to write to you this sometime but there has been nothing worth writing, and even now I know not what to write. We have not long since, heard of the taking of St. Eustatia, it cast a great damp upon the spirits of the dutchmen here; however the latest news from America make up for it for in the English news papers there is paragraph which makes mention that by the latest dispatches from New York they learn that the corps under Col. Tarleton was defeated, but it is not yet confirmed; however if it is true, it is no news to you, but what will be perhaps is the check the English have had in the East Indies, and of the two Colonels Fletcher and Baily one was kill'd and the other taken, they also have lost a great number of men.

Since I begun this letter Pappa is arrived from Amsterdam, he has received two letters from you which came by Col. Laurence, but I was very much disappointed, to find there was none for me; as to Sister, she has not done me the honour of writing me one line since I have been in Europe. The last letter that I recieved was one from you containing some excellent advice[1] for which I am very much obliged to you.

I am now at the most celebrated university in Europe which was founded here for the valour of its inhabitants when it was besieg'd, when they were at war with Spain, it was put to it's choice whether to be exempt from all taxes for a certain number of years, or to have an University founded here, and they wisely choose the latter. I will give you a short description of this city.

Leyden is fortified as are all the other Towns in the seven Provinces, with a strong Rampart of Earth and a very broad Canal, so that it is able to sustain a seige. The Citizens are able to lay the whole Country about them under water, as was done by the advice of the Prince of Orange during the famous Siege which they sustain'd which was in 1574. They had recourse to the desperate Remedy of cutting the Banks of the Maes and Issel, by which all the neighbouring country was turn'd into a kind of Sea, and 1500 Spaniards were drown'd before they could retire. The besieg'd were reduced to extraordinary straits, they were forced to make paper money, which was afterwards chang'd for Silver. They had these Legends upon them, on one side, Haec libertatis ergo, and Pugno pro patria; "These miseries we suffer for the Sake of our Liberty, and in defending our Country." And on the other side were these Initials N.O.U.L.S.G.I.P.A.C. that is Nummus obsessae urbis Lugdunensis sub gubernatione Illustrissimi Principis Auriaci cusus. In English The Money of the besieged city of Leyden, coined during the Government of the most illustrious Prince of Orange. The University was founded about a year after the city's deliverance.

Hengest castle or the Berg said to have been built by Hengest The saxon as a Trophy for his conquest of England is situated in the middle of the city in an Angle formed by the Channels of the Old and New Rhine and is planted with Trees. From the Top of it is an Extensive Prospect of the adjacent Country and Villages, of the Haerlem lake and the Sand hills. Some Antiquarians pretend, that it was built by the Romans as a garrison for one of their Legions. There is a Well here out of which it is said the Inhabitants took a Fish alive when the Place was almost famish'd during the siege, Which was shewn to the Enemy over the walls, in order to discourage the besiegers, by making their condition appear better than it was. This well is now dried up.—The plesantest Street in Leyden is the Rapenburg. It has a fine Canal over which are several handsome bridges. Each side of it is adorned with a Row of lofty Trees and the Streets as well as those of all the other cities of Holland have a small Declivity towards the Canals so that they can never be dirty even after the greatest rains.

The Physick Garden is a curiosity here. The inscription on old Clusius's tomb, flatters him a little.[2] The Poet in extolling this Professor of Botany who died in 1619 says, wittily enough

"Non potuit plures hic quaerere Clusius herbas
Ergo novas campis quaerit Elysiis."

"Since no more herbs the Earth to Clusius yields
New ones he seeks in the Elysian fields."

This is all that is remarkable in this City.[3]
I am your dutiful Son,   John Quincy Adams

RC (Adams Papers).

[1] AA to JQA, 21 Jan., above.
[2] Charles de l'Escluse (1526–1609), generally known as Carolus Clusius, the celebrated botanist, professor at the University of Leyden from 1592 until his death (*Nieuw Ned. Biog. Woordenboek*, 9:150–153).

[3] JQA's historical and topographical matter above was undoubtedly derived from a guidebook, perhaps the one JA purchased in Rotterdam when the Adamses first arrived in the Netherlands (see JQA, Diary, 7 Aug. 1780), but it has not been identified.

James Lovell to Abigail Adams

April 17.1781

By your Letter of the 3d.[1] received this day I find that I have lost the Pleasure of having what you and Mr. Cranch wrote some Time ago respecting your little Invoices. Tho' I make little Progress in forwarding your Property yet my past Notifications will show that I am constantly attentive to the Business. I suspect that Mr. Cranch may have mentioned some Waggons which came to this City with Mr. Dugan's Goods: But I found it dangerous to send small Boxes in those Waggons; and I could not obtain Room for your strong one. The Waggoners would have been glad to get Freight but they were both honest enough to tell me that the uncouth manner in which they had been obliged to place their first Charge would expose all after-loading to be crushed. Each had one Hogshead and one Pipe of Tobacco in his Waggon.

There was one other Opportunity but I was advised not to trust to the Character of the Owner of the Waggon.

I may not have the Chance of seeing Capt. Jones before this Letter goes off, but I will endeavor to obtain all the Information he can give respecting the Invoice. I have so closely packed the Goods, after lessening the Case, that I am unwilling to open it again without I receive some particular Request, from you or some other of the concerned, for some *Part* of the Contents, when a known Conveyance offers.

Mr. G[erry]'s and Mr. P[almer]'s Good's were put up by the Direction of Mr. Ross, not by Mr. Moylan. I have transmitted Letters of Advice and Invoices to my two Friends. I shall write to Mr. Moylan as you desire.

I am very sorry that the Packages delivered to Doctor Winship have not reached you. My Charges to him and his Promises of Care are my only Warrants for sending your Things unboxed. Tho' they are well secured against Friction by the Wrappers, they will be ruined if Rain gets to them. If you had mentioned who has the particular Charge of them at Fishkill, I could have taken Measures by this Post to recommend them strongly to the Attention of a Friend. I will write at Random *to Col. Hughes.*

I will, at more Leisure use Cyphers to answer some of your Questions. I shall only now add assurances of respectful Affection and my best Wishes for your Happiness.   J: L.

RC (Adams Papers).
[1] Not found.

Abigail Adams to John Adams

My Dearest Friend   April 23 1781

You will wonder I suppose to what part of the world all the Letters you have written since the 25 of Sepbr. are gone, that not a line of a later date has reachd me, even up to this 23 day of April. My Heart sickens at the recollection, and I most sensibly feel the sacrifice of my happiness from the Malignant Union of Mars with Belona. My two dear Boys cannot immagine how ardently I long to fold them to my Bosom, or the still dearer parent conceive the flood of tenderness which Breaks the prescribed Bounds and overflows the Heart, when reflection upon the past, and anticipation upon the future unite in the mind of Portia. Unaccustomed to tread the stage of dissipation, I cannot shake of my anxiety for my Country and my dearest connextions, in the *Beau Mond*, whilst the one is Bleading, and the others seperated far, far from me, but in a frugal and republican stile; I pass the lonely Hour, with few enviers and fewer Imitators.[1]

Your predictions with regard to peace and war are verified and the united Provinces are at last obliged to declare themselves. Happy for them if they had sooner attended to the voice of their Friends, they would then I dare venture to affirm been sooner upon their gaurd against the Hostile depredations of Britain, but if the old Batavian Spirit still exists among them, Britain will Rue the Day that in Breach of the Laws of Nations, she fell upon their defenceless dominions, and drew upon her, as it is thought she must, the combined force of all the Neutral powers. If these people do not possess an ambition for conquest, yet they have heretofore exhibited a spirit superior to domination, that Spirit which prompted them to repel the Tyranny of Philip administerd by the cruel Alva, will excite them under superior advantages to Retaliate the Hostilities of the British Alva, that Spirit which prompted from Prince William that Heroick reply, "that he would die in the last Ditch, e'er he would see his Countrys ruin," will cement an indissoluble bond of union between the united States of America and the united Provinces who from a similarity of circumstances have each arrived at Independance disdaining the Bondage and oppression of a Philip and a Gorge.[2]

Our own American affairs wear a more pleasing aspect. Maryland has acceeded to the confederation at the very time when Britain is deludeing herself with the Idea that we are crumbling to peices. New York has given up her claims to Vermont, and a 14tenth State will soon lift her Head under the auspices of Congress.[3] Our Leavies are generally raised for 3 years and on their March to join the main Army. The Spring is advanceing and our Soldiers will have less occasion for cloathing—patience, perseverance and intrepidity have been their Armour and their cloathing through an inclemnant Winter. Who is answerable for the shamefull conduct which deprived them of their outward cloathing which they had reason to expect and justice demanded. I presume not to say, but if the omission has arisen from fraud, negligence or cabal, may the inhumane wretches be exposed to view and meet the infamy they justly merrit.

You will see by the paper inclosed that the Seat of war is chiefly in the Southern States, and there our Enemies by victories and defeats are wasteing daily, whilst they are training to Arms, and inureing to dicipline and hardships those states as they have before our Northern ones, to persue them to Inevitable distruction, and to prove to all Europe the falsity of their assertions, when not a single State submits to their haughty userpations, in all their Boasted conquered dominions.

Our Finnances have been upon a much more respectable footing for some time. Goods of all kinds fell in their prices, and exchange kept at 75 for one for five months. The Capture of Eustatia and the War between Holland and england has raised Goods again Tea in a particular manner to double what it ever has been before, it was down to a hard dollor per pound or 75 it is now at 15 Shillings.

I have thought that a small chest of about one hundred weight of Bohea Tea, would turn to as good an account as any thing you could send me. This Letter is to go by a vessel of Mr. Tracys. If you think it expedient you may order it by her, as it will come freight free if consigned to him, as the other articles were from Bilboa.

The best Green Tea I have ever had was that sent by Davis. If you send again, let it be Suchong, it is not so dear and answers better here. The Bandano hankerchiefs from Holland were the best article for sale I have ever received. The chints you were so kind as to order me by Sampson arrived—safe I cannot say. They were put up with some things which came to Mr. Austins Brother and were so unfortunate as to be wet, and half of them damaged, mildewed and in a manner spoilt. I parted with them in the best manner I could, the damaged for rather more than the sterling cost and the others very well. They were all good as well as handsome which renderd it more unfortunate to have them wet, but the cargo was so in general.—As to my long expected trunk, it has at last arrived in Philadelphia.[4] I am loth to discribe the state of it, because I am loth to make you angry, yet you ought to know it, least the person who put them up should again be imployed by you. I have neither Letter or invoice, which is the first time an omission of this kind has taken place. I cannot determine the price of a single article or know what were really put up, or what omitted. From your Letters alone in which you have repeated that all was orderd which was requested, and the loss of all Dr. Tufts things; leads me to think that the many others which are missing were stolen out. My Muslin hankerchiefs, Aprons, Nabbys plumes, Mr. Tufts Buckles, Brothers velvet, the linings and trimmings for the Gentlemens cloaths are among the missing articles. According to Mr. L[ovel]l['s] invoice for I have not yet seen them. When I found they would be like to go to Philadelphia I requested Mr. L——l to receive them for me when ever they arrived, and it was well he did or what remaind would have been intirely lost. They were put in a Box without any wraper, through the cracks of which you might see the things; they were liable not only to be wet but plunderd, both of which they sufferd. Dr. Winship whom I have seen, says that when Mr. Moylan requested him to take them; he refused them, unless he would repack them, and purchase a hair Trunk for them; he replied that he had no money in his hands, that he had sent the account to you, and you had paid it, and that if he would not take it, he would deliver it to Capt. Jones, which he accordingly did; when Mr. L——l received them together with a Box for Mr. Gerry, they were in a smoaking state. He examined his, found them rotton upon which Mr. L——l unpacked mine and found them so wet as to oblige him to dry every thing by the fire. The linnings, the diaper all damaged, Mrs. Cranchs cambrick mildewed, happily the wollen cloths were only wet, the leather Gloves quite rotton. I could wish you to repeat that article by the first opportunity and order a peice of wollen between every pair as they are the most liable to damage by wet. The Box of china was deliverd safe to Mr. L——l. If this should reach you before the Alliance leaves France be so kind as to order me one half a dozen tombour worked Muslin hankerchiefs, 4 Ells Book Muslin, one pound of white threads, 12 Ells of light crimson caliminco with a peice of coarse cambrick and any light wollen stuff that will answer for winter gowns, half a dozen coulourd plumes and a small Box of flowers for Miss Nabby at her request to her pappa. My chints came just in time to enable me to purchase the 3 part of a Man which fell to my share in the class to which I belonged at the head of which I had the *Honour* to stand. We gave 300 hard Dollors for 3 years, and a third part fell to my share, a third part is paid in hand, the remainder annually. The Town was divided into classes, and in about a months time the men were all raised. 38 fell to the share of this Town.[5]

Poor Mrs. D[an]a says she is taxed to death and she shall be ruined if he stays any longer. What shall I say—why that I have paid 21 hundred pounds since last july, Lawfull money, and have a thousand pound still to pay, and that you have enabled me to do it—but I do not increase in wealth, nor yet diminish the capital.—I have ventured to make some improvements in Husbandry and have a desire to become a purchaser in the State of Vermont. I may possibly run you in debt a hundred dollors for that purpose. Many people are removeing from this Town, and others. Land is sold at a low price, what do you think of a few thousand acres there? I know you would like it, so shall venture the first opportunity a hundred and 20 or 30 dollors will Buy a thousand acres.[6]

I have written very often to you by way of Spain and Bilboa, which places I wish you would try. If you sent me any thing by the Fame, let me know. She is lost or taken—and Mr. Guile we fear in her. Adieu my dear Friend my Love *must* suffice my dear Lads now. I have not time to write to them or Mr. T[haxte]r.

Yours ever yours, Portia

RC (Adams Papers); endorsed: "Portia. April 23. 1781." Enclosed newspaper not found or identified.

[1] Sentence thus punctuated in MS.

[2] Sentence thus punctuated in MS except for closing quotation mark, editorially supplied.

[3] See Isaac Smith Sr. to JA, 27 Feb., above.

[4] See Lovell to AA, 27 Feb., above, and notes and references there.

[5] The following paper, evidently documenting this transaction by which a Braintree man was enlisted and paid for Continental service on a pay-as-you-go basis to avoid further inflation, is in the Adams Papers:

"Braintree April 9th. 1781.

"Recd. of Mrs. Abigail Adams four hundred and thirty Pounds and ten Shillings old Currency, equal to £5–15–10 1/2 hard Money, towards raising a Man for Class No. 7, I say Received in behalf of said Class pr. Richard Cranch."

For the "classing" of inhabitants for tax purposes in towns deficient in their troop quotas, see Mass., *Acts and Laws, Resolves* of Jan. 1780 sess., ch. 161 (Resolve of 26 Feb.); also *Braintree Town Records*, p. 521.

[6] Sentence thus punctuated in MS. It is possible that AA intended to place a full stop after "opportunity."

In 1782 AA acted on her desire, which she had continued to cherish, to purchase wild land as a speculation in Vermont, buying 1,620 acres in Salem township, Orleans co. See AA to JA, 25 April 1782, below, and references cited in note 4 there.

James Lovell to Abigail Adams

Apr. 13. [*i.e.* 23] 1781 [1]

Not receiving any Line from you by this day's post, I recur to your favor of April 3d.[2] already answered in part. I wrote to Col. Hughes to endeavor to forward the two Packages left by Doctor Winship, if he could find where they were deposited. I hope he will have found them and had them cased in Boards.

Capt. J. P. Jones is without Letter or Invoice and supposes they must have been sent by the Alliance. A Vessel is in the River from France in 11 Weeks Passage, perhaps I shall get some Light by her. I assure you I have had some considerable fears of losing *on the Road* what I have to forward. The Tories rise in Insolence of Pillaging. But we have Today Reports of such large Embarkations from New York as will make that City very weak. It is even said that the Refugees are ordered to prepare for Halifax or Georgia.

Be persuaded, amiable Friend, that I will act for you as for myself.

Apr. 14 [*i.e.* 24]

Capt. All has been 9 Weeks from France. He put his Letters ashore at the Cape; perhaps they will be here before the Post goes.

P.M. The Letters are come. None from France, but a short one of Decr. from J. Williams about his *hopes* and *Intentions* of forwarding what had been granted Us months before to cover our naked Soldiers.

We have at last a very long Letter from Mr. Jay. But, your Curiosity, charming Patriot, must await the Return of Mr. ⟨S.A.⟩³ which may precede next Post.

Very sincerely and self-pleasingly yr. Servant,   J L

RC (Adams Papers).

¹ AA suggested in her letter to Lovell of 13 May, below, that the present letter was mistakenly dated, his of 17 April, above, having certainly been written earlier. To this Lovell responded in his of 16 June, below: "My Letter dated April 13. was written the 23," and its

postscript, accordingly, on 24 April.
² Not found.
³ Samuel Adams left Congress for Boston near the end of April or very early in May (Burnett, ed., *Letters of Members*, 6:xlvi).

John Adams to Abigail Adams

My dearest Friend   Amsterdam April 28. 1781

Congress have been pleased to give me so much other Business to do, that I have not Time to write either to Congress, or to private Friends so often as I used.

Having lately received Letters of Credence to their High mightinesses the states General of the United Provinces of the Low Countries and to his most serene Highness the Prince of Orange, I am now fixed to this Country, untill I shall be called away to Conferences for Peace, or recalled by Congress. I have accordingly taken a House in Amsterdam upon the Keysers Gragt i.e. the Emperors Canal, near the Spiegel Straat i.e. the Looking Glass street, so you may Address your Letters to me, there.¹

I have hitherto preserved my Health in this damp Air better than I expected. So have all of us, but Charles who has had a tertian fever but is better.

I hope this People will be in earnest, after the twentyeth of June. Americans are more Attended to and our Cause gains ground here every day. But all Motions are slow here, and much Patience is necessary. I shall now however be more settled in my own Mind having something like a Home. Alass how little like my real home.—What would I give for my dear House keeper. But this is too great a felicity for me.

I dont expect to stay long in Europe.—I really hope I shall not.— Things dont go to my Mind.

Pray get the Dissertation on the Cannon and feudal Law printed in a Pamphlet or in the Newspapers and send them to me by every

Opportunity untill you know that one has arrived. I have particular Reasons for this.² —My Nabby and Tommy, how do they do.³

RC (Adams Papers).

¹ On his return from Leyden to Amsterdam late in February JA gave up his lodgings at Madame Schorn's in "the Agterburgwal by de Hoogstraat" and set up interim headquarters at the Arms of Amsterdam. It appears that there had been some "whisperings" and "remarks" among the Dutch and others about the obscurity or even impropriety of such lodgings for the American minister, whether or not his status was yet officially recognized. See JA, *Diary and Autobiography*, 2:450–451; *Corr. in the Boston Patriot*, p. 345–346. Though JA spent much of his time in March and April at Leyden and The Hague, the question of a suitable residence was very much on his mind, and in letters to the newly formed American firm of Sigourney, Ingraham & Bromfield in Amsterdam, he instructed them to find, rent, furnish, and staff a house "fit for the Hotel des Etats Unis de L'Amerique" (9, 11, 13 April, LbC's in Adams Papers; JA, *Corr. in the Boston Patriot*, p. 426–428). On 27 April he announced to Edmund Jenings: "I have taken an House on Keysers Gragt near the Spiegel Straat, and am about becoming a Citizen of Amsterdam—unless their High mightinesses should pronounce me a Rebel, and expel me their Dominions, which I believe they will not be inclined to do" (Adams Papers). For two views of what is now No. 529 Keizersgracht, one from an engraving in *Het Grachtenboek* ("The Canal Book"), 1771, and the other from a photograph in 1960, see JA, *Diary and Autobiography*, vol. 2, facing p. 322.

² JA's "Dissertation on the Canon and the Feudal Law" (as it came to be called, though he had given it no name) was his first major political tract. It argued on historical and philosophical grounds for the necessity of resistance to tyranny, and was published in installments in the *Boston Gazette* in the year of the Stamp Act, reprinted in the *London Chronicle* before the end of that year, with the title (furnished by Thomas Hollis) it has generally been given since,

and reprinted, still without the author's name, by Hollis in the collection he entitled *The True Sentiments of America*, London, 1768. There were later editions issued in London, 1782, and Philadelphia, 1783, but their bibliographical history is complex, and whether JA directly or indirectly promoted either of them is not clear. See JA, *Diary and Autobiography*, 1:255–258; 3:284; and, for the most accessible text, JA's *Works*, 3:445–464.

³ A background note on how the Dutch drifted into war with England in the winter of 1780–1781 appears in JA's *Diary and Autobiography*, 2:452–453. Late in February, at the very crisis of Anglo-Dutch relations, JA received his powers and instructions to negotiate a treaty of amity and commerce with the Dutch Republic. See above, JA to AA, 11 March, note 2. Despite the deeply divided state of Dutch opinion over whether to fight or humbly submit to England, JA determined to do what he could to obtain recognition of American sovereignty by the Republic, for he now realized that this was an absolute prerequisite to not only a treaty but a loan, all the efforts of Dutch friends to America having so far failed to raise more than insignificant sums.

He chose a characteristic way to proceed, namely through the press. From the end of March through mid-April he spent such time as he could at his sons' lodgings in Leyden composing a paper appealing to the ancient spirit of patriotism among the Dutch people, drawing parallels between their country's successful struggle for independence and America's current struggle, and urging the immediate and future advantages to them of closer commercial relations with the American states. A fellow lodger in the house in the Langebrug at this time was Benjamin Waterhouse, who many years later drew from memory a vivid account of this episode which was to have such momentous results for the United States:

"I never shall forget the day and the circumstances of Mr. Adams's going from Leyden to the Hague with his *Memorial* to their High Mightinesses the States General dated, whether accidentally or by design April 19! I know not. He came down into the front room where we all were—his secretary, two sons, and myself —his coach and four at the door, and he full-dressed even to his sword, when with energetic countenance and protuberant eyes, and holding his memorial in his hand, said to us, in a solemn tone—Young men! remember this day— for this day I go to the Hague to put seed in the ground that may produce GOOD or EVIL—GOD knows which,—and putting the paper into his side-pocket, he steped into his coach, and drove off alone—leaving us his juniors solemnized in thought and anxious, for he had hardly spoken to us for several days before— such was his inexpressible solicitude." (Waterhouse to Levi Woodbury, 20 Feb. 1835, DLC:Woodbury Papers, vol. 16; photoduplicate in Adams Papers Editorial Files.)

This, one of the principal state papers of JA's entire career, appeared as a pamphlet issued at Leyden under the title *A Memorial to Their High Mightinesses the States General of the United Provinces of the Low Countries*, signed and dated by no means accidentally 19 April 1781. Its formal presentation to Dutch officials early in May and its subsequent circulation, in Dutch and French as well as in English, had, however, to await translation and printing, undertaken by JA's friends Dumas and Luzac. Various drafts and copies survive in the Adams Papers and in PCC, No. 84; readily accessible printed texts are in JA, *Works*, 7:396–404, and in Wharton, ed., *Dipl. Corr. Amer. Rev.*, 4:370–376. The story of its presentation and reception has been summarized in JA's *Diary and Autobiography*, 2:457; and see also, for the tussle between JA and the Duc de La Vauguyon, the French minister at The Hague, over JA's mode of proceeding, JA's *Corr. in the Boston Patriot*, p. 431–434. The fruits of the *Memorial* —Dutch recognition and the first Dutch loan—belong to the following year, 1782.

Joseph Gardoqui & Sons to Abigail Adams

Madam   Bilbao the 2d. May 1781

Your much respected and highly Esteemed favour of the 4th of Septr. last[1] we duelly received and after a due acknowledgment for its agreable Contents are not a little sorry to Informe you that it was not in our power to comply with your desire of shipping the articles you are pleased to order by our freind Mr. Smiths Vessell as she putt in at Ferrol and proceeded from thence back to America. However haveing at present the opportunity of the Armed ship Commerce Capt. Ignatius Webber have Taken the freedome of shipping in her directted to the care of Isaac Smith Esqr. a packadge that containes the goods you was pleased to order as you will see by the within Invoice which very cordially wish safe to your hands after a prosperous and pleasing Navigation and that they may merritt your Kind approvation. The bills you was pleased to Inclose have been placed to the Creditt of our very worthy freind the Hble. Mr. Adams Account who have the pleasing satisfaction to hear Enjoys a perfectt Scane of health at Amsterdam on which sincerely congratulate you and beg your Commanding on all occations those who respectfully Subscrive.

Dupl RC (Adams Papers); at head of text: "Mrs. Abigail Adams Braintree." Text of Dupl precedes text of another letter, in a different hand, from the Gardoqui firm to AA, 14 Oct. 1781, q.v. below under that date. Enclosed invoice not found.

¹ Not found.

Abigail Adams to James Lovell

*[Braintree, 10 May 1781]*¹

Upon opening your favour of April 17 my Heart Beat a double stroke when I found that the Letter which I supposed had reachd you was the one captured² in the room of that you received which was what I had supposed lost, but I should have been secure from the knowledge of the writer if Mr. Cranchs Letter and one I wrote at the same time had not accompanied it.³ The Letter which I would not have chosen should have come to any hand but yours, was in reply to two of yours and containd some Stricktures upon the conduct of a Friend.⁴ Least you should imagine it freer than it really was I enclose the coppy. I risk no more should it be captured than what the Enemy already have.—The Letter which occasiond some of the remarks I have not yet seen, tho I find it was published in the Halifax paper as well as Riveingtons.⁵ If what I have heard with regard to its contents is true, I cannot open my lips in defence of a Friend whose character I would wish to justify, nor will I secret from him that it suffers exceedingly even in the Eyes of his Friends from his so long absenting himself from his family. How well he may satisfy her who is nearest concernd I presume not to say, but if she possesses that regard for her partner which I presume she does, she must be exceedingly hurt even by the Speach of the world, if she is otherways sufficiently convinced of the attachment and affections of her partner. I write from a Sense of the feelings which under similar circumstances would harrow up my Soul, and wound with a Bearded Arrow. I have but a very small personal acquaintance with the Lady whom I esteem and commisirate, those who have speak highly of her. I have as little personal acquaintance with the Gentleman connected with her; but it has so happened that I have stood in need of his services, and he has exhibited an assiduity and Friendship in the discharge of them that has bound me to him in the bond of Friendship. Add to this he is the particular Friend and correspondent of him who is dearest to me and for whose sake alone I should Esteem him, but it would mortify me not a little to find I had mistaken a character and in the room of a philosopher, a *man* of the *world* appeard. If I could credit the report [*remainder missing*]

Dft (Adams Papers); text incomplete and without date or indication of addressee; at head of text in CFA's hand: "⟨*March*⟩ May 1781."; see note 1. Enclosure: copy (not found) of AA to Lovell, 17 March, printed above from Dft; see descriptive note there.

¹ Lovell furnished the date of the (missing) RC of this letter in his replies of 29 May and 16 June, both below.
² That is, her letter of 17 March, of which the draft text is printed above and a "coppy" was enclosed in the recipient's copy of the present letter. It was only a presumption by AA that this letter was actually captured.
³ The letters here alluded to (other than AA's of 17 March) have not been found, but see the opening sentences of Lovell to AA, 17 April, above, and 14 May, below.
⁴ That is, Lovell himself.

⁵ Lovell's letter to Elbridge Gerry, 20 Nov. 1780, captured by the British and published in a Halifax paper and in James Rivington's New York *Royal Gazette*, 27 Dec. 1780. From the cryptic and circumlocutory remarks below, it appears that AA, although she had not yet seen the text of this letter, had gathered from common report ("the Speach of the world") that Lovell had alluded in some demeaning way to his wife, Mary (Middleton) Lovell. For what Lovell actually wrote, and his plea in extenuation, see below, Lovell to AA, 16 June, and notes there.

Abigail Adams to James Lovell

May 13th [*1781*]¹

I wrote you by the last post² with a freedom which perhaps you may think I had no right to make use of. I was stimulated to it by many severe speaches that I had heard, and from not knowing myself what to say in paliation of my Friend. All former excuses were worn out by *time* and tho I do not believe the hard things I have heard, I think he ought to suffer any temporary inconvenience which a short absence from the scene of his buisness might subject him to, rather than the world should judge that he was devoid of all domestick attachments.

A report prevails here that the Alliance is arrived at Philadelphia. If so I hope I shall again here from my dear connextions. I have been more unfortunate for six months past than usual. Not a line has reachd me of a Later date than Septbr. The Fame on Board of which was Mr. Guile upon his return from Holland, was taken off Newfoundland and carried to Ireland. By that vessel I had large packets from all my Friends. No vessel has arrived from that port since Davis in November, who threw over all his Letters. Two prizes arrived here last week taken by the Alliance 3 days after she saild from France. If she is come to Philadelphia and means to come round to Boston I would risk what property you have of mine and others in her rather than by land. I hope what private Letters are come will be well gaurded this way. What publick News she bring[s] that may be communicated you will be so good as to write me. A French vessel arrived from Brest with an admiral for Newport, but brought no private Letters. We are longing for News with a hungry avidity. How will Holland realish the hard knocks she has received. Britain has done sufficient to make them feel where it is said they are most Susceptable. She has taken and distroyed so much of their property, that I should suppose they would retaliate with a vengance.

I forgot to mention the receipt of your favour of April 13th it is dated but I believe it was a mistake as the preceeding one was the 17th.[3]

No invoice was ever sent in the Alliance as the Ship was throughly examined by my Friends. This Buisness was transacted much like your continential cloathing, with the same attention and Honesty. In the Name of all concernd I most sincerely thank you for your care and attention as well to others, as to your obliged Friend,

Portia

Dft (Adams Papers); without indication of addressee.

[1] According to Lovell's reply, 29 May, below, the (missing) RC was dated 14 May.

[2] Letter of 10 May, preceding.

[3] Lovell's letter dated 13 April was actually written on 23 April (as he himself was to say in his to AA of 16 June, below) and is printed above under the corrected date.

John Quincy Adams to John Adams

Honour'd Sir   Leyden May 13th 1781

As you may possibly not come here before the 18th I write to know, if I must leave these lodgings at that time, as the month will then be up, and if I stay any longer I must begin another month.

I have finish'd Phaedrus's fables and the lives of Miltiades, Themistocles, Aristides, Pausanias, Cimon, and Lysander; and Am going next upon Alcibiades in Cornelius Nepos, I shall begin upon Alcibiades next.[1] I transcribe and learn also a Greek verb through the Active, Passive and Medium Voices every day.

We have no news here, though as you know Sir, this is a barren place for that. Please to write me them if you have any. I saw Mr. Luzac last evening he desires his respects to you.

I am your dutiful Son,   John Quincy Adams

P.S. I hope brother Charles has got entirely well. Dr. Waterhouse says he gets flesh. I should be very glad if he would write to me.

RC (Adams Papers); addressed: "A Monsieur Monsieur Adams. Sur Le Keizers Gragt prés du Spiegel Straat à Amsterdam"; endorsed: "J. Q. Adams. May. 13. ans. 14. 1781."

¹ Cornelius Nepos was a Roman biographical writer in the first century B.C. JQA was doubtless reading some school text of Nepos' *De viribus illustribus*, of which he acquired his own copy of a Latin and French edition, Paris, 1771, in St. Petersburg later this year (*Catalogue of JQA's Books*, p. 114).

John Adams to John Quincy Adams

My dear Son   Amsterdam, May 14. 1781

I received yours of 13 this morning.

If you have not found a convenient Place to remove into, you may continue in your present Lodgings another Month.

I am glad you have finished Phædrus, and made Such Progress in Nepos, and in Greek.

Amidst your Ardour for Greek and Latin I hope you will not forget your mother Tongue. Read Somewhat in the English Poets every day. You will find them elegant, entertaining and instructive Companions, through your whole Life. In all the Disquisitions you have heard concerning the Happiness of Life, has it ever been recommended to you to read Poetry?

To one who has a Taste, the Poets serve to fill up Time which would otherwise pass in Idleness, Languor, or Vice. You will never be alone, with a Poet in your Poket. You will never have an idle Hour.

How many weary hours have been made alert, how many melancholly ones gay, how many vacant ones useful, to me, in the course of my Life, by this means?

Your Brother grows dayly better but is still weak and pale. He shall write to you, Soon.

Your affectionate Father,   J. Adams

RC (Adams Papers).

James Lovell to Abigail Adams

Noon 14th. of May 1781

By a Letter of the 1st.,¹ this Moment received, I find that my amiable and respected Friend is under the mistake of supposing the Enemy in Possession of one of her former which has reached me, and that I have neglected to answer some others. She will know better before this reaches her. The Enemy have the one which attended Mr.

Cranche's: So that I have no Knowledge of the Mode He or She particularly pointed out for forwarding the Goods in my Possession.[2]

I have had the Satisfaction of knowing that Mr. Hugh Hughes has well guarded, by boxing, what I committed to Doctor Winship and I have this day desired Mr. Brown, who setts off with a Light Waggon, to take the Box from Mr. Hughes and deliver it to Mrs. Lovell who has my former Directions about the Contents which are for different Persons. I was not able to send by Mr. Brown your large Box or the China. He goes greatly loaded from hence, but as he drops part of his Charge at Head Quarters, he can conveniently take what I have mentioned, at Fishkill, if it has not yet been sent on by the Kindness of Mr. Hughes.

The Enemy have published one Letter from Mr. Adams, dated in December[3] and they say they have intercepted a Pacquet from him and Doctor Franklin; but I do not think they say truly. I imagine they have got only that general Letter of News not ordered to be sunk. We have had nothing from Holland a long Time, except something which Mr. Carmichael transmitted in the handwriting of a known Correspondent at the Hague, and which you must have seen republished, I imagine, in your own Gazettes.[4]

I have endured much Pain lately from a Fall: I shall not soon be free from the ill Effects. But I have been very stoical. For it would have been a Shame to groan at what happened, while I reflected that neither Back nor Limb was broken, nor any Joint *absolutely* dislocated. Portia will however do me the Justice to think that neither Pain or Affliction shall make me neglect Endeavors to render her Service in finishing the little Business of sending on her Invoices or rather her *Goods*. I have written for the *Invoices* agreable to her Hints.

I imagine that some of the Articles supposed missing are in the *Band Box*, and that Mr. Wibert may find some Things *within* his Package of Cloth, which was in so good order as not to need opening. I have so thoroughly packed the Case for Transportation, that I do not incline to make a Scrutiny anew of the Contents. D[ea]r Lady, Yrs., JL

RC (Adams Papers).

[1] Not found.

[2] These letters have not been found, or at any rate are not identifiable from the allusions made to them here. See also AA to Lovell, 10 May, above.

[3] Probably JA to Samuel Huntington, 28 Dec. 1780, mentioned more specifically in AA to JA, 28 May, below; see note 2 there.

[4] Probably the letters, not specifically identified, from C. W. F. Dumas that were enclosed in William Carmichael to the Committee of Foreign Affairs, Madrid, 4 March (Wharton, ed., *Dipl. Corr. Amer. Rev.*, 4:272–273).

John Adams to Abigail Adams

My dearest Friend   Amsterdam May 16. 1781

I am now settled at Amsterdam on the Keysers Gragt near the Spiegel Straat. Charles is with me to recover his Health after his fever. John is at Leyden. Mr. Thaxter with me.

De la Motte Piquet has taken half Rodneys Plunder.[1] I know not what other News to write. We hope, that Vessels will soon arrive from Boston. Hope you have received your Boxes by Sampson and Jones. I shall send you, as I can, but you must draw upon me, if you find it necessary.

I am more busy than ever, but to no Effect, at least no immediate Effect.

Oh! Oh! Oh! that you were here, to do the Honours of the United States, and to make the beautifull Scænes with which this Country and Season abounds, agreable to yours forever.

RC (Adams Papers). Written on verso of a canceled "Copy" (in Thaxter's hand) of a note from JA to Hendrik Fagel, 19 April 1781, transmitting JA's Memorial to the States General of that date.

[1] That is, the plunder taken by Rodney following his capture of St. Eustatius earlier this year. See above, Thaxter to AA, 1 April, and note 3 there. JA observed of this event a little later that "the Cards are once more turned against the Gambler; and the [British] Nation has gained nothing but an Addition to their Reputation for Iniquity" (to Pres. Huntington, 29 May, PCC, No. 84, III; Wharton, *Dipl. Corr. Amer. Rev.*, 4:460).

John Quincy Adams to John Adams

Honoured Sir   Leyden May the 17th 1781

I reciev'd this morning your letter of the 14th. in which you speak of Poetry, and although I have not read much of it, yet I always admired it, very much.

I take the Delft Dutch paper to learn to read the language. To day there is a report which I read in it that Admiral Kingsbergen had taken fourteen of the German Transports, but this is only a report.[1]

Inclosed is a letter which I reciev'd this morning, I should have sent it by Mr. Thaxter (who is arrived here with Mr. Guild) but he says that it would be better to send it, this night.[2] I will write to brother Charles by Mr. Thaxter.

I am your dutiful Son,   John Quincy Adams

RC (Adams Papers); addressed: "A Monsieur Monsieur Adams Ministre Plenipotentiaire des etats unis de l'Amerique Sur le Keizers Gragt prés du

Spiegel Straat à Amsterdam"; endorsed in John Thaxter's hand: "Master John 17th. May 1781." For the enclosure see note 2.

¹ The report JQA had read in "the Delft Dutch paper" (on which see JA's reply of 18 May, below) related to Adm. Jan Hendrik van Kinsbergen, soon to be better known for his part in the Dutch naval action against the British at the Doggerbank, Aug. 1781 (*Nieuw Ned.* *Biog. Woordenboek*, 4:839).

² The letter enclosed was a note to JA from the Duc de La Vauguyon, French minister at The Hague, 16 May 1781, acknowledging receipt of copies of JA's *Memorial to . . . the States General* (Adams Papers; JA, *Works*, 7:416).

John Adams to John Quincy Adams

My dear Son   Amsterdam May 18. 1781

I have this Morning received yours inclosing a Letter from the Duke de la Vauguion.¹

Please to inform me in your next, when the Vacation begins. It is my Design that you shall come and spend a Part of the Vacation with me.—I approve very much of your taking the Delft Gazette the Writer of which is a great Master of his Language, and is besides a very good Friend to his Country and to yours.²

You go on, I presume, with your latin Exercises: and I wish to hear of your beginning upon Sallust who is one of the most polished and perfect of the Roman Historians, every Period of whom, and I had almost said every Syllable and every Letter is worth Studying.

In Company with Sallust, Cicero, Tacitus and Livy, you will learn Wisdom and Virtue. You will see them represented, with all the Charms which Language and Imagination can exhibit, and Vice and Folly painted in all their Deformity and Horror.

You will ever remember that all the End of study is to make you a good Man and a useful Citizen.—This will ever be the Sum total of the Advice of your affectionate Father,   John Adams

RC (Adams Papers).

¹ See the preceding letter.
² The "Delft Gazette," which JQA subscribed to and read in order to improve his knowledge of Dutch, was the *Hollandsche Historische Courant*, whose publisher and editor was Wybo Fynje (1750–1809), a former Mennonite minister and a strong adherent of the Dutch Patriot party. In 1775 Fynje had married Emilie, a sister of JA's friend Jean Luzac, publisher of the *Gazette de Leyde*. The Fynjes were forced to flee to Antwerp and then to St. Omer in France following the suppression of the Patriot movement in 1787. With the establishment of the Batavian Republic, Fynje returned to The Hague in 1795 and resumed his journalistic and political activities. (*Nieuw Ned. Biog. Woordenboek*, 1: 906–908; information furnished by C. D. Goudappel, Director, Gemeentear-chief Delft, Netherlands.) In later years JA remembered that it was the "editor of a gazette at Delpht, who had the reputation of one of the most masterly writers in the nation in their own language," who had translated JA's *Memorial* of 1781 for publication in Dutch, but he did not record his name (JA, *Corr. in the Boston Patriot*, p. 430).

John Quincy Adams to John Adams

Honour'd Sir   Leyden May the 19th 1781

I reciev'd this morning your yesterday's favour, in which you say, you want to hear of my beginning in Sallust; I have not begun yet but shall soon; but am for the present continuing in Cornelius Nepos. I have got a fair copy of Phaedrus bound, it is My Master's Translation which if you desire to read, and have time for it, I will send to you.[1]

The Vacancy does not begin at the same time, sometimes it begins the 15th of June, sometimes the 24th, and sometimes the last; I should not desire to stay at Amsterdam above a fortnight then, for if I should stay any longer it might do harm to my Studies, of which I have Just got into a steady course, and my master's manner of teaching I find agree's with me very well.

Perhaps you may remember that you told me before you left this place, that you should give me lessons of Algebra by writing. I am always ready Sir, whenever you have time.

Dr. Waterhouse desires his Compliments to you.

I am you[r] dutiful Son,   John Quincy Adams

P.S. My love, if you please to brother Charles. I should write to him, but I have not time.

RC (Adams Papers); addressed: "A Monsieur Monsieur Adams. Ministre Plenipotentiaire Des Etats Unis de L'Amerique Sur le Keizers Gragt Entre Les Leide et Spiegel Straaten à Amsterdam"; endorsed in John Thaxter's hand: "Mr. J. Q. Adams 19th. May 1781."

[1] In the Adams Papers (M/JQA/23; Microfilms, Reel No. 218) is a bound MS of 100 folios in JQA's hand containing a translation into French of five books of Phædrus' *Fables*. On fol. 1 JQA inscribed the date "February 10th. 81," and on fol. 100, "May 11th 1781." The translation was apparently the work of JQA's language "Master," Wenshing or Wensing, on whom see JQA to JA, 22 Dec. 1780, above. JQA's earlier study of Phædrus is noted at vol. 3:308.

John Quincy Adams to John Adams

Honour'd Sir   Leyden May the 21st 1781

Inclosed are some numbers of the *lettres Hollandoises*.[1] I took them out of thier covers, because I knew they were nothing else, and I could not do them up so well when they were in, however, if you please, I will not take out any more; Mr. Luzac's this day's paper is also inclos'd.

I wrote to brother Charles by Mr. Thaxter, and to you the night before last,[2] but have not yet reciev'd answers to either.

I am, your dutiful Son, John Quincy Adams

RC (Adams Papers); endorsed in John Thaxter's hand: "Master John 21st. May 1781." Enclosures not found, but see note 1.

[1] *Lettres hollandoises, ou correspondance politique sur l'etat présent de l'Europe, notamment de la République des Sept Provinces-Unies,* a journal or news sheet published in Brussels friendly to the American cause; the author or editor was said by Edmund Jenings to be named Rivales (Jenings to JA, 24 Jan., 18 Feb. 1781; Adams Papers). A set of this work with JQA's bookplate, vols. 1–3, 5–7, is in MQA; the whole or parts of vols. 3–4 are in MB (*Catalogue of JA's Library,* p. 145).

[2] JQA's letter to his father of 19 May is above; that to CA has not been found.

Hugh Hughes to Abigail Adams

Madam   Fishkill May 21st. 1781

I do myself the Honour, at the Request of the Honble. James Lovel Esq; Member of Congress, to address two Packages, that were left here by Doctr. Winship, to you. They came to Hand without a Case, which I have order'd made for their Security. They are in Charge of a Mr. Brown, who conducts a Wagon from Philadelphia to Boston, for some Members of Congress and others.

When I began this, Brown was not got here from the Landing. He is now arriv'd and I inclose his Receipt for the Box and its Contents, which I wish safe to Hand.

Lest it should be imagin'd that the Packages had been neglected, I must beg Leave to acquaint you Madam that they were left in Store without my Privity, unless as a Part of Doctr. Winship's Baggage which I never saw, but told him that he was welcome to store it, till he could send for it, which Situation they remain in till I received Mr. Lovell's Requisition to make Inquiry for them, in doing which they were discover'd by the Storekeeper, as above, that is, with the Doctr's. Chest and Trunk &c. They appear'd to be entire, and in tolerable Order, and I hope they have sustain'd no Injury. I beg Pardon for being this tedious, which I should not have been, had I not conceiv'd it an indispensable Duty.

As I perceive by Mr. Lovell's Letter that his Lady has some Interest in the Packages, I beg you will please to communicate the Contents of this to her.

I have the Honour to be, with the greatest Respect, Madam, your most Obedient and very Humble Sert., Hugh Hughes[1]

RC (Adams Papers); at foot of text: "The Honble Mrs. John Adams." Enclosed "Receipt" not found.

[1] Hugh Hughes, mentioned passingly in earlier letters, was a New York officer in the Quartermaster General's department who was stationed on the east side of the Hudson at Fishkill (now Beacon), N.Y. (Heitman, *Register Continental Army*). Lovell had explained the arrangements with Hughes in his letter to AA of 14 May, above.

James Lovell to Abigail Adams

May 21. 1781

I hope you are not still without later Dates from Mr. A's Hand than what we have—Oct. 24.[1] I conclude he was well about the last of Febry., because Mr. Carmichael under Date of March 11th sends us Mr. A's Plan of a Loan to be opened at the House of Nieufville & Son March 1st.[2] We have no Vessels from Holland. Accept of my Conjecture as a Proof of my uniform Wish to contribute to your Ease of Mind and general Happiness.

I have sent an open 3plicate to Mr. A. for Mr. Moylan respecting your Invoice.[3]

Free from Pain, I shall however limp for many a day.

RC (Adams Papers); addressed: "Mrs. A. Adam[s] Brain[tree] near [Boston]"; franked: "Philada. Jas. Lovell." Lower portion of MS torn off, destroying part of address on cover.

[1] JA to Pres. Huntington, 24 Oct. 1780, is in PCC, No. 84, II (printed in Wharton, *Dipl. Corr. Amer. Rev.*, 4:103–104); LbC is in Adams Papers (printed in JA, *Corr. in the Boston Patriot*, p. 259–260).
[2] Carmichael's letter of 11 March was addressed to the Committee of Foreign Affairs and is printed in Wharton, *Dipl. Corr. Amer. Rev.*, 4:279–280. The plan of a loan through the house of Neufville was premature and came to nothing; see JA, *Corr. in the Boston Patriot*, p. 377–378, 398–400.
[3] No such communication has been found. Concerning Moylan and his invoice, see above, Lovell to AA, 27 Feb., and note 1 there.

Benjamin Waterhouse to John Adams

Sir   Leyden 21st of May 1781

Almost every body here is preparing for the fair which opens next Thursday, and as this is Leyden-'*Lection* I was saying to my companion that it was a pity Master Charles was not here that he might see that a Dutchman can be merry when he is resolved upon it. And John seems to wish it so much, that I thought I would write to you and if you had no objection we should have the little Gentlemans company. We thought he would perhaps find some of his Countrymen in Amsterdam who having as much leisure as curiosity would accompany him here. At this time every one turns the best side outwards and the Dutchmen and Women try to look pleasant. The vast number of tents—merchandize—the different nations, together with a multitude of things to be seen as *sights*—would perhaps both please and instruct my little friend. This idea together with that of the pleasure of his company for a day or two induces me to request you would let him come.[1]

It is with no small pleasure I inform you that John adheres to his studies with a constancy rarely seen at that age, and what is happy for him the adding to his knowledge does not diminish his flesh. We have no news. With my best compliments to Mr. Dana and Mr. Thaxter, I remain with great respect your humble servt.,

Benj. Waterhouse

RC (Adams Papers).

[1] It does not appear that CA came to Leyden for the fair. See below, JA to JQA, 30 May, and note there.

John Adams to Abigail Adams

My dearest Friend   Amsterdam May 22 1781

I Yesterday received your Letters by Captain Cazneau and Mr. De Neufville received his, and will accordingly send the Things you wrote for.[1]

You had better pursue this Method and write to Mr. Guardoqui at Bilboa and Mr. De Neufville here for what you want and desire them to draw upon me for the Pay.

I will answer the Letters of my Friends as soon as I can, but I have so many Things upon me at present, that I have not Time. We are all well but Charles, who is yet weak from his Fever, but is getting better daily.

We are anxious to hear further of Green and Cornwallis. Tho Green lost the Field on 15 March, it seems Cornwallis must be in a critical situation.[2]

I know not what this People will do. I believe they will awake, after some time. Amsterdam, Harlem and Dort have represented the Necessity of an Alliance with America but when the rest will be of their Mind, I know not.[3] If they neglect it, they and their Posterity will repent of it.

The Trade will turn away from this Country to France and Spain if the Dutch act so unwise a Part, and indeed, according to every

Appearance, this Country will dwindle away to nothing. Other Powers will draw away all its Commerce. By an early Treaty with America and active Exertions they might save it: but they seem little disposed as yet.

My dear Nabby and Tommy how do they do? Our Parents, our Brothers, sisters and all Friends how are they?

If I could get back again I would never more leave that Country, let who would beg, scold, or threaten.

As to Peace, mark my Words, the English will never make it with Us, while they have a ship or a Regiment in America. If any one asks whether there is like to be Peace, ask in return, whether G. Washington has taken New York, Green Cornwallis and Charlestown, and Nelson Arnold and Portsmouth?

Rodney has lost most of his Statia Booty. De la Motte Piquet has taken it. The English East India Possessions seem to be going to wreck—their Trade is torn to Pieces, but all is not enough.

If Congress and the states execute their Resolution of cutting off all Communication and Commerce, directly and indirectly with America, this will affect them more than any Thing. But how the Authority can prevent British Manufactures from being imported from France, Holland, Brabant &c. Is the Question.[4]

RC (Adams Papers). Partial Tr (MHi:Cranch Papers), in hand of Richard Cranch; see note 4. For an important enclosure, not now with the letter, see note 4 also.

[1] AA wrote JA on 15 Jan. by Cazneau; her letter is printed above. A letter she wrote Jean de Neufville & Son the same day has not been found; see their reply, 25 May, below. A version of her order for goods from the Neufville firm had first been enclosed in her letter to JA of 13 Nov. 1780 and is printed above as an enclosure in that letter.

[2] Although Nathanael Greene "lost the Field" at the battle of Guilford Court House, N.C., the action has generally been accounted an American strategic victory because Cornwallis suffered heavier losses and was obliged to abandon the interior of the state; see Isaac Smith Sr. to JA, 23 May 1781, below.

[3] JA refers to the Amsterdam "Proposition" of 18 May, soon thereafter endorsed by the deputies of Haerlem and Dort (Dordrecht). A French text is in the *Gazette de Leyde*, Supplément, 25 May 1781, and JA sent an English version in his letter to Huntington, 24 May

(PCC: No. 84, III; Wharton, ed., *Dipl. Corr. Amer. Rev.*, 4:431–433). See also Thaxter to AA, 27 May, below.

[4] In her reply to the present letter, AA informed JA that it had been almost exactly a year since the date of the last letter that she had received from him (AA to JA, 29 Sept., below). She promptly shared the letter with the Cranch circle, and Richard Cranch copied most of the text, probably for publication, though it has not been found in print (Tr in MHi:Cranch Papers, omitting only the paragraphs dealing with personal matters). In his letter to JA of 26 Sept., below, Cranch remarks that the present letter enclosed JA's "excellent Address to the States General of the United Provinces" and that he had "put it into the Press." This was the English version of *A Memorial to … the States General*, dated 19 April 1781; it was reprinted in the *Independent Chronicle* of 27 Sept., p. 1, col. 2 – p. 2, col. 3.

Abigail Adams to John Thaxter

My dear Sir   May 23 1781

The sight of your old Friend Mr. Storer will give you sensible pleasure, he means to be the Bearer of this to you. I wish him safe.

I need not add any thing in recommendation to you, who know him so well further than to say his character is not less fair or amiable, than it was when you quitted your native Land. He will I hope continue as free abroad from the fashionable vices of other countries; as he has steared clear of those of his own. He posseses engageing manners, and an Attractive form. I saw the Gloom which spread over the countanances of some of his Female acquaintance here when he bid them adieu, the other day, and as it was a circle of sensible, virtuous Girls, it was a proof of his merit, considering there was no partiality of a particular kind amongst them.[1]

The Gentle Eliza dropt a tear as it brought fresh to her mind the amiable Phylander, the chosen Friend of this young Gentleman—now alas! no more.[2] As to the other Eliza, I believe if their were any Convents in America, she would immediately devote herself. She still excludes herself from company, wears her widow garments, and mourns for the living or dead refusing to be comforted. There is another Lady of the same Name in whose heart it is said your Friend Charles has an Interest. I tell you this that you may decide the matter between you, as all parties are agreed that your Fair American bears that Name. I do not mean any Lady belonging to this Town—I clear the favorite of your youth from the Number.

Not a line from you this age—the climate of the United provinces does not extinguish Friendship, I hope, if unfriendly to Love. I am so anxious to hear from my dear Friends, that every arrival is eagerly sought after, and inquired into, but every one proves a dissapointment to my hopes. I wish you would write journals so far as you could with safety. They would greatly entertain me.

Politicks my Friend—learn them from the statesmen. I have written enough allready. They told us from York that poor Trumble was Executed—I never doubted their good will, tho I never credited the report. May his sufferings teach wisdom to our American youth.[3]

Are you not satisfied with Europe? Do you not wish to return to the wild and native Beauties of America—to the rugged Rocks of B[raintre]e and the contemplative Groves

"Where the free soul looks down to pitty kings."

The season is delightfull, it is the Charming month of May. Who can forbear to join the general smile of Nature?

> "Full of fresh verdure and unnumberd flowers
> The negligence of Nature, wide and wild
> where undisguised by mimic Art she spreads
> unbounded Beauty to the roving Eye."

The cultivated charms of Europe will give you a higher realish for the Natural Scenes of your own country, were it only by way of variety, which Gentlemen [4] are always fond of, but if you wish to connect yourself happily, you must banish all roving Ideas. There is no Country where matrimony is held in higher estimation than your own, where the conjugal union is considerd in a more solemn and sacred light or adhered to with a stricter fidelity. Property is so equally distributed, Nobility excluded, Rank and precidency gained so small a footing amongst us, that Heart for Heart is the only Barter known. The affections have full scope; Decorum alone is necessary.

Prize O! prize the blessing whilst it lasts, e'er Luxury and corruption debases and debauches the natural Innocence and Simplicity of our Land, e'er she eradicates all those tender Sentiments which constitute domestick felicity.

Your Worthy Mother is recovering from a long and painfull disorder with which she has been greatly afflicted through the winter. Your Pappa came very near representing your Native Town this year.[5]— I enjoin it upon my Friend to let no opportunity slip of writing—your Friend Watson[6] would sometimes be able to convey Letters. We long for News from abroad, all intelligence seems to be cut of, 8 months have elapsed since I received a line from Amsterdam. I am wholy uncertain where my Friends are, but think they cannot be in France or I should have heard from them.[7]

All happiness is wished you by your affectionate Friend,

Portia

RC (MB); addressed in AA2's hand: "Mr. John Thaxter Amsterdam"; endorsed: "Mrs. Adams 23d. May 1781." Dft (Adams Papers); varies from RC at a number of points, two of which are recorded in notes below.

[1] Charles Storer (1761–1829), Harvard 1779, a distant family connection of AA, was an intimate of the Adams and Smith family circles in Braintree and Boston and, after arriving in Europe, was at first to join and then replace his friend John Thaxter as JA's private secretary. He was the son of Deacon Ebenezer Storer of Boston by his first marriage and thus a stepson of Hannah (Quincy) Lincoln Storer. See Adams Genealogy and numerous allusions to young Storer in letters that follow, as well as some correspondence between Storer and more immediate members of the Adams family.

[2] The "amiable Phylander" was doubtless Nathaniel Cranch, who had died in an accident in April 1780 when engaged

to his cousin Elizabeth Palmer ("The Gentle Eliza"); see Adams Genealogy on both, and a note on the accident at vol. 3:328–329, above. The other two Elizas mentioned by AA, below, and Thaxter's "Fair American" are too shadowy for certain identification.

[3] By "York" AA means New York, and her source was doubtless one of the loyalist newspapers published there. John Trumbull, who had gone to Europe to pursue his studies in painting, was not executed but had a close call with the law in London. See note at vol. 3:328, above, and John Trumbull, *Autobiog-*

raphy, ed. Theodore Sizer, New Haven, 1953, p. 58 ff.

[4] Dft reads: "which you Gentlemen."

[5] Col. John Thaxter (1721–1802), Harvard 1741, of Hingham, lost his bid for election to the General Court, in which he had served earlier, to Capt. Charles Cushing (Boston *Independent Chronicle,* 7 June 1781, p. 3, col. 1; Sibley-Shipton, *Harvard Graduates,* 11: 69). The elder Thaxter was AA's uncle by marriage; see Adams Genealogy.

[6] Not further identified.

[7] Preceding two sentences not in Dft.

Isaac Smith Sr. to John Adams

Sir   Boston May the 23d. 1781

Not knowing but this may reach you as soon or sooner than a conveyance from Newbury (a ship of the Tracy's Capt. Brown) by whom Mrs. Adams has wrote you—As such I take upon me to trouble you with a few lines, to let you know Mrs. Adams and family were well Yesterday.

We have a ship from Port Loreon [Lorient] last week in 27 days, but as to News we have nothing Material, was in hopes the Dutch had made a decliration but we dont find they have. The Alliance and a large french ship sent in here lately a large privateer, they took on there passuage. Another of which sort they took likewise which they carried with them to Philadelphia. This privateer belonged to Guernsey &c. We are in pain for the Alliance and the Other ship which itt is said are very Valuable, As there are ships superior Cruising of the Delaware, who have taken the Confederacy with the Clothing that has been sometime att Hispaniola and we have lost Our state ship the Protector, Capt. Williams, both ships being carried to N. York. The french are good in coming to Our Assistance, but as they are not superior [by] sea, the british has the Advantage of transporting by water to any part of the Continent which makes the charge to us by land very heavy. Iff we had but a superiority by sea but for One six Months we should be Able to do any thing and every thing we want to do. Iff we could have from Our Allie's, the charge itt might cost in the transporting and maintaining troops Vested in the shiping itt would Answer better purposes, and till then we may linger Out the Warr seven Years longer. The british have kept att Gardner-bay a harbour Opposit to N[ew] London were they lay exposed to any superior force.

The seat of the Warr itt looks likely will be in the southern goverments. As Genl. Phillips, Arnold &c. keep footing in Virginia and go on in the burning way, I have Often thought whether some remonstrance to the Neutral powers representing there barbarous and Unpresidented method of burning private property wherever they go might not have some influence to make them asshamed of there Conduct, but, there late conduct att St. Eustatia gives but little hopes of a reformation. Iff the british Conduct, towards the dutch dont stirr them up to Act with spirit, nothing ever will.

Genl. Cornwallis put Out a pompuss proclimation after the battle with generall Green the 15 March, Offering protection to the Inhabitants when itt was not in his power to defend himself as Genl. Green drove him Out of the Country. Although Cornwallis kept the ground, which is all he had to boast of, Yet as the Old saying is he came off second best as the battle ruined him haveing 700 killed, taken &c. and Green not half the Number. The latest Account from the Southward is that General Green was att Cambden, the garison on his Approach haveing fled.

Here is a ship called the Robin Hood in which Charles Storer, and half a dozen more Young passengers, are going bound to ⟨Gottenburgh⟩ Denmark in there way to Holland.

Mrs. Dana received a letter from Mr. Dana (by the Loryon ship) of the 22d. March. She was well Yesterday.

You would get much the best conveyance by way of Bilbao for any private letters as there is several Armed Vessell's gone there round by the way of the West Indies.

And when you are att leisure iff you would favor me with a line itt would be Agreeable—to Your huml. Servant,   IS

Doctor Tufts is returned a senator in the room of Mr. Nyles.[1]

RC (Adams Papers); endorsed in John Thaxter's hand: "Isaac Smith Esqr. 23d. Feby. [*sic*] 1781."

[1] Cotton Tufts was elected one of the senators for Suffolk co. in the place of Deacon Samuel Niles of Braintree, and sat in the Senate for over a decade (*Boston Gazette*, 4 June, p. 2, col. 2; Sibley-Shipton, *Harvard Graduates*, 12:497). On Niles, JA's early political mentor, see JA, *Diary and Autobiography*, index; Sibley-Shipton, *Harvard Graduates*, 9: 72.

Abigail Adams 2d to John Quincy Adams

Braintree May 24. 1781

And are you really determined my Dear Brother not to condescend to write to your Sister again till She has answered some of your letters.[1]

I must acknowledge myself rather in arrears, but you must consider that you are daily removing from one scene to another, new and pleasing objects continually engage your attention, and furnish you with new subjects and pleasing ideas which if related by you will ever give pleasure to your friends on this Side the water and particularly to your Sister who is so sensible of her own unworthiness as to be partial to the foibles of her Brother. It has hitherto fallen to my lot to pass my time in a very contracted Sphere, I have scarcely visited as many towns as you have kingdoms: your improvements I hope will be in proportion: you have now an opportunity of receiving advantages, which if neglected will ever be out of your power again, and if improved aright may make you an useful member of Society and an ornament to your parents, who watch with attention each improvement, and whose hearts would be wounded by a misconduct, and may it be our joint effort to study their happiness.

The presence of your Pappa is an advantage you cannot realize, he will commend every laudable action and discountenance every foible e'er it grow to a vice, and by a strict attention to his precepts may you reap the promised blessing of length of days.

The account you give us of our little Charles gives pleasure to all that knew him.[2] He was a sweet little fellow when he left us, and I hope neither the Vices of other Climates or the captivating delusions of pleasure will make any impression on his young mind which was the seat of innocence.

We were a few days since relieved from painful anxiety on Mr. Guiles account, hearing he had not met a more dreadfull fate than falling into the hands of the enemy.

This letter will be delivered to you by Mr. Charles Storer who has offered to take letters from Mamma, and intends to reside in Holland.

Please to present duty to my Pappa, and Love to little Charles, from your Sister.

Early Tr (Adams Papers), in JQA's hand; at head of text: "*1. From my Sister.*" This is the first of a series of letters received by JQA that he copied into a letterbook he began shortly after arriving in St. Petersburg in August 1781 (Lb/JQA/1; Adams Papers Microfilms, Reel No. 125). The copies of letters received are interspersed with copies of letters sent.

[1] The only earlier recorded letter of JQA to AA2 is that of 27 Sept. 1778, printed in vol. 3 above. AA2's papers were destroyed by a fire in 1862; see above, vol. 1:xxix–xxx.

[2] This "account," mentioned again in AA to JQA, 26 May, below, appears to be missing.

Abigail Adams to John Adams,
with a List of Articles wanted from Holland

May 25 1781

In this Beautifull month when Nature wears her gayest garb, and animal and vegetable life is diffused on every side, when the Chearfull hand of industery is laying a foundation for a plentifull Harvest who can forbear to rejoice in the Season, or refrain looking "through Nature up to Nature's God?" [1]

"To feel the present Deity and taste
The joy of God, to see a happy World."

While my Heart expands, it sighing seeks its associate and joins its first parent in that Beautifull Discriptive passage of Milton

Sweet is the Breath of morn, her rising sweet,
With charm of earliest Bird; pleasent the Sun,
When first on this delightfull land he spreads
His orient beams, on herb, tree, fruit and flower
Glist'ring with dew; fragrant the fertile earth
After soft showers, and sweet the comeing on
of Gratefull Evening mild; then Silent Night
with this her solemn Bird, and this fair Moon
And these the Gems of heaven, her starry train;
But neither Breath of Morn when she assends
With charm of earliest Birds nor rising Sun
on this delightfull land: nor herb, fruit, flower
Glist'ring with dew; nor fragrance after showers
nor Gratefull Evening mild, nor Silent Night
with this her Solemn Bird, nor Walk by moon
or Glitt'ring Star light, *"without thee is sweet."* [2]

This passage has double charms for me painted by the hand of Truth, and for the same reason that a dear Friend of mine after having viewed a profusion of Beautifull pictures pronounced that which represented the parting of Hector and Andromaque to be worth them all. The journal in which this is mentiond does not add any reason why it was so, but Portia felt its full force, and paid a gratefull tear to the acknowledgment. [3]

This day my dear Friend compleats 8 months since the date of your last Letter, and 5 since it was received. [4] You may judge of my anxiety. I doubt not but you have written many times since but Mars,

Belona and old Neptune are in league against me. I think you must still be in Holland from whence no vessels have arrived since the Declaration of War. Their are some late arrivals from France, but no private Letters. I have had the pleasure of hearing of the Safety of several vessels which went from hence, by which I wrote to you, so that I have reason to think I have communicated pleasure tho I have not been a partaker in the same way. I have just written to you by a vessel of Mr. Tracys, Capt. Brown bound for Amsterdam which I hope will reach you.[5] If you made use of Bilboa your Friends there could forward ten Letters from thence, for one opportunity else where. Many vessels from Boston and Newbury are now bound there.

This will be deliverd to you by Mr. Storer, who is going first to Denmark and who designs to tarry abroad some time. If you had been a resident in your own country it would have been needless for me to have told you that Mr. Storer is a young Gentleman of a Fair character, I need not add amiable manners as those are so discoverable in him upon the slightest acquaintance. You will not fail to notice and patronize him according to his merrit.

We are anxiously waiting for intelligence from abroad. We shall have in the Feild a more respectable army than has appeard there since the commencement of the War and all raised for 3 years or during the war, most of them Men who have served before. The Towns have excerted themselves upon this occasion with a spirit becomeing patriots. We wish for a Naval force superiour to what we have yet had, to act in concert with our Army. We have been flattered from day to day, yet none has arrived, the Enemy exult in the Delay, and are improveing the time to ravage Carolina and Virginia.

We hardly know what to expect from the united Provinces, because we are not fully informd of their Disposition. Britain has struck a blow by the Capture of Eustatia sufficent to arouse and unite them against her, if there still exists that Spirit of Liberty which shone so conspicuous in their Ancestors and which under much greater difficulties led their hardy fore Fathers to reject the tyranny of Philip.

I wish your powers may extend to an Alliance with them, and that you may be as successful against the Artifices of Britain as a former Ambassador was against those of an other Nation when he negotiated a triple Alliance in the course of 5 days with an address which has ever done Honour to his memory. If I was not so nearly connected, I should add, that there is no small similarity in the character of my Friend, and the Gentleman whose memoirs I have read with great pleasure.[6]

Our state affairs I will write you if the vessel does not sail till after Election. Our Friend Mr. C[ranc]h goes from hence rep' by a *unanimous vote*. Dr. T[uft]s of W[eymout]h is chosen Senator, our Govenour and Lieut. Govenour, *as at the begining*. Our poor old currency is Breathing its last gasp. It received a most fatal wound from a collection of near the whole Bodys entering here from the Southward. Having been informed that it was treated here with more respect, and that it could purchase a solid and durable Dress here for 75 paper Dollors, but half the expence it must be at there, [it]⁷ traveld here with its whole train, and being much debauched in its manners communicated the contagion all of a sudden and is universally rejected. It has given us a great Shock. Mr. Storer can give you more information.

I have by two or 3 opportunities acquainted you that I received the calicos you orderd for me by Sampson, tho many of them were much injured by being wet. I have not got my things yet from Philadelphia. I have acquainted you with my misfortune there, oweing to the bad package. I have no invoice from Mr. Moylan or Letter, tho I have reason to think many things have been stolen out as all Dr. T[uft]s are missing, and several of mine according to Mr. L[ovel]ls invoice who was obliged to unpack what remaind and dry them by a fire, most of them much damaged. I have been more particular in other Letters.

Our Friends in general are well, your M[othe]r in a declining way. I rather think the Good Lady will not continue many years, unless Her health mends. I fear not the present. She is anxious to hear from you whilst she lives, but bids me tell you not to expect to see her again. To my dear sons I shall write by this opportunity. I have not received a line from them for this twelvemonth. I hope they continue to behave worthy the Esteem of every body, which will never fail to communicate the greatest pleasure to their affectionate parents. I inclosed an invoice of a few articles by Capt. Brown. I will repeat it here. Any thing in the goods way will be an acceptable remittance to your ever affectionate   Portia

ENCLOSURE⁸

A List of Articles per Capt. Brown. Half a Doz. Tambour worked Muslin hankerchiefs. 9 Ells Book Muslin. 1 pd [*sic*] of white Threads. 12 Ells of light crimson caliminco. 1 peice of coarse cambrick. Any light wollen Stuffs that will answer for winter Gowns. 3 coulourd waveing plumes (all Stolen from Capt. Jones). A small Box of flowers for Miss N[abb]y, with a couple of peices of Genteel Ribbon. 6 Ells of white flowerd Gauze. 1 peice of fine Linnen.

RC (Adams Papers); addressed: "To Honble. John Adams Amsterdam"; endorsed in John Thaxter's hand: "Portia 25th. May 1781." AA's enclosed "List of Articles," printed herewith, is written on verso of a short note from Richard Cranch to her, 10 May 1781 (Adams Papers).

¹ Initial quotation mark supplied.

² These sentiments, quoted with reasonable accuracy, are Eve's in her dialogue with Adam, *Paradise Lost*, bk. IV, lines 641–656.

³ AA alludes to a passage in JA's diary for 20 May 1778, repeated in different language in his Autobiography (*Diary and Autobiography*, 2:313–314; 4:105).

⁴ The latest letter AA had received from JA was that of 25 Sept. 1780, acknowledged in her reply of 25 Dec. 1780, both above. It was September before she received another; see AA to JA, 29 Sept., below.

⁵ AA's last preceding letter to JA was dated 23 April, above, and was "to go by a vessel of Mr. Tracys." Doubtless Tracy's Captain Brown had carried AA's order for goods of which the enclosure in the present letter is a duplicate.

⁶ The allusion is to Sir William Temple's negotiations in the Netherlands,

1668. AA had been reading Temple's *Observations upon the United Provinces*; see her letter to John Thaxter, 5 Feb., above. This essay is in his *Works*, where AA could also have read his letters and memoirs relating to his diplomatic missions. In JA's library in MB is an edition of Temple's *Works* edited by Jonathan Swift, 2 vols., London, 1731. Temple had performed the remarkable feat of negotiating in five days a defensive alliance among England, the United Provinces, and Sweden that protected the Dutch from threatened French aggression, "the commissioners from the seven provinces taking the unprecedented step of signing without previous instruction from the states" (*DNB*, under Sir William Temple).

⁷ Editorially supplied for sense.

⁸ See both descriptive note and note 5 above.

Abigail Adams 2d to John Thaxter

Braintree may 25 1781

My mamma has so often reminded me of a deficiency in politeness in not replying to your letter¹ which is now too long out of date to answer, that I can no longer withstand her frequent solicit[at]ions, and an opportunity offering by Mr. Charles Storer I am prevailed upon to take your attention from more important subjects to the perusal of a letter which will afford no pleasure but as it will give me an opportunity of receiveing an answer.

Were I to form an opinion of the whole circle of Mr. Storers acquaintance by the number of too or three I should judge their regret to be great upon his leaving America. There are so few Gentlemen in these days of modern refinement who arrive at the age of twenty; before they are Characterised for some fashionable vice; and we so rarely meet with persons before that age that pass their time in the rigid Schools of Virtue; that you cannot wonder at the wish exprest for his continuance in his native Country.

Methinks I might have been favoured in the course of eighteen months past with a letter had you wished for a revival of your former correspondence; if it will admit of the term. I can claim no title to such a favour; upon the Score of merit; tho the advantage I might have received would have laid me under a greater obligation then I could have returned.

Our sweet Eliza has for these too years past enjoyed a very unequal State of health; a gloomy disposition of mind has prevailed at times, within these few months her chearfulness has returned; and her health restored in a great degree. A mind so susceptible of the distresses of others as hers; will meet with a greater degree of pain then pleasure in this Life. The greatest pleasure she can receive must result from her own goodness of heart.

The vissit which was proposed my makeing at Hingham before you left us has never been accomplished. Your Mammas ill health this winter has only prevented me. Mr. Rice has at last drawn the prize in the matrimonial Lottery; past a short time in the Society of his Lady; and returned to camp to take a part in the next campaign.[2]

I shall tire your patience with a detail of events perhaps uninteresting to you, whose time is taken up in the important pursuits of buisness or pleasure; but if a few moments can be spared from either or both may I ask it as a favour that they may be employed in pointing out the many foibles that are conspicuous in this letter from your young friend.

RC (Adams Papers; gift of Mrs. Harold Kellock, 1961); addressed: "Mr John Thaxter. Amsterdam."; endorsed: "Miss Adams 25th. May 1781."

[1] No earlier letters from Thaxter to AA2 have been found.
[2] Nathan Rice, a former law clerk of JA's, identified at vol. 1:142, above; see also MHS, *Procs.*, 82 (1970):146. In Feb. 1781 he had married Meriel Leavitt of Hingham (*History of the Town of Hingham, Mass.*, Hingham, 1893, 2: 433).

Jean de Neufville & Son to Abigail Adams, with an Invoice of Goods shipped from Amsterdam

Madam   Amsterdam 25th May 1781

We are honor'd with your Ladyship's letter of the 15th Jany. last,[1] and deem ourselves peculiarly unfortunate, not to have been more happy in the choice of the Color of Silk we sent you. 'Tis the more painful to us, as we can make no amends but by redoubling our attention and Vigilance, In the execution of your future Commands which we set so high a value on that we consider your Continuance of them, Notwithstanding the egregious mistake comitted, as a mark of distinguish'd favour. We flatter ourselves we shall not Incur your Ladyships reprehension in the execution of your last order, having had His Excellency Mr. Adams Sanction, where you required it. This we are certain will ensure Approbation, as We believe him to be as infallible in his choice on trivial Matters; as we know him to be unerring In his Opinion on those of greater Importance: and although he is in that respect above our praise, we cannot withhold our Testimony from that of all who have the honor and happiness of knowing him: with equal truth we repeat the Young Gentlemen, your Amiable Sons bid fair (in good time) to imitate the Virtues &c. of so Noble a Model. We confess the Knowledge of so much intrinsic worth united, exalts our Ideas, on a Cause and a Country that Engrosses our best, and most earnest wishes: so Congenial with your Ladyships, and of all who have proper Ideas on so Sublime a subject. May heaven grant speedily the wished for Boon, as a due Reward to the Superior virtue of the Inhabitants of your States, a relief to the Calamities so long suffered by that part of Mankind which are Involved in the Contest, and as a Benifit to the world in General.

We entertain a due regard of the very flattering opinions Your Ladyship expresses of our principles in the glorious Cause. They are as fix't and unalterable, as we beg you to be assured, Our respectful Attachment to your Ladyship and family is great, having the honor to Subscribe ourselves Your Ladyships Most Obt. Humbl. Servts.,

John de Neufville Son

We address to Isaac Smith Esqr. the sundry articles your last pleased to order us,[2] and have sent said Gentleman the bill of Loading. They are shippd on board the Juno Captn. Haydon. Inclose herein the Invoice amounting to f364:18:—and we annex thereto the produce of the Bill your Ladyship sent us of 100 Dollars at 5£=£500 livres Tournois Negotiated at the Exchange of 51 3/4

$$\begin{array}{ll} \text{Bco. f.215:12:} & 8 \\ \text{agio 4 3/4 f. } 10: & 5: \\ \hline \text{Currency f.225:17:} & 8\,^3 \end{array}$$

The difference between the Cost of the Goods and the proceeds of your Ladyships bill of 100 Dollars we have settled with his Excellency Mr. Adams.

ENCLOSURE[4]

INVOICE of Sundries Shipped on board the Juno William Haydon Commander, bound for Boston. Consign'd to Mr. Isaac Smith Mercht. there, on order, and for Account of the honorable Lady Adams, in Braintree, mark'd, and number'd, as in margin Viz.

No. 1   1 Box Containing

No. 1	2 Damask Table Cloths 5 by 3 1/4 Ell at f.11 1/2				23	
2	2 do. do. 1 1/2 by 3 1/4 [at f.]10 1/4				20	10
3	2 do. do. 3 1/4 by 3 [at f.]7 1/2				15	
4	2 Pack Pins [at f.]3 1/4				6	10
5	1 Pc. 6 1/4 fine Bedtick 36 Ell [at f.]2				72	
	1 very handsome flower'd Persian Carpet 6 by 6 Ells and 36 Ells @ f.3				108	
	1 dark gray muff & Tippet				24	
1 Light gray do. do.					22	10

	f.291	10
Discount 1 PCt on f.183 10s	1	17
	289	17
Box	3	
	292	13

No. 2   1 Box Containing

12 pair blue & white Tea Cups & Saucers @ 6s.		3	12	
6 pint bowls	10	3		
12 fine Cut wine Glasses	16	9	12	
		f.16	4	
Disct 1 PCt		4		
		16		
Boxs &c.		12	16	12

No. 3 1 Pack Containing 2 Setts House brushes @ 42s.		4	4	
Packing Matt		9	4	13
			313	18
Duty Passeport and Officers fees		7	18	
Carriage and boathire		16	8	14
			322	12

Freight @ 12 1/2 PCt 40   6
Primage   5 PCt   2   42   6
                                    f.364 18

Errors excepted.

Amsterdam 30th May 1781.   John de Neufville Son

RC (Adams Papers); addressed "To the Honble Lady Adams   Braintree near Boston. P[er] Gates   Captn. Newman"; postal markings appear to read: "NP/h, 3.8   2/3." Dupl (Adams Papers); addressed as above but with routing: "P[er] Juno   Captn. Haydon." Both RC and Dupl are in a clerk's hand and signed in a different hand. Enclosed invoice is printed herewith; see note 4.

[1] Not found. This missing letter, referred to in AA to JA, 15 Jan. 1781, above, was in answer to Neufville's letter of 2 Sept. 1780, in vol. 3 above.

[2] This order on the Neufville firm, invoice below, had first been sent to JA in AA's letter of 13 Nov. 1780, above, and is printed there as an enclosure.

[3] The net credit in florins purchased by the $100 sent by AA seems to have been arrived at by transferring dollars to livres at 5 for 1, then calculating the rate of exchange from livres to florins at .5175. That sum was then subjected to a bank discount or charge (banco) of 16 2/3 percent. To the discounted figure was then added an allowance (agio) of 4 3/4 percent accruing from the exchange of currencies. The lack of explanation of these charges and allowances suggests that they were standard and would be understood by JA.

[4] The original invoice sent to AA is missing. Text is printed here from a retained copy in DLC:de Neufville Letterbook, 1781–1785, fol. 689, docketed "Invoice of Sundries Shipped by de Neufs. for Acc. of Lady Adams."

Abigail Adams to Charles Adams

My dear Charles   May 26 1781

I am sometimes affraid my dear Boy that you will be spoilt by being a favorite. Praise is a Dangerous Sweet unless properly tempered. If it does not make you arrogant, assuming and self sufficient, but on the contrary fires your Breast with Emulation to become still more worthy and engageing, it may not opperate to your Disadvantage. But if ever you feel your Little Bosom swell with pride and begin to think yourself better than others; you will then become less worthy, and loose those Qualities which now make you valuable. Worthy and amiable as I hope you are, there are still imperfections enough [in] every Humane Being to excite Humility, rather than pride.

If you have made some small attainments in knowledge, yet when you look forward to the immense sum; of which you are still Ignorant, you will find your own, but as a grain of sand, a drop, to the ocean.

If you look into your own Heart, and mind, you will find those amiable Qualities, for which you are beloved and esteemed, to result rather from habit and constitution, than from any solid, and setled principal. But it remains with you to Establish, and confirm that by choise and principal which has hitherto been a natural impulse.

Be modest, be diffident, be circumspect, kind and obligeing. These are Qualities which render youth engageing, and will flourish like a natural plant; in every clime.

I long to receive Letters from you. To hear of your Health and that of your dear pappas, would give me a pleasure that I have not experienced for 8 months.

O My dear children, when shall I fold you to my Bosom again? God only knows and in his own time will I hope return you safe to the Arms of your ever affectionate Mother,   A Adams

RC (Adams Papers).

Abigail Adams to John Quincy Adams

My dear John   May 26 1781

I hope this Letter will be more fortunate than yours have been of late. I know you must have written many times since I had the pleasure of receiving a line from you, for this month completes a year since the date of your last Letter.[1]

Not a line from you or my dear Charles since you arrived in Holland, where I suppose you still are.

I never was more anxious to hear yet not a single vessel arrives from that port, tho several are looked for.

I hope my dear Boy that the universal neatness and Cleanliness, of the people where you reside, will cure you of all your slovenly tricks, and that you will learn from them industery, oconomy and frugality.[2]

I would recommend it to you to become acquainted with the History of their Country; in many respects it is similar to the Revolution of your own. Tyranny and oppresion were the original causes of the revoult of both Countries. It is from a wide and extensive view of mankind that a just and true Estimate can be formed of the powers of Humane Nature. She appears enobled or deformed, as Religion, Goverment, Laws and custom Guide or direct her.

Firce, rude, and savage in the uncultivated desert, Gloomy, Bigoted and Superstitious where Truth is veiled in obscurity and mistery. Ductile, pliant, Elegant and refined—you have seen her in that dress, as well as the active, Bold, hardy and intrepid Garb of your own Country.

Inquire of the Historick page and let your own observations second the inquiry, whence arrises this difference? And when compared, learn to cultivate those dispositions and to practise those Virtues which tend most to the Benifit and happiness of Mankind.

The Great Author of our Religion frequently inculcates universal Benevolence and taught us both by precept and example when he promulgated peace and good will to Man, a doctrine very different from that which actuates the Hostile invaders, and the cruel ravagers of mighty kingdoms and Nations.

I hope you will be very particular when you write, and let me know how you have past your time in the course of the year past.

Your favourable account of your Brother gave me great pleasure—not only as it convinced me that he continues to cultivate that agreable disposition of mind and heart, which so greatly endeared him to his Friends here, but as it was a proof of the Brotherly Love and affection of a son, not less dear to his Parents.

Your Brother Tommy has been very sick with the Rhumatism, taken by going too early into water, by which means he lost the use of his Limbs and a fever ensued. He has however happily recoverd, and learnt wisdom I hope by his sufferings. He hopes soon to write you a Letter. He has a good school and is attentive to his Books.[3] I shall write to your Brother, so shall only add the sincere wishes for your improvement and happiness of your ever affectionate Mother,

A A

RC (Adams Papers). Early Tr (Adams Papers), in JQA's hand; at head of text: "*1. From my Mother*"; see descriptive note on AA2 to JQA, 24 May, above.

[1] This reference to JQA's "last Letter," written at least a year earlier, is too vague to permit identification. From AA's allusion below to JQA's "favourable account" of CA, it would appear that a letter from JQA to AA written in the spring of 1780 is missing.

[2] The foregoing paragraph was silently omitted by CFA when he first printed this letter, in AA, *Letters*, 1848, and again later in JA–AA, *Familiar Letters*.

[3] Preceding three sentences were silently omitted by CFA in printing this letter in the editions named in note 2.

Abigail Adams to John Adams

My dearest Friend   May 27 1781

I have written so largely to you by Mr. Storer[1] who goes in the same vessel, that I should not have taken up my pen again, but in compliance with the request of a Friend whose partner is going abroad, and desires a Letter to you as an introduction. Of Mr. Dexter the Bearer I know nothing but his Name. I have inclosed the Letter which I received from his partner who you know is a valuable Gentleman, and Eminent in his profession.[2]

As Election is not passed I have nothing New to add. My wishes for your Health and happiness and my anxiety to hear from you are an old Story. Should I tender you my warmest affections, they are of a date, almost with my first knowledge of you, and near coeval with my existance, yet not the less valuable I hope to a Heart that know[s] not a change, but is unalterably the treasure of its ever affectionate

Portia

RC (Adams Papers); addressed: "To Honble. John Adams Esqr Amsterdam"; docketed by CFA: "Portia May 27. 1781." Enclosure missing, but see note 2.

[1] Presumaby her letter of 25 May, above.

[2] "Mr. Dexter the Bearer" was Aaron Dexter (1750–1829), Harvard 1776, hon. M.D. 1786; professor of chemistry and materia medica at the Harvard Medical School, 1783–1816 (*Harvard Quinquennial Cat.*; Kelly, *Amer. Medical Biog.*). The enclosed letter from Dexter's "partner" has not been found, but Richard Cranch in his letter to JA, 28 May, below, not only specifies Dexter's errand abroad but identifies his partner as Dr. Thomas Welsh of Boston, a family connection, on whom see a note at vol. 3:78–79, above, and Adams Genealogy.

John Thaxter to Abigail Adams

Madam   Amsterdam May 27th 1781

I have been honoured with your favor of the 5th. February last. It would give me infinite Satisfaction to contribute in any way to your Enquiries into the Religion, Government, manners and Customs of this Country: and in some future Letter I will endeavour to give a small sketch (tho very imperfect) of them. The best History of this Country is in *Dutch*, and according to the Stile of the Nation *unconscionably long*: two insuperable Obstacles to my becoming acquainted with it. There is in English a History of 2 Vols. 8vo. written by Mr. Watson, of the Reign of Philip 2d, which is worth reading, as the Springs and Causes of the Revolution of this Country are in some good measure traced in this work.[1] There are two Histories of this Country in French, which I could wish to have transported to America —that of Mr. Cerisier is by far the best,[2] the other being an Abridgment. Temple's Observations were perhaps calculated for the Meridian of the Times in which he lived.[3] He is not without his Errors, Imperfections and Prejudices: and whatever Credit he may have obtained in England and among Foreigners, this Country allows him but a small share of Merit.

You will learn from your dearest Friend, what he has done respecting his Commission here. The Memorial has been admired and applauded beyond Expectation.[4] The Tories or Anglomanes themselves do not pretend to dislike it, tho' they wish to turn their Eyes from the Glare of Truth. The Deputies of this City, by the express Orders of the Regents, have presented a noble and spirited Proposition as it is called to the States of Holland. They have remonstrated against the Inactivity and Sloth of this Country in a Language, that an ardent Love of their Country, and a disinterested Zeal for its Dignity, Honour and Salvation alone could inspire. They direct their Deputies to endeavour to push on in the Generality a Negotiation with the Court of France, and that such measures may be taken for the future as "to repair the past, and wash out the Shame and Dishonour with which this Country is stained in the Eyes of Foreigners." [5] Tho' nothing is said of America in the Proposition so far as it respects a Negotiation with France, yet one would think if a Negotiation was completed with that Court, this Republick would not object to a better Acquaintance and a more friendly Intercourse with her new born Sister on the other side of the Atlantic. We have a common Enemy, and if She enters into a Treaty with France, why not connect herself with America? It is impossible to foresee what will be the Event. (An old Maid is sometimes coy and shy, as well as a young one. Pray don't show this to any antique Maid, for I shall have my Neck broke if You do.)

The Government and People of this Republick are infinitely more enlightened than formerly upon American affairs. The reason of that is obvious. You well know one whom I think inferior to None in Ability, Zeal and Activity in the service of his Country. You know who has but one Object, the Good of that Country, who is and was ever industrious and indefatigable. It is needless to add—the Man is designated.

The Body of this People are decidedly against England, and their Anger, Rage and Resentment are daily bursting forth in pointed Execrations of their old ally. They are perpetually lashing, pelling[6] and cursing the English in Songs and Ballads—and Americans being sometimes taken for the English in this City are exposed to Insults, until they mention their Country—the Sailors of America more particularly. But all this is only Smoke and Ton[7]—it is not Powder and Ball, the only Arguments to be employed against that mad Enemy to the Rights of Humanity: but it will come to this in time. Meanwhile these are good Symptoms.

Mr. A. has taken a House here, and We are getting affairs into a little Order, but things are not well arranged yet. There is but one of the whole sett of Servants who speaks any French or English, and that one but little of either, so that We do notably indeed with Dutch and German. I have proposed to Mr. A. to get me a Wife as a *real Conveniency*; he approves the matter much, as She might oversee domestic Affairs. If I could find one of about twenty or thirty ton of Gold (for that is the method of Estimation and Value here) I should begin to think a little *soberly* and *seriously* about it; or in other words in "sober sadness." But then it is such a *prodigious Embarrassment* if I should think of returning soon, (for I suppose She would not go with me) that it almost discourages me.

My most affectionate Regards to the young Ladies. I am much obliged by their kind mention of me. I have a Civil Thing or two to say to my "Fair American," but I dare not commit it to writing. You have written that *She* was much gratified at *my Residence* in Holland. I cannot say so much for myself. But how You came by that Piece of Information, Madam, is inconcievable to me. I had presumed that nobody knew my *Flame*, as the Phrase is, and I cannot help suspecting a little mistake in this matter. Who the "fair American" is that has made the declaration I know not: but I am sure that the one I mean would trust me in any Country.

Please to remember me dutifully, respectfully and affectionately where due: I wrote Mrs. C.[8] last December, and propose to write again. I cannot as yet forward any Letters.

I have the honour to be, with the greatest Respect, Madam, your most obedient humble Servant,   J.T.

RC (Adams Papers).

[1] Robert Watson, *The History of the Reign of Philip the Second, King of Spain*, 2 vols., London, 1777. A copy at MQA of the 5th edn., 3 vols., 1794, has JQA's bookplate. JA owned a French translation, 4 vols., Amsterdam, 1778, now in MB (*Catalogue of JA's Library*, p. 262).

[2] On this work see above, JQA to JA, 18 Feb., and note 1 there.

[3] See above, AA to Thaxter, 5 Feb., to which Thaxter is here replying.

[4] On JA's *Memorial* of 19 April, see note 3 on JA to AA, 28 April, above.

[5] See JA to AA, 22 May, and note 3 there.

[6] Pell, an obsolete word meaning to beat or knock violently (*OED*).

[7] Ton, from the French, meaning the vogue or fashion of the moment (same).

[8] Presumably Mary (Smith) Cranch (on whom see Adams Genealogy); the letter has not been found.

Abigail Adams to John Adams

My Dearest Friend   May 28 1781

I could not have conceived that a Letter written upon merely political subjects could have communicated so much pleasure to my Bosom as yours of the 28th of December to the president, of Congress, has given to mine.

This Letter was taken by the Enemy, carried into New York, and published by them, and republished [by] [1] Edes. [2] For what reason the Enemy published it I cannot tell, as it contains nothing which can possibly [injure] [3] us or the writer. It has proved a cordial to my anxious Heart for by it I find you were then living, and in Amsterdam, two facts that I have not received under your own hand for 8 months. This Letter is 3 months later than any which has reachd me.

Dr. Dexter by whom I have before written, has since, been polite enough to visit me, that he might, as he expresses it, have the pleasure to tell you, that he had seen me, and take from me any verbal message, that I would not chuse to write, but my pen must be the faithfull confident of my Heart. I could not say to a stranger, that which I could not write, nor dare I even trust to my pen the fullness of my Heart. You must measure it, by the contents of your own when softned by recollection.

Dr. Dexter appears to be a sensible well bred Gentleman, and will give you much information respecting our state affairs which may not be so prudent to commit to paper. I have written to the House of de Neufvilla for a few articles by an other opportunity and have now inclosed a duplicate.

I intreat you my dearest Friend to forward Letters to the various ports in France as you have some acquaintance with many of them. I should then be able to hear oftner.

june 1

Our Friends from P[lymout]h have made me a visit upon their remove to *Neponset Hill* which they have purchased of Mr. Broom. You will congratulate me I know upon my acquisition in the Neighbourhood, it is a very agreable circumstance. By them I learnt that the late vessels from France had brought them Letters from their Son up to the 10 of March, in which he mentions being with my dear Friend, my Sons, and Mr. T[haxte]r. They have received five Letters, by different vessels yet not a line has yet blest my hand. May I soon be made happy, and the Number compensate for the delay.

I hope you do not think it necessary to continue in Holland through the summer. I am very anxious for your Health—so flat a country will never agree with you. Pray do not be negligent with regard to an article which so nearly concerns the happiness of Your Ever affectionate

Portia

RC (Adams Papers); addressed: "To Honble. john Adams Esqr Amsterdam"; docketed by CFA: "Portia May 28. 1781." Enclosed "duplicate" order on the firm of de Neufville is missing, but a text of it is printed as an enclosure in AA to JA, 25 May, above.

[1] Editorially supplied for a word missing in MS.
[2] The original of JA to Pres. Samuel Huntington, 28 Dec. 1780, was captured at sea and published in the *New York Mercury* extraordinary of 19 April 1781, from which it was reprinted in Edes & Sons' *Boston Gazette*, 28 May, p. 2, col. 3 – p. 3, col. 1. A duplicate is in PCC, No. 84, II; printed in Wharton, ed., *Dipl. Corr. Amer. Rev.*, 4:213.
[3] Editorially supplied for a word missing in MS.

Richard Cranch to John Adams

Dear Bror: Boston May 28th. 1781

Having an Oportunity by Doctor Dexter, now bound to Europe, I gladly embrace it to write you a few Lines. We have been longing to hear from you a great while—not a line received from you or Mr. Thaxter for near six months. A Dutch War—Northern Powers arming for Defence of their Trade &c. are important Events since we last heard from you, which we wish to have an account of from you with your Opinion what the Issue of them will probably be. The Enemy in America are making their efforts in the southern States with various success, *often repulsed* with great loss, but *always victorious*, if you believe Rivington's Gazett. We have some way or other been taught to believe for a number of Months past, that a second Divison of Ships of War and Troops were coming to our assistance from our Illustrious Ally: Such a Belief and Expectation has been very injurious with respect to some of our publick Measures, and we feel a Disappointment with respect to the reinforcement of Ships more especially; as, for want of having more Men of War, those already here have been of little or no Service, being generally kept in Port by a superiour British Fleet. A Superiority by Sea in North America would probably terminate the War gloriously in this Part of the World. Our new Army fills up finely; Government has order'd all the Inhabitants to be Classed according to their Polls and Estates, Poor and Rich together, and each Class is to find a Man for three years or during the War, by which method our Army fills up very fast with fine Men. I mentioned above, the want of a superiour Fleet of Men of War in these Seas; it appears to me that a small Reinforcement in addition to the Ships that are already here would give a decided superiority, and would be of infinite importance to the common Cause, as by that means a few Ships might be spared from time to time, which, in conjunction with our Forces, might easily break up those little Nests that now keep a large Territory almost constantly in an Alarm by means of their paltry Lodgements, as is the Case at Ponobscutt, Chesepeak, &c: And at the same time might clear the Coasts from those small Piqueroons that Harbour there and infest our Trade. Another great Advantage that would arise from having the command of the American Seas would be that of transporting our Stores for the Army &c. as well as the different Produce of the United States, by Water carriage, which would be an amazing Saving in Expence as well as Time, compar'd with the expensive and tedious method of Land Carriage.

To the same want of a superiour Fleet I think we may charge the Loss of our State Ships of War from time to time as the Confederacy lately; and, we fear, the Protector also. 'Tis almost impossible to prevent our Enemies from knowing very soon when any of our State Ships of War sail, and we having no Fleet on the Coast, or, (which is much the same thing) none that is strong enough to venture freely out of Port; the Enemy by means of having a few more Ships are able to dispatch a Ship or two of superiour force after them and so take one by one, our best Ships. It appears to me plainly that our greatest Difficulties and the prolonging of the War is almost entirely owing to the want of having a superiority of Ships of War in these Seas. Had we a sufficient Fleet to cooperate with such an Army as we are now every Day getting into the Field, we might with the Smiles of Heaven, very soon extirpate the Enemy from the United States. My earnest Wish is for a Fleet!

I have mentioned to you that I send this by Doctor Dexter, whome I now take the liberty to recommend to your Notice as a very worthy Man;—he is engaged in Business with our Friend and Cousin Doctor Welsh and two other Gentlemen in a Plan of importing Druggs and Medicines in the wholes[ale] way. Doctor Dexter will bring with him Bills to a large amount to begin with. Your taking Notice of him will give him Rank.

Braintree has honour'd me [this?] year with an *unanimous* Choice to represent them in General Court the following Year. Doctor Cotton Tufts is chosen [sen]ator. I was at Braintree yesterday, when I had the pleasure of seeing your Mother, your Lady and Children, your

Brother and Children, Messrs. J. Quincy, and N. Quincy, Palmer, Wibird &c. all well. Father Smith was well a few Days ago. Coll. Thaxter's Family were well the last time I heard from them.[1]

I hope you will excuse my taking up so much of your valuable Time and believe me to be with every Sentiment of Friendship and Esteem, your affectionate Bror: ———

Please to give my kindest Regards to my dear young Friends Johnney and Charley, and to Mr. Thaxter, (to whome I intend to write by Doctor Dexter.) My dear Mrs. Cranch and Children are well and retain the kindest Wishes for your Happiness. I suppose our little Folks will write by this Oportunity.

RC (Adams Papers); addressed: "His Excellency John Adams Esqre. at Amsterdam. [Per fa]vr. of [Dr. De]xter," followed in another hand by: "Forwarded by Excellency's Most obedt. hume. Servant Aaron Dexter Gottenberg. Augt. 15 1781"; endorsed by John Thaxter: "Mr. Cranch May 28th. 1781." Dft (MHi:Cranch Papers); endorsed: "Rough Draft of a Letter to Bror. Adams. May 28th. 1781." Dft differs from RC in many details, one of which is recorded in note 1.

[1] Dft adds in this paragraph: "I am almost constantly in this Town [i.e. Boston] (excepting Sundays) on Committees of the General Court."

John Adams to John Quincy Adams

My dear Son   Amsterdam May 29 1781

I am two Letters, I believe in your Debt, but I have been too busily engaged, to be able to write you.

I am pleased with the divisions of your time, which you tell your Brother you have lately made, which appears to be a judicious distribution of Study and Exercise, of Labour and Relaxation.[1]

But I want to have you, upon some higher Authors than Phædrus and Nepos. I want to have you upon Demosthenes. The plainer Authors you may learn yourself at any time. I absolutely insist upon it, that you begin upon Demosthenes, and Cicero. I will not be put by. You may learn Greek from Demosthenes and Homer as well as from Isocrates and Lucian—and Latin from Virgil and Cicero as well as Phædrus and Nepos.

What should be the Cause of the Aversion to Demosthenes in the World I know not, unless it is because his sentiments are wise and grand, and he teaches no frivolities.

If there is no other Way, I will take you home, and teach you Demosthenes and Homer myself.

I am your affectionate Father,   John Adams[2]

RC (Adams Papers); at foot of text: "Mr. J. Q. Adams."

¹ JQA's letter to CA on "the divisions of [his, i.e. JQA's] time," probably written on 20 May, has not been found; see JQA to JA, 21 May, above.
² Although CFA did not choose to print this quaint but characteristic letter advising JQA on his Greek and Latin studies, he did permit the publisher or anonymous editor of *Homes of American Statesmen ... by Various Writers*, N.Y., 1854, to make a facsimile of the MS, which appears as a double-page insert with Clarence Cook's account of John Adams in that volume, following p. 150.

James Lovell to Abigail Adams

May 29 1781

Yesterday's Post brought me your Letters of the 10th and 14 with a Copy of March 17. on the Subject of which I shall be particular when I have a proper Opportunity.¹ I have a Friend² to whom I communicate most unreservedly *all* the Ocurrences which tend to govern my Pleasures and my Pains; your Letters will of Course be submitted in that mixt View: I have already hinted their Influence in the latter; so that there is a Chance of some Eclaircissement before I can convey them in whole, should you meet each other.

"You have a very small personal Acquaintance with the Lady whom you esteem and commisserate—you have as little personal Acquaintance with the Gentleman connected with her."³—Had you greater with both, you could not fail to think more highly of the former, and not so well or so ill of the latter as you seem at present to think, if I, who am perfectly intimate with them, may conclude from the Communications which you have lately made to me.—When I write again on this Subject I shall transmit some Anecdotes which you will think interesting to your Friend abroad. I believe I have already told you to see S[amuel] A[dams] as a Preparative.

I please myself with imagining you had Letters by Capt. Porter who appears to have reached Boston the 13th. in 27 Days from France. We are still without a Line from Mr. A or Mr. D[ana] since October.

I shall be attentive to Mr. Cranch if an Occasion offers to Fishkills.

I need not betray the Secrets which I am enjoined to keep. Your Eveship ought to be satisfied with what the Printers are pleased to give to the good People of Boston-Town. Glory or Shame, great in Degree of either Kind, depends upon the Behavior of the Americans in the coming six months, but more especially in the two first. I shudder verily at the Thought. Is it not almost a Resurrection from the Dead that I am looking for?

And now, avaunt ye Emanations of an honest Pen! Come to my aid ye Products of Insincerity! It is not the candid but the sentimental to whom I send you.

"I have the Honor to be with the most perfect Consideration Your Excellency's most obedt. & devoted humble Servant,"

James Lovell

PS By way of Nota Bene Excellency in English is of both Genders.

RC (Adams Papers).

¹ All three of AA's letters here acknowledged are printed above, but that of 14 May appears under the date of her draft, 13 May, the only surviving text. Lovell found "a proper Opportunity" to enter into the subject of AA's reproaches of 17 March in his letter of 16 June, below.
² Mrs. Lovell.
³ Lovell is quoting from AA's letter to him of 10 May, above. The lady and gentleman are of course Lovell and his wife.

John Adams to John Quincy Adams

My dear John   Amsterdam May 30. 1781

If there are any extraordinary Productions of Nature or Art, exhibited, at the Fair of Leyden, write me an Account and a description of them, and insert them in your Journal.¹

There were so many Rarities, at the Fair of Amsterdam, that I think these Fairs worth seeing. A Youth may store his Mind with many new Ideas, and with many usefull Reflections by attending to these Things. To open your Views and enlarge your Ideas of Nature, you ought not to neglect any innocent Opportunity.   J. Adams

RC (Adams Papers).

¹ See Waterhouse to JA, 21 May, above. If JQA followed his father's advice, no record of it appears. No "Journal" kept by him has been found for this period, though he resumed his diary in a new booklet on 9 June (D/JQA/4 in the Adams Papers; Microfilms, Reel No. 7).

Elizabeth Cranch to John Quincy Adams

My Dear Cousin   Braintree May. 1781

How shall I excuse myself for my long neglecting to write to you? Should I offer any other apology, than want of proper abilities, it would be false; and should I offer *that*, which is the only true one, perhaps it might be thought I wished for a compliment. But I had rather my Cousin should have a less favourable opinion of my understanding; than have cause to doubt my regard for him. That regard, joined to your Mama's repeated solicitations and my wishes for that improvement, and entertainment, which I shall receive from your letters, have at last encouraged me to write; and if you should read this letter, let it be with the candour of a Friend, not with the scrutinizing eye of a Critick.

It gives me pain to think that we are deprived of so many of your Letters by means of the frequent capture of Vessels. We have not heard from you but once, since you have been in Holland. We are impatient for some news from you; I hope it will not be a great while yet before we shall have it.

I expect to see you at your return, the *accomplished gentleman*; possessed of all the solidity and resolution of the American, finely polished by the ease, and sprightliness of the French. And may you not be destitute of the greatest of all accomplishments, that which can alone make you amiable, that which constitutes a *Good Man*; a due regard for *Virtue* and Religion. I am sensible my dear Cousin that they are words, which are very seldom, if ever, mentioned in the modern Plan, for what is called a Polite Education. But I dare say they are neither new, or unpleasing Sounds to your Ear. From your Papa (who practises them so well), I do not doubt you often receive the rules for attaining both and from your Mama's Letters (if you are so happy as to receive them) you may collect an excellent System of Morality. Your advantages for improvement are much greater than most young Gentlemen who travel; though they are generally provided with a Tutor, he is not their Parent, and cannot be supposed, to feel so interested for their good behaviour. The advice you receive from your Papa, you are sure, is free from all motives, but such as tend to promote your happiness. Let me beg of you my dear Cousin, by all means and as you prize your's, and the happiness of all your dearest Friends, to regulate your conduct by his precepts invariably— but I must stop and beg you to forgive the earnestness of a Friend and desire you not to impute what I have said to arrogance or self-sufficiency, but to the true motives, which were, my ardent desires to promote your good.

I could wish you to make my most respectful regards acceptable to your Papa and Mr. Thaxter, and my Love to my dear little Charles, (if they still remember me) and if amidst many much more important concerns you should think it proper to favour me with some of the productions of your Pen, I should think myself greatly obliged. May not the time be far distant, when you will all return in safety to your Friends, among which number I hope you include her who is sincerely and affectionately Your's,   E. C.

Early Tr (Adams Papers), in JQA's hand; at head of text: "*1. From Miss E.C.*"; see descriptive note on AA2 to JQA, 24 May, above.

John Adams to Abigail Adams

My dearest Friend   Amsterdam June 16. 1781

Mr. Le Roy the Bearer of this is a native of N. York but has lived nine years in Amsterdam with his Aunt Mrs. Chabanelle, a Lady who with her whole respectable Family, have been vastly civil to me and mine. Our Children have found that House a kind of home. I therefore wish Mr. Le Roy every Respect in America that can be shewn him.[1]

He wishes to form Mercantile Connections in America and therefore, it might be mutually convenient, for him to see your Unkle Smith and Mr. Cranch.

With the tenderest affection, to Miss Nabby and Mr. Thomas, I am, yours,   J. Adams

RC (Adams Papers).

[1] The Adamses had been introduced to the Le Roy-Chabanel circle at Amsterdam at the very outset of their sojourn in the Netherlands. See entries for August and September in JA's *Diary and Autobiography*, 2:446–447. Jacob Le Roy, a native of Rotterdam, had lived for some time in New York in the mid-18th century, and his son Herman was born there. Herman translated into English the questions submitted to JA by the jurist Hendrik Calkoen that led to JA's first propaganda effort in Amsterdam, eventually published as *Twenty-Six Letters, upon Interesting Subjects Respecting the Revolution in America, Written in Holland, in the Year M.DCC.LXXX*, London, 1786 (JA, *Corr. in the Boston Patriot*, p. 194; *Works*, 7:265). Herman returned to America with Gillon in the *South Carolina* in 1781–1782, and formed successive partnerships in

New York City that were long active in developing lands in western New York. The village of Le Roy in Genesee co., N.Y., was named for him. See P. J. van Winter, *Het Aandeel van den Amsterdamschen aan den Opbouw van het Amerikaansche Gemeenebest*, The Hague, 1927–1933, *passim*; John Lincklaen, *Travels in the Years 1791 and 1792 in Pennsylvania, New York and Vermont*, ed. Helen L. Fairchild, N.Y., 1897, p. 141–146; Paul D. Evans, *The Holland Land Company* (Buffalo Historical Society, *Publications*, vol. 28), Buffalo, 1924, *passim*.

JQA's diaries, kept irregularly during 1780 and 1781, show that he and CA were constantly under the care of one or another of the Le Roys and their relative, Mme. V. Chabanel, when not in school or at Leyden.

James Lovell to Abigail Adams

June 16. 1781

I have already acknowledged the Receipt of your Letter of May 10th covering a Copy of March 17th, and accompanied by one of May 14th.[1] I think I told you I would be more particular, at some future Day, in considering certain Parts of them. I meant to do it by Cyphers; but the present Opportunity renders that mode needless. Genl. Ward will probably take a safe Road for himself and consequently for my Scrawl.[2]

"A captured Letter, not to Portia thank Fortune,—published by the Enemy—has made some Talk; let the Writer's Conscience tell him whether any Thing ought to escape his Pen, even to a confidential Friend, that might be just Occasion of Pain to an affectionate Wife." —"I have not yet seen it, I fear it is *not fit I should*."[3]

As to *the* Letter Madam, there is one Expression or rather one Mode of Expression that I wish was not there. I am very unwilling that it should be submitted to the Eye of one so very much my Friend as you profess yourself to be. My Enemies are welcome to read it a thousand Times over. It was an unbecoming Levity, and quite unfit for a "Senator."[4] But it is not that which will give Pain to my affectionate Wife. She will be pained with what you would smile at. For she is more apt to fear than to despise the Enmity of Little-Great-Folks. I should have submitted the Letter, however to your severe anti-shandean Criticism, if I had not thought that an angried Few would have wisely kept from saying any Thing about it, rather than to make spiteful Interpretations of Parts that did not refer to themselves purely to vent that Malice which had been put into a State of Fermentation by Jemmy Rivington's marginal Notes upon those Parts which did really appertain to their Worthyships.[5] I am persuaded Madam I thus hit upon the authors—*original* Authors I mean, of those Suggestions which have troubled you. I did not want to aggrivate their Feelings by giving Communications of what I imagined they would chuse to stifle; that is to say the marginal Notes. By Mr. S[amuel] A[dams] I sent to Mr. G[erry] the original Print. I assure you there is only the Levity of an Hieroglyphic instead of the Words *at home* that I regret.

I must now be very serious. There is in the World, in the Hands of one of my best Friends, a Bond of about 80 Pounds Lawful Money against me, but I have that Amount and more against a Farm mortgaged to me for myself and others, tho' not worth what it is dipped[6] for. This is the whole Connexion I have with Money matters, and a poor one it is, except with my Pay for Time and Service as a Delegate, which ceases *the day I arrive in Boston*, though my Wife and Children will expect to dine the day after and peradventure they will be extravagant enough to expect it the third Day also. I shall not say much about the Probability, that many of those who have dined and supped formerly, often, for a Course of years, elegantly both as to the Table and Sideboard, tho not luxuriously, upon the Product of the exemplary Industry of the *Usher of a Grammar School*, will call to pay their Compliments to *the Honorable Delegate of Congress*, and wellcome him Home, while He poor Wretch cannot in Return offer them a Glass of small Beer to drink in Case of Thirst.

Do those who condemn my Absence mean to take me into their Stores as a Clerk? Will they risk such a Test of my Desire to live with one of the most faithful endearing Wives within the Circle of my whole Acquaintance, the tender and discrete Mother of my numerous Children, the benevolent Neighbour, the chearful sensible Companion of both Sexes.

"I must return if only for a short Visit."[7] Will they be willing to maint...—But, I shall forget who I am writing to, and shall draw upon myself, and not myself only, a Condemnation of a secret Compact against *short* Visits.—I am told that a Dollar and an Half per Day is to cloathe me as a Delegate, and to support the Wife and the seven Children of the same Delegate! Some of my Boys however begin to help me.

And now Madam, do not think that this serious Subject shall prevent my taking Occasion to censure your Sophistry in one part of your Letter.[8]

"What Right has She, who is appropriated, *to appear* lovely or charming in any Eyes but his whose Property she is?" I answer, *all that Right and Title which Virtue inherits above Vice.*

"I am persuaded" says a Lady who had seen much of the World, "that a Woman who is determined to place her Happiness in her Husband's Affections, should abandon the *extravagant Desire of engaging* public Adoration."

I underscore Part to show that it had nothing to do with your own Question above.

But I go further, and say, that the Lady needed not to travel to get double the Wisdom of what she here discovers. She might have sat in her Chamber and known that a Woman who is determined to place her Happiness in her Husband's affections not only "should" but *would* abandon "the extravagant" and even *any* Desire of Engaging "public *Adoration*."[9]

"Portia can join with Juba in the Play." "By Heavens I had rather have that best of Friend's approve my Deeds than Worlds for my Admirers." In Troth a very pretty Scrap of a Play! but quoted very unseasonably. For let me ask may not those very Deeds be approved and the Author of them *consequently* be admired by Thousands and Tens of Thousands; and has not a Wife, as well as a Maid, a Right *thus* "to *appear* lovely and charming to other Eyes than his whose Property she is"? Property! oh the dutch Idea![10]

Besides, Madam, your fine tuned Instrument cannot be an american one; it must be english with which we are at War. It cannot be italien, or it would be more sensibly touched by the *amiable* than by the *lovely*, the first being of roman and the last of british Extract; but otherwise, critically the same.

My Letter dated April 13. was written the 23.[11]—The Duke of *Leinster* not Leominster carried your Letter safely, but she is herself carried into New York.

I begin now to be uneasy about your Goods. Œconomy has banished all Waggoning almost from this City; and if I send by Water to Trenton I know not the Store Keeper's there, so that I shall run new Risques. Perhaps I may hear from you or Mr. Cranch Tomorrow. I am worried by a Paragraph in one of my Son's Letters which mentions your Good's by Doctor Winship being injured by the Rain. It must have been before Mr. Hughes boxed them; and he mentioned no such Thing to me.

I "have received your Letter of March 27[12] (and *worse* ones too) in that Spirit of Friendship with which they flowed from the Pen of Portia."[13] You see nevertheless that I think it a *bad* one and it is that Thought which prevents me from following the Dictates of my own Sincerity in subscribing:

I have not yet worn out the Word MADAM

Your most devoted humble Servant,   J L

RC (Adams Papers).

[1] All the letters mentioned are printed above, that of 14 May under the date of AA's draft, 13 May. Lovell had acknowledged receipt of these in his of 29 May, also above.

[2] AA acknowledged receipt of the present letter, brought by Maj. Gen. Artemas Ward, in her reply of 14 July, below.

[3] Lovell is quoting from AA's letter of 17 March, as he does repeatedly below, not always verbatim and hence sometimes distorting her emphasis if not her meaning.

[4] For a nearly complete printed text of Lovell's letter to Elbridge Gerry of 20 Nov. 1780, intercepted and published by the British in Rivington's New York *Royal Gazette*, 27 Dec. 1780, p. 2, col. 1, see Burnett, ed., *Letters of Members*, 5:451–453. Burnett's text is from the intercepted original in the Sir Henry Clinton Papers in MiU-C, and he locates another MS and another contemporary newspaper printing. He also furnishes excellent explanatory notes on the somewhat cryptic allusions in Lovell's letter to Congressional business, to George Washington, and to John Hancock. But he prints without explaining Lovell's brief paragraph mentioning his wife that had, from what she had heard about it, so perturbed AA and prompted the reproaches in her letter to Lovell of 17 March. This paragraph reads:

" 'Is it not Time to pay a Visit to Mass:'? Does my Wife look as if she wanted a toothless grey headed sciatic Husband *near* her? I am more Benefit to her at a Distance than in ♂ as the Almanac has it."

This is "the unbecoming Levity" toward Mrs. Lovell which had caused so much talk and was all that Lovell admitted to AA he regretted coming to light through the interception and publication of his letter. Specifically, as he explains below, he regretted using "an Hieroglyphic" (i.e. "in ♂") "instead of the Words *at home*." With its mixture of learned and sexually suggestive implications, this was a bit of verbal play very typical of Lovell: in astronomy ♂ is the sign for Mars; in biology it is the male principle.

[5] Rivington's "marginal Notes" were footnotes appended, not to the text of Lovell's letter to Gerry of 20 Nov. 1780, but to *another* Lovell letter intercepted at the same time and printed in the same issue of the *Royal Gazette* (27 Dec. 1780, p. 2, col. 2). This letter was addressed to John Hancock, 21 Nov. 1780; besides dealing with certain financial matters, it tendered Hancock warm congratulations on his recent election as governor under the new Constitution.

The printer commented on Lovell's "duplicity of . . . heart" in toadying to Hancock, since the two men were known to be political enemies, and cast sundry reflections on Lovell's humble origins and doubtful solvency. It should be observed that, since AA had not seen the newspaper text or notes, Lovell's labored explanation must have been largely meaningless to her, except for the revelation that if he gave up his post (and pay) in Congress he would have no means of supporting his family.

[6] See *OED* under *dip*, verb, 7b: "To involve in debt or pecuniary liabilities; to mortgage . . . (*colloq.*)."

[7] Paraphrased from AA's letter to Lovell of 13 May, above.

[8] Of 17 March, to which Lovell now reverts.

[9] Opening quotation mark editorially supplied.

[10] For AA's disapproving response to this phrase, see her reply of 14 July, below.

[11] It is printed above under the corrected date.

[12] Error for March 17.

[13] Quotation marks as in MS, but the opening quotation mark should in fact precede "in that Spirit."

Sarah Sever to Abigail Adams

Kingston June 16th 1781

I am exceedingly oblig'd to Mrs. Adams for her condescention, in the communications she has made in the very kind billet, this day handed me, by Mr. Austin.[1]

I am sincerely pain'd at the disagreable intelligence from my Cousin![2] Poor unfortunate youth! I hope his life is not so near drawing to its close! Just as his conduct merited the approbation of the Judicious; when his freinds might flatter themselves, with the satisfaction he might afford; from his alter'd manners in the morning of life, to be cut of—'twou'd be melancholy! But it might have been still more so!—had the fatal ball snapt the brittle thread, and not have left one moment for reflection,—it might have aggravated the wounds of the sorrowing bosom.—I am very anxious to hear from him; I hope he will be spar'd! Shou'd he suffer an amputation, Tho' 'twill be apparently a severe misfortune, it may prove a blessing.

I am rejoic'd that my Aunt is recovering. It must be ever regreted when eyes so valuable, shall lose their usefulness. Tis no small misfortune to us, the removal of my Uncle's family. But tis a satisfaction my Dear Madam, that the same cause, carrys you an addition of happiness. I expect to be familiariz'd to gloomy scenes; and I hope they will teach me useful lessons.—Mama has been confin'd more than a month to her chamber,—she is very frail and indispos'd. And My brother, who this week puts on a military garb, and leaves us to take the feild, will not hasten her recovery.[3] She and papa join in offering their best regards to Mrs. Adams.

I hope, Madam, you continue to have agreable tidings from your absent freinds. May the period be not far distant, when the Atlantic will no longer separate you from the partner of your heart. May you enjoy many years of domestic felicity in peace and freindship.

Will Mrs. Adams condescend to pardon the presumption of engaging her attention so long, from one so ev'ry way unworthy?—'Tis a proof of her goodness if she does.—Miss Nabby promis'd I shou'd hear from her; she has not been good as her word. I hope we shall have the pleasure of seeing her with Miss Betsy, in the course of the summer. Our alter'd village does not promise many pleasures, but our little power shall be exerted to make it agreable to them.—To see you at Kingston my dear Lady, wou'd make us all very happy.—Will you be pleas'd to make my affectionate regards acceptable to your good sister and family. My love to Miss Nabby, and give me leave to subscribe myself with ev'ry sentiment of respect & esteem, your sincere freind & humble servant,   S. Sever

RC (Adams Papers).

[1] The "very kind billet," presumably from AA, has not been found. The messenger may have been Jonathan Loring Austin, who returned about this time from Europe after being captured by the British; see note on him in vol. 3:262, above, with references there.

The writer of this letter, Sarah Sever (1757–1787), was the daughter of James Warren's sister Sarah (Mrs. William Sever), of Kingston. Though romantically linked with John Thaxter, she married in 1784 the Boston merchant Thomas Russell. See Sibley-Shipton, *Harvard Graduates*, 11:575–578; *Vital Records of Kingston, Massachusetts, to the Year 1850*, Boston, 1911, p. 132,

276; *Mass. Centinel*, 28 Nov. 1787, p. 3, col. 2.

[2] James Warren Jr., identified above, vol. 3:133, was wounded in one or more actions on board the *Alliance*, which had just arrived in battered condition in Boston (*Boston Gazette*, 11 June 1781, p. 2, cols. 1–2; William Bell Clark, *Gallant John Barry*, 1745–1803, N.Y., 1938, p. 224).

[3] James Sever (1761–1845), Harvard 1781, had been commissioned in Feb. 1781 ensign in the 7th Massachusetts regiment (*Mass. Soldiers and Sailors*; Heitman, *Register Continental Army*).

Alice Lee Shippen to Elizabeth Welles Adams

Philadelphia 17. June [1781]

I have long promis'd my self the Honor of a Correspondence with you Madam, and now I cannot in person enquire of your Health and Welfare from Mr. A— your good Spouse, I can no longer deny my self the satisfaction of doing so in this way; and if I can be of the least Service to you here, either by communicating or otherwise, you cannot oblige me more than by commanding me.[1] My Brother A. L— is with us, and with Mr. S— desires to be remember'd in the most respectfull manner to yourself and Mr. A—, on whose safe arrival at Boston I congratulate you Madam, and it gives me great pleasure to hear that the People have Virtue and Discernment enough still to respect and love him: may they long continue to do so; and may he live long, very long, to serve them and enjoy their Gratitude.[2]

The British are making sad Havock in Virginia, they have taken six Members of their Assembly: I am much distress'd lest a Brother I have in that Body should be one of their number. I am sure none of my Brothers will find any Mercy with them. A French Fleet in Virginia now might do every thing we wish, but I despair of such assistance while a certain person is our Minister. He has sent his resignation to Congress; this is probably no more than a State Trick to fix him more firm in the Saddle. He says perhaps he is too Old, but he does not perceive any thing like it himself; and then gives a strong Proof of it by recommending his Grandson as the Person who will, in a Year or two, be most fit for our Plenepotentiary.[3] From this recommendation one or the other of these two things is clear, either Mr. F—'s faculties are impair'd, or he thinks ours are. This same Gentleman is now blackening the Character of Mr. J:A. to Congress more than he did Mr. L—'s, and he has got the french Minister to join him.[4]—I fear I shall quite tire you; I will only beg leave to add that I am with the highest Esteem, Madam, your very humble Servt.,

A:S.

Early Tr (Adams Papers); in the hand of Richard Cranch; at foot of text: "(A. Shippen)." The (missing) RC, "addressed to Mrs. A. but without any christian Name or place of abode," was erroneously delivered to AA in Braintree rather than to its intended recipient, Mrs. Samuel Adams, in Boston. After having had a copy made by her brother-in-law Cranch, AA forwarded the original, with "a proper excuse," to Mrs. Samuel Adams. See letters of AA to James Lovell and to Mrs. Shippen printed below under 30 June.

[1] The writer, Alice (Lee) Shippen (1736–1817), wife of Dr. William Shippen Jr. (1736–1808) of Philadelphia, was the sister of four Lee brothers of

Virginia (Richard Henry, Francis Light-foot, William, and Arthur), all of whom made their mark on Revolution-ary history and appear with more or less prominence in *The Adams Papers*. The Lees' political ties were especially close with Samuel Adams, and only slightly less so with JA; there is a witty saying without a known author to the effect that the American Revolution was the result of a temporary alliance between the Adamses and the Lees.

² Samuel Adams, who had recently left Congress, was now serving as presi-dent of the Massachusetts Senate (*Bos-ton Gazette*, 4 June 1781, p. 2, col. 2).

³ See Benjamin Franklin to Pres. Sam-uel Huntington, 12 March 1781, in Franklin's *Writings*, ed. Smyth, 8:220–223. It hardly needs to be added that Mrs. Shippen's summary at second hand

of Franklin's letter offering his resigna-tion and recommending his grandson, William Temple Franklin, to the further favor of Congress, is not unprejudiced. Congress' reply to Franklin, declining his offer, 19 June, is in JCC, 20:675–676.

⁴ The reference is to Franklin's role in the dispute in the summer of 1780 between JA and Vergennes and its after-effects now current in Congress, whereby, through La Luzerne's influence, JA's powers to negotiate treaties of peace and commerce with Great Britain were re-voked. Mrs. Shippen's term "the french Minister" is ambiguous; it could mean either Vergennes or La Luzerne. See editorial note in vol. 3:390–395, above; Lovell to AA, 26 June, 13 July, 10 Aug.; AA to Lovell, 14 July; all below.

Cotton Tufts to John Adams

Dear S[ir]   Boston June 20. 1781

I am told that a Vessell will this Day sail for Holland. I know not how to neglect so fair an Opportunity of Writing, convinced that a Line from your Friend will be acceptable, if it be only to inform you that we have an Existence in America as an indepen[den]t Nation, that our Commonwealth lives, that our annual Election is Compleated, the Legislative and executive Bodies organized, That our Families and Connections are well and that the Season is truly promising having been blessed with frequent Rains. Our Crops of Grass will be great and the English Grain has a fine Aspect. Great Quantities of the Syberian wheat have been sown this year throughout the State. Hitherto it has succeeded and no blast has happened to it, since its first Introduction in the Country, it is about Six years since any of this Grain was heard of here—a few Quarts was in the Hands of [*blank in MS*] in Portsmouth—last year some Farmers raised 2 or 300 Bushells.¹

The Scituation of our public Affairs is not at present so favourable as I could wish for. For want of naval Assistance, the Enemy have gaind many Advantages, they have bent all their Force to the South-ward, have established Posts at Virginia, North Carolina &c. and are ravaging the Southern States. They have met with many severe Checks, have lost many Men and the Army at South Carolina under Gen. Cornwallis is supposed to be lessened one half—by Battles, Sickness, Desertion &c. Gen. Green has opposed the Enemy with a very inferior Force and under the greatest Embarassments has kept a Body sufficient to prevent the Conquest of those Countries, he has performed Wonders.—The Depreciation of our Paper Currency has been the fatal Source of almost all the Misfortunes We have suffered for several years past. Our Enemies are continually availing themselves of every Advantage that can be obtaind from a fluctuating Currency. They have but too well succeded in their Plans. A late Shock We have sustained, by a sudden Depreciation of the old continental Emission from 75 to 200, 250 and even 300—in one Week it fell from 75 to 150. I flatter myself that this will in the End rather serve than disserve us. It has pretty generally convinced People that We must not any longer depend on a paper Medium, and such Measures are now pursuing and will I hope be carried into effect, as will enable us to conduct our affairs with Stability. It was necessary that we should be severely whipd and a whipping we have had, such as is sensibly felt and will leave a lasting impression. It will purify our Minds, open our Faculties and lead us to guard against those Evils, which must have proved our Ruin if persisted in.

This Morning a Report prevails that the French Fleet and Army under the Command of [*blank in MS*] have retaken St. Lucia. I think there is a great Probability of it. We have had Advice some Days agone, that on the arrival of this Fleet in the West Indies, Rodney was before Martinico, who upon their Appearance, left his Station, attacked the French, found his Fleet unable to cope with the French and ran. The French pursued and cut him off from St. Lucia, took that Opportunity of Landing 4 or 5000 Troops and laid Seige to it.

22d.

By authentic Accounts from the Southward, The Enemy have joined their several Armies at Richmond—to the Number of 6000. Marquiss of Fayette commands our Forces in that Quarter. At present his Army is much inferior to the British. The latter will triumph for a Time; but I trust their Triumphs will be short, as such Measures are taking as will with the Smiles of Providence turn the Scale. While Cornwallis has withdrawn his Army from South Carolina, Genl. Green is taking one Post after another and will soon be master of all their Fortresses except the Capital.

This day a Letter from Genl. Washington to Genl. Heath Dated New Windsor June the 15. 1781, contains the following Intelligence "Since the Enemy formed a Junction of their several Corps in Virginia, nothing material has happened in that Quarter. On the 10th of May Lord Rawden was compelled to evacuate Camden with Precipitation, leaving behind him three of his Officers and 50 Privates so dangerously wounded as to be unable to be removed. On the 11th the strong Post of Orangeburg surrendered to Genl. Sumpter: a Colenel, several Officers and upwards of 80 men were made Prisoners. On the 12th. the garrison of Fort Mott, consisting of 7 officers 12 non commissioned officers and 165 Privates, surrendered by Capitulation to Genl. Marian.

On the 15th Fort Granby capitulated to Lieut. Col. Lee, the Garrison were made Prisoners and consisted of 1 Lieut. Col., 2 Majors, 6 Captains, 6 Lieutenants, 2 Sergt. Majors, 3 Ensigns, 2 Surgeons, 17 Sergeants, 9 Corporals, and 305 Privates. Large Quantities of Provisions were captured at some of the Posts. At the same Time the Posts of Augusta and Ninety Six were invested by Gen. Pickings: and Gen. Greane on the 16th of May had determined to march the Army to expedite their Reduction."[2]

I have wrote to You by 4 or 5 Conveyances but have not been so happy as to receive a Line from you since you left America. Be pleased to remember me to Mr. Thaxter to whom I have repeatedly wrote and have received but one Letter of March 1780. His Parents and Connections are well—Your Family also, on whom I called on Tuesday in my way to this Town, where I am at present stationed and have taken a Post in public Life in compliance with the Call of the Electors of the County of Suffolk.

I am with sincere Regards Yr. affectionate Friend & H Sert.,

C.T.

RC (Adams Papers); endorsed: "Dr. Tufts 20. June 1781."

[1] Sentence thus punctuated in MS.

[2] Washington's letter to Maj. Gen. William Heath, 15 June, is printed in full in Washington's *Writings*, ed. Fitzpatrick, 22:217–218.

Richard Cranch to John Adams

Dear Bror: Boston June 22d 1781

I wrote you by Doctor Dexter on the 28th Ulto. which I hope will come safe to hand. Tho' I have not had the Happiness of a Line from you since you left America yet I shall gladly embrace the Oportunity that now offers (by a Ship bound to Denmark) to write you a few Lines. We have just received Letters from Spain giving an account of the very great successes against the English in India by Hyder

Ali &c.—'Tis remarkable to observe how far the Destruction of the *Indian Weed* at Boston a few Years ago, has operated towards the loss of the very Country itself from whence the Pride of Britain has been so fed and fostered. I mentioned in my last that the Enemy in the southern States were making their Efforts with various success. By a Letter from Genl. Washington to Genl. Heath received yesterday by Express, (which the General was so kind as to read to me) it appears that Genl. Green about the 15th Ulto. had made himself Master of the Enemy's Strong Post at Camden and three other of the strongest Posts that the Enemy held in South Carolina, together with their Stores of Provisions, Cannon and Baggage; and had taken seven or eight Hundred Prisoners. The numbers of Field Officers, Subalterns and Privates are mention'd, but I do not recollect them exactly. Genl. Washington mentions in the same Letter the junction of the Enemy's Forces in a part of Virginia, as being what would give them room to make some partial Depredations at first, but as what will finally prove destructive to them. Genl. Washington has call'd upon this State to fill up its Battallions immediately, which the Court has accordingly order'd to be compleated by the last of this Month. Three Thousand Melitia are also call'd upon from this State for "supporting Communications and for other Purposes," together with Beef &c. for their Support. Above two hundred and fifty Yoke of Oxen and Carriages are now taken up here in this Neighbourhood for transporting Large Mortars and heavy Battering Cannon, and other Warlike Stores from this Place which will set out immediately, some of them this Day; and the like Movements are making in other Parts of this State. What the Plan of our illustrious General is, may be infer'd from the following Passage in his Letter to this Government, dated Weathersfield May 24th 1781.

"In consequence of a Conferance held between his Excellency the Count De Rochambeau and my self at this Place, the French Army will march as soon as Circumstances will admit, and form a junction with the American on the North River. The accomplishment of this Object which we have in contemplation is of the utmost importance to America, and will in all probabillity be attained unless there be a failure on our Part in the number of Men which will be required for the Operation, or the Enemy should withdraw a considerable part of their Force from the Southward. It is in our own Power by proper Exertions to prevent the first—and should the last take place, we shall be amply repaid our Expences by liberating the Southern States where we have found by Experience we are only vulnerable."—"The Enemy counting upon our want of Abillity or upon our want of Energy, have, by repeated Detachments to the southward, reduced themselves in N: York to a situation which invites us to take advantage of it."[1]

We have heard that you have succeeded in Holland in a Loan, thro' the House of Messrs. Deneufville and Son, of about 100,000 Pounds Sterlg.[2] If by means of that Loan you should want to have any Publick Business transacted in this Place I should be glad to be assisting in it. Or if any of your Friends should be inclined to make a Tryal of sending any Merchandize this way on Commission, I should be glad to transact Business in that way for them with the greatest care and Dispatch, and on the most reasonable Terms. I suppose any Goods that are vendable in this Country, and are well bought in Europe, will fetch here double their first Cost in Gold and Silver or Bills of Exchange by the large quantity together; and in smaller quantities such as single Pieces of Linnen &c. three for one. My meaning is that an Invoice of well chosen Goods, that amounted to one hundred Pounds Sterling first Cost at the usual wholesale Price in Europe, would fetch here, from two Hundred to three hundred Pounds of the same Sterling Money in Specie, or in good Bills of Exchange.

I know that the transacting of those Matters lays entirely out of your Line, as well as out of your Inclination; but as you must sometimes mix with the Mercantile World, should a Hint of this kind be drop'd by you it might be of Service to me. Verbum sat &c.

I expect every moment when the Vessell will be under Sail, so that I must in haste conclude, with Love to your dear little Boys and Mr. Thaxter (to whome I wrote two Letters by Doctor Dexter) your affectionate Bror. and humble Servt.,   Richard Cranch

A French Fleet of Transports from Brest under convoy of several Frigates is arrived here within about ten Days past. I hear that all but one are arrived safe, and that one, (being the ship that had most of the Wine on Board) is drove on Shore not far from Plymouth, whether she will be got off or not I dont learn, nor do I know exactly where she is. The Troops that came in this Fleet march'[d] about a Week ago.

RC (Adams Papers); addressed: "To His Excellency John Adams Esqr: to the Care of Messrs: De Neufville and Son, Merchants in Amsterdam."; endorsed by John Thaxter: "Mr. Cranch 22d. June 1781." Dft (MHi:Cranch Papers); endorsed: "Rough Draft of a Letter to Bror. Adams June 22d 1781."

[1] These are extracts from Washington's circular letter to the New England States, 24 May, printed in full in his *Writings*, ed. Fitzpatrick, 22:109–11.

[2] This effort had failed; see above, Lovell to AA, 21 May, and note 2 there.

Abigail Adams to James Lovell

[*Braintree, 23 June 1781*][1]

And is there no medium Sir, between terms which might be mis-construed, and the cold formal adieu of mere ceremony tagd with a title. Your Sentimentilist as you are pleased to stile her[2] prizes the Emanations of a *pure* and friendly Heart, before all the studied com-plasance of a finished courtier.

Uncandid do you say? You never will find Portia so. When the character of the Statesman, the Senator, the Benevolent Philanthro-pist is maintained in its purity the grave parent of children who look up to him for an example for their future conduct should not suffer an impeachment in the Eye of the World, much[3] less should there be just occasion for it.

I will give you a specimen of a conversation that passd not long since between Portia and a Lady of her acquaintance for whom she entertains a high Esteem as one of the best Female characters in America tho Portia would fain believe she errs in judgeing of one character. Cornelia. Have you seen the intercepted Letter of your Friend L[ovel]ls to Mr. G[err]y.[4]—Portia. No Madam but I have heard much of it, and some severe strictures about it. I could wish to see it.— Cornelia. I have read it, and can give you an account of it. It is Eneg-matical, as all his Letters are, but there are some things in it which for decency sake ought never to have been there. Were I his wife they would make me misirable, but I believe he cares little for her.— Portia. O, Madam do not judge so hardly. I have ever thought him to have a high value for her, he has never mentioned her but with respect and tenderness, of which I believe her very deserving.—Cor-nelia. True I am not acquainted with her, but I hear her well Spoken of by every body, and believe her much too good for a Man that can allow his pen such a lisence in writing of her, and add to that can leave her 3 or 4 years together.—[*Portia.*] Pray my dear Madam do not measure a Gentlemans regard for his wife by the last reason given. Is it not misfortune enough to be seperated from our best Friends without the worlds judgeing hardly of us or them for it. How would you wound me should [you] think thus of my own dear partner.—Cor-n[elia]. The case is different with him. It is in the power of one with-out much hazard or risk—but not of the other, and I tell you my Friend that this gentleman whom you think so favourably of, is in my opinion a deciple of Mandivile Nursed in the School of Chester-feild—and looks upon the whole Sex as common prey [or free?] plunder.⁵—Portia. O my dear Madam I cannot think so. Were I once satisfied that such was his sentiments and character, I would Instantly renounce all acquaintance with him. I must condemn the Levity of his pen, but he cannot have a bad Heart. I have but little personal acquaintance with him but I never supposed him a man of the world. I never heard his conjugal character aspersed—did you.—Cornelia. No, only as the world will naturally believe that a Gentleman possessing domestick attachments would visit his family in the course of 4 years, when only 3 hundred miles distant.—Portia. Why Madam he may have reasons which he would not chuse to manifest to the World.—Cornelia. Then let him be uniformly delicate and I will believe them.

Thus ended a conversation but not a conversion. Uncandid as you are pleased to stile Portia, if she had not valued her correspondent for real and substantial virtues of Heart and mind, the just or unjust reflections of the world would have affected her no more than any other vague reports. By giving freedom to her pen and unreservedly censuring what she must ever consider as the Shades of a character she has given proof of a real Friendship which will not be diminished untill she shall be convinced that the character drawn by Cornelia is a just one.—And now Sir for one passage in your Letter which you may well think has not escaped my notice. "When I write again on *this Subject*, I shall transmit some anecdotes which you will think Interesting to your Friend abroad." Now what Inference am I to draw from this? If you mean to retaliate for the pain you say I have given you, by this dark hint, you are mistaken, for my confidence in my Friend abroad is as unbounded as my affection for him which knows no limits. He will not injure me even by a thought. Virtue and principal confirm the Bond which affection first began, and my security depends not upon passion which other objects might more easily excite, but the sober and setled Dictates of Religion and Honour. It is that which cements at the same time that it ensures the affections.

> "There Love his golden shafts employs, there lights
> His *constant Lamp* and waves his purple wings."

I shall not make any inquiry of Mr. S[amuel] A[dams] should I see him, but I hold you in duty bound to explain yourself.—Not a vessel from Holland or a line from that Quarter. My Heart sickens at the recollection. O for the wings of a dove that I might flie away.

Great and important is the day. May America shew herself equal to the call. Our wretched finances undoe us. This Town exerted itself and has forwarded all the Men required and has paid the money required for the Beaf.—What a stupid race are the British retalers of News, to think one sensible American would credit their story of peace makers excluding America, when they would all be glad to hug her.

I hope you have recoverd from your fall, if it was an honest one from your Horse and not down a pair of dark stairs.[6]—I will not receive your sarcasam so have blotted it out, and in lieu of it "read Portias affectionate Friend,"[7] and in return bestow the sincere Emanations of Friendship which glow in the Bosom of
Portia

Dft (Adams Papers); without date or indication of addressee; at head of text in CFA's hand: "May 1781." AA's very careless punctuation, particularly in the dialogue between Cornelia and Portia, has been slightly regularized for clarity.

[1] Lovell's reply of 13 July, below, mentions two letters from AA, dated 10 and 23 June, in language making it clear that the present letter is the second of these two. AA's letter of 10 June has not been found.

[2] In Lovell's letter to AA, 29 May, above, quoted again later in the present letter and alluded to in its leavetaking.

[3] MS: "must."

[4] From AA's characterization of her, from the general tenor of her comments, and from other hints, one may at least guess that "Cornelia" was Mercy Warren, but the identification cannot be established without more evidence than is now available. On "the intercepted

Letter" from Lovell to Gerry, 20 Nov. 1780, see especially AA to Lovell, 17 March and 10 May, and Lovell to AA, 16 June, all above.

[5] The first word in brackets has been editorially supplied for sense; the second word is only partially legible. Another reading of the passage might be: "common prey for plunder."

[6] See Lovell's reply, 13 July, below.

[7] Closing quotation mark editorially supplied. Lovell's "sarcasam" was in the highly formal phrasing of the leavetaking in his letter of 29 May, q.v. above, responding to AA's disapproval of his earlier use of terms of gallantry.

James Lovell to Abigail Adams

June 26. 1781

The Alliance may have brought *you* Letters: neither that nor the Franklin have given *us* any from Mr. Adams. Mr. Dana on the 4th of April resolved to go from Paris to Holland on the Sunday following.[1] He mentions nothing of Mr. A but I send you a Scrap from the Hague[2] which proves the Health of him and his, in a good Degree, March 4th. Any Thing to the contrary would have been mentioned by Mr. Dumas.

There is surely nothing of the Gallant, nothing which need hurt the fine toned Instrument, in this *Solicitude* of mine to administer even the smallest Degree of Satisfaction to a Mind very susceptible of Anxiety, and, a little prone, I fear, to see Harm where Harm is not.

Hague. Dumas. March 5.[3]

His Excellency J. Adams favored me, *Yesterday*, both with his *Visit* and with a Sight of his late Dispatches from your Excellency of December last. I have promised him, in Consequence, what I repeatedly had promised him before; vizt. to assist him with all my Heart and Powers, and I am as sure to have already convinced him of my Zeal in doing so, as in good hope that Things will ripen and our Endeavors be blessed.

There have been some Proceedings nearly affecting Mr. A's public Character. Lest you should be uneasy at Hints catched here and there, I think proper to tell you that a Change of Circumstances in Europe has made it necessary according to the *major* Opinion, to ||be liberal in *discretionary* powers|| and it hath been made Part of the Plan to ||colleague|| the Business in Consequence. I do not think upon the Whole that the latter Circumstance will be the most unpleasing to our Friend; the real Truth being that ||our allies are to rule the roast|| so that the Benefit of the latter Provision will be that the ||insignificance will be in shares.|| This is my poor angry Opinion of the Business.[4]

Now *Woman* be secret.[5]

Y m o m d h St.,   J.L.

Mr. S[amuel] A[dams] will have told you of the two Peices of Business which led to the two Resolves inclosed.

RC (Adams Papers). The enclosed "two Resolves" mentioned in the postscript are not now with the letter. One was the resolution of 10 Jan., forwarded to JA in a letter from Pres. Huntington of that date, approving Vergennes' position on JA's not communicating his powers to the British government (JCC, 19:42; Wharton, ed., *Dipl. Corr. Amer. Rev.*, 4:229). The other enclosure must have related to the actions in Congress in early June modifying JA's instructions as peace minister and joining him in a commission with four others to negotiate peace; see note 4. Four brief passages that appear in cipher in Lovell's letter have here been deciphered between double verticals. In the original, the ciphered passages are marked "A" through "D"; these are Richard Cranch's marks for his decipherment, made at AA's request and surviving as an undated scrap of paper among the Adams Papers. On Lovell's cipher generally, see Appendix to this volume.

[1] See Dana to the President of Congress, 4 April 1781, Wharton, ed., *Dipl. Corr. Amer. Rev.*, 4:349–351.
[2] Incorporated in the text below.
[3] This caption is a marginal gloss in Lovell's letter. The full text of Dumas' letter to the President of Congress of 5 March is printed in Wharton, ed., *Dipl.*

Corr. Amer. Rev., 4:273–274.
[4] Lovell here touches in a very gingerly way on recent actions of Congress that were to have a profound effect on JA's diplomatic career and to embitter him permanently toward those who, in the course of a brief but intense struggle in Congress, had brought them about.

These were, of course, the alterations in his instructions of 1779 as sole minister for peace, whereby he was now empowered to accept a truce under the proffered mediation of Russia and Austria; was ordered "ultimately to govern" himself in everything by the "advice and opinion" of the French court: and, to top off these (to JA at least) degrading instructions, was deprived of his exclusive powers as peace minister by being joined in a commission with four others, namely Jay, Franklin, Laurens, and Jefferson. These and sundry other modifications of the 1779 instructions debated and voted in the first half of June 1781 were the product of a diplomatic stratagem that had been initiated months earlier in the French foreign office and was effected by La Luzerne in Philadelphia through his influence with certain members of Congress who, for varying reasons, held pro-French views and/or distrusted JA's independent views and conduct (his "Stiffness and Tenaciousness of Temper," as John Witherspoon phrased it; Burnett, *Letters of Members*, 7:116). Among them were John Sullivan, James Madison, and John Witherspoon. The circumstances of this maneuver and its sequels are repeatedly touched on in JA's *Diary and Autobiography*; see text and notes in that work at 3:3–4, 104–105; 4:252–253; see also above, vol. 3:231–232. The long series of motions and votes in Congress, as recorded in its Secret Journal, 6–15 June, are given in convenient sequence in Wharton, ed., *Dipl. Corr. Amer. Rev.*, 4:471–481; the drafts and notes of Madison relating to these proceedings are printed in his *Papers*, ed. Hutchinson, 3:133–134, 147–155, with valuable editorial commentary. John Witherspoon's remarkable speech in Congress on 11 (or possibly 9) June should also be consulted (Burnett, ed., *Letters of Members*, 6:115–118); it appears unexceptionably fair-minded toward all the parties in question or contention, including JA. However, later statements by Witherspoon throw a different and possibly sinister light on his and his supporters' motives. William C. Stinchcombe in *The American Revolution and the French Alliance*, Syracuse, 1969, p. 166–168, has discussed this difficult question acutely. Irving Brant, in his *Madison*, vol. 2, ch. 10 ("Clipping Diplomatic Wings") has furnished a lucid and detailed narrative account of what happened in Congress respecting peace policy at this time. But he proceeds on the assumption that nothing Madison did could be wrong, and Stinchcombe's point of view throughout his chapter dealing with this subject is more objective. Another recent account, based on French as well as American sources, is in Morris, *Peacemakers*, p. 210–217. Morris observes that the "stakes" of Vergennes' moves at this time "were nothing less than the control of America's foreign policy.... Lacking all the facts and relying upon the assurances of La Luzerne, the innocent and the corrupted together marched meekly to the slaughter" (p. 210, 213). See also below, Lovell to AA, 13 July, and note 7 there.

[5] This injunction is written lengthwise in the margin beside the preceding paragraph.

Abigail Adams to James Lovell

My dear Sir [Braintree, 30 June 1781][1]

At length the mistery is unravelld, and by a mere accident I have come to the knowledge of what you have more than once hinted at. A Letter of Mrs. Shippen addressed to Mrs. A. but without any christian Name or place of abode,[2] was put into my Hands Supposed for me, I opened and read it half through before I discoverd the mistake. Ought Eve to have laid it by then when so honestly come at? But pay for peeping is an old adage and so have I—for after mentioning our affairs in France and giving a Specimin of the *Abilities* of the present plenipotentiary together with his recommendation of "a mere white curd of asses milk" she adds "this same Gentleman is now blacking the character of Mr. —— to Congress more than he did Mr. S— and he has got the French Minister to join him."[3] This allarmed at the same time that [it] enlightned me. Is Monsieur G—r or L—n meant?[4] If the Latter I am very Sorry that he should become a dupe to the wiles of the Sorcerer, he was no Stranger when he left France to the views and character of the Man and I always supposed him Friendly to my ——.[5] The duce take the Enemy for restraining my pen. I want to ask you a hundred Questions and to have them fully and explicitly answerd. You will send me by the first opportunity the whole of this dark prosess. Was the Man a Gallant I should think he had been monopolising the Women from the enchanter. Was he a Modern Courtier I should think he had outwitted him in court intrigue. Was He a selfish avaritious designing deceitfull Villan I should think he had encroached upon the old Gentlemans perogatives but as he is neither, what can raise his malice against an honest republican? Tis fear, fear, that fear which made the first grand deciver start up in his own shape when touchd by Ithuriel['s] Spear. The honest Zeal of a Man who has no Sinnester views to serve, no Friends to advance to places of profit and Emolument, no ambition to make a fortune with the Spoil of his country, or to eat the Bread of Idleness and dis-sapation—this this man must be crushed, he must be calumniated and abused. It needs great courage Sir to engage in the cause of America, we have not only an open but secret foes to contend with. It comes not unexpected upon me I assure you, he who had unjustly traduced the character of one Man, would not hesitate to attack every one who should obstruct his views and no Man however honest his views and intentions will be safe whilst this Gentleman holds his office. I hope you will be very particular not only in transmitting the accusation but what Effect it has had in your Body, what measures have been taken in consequence, and whether you have acquainted my Friend with it. If not I beg it may be done that he may take proper measures in his defence.—We receive no inteligence from Holland. Mr. D[ana] was in France from November to March when he went to Amsterdam to Mr. A. who was there in March and at the Hague as I learn by a Letter from Young W—n[6] dated 10 of March at Brussels. I suspect Mr. A. is apprehensive of trusting Letters or dispatches by way of France or he would certainly have written by vessels which have come from thence.—You will smile when you see by my last Letter, how much I misunderstood your hints. I believe you did it on purpose. I supposed by what you wrote that some slanderous tongue wished to wound me by reports injurious to the character of my best Friend. He is a good Man, would to Heaven we had none but such in office. You know my Friend that he is a man of principal, and that he will not voilate the dictates of his conscience to Ingratiate himself with a minister, or with your more respected Body.

Yet it wounds me Sir—when he is wounded I bleed. I give up my domestick pleasure and resign the prospect I once had of an independant fortune, and such he could have made in the way of his Buisness. Nor should I grudge the sacrifice, only let not the slanderous arrow, the calumniating stabs of Malice rend in peices an honest character which is all his Ambition.

> Who steals my purse steals trash
> twas mine, tis his and has been slave to thousands
> but he who filches from me my good Name
> takes that which not enriches him
> and makes me poor indeed.

Inclosed is a Letter for Mrs. S[hippe]n. You will be so good as to deliver it and transmit a reply should she ask you. I have invited your good Lady to make me a visit, offerd to send a chaise and Brother C[ranc]h would Gallant her, but she pleads indisposition—the very reason why she ought to come. Do Sir use your influence and request her to visit me. Tell her you know I shall love her as much as I respect her now and that not only for her own sake but for a certain connection that she has who tho some times very sausy yet taking his correction patiently is the more Esteemed by   Portia

Dft (Adams Papers); without date or indication of addressee; at head of text in CFA's hand: "1782." Enclosure in (missing) RC: AA to Alice (Lee) Shippen, 30 June, of which Dft is printed following the present letter.

[1] Date supplied from Lovell's acknowledgments of 17 July and 10 Aug., both below.

[2] Alice (Lee) Shippen to Elizabeth (Welles) Adams, 17 June, q.v. above, with notes there.

[3] Opening quotation mark editorially supplied. "[T]his same Gentleman" is Benjamin Franklin, and the "mere white curd of asses milk" his grandson William Temple Franklin. The blank in this sentence should be filled in with "Adams" (meaning JA). "Mr. S—" is AA's miswriting of "Mr. L—" (Arthur Lee).

[4] AA's question derives from Mrs. Shippen's reference to "the French Minister" as Franklin's accomplice. This left AA puzzled whether the French foreign minister, "Gravier" (i.e. Vergennes), or the French minister to the United States, La Luzerne, was meant. The matter is clarified in Lovell to AA, 13 July, below, and in note 7 there.

[5] Doubtless "husband" is meant.

[6] Winslow Warren; see AA to JA, 28 May, above.

Abigail Adams to Alice Lee Shippen

My dear Madam   Braintree june 30 [*1781*]

Your favour of june 17 was put into my Hands last Evening, and tho not realy intended for me, I cannot but consider it as a fortunate mistake on two accounts not only as it explained to me the machinations of a Man, Grown old in the practise of deception and calumny, but as it give me an opportunity of an epistolary acquaintance with a Lady, whom a dear absent Friend long ago taught me to respect;— my Friend Mr. Lovell had before given me some hints respecting an affair which you speak of more explicitly, but the late captures of the post have taught him caution, and he waited for a private hand to convey to me in full the particulars to which you refer. You Madam who have Sufferd yourself from the unjust aspercions cast upon a much injured Brother can judge of my feelings upon this occasion and they I trust will plead my excuse with you for replying to a Letter which was meant for a Lady of the same name but by mistake was given to me. I shall however forward it with a proper excuse to her.[1] As I am wholy Ignorant of the Nature of the charges which this finished character has exhibited to Congress against my absent Friend, I can only say that those who have no private Interest to serve, no Friends to advance, no Grandson to plenipotentiarise, no Views incompatable with the welfare of their country, will judge I hope more favourably of a Gentleman whose Heart and Mind are truly republican, and who has through a course of years to the great loss of his private Interest sacrificed that and his domestick happiness of which he was not a little fond, to the repeated calls of his country which he ever obeyed, tho I challange his greatest Enemy to Say that he ever sought or in the remotest degree solicited the employments with which he has been honourd. If upright and good intentions with a fair full and diligent discharge of the duties of his office will merit the approbation of his employers I dare say my absent Friend will be able to justify his conduct and to exculpate himself from the Slander of his accuser whose sly secret Malice is of a more dangerous kind than the open attacks of an avowed Enemy. It is some consolation however to have an associate even in misfortune, and my Friends character is not the first which has been immolated by this unprincipeld Gentleman to the Alters of envy, Calumny and disapointed ambition. It has been the Misfortune of America in the unhappy tradigy in which She [has] been engaged, that some of her principle characters have discraged[2] the Scenes. Her Frankling, Dean, and

Arnold may be ranked with her Hutchinson and Galloway. If the Aspercions you mention are such as to obtain the Notice of congress, I hope they will do my Friend the justice to acquaint him with them before they give credit to a Gentleman whom they have long had reason to execrate and who if continued in office will still embarrass their affairs and discourage the faithfullest servants of the publick from engageing in its service.

I mourn my dear Madam with the Cittizens of Virginia their depopulated Towns and dessolated habitations. May it not be the intention of providence that each one of the united states should itself suffer the cruel ravages of the Merciless foe, that they may thus be taught to sympathize with each other, and prize the dear bought blessing earned with the blood of some of their best citizens who with less danger and hazard might not realize the intrinsick value of their Independance. Is the Brother for whom you are Distressd Mr. Richard Henry Lee?[3] I have often heard my Friend express a great regard for him as a Gentleman firm in the Cause of America and an able defender of her Rights.

You will be so good Madam as to present my respectfull Regards to Dr. Lee who did me the Honour of a visit and with whom I have some little acquaintance and pardon the freedom I have taken in replying to a favour designd for an other, but which will not deprive you of a return from her. Permit me Madam the Honour of subscribeing myself with Sentiments of Esteem your Humble Servant,

A Adams

Dft (Adams Papers); at foot of text in AA's hand: "To Mrs S Shippen"; at head of text in CFA's hand: "1782." The (missing) RC was enclosed in the (missing) RC of AA's letter to James Lovell of the present date, of which the Dft is printed above.

[1] Doubtless AA forwarded to Mrs. Samuel Adams the missent original of Mrs. Shippen's letter of 17 June, q.v. above, but neither the original of that letter nor AA's covering note has been found.
[2] Thus in MS, for "disgraced."
[3] AA's conjecture was correct. Richard Henry Lee was serving in the Virginia House of Delegates.

Hugh Hughes to Abigail Adams

Madam   Fishkill, July 1st 1781

I am honoured with your very polite Favour of the 10th of June,[1] which arrived in my Absence.—No Expense has accrued but what you are justly entitled to as the Consort of a Gentlem[an] of distinguished Rank and Merit, in publick Life.

When the other Boxes arrive, they will claim my Attention, as well as any other Commands you may please to favour me with.

As I have the Honour of being known to your Mr. Adams, I beg you would, whenever Opportunity presents, offer my most respectful Regards to him, Madam.

With the greatest Respect, I am, Madam, your most Obedient and very Humble Serv.,   Hugh Hughes

RC (Adams Papers).

[1] Not found; it was in reply to Hughes' letter to AA of 21 May, q.v. above, with note there.

James Lovell to Abigail Adams

Ma'am   July 2d 1781

The Gentleman by whom I meant to send the inclosed was obliged unexpectedly to return to Baltimore. I do not find, upon breaking the Seal that it can give Mr. Rivington much Amusement.

I am sorry to find by this day's Receipt of yours of June 10th.[1] that you had not more Satisfaction from the Arrival of the Alliance.

You will know, by what Genl. Ward had to convey to you,[2] that an Expression in the within Letter was not calculated for you *after* you should have seen what I now[3] observe you have, for *there* was harm in reality, but more grounded in Folly than Viciousness.

Our News from the southward is of the very best but not yet the most authentic.

I will be industrious to forward your Cases. I am much relieved by hearing the Things sent were not wet.

Your humbl*ed* Servt.,   J L.

RC (Adams Papers). Enclosure not identified, but see note 3.

[1] Not found.
[2] Lovell to AA, 16 June, above.
[3] In the MS at this point appears a double-dagger sign and in the margin appears another, accompanied by the figure 5, or possibly the letter S, in parentheses. Since these marks link in some manner the enclosure in the present letter and AA's letter of 10 June, the first of which is unidentified and the second of which is missing, the editors can offer no explanation of their significance. The matter is touched on again in Lovell's letter to AA of 13 July, below, q.v. at note 3.

John Adams to Abigail Adams

My dear Portia   Paris July 11. 1781

I am called to this Place, in the Course of my Duty: but dont conceive from it any hopes of Peace. This desireable object is yet unhappily at a Distance, a long distance I fear.[1]

My dear Charles will go home with Maj. Jackson. Put him to school and keep him steady.—He is a delightfull Child, but has too exquisite sensibility for Europe.[2]

John is gone, a long Journey with Mr. Dana:—he will serve as an Interpreter, ⟨if not a Clerk,⟩ and the Expence will be little more than at Leyden.[3] He will be satiated with travel in his Childhood, and care nothing about it, I hope in his riper Years.

I am distracted with more cares than ever, yet I grow fat. Anxiety is good for my Health I believe.

Oh that I had Wings, that I might fly and bury all my Cares at the Foot of Pens Hill.

RC (Adams Papers).

[1] As the sole American representative in Europe empowered to discuss terms of peace with Great Britain, JA had been summoned to Paris by Vergennes to consult on proposals for a joint Russian and Austrian mediation between the warring powers. He set off from Amsterdam on 2 July and arrived in Paris on the 6th, where he put up at his former residence, the Hôtel de Valois in the Rue de Richelieu; see his account of travel expenses in *Diary and Autobiography*, 2:456–457. Not without justification, JA deeply distrusted the motives not only of the imperial mediators but of Vergennes toward the United States, and for this and other reasons the proposed mediation came to nothing; see same, 2:458, with references there; also the very full treatment of the mediation, its background, and its collapse, in Morris, *Peacemakers*, chs. 8–10.

[2] CA's recent illness is alluded to in John Thaxter to JA, 5 April, above, and in following letters. In his "second autobiography" JA said in explanation of his sending CA home at this time: "My second son, after the departure of his brother, found himself so much alone, that he grew uneasy, and importuned me so tenderly to let him return to America to his mother, that I consented to that, and thus deprived myself of the greatest pleasure I had in life, the society of my children." JA continued: "On or about the 10th [actually, after various and devious maneuvers by the captain, on the 12th] of August, 1781, the South Carolina, commodore Gillon, put to sea from the Texel, with Mr.

Searle, Colonel Trumbull, Major Jackson, Mr. Bromfield, Dr. Waterhouse and Charles Adams on board as passengers." (JA, *Corr. in the Boston Patriot*, p. 572.)

The choice of a ship and commander for CA's conveyance home proved unlucky. After leaving the *South Carolina* in La Coruña in Spain in September, CA sailed home from Bilbao in a different vessel, the *Cicero*, Captain Hugh Hill, which at length reached its home port of Beverly, Mass., on 21 Jan. 1782. CA arrived in Braintree on the 29th. Not until June 1782 did AA receive any of the mail put aboard the *South Carolina* for her ten months earlier. See note on Alexander Gillon under Waterhouse to JA, 26 Dec. 1780, above, with references there; and below, letters to JA and to AA from Gillon, Waterhouse, William Jackson, Richard Cranch, Isaac Smith Sr., and Hugh Hill. AA's final word on the whole subject is in her letter to JA, 17 June 1782, also below.

Major William Jackson (1759–1828), under whose particular care JA had placed CA during the voyage, was a Charlestonian who had served under Maj. Gen. Benjamin Lincoln in the latter's southern campaign and had come to Europe with John Laurens' mission to obtain further aid for the American military effort. JA had recently told Pres. Huntington that "Major Jackson has conducted through the whole of his Residence here [in Amsterdam], as far as I have been able to observe, with great Activity and Accuracy in Business, and an exemplary Zeal for the public Service" (27 June 1781, PCC, No. 84,

III; Wharton, ed., *Dipl. Corr. Amer. Rev.,*
4:522). Some of the military goods,
obtained in the Netherlands, were on
board the *South Carolina* when it sailed
surreptitiously from the Texel in August.
The erratic conduct of Gillon led to an
early and bitter quarrel between him
and Jackson; they parted in Spain and
afterward fought a duel in America, in
which Jackson was wounded; see Jackson's correspondence with JA, Aug.–Dec.
1781, and AA to John Thaxter, 18 July
1782, below. Jackson, who became secretary to Washington when President
and afterward surveyor of customs in
Philadelphia, is best remembered as
secretary of the Federal Convention of
1787 (*DAB*; JQA, *Memoirs*, 4:174–
175).

³ This first allusion by JA to JQA's
departure for St. Petersburg was written
on JQA's fourteenth birthday. JQA had
left Amsterdam on 7 July to join Francis
Dana in Utrecht, after JA had already
left for Paris; see JQA, *Diary*, 7 July
et seq., for the overland route that he
and Dana followed through Germany
and Poland to Riga, Narva, and St.
Petersburg, where they arrived on 27
August.

On Dana's mission as the first American minister appointed to Russia but
never accredited by that court, see above,
Lovell to AA, 8 Jan., note 5, and references there. JA's recollections in old
age, not always reliable in details but
in this case correct in general substance,
throw light on the motives of those involved in this unusual and unexpected
incident:

"Congress had ordered [Francis Dana]
to go to St. Petersburg, and had sent him
a commission as their minister, with instructions to conclude a treaty of friendship and commerce with the empress of
Russia; but they had given him no secretary of legation, nor made any provision for a private secretary, or even a
copying clerk. They had, moreover . . .
reduced Mr. Dana's compensation below
that of the other ministers. Mr. Dana
had taken pains to persuade some gentlemen to accompany him, but could find
none that would consent to go. He had
before him the dreary prospect of an
immense journey by land, through Holland, Germany, Denmark, and he knew

not how many other nations, of whose
languages he knew not one word; and in
the French, which was the travelling
language of Europe, he was yet but a
student. In this situation, he requested
me to let him have my oldest son, John
Quincy Adams, for a companion and a
private secretary or clerk. The youth was,
in conversation, a ready interpreter of
French for an American, and of English
for a Frenchman; he could easily translate in writing, as Mr. Dana had seen,
any state paper. He wrote a fair hand,
and could copy letters, or any other papers, as well as any other man; and he
had the necessary patience of application
to any of these services. I was at first very
averse to the proposition, but from regard
to Mr. Dana, at last consented. I would
not however, burthen Mr. Dana with his
expenses, but advanced him money for
that purpose, and desired Mr. Dana to
draw upon me for more when that should
be expended, which he did. He returned
from Russia before Mr. Dana was recalled, and in this interval, Mr. Dana
must have been put to other expenses
for clerkship. Mr. Dana agreed with me
in opinion that congress would finally
make him a grant for a private secretary
at least, and in that case he was to pay
me the money I had advanced, or should
advance for expenses, and nothing more.
All this I presume was known to congress, when they made the grant to Mr.
Dana, not for the form but for the substance, for it was Mr. Dana's right. When
Mr. Dana received the grant from Congress, he returned me the sums I had
advanced for expenses and no more.
Neither the father nor the son ever received any thing for services." (JA, *Corr.
in the Boston Patriot*, p. 570–571.)

In Dana's Account with the United
States, rendered 30 Aug. 1785, the sum
requested for "Mr. John Quincy Adams's
Expences in his Journey with Mr. Dana
to Petersburgh during his Residence there
as Mr. Dana's Private Secretary and his
return to the Hague" is given as £357
16s 9d (DNA:RG 39, Foreign Ledgers,
Public Agents in Europe, 1776–1787,
p. 364). The sum finally allowed when
Dana's accounts were settled in 1787
was $2,410 3/19 (PCC, No. 122, Book
of Resolves of the Office of Foreign Affairs, 1785–1789, p. 101).

James Lovell to Abigail Adams

Ma'am   July 13. 1781

I have already acknowledged the Receipt of your Favour of June
10th.[1] Severely as it concluded in Regard to my Reputation I did not
arraign its Justice, but wrote an ingenuous Confession, similar to one
I had before made by the Opportunity of Genl. Ward.[2] I thought your
Conclusion was founded upon a natural Construction of what you
had been reading.[3] I venerated the Purity of your Sentiments. I was
persuaded that no *unkind Suspicions* guided your Pen. But your
Letter of the 23d. of that month wears a different Complexion from
the former. My Fall, Ma'am was not from a Horse, but still it was an
"honest" one. I had been engaged in the most benevolent Way, at
my Pen for hours that Evening, witness, among others my Letter to
Mr. Thos. Russel and Mr. Nathl. Barber April 24th. I was forced
out, in the Rain, to procure Money for a Person who wanted it much
against the Dawn of next Morning. I found when abroad that I had
misguided a Stranger as to the Lodging of the Gentleman from whom
I was to receive the Money. I meant to rectify that Error by taking
the Stranger with me. I suddenly crossed the Street where I was, at
right Angle; and looking up under my flopped Hatt saw a Vacancy
immediately before me, which I took to be an Alley I had often gone
through; but I found that a Shop had been drawn away and a Cellar
10 feet deep had been dug to receive me. The Consequences were
nearly mortal. I had delivered my Letters at the Office. The giving of
early Intelligence to Mr. R of the miserable State of his captive Unkle
was *honest* Employment. The Endeavour to prevent an *abrupt* Notice
to Mr. B of the death of an amiable Son was equally *honest*. The
Seeking of money for one of my *Creditors* who was then in *want* of
Cash, and the putting of a Stranger into the *right* Way were both of
them honest Works. But, as the Honesty of my Pursuits was no
Security against a Fall, neither has it been a Preventive against false
Constructions of that Destiny. Michael Morgan Obrian, most *natu-*
rally indeed, concluded that I had staggered sideways drunken into
the Dock. Some, *as naturally*, and One *against* Nature have supposed
I fell *dis*honestly down a *Pair* of *dark Stairs*. I have Hopes of being
intirely free from Lameness in the Course of the Summer; and I am
sure that Portia will rejoice at such an Event as my *walking rightly*
for the Rest of my Life.

Give my Compliments to your *amorous* Friend Cornelia. I hope
her Husband never leaves her for a Night. I presume she holds the

general opinion that *Friendship* may be even encreased by Seperation of the Parties; tho, differently from some of Us, she thinks bodily Presence essential to *Love*. She may be assured that there is that mixture of Friendship and Love in the Affection which unites Mrs. L and Me that Presence does not burn up the former, nor Absence congeal the Latter.

I send you an Extract that will prove the confidential Sincerity of my former Letters to you. I would not wish that any other should see it. The Friends she alludes to are perhaps now my Enemies. I *sacrifice* to my Value for *your* Good Opinion.[4]

Yes, I am "Portia's affectionate Friend," and I did *not* "mean to retaliate for the Pain she had given me." I *"could"* not, I *"would"* not. Led astray by Cornelia's Fancy, your Mind had taken a *"dark"* Turn, and you found dreadful Things in an innocent Phraise *"on this subject."* Why, Ma'am, in my Thoughts the Subject simply was ABSENCE; and compoundly long Absence, but in yours it was a BREACH OF THE COMMANDMENTS and WHAT NOT.[5]

I have no Copy of any Letter to you but I imagine I was not very unconnected or enigmatical. If you had ventured to converse with Mr. S[amuel] A[dams] you would have found that your *All* is not servile enough to gain the unbounded Affection of the foreign Court at which he resided when he had the Correspondence which produced the two Resolves of Congress already communicated to you.[6] You would have found that ||Gravier|| wrote two Letters in a Pet against Mr. A to ||old Fkln|| and that the latter had also written a most unkind and stabbing one hither; which he was under no necessity of doing, as he needed only to have transmitted the Papers given to him, for the Purpose, by the former. This Knowledge would have prepared you for my last Letter in Cyphers; and for the Information that Mr. A has now ||no *distinct* powers.||[7] I shall write minutely in Cyphers *"on this Subject"* to S.A. and you *must* have it at 2d. hand.[8] I will only say for your Satisfaction that I cannot accuse any one or more of any want of Esteem for Mr. A, but I see him indelicately handled by Means of wrong measures on a general Scale.

That I may be more at Leisure to be attentive *only* to senatorial Subjects, I will now close the former by telling you that Mrs. L added in her Letter "I think, however, you will be obliged to come and *show yourself* this Fall."—This you will find is enough, tho it is not founded in her Wishes but in her Fears. The enevitable ill Consequences which I have proved to you, and the almost enevitable ones which I was afraid to name to you or to your Husband, who glories in what I should be sorry for, will not deter me from obeying this *Half-*Call, which is what I have never had before since I quitted Home.—I add also—That *the* Expression, which I wish had never seen Light, was in Fact the Fruit of a Desire to pass a Compliment upon the Figure and Portrait which Mr. G[erry] had drawn in his Letter, it was indiscretely worded and was very liable to the worst Interpretation by any one whose Mind was in the least Measure predisposed to make it.—What is the most decent *Day Labour* you can think of for me while I am there? [9]

I do not find Opportunity to send your Boxes. I wish you would keep a good Account of what I sent: for really I cannot tell. I think I wrote you exactly at the Time of sending. Mr. Moylan perhaps will give an Invoice some Time or other. J. P. Jones is on the Road and will see you.

RC (Adams Papers); contains ciphered passages which are here deciphered between double verticals. (On Lovell's cipher, see Appendix to this volume.) Enclosure: extract from a letter of Mrs. Lovell to James Lovell, not found. MS of the present letter consists of two small sheets each folded into four pages. At some point in the past, before CFA had the letters received by AA in the 1780's bound up, the second sheet was by mistake attached to Lovell's letter to her of 15 Sept. (below), the MS of which has a similar physical appearance; and in the Adams Papers Microfilms it will be found there instead of in its proper place as the second sheet of the present letter. Because of this mistake a key paragraph, beginning "I have no Copy of any Letter to you," was printed by Burnett in *Letters of Members*, 6:219, under the later and wrong date.

[1] Not found. Lovell had acknowledged its receipt in his reply of 2 July, above.

[2] Lovell to AA, 16 June, above.

[3] In the MS at this point appears the figure 5, or possibly a capital S, in parentheses. This parallels the use of the same symbol in a cryptic passage in Lovell's letter to AA of 2 July, above, q.v. at note 3.

[4] Thus apparently in MS, although because of ink marks that may be blots it is not clear whether a full stop, a colon, or no punctuation at all was intended by Lovell after the word "Enemies." Here the first sheet of Lovell's MS ends; see descriptive note.

[5] In the foregoing paragraph Lovell is echoing and answering AA's letter to him of 23 June, above, particularly its animadversions on his letter to her of 29 May, also above.

[6] Sent in Lovell to AA, 26 June, q.v. above.

[7] Lovell here returns to, and under the protection of ciphered phrases is a little more explicit about, what was currently happening to French-American relations in Paris and Philadelphia. The immediate background is given in his letter to AA, 26 June, above; see especially note 4 there on Congress' alteration of JA's peace instructions and its joining him with other commissioners in the peace negotiation. The incidents which led up to these actions, and which Lovell refers to here, nearly a whole year later, are set forth above in note 5 on Thaxter to JA, 7 Aug. 1780 (vol. 3:390–395).

"Gravier" is the family name of the French foreign minister, the Comte de Vergennes. His "two Letters [written] in a Pet against [JA] to old F[ran]kl[i]n" are (1) that dated 30 June 1780, disagreeing with JA's support of Congress' new monetary policy and requesting Congress' reconsideration of that policy (Wharton, ed., *Dipl. Corr. Amer. Rev.*, 3:827); and (2) that dated 31 July 1780, enclosing the mass of his recent correspondence with JA on other topics in dispute between them, and demanding that the whole of it be submitted to Congress for appropriate action, by which Vergennes certainly meant a reprimand (same, 4: 18–19; text of French original quoted at vol. 3:392, above). Franklin's "unkind and stabbing" letter transmitting the documents to Congress is dated 9 Aug. 1780 and is the fullest comment Franklin ever permitted himself to make on JA's conduct as a diplomat, contrasting it with his own more accommodating approach to the French court and condemning the whole concept of what has come to be known as "militia diplomacy." The original is in PCC, No. 82, I; it is printed in Franklin's *Writings*, ed. Smyth, 8:124–130 (see esp. p. 126–128); a normalized text is in Wharton, ed., *Dipl. Corr. Amer. Rev.*, 4:21–25 (see esp. p. 22–23). Relevant portions are quoted in vol. 3:394, above, but to understand the deepening embitterment between the partisans of JA and of Franklin on both sides of the Atlantic, the whole passage dealing with JA should be read and pondered.

Just how Franklin's remarks got into circulation at this time in Boston and vicinity is not known, but letters that follow in the present volume make clear that they indeed did and that they stirred up strong feelings there. See AA to Lovell, 14 July; Richard Cranch to JA, 16 July; AA to Elbridge Gerry, 20 July; Gerry to AA, 30 July; all below.

Congress had considered the JA-Vergennes exchanges on 26 Dec. 1780, together with numerous dispatches from JA dating between the previous July and October (JCC, 18:1194). Not a word was recorded at this time concerning Franklin's dispatch of 9 Aug., which according to the *Journals* was not read in Congress until 19 Feb. 1781, together with other Franklin letters and enclosures (same, 19:174). While a good deal of discussion "out-of-doors" must have followed from the revelation of the disputes between JA and Vergennes, Congress officially noticed only three of the letters read in December, namely JA to Vergennes, 17 and 26 July, and

Vergennes to JA, 25 July, in which JA had asked leave to communicate to the British ministry his powers to negotiate a commercial treaty, and Vergennes had refused to give such leave (texts in Wharton, ed., *Dipl. Corr. Amer. Rev.*, 3:861–863; 4:3–6, 7–11). A committee consisting of Thomas Burke, John Witherspoon, and James Duane was appointed to report on these letters (JCC, 18:1194), and on 10 Jan. it brought in a draft of a letter which was agreed to and sent over Pres. Huntington's signature to JA on that day (same, 19:41–42). Although the letter recognized the "zeal and assiduity" displayed by JA in his request of Vergennes, it amounted to a rebuke because it approved Vergennes' reasons for refusing the request (Adams Papers; printed in JA, *Works*, 7:353; JCC, 19:42).

During the following months La Luzerne, under guidance from Vergennes that was hardly needed, conducted his campaign among friendly delegates in Congress that culminated in the measures taken by that body in June to curb JA's freedom of action. A further measure to the same effect was taken the day before Lovell dated the present letter. This was the outright revocation of JA's commission and instructions to negotiate a treaty of commerce with Great Britain, issued to him in Sept.–Oct. 1779 simultaneously with his peace commission (see *Diary and Autobiography*, 4:179–180, 183–184; see also vol. 3:230–233, above). The immediate initiative for this had come from the committee of conference with La Luzerne in May, and an attempt was made on 19 June to transfer these powers from JA to the five newly named peace commissioners (of whom JA was one), but this failed at the moment (JCC, 20:619, 676). After further maneuvers which cannot be traced here, James Madison moved on 12 July that JA's commercial powers be revoked and that, among other things, the peace commissioners be instructed to place the territorial claims of the United States all the way to the Mississippi on an equal footing with its claims to the Atlantic fisheries—neither of these claims being any longer ultimatums because of the alterations in the instructions for peace and the contemplated revocation of JA's commission to negotiate a treaty of commerce. This motion passed by a large majority, only the New England delegates dissenting (same, 713–714, 746–747; Madison, *Papers*, ed. Hutchinson, 3:188–189). Madison's multiple and complex motives have been discussed by Brant in his *Madison*, 2:143–145, from Madison's point of view. Justly or not, Madison had by this time come to distrust JA's egotism and impulsiveness, his New Englandism, and his suspected partiality for British as opposed to French interests. Subsequent events deepened Madison's prejudices toward JA, as will later appear.

JA's view of these transactions was that they constituted the most humiliating stroke ever dealt him in the house of his supposed friends. See his confidential conversation in Jan. 1783 with Benjamin Vaughan as recorded in *Diary and Autobiography*, 3:103–105; also his letter to Secretary R. R. Livingston, 5 Feb. 1783, in which he endeavored to reconstruct Congress' motives, as shaped by French intrigue, and to show how mistaken they were (LbC, Adams Papers; JA, *Works*, 8:33–40).

⁸ No letter from Lovell to Samuel Adams on this subject at this time has been found. In forwarding to JA the resolution of 12 July, Lovell was laconic in his official note for the Committee of Foreign Affairs, but he added a "private" postscript, partly in cipher, that was more revealing:

"The whole of the Proceedings here in regard to your two Commissions are, I think, ‖ill-judged but‖ I persuade myself no ‖dishonou[r] int‖ended[. T]he business greatly in every View ‖chagrins me.‖ [T]his you will have learnt from my former Letters written in an half-light" (21 July, Adams Papers; JA, *Works*, 7:453; Burnett, ed., *Letters of Members*, 6:151).

⁹ The allusions in this paragraph can be only partially clarified. The "ill Consequences" of Lovell's now seriously contemplated return home would be poverty, which JA might glory in but Lovell would not. It would appear from this and similar remarks elsewhere in Lovell's correspondence that he feared outright impoverishment if he gave up his seat in Congress. (See especially Lovell to Gerry, 13 July and 14 Sept., MHi:Gerry-Knight Coll.; and Lovell to AA, 10 Aug., below.) The letter from Gerry to Lovell here mentioned must have been one of the several acknowledged in Lovell's by now notorious intercepted reply of 20 Nov. 1780 (see AA to Lovell, 17 March, above, and notes and references there).

Abigail Adams to James Lovell

My dear Sir   July [14]th 1781¹

Your favour by General Ward² was not deliverd me till this day or I should have replied to it by the last post; the Generous acknowledgement of having tran[s]gressed forbids any further recrimination even tho I had more than the Right of a Friend. The serious part of your Letter drew a tear from the Eye of Portia. She wished for ability she wished for power to make happy the Man who so richly deserved far better treatment than he had ever yet met with. The pittance you mention, is meaner than my Immagination could possibly form tho I have had sufficient Specimins of it here to fore but it must and shall be enlarged if the Friends to whom Portia is determined to apply have any influence in a Body who too often strain at a knat while they gulph down a camel with great facility.

I am gratified however to have from your own Hand arguments

to rectify the Ideas of some who I really believe your Friends, but who not knowing or fully attending to the circumstances you mention, have been left to wonder at a conduct they could not account for. The affectionate regard you profess for a Lady who I believe every way deserving of it, intirely banishes from my mind the insinuations of Cornelia, and I could wish that Letter might not be submitted as you tell me others have been,[3] least it should unnecessaryly give pain to a Lady I must more and more Esteem—and with whom I am determined to cultivate a more particular acquaintance. Possibly I may be able to render her some small services. I cannot be so particular as I wish because this must take its chance by the post. I will not thank you for your comments upon my Letter of March 17th. They are not generous. However as I have never spaired my correspondent when I thought him wrong, I will suppose that he really believed Portia deserving the censure he has bestowed.—"Dutch Idea" abominable. You know I meant by the Word property, only an exclusive right, a possession held in ones own right.[4] Will you please to consult Johnson upon the term?—Still more Sophistical is your comment upon the fine tuned Instrument. If I did not know you I should suppose you a practiseing Attorney. There is one thing however that sticks a little hardly by me—"I am very unwilling that it should be submitted to the Eye of one so *very much* my Friend as *you profess yourself to be.*" This looks like such a distrust of my sincerity as wounds me. There are some other strokes to which I am not callous, but can forgive them considering the freedom I have exercised in my own remarks.

Will you balance accounts? and we will begin a New Score upon the old Stock of Friendship. I do not pretend to exculpate from censure what I really thought deserving of it, but only the doubtfull right I had to use it as it did not at that time particularly affect me.

You have not fulfilled one part of your promise which was to transmit to me some Annecdotes respecting my Friend abroad and as a preparitive I was to see Mr. ———.[5] I have [now?][6] *received my preparitive.* In the Name of Indignation can there be any thing more diabolical than what is put into my Hands? False insinuating disembling wretch —is it for this your Grey Head is spaired—is this the language of courts?—is this the reward of an Independant Spirit, and patriotick virtue? Shall the Zealous and Strenuous asserter of his countrys rights be sacrificed to a court Sycophant? This finished Courtier has first practised his Arts upon the M[iniste]r till he has instilled into his mind the most ungenerous prejudices, played over the same Game he practised against Dr. L[ee] by reporting Speaches I dare say that were never made, or taking them seperately from what might be connected with them and therby rendering offensive what in an other view might be quite harmless—and having gained his point there, is now in the most specious manner crocodile like whining over the prey he means to devour, to your Body who if they mean peace and good will to their country will immediately accept a resignation which it is said he has tendered but for Heavens sake do not join him in commission with my Friend, they cannot act in concert, after such a proof of jealousy, envy and malice can you suppose it?[7]

Join to him an upright honest Man of real abilities and he will thank you for an assistant should a negotiation commence, but do not *Saddle* him with a Man who looks no further than the present state of existance for a retribution of his virtues or his vices, but who considering this world as the summum bonum of Man might I think have a little more regard to the happiness of his fellow Mortals in the present state, and not quite so willing to relinquish their Natural Rights. One will speak a bold and firm language becomeing a free sovereign and Independant Nation, the other will be indesisive yealding fauning flattering. Are these consistant qualities? Very justly does he observe that they do not always hold the same language and the one may erase the impressions of the other.—If after all the Efforts of the Friends of Liberty C[ongre]ss should join them you may be assured my Friend will resign his commission. I shall intreat him to, but he will not want persuasion. He shall not share if I can prevent it in the disgrace which will most assuredly fall upon these States. Humiliating thought, that so much Blood and treasure should be sacrificed to state intrigues and our negotiation disgraced by a Man—but I will believe a more virtuous Majority exists among you. I ask not the support of my Friend because he is my Friend—I ask it no further than as you find he persues the best Good of his country, than as you find he acts a disinterested part ⟨*considering himself only as one individual of the many he represents*⟩.

Dft (Adams Papers); without indication of addressee; text probably incomplete, breaking off above the middle of last page of MS and without leavetaking.

[1] Day of the month, left blank by AA, supplied from Lovell's acknowledgment of receipt of this letter in his reply of 10 Aug., below.

[2] Dated 16 June, above.

[3] The "Lady" is Mrs. Lovell, and "that Letter" (which AA did not wish to have "submitted" to Mrs. Lovell) is AA's to Lovell, 23 June, above.

[4] On the "Dutch Idea" see Lovell to AA, 16 June, above, at note 10.

[5] Samuel Adams; see Lovell to AA, 29 May, above.

[6] AA wrote "&."

[7] Sentence thus punctuated in MS. The allusions in this paragraph will not

be clear unless read in the light of a number of letters that precede. The "False ... wretch" is Franklin, and what had been put into AA's hands—her "preparitive"—was a text of Franklin's letter to Congress of 9 Aug. 1780, which took the French side in the dispute between JA and Vergennes and which Lovell characterized as "most unkind and stabbing" toward JA (Lovell to AA, preceding; see note 7 there; and see also vol. 3:394–395, above).

AA's term "the M[iniste]r" (on whom Franklin had "practised his Arts") echoes phrasing used in Mrs. Shippen's letter to Mrs. Samuel Adams, 17 June, above, and means Vergennes. See notes on AA to Lovell, 30 June, and Lovell to AA, 13 July, both above.

Richard Cranch to John Adams

Dear Sir   Boston July 16th 1781

I have enclosed to you a Copy of certain Letters lately transmitted to Congress by B:F: Esqr.—Copies of them having been sent from ⟨Congress⟩ Philadelphia to your Friends here, I tho't it my Duty to let you know as soon as possible what treatment you receive from that Gentleman. I have heard (sub rosae) that influence has been used in a certain ⟨Place⟩ august Assembly to have the ⟨*Regulator of Heaven's Artillery*⟩ Conductor of Lightning joined with you in ⟨*a certain Negotiation*⟩ bearing the Olive Branch. This Time may discover. I know not whether you have ever seen an Order of Congress of Decr. 12th. 1780. I have enclos'd a Copy of it as sent to your Dear Lady. I suppose it referrs to the same Subject when transmitted by you to Congress, which is now said to have given such offence elsewhere.[1]

I have wrote you often, particularly by Doctor Dexter on the 28th of May, and again largly by a Vessell bound to Denmark on the 22d of June: And tho' I have never yet had the happyness of receiving a Line from you since you left us, yet I shall embrace every Oportunity, of writing to you, believing that you have written to me tho' I have been so unhappy as not to have received your Letters.

The General Court is now prorogued untill the 3d Wednesday in September sufficient Provision having been first made for filling up what is yet wanting in our Quota of the Continental Army; and also for sending into the Field immediately 3,200 Melitia from this Commonwealth to assist in the present Campaign on the North River &c. As I wrote you before, so I must still lament the want of a sufficient number of Ships of War on this Coast. For want of a very few More Ships those that are here already can do little or no service, being too weak to venture far out of Port. By this means the Enemys Ships of every sort on the Coast of Virginia and the Carolinas can with safety by water carriage facilitate every movement of their Army without interruption, while our Troops and those of our Generous Allies under that best of Men and of Generals, the Marquis de la Fayett and other excellent Commanders, are subjected to the slow tiresom and expensive Modes of Land Carriage by which all their Plans for our defence are [retarded?] and often rendered abortive. You that are placed nearer the Centre of the grand System can perhaps discover the Wisdom of this Conduct as it regards the whole, while to us who view but detached Parts it appears like a most fatal Failure in the management of the American War.

I saw your dear Lady and Children Yesterday, who with your Mother and Brother &c. are all well. My Dear Partner and Children are in usual Health, and join with me in the tenderest sentiments of Love and Friendship to you, your dear little Boys, and Mr. Thaxter. We have not heard from you for above eight Months (if I recollect right) a tedious Period! especially to those whose "Love is without Dissimulation," among whome I hope you will always find him who in Days of Yore signed himself   Damon

Dft (MHi:Cranch Papers); endorsed by Richard Cranch: "Rough draft of a Letter to Bror. Adams July 16th. 1781 by Capt. Davis bound to Amsterdam (Suppos'd to be taken.)." Written on a folio sheet, on verso of which is a canceled draft in Cranch's hand of a Massachusetts House of Representatives committee report on printing the resolves of the General Court. For the enclosures in the (missing) RC, see note 1.

¹ At least two of Cranch's enclosures, though not found, are clearly identifiable: (1) a copy of Franklin's letter to Pres. Huntington, 9 Aug. 1780, enclosing copies of JA's recent correspondence with Vergennes and commenting unfavorably on JA's high tone toward the French court; see above, Lovell to AA, 13 July, note 7, and vol. 3:394–395; (2) a copy of Congress' resolution of 12 Dec. 1780 approving JA's letter to Vergennes of 26 June 1780, which had defended the new monetary policy of Congress against Vergennes' criticisms; see vol. 3:391–392. JA's letter had been read in Congress on 30 Nov. and referred to a committee of three, Lovell chairman; the committee reported on 6 Dec. but action was postponed; and on the 12th Congress ordered "That the said letter be referred to the Committee of Foreign Affairs, and that they be instructed to inform Mr. Adams of the satisfaction which Congress receives from his industrious attention to the interests and honor of these United States abroad, especially in the transactions communicated to them by that letter" (JCC, 18:1107, 1123, 1147).

John Thaxter to John Adams

Sir   Amsterdam 16th July 1781

I have the honor to inclose You the 23d. No. of the Politique Hollandais.¹

I have this moment heard of your safe arrival, and of your good health and Spirits, which is a vast addition to my happiness. I had a hint of your visit at P[aris], and altho' some Folks are surprized at the peculiar Nature of it, yet I am persuaded that Chaleur and froideur can exist politically, if not naturally, together.

I have the honor to be, with the most respectful Attachment, Sir, your most humble Servant, John Thaxter

RC (Adams Papers). For the (missing) enclosure see note 1.

[1] The weekly journal published by JA's friend A. M. Cerisier at Amsterdam.

James Lovell to Abigail Adams

July 17. 1781

The Dates of my Letters connected with the Time of the Receipt of yours are become somewhat essential towards a right Judgement of my Character, so much called in Question lately by the CENSORIOUS. Though John Paul Jones may not even yet have left the City you will sometime or other find what I wrote to go by a Mr. Anderson and afterward delivered to the said Chevalier Jones. You will also find by Mr. Jeremiah Allen or by a Post my Comments in Season upon your Frightability at the Expression *"on this Subject."* [1] Since that Season I have received your Letter of June 30th brought yesterday by the Post. I translated two letters for Mr. S[amuel] A[dams] and he took a Copy of a 3d which was in english relative to the Subject of your Anxiety.[2] It would be a very laborious Task indeed to copy more than those; which being considered with what I have already sent you will give a full Comprehension of the Scene. You *must* talk with S A who will communicate what he knows.

I delivered yours to Mrs. Sh[ippe]n [3] who is greatly pleased at her own Profit from your mistake.

Every Civility to Mrs. L[ovell] excites my Gratitude doubly to what the same Conduct immediately towards myself effects. There is a peculiarly obliging Tenderness in your Argument for her complying with your Invitation. But I cannot press her to comply; and I cannot be deceitful enough to conceal my selfish Reasons. The dear Woman *now* has the most just Persuasion of the Countinuance of an Affection towards her which constitutes great Part of her Happiness. I should be sorry to have that Persuasion poisoned *accidentally* by any Cornelia. The Suggestions of *"trifling"* People have not injured me. The same from *"one of the best Characters"* might embitter some of my future Days. The Ingenuous will always "take Correction patiently" when *Justice* lays it on. Censoriousness cannot prove itself to be even a distant Branch of the Family of Justice.

With much Esteem Yr. Frd.,   J L

RC (Adams Papers).

¹ See Lovell to AA, 29 May, and AA is now identifiable.
to Lovell, 23 June, both above.   ³ AA to Alice Lee Shippen, 30 June,
² None of the three letters alluded to above.

Abigail Adams to Elbridge Gerry

Sir   Braintree july 20. 1781 ¹

When I looked for your Name among those who form the Representative Body of the people this year I could not find it. I sought for it with the Senate, but was still more dissapointed. I however had the pleasure of finding it amongst the delegates of this Commonwealth to Congress, where I flatter myself you will still do us Honour which posterity will gratefully acknowledge; and the virtuous few now confess. But as you are no worshiper of the rising Sun, or Adulator at the shrine of power, you must expect with others, who possess an Independant Spirit, to be viewed in the shade, to be eyed askance, to be malign'ed and to have your Good evil spoken of. But let not this Sir discourage you in the arduous Buisness. I hope America has not yet arrived at so great a pitch of degeneracy as to be given up by those alone who can save her; I mean the disinterested patriot—who possessing an unconfined Benevolence will persevere in the path of his duty. Tho the Ingratitude of his constituents and the Malevolence of his Enemies should conspire against him, he will feel within himself the best Intimations of his duty, and he will look for no external Motive.

History informs us that the single virtue of Cato, upheld the Roman Empire for a time, and a Righteous few might have saved from the impending Wrath of an offended deity the Ancient cities of Sodom and Gomorah. Why then my dear Sir, may I ask you, do you wish to withdraw yourself from publick Life?

You have supported the cause of America with zeal with ardour and fidelity, but you have not met even with the gratitude of your fellow citizens—in that you do not stand alone.

You have a mind too Liberal to consider yourself only as an Individual, and not to regard both your Country and posterity—and in that view I know you must be anxiously concerned when you consider the undue Influence excercised in her Supreme Counsels. You can be no stranger I dare say Sir, to matters of the Highest importance to the

future welfare of America as a Nation; being now before her Repre-
sentitives—and that she stands in need of the collected wisdom of the
United States, and the Integrity of her most virtuous members.

I will not deny Sir, that personally I feel myself much Interested
in your attendance there. I fear there is a spirit prevailing, too powerfull for those who wish our prosperity; and would seek our best Interests. Mr. L⟨ove⟩ll and Mr. A⟨dam⟩s have informed you I suppose
of the Intrigues and malicious aspersions of my absent Friends character, if they have not, I will forward to you a coppy of a Letter which
will not want any comment of mine.[2]

The plan which appears to be adopted both at Home and abroad,
is a servile adulation and complasance to the Court of our Allies,
even to the giving up some of our most valuable privileges. The Independant Spirit of your Friend, abroad, does not coinside with the
selfish views and inordinate ambition of your Minister, who in consequence of it, is determined upon his distruction. Stung with envy
at a merit he cannot emulate, he is allarmed with the apprehension
of losing the Honour of some Brilliant action; and is useing his endeavours that every enterprize shall miscarry, in which he has not
the command. To Effect this purpose he has insinuated into the minds
of those in power the falsest prejudices against your Friend, and they
have so far influenced the united Counsels of these States, as to induce them to join this unprincipled Man, in Commission with him
for future Negotiations. If Congress had thought proper to have
joined any Gentleman of real abilities and integrity with our Friend,
who could have acted in concert with him; he would have gratefully
received his assistance—but to clog him with a Man, who has shewn
himself so Enimical to him, who has discovered the marks of a little
and narrow Spirit by his malicious aspersions, and ungenerous insinuations, and whose measures for a long time they have had no
reason to be gratified with, is such a proof to me of what my absent
Friend has reason to expect, and what you know Sir, I very early
feared; that I can see nothing but dishonour, and disgrace attending
his most faithfull, and zealous exertions for the welfare of his Country.

These Ideas fill me with the deepest concern. Will you suffer
Female influence so far to operate upon you; as to step forth and lend
your aid to rescue your Country and your Friend, without inquiring

"What can Cato do
Against a World, a base degenerate World
which courts a yoke and bows its Neck to Bondage."

There is a very serious Light in which this matter is to be viewed; the serious light in which a late distinguished Modern writer expresses it—"that we are all embarked on the same Bottom, and if our Country sinks, we must Sink with it."

Your acknowledged Friendship and former politeness has led me to the freedom of this address, and prevents my asking an excuse which I should otherways think necessary for her who has the Honour to subscribe herself your Friend and Humble Servant,   Portia

PS   The communication of the minister at Versails being joined with my Friend was made in confidence—I wish it may not be mentiond at present.

RC (PPAmP); endorsed: "Braintree Lettr Mrs. Adams July 20 1781 & Ansr. July 30."

[1] It seems likely that AA did not finish, or at any rate did not send, this letter on the day that it is dated but, rather, some days later. See her remark in the following letter to Lovell about deliberating "some time" before writing Gerry, and her acknowledgment of Gerry's "very quick reply" of 30 July (to Gerry, 4 Aug., below). Ten days between Marblehead and Braintree could not by any standard be called "quick."

[2] Which particular letter is meant, among the numerous ones revelatory of recent proposals and actions at Paris and Philadelphia to put restraints on JA, is not perfectly certain. In his reply of 30 July, below, Gerry assumed that AA meant Franklin's letter of 9 Aug. 1780, on which see above, Cranch to AA, 16 July, and note 1 there.

Abigail Adams to James Lovell

[Braintree, 20 July – 6 August 1781] [1]

Your two Letters of june 26 and july 2d came safe to hand together with the resolves which would gratify me if there was a sufficient stability in the Body which confer'd it to render it truly honorary, but the Letter of Janry. 10th strikes me very dissagreably and is highly tinctured with parissian influence. [2] It bears a striking likeness of a servility to a court that ought not to have so undue an influence upon an Independant Nation. ⟨*Are we not throwing ourselves into hands and rendering ourselves subject*⟩ If ever America stood in need of wise Heads and virtuous Hearts it is at this juncture. The ship wants skilfull hands, your old sea men are chiefly retired, your Hands are new and inexperienced. Sylla is on one Side and Caribdis on the other—how will you Stear between them? In avoiding the rocks you are in danger of being swallowed up in the sands. I am greatly agitated at your movements. I see nothing but dishonour and disgrace in the union of —— with ——. [3] I wish I had sooner been apprized of the design. You most assuredly have a party who do not mean the best welfare of their country by this movement. You or Rivington will have my mind upon the Subject before this reaches you. If the union is still undecided let me beg you to oppose it with all your influence. I wish your Friend G[err]y was with you. He is I hear unwilling to continue to be *one of you*. I will try persuasion upon him, and see if Female influence has any force with him.[4]

Three post days have passed since I received a line from you. You will see by the date of this Letter that I designed you a speedy reply to your favours but I really felt so unhappy and my mind was so intent upon consequences that I threw down my pen. I deliberated some time then took it up and wrote to our Friend G[err]y. He very obligeingly replied to me, and assured me that he would not decline a publick station whilst there was any prospect of rendering Service to his country. He informed me that by a Late Letter from Mr. L[ovell] he expected him soon in B[osto]n and that we should then be better able to judge from his information of the late measures of C[ongress].[5] This has been the true reason why I did not write by the two last posts as I had no inclination my Letters should fall into other Hands than those for which they were designed, but hearing nothing further I shall venture to forward this, requesting you to communicate to me the whole Fraternity to whom our Friend is joined, for what reason the comercial part of his commission is taken from him. Is it because he has enterd into no private contracts nor laid any plan for a fortune for himself and others who wish to be connected with those who will? I will tell you Sir the consequence of the late movements. If British Ships and old Neptune are not more intent upon dissapointing me than C[ongres]s I shall in the course of six months embrace my Dear Friend in his own native land. He will have no part in executing orders dishonorary to his country. One path is plain before him. He can and he will resign his commission. This his Enemies know and they will effect their purpose. I could (said he to a Friend upon an occasion not unlike the present) return to my practise at the Bar and make fortunes for my children and be happier and be really more respected than I can in the hazardous tormenting employments into which C[ongress] have always put me. I can be easy even under the marks of disgrace they put upon me, but they may depend upon it, they either mistake their own Interest in putting me into these employments, or in putting these Brands upon me—one or the other.[6] Time Sir will determine which of these predictions are true.

> "All humane virtue to its latest Breath
> Finds envy never conquer'd but by death."

I hope you received all my late Letters. Yet I know not how to account for not hearing from you unless you are realy returning to your Family and Friends, and in that Number I flatter myself you will ever consider   Portia

Dft (Adams Papers); without date or indication of addressee; at head of text in CFA's hand: "1782"; see note 1.

[1] The dates on which the first part and the longer continuation of this letter were written are established from the postscript of Lovell's letter to AA of 4 Aug. [i.e. Sept.], below: "Your Letter of July 20 / Aug. 6 reached me yesterday." In the interval between beginning her present letter and completing it (see note 4), she had written a letter to Gerry bearing date of 20 July (preceding, but probably not sent until some days later) and had received Gerry's answer of 30 July, below.

[2] Sent in Lovell's letter to AA of 26 June, above; see descriptive note there.

[3] Adams (JA) and Franklin must be meant.

[4] The foregoing was presumably written on the day this letter was dated. What follows was written with a different pen on 6 Aug.; see note 1.

[5] See AA to Gerry, 20 July, preceding; Gerry to AA, 30 July, below.

[6] AA is quoting from a letter written by JA to Elbridge Gerry, 18 Oct. 1779 (LbC, Adams Papers), which JA marked "Secret as the Grave" and then apparently did not send. See a longer passage from this letter quoted by AA in her letter to Gerry of 4 Aug., below; AA there says that the letter was never sent.

John Thaxter to Abigail Adams

Madam   Amsterdam 21st. July 1781

Ten months have I been waiting for an opportunity to forward my Letters, but none has presented, which of Course leaves an immense budget of Trumpery on hand.[1] I know not whether to continue writing or begin burning.

You will find by the inclosed Gazette Madam, an Account of our Celebration of the Anniversary of Independence. Every thing was conducted with the utmost order and decency—in one word, We were merry and wise.[2]

Mr. A. left this place the 2d. of this month for Paris. Mr. D. and your Son John set out on their Journey for Petersbourg the 7th of this month; Master Charles and I keep House together, with one Man Servant and three Women Servants.

Mr. Guild has this moment come in to see me. I never in my life saw a Man more matrimonially mad, and more impatient to get home. I am as impatient as he can be to be here, and really he has talked, preached, and dwelt so everlastingly upon Matrimony, that I feel my head and heart not a little deranged, and have almost fallen into that *infirmity* of Madness with him. Is all this Sympathy, Compassion, fellow feeling or personal Propensity to that State of life? I have at this moment the Care of a Family, and am at the head of it, without Wife and without Children—or in other words a Batchelor learning to keep House, the Expences of a Family &c. &c., which I hope will be some recommendation of me to my *"Fair American."* I think I do tolerably well, at least I may say so, for there is nobody either to contradict me or stand Trumpeter for me.

I intended to have wrote a long Letter when I begun; but since writing the above I have had a hint to close immediately, but cannot do it without informing You, that Mr. A. is in good health and Spirits at Paris, as I am just informed by a Person directly from thence. Pray acquaint my dear Parents and family that I am very well at present— I have not time to add a line to them. Oh! how happy should I be to embrace this Opportunity to go home, or some where out of this Capitol of Mammon. I never was so thoroughly tired of any Spot of Creation as this Atom stolen from the dominion of Neptune. I cannot live here I think.—'Till within this fortnight I have not been too well, nor very sick, but I impute it in part to the want of an old Companion, the Salt Rheum, which however has at length returned to renew its acquaintance.

Remember me, Madam, respectfully and affectionately where due, and believe me to be, with the most perfect Respect & Esteem, your most obedient & obliged humble Servant, JT.

RC (Adams Papers). Enclosure not found, but see note 2.

[1] In her letter to Thaxter of 8 Dec. 1780, above, AA acknowledged several letters from him, the latest dated 3 Sept. 1780 (not found). None from him were acknowledged in subsequent letters from her up to the present date, though several are in the Adams Papers and are printed above. They were perhaps all sent together with the present letter.

[2] There is a very full and engaging account of this celebration, which lasted from dawn till midnight, reprinted from an Amsterdam paper, in the *Boston Gazette*, 24 Sept. 1781, p. 3, cols. 1–2. It is also mentioned by JQA in his Diary under 4 July, although he and CA did not attend.

Jean de Neufville & Son to Abigail Adams

Madam   Amstm. 25th July 1781

We regret that your Ladyship's letter of 25th April[1] should not have Came to our hands soon enough to have prevented our executing your orders p[er] the Ship Juno, in Lieu of that of our good friends Messrs. N. & T. Tracey (the Minerva) as a freight of 12 1/2 PCt. is an object worth saving. But they were Shipped as early as the 25 May, and we were in hopes you would have received them before now, but the ship on board which they are, having waited for the

Convoy of a Large Frigate going to your Continent, prevented its departure till now.[2]

We are very Sencible of what America must expect from us, and feel too much for its disappointment at our tardiness in Seeking revenge for Such attrocious Insults, and Injuries. It has been a Subject of wonder to Europe, also, and to ourselves a Cause of painfull Sensation though we are Still persuaded we shall see our nation fully avenged. The Slowness of measures here having been more owing to the banefull influence of a Court, then to a want of proper Spirit in the nation, who on the Contrary gave us to dread from their resentment against Some Leaders, the most dreadful Consequences. True patriotism however Seems to gain the ascendancy with us, from which we hope the happiest effects will result, and finally that Iniquitous and haughty power (in Lieu of bringing the world at her feet to unconditional Submission) be punished for the wickedness of her measures.

It now is in the State of a ruined Gamester throwing its last Stake Neck or nothing: All in the East Indies is in as forlorn a State as in America. In short their Situation in all quarters is so deplorable that tho' an honest Brittain Cannot behold it without weeping he sees no Safety for himself or posterity from being enslaved but by further disgrace and ruin to their arms in hopes the remaining virtue left amongst them will at Last from despair unite in attempting to drag from the Seat of power the wretches who have perverted it, to their ruin, by every Corruption. May the good genius of your rising States ward them from every kind of it, and preserve their virtue and may our former one be restored to us, that we may be the more worthy of that union we so earnestly wish for, and to which we direct all our Labours. We flatter ourselves it is not far off. Tho' it will not add to our attachment or devotion to America, we believe it will to the energy of our assurances of that respect with which we have the honor to be most respectfully, Your Ladyships Most obt. hume. servts.,

John de Neufville & Son

RC (Adams Papers); in a clerical hand, signed by a member of the firm; at foot of text: "The honorble. Lady Adams." Another RC (Adams Papers), marked "Triplicate" at head of text.

[1] Not found.
[2] See Jean de Neufville & Son to AA, 25 May, above, and enclosed invoice and notes there.

to their swords.) if Independance is not made the Basis — ardently as
I long for the return of my dearest friend, I cannot feel the least inclination
to a peace but upon the most liberal foundation — patriotism in the
female sex is the most disinterested of all virtues — excluded from honours
and from offices, we cannot attach ourselves to the state or government from
having held a place of Eminence — even in the freed countrys our property
is subject to the controul & disposal of our partners. to whom the Laws have
given a soveriegn authority — Deprived of a voice in Legislation, obliged to
submit to those Laws which are imposed upon us, is it not sufficient to make
us indifferent to the publick welfare ? get all History & every age exhibit
Instances of patriotick virtue in the female Sex; which considering
our situation equals the most Heroick of yours — "a late writer observes
that as citizens we are called upon to exhibit our fortitude, for when you
offer your Blood to the State — it is ours — in giving it our Sons and Husbands
we give more than ourselves — you can only die on the field of Battle —
but we have the missfortune to Survive those whom we Love most,,

I will take praise to myself — I feel
that it is my due, for having Sacrificed so large a portion of my peace
and happiness to promote the welfare of my country which I hope for
many years to come will reap the benifit, tho it is more than probable
ammindfull of the hand that blessed them — your friends complain that
you do not write to them — I say all I can in excuse — but I wish you
to notice them all — and in a particular manner to continue your
affectionate Regard and attachment
to portia

Black and white gauges
and gauge hankerchiefs (the best articles imported)
tapes quality bindings shoe binding
Low priced linen, Black caliminco red tammies
fine threads low priced calicos ribbons

I. "PATRIOTISM IN THE FEMALE SEX IS THE MOST DISINTERESTED
OF ALL VIRTUES"
See page vii

2. "INQUIRE OF THE HISTORICK PAGE AND LET YOUR OWN OBSERVATIONS
SECOND THE INQUIRY"

See page vii

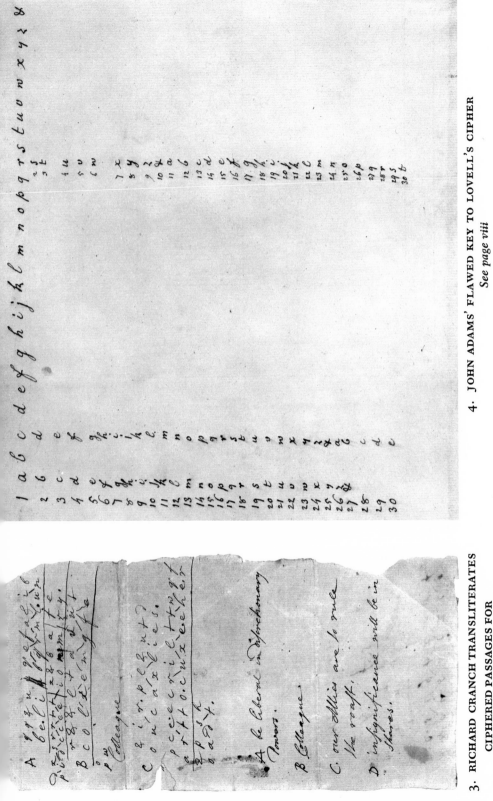

3. RICHARD CRANCH TRANSLITERATES
CIPHERED PASSAGES FOR
ABIGAIL ADAMS
See page viii

4. JOHN ADAMS' FLAWED KEY TO LOVELL'S CIPHER
See page viii

5. THE HUTCHINSON-WARREN HOUSE ON MILTON HILL
See page ix

6. "VIEW TOWARD THE BAR OF BILBAO," 1781, BY JOHN TRUMBULL
See page x

Elbridge Gerry to Abigail Adams

My dear Madam   Marblehead July 30 1781

I have been honored with your Letter of the 20th Instant, on a Matter of the highest Concern to the Continent, as well as to our mutual Friend, who represents it in Europe.

Previous to the Receipt of the Letter I saw a Copy of one from Dr. F[ranklin] to C[ongress],[1] and was soon after confidentially informed by a Gentleman at the southard of the proceedings thereon, which I confess have given me the greatest Pain and uneasiness. I cannot write so freely, Madam, as I shall confer with You, at a convenient Opportunity; but thus much I am greived to impart, that the Decree is past for revoking all the former Powers of our Friend, and for appointing him to execute new Instructions, with a Fraternity, some of whom to injure him, would I fear go greater Lengths than Judas did, to betray his Lord.[2]

I think it no difficult Task to trace the Vestiges of an undue Influence, which dared to approach our publick Councils as early as the period of the first Instructions, and which appears to me, for political purposes foreign to the Interest of America, to have produced a deep layed Plan for removing a Gentleman from office, upon whom alone many of the States could rely for obtaining a safe and honorable Peace.

If I have a right Idea of the last Powers, there can be no great Honor in executing them, either seperately or jointly; and the only object worth contending for in C[ongress] will be, a Revocation of these, and a Confirmation of the former Instructions with one Minister to execute them: but it is a Matter of Doubt in my Mind, whether the proceedings of C[ongress] have not made such a Measure altogether impracticable.

We shall however, Madam, be better able to judge understandingly, on the Return of Mr. L[ovell] who in his last Letter proposed soon to be in Boston: and altho the Times may justify the Sentiment that "the Post of Honor is a private Station"[3] I shall not decline a publick one, whilst there is the least prospect of serving my Country on so important an occasion. I need not add Madam that nothing will afford me greater pleasure than an opportunity of rendering Services to Yourself and Family, and that I have the Honor to be with the sincerest Esteem your most obedt. & very hum. sert:,   E. Gerry

RC (Adams Papers); at foot of text: "Portia." Dft (MHi:Gerry-Knight

Collection). Only one of the numerous cancellations and alterations in Dft has been noted below.

[1] Franklin's controversial letter to Huntington, 9 Aug. 1780, criticizing JA's conduct toward Vergennes; see above, Lovell to AA, 13 July, and note 7 there. Gerry's allusion makes clear that copies of Franklin's letter were sent to Boston at this time through more than one channel.

[2] In a letter of the present date to Lovell (Dft, heavily corrected, on verso of Lovell to Gerry, 17 June 1781, MHi: Gerry-Knight Coll.), Gerry wrote: "I have seen a Copy of the Letter from ⟨Doctor Franklin⟩ to ⟨Congress⟩ respecting ⟨Mr. J. Adams⟩ *and fear* that his Zeal for his Country has *far exceeded his usual Caution.* Be that as it may I *feel a deep Concern for* our worthy Friend, and *apprehend that the* ⟨ungrateful and⟩ *ungenerous Treatment* he has received will be *productive of Disgrace and irreparable Injury* to his Country. ⟨Gerard⟩ You well remember was ever against *our saving the Fishery,* and as he received his *Instructions* from the ⟨Court of France⟩, is it not probable they have *layed a plan to oust Mr. ⟨Adams⟩* in order to carry their Measures into Effect." Whether the names stricken by Gerry in his Dft, and which appear here as cancellations, were replaced in RC with identifying initials, were written in cipher in keeping with Lovell's usage in his letter on recto, or were left blank to be supplied by Lovell, cannot be known.

[3] In Dft, Gerry at this point wrote and then cancelled: "I would chearfully make a Tour to the southard."

Abigail Adams to John Adams

August 1 1781

O that I could realize the agreable reverie of the last Night when my dear Friend presented himself and two Son[s] safely returnd to the Arms of the affectionate wife and Mother. Cruel that I should wake only to experience a renual of my daily solicitude. The next month will compleat a whole year since a single Line from your Hand has reachd the longing Eyes of Portia. No vessels have arrived here since the declaration of war from Holland. Congress have no dispatches later than october from you. I hope and hope till hope is swallowed up in the victory of Dispair. I then consider all my anxiety as vain since I cannot benifit any one by it, or alter the established order of things. I cannot relieve your mind from the burden of publick cares, or at this distance alleviate the anxiety of your Heart, tho ever so much distressed for the welfare of your Native land or protect you from the Slanderous arrow that flieth in Secret, a Specimin of which you will find inclosed in a Letter from Mr. C[ranc]h[1] but which you must I think have received before as many coppies have been sent. My Indig[nation] is too big for utterance.

> Falsehood and fraud shoot up in ev'ry soil
> The product of all climes—Rome had its Cea[sar.]

I will not comment upon this low this dirty this Infamous t[his] diabolical peice of envy and malice as I have already do[ne] it where I thought I might be of service—to your two Friends L[ovell] and G[err]y.

> True consious Honour is to know no Sin—

and the firm patriot whose views extend to the welfare of Mankind tho obstructed by faction and vice, tho crossed by fortune, tho wounded by calumny and reproach, shall find in the end that his generous Labour is not lost—even tho he meets with no other reward than that self approveing hour, which the poet tells us [outweighs?] whole years of stupid starers and of loud Huz[zas.]

When ever any opportunity occurs write, and write me a volume to amuse, to comfort and inform me. I turn to the loved pages of former days and read them with delight. They are all my comfort, all my consolation in the long long [in]terval of time that I have not received a line. Should I name my dear Boys a tear will flow with the Ink—not a line have I received from them for more than a Year. May they be their Fathers comfort and their Mothers delight.

No very important military events have taken place since I wrote you last which was by Capt. Young to Bilboa. Green is driving Cornwallis acting with much Spirit and viggour. We are here looking upon each other in a mere maze. Our old currency died suddenly, the carkases remain in the hands of individuals, no Burial having been yet provided for it. The New was in Good repute for a time, but all of a Sudden and in one day followed [its] Elder Brother—so that with old and New in my hand, I can not purchase a single Sixpence worth of any thing yet taxes must be paid, men must be raised for Road Island and West Point and paid too, yet the profits of what each one has sold for paper avails them not. This was a stroke of our Enemies by employing Emissaries to depreciate it who were detected and put into jail. Barter and hard money is now the only trade. The strugle will be to supply our army. How after having sold our commodities for paper we can raise hard money to pay the next demand which must be speedy, I know not. I had collected a sufficient Sum of paper to pay a very large tax which the last Session of the court levied. It now will avail me not a groat. I mentioned in a former Letter that [I] wished you to send me a chest of Bohea tea by any vessel of Mr. Tracys or Smiths.[2] It would turn into money quicker [*remainder missing*]

Dft (Adams Papers); incomplete. The MS is worn and torn along one edge, requiring a number of words to be partly or wholly supplied by editorial conjecture.

¹ Franklin's letter to Huntington of 9 Aug. 1780, a copy of which was enclosed in Richard Cranch to JA, 16 July, q.v. above.
² AA to JA, 23 April, above.

Abigail Adams to Elbridge Gerry

*[Braintree, 4 August 1781]*¹

The very quick reply with wish [which] you honourd my Letter together with the Friendly contents of your polite favour demand my acknowledgement.²

If you Sir as a patriot and a Friend feel for the injurys offerd to your Country and the disgrace with which those in power are endeavouring to load our Friend, you may easily judge of the anxiety of one whose happiness is so interwoven and blended with the injured, that he cannot receive a wound at which the other does not blead.

I presume not to judge of all the consequences which will follow the late determinations of C[ongress]. One only I am satisfied in. If our Friend is cloged and embarrassed as you hint, if his instruction[s] are such as he ought not consistant with the Good of his country and the duty he owes to it, to execute, he will resign his commission and return to his native country.

Here Sir I will give you a few extracts which will shew you his Sentiments not upon the present, but upon his Situation when he returnd from Europe, which you know was not then very Eligible. They were written in a confidential Letter to you, but some parts of the Letter was written with so much freedom that he thought proper to surpress it.³ In speaking of the Jealousy which he had ever observed in C[ongress] of the Massachusetts, he adds "Is it possible that C[ongress] should be respected if she suffers those Men upon whom she has as her records shew most depended from the begining, those Men who had a chief hand in forming her Navy and Army, who have supported her Independance, who have promoted and formed her alliances, to be slandered and disgraced. These things are of more importance in Europe than here to the publick but they [are] of too much here to be neglected. If the Mass[achusetts] is to be made the But and Sport in the Manner it has been you will soon see it abandoned by all Men of Spirit, or you will See it break the union. For myself I care nothing at all, for my children I care but little for these things, but for the publick I care much. It is really important that congress should not dishonour their own members without cause and is really Important that the Members of Mass Bay should support each others honours and characters. I could return to my practise at the Bar, and make fortunes for my children, and be happier and really more respected than I can in the hazardous tormenting employments into which Congress have always put me. I can be easy even under the marks of disgrace they put upon me but they may depend upon it they either mistake their own Interest in putting me into these employments or in putting these Brands upon me."

Time will shew which of his predictions are true. If our Friend Mr. L[ovel]l returns I shall be fully informed, he has often refered me for information to Mr. A. but that Gentleman is so much ingrossed that I cannot get him even to spend one day with me. Have only been able to see him for half an hour and that in company. I shall be happy sir to see you at Braintree, whenever it suits your convenience; I doubt not of your Friendship or of your assiduity to support my Friend in every measure He may persue for the benifit of his country, but by your Letter and Mr. L[ovel]ls late hints I fear it is wholy out of his power. He will immediately upon the recept of the new plan feel his dissagreable Situation and I am pained when I reflect upon the anxiety it will give him. He must and will quit a Situation in which he cannot act with Honour, this his enimies know and they will assuredly answer their end. Those who wish well to their country must mourn the corrupt influence that has poisoned the fountain of power from whence issue Streams which Instead of nourtering and refreshing these Infant States are like to prove as Banefull as the ten fold plagues of Egypt. If you should receive any further information from your Friends at Congress respecting these matters I should take it as a favour if you would communicate them to Sir Your obliged Friend & humble Servant, Portia

Dft (Adams Papers); written on discarded cover sheets of old letters, one bearing the address "Mr. John Thaxter   Paris"; docketed by CFA at head of text: "1781?"

[1] Dated from Gerry's acknowledgment, 31 Aug. (below), of the (missing) RC.
[2] AA to Gerry, 20 July (which may not have been sent until some days later), and Gerry's reply, 30 July, both above.
[3] JA to Gerry, 18 Oct. 1779 (LbC, Adams Papers), marked "Secret as the Grave" and then, according to AA, not sent; see above, AA to Lovell, 20 July–6 Aug., and note 6 there. Quotation marks have here been editorially supplied, but it should be noted that AA quotes JA's letterbook text freely and with her own improvements in phrasing.

James Lovell to Abigail Adams

Aug. 10. 1781

I am persuaded to believe that I have acknowledged the Receipt of your Favor of June 30th tho it is not so endorsed.[1] I think I recollect to have discovered my Unwillingness to persuade my dearest Friend, my affectionate, faithful, generous-spirited Maria to put herself in the Way of a Meeting with a Stranger prejudiced against me and perhaps prompt to utter her Prejudices. I am sure such Ideas rose in my Mind when I first read your Wishes that I should urge an Acceptance of your Invitation, given I am sure, in unfeigned Politeness and pressed afterwards for a most benevolent Purpose. I thank you cordially for your kind Intentions. But I maintain my former Judgment of the Consequences. I hope you see enough of my Temper to prevent you from ever giving me the real Name of Cornelia or Clarinda or whatever C. it was mentioned in one of your Letters, now in Boston. The good Opinion and Confidence of Mrs. L is one of the Chief of the very few Things that are to constitute my Happiness for the short years I may have to live.

I have made Communications to Mr. S[amuel] A[dams] if not to you that will answer all those Questions which you was restrained from asking thro' Fear of Rivington. I do really think that no Pique or ill Will against your Mr. A— exists here. Whatever has been done that can excite a Suspicion of the Kind has sprung out of mistaken Principles of general Policy. I am not induced to suppose La Luzerne otherways than friendly and respectful; But when he has, agreably to what Vergennes wrote to him, desired Instructions to our Negotiator to act cordially and unreservedly with those of France, the Measures adopted here, in Consequence, have exceeded his Expectations.

I wish you not to suffer any Vexation of Mind beyond what I do myself. There is no such Idea here as any Criminality in Mr. A—. He is much esteemed. But such is the uncouth way of Proceeding here at Times that unintended Chagrin must arise. Doctor F[ranklin] is experiencing very much I am persuaded on the Appointment of J. Laurens. It is *therefore* that he has asked for Retirement rather than because of his age.

I am to acknowledge the Receipt of your very kind Epistle of July 14 received the 23d. Your Tenderness will betray you into an Indiscretion if you press your Friends as you proposed.[2] There has been a Disposition in the Court to make a Distinction in my Favor. They have done it in more Instances than one, without giving Offence to any of my Colleagues. I have no Right to complain beyond what the Rest have. A Batchelor or a Man with a very small Family can afford to serve. There are 3 of the former and 1 of the latter in our List. I know not Genl. Ward's Number. Those with *many* may *refuse* to accept when chosen.

I do not recollect what I have written to make you judge so severely of the *Pittance*. But be it what it may, it cannot be now altered. In short it is so involved in the Cloud of Calculation in the Case of Mr. Gerry who was 3 Years here that I doubt whether any Member of the Assembly can tell what has been given per day to the Delegates for their Time and Service, exclusive of Expences. It is a Fact that modest Œconomical Connecticutt has never given less than 3 Spanish or an Equivalent, from the first Congress till this day.—It is my Mishap that I am not what your Ladyship maliciously, in Appearance, wished to call me—"a practicing Attorney."

I really do not foresee how I am to begin the World at 42 without any of what are called the 3 learned Professions, without Farm or Stock for Trade; and yet if you will believe me I do not feel distressed, for, tho slandrous Females will speak slightly of my Morality I know that I am one of the most religious Men in the World. I am in perpetual Adoration of the SUPREME who sent me into this STATE of EXISTENCE and who has given me the Will to labour. While he continues my Health therefore I can maintain more than one especially on the other Side of the Alleghenny Mountains, near the Ohio.

I think that Cornwallis must be on his Way to New York and that the Embarkation in the Cheseapeak was only amusing the Neighbourhood by sailing up and down till the Capital Ships of Convoy should appear at the Capes.

I am, dear Madam, respectfully Your Friend,   J L

RC (Adams Papers).

[1] Lovell had acknowledged AA's letter of 30 June, above, in his of 17 July, also above.

[2] For a raise in Lovell's pay as a delegate to Congress; see AA's letter to him of 14 July, above.

James Lovell to Abigail Adams

20th Aug. [17]81

I am too ill to write much. Your Ease of Mind is what I wish to promote by confirming what I have before said vizt. That Mr. A[dams] was greatly esteemed here tho' we have an odd way of discovering it sometimes. He is sole Minister Plenipo to form a triple Alliance between Holland, France and these United States with Discretion to make it Quadruple by joining Spain—for the Purpose of our Independ[ence] and finishing the War.[1]

Should a french Fleet be on this Coast, I shall have Opportunity to send your Things by Water.

Adieu.   JL

A Cold Scrawl for a Man in a Fever. I have quite forgot what Word I *may* use. What I may *not* is at my Pen's End.

RC (Adams Papers).

[1] This project, which in the end had no material result, was set in motion by La Luzerne, no doubt under direction from Paris. The original of JA's commission, endorsed by him "Commission of 16. August 1781.—to negotiate a triple or quadruple Alliance," is in Adams Papers, together with his instructions, endorsed "Instructions of Aug. 16. Holland." For the background and printed texts see JCC, 21:846–848, 859, 876–880; Wharton, ed., *Dipl. Corr. Amer. Rev.*, 4:636–638. See also Elbridge Gerry's comment in his letter to AA, 31 Aug., below.

James Lovell to Abigail Adams

Aug. 23. 1781

I feared moths—have opened your Goods—aired and shook the Wollens—added good Tobacco leaves and again secured them for Transportation. I shall put Clamps to the Chest and send it to the Store of the Deputy Commissary General [1] where Mr. Jno. Checkley will secure the first good public or private Carriage to Mr. Hughes or to Boston.

I mentioned Gauze for Mr. Tufts. You say he misses some gauze Handkerchiefs. These are Handkerchiefs and not simply Gauze. I discover no other Relief to your Fears than that there are Serge and Buttons and Twist for Mr. Wibert and some *Satinett* or *like it* for *Small Cloaths*. They were within the Cloath which needed not opening at first. I am recovered from a slight Fever; have been abroad; and am again going to deliver this mark of my Devo—no, no! Lov—worse and worse! my humble Desires to serve you,—flat as Dishwater! my Respect, Madam, my affectionate Esteem Ma'am—   JL

RC (Adams Papers).

[1] The deputy commissary general of prisoners, as the following letter makes clear. He was Col. Abraham Skinner, a Pennsylvania officer (Heitman, *Register Continental Army*).

James Lovell to Abigail Adams

August 24, 1781

After giving a few Lines for you yesterday to the Commissary

General of Prisoners who was going for Boston; I held Conversation with a Capt. Mason who had just landed from a Flag of Truce of Bermuda. He sailed from the Texel May 29 was taken close off the Capes of Delaware, after about 8 weeks passage and carried to the island from whence he is now arrived on parole to release another Captain for a balance. He had lately before sailing from Holland, dined with Mr. Adams and his family, who were all well. This gentleman brought out from the Texel the quantity of a barrel of letters, but was obliged to sink them on the 8th of June, when he was brought to by the Suffolk man of war, and endured a search and examination for 5 hours, but was not discovered to be an American vessel. The Suffolk was with three other ships of the line convoying 65 merchantmen from Jamaica, and had, a few days before, taken, after 3 hours engagement, *the Marquis de Fayette* a 44 gun ship with our cloathing, &c.

Capt. Mason mentions that about three days before he left Holland Mr. Adams had made a very great change as to an exhibition of character, had taken a large house, proper equipage and servants; and it was not doubted to be according to the wishes and designs of their High Mightinesses.[1] I conclude from my memorandum book that Mr. A. must have received at that Period our Resolves and Instructions respecting the Completion of the Union, March 1st. by the signature of Maryland to the articles.

You may expect Commod: Gillon momently in a ship of 24 42 pounders on one deck. There is also a Capt. Eden or something like it bound for Boston. People connected Mr. a's appearance with a certain proceeding of Gillon, and judged both originating in the Government there. Gillon very suddenly unloaded known *private* property and received other Goods at the same Hours, one Shallop going and another coming constantly. *The* memorial of mr. a is spoken of by Capt. Mason, as it is by Mr. Carmichael, very familiarly, both conceiving we have it amongst us, but we only see it hinted at sneeringly in British papers. Is not this vexatious to us Evites?

I hope the Children with you, and their Mama enjoy perfect Health. *They* have much of my Love. There is a Cnot of Emphasis and Grammar which may amuse the Teeth of any one of the C's of your Circle who chuses to search for mischief.

I am induced, upon second thought, to repeat what may lag on the road with Col. Skinner.

Upon reviewing and securing your Goods against moths, I found that instead of *Gauze* I might have said *Gauze Handkerchiefs* for D.

Tafts: that there are Buttons, Twist, Serge and something of the Sattinet kind for Mr. Wibert found within his Cloth.

Rationally respectfully, Mistriss Adams's humble Servant,

J S———²

MS not found. Printed from Rivington's New York *Royal Gazette*, 8 Sept. 1781, p. 2, col. 4 – p. 3, col. 1. Without indication of place, without salutation, and with an obvious misreading of its initialed signature, the letter appears with a number of others in Rivington's paper under the heading "Part of the Contents of a new Rebel Mail (being the Fifth) which was taken by a party of Refugees, On Tuesday last" (i.e. on 4 Sept.).

¹ In a letter to Mrs. Francis Dana of 23 Aug. which was captured in the same mail and published in Rivington's New York *Royal Gazette* of 12 Sept., Lovell elaborated as follows:

"Within half a week of the sailing of Captain Mason from the Texel Mr. Adams had gone into a vast change of Living; from a course of private Lodging with command of two rooms, He took a grand House rolled his Chariot multiplied his Servants and put on the minister plenipo: without any other Explanation than what the free publication of his memorial in all the Gazettes naturally gave. The general persuasion was that their High mightinesses were fully decided to declare in our favour." (Burnett, ed., *Letters of Members*, 6:194.)

² A misreading by Rivington's printer of "J L———," as Lovell himself pointed out in his letter to AA of 15 Sept., below.

John Thaxter to Abigail Adams 2d

Amsterdam 25th August 1781

I was yesterday honoured with a Letter from Braintree dated the 25th of May last, and tho' an anonymous one, yet the hand writing, connected with other Circumstances, warranted my subjoining the Signature of the amiable and accomplished Daughter of one of the first Ladies of the Age, to whose Goodness added to your Politeness I am indebted for this mark of Attention. I have embraced the first moment to acknowledge the Receipt of so unexpected a favor, and to assure You of my readiness to commence, renew or "revive" a Correspondence. Indeed it has been so rare for me to converse or even to speak with a Lady, to write to or receive from one a Letter, for these two years past, that I esteem any Civility or attention from them, an Instance of Compassion to one who was formerly very happy with the fair Circle of his female Acquaintance.

My worthy friend Mr. Storer, who forwarded your kind favor, is safely arrived at Gottenbourg, and he is expected in this City every moment. I am impatient to take him by the hand. I can easily concieve that the absence of so amiable a Character will be exceedingly regretted by his Friends, and by the fair particularly. Europe may be a good School for an exterior Polish: but Morality is a plant of slow Growth in this quarter of the Globe, where the polite and fashionable Vices of the Age have but too much extinguished the sentiment of it, and given an air of Awkwardness to Virtue. A good Education in our own Country is not an object of difficult Acquisition. An easy deportment and graceful Address are the fine polishes of a polite and may be of a virtuous and good moral Character: but the Graces and Virtues are not always united. When they do harmonize, they add a mutual Lustre to each other, and form one of the most pleasing Spectacles in Life.

The tender the gentle Eliza, "whose Mind is Virtue by the Graces drest," as your good Mamma has observed, has had a Share of my sincerest and tenderest Pity during her Indisposition. I am very happy to find by your Letter, that She has recovered her Chearfulness and her health to so great a degree—be good enough to wish her affectionately for me a long Continuance of both.

You have informed me that Mr. Rice has at last drawn the Prize in the matrimonial Lottery—the happier he. Of all Lotteries this is the most hazardous. And being at all times unlucky, is a sufficient Objection with me to putting any thing to the Risque. However I am not too envious to wish any one success in this Wheel of Fortune.

You have closed a charming Letter, by calling me off from "my more important Business or Pleasures to point out the foibles of it." I am almost tempted to scold at You for endeavouring to make me a Scrutinizer or critical Reviewer and sarcastically giving me an air of Importance. My pleasures are few but the most "important" of them is writing to my dear Friends on the other side of the Atlantic, whom may God bless and preserve. I cannot undertake the office of a Critic. To point out *Foibles and Faults* where *none* exist, is the mark of an ignorant, envious, ill-natured one, a Character which I hope no one will fix upon me.

If a Correspondence with You can give You the least pleasure or entertainment, I shall be happy to be ranked in the Class of them, and will not suffer another eighteen Months to pass away, without convincing You that You have a Correspondent in the old World. I shall make but an indifferent figure among your others, but that shall not discourage me. As to scores and Ballances of Merit, I make no pretensions.

Remember me dutifully and respectfully to all friends at Braintree, Weymouth and Boston, and believe me to be, with sincere Esteem, your affectionate Friend and Hbl. Servant, JT

An abundance of Love to all the young Ladies of my Acquaintance, and particularly to my fair American, if it is yet discovered who She is.

RC (MHi:Thaxter Papers); at foot of text: "Miss Nabby Adams."

John Boylston to John Adams

Dear Sir   August 31st. 1781

You may possibly wonder at my *Silence in* not *writing you* during so long a period and which might yet have continu'd from the danger which attends it did not the cruelty and injustice of this Govt. impel me to sollicit you and Doctor F[ran]k[li]n to use your utmost interest with the Court of V[e]rs[ail]les to take the American Prisoners under its immediate Protection by insisting on a Cartel for exchanging them forthwith and liberating them from the vindictive Confinement many of them have suffer'd for three years past which has induc'd many (despairing of relief) to enter in the Navy and which is the ultimate motive of this treatment.[1]

There are at present in Forton jayl only, above 500 for whose particular situation I wish to refer you to the Revd. Thos. Wren at Portsmouth[2] who merits the highest praise for his constant and unwearied attendance in distributing the charitable Contributions hitherto collected for their relief, and in which I have not been wholly useless, altho' am mortified to find it now grows very cold and languid which requires your utmost speedy exertions to prevent the consequences in their seduction thro want of proper necessaries.—I am here much vex'd to find those necessaries considerably abridg'd by the infamous Peculation of T. D[ig]gs in having withheld several sums received from Doctor F—k—n, besides several other considerable Private Donations which I am inform'd the said D—gs has receiv'd for their relief.[3] He is one of that description I had in veiw when I formerly wrote you my Sentiments[4] that no other than persons of establish'd reputation and property should be any ways employ'd in the Affairs of America.—The severe treatment which many have suffer'd here for illicit Correspondence may apologize for the omission of Place and Signature hereto, but which you may supply from the recollection of my having formerly sent you the Arms of B[oylston].[5]— I should be extreamly happy to hear of your success in the above application which will greatly adorn your Embassy and procure you much Merit. If you favour me with a Line in answer take good care it is under safe Conduct as my Letters are often open'd.

Ardently wishing you all health & prosperity, I am

RC (Adams Papers); docketed by CFA at head of text: "from ⟨Dr. Bancroft⟩ J. Boylston."

[1] John Boylston (1709–1795), son of the famous Dr. Zabdiel Boylston and first cousin of JA's mother. He had been a merchant in Boston and is depicted in JA's diary in the 1760's as a lively but somewhat affected conversationalist (*Diary and Autobiography*, 1:293–294). By 1771 he had taken up residence in London, and he remained in England for the rest of his life, though with misgivings because (despite statements commonly made to the contrary, including notes in the present edition) he seems always to have been more of an American patriot than a loyalist at heart. His correspondence with the Smith family in Boston (MHi:Smith-Carter Papers) shows that he remained sympathetic with the American cause and that he continued his charitable activities in Massachusetts, through intermediaries, during and after the war. In the Franklin Papers are letters respecting his proposal in 1778 to take an oath and give security in order to return to America (*Cal. Franklin Papers, A.P.S.,* 4:272, 274), but this did not occur. In a letter to JA, 28 June 1782 (below), Boylston heatedly denied he was in any sense a loyalist "Refugee," having "ever been constantly and invariably attach'd to the cause and interest of my native Country." In his reply of 5 July 1782 (also below), JA assured Boylston that "I have long known your Sentiments to be favourable to your native Country, as well as to Liberty in General."

When JA and JQA came to England late in 1783, Boylston was established in prosperous retirement at Bath, where he entertained his relatives handsomely, as he again did JA and AA some years later (JA, *Diary and Autobiography,* 3:151; AA to Mary Smith Cranch, 20 Jan. 1787 [MWA]). As the present and later letters relate, Boylston was active in efforts to relieve the distresses of American seamen imprisoned in England. See further, Adams Genealogy.

On the whole subject of American seamen in British prisons during the war, particularly Forton Prison at Portsmouth and Mill Prison at Plymouth, their treatment, British policy relating thereto, and humanitarian efforts by both Americans and British, see the authoritative and well-documented articles by John K. Alexander, " 'American Privateersmen in the Mill Prison during 1777–1782': An Evaluation," *Essex Inst., Hist. Colls.,* 102:318–340 (Oct. 1966); and "Forton Prison during the American Revolution . . . ," same, vol. 103:365–389 (Oct. 1967).

On JA's activities in behalf of captured American seamen in general, and of a number of Braintree men at Mill Prison in particular, see below, AA to JA, 9 Dec. 1781, and note 3 there.

[2] Rev. Thomas Wren (1725–1787), a dissenting minister in Portsmouth who administered relief to Americans in Forton Prison and whose zeal in their behalf was said to be "prodigious." According to John K. Alexander, Wren "mixed a little treason with his humanity" in helping escapees get out of England (*Essex Inst., Hist. Colls.,* 103:383 [Oct. 1967]). Franklin, with whom Wren corresponded, recommended that Congress officially thank "this good Man" and that he be given an honorary degree by "some of our Universities." Congress did thank him, and the College of New Jersey awarded him a doctorate of divinity in 1783 (Franklin, *Writings,* ed. Smyth, 9:72, 124; JCC, 25:588, 619, 632). There is correspondence between JA and Wren in the Adams Papers; and in the *Gentleman's Magazine* for Nov. 1787 there is a long and eulogistic obituary (57:1026–1027).

[3] Thomas Digges (1742–1821), a Marylander in England who had a very checkered career that has been traced in great detail by William Bell Clark in his article "In Defense of Thomas Digges," *PMHB,* 77:381–438 (Oct. 1953). Although Digges has long been condemned as a double agent as well as an embezzler of funds raised to aid American prisoners in England, Clark has established that he was never in the pay of the British and that his embezzling was the last resort of a man in great difficulties and by no means on the grand scale that Franklin and others believed. Digges was a secret correspondent of JA under a

great variety of pseudonyms.

⁴ Letter not found.

⁵ No earlier communication from John Boylston to JA has been found. There can be no certainty whether the Boylston arms which Boylston "formerly sent" was in the form of a seal or on paper. However, by 1782 JA did have in his possession a seal bearing the Boylston arms and perhaps a drawing or engraving as well. Following American recognition by the States General in April 1782, JA as minister plenipotentiary had occasion to frame a form of passport for issuance. He chose to imitate closely the one devised by Franklin in Passy in 1780, substituting for the coat of arms Franklin had used to give the document an official character, the coat of arms of the Boylston family (the woodblock of the coat of arms he had made is in MHi and is illustrated in Boston Athenæum, *Catalogue of JQA's Books*, facing p. 136; the passport utilizing it is reproduced in the present volume). In November of the same year in affixing his signature to the Preliminary Treaty with Great Britain, JA used a seal in cornelian and gold of the Boylston arms, thenceforward known in the family as the Treaty Seal (the seal, now a part of the family memorabilia at the Adams National Historic Site, Quincy, was given by JA to JQA and by JQA in trust to CFA on the baptism of JQA2; the seal is illustrated in *Catalogue of JQA's Books*, facing p. 135).

AA had used a seal of the Boylston arms, presumably left in her care in Braintree, on the cover of her letter to JA aboard the *Sensible*, 14 Nov. 1779; see vol. 3:234, note. This tends to support HA2's assertion that the seal had come to JA from his mother, Susanna Boylston (Boston Athenæum, *Catalogue*

of *JQA's Books*, p. 136). However, it seems unlikely that AA would have sent the seal to JA in Europe in the interim, and no instances are presently known of JA's employment of a Boylston seal in Europe before the use in 1782 described above. One possible explanation is that the Boylston seal that JA affixed to the Preliminary Treaty may have been the "Boylston Arms" sent to him by John Boylston, who was unmarried and in 1781 over seventy years of age. There would then have been two seals of the Boylston arms in the possession of the Adams family, but only one remains.

Between 1783 and 1785, JA, in devising a seal to commemorate his signing of the treaties, adapted the Boylston seal by having the three roundels, earlier blank, replaced with roundels bearing respectively a lion, a fleur-de-lis, and a lion. Later Adamses incorporated the Boylston arms, as adapted, in a variety of ways in their seals and bookplates (Boston Athenæum, *Catalogue of JQA's Books*, p. 136–148; see also JQA, Diary, 26 Oct. 1827, 3 Sept. 1836, 4 Nov. 1841; JQA to CFA, 28 Feb. 1831, 27 Oct. 1833 [Adams Papers]). When a bookplate for Ward Nicholas Boylston's benefactions to the Boston Medical Library was devised, the coat of arms used was in the form as adapted by JA.

In the Boylston arms the shield consists of six silver (white) crosses crosslet fitché, arranged 3, 2, 1, on a red field, above which, in chief, on a field of gold or yellow are three black roundels or pellets. The crest above shows a lion, passant guardant, holding in his dexter paw an angled cross crosslet fitché of the type on the shield (Charles K. Bolton, *Bolton's American Armory*, Boston, 1927, p. 1, 20).

Elbridge Gerry to Abigail Adams

My dear Madam   Marblehead August 31. 1781

Agreable to the Request contained in your Letter of the 4th, I have the Pleasure of transmitting You some further Intelligence, respecting our Friend in Europe, received last Evening in a Letter from Philadelphia. Mr. L[ovell] says "Mr. J.A. is sole Plenipo[tentiary] for forming a triple Alliance between Holland, France, and America, for bringing the War to a speedy Issue. Spain may make it quadruple." [1] I conceive not however, that either Mr. A[dams] or the State is obliged to C[ongress] for their last Appointment; which was probably made for the double purpose of reconciling him to the extraordinary Revocation of his former Powers, and of preventing an Enquiry into the Injuries which the State has Reason to apprehend from an Alteration of his first Instructions. I hope nevertheless, that some Gentlemen of ability and Leisure will investigate the Matter, and remain Madam with the sincerest Esteem your assured Friend & most hum. Sert.,

G.

RC (Adams Papers); addressed: "His Excellency John Adams Esqr. to the Care of his Lady at Braintree to be left with Isaac Smith Esqr. Boston"; at foot of text: "Portia."

[1] See above, Lovell to AA, 20 Aug., and note there.

Alice Lee Shippen to Abigail Adams

Philadelphia August 1781

I rejoice at any circumstance that begins a correspondence with a lady whose acquaintance I have long wish'd for; but am sorry the contents of my letter must have given you pain.[1] I would much rather endeavor to console you, but am sure your own good sense will suggest to you every consolation. I can truly sympathize with you Madam. I have learnt to mourn for injured worth and merit, your case indeed is not singular, my amiable brothers are as you observe fellow sufferers, they have sacrificed every other prospect for the sole one of serving their Country, and how are they rewarded! and what is worst of all, how are they tied up from the sweet service of America! I will not trouble you with details, or "I could a tale unfold," but suffice it to say that the wounds we receive are deeper, because they wound our Country, the honest men of America are her barriers, they must be pull'd down, before she can be destroyed. Money and power are now in the hands of bad men, and there is no popular Ear. You are acquainted by this time with particulars. It is a little surprizing is it not that Congress should have join'd Dr. Franklin in commission with your Friend after what has pass'd; Can harmony be expected by joining a mans calumniator with him? It is certainly putting your friend in a disagreable situation, 'tis most probable if an advantageous peace should be negociated, Dr. Franklin will take the credit: if otherwise, he will throw the blame on him he has already marked out; but my dear Madam, the slander of corrupt men in a corrupt age, is better than their praise. The Dr. appears to be no respecter of persons, he breaks through every tye of gratitude, and of Country, all his affections centre in one character. He loves a knave wherever he finds him.

Genl. Sullivan is on his return to New Hampshire. I hope he does not deserve what is generally said of him here, that he is under French influence, surely if it be true, he is most unfit for the Councils of America. I am not surpriz'd that the French should interfere, but am both astonished and grieved that any in our Councils should have adopted the weak policy of being governed by them.[2]

It was my brother R. H. Lee for whom I expressed my anxiety, several Tories laid in ambush for him, but were providentially dissappointed: 15 of them are taken, but I have not yet heard their fate. The Enemy have taken 50 Negroes from my brother Williams estate in Virginia—but this is a small part of what he has lost in this contest.

Dr. Cutting will do me the favor to take care of this letter, he is returning to his native country with the good wishes of every honest, sensible acquaintance wherever he has been.[3] His friends are purchased by merit, for he has made no money in the public Service to purchase them with. I refer you to this Gentleman for the news of the day.

Our friend Mr. Lovell delivered your polite letter with his own hand. I thank you, Madam, for the obliging things you are pleased to say in it. My brother A. Lee begs me to return you his most respectful compliments. And I beg you will believe, I always pray that yourself and worthy friend may long continue the ornaments of your Country.

I have the honor to be, with great respect your much obliged humble Servant,   A H Shippen

RC (Adams Papers); text in an amanuensis' hand; signed by Mrs. Shippen, whose full maiden name was Alice Harriet Lee.

[1] See Alice Lee Shippen to Elizabeth Welles Adams, 17 June, above.

[2] This is the earliest reference in the Adams Papers to a subject long and bitterly debated in the 19th century among partisans for and against John Sullivan, and now definitely resolved against him. Maj. Gen. Sullivan retired from the army late in 1779 and served as a New Hampshire delegate in Congress, 1780–1781. Here he was on the most intimate terms with the French minister, La Luzerne, and followed a vigorously pro-

French (that is to say, anti-Adams) line in his votes relating to foreign affairs. The latest student of Franco-American relations during the Revolution, William C. Stinchcombe, adduces evidence from both the official and personal papers of La Luzerne to show that Sullivan was in the pay of the French foreign office from 1780 to at least 1784 (*The American Revolution and the French Alliance*, Syracuse, 1969, p. 163 and note); see also William E. O'Donnell, *The Chevalier de La Luzerne*, Bruges, 1938, p.

63–65, 171; Charles P. Whittemore, *A General of the Revolution: John Sullivan of New Hampshire*, N.Y. and London, 1961, ch. 11, which offers some palliatives but by no means exculpates Sullivan; Morris, *Peacemakers*, p. 210 ff.; and Sibley-Shipton, *Harvard Graduates*, 14:332–334.

[3] Dr. John Brown Cutting served as apothecary general in the eastern and middle departments of the Continental Army hospital establishment, 1777–1780 (Heitman, *Register Continental Army*). According to Heitman, Cutting was a New Yorker, not a New Englander.

John Thaxter to Abigail Adams

Madam   Amsterdam August   1781

I am almost ashamed to intrude another Letter by this Conveyance, which, if it should prove a safe one, will throw into your hands an Abundance of trumpery from me, sufficient for one Year.

Accept my thanks, Madam, for your Goodness in forwarding my Sister's Letter to me. I feel myself much obliged by your kind attention to me in this way, and particularly for *not reading the Letter* which You broke open from the best motives. I confess with great Candor, Madam, I had given just Cause for Retaliation: but I felt myself justified in breaking the Seals of your Letters in the Absence of your best Friend, from his Instructions to and Confidence in me. Add to this, an irresistible Inclination to profit of every line from so instructive and so elegant a Pen.—But the Moment You signify your displeasure at such a freedom, I will make a point of disobeying his directions, rather than incur your Censure.

It is near eight Months since the English declared War against this Republick, and the Dutch have done nothing. There may have been one or two Privateers at sea, and they have a small fleet out at present. The most shameful Sloth and the most disgraceful Inactivity have marked their whole Conduct: such are the Principles, systems and Interests of the different Cities and Provinces, there are so many who have Money in the English Funds, ⟨*they are so hampered with a Love of . . .*⟩[1] so much Jealousy of one another, ⟨*so many Anglomanes in and out of Government,*⟩ so many Altercations about augmenting their Army and Navy, so much Crimination and Recrimination, such shifting of Faults from one quarter to another, ⟨*so much Avarice, so little Love of Country and public Spirit, and so little of any thing . . .*⟩;[2] that it will be a long time perhaps before any thing is done to purpose. There must be a great Revolution within before there is much War without. I have written very freely, Madam, and I pray You to take particular Care of this Letter. The Americans that are here feel more for the Injuries and Insults this Country has recieved from England, than the Dutch themselves—but I will quit the subject, and I wish to Heaven I was going to quit the Country. There are many worthy Characters in the Republic, real Patriots, and they are pitied, but at large (the Country in general I mean), they have experienced as small a share of that tender sentiment as they deserve. Perhaps they mean to stand still and see their Salvation. May it come to them in due Season.

You will please to present my Duty and Respects where due, and to remember me affectionately to your family.

I have the Honor to be, with the most perfect Respect, Madam, your most obedient and much obliged humble Servant,   JT[3]

RC (Adams Papers). Two passages, heavily scored out because Thaxter evidently thought them too "freely" critical of the Dutch to be entrusted to any eye at all, have been only partially reconstructed editorially.

[1] Remainder of scored-out passage, some eight or ten words, illegible.
[2] One or two scored-out words illegible.
[3] The initialed signature is a monogram.

John Quincy Adams to John Adams

O.S. St Petersburg August 21st 1781

Honour'd Sir   [*1 September* 1781 N.S.][1]

We arrived here on Monday the 16/27 instant having left Amsterdam the N.S. 7th of July And rode the greatest part of the way day and night. The distance is about 2400 English Miles.[2]

The first place of any consequence we stopp'd at was Berlin the capital of the king of Prussia's Dominions; this is a very pretty town, much more so than Paris, or London as Mr. Dana says; but it will be still more so if the present King's plan is adopted by his successor, for wherever there is a row of low, small houses he sends the owners out of them, pulls them down and has large, elegant houses built in the same place and then sends the owners in again. But notwithstanding this, he is not beloved in Berlin, and every body says publicly what he pleases against the king; but as long as they do not go any farther than words, he don't take any notice of it but says that as long as they give him all he asks, they may say what they will.

But they have a great reason to complain of him, for he certainly treats them like Slaves; Among other things, if a farmer has two or more sons the eldest[3] inherits all the land and all the others (when of age) are soldiers for life at a gros and a half which is about two pence sterling per day, and they must with that find their own provisions; if a farmer has but one Son He inherits his land; whenever a

Vacation happens in any regiment, he chuses one of his subjects to fill the place and this subject from that time becomes a soldier for life; every body that is tall enough is subject to this law. In peace time the Native troops are disbanded Nine months in a year, and in all that time their pay ceases and they must get their living as they can.

There is nothing very remarkable in Dantzic, Konigsberg, or Riga; in coming to this last we pass'd thro' Courland, a province which does strictly speaking belong to Poland but Russia has much more influence there than Poland itself in that Province. All the Farmers are in the most abject slavery, they are bought and sold like so many beasts, and are sometimes even chang'd for dogs or horses. Their masters have even the right of life and death over them, and if they kill one of them they are only obliged to pay a trifling fine; they may buy themselves but their masters in general take care not to let them grow rich enough for that; if any body buys land there he must buy all the slaves that are *upon it.*

Narva is the last place which we stopp'd at before our arrival here, it is a small, insignificant town but will be always famous for the battle fought there.⁴ As to this place, I have not been here long enough to know much about it, but by what we have seen of it I think it to be still handsomer than Berlin. The streets are large and the houses very well built but it is not yet half finish'd and will require another century to be render'd compleat.

Just before we got to Berlin, by the carelessness of a postillion our carriage overset and broke so that Mr. Dana was obliged to buy another there but luckily no body was hurt by the fall.

Nothing else Extraordinary befel us on our journey.

I am your dutiful Son, John Q. Adams

RC (Adams Papers); addressed: "A Son Excellence Monsieur Adams Ministre Plenipotentiare des Etats-Unis de L'Amerique à Amsterdam."; endorsed: "J. Q. Adams 21. Aug. Ansd. 15. Decr. 1781." LbC (Adams Papers); the first true letterbook entry in Lb/JQA/1 (Adams Papers, Microfilms, Reel No. 125); see descriptive note on AA2 to JQA, 24 May, above.

¹ Adams Papers editorial style requires adhering to new style dates (eleven days later than old style) when either old style is known to have been used or double dates appear in the documents. This is one of the rare cases when JQA gives an old style date only.

² For the circumstances leading to this journey, see above, JA to AA, 11 July, and note 3 there. For Dana's and JQA's itinerary across Europe see JQA, Diary, 7 July – 27 Aug. 1781; Francis Dana, Journal from Amsterdam to St. Petersburg, July–Aug. 1781 (MHi:Dana Papers); Dana to JA, 28 Aug. / 8 Sept. 1781 (Adams Papers; JA, *Works,* 7:461–463).

³ Two words supplied from LbC; RC torn by seal.

⁴ Charles XII of Sweden defeated a greatly superior force of Russians at Narva in 1700.

James Lovell to Abigail Adams

Aug. [*i.e.* September] 4th. 1781 [1]

Supposing Col. Laurens to have arrived at Rh. Island, I was greatly chagrined when he told me he had no Letters for you; and I was searching his papers to pick from them all the Comfort I could, to be transmitted to Braintree, when I found he had landed at Boston and had sent you a Message of what Satisfaction he could furnish relative to your dear Partner and your Children. What I told you from *Mason* was indubitably true being all in the Train of natural Consequence to what is now communicated to us. [2]

We are, at this present Writing, in high Glee with our General in the City and the french Troops encamped on the Commons, and with the Log Book of a Vessel this Afternoon, putting the highest probability of compleat Success upon the present military Movements. [3] I want only my Spectacles which are left at the State House to make me quite happy by enabling me to prosecute the pleasing Task of Correspondence with *one of* the ——est and ——est and ——est Women. I am sure Madam there is nothing of Flattery or *im*proper Affection in those half written Epithets though they partake of the superlative Degree. I am equally sure that the Spirit of Misinterpretation of any one of your Circle can find no Malice there: It is impossible for a single Heart in this City to feel malicious while the Bells are so sweetly chiming—always however excepting the Hearts of the Tories.

JL

Your Letter of July 20 / Aug. 6 reached me yesterday.

RC (Adams Papers).

[1] Date corrected from internal evidence and the sequence of AA-Lovell letters and replies.

[2] See Lovell's (intercepted) letter to AA of 24 Aug., above.

[3] Rochambeau's army, together with a part of Washington's army, marched through Philadelphia on their progress south to Yorktown on 3 to 5 September. For the excitement this martial display stirred in that city see letters in Burnett, ed., *Letters of Members*, 6:205–207.

Abigail Adams to James Lovell

Sepber 12 1781

I cannot swallow your prohibition with a good grace and yet I am glad I know the real cause of Marias Silence to my repeated invitation. [1] On one account I could have wished that the Letter containing the conference between Portia and Cornelia might not have been communicated.[2] Portia is loth that Maria should be witness to the freedom of her pen least unknowing to all the circumstances which have calld it forth she should judge hardly of her intentions.—Of her Friend she is not affraid, yet when she sees him so nearly touched she feels both pain and pleasure. In the anxiety he discovers, he gives full proof of the Sincerity of his attachment where alone it is due, and if he feels a pain let it serve to Gaurd his words and actions with the Strictest Scrutiny. The unhappy of every denomination have a claim upon a Benevolent Heart—yet I know not, if that very principal which leads us to sympathize with the afflicted may not so deeply Interest a Generous mind, as to be miscontrued by a world too apt to judge more by outward appearance than to trace the real Source from whence they Spring.

I had no thoughts of entering deeply or so seriously into matters which personally so little concernd me as I find I have insensibly been drawn into, but if you have no other cause for uneasyness than what has fallen from my pen let not that wound you. You have sometimes given a latitude to your pen which I thought exceptionable and I have ever told you so with the fredom of a Friend. At the same time I could not hear unkind or injurious reflections and insinuations without hinting them to you—and wishing you to remove one great cause from whence I supposed them to arise. But no intimation could have possibly escaped me where I know you to repose your utmost confidence. Maria therefore might have visited B———n[3] unpoisoned even by Cornelia who is not a resident here and who had she been would not have wounded her. But to be very sincere Sir I do not think female Slander has been the busyest—you might possibly find it in the city where you reside. I wish to close a subject upon which too much has prehaps been already written by one who has no other claim to attention than Friendship may demand and who thinks too favourably of the party to give credit to more than *a degree of imprudence*. If I was possessd of Parissian delicacy I might notice your *consequences*, but as I am not I can only advise to discretion.[4]

I freely own I should have been made misirable for a time under certain circumstances. Too great anxiety put a period to the existance of one at the very time you have hinted at and came nigh finishing the other.

Heaven only knows what might have been the concequences under a still greater degree of anxiety.

Are you very sick?—poor Maria—how anxious must She feel. Why did you not leave that pestilential air before this Sickly Season. You have scarcly ever escaped—why will you not learn prudence? Have you a good Nurse? You ought to have. I know from the Benevolence of your own Heart you would make a good one. Gladly would Portia administer to your relief were you within her reach. Tis due to the Friendly hand which neither pain or Sickness could ever restrain from affording ease and satisfaction to a mind possibly too anxious—and it has done so in the assureances given that no ill will presided in your assembly whose measures have lately given me pain. For myself I have little ambition or pride—for my *Husband* I freely own I have much. With him this rustick cottage would yeald me all that high fancy forms or lavish hearts could wish—Truth Goodness honour Harmony and Love—Retirement rural quiet Friendship Books—ease and alternate Labour—usefull life—progressive Virtue, and approveing Heaven.

But [since] [5] the stormy Scenes of life have disturbed this peacefull tranquility and calld him forth a principal actor upon the Stage, my ambition is that he exhibits there a character which shall do Honour to his country whilst he secures to it Freedom, independance, and fame. And whilst he is invariably persueing its best Interest divested as I know him to be of self Interested views and private Emolument, Gaurd and protect his Honour ye who ought to be a terror to evil doers and a praise to those who do well.

You will have received Col. Laurence [John Laurens] before this reaches you. I was much dissapointed in not hearing from his transatlantick Excellency as the British call him by Col. Laurence. I hope however that congress have dispatches from him. Mr. L[aurenc]e is a Gentleman of so much dispatch that I had no opportunity to see him. We have some curious publications in our papers since his arrival which I believe with discretion.

I hope he has succeeded well, if he has not I dare say it has not been oweing to want of zeal, firmness or industry. If any thing is communicable I hope you will be well enough to let me hear from you. I shall be very anxious till I do for I assure you I feel much Interested in your Health and happiness a large share of which is most sincerely wished you by your ever affectionate Friend,   Portia

Dft (Adams Papers); without indication of addressee; docketed by CFA at head of text with date only.

[1] See Lovell to AA, 17 July, above.
[2] AA to Lovell, 23 June, above.
[3] Thus in MS, but AA must have meant Braintree, where this letter was written, not Boston, where Mrs. Lovell lived.
[4] This and what follows in the next two brief paragraphs is cryptic but apparently echoes sentiments in the first paragraph of Lovell to AA, 10 Aug., above.
[5] Word editorially supplied.

Isaac Smith Sr. to John Adams

Boston Sept. 13th. 1781

Itt is sometime since any of your friends have had a line from you though many Vessells have Arrived from France by which conveyance they have been expecting letters from you.

There has been Three frigates with money, some for the Congress, and Cloathing. The Marquis Lafaett that had a quantity of Cloathing is supposd to have founderd.

We have been very much troubeld on Our Eastern Coast and have lost some very Valuable Vessells taken in Our bay. A french frigate about Ten days ago coming from Piscataqua haveing a Mast ship under convoy was taken by a 50 Gun ship after a very smart engagement. The Mast ship escapd.

Last week Traitor Arnold and a Colo. Mongomery came Over from N York to N London with about 1400 and burnt about 120. houses &c. before Assistance could be had. They took the fort commanded by a Colo. Ledger who defended itt as long as he was Able and then surrended (he delivered his sword up to the surviveing officer Colo. Ayre [Eyre] & C. Montgomery ⟨*being kild*⟩), after which he with about 70. were put to the sword. They find they cant conquer so go upon distroying property.

But that method dont make proselids for a Gentleman from Virginia tells me all the time they have been there their has not three Inhabitants joyned them. On the Contrary, every One that was before in their favor have become the greatest Wiggs, Scotchmen likewise.

There is Advise of a Vessell from Holland being taken and carried into Bermuda, belonging to Philadelphia which itts said left Holland the 16th. June.

Count Degass [de Grasse] Arrived att Virginia the 24th. Ulto. with ⟨36⟩ sail of the line. Genl. Washington with part of his Army and Count Deshombo [de Rochambeau] are gone to Virginia, with a view, iff the french can get the Mastery by Sea, to see Cornwallis.

I am Sr. Yr. Most O. Servt.,   Isaac Smith

Last sabbath a Certain worthy Old Doctor C   y[1] exprest himself Good Lord iff thou pleasest to continue the Warr let Our enemies fite like Men and not Act as savages and brute beasts.

PS   17th. We have Authentick Accounts from Genl. Green that on the 18th August he had an engagement near Charlestown, defeated the whole party took 150 prisoners besides which were 140. horse— the chief of these baggage and Waggons in which were 720 Guineas which he distributed Among his soilders—burnt 5 Vessells with store; and drove the remainder of what of the party[2] into Charlestown, so that he is in possession of that Country except Charlestown and Oranburgh. To day an express is Arrived with Advise of Count De Grasse arriveing att Virginia the 26th. Ulto. landed 3,000 Troops, had 28 sail of the line. Count De Gassee took a packet from Carolinia with Lord Rawden on board bound to England.

There has been an Engagement between Count Degass, and Graves Wood[3] &c. which went from N York with 21 sail of the line and a Number of frigates off the Capes of Virginia the 5th. Instant, but have not been Able to here how itt has ended.

As Count Degass had sent some of his ships up the river and Barraas with 7 ships from Rd. Island not joyned him am Affraid how matters are. The latter, there is some danger of the English falling in with seperate, but hope Otherwise.

As we have no Vessell bound to Holland, did not know but the[4] way I forward this might reach you as soon as any Other some part of the intelligence being of a publick and something interesting.— Judge Cranch from home to day all well.

21st.

Genl. Washington and Count Deshombo went down the Elk the 8th. with 8,000 Troops.

22d.

This Morning letters by Capt. Newman Arrived in Town. Your publick Letters are going forward by Express. Your Letter Judge Cranch carries this Afternoon to Mrs. Adams.[5]

RC (Adams Papers); endorsed by John Thaxter: "Isaac Smith Esqr. 13th. Septr. 1781."

[1] Presumably Rev. Charles Chauncy (1705-1787), minister of the First Church in Boston for sixty years.

[2] Thus in MS.

[3] Smith's error for Adm. Samuel Hood (later Viscount Hood), who commanded the rear of Adm. Thomas Graves' fleet in the Battle of the Capes, which resulted in the French under de Grasse retaining command of the Virginia coast.

[4] MS: "they."

[5] JA to AA, 22 May, above; see AA's reply, 29 Sept., below.

James Lovell to Abigail Adams

Madam   Sepr. 15. 1781

Under a Date of Aug. 24 I did myself the Pleasure to endeavour to convey to you later Information respecting your dear Connection in

Holland than you had before received, but my Letter was with others carried to New York.[1] Mr. Adams and Family were well May 28th; and he had a few Days before taken upon himself much more of public Character than at any prior Time. Instead of Lodgings he took an House with Equipage and Servants in Proportion. It was judged to be according to the Wishes of the Dutch Government. Capt. Mason who gave me the Information had been captured so that he cautiously sunk all his Dispatches. I do not find any Particulars by Mr. Laurens worth communicating in regard to the Affairs of Holland. I have before me a Letter of Mr. Adams to him dated May 8th. in which he says: "I have communicated my Credentials to the States General, who after the Deliberations which the Form of their Constitution requires will determine whether they can receive them or not. It will probably be *long* before they decide."[2] His Change in Appearance towards the End of the Month makes me conjecture he was a little mistaken. He must in a few Days after Writing have received our Resolves passed March 1st. upon the compleat Signature of the Articles of Confederation, which gave him new Confidence.

Perhaps before the Chevalier L'Etombe, the Bearer, leaves Philadelphia we may have Something authentic from Cheseapeak of the agreable Kind: I will not give you *Baltimore Reports*, which are become proverbial, for Falsities.

Rivington got so little by the late Capture of our Mail, that he was induced to misspell, mispoint, and misletter to afford Amusement to his Customers by the Assurance of a *literatim* and *verbatim* publication. My Letter is printed without being directed to any Body and is signed J.S.

I imprudently mentioned that you might momently expect Commodore Gillon, and a Capt. Eden at Boston. I now hope they are arrived.

I wish you every Happiness and am with much Esteem Your humble Servant, JL

RC (Adams Papers). In the Adams Papers as arranged and bound up by the family in the 19th century, the second sheet of Lovell's letter to AA of 13 July (above; see descriptive note there) was placed with the present letter as if it were a continuation of it; and a paragraph of the supposed continuation was printed by Burnett in his *Letters of Members*, 6:219, under the later and wrong date.

[1] This letter is printed above under its date from Rivington's *Royal Gazette*, the only known surviving text; see notes there.

[2] Quoted from JA to John Laurens, 8 May (LbC, Adams Papers). The complete text is in JA, *Works*, 7:415–416.

John Quincy Adams to John Thaxter

Sir   St: Petersbourg September 8/19 1781

We arriv'd here the 16th of August old stile,[1] (which is universally used yet, all over this Country;) having left Berlin, the 2d. of the same month, new stile, and rode the whole way, day and night, stopping only at the principal towns which lay in our way, viz: at Dantzic, three days, at Konigsberg, one, at Memel, one night, at Riga, four days, and at Narva, two: between these places, which are distant from one another, from one to four hundred English Miles there is hardly a Village to be seen. The whole route from Berlin here may be call'd a barren desart; and except a few places in Pomerania, Courland and Livonia, the road is pretty much like that between Bayonne and Bordeaux. When we left Prussia we entered into the province of Courland, which belongs to Poland, here all the Farmers are in the greatest slavery imaginable, their masters having the right of life and death over them, which they have not in Russia, tho' the common people are all Slaves.

The city of Petersbourg is the finest I ever saw, it is by far superior to Paris, both for the breadth of its streets, and the elegance of the private buildings, which are for the most part made of brick, and plastered over in imitation of Stone; but the police of the city is very bad, for almost every night, we hear of some robbery or murder committed.

As to the climate, the season is not yet far enough advanced for us to be able to form a judgement about it, but as yet, we don't find that it is colder here than it is in our country at this time; they have but little Sun here in the winter, for on the shortest day of the year it is but five hours and a half above the horizon, and on the longest it is eighteen and a half.

The common people here wear almost universally long beards, that is, the men; and in the summer cloth gowns which come down to their knees, and in the winter sheep skin ones, and most commonly boots. The people of fashion wear cloth clothes winter and summer, but in the winter when they go out, they put on furs, and boots lined with flannel, which they slip off as soon as they go into a house.

I am Sir, your most obedient and most humble Servant.

LbC (Adams Papers).

[1] 27 Aug. new style.

Abigail Adams to James Lovell

20[?] Sepbr. [1781][1]

In truth Friend thou art a Queer Being—laugh where I must, be candid where I can.—Your pictures are Hogarths. I shall find you out by and by—I will not Build upon other peoples judgements. My *philosopher* (I like the Name exceedingly) used to say I was a physiognomist. I have tried not unsuccessfully to find out the Heart of many a one by the countanance. I do not recollect that I ever had that opportunity with my correspondent, twice only in my life do I remember to have seen him, and then my harp was so hung upon the willows that I cared not whose face was sweet or sour. Yet do I remember the traits of Friendship and Benevolence were so conspicuous that they demanded a return in kind, and something like compassion, pitty, commisiration, call it by what Name you please I remember to have felt for the unjust sufferings of a worthy Man. But I did not study the Eye that best Index to the mind to find out how much of Rogury there was in the Heart, so here I have been these four years obtaining by peacemeal what I could have learnt in half an hour.

You may easily suppose that I have before me your Letters of August 4th and 23 and Sepbr. 10th[2] but where the inteligence is which you say you told me from Mason I know not. Possibly Rivington may give it to me.[3] I suspect it was with the captured post. I perceive you are up in alt with your Superlatives. So am I. Rejoice with me, for I have got a Letter at last. My Dear Friend well—that is a cordial to my Heart. Longs to come home to his American dame—for all the French Spanish Dutch Madams. That is flattering to my vanity—but he does not say so. I only find it out by his saying if he once gets back he will never leave me again. If I ever live to see that *once* I will hold him to his word. My dear Charles, sweet Boy, been sick of a Fever, and no Mother at hand to nurse and administer to the dear fondling. How does this inteligence soften every fibre and improve the Mothers sad Capacity of pain.

Thus do I run on because I know you take an Interest in my happiness and because I know I can make you feel. I hate an unfealing mortal. The passions are common to us all, but the lively sweet affection[s] are the portion only of a chosen few. I rejoice to find you have recoverd your Health and Spirits. Maria too tells me she has been sick, by Sympathy I suppose—that she will come and see me as soon as she can ride. The embargo is taken of[f] I find. If she comes suppose I should make an exchange, give her my Letters for hers. No I wont, I will keep them for—for—there would be too much honey for me who have no right to it.—Laugh and Satirize as much as you please. I Laugh with you to see what a figure your inventive Genious makes in picking up terms—tis necessary to keep a Watchfull Eye over you.

Now to be a little serious, I think my good Gentleman is not very well pleased with the slow movements of the Mynheres—they do not accord with his feelings. He has no doubt forwarded his memorial with his Letters.[4] The date of mine is the 22 of May. If any thing of a later date is sent to Congress, I wish you to transmit it by a private hand, I fear the post. We are in great hopes and high expectations of good News from the South. May it be better than our deserts or our hopes will again be Blasted. This vessel brings us News of a Naval engagement between Sir Peter Parker and some dutch Ships. You will have it in the papers. Many thanks for your attention to my and others things. If I had known of your Intention of again opening them I should have requested you to have kept out the white cloth and blew Sasnet to have forwarded provided an opportunity had offered. The rest may take their chance when they can.

I did not misapply Cornelia for Portia. I new it to be no fiction. There realy existed the Dialogue I related and nearly in the same words as I could recollect.

Dft (Adams Papers); without indication of addressee; CFA added "1781" to AA's incomplete date. Written on both sides of a folio cover sheet of a letter, date unknown, sent and franked by James Lovell in Philadelphia to AA in Braintree "To the Care of Isaac Smith Esq Boston." AA's extremely careless punctuation has been slightly regularized for clarity.

[1] The real date of this letter is questionable. AA clearly wrote "20 Sepbr." at head of Dft, but in the course of it she mentions receiving "a Letter at last" from JA and specifically identifies his letter as that of 22 May, above. That letter came by Capt. Joseph Newman in the *Gates*, the precise date of whose arrival in Newburyport, 21 Sept., we know from the *Boston Gazette* of 24 Sept. (p. 3, col. 1), and whose mail reached Boston on 22 Sept. (see the last postscript in Isaac Smith Sr.'s letter to JA, 13–22 Sept., above; also Richard Cranch to JA, 26 Sept., below). In replying to AA on 9 Oct., below, Lovell speaks of "your Favour of Sepr. 26th," for which date *no* letter of hers, either

Dft or RC, has been found, and both there and in subsequent acknowledgments (29 Nov., 4 Dec., both below) Lovell, though echoing some points in the present letter, mentions others *not* in the text as we have it. The best explanation that can be offered is that AA did indeed misdate her Dft (20 for 26 Sept.) and that in the (missing) RC she extended the text and dealt with matters, or raised questions, not in Dft. Both were common enough practices with her, but the evidence available at this time is sufficient only to question, not to redate, the present letter.

[2] These letters are all in the Adams Papers. That of 4 Aug. was really written on 4 Sept. and is printed above under

its correct date. That of 23 Aug. is also printed above. That of 10 Sept., in a Shandean vein but of little substance, is omitted here.

³ This was correct. See Lovell's (in-tercepted) letter to AA of 24 Aug., above.

⁴ That is, in his letters to Congress which had come in the *Gates* and were being forwarded from Boston.

Richard Cranch to John Adams

Hond. and dear Sir   Boston Sepr: 26th. 1781

Tho' I have often wrote to your Excellency, yet I have not had the Happiness of a Line from you since you left us. I have this Day heard that Mr. Codman, who had his mercantile Education under our worthy Uncle Isaac Smith Esqr, will sail tomorrow Morning for Spain.¹ I therefore take the liberty of sending a few Lines by him, tho' the Conveyance be somewhat circuitous.

Our Affairs at the Southward wear a very pleasing Aspect at present. The French Fleet under the Count De Grass, consisting of twenty-eight Sail of the Line arrived lately at Chessepeak-Bay, and landed three Thousand Men in James River, to reinforce the Marquis De Fayett. General Washington and the Count De Rochambeau with eight Thousand French and American Regular Troops arrived at the Head of Elk, from Rhode Island and North River about the 8th. Instant, where every thing was ready to carry them down the Bay to assist in the great Cause of taking Lord Cornwallis and his Army, and so to free Virginia and the southern States;—an Event that seems in the highest degree probable, nay, we hear from various Quarters that Cornwallis has already proposed Terms on which he would surrender, but which are not accepted. Genl. Green has driven all the Troops that remain in South Carolina, into Charlstown; so that the English hold no other Post in that State at present. Lord Rawdon himself, with a number of others, was taken Prisoner by the Count De Grass's Fleet in their Passage to Virginia: He was on board a Pacquet bound to England. The General Court, now sitting here, received Information yesterday from Genl. Parsons near N. York, that a large Embarkation is taking place at New York, but he could not learn where they were destin'd. Capt. Newman in the Brig Gates from Amsterdam arrived at Newbury Port last Week in five Weeks. Your Lady received by him your Letter of the 22d of May inclosing your excellent Address to the States General of the United Provinces. I have put it into the Press, and it will be out tomorrow.² I had a few Days before met with the same in French, and had just finished a Translation of it when yours came to hand. I have not yet seen Mr.

Brush who came Passenger in Capt. Newman, but I hear he brings information that your dear Johnney is gone to Petersbourg with Mr. Dana, and that Master Charles is coming home in Comr. Gellion [Gillon]. I want much to see Mr. Brush, that I may hear more particularly.[3] Your most amiable Lady and Children were well to day, when I received a Line from her,[4] dictated by unaffected Tenderness to you and the dear Little Boys, requesting me to see Mr. Brush and enquire every thing that he knows concerning you and them. I have not yet been happy enough to see him.—We have not received a Line from you since last October, except the Letter mentioned above.

The Action between the Dutch Squadron and Admiral Parker on the 5th. Ulto., is worthy the antient Batavian Spirit. I long to see that Spirit fully rouz'd. Time will not permit me to enlarge. I must however give you the Pleasure of letting you know that we are all well in the several Families of Braintree, Weymouth, Hingham &c. longing for the arrival of Comr. Gellion, Capt. Hayden, &c.; when we hope to hear more particularly from you, Cousin Thaxter, &c. In Expectation of which I remain with the highest Esteem and warmest Affection your obliged Friend and Bror.,   Richard Cranch

Please to present my kind Regards to Mr. Thaxter and tell him I have wrote to him several times, but have never received an Answer. I fear most of my Letters to You and Him have miscarried.[5]

P.S. Should the fate of War throw Mr. Codman in your way, and he should want your Assistance I would warmly recommend him as a young Gentleman of a good Family, and worthy of your Notice. His Brother is Partner with Cousin Billy Smith.

Thursday Morning. 8. o'Clock. As Mr. Codman is not yet gone on board I have enclos'd this day's Paper.[6]

RC (Adams Papers); addressed: "To His Excellency John Adams Esqr: Minister from the United States of America to the States Genll: of the United Provinces. Residing at the Hague."; stamped postal mark: "ASTURIAS"; endorsed: "Mr. Cranch Sept. 26. 1781." Dft (MHi:Cranch Papers); written on both the blank and printed sides of a broadside resolve of the General Court, "State of Massachusetts-Bay. In the House of Representatives, June 8, 1779," instructing towns to settle their accounts with the State for payment to soldiers' families. Dft omits a portion of the postscripts; see note 5. For the (missing) enclosure in RC, see note 2.

[1] Stephen or Richard Codman, both Boston merchants and younger sons of John Codman Sr., whose eldest son, John Jr., was a business partner of AA's "Cousin Billy Smith," as mentioned in the postscript to this letter. See Cora Codman Wolcott, *The Codmans of Charlestown and Boston, 1637–1929*, Brookline, 1930, p. 63–66.

[2] JA's *Memorial* of 19 April 1781 was

printed in the *Independent Chronicle* of 27 Sept., p. 1–2, and a copy of that issue of the paper was enclosed in Cranch's letter, as the postscript states.

³ Eliphalet Brush is repeatedly mentioned as a member of the growing American circle in Amsterdam in JQA's Diary, 10 June *et seq.*, and was present at the Fourth of July celebration held there this year. He brought JA's dispatches for Congress in the *Gates* and is the only

passenger noted in the *Boston Gazette's* account of the arrival of that vessel (24 Sept., p. 3, col. 1). The *Gazette* identifies him as "of the State of New York." Brush called on AA and furnished her with much-wanted family news; see AA to JA, 29 Sept., below.

⁴ Not found.
⁵ Dft ends at this point.
⁶ See note 2.

William Jackson to John Adams

Corunna September 26. 1781

Lest the date of my letter should alarm your Excellency, I am happy in prefacing it with an assurance that your dear little Boy, who is now at my elbow, is perfectly well.

Mr. Gillon (to the baseness of whose character no term of reproach is equal) has, after adding insult to injury landed us in Spain. I would enter into the detail of his unparalleled villainies—but the late hour at which I write obliges me to defer it until the next post.[1] Colonel Searle, Colonel Trumbull, and myself propose going to France on board a frigate which will sail in twelve or fourteen days. I shall take Charles with me, and should your Excellency honor me with farther instructions respecting him, I will follow them with pleasure and punctuality. You will please to forward these instructions to your Correspondents at the different Ports in France, as it is not yet known to which the Ship goes.

I shall do myself the honor to write you fully by the next post. Your goodness must excuse my present brevity. I was unwilling to lose the first conveyance to announce our situation—and the extreme hurry in which I write will scarce admit my adding Colonel Searle's, Col. Trumbull's and my own affectionate and respectful compliments to your Excellency and Mr. Thaxter.—Be assured your Son's happiness will be my peculiar care—he has, and continues to read french and english to me daily, and is in every respect the Boy you would wish him to be, endearing himself to every-body.

I am with the most perfect esteem and respect, Dear Sir, Your most obedt. Servant and sincere friend,   W. Jackson

RC (Adams Papers).

[1] For the background of the remarkable voyage of the *South Carolina*, which sailed surreptitiously under the command of Alexander Gillon from the Texel on 12 Aug., with CA, Capt. Joshua Barney, William Jackson, James Searle, John

Trumbull, and Benjamin Waterhouse, among others, as passengers, see above, Waterhouse to JA, 26 Dec. 1780, note 4; JA to AA, 11 July 1781, and note 2 there. Gillon had wandered in the North Sea for weeks, circumnavigated the British Isles, and at length put into La Coruña in Spain for want of water and provisions to make the Atlantic crossing. During one storm that was encountered, Joshua Barney had had to take command to save the vessel (John Trumbull, *Autobiography*, ed. Theodore Sizer, New Haven, 1953, p. 76). In this or another storm the vessel also suffered some damage and therefore required repairs. At La Coruña, CA, under Jackson's care, together with some of the other passengers, left the *South Carolina* and sought other transportation home. Waterhouse elected to continue with Gillon and had further adventures in the West Indies. These sequels will unfold in the correspondence, during the next nine months, of Jackson, Waterhouse, Capt. Hugh Hill of the *Cicero* (which ultimately brought CA home), and Isaac Smith Sr. with JA and AA, and between JA and AA, who both were to go months without word of CA's whereabouts.

Abigail Adams to John Adams

My dearest Friend   Sepbr. 29 1781

Three days only did it want of a year from the date of your last Letter,[1] when I received by Capt. Newman in the Brig Gates your welcome favour of May 22d.

By various ways I had collected some little intelligence of you, but for six months past my Heart had known but little ease—not a line had reachd me from you, not a syllable from my children—and whether living or dead I could not hear. That you have written many times, I doubted not, but such is the chance of War; and such the misfortune attending a communication between absent Friends.

I learn by Mr. Brush, that Mr. Dana is gone to Petersburgh, and with him Master John. For this I am not sorry. Mr. Danas care and attention to him, I shall be well satisfied in—and Russia is an Empire I should be very fond of his visiting. My dear Charles I hear is comeing home with Gillion.

I know not your motives for sending him but dare say you have weighty reasons. That of his Health is alone sufficient, if the low countries are as prejudicial to him, as I fear they are—and will be to his Father too. Why did you not write me about it? At first I learnt it, only by hearing of a list of passengers who were to come in the Indian,[2] amongst which was a son of Mr. A—s. This made me very uneasy—I had a thousand fears and apprehensions. Nor shall I be much at ease, you may well suppose, untill I hear of her arrival. I fear she will be an object, for the British to persue. The Event I must commit to the Supreme Ruler of the universe.—Our Friends here are all well, your Mother has recoverd beyond my expectation, my Father too is in good Health for his years. Both our parents remember you with affection.

General Green, is making the Requisition you require, and setling the preliminarys for a Peace, by extirpating the British force from Carolina. We are from the present prospect of affairs in daily expectation that Cornwallis will meet the Fate of Burgoine. God Grant it— and that this winter may produce to America an *honorable Peace.* But my fears are well grounded when I add, that some of your Colleagues are unfit for the Buisness and I really am in suspence whether you will hold your Garbled commission, for reasons to which you will be no stranger before this reaches you. But if you resign, I am not the only person by hundreds who dread the consequences, as it is probable you will find, from instructions which I hear are to be sent, from several States to their delegates in Congress. You have a delicate part to act. You will do what you esteem to be your duty, I doubt not; fearless of consequences, and futurity will discriminate the Honest Man from the knave tho the present Generation seem little disposed to.

I cannot write so freely as I wish. Your Memorial is in high estimation here.

So you have set down at Amsterdam in the House keeping way. What if I should take a trip across the Atlantick? I tell Mrs. Dana we should pass very well for Natives.—I have received a very polite Letter from Mr. DeNeufvilla.[3] How did this Man discover, that extolling my Husband was the sweetest Musick in my ears? He has certainly touched the key which vibrates Harmony to me!

I think I have requested you to send me a chest of Bohea Tea, by any vessel of Mr. Tracys. Do not think me extravagant—I economize with the utmost Frugality I am capable of, but our Taxes are so high, and so numerous, that I know not which way to turn. I paied 60 hard dollars this week for a State and county Rate. I have 30 more to pay immediately for hireing a Man for 6 months in the Service, and a very large town tax, now comeing out. Hard Money is our only currency. I have a sum of old and new paper which lies by me useless at present. Goods of the West India kind are low as ever they were— Bills Sell greatly below par. Hard money is very scarce, but I hope never to see an other paper Medium. Difficult as the times are, and dull as Buisness is, we are in a better situation than we were before.

Where is my Friend Mr. Thaxter? that not a line has reachd me from him? His Friends are all well, but longing and impatient to hear from him. We see by the paper that he was well enough to celebrate independence on the fourth of july.[4]—The Robinhood had Letters to all my Friends which I hope you have received. I send many to Bilboa, do you get any from thence, pray write to me by way of France and Bilboa.

This is to go by a Brig to France which I heard of but yesterday. You have I suppose received a commission for forming a Quadrupple alliance—such an one is made out.

O my dear Friend, how far distant is the day when I may expect to receive you in your Native Land?

Haughty Britain sheath your sword in pitty to yourselves. Let not an other village be added to the long list of your depredations. The Nations around you shudder at your crimes. Unhappy New London Named after your capital—may she close the devastation.

How many tender Sentiments rise to mind when about to bid you adieu. Shall I express them or comprise them all in the assurance of being ever Ever Yours,   Portia

RC (Adams Papers); endorsed by John Thaxter: "Portia Septr. 29. 1781."

[1] His letter of 25 Sept. 1780, acknowledged by AA in her reply of 25 Dec. 1780, both above.

[2] The original name of the frigate which Commodore Gillon had obtained from the French government and renamed the *South Carolina* was *L'Indien*

(*So. Car. Hist. & Geneal. Mag.*, 9:199–200 [Oct. 1908]).

[3] Of 25 May, above. The original came by Capt. Newman in the *Gates*.

[4] See above, John Thaxter to AA, 21 July, and note 2 there. This letter had obviously not yet been received.

Benjamin Waterhouse to John Adams

Dear Sir   Corunna Septr. 30th. 1781

I imagine You heard by the last Post of our being at this Place, and the reasons of our coming here. It is a great disappointment to Us all; yet the danger of our proceeding in the Condition We were in and the hopes of getting out soon, ought to make Us content.

You already know I believe that there has been a very unfortunate difference between two of the Passengers [1] and our Commodore, which has been carried to very great lengths indeed—a private pique has been tortured into a public affair, and matters have gone near to the destruction of our Ship. Affairs however have a better Aspect at present, and I fully believe We shall proceed on to America in a Week or ten days. I am mortified, grievously mortified, that We should injure ourselves in a foreign Country by our little private Animosities. If You ask me what gave rise to this difference? I answer I cannot positively say—various Reasons have been assigned for it. Whatever they may be You will think with me that this place or any other out of America are unfit for settling them, more especially if they any how concern public Affairs. Major Jackson takes Charles with him; as he says he has the absolute Charge of him, I cannot interpose. The Commodore was in some difficulty how to act on this head: he has done however as I should have done under the like Circumstances. If We arrive safe I shall not fail to acquaint his Mother with the reasons for his not coming at the same time I did. I have suffered much Anxiety and Mortification in this dispute, altho' I have not been immediately concerned. Mr. Van Haslet, Le Roy, Bromfield, Brailsford and myself have private Lodgings ashore, where We enjoy Peace and Quietness, and here We chearfully wait until We are called on board again, which I hope will be soon, unless another cruel step should be taken to detain Us and ruin the Ship.

We shall not get the Repairs We wished for, but shall patch up our defects as well as We can. If You wish to know why We proceed to sea at this season without thorough Repairs and ample provisions, I must refer You to Colo. James Searle and Major William Jackson, who I believe are the only People in the World capable of informing You.

With great Respect I am your obliged Friend,   B. Waterhouse

Early Tr (PPAmP); in the hand of John Thaxter, who wrote at head of text: "Copy of a Letter from Dr. Waterhouse to Mr. Adams." The reasons for making this copy (now the only known text) are unknown.

[1] William Jackson and James Searle.

James Lovell to Abigail Adams

Octr. 5. 1781

I doubt not Madam, you have Letters from Mr. Adams of later Date than what we have received but that Fact will not prevent your Expectations of Something from me in the Way of retailed Politicks:— He has sent as I imagine but few duplicates of what are actually on Board Gillon. He dated May 16 and Augst. 3d. from Amsterdam, July 11. 14. 15 from Paris.[1] He thinks Britain altogether insincere as to honorable Peace. He sees in Holland the almost absolute Certainty of ‖no Loan till‖ our Independence ‖is‖ acknowledged by the States General — ‖a distant Period.‖

The other day Mr. Cumberland Dugan sent a Wagon from hence to Boston. He made me hope for a Chance of conveying at least a Part of your Goods, but found it impossible, finally, being obliged to load 400 lb. more than his first Contract. I had the large Chest hooped with Iron, and I hope soon to get an Opportunity of sending it.

I wish you every Happiness being with much Esteem, Madam, Your humble Servant, JL

RC (Adams Papers). Words in cipher have been deciphered between double verticals; in MS they are interlined in the hand of Richard Cranch. On Lovell's cipher see Appendix to this volume.

[1] RC's of the letters mentioned, all addressed to the President of Congress and including two of the first date (16 May), are in PCC, No. 84, III; LbC's are in JA's letterbooks in use at the time (Lb/JA/16–17; Microfilms, Reel Nos. 104–105); printed texts are in Wharton, ed., *Dipl. Corr. Amer. Rev.*, 4:419–421, 560–561, 574, 575–576, 619–621.

John Adams to Abigail Adams

My dearest Friend   Amsterdam October 9. 1781

This is the first Time, I have been able to write you, since my Sickness.—Soon after my Return from Paris, I was seized with a Fever, of which, as the Weather was and had long been uncommonly warm, I took little notice, but it increased very slowly, and regularly, untill it was found to be a nervous Fever, of a dangerous kind, bordering upon putrid. It seized upon my head, in such a manner that for five or six days I was lost, and so insensible to the Operations of the Physicians and surgeons, as to have lost the memory of them. My Friends were so good as to send me an excellent Physician and Surgeon, whose Skill and faithfull Attention with the Blessing of Heaven, have saved my Life. The Physicians Name is Osterdike.[1] The surgeon the same, who cured Charles, of his Wound.[2] I am, however still weak, and whether I shall be able to recover my Health among the pestilential Vapours from these stagnant Waters, I know not.[3]

I hope Charles is well and happy with you, by this Time. He sailed with Commodore Gillon seven Weeks ago. We have no News from Mr. Dana and his young Fellow Traveller, since they left Berlin.

The Pamphlet inclosed, is a Dutch Translation of the Abby Raynals History of the American Revolution. It is a Curiosity for you to lay up.[4]

With Sentiments and Affections that I cannot express, Yours.

RC (Adams Papers). For the enclosure see note 4.

[1] Nicolaas George Oosterdijk (1740–1817), professor of medical theory at Leyden from 1775 (*Nieuw Ned. Biog. Woordenboek*, 3:935–936).

[2] The surgeon is unidentified. CA had been ill in the spring, and it was in part for this reason that he was being sent home, but the editors have found no other allusions to a "Wound" he had sustained.

³ AA did not learn of JA's illness for a long time to come, because this letter was not received for many months; her first reference to the news in it was in her letter to JA of 17 March 1782, below.

JA had returned to Amsterdam from Paris by the end of July. On 24 Aug. he received a letter from Franklin dated on the 16th enclosing a packet from Congress that contained JA's new joint commission and instructions to treat of peace as adopted by Congress in June (Adams Papers; JA, *Works*, 7:456–457). JA replied next day, 25 Aug. (Adams Papers; JA, *Works*, 7:459–461); but on 4 Oct. he wrote again to Franklin in a letter that began: "Since the 25th of August, when I had the honor to write You, this is the first Time that I have taken a Pen in hand to write to any body, having been confined and reduced too low to do any kind of business by a nervous Fever" (PPAmP:Franklin Papers; printed from LbC, Adams Papers, in JA, *Works*, 7:465–466). The letter sent to Franklin is, however, actually in John Thaxter's hand and only signed by JA, as are the two or three other letters sent over his name during the preceding six weeks.

The illness was severe. In apology for having lately written so little to Congress, JA told Pres. Thomas McKean on 15 Oct.:

"[N]ot long after I got home I found myself attacked by a Fever, of which at first I made light, but which increased very gradually and slowly, until it was found to be a nervous Fever of a very malignant kind, and so violent as to de-

prive me of almost all sensibility for four or five days, and all those who cared any thing about me, of the hopes of my life. By the help however of great skill and all powerful Bark I am still alive, but this is the first time I have felt the Courage to attempt to write to Congress. Absence and Sickness are my Apologies to Congress for the few Letters they will receive from me since June.

"Whether it was the uncommon Heat of the Summer, or whether it was the Mass of pestilential Exhalations from the stagnant Waters of this Country that brought this disorder upon me, I know not: but I have every Reason to apprehend, that I shall not be able to re-establish my Health in this Country. A Constitution ever infirm, and almost half an hundred Years old, cannot expect to fare very well amidst such cold damps and putrid Steams as arise from the immense quantities of dead Water that surround it." (PCC, No. 84, III; Wharton, ed., *Dipl. Corr. Amer. Rev.*, 4:780.)

For his later recollection of this illness, see JA, *Corr. in the Boston Patriot*, p. 148, in which he says it resulted from "Anxiety concerning the state of my affairs in Holland," the "unwholesome damps of the night," and "excessive fatigue" from travel and work, and "brought me as near to death as any man ever approached without being grasped in his arms."

⁴ Abbé Guillaume Thomas François Raynal, *Staatsomwenteling van Amerika. Uit het Fransch*, Amsterdam, 1781. Two copies are among JA's books in MB (*Catalogue of JA's Library*, p. 208).

James Lovell to Abigail Adams

Philada. Octr. 9th [1781]

Yesterday's Post brought me your Favour of Sepr. 26th.¹ Your dear Boy Charles should most certainly have had half of the Bed of one of his *Father's* devoted Friends here, if the Winds had so directed the Ship's Course in which he is a Passenger; but I am told she is arrived at Falmouth in Casco Bay. I wish you an happy Meeting with him. I shall be rejoyced to find that the Voyage has been beneficial to his Constitution.

I have already given you the dates of Mr. A's Letters which came by Newman: viz. May 16. July 11. 14. 15. Aug. 3d.[2] In the 1st he says

"This Country is indeed in a melancholy Situation — sunk in Ease, devoted to the Pursuits of Gain, over-shadowed on all sides by more powerful Neighbours, unanimated by a Love of military Glory or any aspiring spirit, feeling little Enthusiasm for the Public, terrified at the Loss of an old Friend and equally terrified at the Prospect of being obliged to form Connexions with a new one, encumbered with a complicated and perplexed Constitution, divided among themselves in Interest and Sentiment, they seem afraid of every Thing. Success on the Part of France, Spain, and especially of America raises their Spirits and advances the Good Cause some what; but Reverses seem to sink them much more." He adds "The War has occasioned such a Stagnation of Business and thrown such Numbers of People out of Employment that I think it is impossible Things should remain long in the present insipid state. One System or another will be pursued. One Party or another will prevail; much will depend on the Events of the War. We have one Security, and I fear but one; and that is the domineering Character of the English who will make Peace with the Republic upon no other Terms than her joining them against all their Enemies in the War; and This, I think, it is impossible she ever should do."

It is to be hoped that the Events of this Campaign will be such as to influence Holland and even Britain to do us Justice. There has been a most severe Engagement on the 8th. of Sepr. in South Carolina.[3] I think I shall be able to send a printed account to Boston by the Bearer of this. It has been spoken of, here for some days; and this Evening Gen. Green's Thanks to his Army are brought to Philada. by a Gentleman of good Character. It is said the Enemy are Sufferers to the Amount of 1100 and our Army to 500. These Numbers being for killed, wounded and missing.—In Virginia Things are proceeding surely and faster than we had a Right to expect.

I have been chagrined about your Goods the last Week. I hoped to send them by two different Opportunities being promised a Chance. I weighed them and bound the heaviest with Iron Hoops ready for loading, but the Waggoners could not take the Charge. I cannot without great Trouble and Injury to the Chest take out the white Broad-Cloth. I will double my Diligence to send the Whole.

Your Attentions to Mrs. Lovell prejudice me so much in your Favour that I can let you call me "queer" or any Thing else that hits your Fancy, provided always that you do not call or even think me *deceitful* when I profess myself with affectionate Respect Madam your Friend & humble Servant, JL

Perhaps after my Profession of Respect it will [be] incongruous to hint that you also Madam are a "queer Being." I verily believe you would be willing to hear any one call your best Friend, "old Darby," rather than to hear it said he appears lively as Chesterfield. You talk of your *Philosopher* and his *Dame*. Why, Nothing was farther from my Intention than your sprightly Husband when I wrote of *your Philosopher*. No, No, he is too modern to be adduced in the Reasoning I sent you. It was your "Antient," Ma'am, that had been held up to me as a Pattern, That Wiseacre, who, "had he lived in the House or Family" &c. &c.

Take the Song of Darby and Joan in Hand and stand before your looking Glass to find the Resemblance;—a pretty *Dame Adams* indeed![4]

You "did not misapply Cornelia for Portia." But, you did, most assuredly. "There was no Fiction in the Story." "The Dialogue really existed as related." I supposed so; and therefore all the little malicious Things I have written were intended [for] Cornelia and not for Portia.

RC (Adams Papers).

[1] Probably the (missing) RC of the (incomplete?) Dft of AA's letter dated 20 Sept., above. Certainly that letter is referred to in the present one, but whether an AA letter of 26 Sept. was also written and is now missing, is not clear.

[2] These letters are accounted for in note 1 on Lovell to AA, 5 Oct., above.

[3] Battle of Eutaw Springs.

[4] Darby and Joan: "A jocose appellation for an attached husband and wife who are 'all in all to each other', especially in advanced years and in humble life"; the names derive from the central figures in a song or ballad published in the *Gentleman's Magazine* in 1735 (OED).

Joseph Gardoqui & Sons to Abigail Adams

Madam the 14th. Octovr. 1781

Since the above duplicatte of our last Respectts to you[1] has Kissed our hands your allways obliging Esteemed favour of the 18th. Jully[2] and therewith your Remmittance for Livers 300 on Paris which in Repply have the pleasure to Informe you has by us been punctually forwarded for Acceptance, as such when in Cash your Account with us will be creditted for the same at the Exchange of 76 Souls per current dollar in Riales 1188 & 29 mrs. of Vellon[3] which if Right be pleased to notte in Conformity with us.

The Brigg Boston Packett Capt. White putt in at Coruna, by

contrary winds from whence we Expectt her hourly, and as you are pleased to directt our shipping the Ammount of the above bill in Sundry goods in her the present Chiefly serves to advice you that it will be with pleasure punctually Comply'd with, by those who Salutting you with due Respectts Subscrive with the highest Reggard & Esteem, Madam, your mt. obt. hble. Servts.,

Joseph Gardoqui & sons

RC (Adams Papers). Follows on same sheet of paper (though it is in a different hand) text of Dupl RC of Gardoqui & Sons to AA, 2 May 1781, q.v. above under that date.

[1] See descriptive note.
[2] Not found.
[3] That is, 1188 reals and 29 maravedis of vellon (or billon), a form of Spanish currency (Patrick Kelly, *The Universal Cambist and Commercial Instructor*, 2d edn., London, 1826, 1:316–318).

John Adams to William Jackson

Amsterdam Oct. 20. 1781

Your Letter, Sir, of the 26 Ult. I received last night, and should have [been] astonished at its date and Contents if I had not seen yours to Mr. De Neufville, of the same date, which he received three days before.

I had ever[1] taken Mr. Gillon, for a Man of Honour, drawn insensibly into difficulties by a Train of Disappointments: but I cannot reconcile his Conduct upon this occasion.—But it is to no Purpose to enlarge upon this Subject.—What is become of the Dispatches to Congress? There were on board half a Cart Load from me. All my Letters to Congress for 6 or 8 months were there.

Your Account of the Health, and especially of the good Behaviour of my dear Charles, gives me great Pleasure.

I can give you, no Instructions what to do with him. If you have a Prospect, of a Passage soon to America, and can conveniently, take him with you, I suppose that would be most agreable to him. In this Case, if you go to Paris, I wish you would leave him in the meantime, in the Care of Mr. Johnson or Mr. Williams at Nantes, or Mr. Cummings at L'orient,[2] desire those Gentlemen to give him a Latin or a French Master, and draw upon me for the Expence. But if you should come to Amsterdam, bring him with you: but in this Case Mr. Charles must lay aside his Thoughts of going to America, untill I go.

I am extreamly sorry you are likely to be embarrassed with the Care of this Child, in Addition to all your other Vexations.

My best Regards to Mr. Searle and Coll. Trumbull. I have received some Letters for Mr. Searle from his Excellency Governor Reed. Should be glad of Mr. Searles directions where to send them.

With great Esteem, I have the Honour to be Sir your most obedient & obliged humb. sert.

Pray what do you intend to do, with the Continental Goods left here?

LbC (Adams Papers).

[1] MS apparently reads "even."

[2] Joshua Johnson (1742–1802), of Maryland and London, whose daughter Louisa Catherine (LCA) was in 1797 to become the wife of JQA; the Johnsons resided at Nantes during the later years of the war, and JA and JQA became familiar with their household there when awaiting passage to America in the spring of 1779 (JA, *Diary and Autobiography*, 2:300, 357–359; Adams Genealogy).

Jonathan Williams (1750–1815), a merchant at Nantes, identified in vol. 3:72, above.

James Cummings, an American merchant at Lorient (JA, *Diary and Autobiography*, 2:357, 370; George H. Lincoln, *A Calendar of John Paul Jones Manuscripts in the Library of Congress*, Washington, 1903, p. 159).

Abigail Adams to John Adams

My dearest Friend   October 21. 1781

It is now four weeks since Capt. Newman arrived in the Brig Gates and brought me your Letter of the 22d of May. It wanted but a few days of a year from the date of your last when this reached me.[1] Time which is said to soften and alleviate Sorrow, encreases anxiety when connected with expectation. This I hourly experience, and more particularly, since Mr. Brush acquainted me that my dear Charles was on Board Commodore Gillion.

3 frigates of the Enemies and a 50 Gun Ship the Chatham, are cruising upon our Coast for the vessels which are expected from Holland. I tremble for the dangers to which he may be exposed from the Enemy, and of our coast, if he should not speedily arrive, but there is one consolation to which I must ever resort, in all my anxietyes. I thank Heaven who has given me to believe in a superintending providence Guiding and Governing all things in infinate wisdom and "to look through and trust the Ruler of the Skye."

From Mr. Brush I learnt something of your domestick affairs— that you had taken a House in Amsterdam, that you had Sent our eldest Son to Petersburgh with Mr. Dana, and Charles Home on account of his Health—and the desire he had to return again to his native Country, which must have been great indeed to induce the poor fellow to cross the atlantick without Father or Brother. How much does the anxious Heart of a Mother feel upon this occasion. No doubt you have some kind Friends, to whose care you have entrusted him, but I should have felt easier if you had written to me about it.

The Cheval[ier] L'Etomb arrived here and did me the honour of a visit soon after.[2] He brought me your favour from Leyden dated March 11th. He has kindly offerd me a safe conveyance of my Letters, by covering them himself to you, and by particular orders which he has promised to give about them. If you should write by way of France I could wish you would send under cover to him. I am not without Suspicion that you have written by way of France, and that they have been stoped. I know not how else, to account for my not hearing from you for so long a space of time. No doubt their are British Emissaries and American knaves employed for that purpose. I am told D—n is in Holland—for no good I dare say.[3] The whole junto will be soon known in America for a set of wicked unprincipled debauched wretches, from the old Deceiver down to the young Cockatrice.

You flatter me with a pleasing Illusion that if ever you see your Native land again you will not quit it. If you once see it at peace, I should hope you would not, but untill then, I can have little faith in the promise—for tho you should return with that desireable object unaccomplished, the same principle which first led you to quit your family and Friends would opperate again, when ever you could be brought to believe that you could render your Country more Service abroad than at Home; altho providence has been pleased to seperate us, it is not with the mortifying reflection that you quited your Native Land through fear, malice or Ill Will towards it, but by the unanimous voice of a free people you were deputed to give peace to Britain. Her haughty and unjust principles and sentiments have heitherto obstructed the Benevolent wishes of the United States.—Some late measures of [Congress][4] have led the Friends of American Freedom to fear that an undue influence presides in her C[ounci]ls, and that partiality will confer the recompence due to virtue upon elegant and polished vice—that complasance is preferred to honest zeal, adulation, to Truth, and meaness of Spirit, to Elevation of Soul. Are We an Independant Nation? If we are, why not speak a language becomeing a free people?

You will receive dispatches no doubt before this will reach you that will serve to explain what I have said. You will see with whom and what you are colleagued. Some you can have little hopes of assistance from, considering their present situation—and some will have no Inclination, but to obstruct your measures.

But at present I see no prospect of your negotiating jointly or seperately. Yet Cornwallis is in a most deplorable situation, his out works all taken, himself cooped up, and must be necessitated to surrender with his army soon from present appearences. Green is fighting like a Hero, as he is. I believe he has fought more Battles than any General in the Army, and has been as successfull. Our affairs look Brilliant I assure you.

My dear dearest Friend write by every opportunity, why not by Bilboa. It is as good and safe a way as any I know of. Do not if you can possibly prevent it, let me pass such an other twelve month as the year past. I have sighd enough to have borne your Letters over could they have reachd you.—My Charles, o when shall I see him. May no misfortune befall him prays your ever Ever affectionate

Portia

RC (Adams Papers); endorsed by John Thaxter: "Portia 21st. Octr. 1781," and by JA: "ansd. Decr. 2."

[1] See above, AA to JA, 29 Sept., and note 1 there.

[2] P. A. J. de Létombe, French consul; see above, vol. 3:287.

[3] AA must mean Silas Deane, who has appeared with some frequency in the *Adams Family Correspondence* and more often in JA's *Diary and Autobiography*. Deane had returned to France in the summer of 1780, reaching Paris soon after JA left that city for Amsterdam, and resumed his residence with Franklin at Passy (*Deane Papers*, 4:174, 190, 218). He spent some weeks in the Netherlands early in 1781, and apparently paid another brief visit there in the summer of that year (same, 4:274–275, 287, 290; 5:30), but he seems otherwise to have been steadily in Paris. He had come back to Europe ostensibly to settle his accounts with Congress as a joint commissioner, but he was much occupied with fruitless commercial ventures of his own and with long letters of apologetics that by May 1781 turned into arguments for renouncing American independence as a hopeless cause. A number of these letters written to Deane's friends in America may have been paid for and were certainly circulated by the British government; the tory printer James Rivington was beginning to publish them, as if intercepted, at just this time in his New York *Royal Gazette*, Oct.–Dec. 1781 (same, 4:311–315, 500–505, and *passim*; see also AA to JA, 23 Dec., below; and Burnett, ed., *Letters of Members*, 6:262–263). At about the same time Deane left Paris, "distressed both in mind and circumstances" according to Franklin, to live in Ghent, where he remained until he went to England for his final tragic years early in 1783 (*Deane Papers*, 4:491, 497; 5:70, 145). On the subject of Deane's character, wanderings, and lurid last years, see Julian P. Boyd: "Silas Deane: Death by a Kindly Teacher of Treason?" *WMQ*, 3d ser., 16:164–187, 318–342, 515–550 (April, July, Oct. 1959).

[4] Blank in MS.

John Adams to Abigail Adams

My dearest Friend   Amsterdam Oct. 21. 1781

I have not yet seen the Work from whence the inclosed Extracts were made. A set is on the Road, a Present from the Friend of Man, to me. Meantime a Friend at a Distance who has a Set has sent me these Extracts.[1] They are worth printing in the Gazette, not to gratify the Vanity of an Individual so much as for the noble Testimony of a Character so much respected as that of Mr. Hollis in favour of our Schools and System of Education. I think too his sentiments that an Agent should stay but 3 years applicable to Congress Ministers, according to which Rule, my time is out.

I have great Occasion for a few of the New England shillings. Pray send me, half a dozen if you can procure them by different Occasions.[2]

With never ceasing affection, yours.

RC (Adams Papers). For the enclosure see note 1.

[1] The "Extracts" (of which JA enclosed a copy in his own hand, now in MHi:Cranch Papers, under date of 1781) were originally furnished by Edmund Jenings in his letter to JA from Brussels, 17 Sept. (Adams Papers). Jenings' letter devoted three of its six folio pages to two quotations from [Francis Blackburne,] *Memoirs of Thomas Hollis, Esq.,* London, 1780, a work in two large and elegant quarto volumes containing numerous engravings. (On JA and Hollis see index to JA's *Diary and Autobiography.*) The first quoted passage from the *Memoirs,* 1:400–401, relates to the publication and authorship and extols the substance of JA's anonymous essays, originally published in the *Boston Gazette* in 1765 and reprinted in London by Hollis in 1768 under the title *Dissertation on the Canon and the Feudal Law.* It concludes with the text of a brief letter Hollis addressed to the Empress Catherine of Russia in 1768, transmitting a passage from the *Dissertation*

in praise of the New England plan of education at public expense. The second passage from the *Memoirs,* 1:416–417, quoted in Jenings' letter is from a letter written by Hollis to the Boston clergyman Andrew Eliot Sr., 10 May 1769, and deals chiefly with the qualifications of a colonial agent, mentioning JA as a person well qualified.

After some difficulties, JA obtained a set of Hollis' *Memoirs;* see JA to Jenings, 9 Oct., 28 Dec. (both in Adams Papers). Volume 2 of this set survives among JA's books in MB (*Catalogue of JA's Library,* p. 28).

[2] In his letter to JA of 17 Sept., cited in note 1, Jenings had mentioned that Thomas Brand Hollis, heir of Thomas Hollis (see JA, *Diary and Autobiography,* 3:188), desired a specimen of early Massachusetts coinage. It was JA's intent to send one to supply this want. He repeated his request in his (2d) letter to AA of 4 Jan. 1782, below.

John Quincy Adams to Abigail Adams

St. Petersbourg October 12 Old Style

Honoured Mamma   [*October*] 23 N.S. 1781

I am afraid you will think I was negligent in not writing more than I did by so good an opportunity as my brother Charles, but I hope you will excuse me as a journey of two thousand of our miles of which I had not the least thought a week before I set out was the only reason for it, so that I had not time to write before I left Holland, as all my time was employed in getting ready to go.

We left Amsterdam the 7th of July and arrived here the 16/27 of August: and I have not yet had an opportunity of writing, but as now a very good one presents itself[1] I cannot let it slip without writing you, to tell you at least that I am well and that I have got to the end of my Journey without any accident, except having been overset once in the carriage, but luckily nobody was hurt.

Voltaire in his history of Russia gives the following description of this city, by which you will be able to form an opinion of the place where we are.

"The city of Petersbourg is situated upon the gulf of Cronstadt, in the midst of nine branches of rivers, by which it's different quarters are divided. The center of the town is occupied by a very strong castle upon an island formed by the great arm of the Neva. The rivers are branched out into seven canals which wash the walls of One of the imperial palaces, of the admiralty, of the dockyard for the gallies, and of several manufactories. The city is embellished by five and thirty large churches among which are five for foreigners; Roman Catholic's, Calvinists and Lutherans. These five temples are monuments of the spirit of toleration, and an example to other nations. There are five imperial palace[s]; the old one, called the Summer Palace, situate on the river Neva is bordered by a handsome stone ballustrade along the river side. The new Summer Palace, near the triumphal gate, is one of the most beautiful pieces of architecture in Europe. The admiralty, the school for the instruction of cadets, the imperial colleges, the academy of sciences, the exchange, the merchants warehouses, the dock-yard belonging to the gallies, are all magnificent structures. The town-house, or guild hall, the public dispensary, where the vessels are all made of porcelaine; the magazine belonging to the court, the foundery, the arsenal, the bridges, the market-place, the public squares, the caserns for the guards of horse and foot, contribute to the embellishment, as well as to the security of this metropolis. They reckon at St. Petersbourg at present no less than four hundred thousand souls. Round the town there are villa's or country-houses surprizingly magnificent: some of them have *jet d'eaus* or water-works, far superior to those of Versailles. There was nothing of all this in 1702, it being then an impassable morass."²

I have not time to write any more at present, and must conclude by subscribing myself your most dutiful Son,   John Q. Adams

RC and LbC (Adams Papers).

¹ This letter was doubtless brought from St. Petersburg to Amsterdam, for posting there, by Stephen Sayre, who brought JQA's letter of this date to JA, following; see JA's reply to JQA, 15 Dec., below.

² Copied and translated by JQA from the first chapter of Voltaire's *Histoire de l'empire de Russie sous Pierre le grand.* JQA's copy of this work, 2 vols., n.p., 1759–1763, remains among his books in MBAt and bears a few corrections and annotations apparently in his hand. According to notes on the front flyleaves, JQA paid 5 guilders and 2 stivers for the first volume and 3 guilders and 10

stivers for the second, on 13 July 1781. His diary records that on that day he traveled from Cologne to Coblentz, and so he either paid a German bookseller in Dutch currency or erred by a few days in recording the date of his purchase. At any rate, the book was acquired for study as JQA started on his journey to St. Petersburg. A notation in vol. 2 indicates that binding the volumes cost him "80 Cop[eks]." Though done in Russia, the bindings, in the French style of the period, are among the handsomest in JQA's library and are still in pristine condition.

John Quincy Adams to John Adams

Honoured Sir   St. Petersbourg October 12/23 1781

I wrote you just after I arrived here,¹ and gave you a short sketch of my Journey from Amsterdam to this Place, and promised you in my next a description of this city, but I dont find any thing more than what Voltaire says of it in his history of Russia nor even quite so much, for according to his description, the city is situated upon the Gulf of Cronstadt in the midst of nine branches of rivers, which divide its different quarters. Seven of these nine branches of rivers are nothing more than creeks made into canals about as wide as the cingel at Amsterdam, the rest of his description is pretty exact.

I left at Amsterdam Littleton's Latin and English Dictionary which Dr. Waterhouse gave me;² if I should stay here, I should be glad if you would send it to me by the first vessel that shall come here in the spring, as I can't get here any good dictionary either French and Latin or English and Latin. Indeed this is not a very good place for learning the Latin and Greek Languages, as there is no academy or school here, and but very few private teachers who demand at the rate of 90 pounds Sterling a year, for an hour and a half each day. Mr. Dana don't chuse to employ any at that extravagant price without your positive orders, but I hope I shall be able to go on alone.

The night before last it froze hard; and yesterday it snow'd a little for the first time. It snows at present; by this you see how soon the winter begins with us here, we dont find as yet that it is colder than it is sometimes in America at this time.

I am your dutiful Son,   John Q. Adams

RC (Adams Papers); endorsed: "J. Q. Adams. Oct. 12. ansd. Decr. 15. 1781." LbC (Adams Papers). JA's reply, 15 Dec., below, indicates that JQA's letter was brought from St. Petersburg to Amsterdam by Stephen Sayre.

[1] Letter of 21 Aug. / 1 Sept., above.
[2] Adam Littleton, *Latin Dictionary*, 6th edn., London, 1735, now among JQA's books in MBAt, bearing JQA's autograph and the date 1781 on a flyleaf.

William Jackson to John Adams

Dear Sir   Bilboa October 26. 1781

I had the honor to address your Excellency from Corunna on the 26 of last month, in which letter I promised myself the pleasure of writing you more fully in a few days—but an opportunity offering unexpectedly for this place, from whence I propose embarking for America I embraced it. Our passage from Corunna has been uncommonly long owing to a continued contrary wind, which obliged us to make a second port. As the Vessel in which we shall go to America is a remarkable fast Sailer, quite new, well armed, (having cruised as a privateer on the English coast during the summer) and commanded by a very good Man, I purpose in compliance with your Son's very earnest request to take him with me, unless You should dispose otherwise. The Ship we shall sail in is the Cicero of 20 guns, Captain Hill, belonging to Mr. Cabot of Beverley.[1] I hope this measure, which is dictated by the warmest wish of friendship will meet your Excellency's approbation. The Ship is indeed one of the very best I ever saw, and I do not conceive there is more risque, than there was in going on board the South Carolina. Charles is very anxious to go to America. He says his younger Brother will be greatly before him in his education if he remains in Europe, and he begs I will not by any means leave him.

As the Ship will not sail before the 16 or 18 of November I shall expect to receive your Excellency's orders.[2] In the mean time I beg you will be persuaded that my best attention shall be bestowed upon your Son. He writes and reads to me daily. I will give him every instruction in my power, and by an assiduous care endeavor to compensate other deficiencies as a preceptor. He is now reading, in english, Dr. Robertson's history of America.[3] I have requested him by the next post to collect the general heads of the first volume, and make them the subject of a letter. Don Quixote is the book which he reads in french[4]—and I believe, if Sancho's principles of government equalled the Constitution of Massachusetts, Charles might soon emulate his Sire as a Law giver. Those two books being both elegant and entertaining he reads them with pleasure, and I believe will improve his english considerably, while he retains his french. His health is very good, and he takes sufficient exercise and moderate diet to preserve it so.

The recital of Mr. Gillon's unvaried villanies has already employed a great part of my time, and a minute detail of them requires infinitely more patience than the retrospect affords me. But it is proper and necessary that your Excellency should be informed of some circumstances, and I must beg leave to trespass on your leisure with a narration of them.

The violation of his contract with Colonel Laurens by refusing to carry in his own ship the cloathing purchased for the Continent, your Excellency is already acquainted with. The manner in which he pretended to remedy this breach of faith by chartering two other ships you are likewise informed of. I will therefore begin with the relation of his conduct from the 7 of August upon which day he weighed anchor in the Texel under a pretence of trying how the frigate sailed. But as soon as he had passed the Dutch-fleet and cleared the shoals he informed me that it was his intention to put to sea. I expressed my astonishment and exclaimed against the measure. He told me he meant to wait off the Texel for his Convoy, but it was necessary he should leave the port. I now found that his debts (notwithstanding the solemn assurances repeated in his contract) had accumulated far beyond his resources, and that he was resolved, in order to elude his Creditors, at once to prostitute the honor and sacrifice the dearest interests of America. I intreated and threatned him alternately with the consequences of his neglecting to convoy these Ships. Colonel Searle joined me in representing to him the fatal effects, which must ensue to America in the disappointment of this cloathing. Every argument was urged, every means tried, but all in vain. He even refused, as Mr. de Neufville may have informed you to execute the Charters for the Vessels which he had taken up, and finally he resolved to leave the coast although his Officers had requested that the Ship might return, and they would wait for the Convoy. But this he evaded by ordering the Ship, when informed how the Texel bore from the mast-head, to be kept [on] such a course as brought us greatly to leeward of it, and then he gave directions to proceed to America. But this was by no means what he designed, for his baseness has been conducted upon a systematical scale, nor did it end here. He would not permit me to send a letter to your Excellency which I had wrote to request, as I now do, that you would be pleased to give such directions for the disposal of the Continental property as you should think best,[5] and another to Messrs. de Neufville & Son, by a Neutral Ship which we spoke at sea, bound to Amsterdam—and by which Vessel he himself wrote to Holland.

After cruising four weeks on the coast of Ireland and near the Eng[lish] channel he put into Corunna, and there we experienced a treatment which even exceeded the common audacity that characterises this base Man. He positively refused Col. Trumbull, Col. Searle, and Myself permission to go on shore, and actually detained us prisoners upwards of twenty four hours, and had it not been for the interference of the Captain of a french Man of War then in port, with whom I was acquainted in America, it is my belief he would have continued us confined. He refused to deliver some trunks belonging to Colonel Searle, which obliged him to stay at Corunna, until Mr. Carmichael arrives, as Col. Searle had requested Mr. Jay to send that Gentleman. In short to enumerate all the base actions of Mr. Gillon sense we left the Texel would require a Volume. He has detained the Masters of Vessels who had escaped from Prison in England and embarked with him as Passengers for America, telling them that they should not leave his Ship while he commanded her. Some of them have escaped, and are now here; but they were obliged to abandon their clothes to obtain their liberty.

I shall do myself the pleasure to write your Excellency in a few days. I beg that you will present my best compliments to Mr. Thaxter, and that you will believe me to be with profound respect, and esteem, Dear Sir, Your Excellency's most obedient, humble Servant,

Wm. Jackson

RC (Adams Papers); endorsed: "Majr. Jackson.   ansd. 14 Nov. 1781."

[1] Concerning the ship *Cicero*, of 300 tons, 16 guns, and 60 men, commanded by Hugh Hill and owned by Andrew Cabot and others, of Beverly, see Gardner W. Allen, *Massachusetts Privateers* of the Revolution (MHS, *Colls.*, 77 [1927]), p. 99. The tonnage and number of guns and crew vary in other sources.

[2] See JA's reply, 14 Nov., below. The

Cicero did not sail from Bilbao until about 10 Dec.; see Isaac Smith to JA, 23 Jan. 1782, below, and note 1 there.

Jackson does not mention here an adventure of his with CA in the passage between La Coruña and Bilbao, which accounted in good part for their detainment so long in Spain and Spanish waters. This is related in colorful detail by John Trumbull in his *Autobiography*, ed. Sizer, 1953, p. 78–79. Trumbull reports that, on finding the *Cicero* at La Coruña readying to sail for Bilbao and then for America, he, Jackson, CA, and some other passengers from the *South Carolina*

"endeavored to get a passage to Bilboa, on board of this ship, and were permitted to go on board of their prize, a fine British Lisbon packet. The usual time required to run from Corunna to Bilboa was two or three days. We were again unfortunate; the wind being east, dead a-head, we were twenty one days in making the passage, and, as if Jonas himself had been among us, at the end of eighteen days, we fell in with a little fleet of Spanish coasters and fishermen, running to the westward before the wind, who told us that when off the bar of Bilboa, they had seen a ship and two brigs, which they believed to be British cruisers, and cautioned us to keep a good look-out. Capt. Hill of the Cicero, immediately hailed his prize, a ship of sixteen guns, which was also in company, and directed them to keep close to him, and prepare to meet an enemy. At sunset we saw what appeared to be the force described, and about midnight found we were within hail. The Cicero ran close alongside of the ship, and hailed her in English—no answer; in French—no answer. The men, who were at their guns, impatient of delay, did not wait for orders, but poured in their broadside; the hostile squadron (as we supposed them) separated, and made all sail in different directions, when a boat from the large ship came alongside with her captain, a Spaniard, who informed us that they were Spanish vessels from St. Sebastians, bound to the West Indies—that his ship was very much cut in her rigging, but happily, no lives lost. He

had mistaken us for British vessels, and was delighted to find his mistake. We apologized for ours, offered assistance, &c. and we parted most amicably. Soon after, we entered the river of Bilbao, and ran up to Porto Galette. The disabled ship with her comrades put into Corunna, where it was found that one of our nine pound shot had wounded the mainmast of our antagonist so severely, that it was necessary to take it (the mast) out, and put in a new one. This was not the work of a day, and her consorts were detained until their flag ship was ready. In the mean time, we had almost completed taking in our cargo at Bilboa, when a messenger from Madrid arrived, with orders to unhang the rudders of all American ships in the port, until the bill for repairs of the wounded ship, demurrage of her consorts, &c. &c., was paid. We were thus detained in Bilboa until the 10th of December, and even then had to encounter one more vexation and delay."

³ JA owned a set of William Robertson's *History of America*, 3d edn., 3 vols., London, 1780, and two editions in French, all surviving among his books in MB (*Catalogue of JA's Library*, p. 214). Other, later editions in English of this very widely read work are in the Stone Library (MQA).

⁴ JA owned a French translation of Cervantes' *Histoire de l'admirable Don Quichotte de la Manche*, nouv. édn., 6 vols., Paris, 1768, of which only the first volume survives among his books in MB (*Catalogue of JA's Library*, p. 47). In the Stone Library (MQA) are two other editions in French, published at The Hague, 1768 and 1773 respectively, both in six volumes.

⁵ See JA's reply to Jackson, 14 Nov., below. On 12 Aug., Jackson had written to JA from "On board the South Carolina," sending his respects and little more, explaining: "I am scarce allowed time by Mr. Thaxter's immediate departure to bid Your Excellency farewell in this abrupt manner" (Adams Papers). Thaxter had come aboard to place CA under Jackson's care. Jackson's letter is helpful in fixing the date of Gillon's final departure from Dutch waters.

Cotton Tufts to John Adams

Dear Sir   Boston Octobr. 29. 1781

In my last I informed You of the Enemy's taking a Post in Virginia.[1] At that Time they were in possession of Georgia and Charlestown and had overrun the greater part of S. Carolina. I have the Pleasure to inform You, That American Government is now again settled in Georgia, that the Enemy are confined to Charlestown in S. Carolina and that on the 18th. Inst. York Town and Gloucester the only places in Virginia the Enemy were in possession of there, surrenderd with the Army under Command of Genl. Cornwallis to our illustrious Genl. Washington. Count de Grasse commanded by Water with a Fleet of 36 Sail of Men of War. 1 Ship of 44 Guns, 1 of 32, some smaller Armd Vessells and 100 Sail of Transports were captured also 9000 Soldiers and Seamen composing the Garrison.—Count De Grasse arrived in the Chesapeak in the Beginning of September. The British Fleet consisting of 18 or 20 Ships of the Line followed De Grasse, attacked him, receivd a severe drubbing, lost one or more Ships and returned to New York sadly maimed. The particulars of this Engagement youll probably have before this reaches You.

I have not Time to give You particulars; arriving in Town this Afternoon and hearing that a French Frigate was under sailing orders, stole a Moment just to give You this Information (which may be relied on for Truth) and also to tell You that Your Family was this Morning well. Mrs. Adams received some Articles by Brown and Skinner who are arrived.[2] Newman also has arrived and last Night Somes from Copinhagen came into port.

Fine Crops this Year—Plenty of Provisions—Paper Money abolished &c. Yr. Affct. Friend & Obt. Sert.,   C.T.

RC (Adams Papers).

[1] See Tufts to JA, 20 June, above.
[2] Brown and Skinner were captains of vessels that had arrived from Amsterdam at Cape Ann and Boston respectively on 20 Oct. or a day or two later (Boston *Independent Chronicle*, 25 Oct. 1781, p. 3, col. 3).

Richard Cranch to John Adams

Dear Bror.   Boston Octr. 30th. 1781

I am just come from Braintree, and hear a Vessell is to sail for France directly: I have only time to enclose you two Hand-Bills, on the Contents of which I heartily congratulate you.[1]—American Affairs never wore a more agreeable Aspect than at present. I want to hear how this News will be relish'd at St. James's.

Captains Brown, and Skinner are arriv'd from Amsterdam last Week, and Capt. Newman about three Weeks ago. Hayden was parted within the North Sea soon after they sailed. Mr. J. Temple[2] and Mr. Guild came Passengers in Capt. Brown who arriv'd at Cape Ann. Have seen both of them, but they bro't no letters to Town with them from you or Mr. Thaxter. Mr. Temple supposes there are Letters on board, but they are to be sent to Newbury to Mr. Tracy. A few Things for your Lady are come to hand by Capt. Skinner. We long to hear from Cousn. Charley who is suppos'd to be on board the Frigate.

Your Daughter is in town at Doctr. Welsh's. I saw her this Morning. Your dear Lady was well yesterday and Master Tommy also. I have only time to say that we are all well, and that I am with every sentiment of Esteem and Respect your affectionate Bror.,

Richard Cranch

Dft or FC (MHi:Cranch Papers); endorsed by Cranch: "Copy of a Lettr. to Bror. Adams Octr. 30th. 1781." For the enclosures, not found, see note 1.

[1] These doubtless related to Cornwallis' surrender and Greene's victories in the South. See Ford, *Mass. Broadsides*, Nos. 2282, 2312, &c.

[2] For more on the arrival and condu t of John (later Sir John) Temple (1731–1798), see Cranch to JA, 3 Nov., following. This was the beginning of a protracted controversy over the real motives for the return of Temple, who was James Bowdoin's son-in-law and, from 1785, British consul general in New York. See various references to him in JA, *Diary and Autobiography*; Cotton Tufts to JA, 26 Sept. 1782, below; and, for a connected account, Lewis Einstein, *Divided Loyalties*, Boston and N.Y., 1933, ch. 3.

Richard Cranch to John Adams

Dear Bror.   Boston Novr. 3d 1781

By Capt. Haydon who arrived here the day before yesterday I received a Pacquet of News-Papers and Pamphlets from you, also I received two other Pacquets by Capt. Brown a few Days ago, for which I thank you. I had however the mortification of not finding a Line in either of them from you or Mr. Thaxter. I have wrote you often but have not had the Happiness of receiving a Letter from you since you left America. I have just now heard of a Vessell at Newbury that is now waiting for a Wind to sail for Holland, I shall endeavour to send this by her.

I heartily congratulate you on the great and important Event, the taking of Lord Cornwallis and his whole Army. They surrender'd Prisoners of War on the 18th. of October. Though we have not yet received the News under the Signature of Charles Thomson, yet we have it from publick Officers of distinction by Express. One Letter in particular from Coll. Cobb Aid de Camp to his Excellency Genl. Washington, dated at York-Town, the very Place where the Army surrender'd, mentions that Lord Cornwallis is to return to England on his Parole not to serve in the War untill he is exchang'd, that the Officers had their private Baggage given them, and were with the Army to remain Prisoners of War untill an Exchange shall take place. —How will this News relish at St. James's?—Genl. Green as you will see by the inclosed Paper, has done Wonders in South Carolina. As soon as Lord Cornwallis had surrender'd, Genl. Washington (as I am inform'd) sent off on Horsback a strong Reinforcement of light Troops to strengthen Genl. Green, so that the Remains of the broken British Army in that Quarter will probably soon melt away.

I suppose you have heard that Paper Money, which has made such a Noise in Europe, and from the Depreciation of which England has expected such great things, is now done with in this Commonwealth. We have a Tax now gone out sufficient to draw in the whole of the Bills of the New Emission that have been issued by this State, and which are not to be re-issued, but to be destroy'd. And another Tax for three hundred Thousand Pounds in hard Money to be collected in Lieu thereof for the Purposes of Government. This is a great Effort, but I think we shall be able to bear it; for, it appears by the new Valuation which pass'd this present Session, that the Property and Polls in this Commonwealth are much increased since the last Valuation in 1778 notwithstanding the great Expences of the War: particularly we find that we have now in this State many thousand Horn'd Cattle more than we had in 1778 when the last Valuation was taken, notwithstanding the amazing Quantities of Beef supply'd for the Army. And the Harvests in the United States this Year have been perhaps the plentyest ever known.—May our Hearts be duely affected with Gratitude to the great Ruler of the World for his unspeakable Favours!

I have received by Capt. Haydon a Letter and an Invoice of Merchandize sent to my Care by Mr. Joseph Mandrillon.[1] I have wrote him a Letter by this Conveyance, directed to the Care of Messrs. De Neufville and Son. I should be glad you would please to inform him that I shall take the utmost care in disposing of the Goods for him to the best advantage, and shall make the Returns as soon as possible. The Goods are not yet out of the Ship. I am much oblig'd to you for this beginning of Commission-Business, as I learn by his

Letter that I am indebted to your Friendship for it.—Your Character and Connexions might be of most essential Service to me and my Family, by your only mentioning my Name to such Gentlemen as may have publick Business to transact here respecting publick Supplies for this State or for the Continent; or to such Gentlemen in Trade as may be disposed to send Effects here to be sold on Commission. My Connexion with the General Court and the Court of Common-Pleas keeps me almost constantly in this Town on publick Business, Committees &c, and Uncle Smith's Warehouse is always ready for taking in any Merchandize that may be sent to me. I shall spare no Pains to give Satisfaction in making the best and quickest Returns.

In Capt. Brown came Passengers John Temple † Esqr. and Mr. Guild. We hear by a Passenger that came in Capt. Skinner that your dear Little Charley is on board the Frigate Capt. Guillon, and are anxious to hear from him, as the People who came in the Ships lately arriv'd mention a dangerous Storm having happen'd on the Coast of Holland while Capt. Guillon was out on a short Cruise a few Days before they sailed. I hope Providence has preserved him and will preserve him. We long to hear how Master John likes the Northern Regions. He will be the greatest American Traveller of his Age. Your amiable Daughter is at present at Mr. S. A. Otis's in this Town.[2] Your Lady and Master Tommy, and your Mother and Brother were all well last Monday when I left Braintree, as were also our other Friends at Braintree, Weymouth, Hingham &c. Please to give my kindest Regards to Mr. Thaxter and tell him that I have wrote him several Letters, and should think my self happy in receiving a Line from him. I fear many of our Letters on both sides have miscaried. I hope you will excuse the tedious Length of this Letter, and believe me to be with the highest Esteem your affectionate Bror.,

Richard Cranch

† This Gentleman has given great umbrage by going over to London in the manner he did. He has been under Examination before the Governor and Councill, who are unsatisfied with his Conduct, and sent his Defence in Writing down to the House. The two Houses have sent it back to the Executive. I don't know what will be the end of it.

I suppose you have heard that our University has conferr'd the Degree of Doctor of Laws on You.[3] I congratulate you on it, tho' I think the University receives therby a greater Honour than it gives.

The Vessells lately arriv'd from Holland are commanded by the

Captains Newman, Brown, Skinner and Haydon. I don't remember any others.

RC (Adams Papers). The "inclosed Paper" has not been identified. This letter after some vicissitudes was not dispatched until 31 Jan. 1782 or later, when Cranch sent it with his letter to JA of that date, below.

[1] An Amsterdammer of French origin who was both a merchant and a writer on political and geographical subjects. Correspondence between JA and Mandrillon, 1780–1790 (Adams Papers), deals chiefly with books, maps, and the like. Mandrillon, strongly pro-American, was also a correspondent of George Washington; see Washington, *Writings*, ed. Fitzpatrick, 27:499–500; 30:68–69, 136.

[2] Samuel Allyne Otis; identified at vol. 3:155, above.

[3] At Commencement in July 1781, the Harvard Corporation voted to confer the honorary degree of LL.D. on JA, the Chevalier de La Luzerne, and Arthur Lee, among others. But perhaps because the office of president was vacant, there was no public announcement of these honors until after a new president, Rev. Joseph Willard, was elected. Willard made the announcement at his installation on 19 Dec. 1781, but with respect to at least JA no action followed until 1 April 1783, when the Corporation voted "That the Diploma for a Doctorate of Laws, conferred on His Excellency John Adams Esqr., some time since, be immediately engrossed, and the seal enclosed in a silver box." The diploma, bearing the date of 19 Dec. 1781 and with its seal enclosed in a silver box, remains among the Adams Papers. But JA did not receive it for more than a year, when AA sailed to Europe and brought it, together with a letter from the Corporation, 8 June 1784, requesting his aid in raising funds for Harvard in Europe. JA warmly acknowledged the honor that had been paid him but discouraged any notion of "pecuniary Advantage" to Harvard from solicitation in Europe (to Joseph Willard, 8 Sept. 1784, MH-Ar:Corporation Papers). For an account of this affair, with some of the documentation, see William Coolidge Lane's remarks in Col. Soc. Mass., *Pubns.*, 13 (1912):112–117.

John Adams to William Jackson

Dr. Sir   Amsterdam November 14. 1781

Last night I had the Honour of your Favour of 26 of October[1] and congratulate you on your Arrival at Bilbao and your agreable Prospect of a Passage to America. I thank you sir, for your kind Attention to my Son, and wish you to take him home with you. Mr. Guardoqui will be so good as to furnish Charles with Stores, and draw upon me.

What can be done with the Continental Property I know not, unless Dr. Franklin will advance Money to charter Vessells to send them along to take their fate, at all hazards. We shall do the best We can, but it is a melancholly and affecting Dissappointment.—I presume, you will be saild, before this reaches Spain, or I should be more particular. I have the Honour to be, Sir, your most obedient humble servant,   J. Adams

RC (DNA:PCC, No. 84, III); endorsed: "from J. Adams Novr. 14. 1781 received November 28. 1781." LbC (Adams Papers); in John Thaxter's hand.

¹ Above.

Abigail Adams to James Lovell

November 15th 1781

There is a Lust in Man no Charm can tame
of loudly publishing his Neighbours Shame
on Eagles wings immortal scandles fly
whilst virtuous actions are but born and die.

Do you know a Man by the Name of *More*[?] What is his character?¹

I have never replied to your favour of october 9th. I felt a reluctance at writing. Yet I love your Letters when they are not too sausy, or do not border upon what I never will pardon or forgive. I cannot withdraw my esteem from the writter, yet if his Friends do not tell him how much his character suffers, they do not act the part of Friends in that particular. Massachusets air can alone purify it. I never meant to have touched so dissagreable a string again. There is but one thing wanting to have put a final stop to it, a conviction of the cause'es realy existing. If ever that takes place do not recollect that you ever knew Portia, for she will blot from her memory every vestage of a character in which she has been so much deceived.²

At length Sir I have heard [of] Gillion after many terrors on account of the storm which took place after he saild. A vessel from Bilboa last night arrived brings word that he put into Corruna in Spain—no further particulars yet come to hand. She is certainly bound to your port. Mr. Guile who arrived in Brown about 3 weeks ago embarked on Board the frigate, but went on shore for one Night. She saild and left him, from him I learnt her orders were to go to Philadelphia, from whence I hope to hear of her arrival soon, and of my dear Boys safety.

I congratulate you Sir upon the Capture of Cornwallis and upon every other important and favorable event which has taken place since I wrote you last. There may possibly be some opportunity opened by water for a safe conveyance of the articles about which you have already taken much trouble. If there should I would rather risk the Box of china that way than by land.—I will subscribe myself what I now am and ever wish to be your *real Friend,*   Portia

Dft (Adams Papers); without indication of addressee. At head of text CFA misassigned the date as "October 15. 1781."

¹ See Lovell's answer, 4 Dec., below.
² This cryptic paragraph, involving a further charge against Lovell's character, is clarified in AA to Lovell, 8? Jan. 1782, below; see note 3 there.

James Lovell to Abigail Adams

Madam   Philada. Novr. 26th. 1781

I shall have an excellent Opportunity to send those Articles of yours, which have been long under my Care, by a Waggon of Genl. Lincoln going in a few days to Boston and perhaps also to Hingham. I feel a Sort of Mortification, at the Air of Negligence which seems to be thrown over my past Endeavors to serve you, by this early Execution of the Promises which our good Friend Lincoln made to you or Mr. Cranch not long ago. The Articles will now go by one of the very best Conveyances both as to Honesty and Carefulness in the Waggoner.

You will be quite particular in making out Invoices of the Contents of the Case as they come to Sight. I doubt not you will find my first Suspicions of a Loss confirmed, when you get Invoices from Europe. All I can say is that while the Boxes were open in my Room, I always turned the Key and pocketed it, when I went out.

Your most humble Servant,   James Lovell

Decr. 2d. 1781

P.S.   The Goods are gone. I shall write to Col. Crafts to give you notice of the Arrival of the Waggon in Boston, if it should not proceed to Hingham.

RC (Adams Papers); addressed: "Mrs. A. Adams   Braintree"; franked: "Philada. Jas. Lovell."

James Lovell to Abigail Adams

Madam   Novr. 29 1781

My Almanac says that I wrote to you on the 9th. of October, but your Favour of Sepr. 26.¹ received the 8th. of Octr. is not endorsed *answered.* Is this the Reason of your Silence? Or, Heaven forbid it! are you sick? At best, I fear you are in Distress.—Mr. Adams was well late in Augst., but I cannot conceal my anxieties about your second Son, who was to take Passage with Gillon. That Frigate which was to bring him was forced out to Sea without taking the Merchantmen under Convoy, which had been loaded with a View of having her

245

Protection. 13 Weeks have elapsed since. I do not however despair of her Arrival. I only deal justly by you in giving the real State of the Case that your Hopes may be duely regulated.

I do not now *answer* your Letter. I write for Post Conveyance and am not in the Humour to use Cyphers.

I find by a Letter of Sepr. 13th. from Doctr. Franklin that Mr. Adams had received our Proceedings of June before the Doctor's Communication of them:[2] I mean those Proceedings to which you refer in your Letter now before me. I wish much to learn the Effect upon his *Philosop[h]y*. I feel Satisfaction in thinking him a much *calmer* Man than myself. Whatever he determines will be well weighed. He is practised in sacrificing his personal Feelings and Interest to his Country.

I have received some Gazettes from him without a Line of Epistle. This is not the only Reason I have for thinking that my Letters Via France do not reach his Eye.

I hope you are not very ill. You are surely not very well. Yr. m h Servant, J. L.

RC (Adams Papers); addressed: "Mrs. A Adams   Braintree."

[1] Perhaps the same as her draft letter of 20 Sept., printed above under that date; see note 1 there.

[2] See Franklin to Congress, 13 Sept., Wharton, ed., *Dipl. Corr. Amer. Rev.*, 4:709–710.

Joseph Gardoqui & Sons to Abigail Adams

Madam   Bilbao the 30th. Novr. 1781

We beg leave to Trouble you above with duplicate of our last Respectts to you,[1] and as have had since the very high pleasure and satisfaction of seeing with us your worthy Amable little Son Mr. Charles Adams under the Care of Major Jakson Intending boath to Returne home on Board the Armed Ship the Cicero Capt. Hugh Hill, have with the Majors advice Taken the liberty of altering your dispositions, accordingly have Instead of shipping the order you was pleased to give us on Board the Boston Packett Capt White, Embarkt the same under the Immediate care of your little Dear Son on the above Vessell the Cicero as you will see per the within Invoice and bill of loading which Request the favour of your ordering it to be Examined and if without Errors to place its ammount to our Credit In Riales 914 & 10 mrs. of Vn.[2] We most affectionately wish that your dear little Darling may present you in full health the Articles contained in the Invoice after a safe prosperous and pleasing Passage of 30 days, which will be the highest Satisfaction to those who have the honour of subscriving with the most profound Respectts of Esteem Madam your mt. obt. hble. Serts.,　　　　　　　　　　Joseph Gardoqui & sons

RC (Adams Papers); at foot of text: "Originall per Hill, Copy per Dixzy"; see note 1. Enclosed "Invoice and bill of loading" not found.

[1] That is, a duplicate of their letter to AA of 14 Oct., above. No duplicate has been found; nor is it clear whether the present letter is the "Originall" sent by Hill or the "Copy" sent by "Dixzy," presumably Capt. John Dixey of Newburyport (Gardner W. Allen, *Massachusetts Privateers of the Revolution* [MHS, *Colls.*, 77 (1927):246]).

[2] Maravedis of vellon; see Gardoqui & Sons to AA, 14 Oct., above.

William Jackson to John Adams

Dear Sir　　　　　　　　　　　　　Bilbao November 30. 1781

The last post brought me your Excellency's letter of the 14. I hope Doctor Franklin will be fully in sentiment with you respecting the disposition of the Continental property, and I am happy in anticipating the pleasing close, which may still attend this hitherto unfortunate business.

Previous to the receipt of your last letter I had drawn upon Messrs. de Neufville & Son for a sum of money to supply Colonel Trumbull and Doctor Browne,[1] and I apportioned two hundred & fifty guilders for Charles's use. This is considerably more than was necessary to defray his expences, but in case of accident at sea it would be proper he should have a little money. When we arrive I shall do myself the honor to wait upon Mrs. Adams, and I will then pay her the surplus.

It is no compliment paid to Charles when I assure your Excellency that his behaviour is unexceptionably good. He reads as much as I wish him to do both in french and English. His writing is considerably improved and his spelling tolerably correct.

I shall continue to give him every instruction in my power. During the passage we propose to read latin.

I felicitate your Excellency upon the very acceptable news of Cornwallis's capture, which we celebrated here yesterday with singular satisfaction.

I most sincerely wish you a perfect restoration of health and the full enjoyment of every blessing which can render life estimable. Your Excellency will do me justice by believing me at all times to be, with the most perfect esteem and profound respect, your most obedient, humble Servant,　　　　　　　　　　　　　W Jackson

247

RC (Adams Papers); endorsed: "Major Jackson Nov. 30. 1781."
[1] Browne has not been further identified.

John Adams to William Jackson

Sir   Amsterdam Dcr. 1. 1781

Last night I received yours of the 12 Novr. and am very sorry to find, that you were not likely to sail as you expected.[1] My dear Mrs. Adams has heard that Charles is coming home in Gillon and has a Thousand Anxieties about him which will increase every Moment untill his Arrival, but when We trust ourselves to Winds and Waves We must be patient under their Caprices.

I thank you for the good News, by this Time you will have learned better. I give you Joy of it, all, Coll. Trumbull, Capt. Hill, Messrs. Gardoqui and every one who has Feelings for America, and for injured Innocence, not forgetting my dear Charles, from whom I have received two or three very pretty Letters.[2] I thank you for your kind Care of him. Beg Mr. Gardoqui to let him have any Thing he may want and draw upon me for it.

The Infant Hercules will go through all the twelve Labours, as tryumphantly as he has strangled the two serpents Burgoine and Cornwallis.

The continental goods are left in such a Situation, that I see no Possibility of getting them to America, this Season. I am doing all I can to get them sent or sold, or any Way disposed of, to prevent a total Loss, but they are detained for freight, Damages and nobody knows what. Very unjustly, and I have no Money to make the dull Jacks go.

LbC (Adams Papers).

[1] Jackson had written to JA from Bilbao on 12 Nov. (Adams Papers), saying that the *Cicero* would not sail on the 16th as he had hoped, because "a sudden fresh in the river, which impedes the ship's loading, will oblige us to wait for the next spring-tide." (For details on the sailing, on or about 10 Dec., see John Trumbull's account, quoted below at Isaac Smith Sr. to JA, 23 Jan. 1782, note 1.) Jackson added the news from America that Cornwallis had offered to capitulate and reported that CA "is very well."

[2] None of these has been found.

Elizabeth Ellery Dana to Abigail Adams

My Dear Madam   Cambridge Dec. 1. 1781

This is the first opportunity I have had since my Journey of congratulating you upon your dear Sons safe arrival in Spain, and hope it will not be long before you have the happiness of seeing him. The frequent arrivals lately from Europe have I hope made you happy in letters from Mr. Adams. Mr. Dana I hear nothing of by letter. Mr. Guild informed me that he left Amsterdam for Russia in July and your Son with him which I was much pleased with hearing.

Before I went to Portsmouth I heared that I was to be so highly favored as to have a visit from you this fall. I was very sorry that my Journey deprived me of that pleasure, but flattered myself that upon my return I should have seen you. But Miss Dana[1] lying dangerously ill of the Throat distemper when I returned prevented my writing to you. She is now better and the season pleasant Must hope that Miss Nabby and you will make us a visit. The Judge[2] and young ladies respect [request?] my love to Miss Nabby and Master Tom. Your affectionate friend and Sister,   Eliza Dana

RC (Adams Papers).

[1] Lydia Dana, afterward Mrs. John Hastings, sister of Francis Dana (Elizabeth Ellery Dana, *The Dana Family in America*, Cambridge, 1956, p. 474).

[2] Presumably Judge Edmund Trowbridge, of Cambridge, uncle of Francis Dana (Sibley-Shipton, *Harvard Graduates*, 8:507–520).

John Adams to Abigail Adams

My dearest Friend   Amsterdam Decr. 2 1781

Your favours of September 29 and Oct. 21. are before me. I avoided saying any Thing about Charles, to save you the Anxiety, which I fear you will now feel in its greatest severity a long time. I thought he would go directly home, in a short Passage, in the best Opportunity which would probably ever present. But I am disappointed. Charles is at Bilbao with Major Jackson and Coll. Trumbull who take the best care of his Education as well as his Health and Behaviour. They are to go home in Captain Hill in a good Vessell of 20 Guns. Charles's health was so much affected by this tainted Atmosphere, and he had set his heart so much upon going home in Gillon that it would have broken it, to have refused him.—I desire I may never again have the Weakness to bring a Child to Europe. They are infinitely better at home.—We have all been sick here, myself, Mr. Thaxter, Stephens and another servant, but are all better. Mr. Thaxters Indisposition has been slight and short, mine and Stevens's long and severe.

I beg you would not flatter yourself with hopes of Peace. There will be no such Thing for several years.

Dont distress yourself neither about any malicious Attempts to injure me in the Estimation of my Countrymen. Let them take their Course and go the Length of their Tether. They will never hurt your Husband, whose Character is fortified with a shield of Innocence and Honour ten thousandfold stronger than brass or Iron. The contemptible Essays made by you know whom, will only tend to their own Confusion. My Letters have shewn them their own Ignorance ⟨and Folly⟩, a sight they could not bear. Say as little about it as I do. It has already brought them into the true system and that system is tryumphant. I laugh, and will laugh before all Posterity at their impotent ⟨, *despicable, ridiculous folly*⟩ Rage and Envy. They could not help blushing themselves if they were to review their Conduct.

Dear Tom thy Letter[1] does thee much honour. Thy Brother Charles shall teach thee french and Dutch, at home. I wish I could get time to correspond with thee and thy sister, more regularly, but I cannot. I must trust Providence and thine excellent Mamma for the Education of my Children.

Mr. Dana and our son are well, at P[etersburg].

Hayden has some things for you. Hope he is arrived. I am sorry to learn you have a sum of Paper—how could you be so imprudent? You must be frugal, I assure you. Your Children will be poorly off. I can but barely live in the manner that is indispensibly demanded of me by every Body. Living is dear indeed here.

My Children will not be so well left by their father as he was by his. They will be infected with the Examples and Habits and Taste for Expensive Living, without the means. He was not.

My Children, shall never have the smallest soil of dishonour or disgrace brought upon them by their father, no not to please Ministers, Kings, or Nations.

At the Expence of a little of this my Children might perhaps ride at their Ease through Life, but dearly as I love them they shall live in the service of their Country, in her Navy, her Army, or even out of either in the extreamest Degree of Poverty before I will depart in the smallest Iota from my Sentiments of Honour and Delicacy, for I, even I, have sentiments of Delicacy, as exquisite as the proudest Minister that ever served a Monarch. They may not be exactly like those of some Ministers.

I beg you would excuse me to my dear Friends, to whom I cannot write so often as I wish. I have indispensible Duties which take up all my time, and require more than I have.

General Washington has done me great Honour, and much public service by sending me, authentic Accounts of his own and Gen. Greens last great Actions.[2] They are in the Way to negotiate Peace, it lies wholly with them. No other Ministers but they and their Colleagues in the Army can accomplish the great Event.

I am keeping House, but I want an Housekeeper. What a fine Affair it would be if We could flit across the Atlantic as they say the Angels do from Planet to Planet. I would dart to Pens hill and bring you over on my Wings. But alass We must keep house seperately for some time.

But one thing I am determined on. If God should please to restore me once more to your fireside, I will never again leave it without your Ladyships Company. No not even to go to Congress at Philadelphia, and there I am determined to go if I can make Interest enough to get chosen, whenever I return.

I would give a Million sterling that you were here—and could Afford it as well as G. Britain can the thirty Millions she must spend the ensuing Year to compleat her own Ruin.

Farewell. Farewell.

RC (Adams Papers).

[1] Not found.
[2] George Washington to JA, 22 Oct., with two enclosures (Adams Papers; text of letter printed in JA, *Works*, 7:475, and in Washington, *Writings*, ed. Fitzpatrick, 23:253–254).

John Thaxter to Abigail Adams

Amsterdam Decr. 2d. 1781

'Tis a pleasing Reflexion to one absent, that his Correspondence with his friends meets with no untoward Accidents, even though the subject matter of his Scralls should be in a stile little interesting or entertaining. But I am deprived of even this satisfaction, for almost all my Letters are on board the Indian.[1] It is needless for me to add an Apology after this, especially as Newman, Brown, Skinner, Hayden &c. were to have sailed under Convoy of this same Indian. I had the honor to write You by a Brig bound to Philadelphia commanded by Capt. Reeler, which sailed in Septr. or October. I also answered a polite Letter from Miss N[abb]y by the same Opportunity.[2] I hope they will arrive safe. If they do not, I hope my dear friends will pardon my [not] attempting any thing further against so decisive a fatality.

With the most unfeigned Joy, I congratulate You at this late period on the glorious News of the surrender of Cornwallis. It is an Event that has acquired much Reputation to our Arms in Europe; nor has the humidity of this Climate prevented its Inhabitants from exhibiting some symptoms of Life and Warmth on the Occasion. Indeed I must say that this is a peculiar People; but whether zealous of good Works or saved of the Lord, is not for me to determine.

I believe I promised You, Madam, in a former Letter to transmit You some Account of this Country. What Demon of Madness or Folly seized me at that time, to precipitate myself into so rash an Engagement I know not. I am totally unequal to the Task. I was certainly mad or in Love or something quite as distracted as either, to promise an undertaking of this kind. I beg You to have the Goodness to excuse me, and to apply to your dearest friend, who will throw more light on this subject in one Line, than I could do in many pages of my flummery.

Thus much I must say for this Country, that upon this Occasion (I mean the last Surrender) they have discovered much Joy and satisfaction. Some are affected to America upon principles which a Love of Liberty and an attachment to the Dignity and Rights of Humanity alone can inspire. These are few in number. Others would love Us if they had less Money in the English funds. Some are too rich to trouble their heads about America—others too poor, tho' perhaps well disposed, to aid her. Some would trade if they dare. Others are governed by the immense profits in view. As to national Affection, extended one Jot or tittle farther than an Idea of Gain, it is a mere Chimera. Nations collectively are not capable of this noble Sentiment, and Policy is often employed to smother and extinguish the first dawnings of it. The History of the Policy of most Governments seems to be little else than a portrait of the worst passions of the human Heart, a Compound of the Intrigues, Subtleties, Subterfuges and Caprices of the weak, the wicked, and the great, and the Blood and Treasure of poor miserable Mankind must flow in Torrents to support their nefarious System. Such is the Lot of Humanity. Who can mend it? I know not.

I have not as yet seen my dear Friend Mr. Storer. I am impatient to see him, and not less so to enquire of him, which of the Betsy's it is that belongs to me, as all parties are agreed, You inform me, Madam, that it is one of that Name. I beseech You to gratify my Curiosity in sending me her Name: otherwise I shall be fidgeting for six Months and perhaps fall in Love with some one of that Name upon the Strength of it.—Are none of the young Ladies of B[raintre]e about entering into Wedlock or courted? For Heaven's sake what do the young Gentlemen mean? Are there not five Suitors to be found, possessed of Accomplishments and Virtues sufficient to render themselves agreable to the amiable five, who live at the foot of Penns Hill, by the Church, down a Hill and on the Farms? If I saw the least possible Chance for myself; if I was not so old and advanced in life as to be *indifferent*; if I had not set my Heart upon living in the Woods upon my Return, I would begin to make *Propositions* at least to one. My best Love to them all. God bless them with good Husbands. Much Duty and Respect where due. With the most perfect Esteem, I have the honour to be, Madam, your most humble Servant,

North Common[3]

Excuse haste and Errors and so much of love affairs.

RC (Adams Papers).

[1] That is, the *South Carolina*; its name under French ownership had been *L'Indien*.

[2] Thaxter to AA, without day, Aug.; and to AA2, 25 Aug.; both above.

[3] What prompted Thaxter to adopt this pseudonym, briefly, is not known. Later he occasionally used another, "J. North," in writing AA.

James Lovell to Abigail Adams

Decr. 4th. 1781

In answer to some Questions contained in your Letter of Sepr. 26[1] you may know that Mr. Laurens might ‖pay any sum up to five hundred po[unds]‖ s[terling] therefore the same is now to be done at discretion. ‖F. Dana is‖ *accompanied* under somewhat similar discretionary stipulations. Indeed you are mistaken about the Scales. I should be happy to be *sure* of what you only *conjecture*. I mean that ‖J. Jay goes.‖

The Boston Papers first and afterwards your Letter of Novr. 15 made me yesterday very happy after eight and forty hours of most painful Condolance with your Family upon information given to Genl. Lincoln by his Son from Cambridge under date of the 17th.[2] I will permit my dull Thoughts under a former date[3] to go on that you may the better judge of my present Joy. You will yet embrace your dear Charles whom I had buried under the Waves without daring to tell you the whole of my Imaginations.

I have already mentioned the Goodness and Punctuality of Genl. Lincoln by which my honest tho ineficacious Endeavours to serve you are intirely eclipsed. You will look to Col. Crafts for what has been long under my Care.[4]

There is in this City a Gentleman by the Name of Philmore.[5] I know not that I have ever seen him; but I have been accustomed on hearing his Name mentioned to suppose it Philip *More*. Mr. Osgood[6] tells me he spoke with a Man at a Tavron here by the Name of More, and if I recollect right I sought the same Person to be the Bearer of some Letters to Boston but found he was gone to Baltimore. As to his Character Mr. O supposes him to be one of the Chiefs of that honest industrious Class who have made the Roads smoke for two or three Years by their Changes and Exchanges. If I saw him, I have forgot it. But, my esteemed Friend, what is he *more* or *less* to me than any other of his Tribe or Name?

"You had not replied to mine of Oct. 9. You had felt a Reluctance at Writing."[7] You do not say at answering or noticing *it*. Yet your following Expressions excite an Idea of the Kind, and have in them a sort of Asperity which I own I never expected to experience *again* after the date of some of your former Letters. I have not a Copy of any one Line that I have ever written to you; nor do I recollect that I have at any Time made a Copy; so that I know not whether the Scrawl of Octr. 9th. was a simple one or whether it had any Thing about it that you could conceive was intended as a "Border." Be assured of my settled deliberate Resolution not to waste a drop of Ink or injure the Fibre of a Quill in that Way.—I presume you can turn your Eye upon what is before me of Novr. 15. You have said too little or too much: I think the former. I must know *More*, or you will "not act the part of a Friend in that particular." I have a Right to conclude that some Circumstances have retarded the Progress of your (friendly) Pen if "only *one* is wanting to put a *final* Stop to it." I am very uneasy at this same Letter of yours of Novr. 15th. And my present Circumstances make that Assertion convey the most respectful Compliment that I have ever paid you. For you are to know that I am so far pressed with what I call *real substantial* Misfortune, the End of which I do not foresee, that a Letter verbatim like yours from any other Pen *but one* on Earth would not have been read a second Time over, much less would it have found Room to have operated in my Head or Breast. Your good Sense and your Friendship make the second Claim to my Attention after that Sovereign one which Mrs. Lovell secures by an avowed, uniform, unabating Love and a prudent Confidence which is sure not to be abused.

Must I become the Slave to *Opinions*? You betray me Madam. You have almost brought me to think that the *Breath* of a Villain is an Object for my Resentment.

RC (Adams Papers). Passages within double verticals have been deciphered from Lovell's cipher, on which see Appendix to this volume.

[1] No letter of this date from AA to Lovell has been found, but an apparently incomplete Dft of it, dated 20 Sept., is printed above under the latter date; see note 1 there. AA's "Questions," here answered by Lovell, are not in AA's Dft. They must have related to the sums allotted by Congress to JA and to Dana for payment of secretaries, and whether John Jay would attend the peace negotiations at Paris.

[2] "As I was coming out of Boston yesterday Col. Crafts informed me that a ship had just arrived from France and brought an account that the Carolina frigate was wrecked on the coast of Holland and that the Captain of the ship had on board a list of the people that were lost. Jackson, John Trumbull and a son of Mr. Adams' were among the number" (Benjamin Lincoln Jr. to Gen. Benjamin Lincoln, Cambridge, 17 Nov., MHi:Lincoln Papers). AA had, however, already written Lovell on 15 Nov. (though it reached him later than Lincoln's report) that the *South Carolina* had put into La Coruña in Spain.

[3] Lovell to AA, 29 Nov., above.

[4] See Lovell to AA, 26 Nov.–2 Dec., above.

[5] Lovell is here responding to a query in AA's letter to him of 15 Nov., above. Philip More (or Philmore?) has not been further identified.

[6] Samuel Osgood (1748–1813), a Massachusetts delegate to the Continental Congress, 1780–1784 (*Biog. Dir. Cong.*).

[7] Lovell here paraphrases AA's letter to him of 15 Nov., q.v. above.

Abigail Adams to John Adams

My Dearest Friend   December 9 1781

I hear the Alliance is again going to France with the Marquis Fayett and the Count de Noiales.[1] I will not envy the Marquis the pleasure of Annually visiting his family, considering the risk he runs in doing it. Besides he deserves the good wishes of every American and a large portion of the Honours and applause of his own Country.

He returns with the additional Merrit of Laurels won at York Town by the Capture of a whole British Army. America may boast that she has accomplished what no power before her ever did, contending with Britain—Captured two of their celebrated Generals and each [with] an Army of thousands of veteran Troops to support them. This Event whilst it must fill Britain with despondency, will draw the union already formed still closer and give us additional Allies; if properly improved must render a negotiation easier and more advantageous to America.

But I cannot reflect much upon publick affairs; untill I have unburthend the load of my own Heart. Where shall I begin my list of Grievences? Not by accusations, but lamentations. My first is that I do not hear from you. A few lines only dated in April and May, have come to hand for 15 Months. You do not mention receiving any from me, except by Capt. Caznew, tho I wrote by Col. Laurence, by Capt. Brown, by Mr. Storer, Dexter and many others. By Babson to Bilboa by Trash, and several times by way of France.[2] You will refer me to Gillion I suppose. Gillion has acted a base part, of which no doubt you are long e'er now apprized. You had great reason to suppose that he would reach America, as soon or sooner than the Merchant vessels and placed much confidence in him, by the treasure you permited to go on Board of him. Ah! how great has my anxiety been, what have I not sufferd since I heard my dear Charles was on Board and no intelligence to be procured of the vessel for 4 months after she saild. Most people concluded that she was founderd at Sea, as she sailed before a voilent Storm. Only 3 weeks ago did I hear the contrary. My unkle dispatchd a Messenger the Moment a vessel from Bilboa arrived with the happy tidings that She was safe at Corruna, that the passenger[s] had all left the Ship in consequence of Gillions conduct, and were arrived at Bilboa. The vessel saild the day that the passengers arrived at Bilboa so that no Letters came by Capt. Lovett but a Dr. Sands reports that he saw a child whom they told him was yours and that he was well. This was a cordil to my dejected Spirits. I know not what to wish for. Should he attempt to come at this Season upon this coast, it has more Horrours than I have fortitude. I am still distresst. I must resign him to the kind protecting Hand of that Being who hath heitherto preserved him, and submit to what ever dispensation is alloted me.

What is the matter with Mr. T[haxte]r, has he forgotten all his American Friends, that out of four vessels which have arrived, not a line is to be found on Board of one of them from him?

I could Quarrell with the climate, but surely if it is subject to the Ague, there is a fever fit as well as the cold one. Mr. Guile tells me he was charged with Letters, but left them with his other things on Board the frigate, She gave him the Slip, he stept on Board Capt. Brown and happily arrived safe. From him I have learnt many things respecting my dear connextions, but still I long for that free communication which I see but little prospect of obtaining. Let me again intreat you to write by way of Guardoca, Bilboa is as safe a conveyance as any I know of.—Ah my dear John, where are you— in so remote a part of the Globe that I fear I shall not hear a Syllable from you.—Pray write me all the intelligence you get from him, send me his Letters to you. Do you know I have not a line from him for a year and half.—Alass my dear I am much afflicted with a disorder call'd the *Heartach*, nor can any remedy be found in America, it must be collected from Holland, Petersburgh and Bilboa.—And now having recited my Greifs and complaints, the next in place are those of my Neighbours. I have been applied to by the parents of several Braintree youth to write to you in their behalf, requesting your aid and assistance if it is in your power to afford it. Capt. Cathcart in the privateer Essex from Salem, went out on a cruise last April into the Channel of England, and was on the 10 of June So unfortunate as to be taken and carried into Ireland, the officers were confined there, but the Sailors were sent prisoners to Plimouth jail 12 of whom are from this Town, a list of whom I inclose. The Friends of these people have received Intelligence by way of an officer who belonged to the *Protector*, and who escaped from the jail; that in August last they were all alive, several of them very destitute of cloathing, having taken but a few with them, and those for the Summer, particularly Ned Savils and Jobe Feild. There request is that if you can, you would render them some assistance, if not by procuring an exchange, that you would get them supplied with necessary cloathing.

I have told them that you would do all in your power for them, but what that would be I could not say. Their Friends here are all well, many of them greatly distresst for their Children, and in a particular manner the Mother of Jeriah Bass.

I wish you to be very particular in letting me know by various opportunities and ways, after the recept of this, whether you have been able to do any thing for them, that I may relieve the minds of these distresst parents. The Capt. got home about 3 months ago, by escapeing to France, but could give no account of his Men after they were taken.[3]

Two years my dearest Friend have passd away since you left your Native land. Will you not return e'er the close of an other year? I will purchase you a retreat in the woods of Virmont and retire with you from the vexations, toils and hazards of publick Life. Do you not sometimes sigh for such a Seclusion—publick peace and domestick happiness,

> "an elegant Sufficency, content
> Retirement, Rural quiet, Friendship, Books
> Ease and alternate Labour, usefull Life
> progressive Virtue and approveing Heaven."

May the time, the happy time soon arrive when we may realize these blessings so elegantly discribed by Thomson, for tho many of your country Men talk in a different Stile with regard to their intentions, and express their wishes to see you in a conspicuous point of view in your own State, I feel no ambition for a share of it. I know the voice of Fame to be a mere weathercock, unstable as Water and fleeting as a Shadow. Yet I have pride, I know I have a large portion of it.

I very fortunately received by the Apollo, by the Juno and by the Minerva the things you sent me, all in good order.

They will enable me to do I hope without drawing upon you, provided I can part with them, but Money is so scarce and taxes so high, that few purchasers are found. Goods will not double, yet they are better than drawing Bills, as they cannot be sold but with a large discount. I could not get more than 90 for a hundred Dollers, should I attempt it.

I shall inclose an invoice to the House of Ingraham Bromfild,[4] and one to de Neufvilla. There is nothing from Bilboa that can be imported with advantage, hankerchiefs are sold here at 7 dollers & half per dozen. There are some articles which would be advantageous from Holland, but Goods there run high, and the retailing vendues which are tolerated here ruin the Shopkeepers. The articles put up, by the American House were better in Quality, for the price than those by the House of de Neufvilla. Small articles have the best profit, Gauze, ribbons, feathers and flowers to make the Ladies Gay, have the best advance. There are some articles which come from India I should suppose would be lower priced than many others—bengalls,[5] Nankeens, persian Silk and Bandano hankerchiefs, but the House of Bromfeild & C[o]. know best what articles will suit here.

I have been fortunate and unfortunate. The things which came in Jones remain at Philadelphia yet.

Our Friends here are all well. Your Mother is rather in better Health, and my Father is yet sprightly. Believe me with more affection than Words can express ever Ever Yours,   Portia

P.S.   I have inclosed a memorandum of some articles. I have not written to any one about them. You will give it to whom you think best and send it when you can. I shall in some future Letter mention a list of articles which I wish you to bring home with you whenever the happy time comes, but which I do not want without you. Adieu.

RC (Adams Papers); endorsed by John Thaxter: "Portia 9. & 23d. Decr. 1781 inclosing Dean's Letter." It was in her letter of 23 Dec., q.v. below, that AA enclosed Silas Deane's letter. The enclosures mentioned in her present letter and its postscript have not been found.

[1] Louis Marie, Vicomte de Noailles, who served with Rochambeau, was La- fayette's brother-in-law; see sketch in JA, *Diary and Autobiography*, 4:85.

[2] Punctuation as in MS.

[3] Although the list enclosed by AA of the Braintree sailors who were made prisoners and sent to Mill Prison at Plymouth after capture of the *Essex* by the English privateer *Queen Charlotte* has not been found, it may be reconstructed by adding to the names of Jeriah Bass, Job Field, and Edward Savil, named in this letter, those of two Beales (Nathanael and another), Gridley and Lemuel Clark, Samuel Curtis, Lewis Glover, William Horton, Briant Newcombe, and Thomas Vinton. (The documents on which the present note is based are listed in a single sequence in a separate paragraph below.)

Before AA wrote, JA had already been apprised by five of the men themselves of their plight, had been requested by them to provide for their relief, and had responded promptly by sending them two guineas apiece through Edmund Jenings in Brussels for disbursement through Jenings' friend Michael Sawrey, a benevolently inclined merchant who lived in Plymouth. Before or at about the same time JA received AA's appeal, he had also heard directly from two more of the Braintree lads, had had letters singly or jointly from the parents of the rest of the twelve, and had received a plea for additional aid from the five he had supplied in October. To these requests, JA responded by having Jenings transmit, as he had before, 40s sterling to each of eight of the men, including two who had shared in the earlier distribution. At the same time he asked that Sawrey inform him through Jenings whether these or any of the others "befriended before" were in need of more and how much. Sawrey responded with a list of seven: Bass, the two Clarks, Curtis, Glover, Horton, and Vinton. JA advanced additional sums then or later, so that all or most of the twelve had received £4 or more each from him before their return to Braintree.

The letters to JA from the Braintree prisoners and their families in 1781–1782 make clear that all the financial aid given by JA was on the express promise of reimbursement. Since he had no public funds available for this purpose, the advances were out of his own funds. Most of the recipients attempted to repay AA, who put them off while awaiting instructions from her husband.

Although JA did not himself acknowledge to AA until Sept. 1782 that he had responded to her appeal in behalf of the prisoners, word of his "Benevolent exertions and generous aid" reached her through their families in July and August. By that time, "enlargement" or exchange of all twelve (whether or not by JA's efforts is not clear) had taken place, and by October eleven of them had reached Braintree.

Two additional prisoners at Plymouth, Capt. John Manley and Capt. Silas Talbot, apparently were added by Sawrey in the fall of 1781 to those JA had named to receive disbursements. What was evidently still another group, of whom the grandson of Rev. Charles Chauncy of Boston was one, escaped to the Netherlands in the summer of 1781 and were there given money and aid by JA. Beyond these instances, JA responded, without apparent success, to appeals in 1781–1782 to locate and aid in having exchanged, Benjamin Brackett, fifteen-year-old nephew of Joshua Brackett of Boston, and a Capt. Armstrong, friend of Tristram Dalton of Newburyport. It is edifying to find that two of the prisoners aided by JA while in the Netherlands turned up aboard the *Active* when AA sailed from Boston to Europe in that vessel in 1784. Dr. Chauncy's grandson, "A likely young fellow whose countanance is a good Letter of recommendation," was serving as second mate of the *Active*; and Job Field, a seaman "whose place on board the ship I had procured for him," AA recorded, was so "Handy, attentive, obligeing and kind, [and so] excellent [a] Nurse, [that] we all prized him" (AA, Diary, June–July 1784, in JA, *Diary and Autobiography*, 3:155, 162).

The documents on which the above account is based are listed in chronological order herewith. All are in the Adams Papers, and the letters between JA and AA that fall within the time span of the present volume are printed herein. Job Field et al. to JA, 8 Sept.; JA to Job Field et al., 24 Oct., LbC; JA to Edmund Jenings, 24 Oct.; Jenings to JA, 28 Oct., 26 Nov.; JA to Jenings, 29 Nov.; Samuel Bass 2d to JA, 13 Dec.; Joshua Brackett to JA, 15 Dec.; Thomas Vinton Jr. to JA, 20 Dec. 1781. Thomas Vinton Jr. to JA, 5 Feb.; Edward Savil et al. to JA, 14 Feb.; JA to Jenings, 21 Feb.; Jenings to JA, 31 March, 6 June; AA to JA, 17 July, 5 Aug., 3 Sept.; JA to AA 17 Sept.; AA to JA, 25 Oct.; Tristram Dalton to JA, 26 Oct. 1782. AA recounts taking tea with Michael Sawrey and his wife when the Adamses visited Plymouth, England, in 1787 (AA to Mary Smith Cranch, 15 Sept. 1787, MWA; quoted in JA, *Diary and Autobiography*, 3:209).

JA's concern with the plight of prisoners was of long duration. In the early days of hostilities he had been exercised over the reported treatment accorded prisoners of war taken by British troops in America; while in France in 1778 he had with Franklin and Arthur Lee dispatched to the British Ministry numerous protests against the treatment of prisoners in British hands and proposals for exchange of naval prisoners. While awaiting the sailing of the *Alliance* at Nantes in 1779 he had overseen an exchange; again at Bilbao in early 1780 he had undertaken to see that American prisoners escaped from Portugal received proper clothing. See above, vol. 2:224–226, 230–231; JA, *Diary and Autobiography*, 2:358–359, 432; 4:127–128, 138–139, 236, and index under Prisoners of War.

During his mission to the Netherlands JA's problem with prisoners and former prisoners of war became more acute. The nature of this problem is epitomized and illuminated in the case of Thomas Beer and his family, which JA had recently had to deal with. Beer was not an American or a prisoner but an Englishman who had "been obliged to flee from England on account of his having assisted the American prisoners to Escape." So Francis Coffyn wrote JA from Dunkirk on 2 Oct. 1781, adding that, on advice from Franklin in Paris, Coffyn had paid Beer "ten Guineas to help him to Holland, with his wife and two young children; I hope your Excellency will be pleased to recommand him and get him Employed in the Rope makers business in which he seems to be Expert, as he was one of the Surveyors in the King of England's yards; to facili-

tate his passage to America" (Adams Papers). On 18 Oct. JA wrote from Amsterdam to Franklin:

"Thomas Beer, with his Wife and two small Children, came to my House, this Forenoon, and presented me, a Letter from Mr. Coffyn of Dunkirk ... recommending Beer to me as a Person who had been obliged to flee from England, for having assisted American Prisoners to escape; and inclosing a Copy of a Letter from your Excellency to Mr. Coffyn of 22 of August, advising Beer to go to Holland, where your Excellency imagined there was great demand for all Kind of Workmen, who are usefull in fitting out ships, ... and requesting Mr. Coffyn, for the future to send the Prisoners, to my Care, at Amsterdam, and to desire his Friend, at Ostend, to give them the same direction.

"As to Beer, I know not what to do with him. He has spent his last Guilder, and the Man, Woman and Children all looked as if they had been weeping, over their Distresses in deplorable Misery. I gave him some Money, to feed his Children a night or two and went out to see, if I could get him Work with a Rope Maker. But I was told that your Excellency was much mistaken.... That Navigation being in a manner stopped, such Tradesmen had the least to do of any, and particularly the Rope Makers complained of Want of Work more than ever and more than any other set of Tradesmen. However, a Gentleman will enquire if he can find a Place for him.

"I have no Objection to American Prisoners coming this Way, and shall continue to do any Thing in my Power, as I have done, to solace them in their distress. I have now for a Year past, relieved considerable Numbers who have escaped from England, with small Sums, and with my best endeavours [tried] to procure them Employment and Passages.

"But your Excellency is very sensible I have no publick Money in my Hands, and that therefore, the small sums of Money, which I have been able to furnish them must have been out of my own Pockett. This Resource is likely to fail very soon, if my Salary is not to be paid me, in future.

"If your Excellency would give me

your Consent that I should take up small Sums of Money, of M[ess]rs. Fizeau and Grand, &c., for the Purpose of assisting our Countrymen who escape from Prison, I should esteem myself honoured by this Trust, for none of my Time, is spent with more Pleasure than that which is devoted to the Consolation of these Prisoners.—The Masters of Vessels have hitherto been very good in giving Passages, and We have made various shifts to dispose of such as have been here, and have succeeded so as to give tolerable Satisfaction but we should do much better if We had a little more Money.

"I have often told your Excellency, that the House of De Neufville & son had received a few thousand Guilders, upon the Loan Opened by me in behalf of the United States.—I have not yet touched this Money, because I thought it should lie, to answer Bills of Exchange upon the Draughts of Congress: But as there is so little, if your Excellency would advise me to it, I would devote it to lie for the Benefit of the poor Prisoners, and would make it go as far, in relieving their distresses as I could."

(LbC in JA's hand, Adams Papers; RC in John Thaxter's hand, PPAmP.)

⁴ This American mercantile firm in Amsterdam had originated earlier this year as Sigourney, Ingraham & Bromfield; see JA, *Diary and Autobiography*, 2:453–454 and *passim*.

⁵ "[P]iece goods (apparently of different kinds) exported from Bengal to England in the 17 c." (*OED*), and evidently to Europe generally in the 18th century.

Abigail Adams to John Thaxter

My dear Sir   December 9 1781

I do not take up my pen by way of reply to any Letter of yours— that is not in my power. 15 Months have elapsed since the date of your last.¹ I must take you a little to task to give you an opportunity of justifying yourself. Here are no less than 3 of the Heathen deities arrived from your port without a single Syllable from You. Minerva— surely it is her peculiar province to communicate Wisdom, yet she is as silent as Apollo whom I consulted upon the occasion, but both of them affirm that they know nothing of you. Juno indeed produced your Hand writing, as a cover to some Newspapers and pamphlets which is all that could be obtained from her. I cannot reconcile this with your former punctuality. It is true I have no more reason to complain, than your other Friends, but we all look sober about it, I assure you: and the more so for hearing that you are not well; and that your wishes are to return to America. I hope you are not so uneasy as to opperate upon your Health; if that is the case, loth as I know my dear Friend would be to part with you, he would not detain you, if you once made known your desires; I have not told your Friends all I have heard upon this subject as I fear it would give them uneasyness.

You will have heard before this reaches you of the strange part Gillion has acted; my dear Charles is at Bilboa, and must exchange September for Jan'ry or Febry., a dreadful Season to come upon this coast. The Letters which were put on Board of him must be still with him, if any were committed to his care. I do not think he means to come to America soon.

I hope you have been made very happy by the agreable tiding from America. The aspect of our affairs is Brightned, an other British Army is added to our Glorious exploits and conquests, with an abhored, because a merciless and cruel Captive General to swell our triumphs. The Month of October is a memorable one to America, and a fatal one to Britain. Will she can she still persist in her wanton cruelties, in her mad projects of domination, whilst she is crumbling to attoms? Will not the united provinces be proud to allye themselves to our vallient states—will they not acknowledge our Independance and claim kindred with us? Is there any prospect of peace? May a Glorious one incircle us with its blessings before an other year Elapses, but I fear from certain movements to which I suppose you are no Stranger that it may not be all we wish. Yet the Capture of Cornwallis must opperate in our favour.

Most of the Ladies of your acquaintance still remain Single. Several whom you left just rising into notice now figure with Eclat. You are not forgotten amongst them. I often hear your name mentiond with much esteem, an Epethet well suited to the tempreture of the low Countries.

Master Tommy desires me to remember to insert his affectionate regard to you, and Miss Nabby looks it, tho not articulated.

Your Friends were all well last week when your Brother was here. Your Sister Celia spent a fortnight here in the last month, and Miss Nancy[2] is expected this Week to spend a month or two. Your Friend Abel Alleyne is sailed for Antigue and from thence designs for Barbados. Provisions plenty here, money a scarce commodity indeed, taxes, exorbitant. Luxery still prevailing in Building, furniture, Equipage, and dress. The scarcity of cash will Lessen it with some, but many realized their enormous sums of paper.

Let me beg of you to be punctual in writing and let no opportunity slip by which you may convey comfort and satisfaction to your Friends particularly to your ever affectionate Friend,   Portia

RC (MB); addressed: "Mr. John Thaxter   Amsterdam"; endorsed: "Mrs. Adams 9th. Decr. 1781."

[1] AA must allude to a letter or letters from Thaxter dated at Paris, 19 and 20 Sept. 1780, both in vol. 3 above. Thaxter had written her a number of times in 1781, and most of these letters are printed in the present volume, but some had been delayed in the sending and she had as yet received none of them.

See above, Thaxter to AA, 21 July, and note 1 there.

²Presumably Hannah, John Thaxter's

other sister, identified above at vol. 3:43; see Adams Genealogy.

John Adams to John Quincy Adams

My dear Son   Amsterdam Decr. 14. 1781

Your Letter of 21 Aug. O.S.¹ the first I have received, reached me only two or three days ago.

I am pleased to see, your hand Writing improve, as well as your Judgment ripen, as you travel. But I am above all happy to find that your Behaviour has been such as to gain the Confidence of M[r]. D[ana] so far as to employ you in copying. This Employment requires a great degree of Patience and Steadiness as well as care. It will be of vast Use to you, to be admitted thus early into Business, especially into Business of such Importance.

Make it a Rule, my dear Son, To loose no Time. There is not a moral Precept, of clearer Obligation, or of greater Import. Make it the grand Maxim of your Life, and it cannot fail to be happy, and usefull to the World.

You have my Consent to have any Masters, which Mr. D. thinks proper for you. But you will have none, upon whom I shall depend so much as upon him. He will form your moral and political Principles, and give you a Taste for Letters as well as Business, if you can but be so wise and happy as to continue to deserve his Confidence, and be admitted to assist him, in Copying his Business.

I have Letters from your Mother who sends you her Blessing and your youngest Brother who sends you his Love.²

Charles writes me from Bilbao 24 Nov.³ expecting to sail the next Week, he desires his Love to you, and his affectionate Respects to Mr. D.

Write me often. Let me know the State of Education and Letters in St. Petersbg. Pray do you hear any Thing of a Passage by Land, from Russia to America? What Discoveries have been made?

It is not necessary to add my Name, when I assure you of my Affection.

RC (Adams Papers). Early Tr (Adams Papers), in JQA's hand.

¹That is, 1 Sept. N.S.; printed above under that date.
²No letter from TBA to JA at this period has been found.
³Letter not found.

John Adams to John Quincy Adams

My dear Child   Amsterdam Decr. 15. 1781

This day Mr. Sayre arrived,[1] with your Letter of the 12/23 of October. Yours of August I answered, Yesterday.

You have not informed me whether the Houses are built of Brick, Stone or Wood. Whether they are seven stories high or only one. How they are glazed, whether they have chimneys as in Spain. What publick Buildings, what Maison de Ville or state house. What Churches? What Palaces? What Statuary, what Paintings, Musick, Spectacles, &c. You have said nothing of the Religion of the Country, whether it is Catholick or Protestant. What is the national Church. Whether there are many Sectaries. Whether there is a Toleration of various Religions &c.

I think the Price for a Master is intolerable. If there is no Academy, nor School, nor a Master to be had, I really dont know what to say to your staying in Russia. You had better be at Leyden where you might be in a regular course of Education. You might come in the Spring in a Russian, Sweedish or Prussian Vessell, to Embden perhaps or Hamborough, and from thence here, in a neutral Bottom still. I am afraid of your being too troublesome to Mr. D[ana].

However, I rely upon it that you follow your Studies with your wonted Assiduity. It is strange if no Dictionary can be found in French nor English.

I dont perceive that you take Pains enough with your Hand Writing. Believe me, from Experience, if you now in your Youth resolutely conquer your impatience, and resolve never to write the most familiar Letter or trifling Card, with[2] Attention and care, it will save you a vast deal of Time and Trouble too, every day of your whole Life. When the habit is got, it is easier to write well than ill, but this Habit is only to be acquired, in early life.

God bless my dear Son, and preserve his Health and his Manners, from the numberless dangers, that surround Us, wherever We go in this World. So prays your affectionate Father,   J. Adams

RC (Adams Papers). Early Tr (Adams Papers), in JQA's hand.

[1] Stephen Sayre (1736–1818), Princeton 1757, was an international adventurer and free-lance diplomat who had spent more than a year in St. Petersburg intriguing to promote U.S.–Russian trade and his own fortune. The most recent biographical account of Sayre is in Sibley-Shipton, *Harvard Graduates* (he held a Harvard M.A.), 14:204–215. Still valuable is Julian P. Boyd, "The Remarkable Adventures of Stephen Sayre," *Princeton Univ. Libr. Chronicle*, 2:51–64 (Feb. 1941). The article by David W. Griffiths, "American

Commercial Diplomacy in Russia, 1780–1783," *WMQ*, 3d ser., 27:379–410 (April 1970), is informative on Sayre's Russian mission; see esp. p. 384–389.

[2] Thus in RC, and so copied by JQA in Tr. In printing this letter in an appendix to AA's *Letters*, 1848, p. 424, CFA silently corrected "with" to "without."

John Adams to Abigail Adams

My dearest friend   Amsterdam Decr. 18 1781

I have Letters from Mr. Dana and his young Attendant, at St. Petersbourg. Both well and in good Spirits. Letters to Mrs. D. and to you go by Captn. Troubridge and by Dr. Dexter.

I have no certain News, as yet of Charles's Sailing from Bilbao, but I presume he is sailed. You will have suffered great Anxiety on his Account, but I pray he may arrive safe. I acted for the best when I consented he should go in Gillon, little expecting that he would be landed in Spain again. Keep him to his studies and send him to Colledge, where I wish his Brother John was.

My Health is feeble, but better than it was. I am busy, enough, yet not to much perceptible Purpose as yet. There is no Prospect at all of Peace. Let our People take Care of their Trade and Privateers, next year. They have not much of a Land War to fear.

General Washington, has struck the most sublime stroke of all in that Article of the Capitulation, which reserves the Tories for Tryal by their Peers. This has struck Toryism dumb and dead. I expect that all the Rancour of the Refugees will be poured out upon Cornwallis for it.[1]

Our Ennemies now really stand in a ridiculous Light. They feel it but cannot take the Resolution to be wise.

The Romans never saw but one caudine Forks in their whole History. Americans have shewn the Britains two, in one War.—But they must do more. Remember, you never will have Peace, while the Britains have a Company of Soldiers at Liberty, within the United States. New York must be taken, or you will never have Peace.—All in good time.

The British Army Estimates are the same as last Year, the Navy less by several ships of the Line. What can these People hope for.

I fancy the southern states will hold their Heads very high. They have a right. They will scarcely be overrun again I believe, even in the hasty manner of Cornwallis. Burgoine dont seem to be affronted that his Nose is out of Joint. He is in good Spirits. Experience has convinced him.—So I hope it has Cornwallis, that the American War is impracticable. The flour, the Choice of the British Army was with him.

The K[ing] of Eng[land] consoles his People under all their Disgraces, Disasters, and dismal Prospects, by telling them that they are brave and free. It is a pity for him that he did not allow the Americans to be so Seven Years ago. But the great designs of Providence must be accomplished. Great Indeed! The Progres of Society, will be accellerated by Centuries by this Rev[olution]. The Emperor of Germany is adopting as fast as he can American Ideas of Toleration and religious Liberty, and it will become the fashionable system of all Europe very soon. Light Spreads from the day Spring in the West, and may it shine more and more until the perfect day.

Duty to Parents, Love to Brothers, sisters and Children. It is not in the Power of Worlds[2] to express the Tenderness with which I bid you farewell.

RC (Adams Papers).

[1] "Article X [of the Articles of Capitulation at Yorktown, 19 Oct. 1781]. Natives or inhabitants of different parts of this country, at present in York or Gloucester, are not to be punished for having joined the British army.

"This article cannot be assented to, being altogether of civil resort." (Washington, *Writings*, ed. Sparks, 8:535.)

Cornwallis' acceptance of the Allies' negative of this article, thereby abandoning the loyalists with the British army "to the power of an inveterate, implacable enemy" (to use Sir Henry Clinton's words), outraged George III and became one of the issues in the bitter controversy between Cornwallis and Clinton. See Benjamin Franklin Stevens, ed., *The Campaign in Virginia, 1781 ...*, London, 1888, 1:44, 199 ff.; 2:202; William B. Willcox, ed., *The American Rebellion: Sir Henry Clinton's Narrative of His Campaigns, 1775–1782*, New Haven, 1954, p. 352–353, 582–583, 592–594, 597–598.

[2] Thus in MS.

John Adams to Richard Cranch

My dear Brother   Amsterdam Decr. 18 1781

I send you a Volume of Politics. A Second Volume will be ready in 6 or 7 Weeks.—You will hear more about this Paper, in time.[1]

I have received several kind Letters from you. Pray continue to write me, altho you should be disappointed of my Answers. I have noted your Desire, in one of them and have taken such measures as I could, but fear you have received nothing as yet, although some have been sent.[2] Little can be done in this Way. This Country begins to think seriously of Us but they must think a long time, you know.

There is no Prospect of Peace. Let our Country men look to their Trade and Privateers, for I suspect the English will strain every Nerve, to hurt them in this Way finding so many Caudine Forks in the Land War. The English are amuzing the Dutch with insidious Proposals of a seperate Peace. But I am perswaded no such Thing can take Place. A Quadruple Alliance would be much more for the Honour and Interest of this Rep[ublic] but whether they will think so time must discover.

The Emperor has acceded to the armed Neutrality: so that all the Powers of the World, are either at War with England or pledged to be Neutral. The King of Prussia acceded sometime ago.

The Brit[ish] Ministry seem to give over the Ideas of Conquest. By their Speeches in Parliament, their Hopes are extinct. Yet perhaps this may be a feint. It is impossible however, that they should do much. The People are meeting and making a Bustle, but all will evaperate in a few frothy Speeches, and fruitless Remonstrances.

Our Allies have at last found the true Method of obtaining Tryumphs. If they pursue the Plan the War will be easy.

The British Navy will be much weaker next year than this. Their Army is not proposed to be stronger, and they will not find it in fact, near so strong.

Let Dr. Cooper read the Politique Hollandais, and tell him that I will send him his sermon and the Governors Speech and the Massachusetts Constitution, translated into Dutch, as soon as I can. The Translation is published with an elegant Comparison between the Mass[achusetts] Constitution and that of this Rep[ublic].[3]

Remember me to every Body.   Your affectionate Brother

RC (MHi: Washburn Collection); endorsed: "Letter from Bror. Adams Decr. 18th. 1781 (from Amsterdam)." For the accompanying "Volume" see note 1.

[1] Evidently the "Volume" sent was the first volume of *Le politique hollandais*, issued at Amsterdam late in 1781 and mentioned by name in the last paragraph of this letter. The editor of this pro-French, pro-American, anti-Orangist weekly periodical was JA's friend A. M. Cerisier, identified above in this volume; for a fuller account of him and his journal, see JA, *Diary and Autobiography*, 2:453–454.

[2] See Cranch to JA, 22 June and 3 Nov., both above.

[3] JA alludes to a collection of documents relative to the American Revolution translated and edited pseudonymously by the Patriot writer and clergyman Francis Adrian Van der Kemp (1752–1829), on whom see further, JA, *Diary and Autobiography*, 2:456. Entitled *Verzameling der Stukken tot de dertien Vereenigde Staeten van Noord-Amerika betrekkelijk*, Leyden, 1781, it contained among other things (in part furnished by JA) a text of the Massachusetts Constitution of 1780; Rev. Samuel Cooper's *Sermon Preached ... October 25, 1780*, Boston, 1780; and Governor John Hancock's speech at the opening of the first session of the Massachusetts legislature under the new constitution, 31 Oct. 1780. JA's copies are in MB (*Catalogue of JA's Library*, p. 255). See also Van der Kemp to JA, 26 Nov., and Jean Luzac to JA, 10 Dec. 1781, both in Adams Papers; and Van der Kemp, *Autobiography*, p. 44–45, 214.

John Thaxter to Abigail Adams

Madam   Amsterdam Decr. 19th. 1781

By the last Mails came the King's Speech, the Address of the two Houses in answer, and the debates in Parliament. His most gracious Majesty is sorry, that the Americans and French have catched one of his flying Generals with an Army, because the *Rectitude* of his Cause entitled him to better luck. He tells his Parliament the Rebellion is still fomented, and that his Subjects continue in that state of delusion, that the Bravery of his fleets and Armies was to have removed seven Years agone. He seems to be anxious about America, and wishes to bring them back to that happy state which their former Obedience placed them in. Never mind it, my Lords and Gentlemen, to be sure it has been rather a bad season for Us, and I am sorry for it, but next Year, if You will keep the Purse full, I will rely with a firm Confidence upon the Assistance of divine Providence, the Justice of my Cause, and the Bravery of my fleets and Armies, and do great things. What solemn Mockery coupled with a most ridiculous Farce? This, Madam, is the Language of a Monarch, who has had seven Years Experience of the most pointed Indignation of Heaven against his despotic Projects; seven Years experience of the Iniquity of his Cause, and an equal peri[o]d of the most convincing proofs, that neither the Bravery or Skill of his fleets and armies are adequate to the Task of subduing a People determined to assert the Rights and Dignity of human Nature, and to be free. Yet with this Torrent of Evidence, he means to go on, as if abandoned by that Providence on which he affects to rely. He is now flattering his People with the Epithets of "brave and free." America will hear much of large Armies — perhaps 20 or 25,000 men—large fleets &c. &c. being to be sent out next Spring by England. But these Men are all to be raised by the way, which will take six or seven Years at least. They cannot fit out a larger fleet than last Year: and this Fleet must be divided in proportion to their Objects and Number of Places to guard and relieve, which have increased much. In the debates of Parliament their fleet is stated to be only seventy nine Ships of the Line—this is not contradicted. France alone has seventy-one, Spain near sixty, and Holland between twenty and thirty. The fleet of England is not in general well manned—many of their ships very old—their standing Army is very small. Supposing the whole regular Army of the three Kingdoms were sent out, it would not replace the losses they sustained last Year in America, the West Indies &c. Altho' We need be under no apprehension at all of any force they can send out next Spring, (which cannot but be small) yet We ought not to relax in the least in our Exertions by Sea and Land, and more especially by Sea; for these Gentry have been so buffetted in this War, so baffled and disappointed in their Expectations, that they will never make Peace 'till they can no longer make War. Commerce is the Heart of the Kingdom, and Blood drawn from this Source will create sensations that will bring them at least to Reflection. Nothing like Privateering for this purpose.

I have become acquainted with an amiable Circle of Ladies in this City. I pay my Respects to them now and then, for the pleasure of their good Company, an improvement in the French Language, and to divert a little Gloom and Melancholy, which this horrible Climate casts over me at times. Three or four of them are handsome, and the rest very agreable, but make no pretensions to Beauty. I find much formality and Ceremony in families that are most intimate, which gives an appearance of an introduction to their most familiar Visits. However they are very sociable and one finds a display of good humour in their Company. The Ladies always salute each other upon entering and parting when they make Visits: And where I dared, I have endeavoured to introduce the practice of Gentlemen's (as far as respected me) making Use of the same feeling Expression of Respect towards the Ladies.

Much Duty and Love where due. I have the honor to be, with the most perfect Esteem & Respect, Madam, your most humble Servant,

North Common

RC (Adams Papers).

John Thaxter to John Quincy Adams

Mon cher Ami   Amsterdam ce 22. Decembre 1781

J'ai bien-recu les Lettres que vous m'avez fait l'honneur de m'ecrire de Francfort et de Berlin.[1] Votre Lettre de St. Petersbourg sous la date de 8/19 7bre. est aussi parvenue. Je vous suis très obligé pour toutes les trois. J'ai été fort content de vos observations sur le Caractere, les manieres et les coutumes des Peuples de ces pays dans lequels vous avez voyagé: et je vous prie de vouloir bien m'envoyer de tems en tems quelques morceaux de votre Journal, parce que je suis persuadé que c'est plein des remarques et des choses extrémement interressantes. Je suis étonné que vous navez pas trouvé plus des Villes entre Berlin et St. Petersbourg, et que le terrein est si stérile. Com-

269

ment trouvez vous les Villes de Dantzic, de Konigsberg, de Memel, de Riga, de Narva, et enfin la grande Ville de St. Petersbourg? Monsieur D[ana] a remarqué dans ses Lettres que cette derniere Ville etoit la plus belle et la plus magnifique du monde. Ayez la bonte de m'ecrire tout ce que vous pensez ou remarquez de cette Ville.

J'espere que Monsieur votre Frere est parti de Bilbao. Vous savez bien qu'il est parti d'ici premierement dans la Sud Caroline et qu'il est arrivé a Corogne en Espagne dans le mois de 7bre. Après il se trouvoit abord d'un Corsaire Americain destiné a Bilbao, où il est heureusment arrivé. Nos dernieres Lettres de cet endroit-la sont sous la date de 30. Novembre, et ces Messieurs, qui sont là, ecrivoient qu'ils doivent partir sur le champ, tellement que nous attendons la nouvelle de leur départ incessament.[2]

Je vous felicite très sincerement sur la prise de Milord Cornwallis avec toute son Armée: c'est un evénément très important pour notre chere patrie.

J'espere que vous trouvez votre situation très agreable et avantageuse. Prenez garde de votre santé. Suivez assidument vos études et je vous conseille en ami a suivre les conseils de Monsieur D. dans toutes choses. Croyez moi, mon cher, qu'il est votre meilleur Ami dans ce pays-la. Il n'y a personne plus capable que lui, ou plus prêt de vous aider et conseiller en tout ce qui vous regarde. Fait bien des Complimens a Mr. D. Tous vos Amis m'ont prie de vous faire leurs Complimens. Soyez assuré de mon affection pour vous et croyez moi que je suis très sincerement votre fidele Ami et Serviteur.

Voila une Lettre pleine des fautes[3]—n'importe. Peut-être vous pouvez la comprendre; mais si vous ne pouvez pas, dit moi franchement.—Adieu.

RC (Adams Papers); addressed: "A Monsieur Monsieur J. Q. Adams à St. Petersbourg"; endorsed: "Mr. J. Thaxter's Letter recd. January 2/13 1782. dated Decr. 22. 1781. No. 1. answered Jan'y 2/13 1782"; docketed in JQA's more mature hand: "J. Thaxter 22 Decr: 1781." Early Tr (Adams Papers), in JQA's hand; see note 3.

[1] Not found.
[2] See William Jackson to JA, Bilbao, 30 Nov., above.
[3] In the early Tr (i.e. in copying the text into his letterbook) JQA corrected some of Thaxter's misspellings and grammatical errors and supplied numerous missing accent marks.

Abigail Adams to John Adams

My Dearest Friend   December 23. 1781

I knew not untill half an hour ago that Mr. Guile intended for Europe, he did not know it himself, it was a suden movement. He has not been able to come [up?] as the vessel is expected to sail to-morrow, the Marquis and Count are already gone on Board. I have written by them,[1] but should have been more full and particuliar by Mr. Guile if I had sooner known of his intention.

He can give you a full and particular account of our Situation at present.[2] I need say nothing on that Head. He can tell you how anxious we have all been for my dear Boy, of whom I hear nothing further since his arrival at Bilboa. He can tell you how much diss-apointed I was that he should have [had] all his papers on Board Gillion so that not one line reachd me. I have not a syllable of a later date than *May*. It seems as if a fatality attended all our exertions for cloathing, and for intelligence. I have so short warning that I have not a line for my Russian vissiter, have you heard from him? When O when shall I?

I hope you enjoy your Health. I am anxious for you. My own I find infirm enough, my Nervous System is too easily agitated. I am frequently confined by slight indispositions to which I was always subject. I hope you have not experienced so much anxiety for our dear little Boy, as I have. It is not over. I fear the Dangers of our coast, every Storm agitates me least he should be comeing upon the coast.

I have written to you already that the things you orderd me all came safe to hand by the Minerva, by the Apollo and the Juno.

I have inclosed by the Count an invoice but have not written to any Body but to you about the articles.

I also inclose to you a coppy of a Letter, said to have been published abroad. You may have seen it before, but if you have not, it is a curi-osity.[3] There is a great scarcity of Money here, and will be a greater I believe when our taxes are paid. I shall not draw upon you if you can continue to make me remittances as you have done. I enter not into the present stile and mode of living. The whole of your Sallery would be inadequate to the expence in which some live now, in furni-ture, equipage, cloathing and feasting, who were not worth ten Spanish milld Dollors when the war commenced. But this rant can-not last long, they must again descend to their nothingness.

271

Excuse this hasty Scrawl. I would not that Mr. Guile should go without a line. Believe me at all times most assuredly yours.

Inclosed is a letter. You will understand more about it when you receive my Letter by the Count de Noiales.[4]

RC (Adams Papers); docketed by CFA: "A.A. Decr. 23. 1781." John Thaxter's endorsement of this letter, "Portia 9. & 23d. Decr. 1781 inclosing Dean's Letter," appears on cover of AA to JA, 9 Dec., above, which was sent by the same vessel, the *Alliance*, but by a different hand, the Vicomte de Noailles. For the enclosures see notes 3 and 4.

[1] AA to JA, 9 Dec., above.
[2] See Benjamin Guild to JA, Lorient, 18 Jan. 1782 (Adams Papers).
[3] This "coppy of a Letter," mentioned in Thaxter's endorsement as "Dean's," was probably Silas Deane's letter to William Duer, Paris, 14 June 1781, a contemporary copy of which in an unidentified hand is in the Adams Papers and cannot be otherwise accounted for. This was one of the purportedly intercepted letters Deane wrote at this time to American friends criticizing American policy and discouraging the idea of independence; see AA to JA, 21 Oct., above, and note 3 there. A text of Deane's letter is printed in *Deane Papers*, 4:424–429.
[4] Probably the enclosure, not now precisely identifiable, was a letter to JA from one of the parents of the Braintree seamen held captive in the Mill Prison, Plymouth; see AA to JA, 9 Dec., above, and note 3 there.

John Adams to Abigail Adams

My dearest Friend   Amsterdam Jany. 4. 1782

My Health is returning to me by degrees, and I hope to be fully reestablished by the Help of constant Exercise, and great Care, but I want the Consolations of my family.—Alass! When shall I have it.

Charles I presume is sailed in the Cicero from Bilbao, and John is well with Mr. D[ana] at Pete[r]sbourg.

The political Questions here are, a seperate Peace with England and the Mediation of Russia on one Hand and an Alliance with France, Spain and America on the other. The Deliberations will be as long as possible—and the Result nobody can guess.

My Blessing to my Children, Duty to Parents, Affection to Friends, &c.

Yours forever,   J. Adams

RC (Adams Papers). There is no evidence, external or internal, indicating which of JA's two letters to AA bearing the present date was written first.

John Adams to Abigail Adams

My dearest Friend   Amsterdam Jan. 4. 1782

I hope, Charles is at home by this time or that he will be in a few days. I presume he sailed from Bilbao in the Cicero, with M[ajor]

Jackson and Mr. Trumbul, one of the first days of december yet I have no certain news of his sailing at all. John is well with Mr. D[ana] at Petersbourg.

I cannot tell you any News—there are great questions upon the Tapis here, but how they will be decided, I know not.—This Rep[ublic] is a Jilt. When you think you have her Affections, all at once you find you have been deceiv'd.

There is not so much as a Talk of a general Peace, nor is there any one who believes in a seperate Peace bet[ween] England and Holland.

Take Care of the War of Ports which the English talk of. Perhaps Falmouth, perhaps Rhode Island. Look to Privateers and trade.

Let not a Bow be unstrung. There will be, there can be no Peace.

I hope Hayden, who had some things for you, is arrived.

I shall not be able to send any thing more I am afraid untill next summer.

My Blessing to my Daughter and Son, my Duty to Parents and Affection to Brothers and Sisters.

Pray send me, half a dozen, N.E. shillings by different Opportunities, if you can find them.[1]

Most affectionately Yours,   J.A.

RC (Adams Papers).

[1] See above, JA to AA, 21 Oct. 1781 and note 2 there.

Abigail Adams to James Lovell

[Braintree 8? January 1782][1]

Yes I have been Sick confined to my chamber with a slow fever. I have been unhappy through anxiety for my dear Boy, and still am apprehensive of our terrible coast should he come upon it, besides the tormenting cruizers infest our Bay with impuinity and take every thing. You have heard I suppose that the passengers all left the Ship and went to Bilboa upon Gillions abusive treatment of them. My Son was arrived there the day the vessel which brought the News sailed, since which time have heard nothing from thence. The sympathetick part you took in my suposed loss, bespeaks a feeling Heart. I thank Heaven I have not yet been called to taste the bitter cup.

Your kind endeavours have at last happily succeeded and the Boxes have arrived in safety, all the articles in much better Situation than I expected. The contents agree with your former invoice tho not with Mr. A—s memorandom—the china came all safe, one plate and Glass excepted, which for such a journey is trifling indeed. I shall acknowledge General Lincolns kind attention by a few lines to him.[2]

You Query why Portia has not written to you as usual. The real reason was that she was perplexed. The character which she supposed she had in former times corresponded with, was that of a Man of Honour in publick and in private Life, sincere in his professions a Strickt observer of his *vows*, faithfull to his promisses—in one word a Moral and a Religious Man. Shall the cruel tongue of Slander impeach and abuse this character by reporting that the most sacred of vows is voilated, that a House of bad fame is the residence, and a M[istre]ss the *Bosom associate. Truth* is the one thing wanting to forever withhold a pen.[3]

An infamous falsehood I would believe it. My reason for inquiring a character was founded upon the report. Sure I am I sought it not. Since the recept of your last, I have endeavourd to come at the report in such a manner as should give you Satisfaction, this is the reason why I have delayed writing but as I did not chuse to inquire but in a transient manner, I have not been able to obtain it. I observed to you in my last that Massachusets air was necessary for you. I still think so, as it would be the most effectual way to silence the abuse which for near a year has circulated. I know your former reasons will recur and perhaps with more force than ever. Indeed I pitty you. If cruelly used, my Heart Bleads for your troubles, and *for your real and substantial misfortunes.* I suppose I know your meaning.

Post conveyances are so doubtfull and have been so dangerous that I cannot write freely neither upon publick or private affairs.

You had as good be in Europe as Pensilvana for all the intelligence we have from Congress. No journals, no news papers and very few Letters pass. Deans is taking great Latitudes, one would think him a pensioned hireling by his Letters. Would to Heaven that the whole of his Letters could be proved as false as the greater part of them, but are there not some Sorrowfull Truths?

Sir   Janry 8. 1782

Whilst I acknowledge your kind attention to a couple of Boxes in which I was interested and which you was kind enough to forward with Safety by your waggon to Boston, I would not omit congratulating you upon your late honorable appointment which gives universal Satisfaction in your native State at the same time that it demonstrates the Sense which your Country entertain of your meritorious Services. It gives a pleasing prospect to those who wish her prosperity to see those advanced to office whos virtue and independant Spirit have uniformly shone from the begining of this unhappy contest.[4]

Dft (Adams Papers).

[1] Date supplied from continuation; AA may of course have begun her letter on an earlier date.

[2] This acknowledgment has not been found.

[3] The charge of immorality against Lovell, darkly alluded to in AA's letter to him of 15 Nov. 1781, above, was one that recurred more than once in his career, with or without justification, from his undergraduate days on. See Sibley-Shipton, *Harvard Graduates*, 14:31, 33. It may have been revived at this time in conjunction with his intercepted letters and his five-year absence from his family. Possibly it influenced his decision to return home for a visit at just this time; see Lovell to AA, 28 Feb., below.

[4] Lovell's new post was that of "continential Receiver of taxes" in Massachusetts, according to AA's letter to JA of 10 April, below. Lovell took up his duties after quitting Congress for good in that month (Burnett, ed., *Letters of Members*, 6:xlvi, 328 and note). The office was regarded as a gift of Robert Morris, Congress' Superintendent of Finance, and Rev. William Gordon said he must now consider Lovell "as a Deserter from the cause of liberty, as a place man" (to Horatio Gates, 24 Jan. 1783 [error for 1782], MHS, *Procs.*, 63 [1929–1930]:480). It was true that Lovell was to live the rest of his life on the public bounty, showing great political agility in obtaining successive state and federal offices under different governors and national administrations. The chronology of these appointments and of Lovell's tenure of them is at best confusing, but see the sketch of Lovell in Sibley-Shipton, *Harvard Graduates*, 14:31–48, for the most nearly satisfactory account.

John Quincy Adams to John Adams

Honoured Sir   St. Petersbourg Jany. 1/12 1782

Last night I received your letters of the 14th and 15th. You make me a great number of questions at a time, but I will answer them as well as I can.[1]

The Houses are for the most part built of Brick, and plastered over. They are from two to four Stories high. They are glazed with large panes as in France, and in the winter they have double windows which are taken down in the Spring, that is, in the Months of May or June. They have no Chimneys, but Stoves of which I have given a description to Mr. Thaxter.[2] I dont know anything about their State-house, but I beleive it is nothing extraordinary. Voltaire says there are thirty-five Churches here, but I believe if anybody had set him about finding them out he would have found it very difficult; there is a church building here upon the plan of St. Peter's at Rome; It was to be entirely finish'd in fifteen years, has been already work'd upon twenty five, and is far from being half done. There are two Palaces in the city, in one of which her Majesty resides in the winter, and is call'd the summer[3] Palace. The Empress stays all summer at a palace called

Czarskozelo about twenty five English Miles from the city. There is no famous Statuary or Paintings, that I know of. There are concerts once a week in several places. There is a German, an Italian and a French Comedy here. The last is in the Empress's Palace.

The Religion is neither Roman Catholic nor Protestant, but as Voltaire has in his history of Peter the great, treated upon that subject, I will give you what he says about it.

"La Religion de L'Etat, says he, fut toujours depuis le onzieme siecle, celle qu'on nomme Grecque, par opposition a la Latine: mais il y avait plus de pays Mahometans et de Payens que de Chrétiens. La Sibérie jusqu'a la Chine etait idolatre; et dans plus d'une province toute espece de Religion etait inconnue.

"Le Christianisme ne fut reçu que trés tard dans la Russie, ainsi que dans tous les autres pays du Nord. On prétend qu'une Princesse nommée Olha l'y introduisit á la fin du dixieme siécle. Cette princesse Olha ajoute-t'on, se fit baptiser à Constantinople. Son exemple ne fit pas d'abord un grand nombre de proselytes; son fils Stowastoslaw qui regna long tems ne pensa point du tout comme sa mere; mais son petit fils Volodimer, né d'une concubine, ayant assassiné son frere pour regner, et ayant recherché l'alliance de l'Empereur de Constantinople Basile, ne l'obtint qu'a condition qu'il se serait baptiser; c'est a cette époque de l'anneé 987. que la Religion grecque commenca en effet a s'etablir en Russie.

"Il y eut toujours, depuis la naissance du Christianisme en Russie, quelques sectes, ainsi que dans les autres etats; car les sectes sont souvent le fruit de l'ignorance, aussi bien que de la science pretendue. Mais la Russie est le seul grand etat Chretien où la Religion n'ait pas excité de guerres civiles, quoiqu'elle ait produit quelques tumultes.

"La secte de ces Roskolniki composée aujourd'hui d'environ deux mille males, est la plus ancienne; elle s'etablit dès le douzieme siècle par des zélés qui avaient quelque connaissance du nouveau testament; ils eurent, et ont encore la pretention de tous les sectaires, celle de le suivre à la lettre, accusant tous les autres Chrétiens de relachement, ne voulant point souffrir qu'un pretre qui a bu de l'eau de vie, confere le bâteme, assurant avec Jesus-Christ, qu'il n'y a ni premier ni dernier parmi les fideles, et surtout qu'un fidele peut se tuer pour l'amour de son Sauveur. C'est selon eux un très grand peché de dire alleluja trois fois, il ne faut le dire que deux, et ne donner jamais la bénédiction qu'avec trois doigts. Nulle societé, d'ailleurs, n'est ni plus regleé, ni plus sévere dans ses moeurs: ils vivent comme les Quakers, mais ils n'admettent point comme eux les autres Chrétiens dans leurs assembleés, c'est ce qui fait que les autres leur ont imputé toutes les abominations dont les Payens accuserent les premiers Galiléens, dont ceux-ci a chargerent les Gnostiques, dont les Catholiques ont chargés les Protestans. On leur a souvent imputé d'egorger un enfant, de boire son sang, et de se mêler ensemble dans leurs ceremonies secrettes sans distinction de parenté, d'age, ni même de sexe. Quelquefois on les a persecutés: ils se sont alors enfermés dans leurs bourgades, ont mis le feu à leurs maisons, et se sont jettés dans les flammes.

"Au reste, il n'y a dans un si vaste Empire que vingt huit Siéges Episcopaux, et du tems de Pierre on n'en comptait que vingt deux: ce petit nombre etait peut-être une des raisons qui avaient tenu l'Eglise Russe en Paix. Cette Eglise d'ailleurs etait si peu instruite, que le Czar Fédor frére de Pierre Le Grand, fut le premier qui introduisit le plein chant chéz elle.

"Fédor et surtout Pierre, admirent indifféremment dans leurs armées et dans leurs conseils ceux du rite Grec, Latin, Luthérien, Calviniste: ils laisserent a chacun la liberté de servir Dieu suivant sa conscience, pourvu que l'etat fut bien servi.

"Il n'y a jamais eu en Russie d'etablissement pour les juifs, comme ils en ont dans tant d'etats de l'Europe depuis Constantinople jusquà Rome. De toutes les Eglise Grecques la Russe est la seule, qui ne voye pas des Synagogues à coté de ses temples."[4]

I don't wonder that you find it Strange that there is no good Dictionary to be had, but there is nobody here but Princes and Slaves; the Slaves cannot have their children instructed, and the nobility that chuse to have their's send them into foreign countries. There is not one school to be found in the whole city.

I am your dutiful Son.

P.S. Please to present my respects to Messrs. Deneufville and to all friends.

RC (Adams Papers); endorsed: "J.Q.Adams. ansd. 5. Feb. 1782." LbC (Adams Papers).

[1] JA's letters to JQA of 14 and 15 Dec. 1781 are both above. From a letter Francis Dana wrote JA on 31 Dec. 1781 / 11 Jan. 1782 (Adams Papers), it appears that he too had read these, and he had this to say in response to JA's concern over JQA's studies and his possibly being "troublesome" to Dana: "My ward is not troublesome to me. I shou'd be unhappy to be deprived of him, and yet I am very anxious about his education. Here there are neither schools, instructors, or Books. A good Latin Dictionary is not to be got in this City. Had he finished his classical studies I shoud meet with no difficulty in his future education. I wou'd superintend and direct that in the course you wou'd choose and point out. I cou'd not indeed do without him unless a certain person cou'd replace him."

[2] In the letter immediately following.

[3] This slip of the pen occurs also in LbC.

[4] Copied, with silent deletion of some phrases, sentences, and paragraphs, from Voltaire's *Histoire de l'empire de Russie sous Pierre le grand,* 2 vols, n.p., 1759–1763, p. 65–73. Concerning JQA's purchase of a copy of this work, now among his books in MBAt, see above, JQA to AA, 23 Oct. 1781, note 2.

John Quincy Adams to John Thaxter

Mon cher Monsieur   A St: Petersbourg ce 2/13 Janvier 1782

Je viens de recevoir la lettre que vous m'avez fait l'honneur de m'écrire le 22 du mois passé et je suis bien embarassé pour vous repondre. Car vous écrivez le Francais comme un Parisien, en sorte que j'ai peur de m'engager avec une personne de votre force; Mais il le faut bien, et je vous écrirai comme je pourrai.

Je vous enverrais bien quelques morceaux de mon Journal, mais je l'ai discontinué depuis mon arriveé ici,[1] et je vous ai donné le précis de mon voiage dans mes lettres précédentes.[2] Vous me démandéz comment je trouve les villes de Dantzic, Konigsberg &c. Il ny a rien de curieux dans toutes ces villes. Pour la grande ville dans laquelle j'ai présentement l'honneur de résider, les maisons sont bien baties et les Rues larges, Mais il n'y a pas encore de Portes; il n'y a pas grande chose à voir, si ce n'est un cabinet d'histoire naturelle qu'on dit être très belle; nous ne l'avons pas encore vu mais nous espèrons le voir un de ces jours. Vous savéz qu'il ne fait pas trop chaud dans ce pays ci en hiver, et le Soleil est presque aussi prodigue de ses raions qu'en Hollande. Mais je vous dirai qu'on vit ici aussi chaudement qu'en aucun pays. Car dans chaque chambre, ils ont un poël (quelquefois deux) gros comme quatre qu'ils remplissent tous les matins de bois et quand il est bien brulé en charbon, et qu'il ne fume plus ils ferment la porte du poël: ils ont aussi dans le poël une porte qui va au trou de la chéminée, on couvre ce trou de sorte que la chaleur ne pouvant sortir par la cheminée donne toute sa force dans la chambre; mais ces poëls sont fort mal sains; surtout pour les étrangers, et si on ferme le trou de la cheminée avant que le bois est bien brulé on risque de se suffoquer ce qui arrive quelquefois. Pour se garantir du froid dehors des maisons on a des pelisses de peaux de Castor, de Zibeline, d'ours, de Renard, de Loup, de Chien, ou de mouton; ces trois derniers sont fort commun, les autres sont très cher, mais on ne peut absolument pas s'en passer, car la chaleur ordinaire des chambres est de 14 or 15 dégrès dessus de la glace et il a déja fait ici cet hiver 28 dégrès dessous la glace deux fois, ainsi vous pouvez imaginer qu'en sortant d'une chambre, et rencontrant 42 dégrès de différence il faut autre chose qu'un surtout de drap. On porte aussi des bottes doublées de laine dans les quelles les souliers entrent aussi; et aussi tôt qu'on entre dans une maison on s'en débarasse.

Mon frere a donc revu l'Espagne....³ J'aurai mieux aimé entendre son arrivée en Amerique.

Je vous suis trés obligé pour vos bons conseils et je tacherai de m'y conformer; pour ce qui est de ma situation, je ne puis pas dire qu'elle est bien avantageuse, car il ny a ni college ni maitre particulier ni bon Dictionnaire pour le Latin ou le Grec.

Mr. D[ana] vous écrira peut être la prochaine poste. Faites bien mes respects a Madame Chabanel et á sa famille; j'espere que vous me feréz l'honneur de m'ecrire de tems en tems.

Je suis vôtre tres humble et tres obéissant serviteur.

P.S.   A propos, j'ai oublié de vous souhaiter une bonne et heureuse nouvelle année.

LbC (Adams Papers).

¹ JQA's MS Diary covers in some detail his journey from the Netherlands to Russia, but breaks off on the day of his arrival in St. Petersburg, 27 Aug. 1781, and does not resume until 27 Jan. 1782.

² The only surviving letter from JQA to Thaxter since the former's departure from Amsterdam is that dated from St. Petersburg, 8/19 Sept. 1781, above.

³ Suspension points in MS.

Isaac Smith Sr. to John Adams

Boston January the 23d. 1782

In Haveing an Opportunity by Via Bilbao, I have the pleasure of communicating to you the Arrival of your son Charles, after a passage of 45 days from Bilbao.¹—The ship Robinhood that Charles Storer &c. went in is Arrived from Gottenburgh, in 45 days likewize a Brig att Providence from france by which we here the News of the Capture of Cornwallis had reacht there.

The Congress has past an Act prohibiting any british goods of any kind being imported after the first March, and in case the Owner cannot prove them (not to be british) they are forfeited, let them come from any ports whatever, or by any Neutral power whatever—which is a pitty was not done sooner.

As there is a person in Town that has considerable of goods from his father in London.²—I hope the recapture of St. Eustatius will put some New life into the Dutch. The British frigates have done more damage to Our trade the last season than any time since the War. That confounded Penobscot is a handy resort.—Your family and friends are well. Itts very happy the Cicero Arrived as she did as the next day came On a very bad snow storm and has continued two days, which has prevented Charles from coming to Town.

As to News we have had nothing from Genl. Green for some Months. A reinforcement is gone from York to Carolinia.

I am Sr. Yr. [humble?] servant,   Isaac Smith

RC (Adams Papers).

[1] Richard Cranch in the following letter to JA says "51 Days" from Bilbao to Beverly, the *Cicero*'s home port, where she arrived on 21 Jan. (Gardner W. Allen, *Massachusetts Privateers of the Revolution*, MHS, *Colls.*, 77 [1927]: 99). Smith would appear to be nearer the mark, if the narrative of John Trumbull, a fellow passenger of CA, is trustworthy—though that narrative is a little confusing about dates (see below). For the events leading up to the *Cicero*'s departure from Bilbao, see William Jackson to JA, 26 Oct. 1781, above, and Trumbull's account as quoted in note 2 there; also JA to Jackson, 1 Dec. 1781, note 1. Trumbull states that the passengers who had left the *South Carolina* in La Coruña and made their difficult way to Bilbao "were detained" in that port "until the 10th of December," and then continues (*Autobiography*, ed. Sizer, 1953, p. 79–81):

"At the entrance of the river of Bilboa is a bar, on which the water is so shallow, that a ship of the Cicero's size can pass over, only at spring tides. When we dropped down from Porto Galette, we found the wind at the mouth of the river, blowing fresh from the north-ward, which caused such a heavy surf upon the bar, that it was impossible to take the ship over. We were obliged to wait until the wind lulled, and then the pilot insisted that he could not take her over safely, until the next spring tide. Several of the passengers thought it was folly to remain on board, consuming the ship's stores, and proposed to the captain that we would go back to Bilboa for a few days. He acceded, promising to send up a boat for us, whenever he might have a prospect of getting to sea. We went, and amused ourselves among the friends we had made; on the third or fourth day, we were walking with some ladies in the Alameda, a public walk which ran upon the bank of the river, when we espied a boat coming up with sails and oars, which we recognized as being from below. One of her men sprang on shore, and ran to us, with the information that the Cicero, and other vessels, had got over the bar that morning at eight o'clock, and were standing out to sea, with a fair wind—that Capt. Hill desired us to make all possible haste to get on board—that he would stand off and on for a few hours, but not long, as he could not justify it to his owners. We, of course, made all possible haste, but the distance from town was eight or nine miles, and when we got down, it was near three o'clock, and the ship was out of sight. We obtained a spy-glass, ran to the top of the house, and could thence discern a ship in the offing, apparently standing in. We persuaded ourselves that it must be the Cicero, and bid for a boat and crew to put us on board. The pilots made great difficulty—the sea was very rough—the ship was too far out—perhaps it was not the Cicero— they thought it was not; all this was said to work up the price. On the other hand, we were desperate; among us we could not muster twenty guineas to carry us through the winter, and the bargain was at last made, at a price which nearly emptied all our pockets, and before sunset we got on board the Cicero, in the Bay of Biscay, two or three leagues from land. The mountains of Asturia were already covered with snow, but the wind was fair, and we went on our way rejoicing.

"No accident befel, until the last day of our passage. We saw the land of America, (the Blue Hills of Milton, near Boston,) in the afternoon of a beautiful day in January; at six o'clock, P.M., we laid the ship's head to the eastward, and stood off under easy sail until midnight, when we hove about, and stood in to the westward, under the same sail, expecting to find ourselves at sunrise, at about the same distance from the land, and all was joy and merriment on board, at the near approach of home. One honest old tar was happily on the lookout, and at three o'clock sung out from the forecastle, 'breakers! breakers! close under our bow, and right ahead!' He was just in time; the crew, though merry, were obedient, and flew upon deck in time to escape the danger. We found we were close upon the rocks of Cape Ann. We must have been drifted by a very strong current, for our course had been judicious, and could never have brought the ship there. Before noon, we were safe in the port of Beverly, where we found eleven other ships, all larger and finer vessels than the Cicero—all belonging to the same owners, the brothers Cabot—laid up for the winter. Yet such are the vicissitudes of war and the elements, that before the close of the

year they were all lost by capture or wreck, and the house of Cabot had not a single ship afloat upon the ocean. In the evening, after we got into port, a snow storm came on, with a heavy gale from the eastward. The roads were so completely blocked up with snow, that they were impassable, and we did not get up to Boston until the third day; but, *per tot discrimina rerum,* I was at last safe on American land, and most truly thankful."

Unfortunately it is not clear whether Trumbull's single specifically mentioned date of 10 Dec. is intended to be that of the *Cicero*'s actual departure or the date *after which* he spent three or four days in the city before hearing of the ship's sudden sailing and having to overtake her in the bay. From 10 Dec. to 21 Jan. would be 43 days for the Atlantic voyage.

[2] Thus in MS, but it would appear that this fragmentary sentence is really the concluding part of the sentence ending the preceding paragraph.

Richard Cranch to John Adams

Dear Bror.   Boston Jany. 31st. 1782

I have the happiness to inform you that your Son Charles arriv'd at Beverly from Bilboa last Week, in the Ship Cicero, after a Passage of 51 Days.[1] He is in fine Health and behaves himself with such good Breeding as gives pleasure to all his Acquaintance. He return'd to Braintree the day before Yesterday where he found his joyfull Mother and Brother and Sister all well. His Trunk and Things are not yet got to Braintree so that I have not the pleasure of knowing what Letters you have sent, but hope I may have one, as I have not yet received a Line from You or Mr. Thaxter since you left us. I wrote you just after the taking of Genl. Cornwallis, but the Vessell after several weeks absence put back again.[2] I put the Letters afterwards into the Hands of a Gentleman who expected to sail for Holland by way of Virginia, and as he is not yet gone I take the freedom of desiring him to wait upon you with them (tho' they are something antiquated) and with this also; knowing that you must be anxious for your dear little Boy untill you hear of his arrival. I long to hear from Master John, how he likes his Tour to Petersbourg &c. Your Mother, Brother, Father Smith, Uncle Quincy, Uncle Thaxter, Uncle Smith &c. &c.

and their Families are all well. I wrote to Cousin Thaxter by the Count De Noailles, which I hope he has received. We have no News since the retaking of St. Eustatia by the French. This was a brilliant Coup De Main. The General Court are now sitting here, and now batteling of it whether an Excise Act pass'd last Session shall be repeal'd or not. "Much may be said on both Sides."

I received by Capt. Hayden the Things consign'd to me by Monsr. Mandrillon, they all came safe except the Glass-ware which was much broken. I have not yet sold them, as I could not get a Price that suited me. I hope soon to make him a Remittance. Hayden arriv'd so long after the other Ships that the Market was supply'd for that Season before the Goods came to hand. I have wrote to him, and shall write to him again by the first Oportunity. I have never received the Letters that he mention'd to me as being sent by Commodore Guillon. Should be glad you would please to present my most respectfull Compliments to him and let him know that I shall do every thing in my Power to serve his Interest. We have been very anxious on Account of your Health, having heard that you have been very Sick, but Master Charles has reliev'd us by informing us that he had received Letters from you of a later Date, and that you was recover'd.

Mr. Sherburn, who has been so obliging as to promise to deliver this and the other Letter to you if he arrives safe to Holland, is a Gentleman who has signalized himself in behalf of his Country, and lost a Limb in the Expedition on Rhode Island.[3] I have heard a good Character of him, but have not the pleasure of a Particular Acquaintance with him. He says he is going on board directly, so that I have only time to add that I am with every Sentiment of Esteem and Friendship, your affectionate Bror.,   Richard Cranch

Mrs. Cranch and our Children are well.

RC (Adams Papers).

[1] See, however, Isaac Smith Sr. to JA, preceding, and note 1 there.

[2] See Cranch to JA, 3 Nov. 1781, and descriptive note there.

[3] John Samuel Sherburne, an officer in the New Hampshire militia, who lost a leg at Quaker Hill, R.I., Aug. 1778 (Heitman, *Register Continental Army*).

John Adams to John Quincy Adams

My dear Boy   Feb. 5. 1782

Yesterday I received your Letter of Jany. 1/12, and thank you for your account of the Place where you are.

I will send you a Dictionary, as soon as I can, but it will be a long time before you can have it. I am very anxious for your Studies. Write me what Books You can procure there, and what others you want.

I am much pleased with your Letter to Mr. Thaxter,[1] but it is a Mortification to me to find that you write better, in a foreign Language than in your mother Tongue. Your Letters discover a Judgment, beyond your Age, but your Style is not yet formed in french or English.

You must study accurately the best Writers in both, and endeavour to penetrate into their Spirit, to warm your Imagination with theirs, to inkindle the flame of Wit by their Fires and to watch the Delicacies in the Turn of Phrases and Periods which constitute the Charms of style.

I have a Letter from your Mamma, 23d Jany.[2] All friends well.

With her Blessing to you, She sends her Wishes to hear from you, as often as you can write.

Your Brother was not arrived, on Christmas day when the Alliance Sailed.

Your Account of the Difference in the Air, in and out of your Chamber, allarms me for your Health but more especially for Your Patrons.[3] You must take Care, not to make the Air of your Chamber too hot, and to change it often, otherwise your Friends Health will suffer immediately and yours after a little time, perhaps more than his.

Pray, what is the Language of the Russians?

Do you find any Company? Have you formed any Acquaintances of your own Countrymen, there are none I suppose. Of Englishmen you should beware; Frenchmen probably many. It must be an unsociable dull Life to a young Man, if you have not some Acquaintances. Alass! I regret that the Friendships of your Childhood cannot be made among your own Country men. And I regret your Loss of the glorious Advantages for classical studies at Leyden.

Your affectionate Father.

RC (Adams Papers). Early Tr (Adams Papers), in JQA's hand.

[1] Dated 2/13 Jan., above.
[2] Error for 23 Dec. 1781, above.
[3] That is, for the health of your patron, Francis Dana.

James Lovell to Abigail Adams

Feb. 28. 1782

"Mr. Lovell, do let me entreat you, this thirtieth time, to write a few Lines to Mrs. Adams. Are you not clearly convinced that it is in vain for you to determine, as you have done, day after day, that you will go to see her? You are betrayed, by a thousand Interruptions, not merely into Unpoliteness, but really into Ingratitude to that Lady. If you do not feel for yourself, I pray you to convince her that I am not insensible to her repeated kind Invitations and other Proofs of her friendly Thoughtfulness of me."

Stop, prithee, stop, Mary. I will write, this moment. Thou art indeed a good Woman. What Pity 'tis, as *Some Folks* think, that you have not a better Husband! [1]

And now, my esteemed Friend, do you not willingly conceive that it is very difficult for me to seize Hours sufficient to secure the great Pleasure of seeing you at Braintree.

Be assured that I am not yet so quit of pressing Business as to have found Leisure to visit at the South West or North parts of this Town many Friends of my early Love or my later Gratitude.

I have many Things to tell; many also to ask about. I will not omit any possible Opportunity of doing both within the next Fortnight.[2] In the mean time, be assured of the Reality of that Regard which is now jointly professed by, Madam, Your obliged Friends,

J. & M. Lovell [3]

RC (Adams Papers).

[1] Lovell was in Boston on leave from Congress for the first time in five years. He had last attended Congress on 23 Jan. and later returned for a brief period of service, 3–16 April, but thereafter took up the duties of his new appointment as Continental receiver of taxes in Massachusetts. See above, AA to Lovell, 8? Jan., and note 4 there.

[2] Whether or not the Lovells visited AA at this time does not appear.

[3] Text and signature are in Lovell's hand.

Abigail Adams to Elizabeth Smith Shaw

My dear sister   [*Braintree, February–March* 1782][1]

I yesterday received a congratulatory Letter from you,[2] upon the safe arrival of my dear Charles, an event which has relieved me from many anxieties and filld my Heart with gratitude to that gracious Being who protected him from the perils of the deep, and from the hostile foe, who raised him from Sickness and has restored him to his Native Land, undepraved in his mind and morals, by the facinating allurements of vice, decked in Foreign garbs—and this I assure you I esteem not among the least favours with which his absence has been distinguished.

The fond Mother would tell you that you may find in him the

same solid sober discreet Qualities that he carried abroad with a modesty bordering upon diffidence, no ways inclined to relate his adventures but as you question him concerning them—perfectly attached to the modest republican Stile of Life, as tho he had never experienced any other. As to any alteration in his person, I perceive none but growth which has not been rapid. If no unforeseen disaster prevents I hope to bring him to visit you in the course of the Spring. He desires his duty to you, and love to his unknown cousins.

I wrote you a long Letter a months ago,[3] but thought to coppy it as it was very carelessly written. I was that Night calld to attend the Sick and I greatly feared dying Bed of our worthy Brother Cranch. For ten days I beheld him in this critical state. Encompassed with my own anxiety, and the anguish of his whole family, I was greatly distresst. Gracious Heaven has restored the good Man to his family and Friends who were trembling least he should cease to be and the faithfull faill[4] from among the children of Men. Whilst I attended round his Bed, I could not avoid often looking abroad and in imagination beholding my dearest Friend laid upon his sick Bed unattended by the wife, the sister or daughter, whose constant and solicitous care and attention might mitigate the riggour of the fever, and alleviate the pain—but with strangers and in a foreign Land my dear Friend has experienced a most severe sickness. In November he wrote to Charles in Bilboa[5] that he was recovering from a fever which had left him very weak and lame, and this is the latest intelligence I have received.

You may well suppose me anxious. My Heart sometimes misgives me. I long yet fear to hear. I have one only confidence to repair to. Shall not the judge of all the earth do right and have I not experienced signal favours—shall I distrust his providentiall care?

I am sorry to hear you complain as the Spring approaches. You have but a slender constitution. I would advise you to a free use of the Bark and a journey. I hope you are not in the increasing way, as I think your Health ill able to bear it. We have none of us nursing constitutions—twice my life was nearly sacrificed to it.

Is our intelligence true that you are like to have cousin B——y[6] for a Neighbour. I hope it will prove for her happiness and then I shall most sincerely rejoice in it. Mrs. Gray is like soon to confirm the observation that there scarce was ever any such thing under the Sun as an inconsolable widow. Grief is no incurable disease; but time, patience and a little philosophy with the help of humane fraility and address will do the Buisness. She is however like to be joined to one of the most amiable of Men, which is too great a temptation to be over balanced by the Sum total of 5 children.[7]

Let me hear from you oftner my Sister. I really am conscience smitten at my neglect. A Good example will awaken my future attention and produce the consequent reformation of your ever affectionate Sister,

A A

Dft (Adams Papers); without date or indication of addressee; docketed by CFA: "1782."

[1] Dated thus approximately from the references to CA's return home from Europe (late January); to the imminent Otis-Gray marriage (see note 7, below); and to the recovery of Richard Cranch, also reported in AA to JA, March 17–25, below.

[2] Letter not found.

[3] Thus in MS. Letter not found.

[4] Thus in MS.

[5] Letter not found.

[6] Not identified. The Shaws lived in Haverhill.

[7] Mary, or Polly (Smith) Gray, cousin of AA and Mrs. Shaw, widowed in 1779, was to marry the widower Samuel Allyne Otis on 28 March 1782. See Adams Genealogy under both names.

John Quincy Adams to John Adams

St. Petersbourg

Honoured Sir   February 21 / March 4 1782

I receiv'd three days agone your favour of Feby. 5th. I have found a good Latin and french Dictionary, but I should be glad to have one Latin and English, because I am obliged at present to translate every thing into French, unless I translate the words twice; by which, (besides it's being very troublesome), the sense of the Latin will be often lost. I can get any Latin books here that I want. I have finished Cornelius Nepos, and have translated Cicero's first oration against Catilina.

I have not made many acquaintances here, but there is a subscription Library of English books, to which Mr. D[ana] has subscribed, so that I have as much as I want, to read. I have lately finished Hume's history of England and am at present reading Mrs. Macaulay's.[1] In the third volume of Hume's history I find an exact description of the present state of this Country in these few lines.

"If we consider the antient state of Europe, we shall find that the far greater part of the society were every where bereaved of their *personal* liberty and lived entirely at the will of their masters. Everyone that was not noble was a slave. The peasants were sold along with the land. The few inhabitants of cities were not in a better condition. Even the gentry themselves were subjected to a long train of subordination, under the greater barons or chief vassals of the crown, who tho' seemingly plac'd in a high state of splendor, yet, having but a slender protection, of the law, were exposed to every tempest of state, and by the precarious condition in which they lived, paid dearly for the power of oppressing and tyrannizing over their inferiors."

Please to give my duty to Mamma whenever you write. I will write to her as often as I can.

We have had here lately some days exceeding cold. Reaumur's Thermometer has been as low as 32 degrees below the degree of freezing but it thaws at present, and it is likely we shall not have again this winter such severe cold weather. We open a window every morning for about a half an hour, so that we always have fresh air in our chambers.

You ask me in your letter, what is the Language of the Russians? Voltaire says, "Un Grec fut premier Métropolitain de Russie ou Patriarche. C'est déla que les Russes ont adopté dans leur langue un alphabet tiré du Grec; ils y auraient gagné si le fond de leur langue qui est la Slavone, n'était toujours demeuré le même, à quelques mots près, qui concernent leur Liturgie et leur Hiérarchie." [2] To this may be added that their alphabet is composed of 36 letters. But all the nobility speak French and German.

I am your dutiful Son,   J. Q. A.

P.S. Please to present my respects to Mr. Thaxter, and to all Friends. Mr. D. is well and writes by this post.

RC (Adams Papers); addressed: "A Son Excellence Mr: Adams. Ministre Plenipotentiaire des Etats Unis de l'Amérique. à Amsterdam." LbC (Adams Papers).

[1] Catharine (Sawbridge) Macaulay's massive *History of England, from the Accession of James I to That of the Brunswick Line*, 1763–1783, was considered an antidote to David Hume's *History of England . . . to the Revolution in 1688*, 1754–1761. Hume's *England* was frequently reprinted, and a number of editions were owned by the Adamses. JQA had borrowed the eight-volume set of Hume he was reading from "the English Library" in St. Petersburg (JQA, Diary, 4, 18, 24 Feb. 1782), and the Macaulay *History* from the same source (same, 25 Feb.). The Diary also indicates that he had located some booksellers' shops and was making frequent book purchases.

On Mrs. Macaulay's reputation as an historian and JA's early correspondence with her, see above, vol. l:xiii, and references there.

[2] Quoted by JQA from his copy (in MBAt) of Voltaire's *Histoire de l'empire de Russie sous Pierre le grand*, n.p., 1759–1763, 1:67.

John Thaxter to Abigail Adams

Madam   Amsterdam 7th. March 1782

Your favor of the 9th. of December last informs me of the Arrival of the Apollo, Minerva, and Juno, three of fabulous Divinity who know nothing of me You observe. I do not wish to altercate even with Gods, much less with Goddesses: but I have a Right to quarrel with the Destinies, or bad Men, and there is but little benefit, I fear, arising from Contests of this kind. What am I to do with such respectable Evidence against me? Conscious of an exact Punctuality in my Correspondence, I have no Occasion to have Recourse to the miserable Subterfuges of the Lovers of Apology for my Justification.— In one Word, all my Letters to You, Madam, and all my Friends were put on board Gillon, who was to have convoyed Minerva, Apollo, Juno and several other Vessels from this Port. I thought that Ship was the safest opportunity, and therefore put all my Letters for eight or nine Months on board of her. I pray You to be assured, Madam, that I have omitted no opportunity in writing to You, and that I am too sincere an Admirer of every Trait of your Pen, which never fails of Instruction or Improvement, to be ever culpable in this Respect. I am doubly obliged by your last favor, as it flowed from a Principle of Benevolence, which has ever distinguished and done Honor to the Heart of Mrs. A. Indeed, Madam, I confess You had Reason to suspect me of Inattention or Indolence; but your Goodness has spared me the Reproach.

I wish to return to America, as You have heard: but this does not affect my Health, and I apprehend You have heard more respecting my Health than is true. I have enjoyed as great a share of this Blessing as most Foreigners do. This City I believe is the most unhealthy Spot of the seven Provinces: but We shall soon go to the Hague to live, which is infinitely more healthy. It is not however the pure Atmosphere of America.

The News of the Surrender of Cornwallis produced an agreable Sensation here. I have the honor to congratulate You, Madam, upon the entire Reduction of the Island of Minorca, which is another humiliating Event for poor old England, for they have puffed a long time about its Impregnability, its excellent State of Defence &c. &c. à la mode Angloise. The few wise men of that Country see their Kingdom crumbling to Atoms and lament it: but Wisdom and Virtue are too feeble to stem the overbearing Torrent of Corruption and

Venality. All the noble Virtues which formerly distinguished that Kingdom are lost in the infamous Vortex of ministerial Bribery.

Genl. Conway has moved in the House of Commons, that they should resolve to pursue the American War no longer by Force, and his Motion was carried by a Majority of nineteen against the Minister —a grand Triumph for Opposition. The House have resolved to wait upon his Majesty with an Address, shewing that an offensive War in America, to the End to reduce to submission the revolted Colonies by *Force*, tends only to weaken the Efforts of this Country against its *European Enemies*, and in the present Circumstances to increase the mutual Enmity, so fatal to the Interests of Great Britain and America.[1]

The Lord Mayor, Alderman[2] and Common Council of London presented a Petition to the House of Commons, to pray them to interpose to put an End to the American War—a most deplorable, lamentable, dismal, ghastly Petition it is—full of Horror and Spleen. It was presented before the Resolution passed, and perhaps contributed much to the Success of Conways Motion. Peace with America, Peace with America is said to be the universal Cry at present in England. It is said there has been Illuminations, Bonfires &c. &c. on the Occasion of the Success of Conway's Motion. What a Nation! Crucify and pacify almost in the same Breath. There is nothing too absurd and inconsistant for them. In one moment rending the Sky and confounding Heaven and Earth in their mad Acclamations of Joy for burning a poor defenceless American Village and massacring its Inhabitants, and in the next cursing and consigning their Ministry to Perdition for carrying on the American War.—And what is to become of Conway's Motion for Peace with America? Quit the American War, to fight France, Spain and Holland, their European Enemies. This seems to be the drift of the Motion, and perhaps America is to be again insulted with Peace making pardoning Commissioners. A seperate Peace is their Object. Nothing can be more insidious than this, and I rest happy in the Persuasion, that there is too much Wisdom in our Councils and Rulers to be duped by such a semblance of friendly Policy, and too sacred a Regard to the Virgin Faith of America to ever suffer it to be spotted by the Intrigues of a British Court, or the still more dangerous Efforts of those who, apparently opposed to the Court and under the Mask of Friendship to America, are secretly and perhaps more surely pursuing the same villanous Policy of a seperate Peace.

Whether Conway's Object was to get rid of the present Ministry, to make Room for Opposition to wriggle themselves in, or to make a seperate Peace, or to prepare the Minds of the People to a general Peace, by holding up the Idea of seperate Peace as some think I am not able to say. The Situation of the Kingdom is deplorable enough to make them wish for general Pacification; but they love France and Spain too well to quit them yet, and I cannot help thinking they mean to try for a seperate Peace. America ought to be upon her Guard and not to relax one Iota, but to dispise such an offer. Let them acknowledge the Independence of America and invite her to assist in making a general Peace, and not pursue a mean, dirty tricking Policy. But to quit a Country which no American has any Occasion to love, and to return to this. They begin to think somewhat in this Country of acknowledging our Independence. Friesland has taken the Provincial Resolution to acknowledge it and to admit your dearest Friend to an Audience, and have instructed their Deputies in the States General to move it. Guelderland is thinking about, and Holland is seriously deliberating upon it.[3] Things look well at present and perhaps a few Weeks will decide what Character America is considered in in this Country. I am not sure of it, for every thing is fluctuating here, and Fear does more in five Minutes than all the Rhetorick and Oratory of Demosthenes could do in as many Years. There cannot be a more excellent Opening than the present. If they do not make a Bargain now, it is impossible to foresee when they will. England can't hurt them now, for their Lion has lost too many of his Teeth and is too old. For my own Part, I am an Infidel. I pray they may help my Unbelief.

I hope You have had the Happiness of embracing your dear Charles long since. He is an amiable little fellow and has left a charming Character and many admiring Friends in Europe. My most affectionate Regards to him, your equally dear and amiable Nabby and Master Thommy.

I am grieved that so many of the young Ladies of my Acquaintance remain single. You observe that most of them are so, and that several who were first rising into Notice when I left home now figure with Eclat. I am charmed to occupy a Place in their Esteem, for I *love* and esteem them most sincerely, and the first Wish of my Heart is to conduct one of them to the sacred Altar, and pledge an everlasting Affection and Fidelity to her: a pretty loving warm Speech indeed for so cold and humid a Country as Holland. I am not quite out of the Reach of the Influence of this same Passion of Love neither. My tenderest Regards to them all if You please, and to any one [in] particular that You choose. It will do her nor me any harm at this distance.—Duty and Respects as due.—With the most perfect Respect & Esteem, I have the honor to be, Madam, your most obedient & most humble Servant, North Common

Saturday. March 23d.

I designedly left my Letter unclosed, in expectation of some Event worth communicating; for the Occurrences of every day are more or less interesting at present in this Country. I had no Idea however of so soon congratulating You upon so pleasing an Event, as the Acknowledgment of American Independence by the Province of Holland. Ten out of eighteen Cities declared in favor of the Measure last Thursday, and the remaining eight will give their Opinion on Wednesday next perhaps. The Reason for their not coming to a decision on the day with the other ten, was, that they had not recieved their Instructions at that time. Altho' ten Cities are a plurality of Voices, yet it is expected that the other Cities will conform to the Resolution of the ten, which were the most opulent and respectable. I wish ardently for Unanimity, for this Spirit in a good Work is a source of pleasing Sensations.

The Merchants of several Cities have contributed much to the Acceleration of this Business by their Petitions to their Regencies, the States of Holland and the States General. Amsterdam, besides petitioning their Regency, joined with Haerlem and Leyden in a Request to the States of Holland and the States General. Never was more Ardor and Zeal discoverd than in signing the Petitions. Between four and five hundred merchants &ca. signed that to the States of Holland and the States General.[4] Twice as many would have signed if necessary. (When the Deputies of this City in the States of Holland acquainted the *great* Man of this Country of the Resolution their Regency had taken respecting American Independence, he said, "Gentlemen, I have still some difficulties on my Mind, but I shall not attempt to oppose You.")[5] But this by the Bye. This answer You will be pleased to communicate only to a few discreet Friends. The Grand Pensionary of Holland[6] promised to promote the Business all in his Power, which is another Secret. Thus have I given You, Madam, a short Sketch of the state of Affairs in this Country. You will doubtless conclude, that Mr. A. will soon be admitted to an Audience, and a Treaty formed. But there are five other Provinces in the Rear, who have not yet explained themselves upon the great Question. However the general Opinion is, that they will follow without much Hesitation, and indeed several of them have discovered good dispositions, Guelderland in particular, who delayed on account of the Maritime Provinces not having declared themselves in favor of a Measure, in which they were more immediately interested. This Objection is now removed. Be not too sanguine in your Expectations. An Event at present unforeseen may still prevent the friendly Embrace—some Northern Blast, or some Demon of Discord from Britain may yet disappoint our well grounded Expectations. I will hope for the best: but to wait the Issue with *Dutch Patience* would be a progress in this Virtue as yet unattained to by him, who is with all possible Respect & Consideration, Madam, your Most Ob. & very Hbl. Servt.,   N. C.

RC (Adams Papers).

[1] On Henry Seymour Conway's famous motion against continuing the war in America, introduced in the House of Commons on 22 Feb. and defeated by one vote only, reintroduced in a more elaborate form on the 27th and carried by 234 to 215 votes, the reluctant response to it by George III, and the "general demonstrations of joy" with which it was greeted by the public, see *Ann. Register for 1782*, p. 168–172, and the more personal but incisive account in Horace Walpole, *Last Journals during the Reign of George III*, ed. A. Francis Steuart, London and N.Y., 1910, 2:406–413. (In Walpole's account Conway is represented as having heard that "Lawrence [i.e. Henry Laurens], formerly President of the Congress," and "another person in Holland," were available and empowered to treat for peace with Great Britain.) Thus JA's existence and powers were known in London but not his name! It is to be noted, however, that, in spite of popular impressions to the contrary, Conway's winning motion of 27 Feb. was not meant by him to announce the opening of peace negotiations with America, to say nothing of a British surrender there. It was intended, rather, to force the ministry to give up further offensive operations looking toward a conquest of America, in order to strengthen England's hand against her European enemies. See Ian R. Christie, *The End of North's Ministry, 1780–1782*, London and N.Y., 1958, p. 319–321.

[2] Thus in MS.

[3] These were very recent developments, and others of the same import were to follow rapidly, as related below in the addition to Thaxter's present letter. Editorial notes on Dutch recognition of American independence appear under JA's letter to AA of 1 April and Thaxter's letter to JA, 20 April, both below.

[4] Texts of these petitions, without the names of the signers, are printed in JA's compilation entitled *A Collection of State-Papers, Relative to the First Acknowledgment of the Sovereignty [!] of the United States of America ...*, The Hague, 1782, p. 26 ff. Most of them were prepared or inspired by Dutch friends of JA. See JA, *Diary and Autobiography*, 2:ix–x, facing p. 323; 3:4.

[5] Presumably Thaxter is quoting Willem V, Prince of Orange and Stadholder of the United Provinces of the Netherlands. "[T]he Prince has declared that he has no hopes of resisting the Torrent and therefore that he shall not attempt it" (JA to Franklin, 26 March 1782, LbC, Adams Papers; JA, *Works*, 7:555).

[6] Pieter van Bleiswyck (1724–1790), who was a correspondent of JA and is mentioned with some frequency in his *Diary and Autobiography*.

Abigail Adams to John Adams

My Dearest Friend   March 17th 1782

Altho I know not of a single opportunity by which I can convey to You my constant anxiety and solicitude for your Health; or obtain from you any knowledge of your present situation, yet I cannot refrain writing my sentiments upon the knowledge I have been able to obtain concerning you here. There has been a motion in C[ongre]ss to recall all their M[inisters] and s[ecretaries] except at V[ersaille]s but it did not obtain.

I have been in daily expectation for months past, that Letters would arrive from you requesting leave to resign your employments; and return again to your Native Land, assured at least of finding one Friend in the Bosom of *Portia*, who is sick, sick of a world in which selfishness predominates, who is sick of counsels unstable as the wind, and of a servility to which she hopes your mind, will never bend.

Most sincerely can she unite with you in the wish of a sequestered Life, the shades of Virmont, the uncultivated Heath are preferable in her mind to the servility of a court.

Some writer observes "that censure is a tax that a Man pays the publick for being eminent."[1] It is in the power of every Man to preserve his probity; but no man living has it in his power to say that he can preserve his reputation. Is it not in your power to withdraw yourself from a situation in which you are certain, no honour can be obtained to yourself or Country? Why Letters have not reached America from you as well as from the minister at Versails, and Madrid since the extrodonary revocation of former powers, I cannot devine— unless purposely stoped by Intrigues and Cabals. The minister at Madrid has done himself and country Honour by refuseing to take a part in the New instructions.[2]

What changes may have taken place in the cabinets abroad since the Capture of Cornwallis, we have not yet learnt. If America does not improve it to her own advantage, she is deficient in that Spirit of Independance which has on former occasions distinguished her.

It is true that her Finances are rather in an unpleasent state. Her Faith has been so often pledged, and having no stable funds, it has been so often forfeited to the undoing of those who confided most, that their is a distrust amongst her best Friends; C[ongres]s have not been able to obtain an impost of 5 per cent which was recommended to be laid upon the importation of all Foreign articles, salt and military stores excepted, for the purpose of raising a revenue to be at the sole disposal of C[ongre]ss.

March 25th

Thus far I wrote and laid by my pen untill I could hear of an opportunity of conveyance. By a Letter last evening received from my unkle I was informed of a vessel soon to sail for France.[3] I reasume my pen, but my trembling anxious Heart scarcly knows what to dictate to it. Should I discribe all that has passd within it, since I heard of your illness, you would pitty its distresses. I fear the anxiety you have felt for the disgracefull concequences which your [country][4] was about to involve itself in, have affected your Health and impaired, your constitution. I well know how Essential the Honour and dignity of your country, its Independance and safety is, to your peace of mind and your happiness; if that cannot be promoted under present circumstances, let me intreat you to withdraw. Let me beg of you to resign; your Health suffers; my Health suffers from a dejection of Spirits which I cannot overcome—

> "O thou whose Friendship is my joy and pride
> Whose Virtues warm me; and whose precepts guide
> Say A. amidst the toils of anxious State
> does not thy secreet soul desire retreat?
> dost thou not wish the task, the duty done
> Thy Busy life at length might be thy own
> that to thy Loved philosophy resign'd
> No care might ruffle thy unbended mind?"

It is this hope, this distant Idea that cheers my languid spirits and supports me through domestick perplexities. I mentioned to you that I had received no Letters from you of a later date than July, and in a former Letter I acquainted you that our dear Charles arrived here in January in good Health,[5] and by him I first learnt that you had been sick. My Friends were not Ignorant of it, having some months before been made acquainted with it; by Letters from Mr. Ingraham to Mr. Daws, but they had carefully concealed it from me, knowing the distress it would give me, and supposeing it would be long before I should hear again from you. Your Letter to Charles in Bilboa greatly alarmed me.[6] God Grant that you may have recoverd your Health, and preserve a Life essential to the happiness of Portia. What a cordial, what a comfort would a Letter, with the happy tidings of your returned Health prove to the distressed Bosom of Portia. Heaven grant it speedily.

Charles is perfectly happy in his safe return, to his dear Native Land, to which he appears the more attached from having visited foreign climes. May the promiseing dawn of future usefullness grow with his Growth and strengthen with his Strength whilst it sweetens the declining Life of those to whom he is most dear.

Major Jackson to whose care you intrusted him, was high in his praises'es and commendations. As I did not know in what situation he was placed, I inquired of Major Jackson. He informd me that when he arrived at Bilboa he drew a Bill upon you for money to answer his expences, that he had kept an account of Charles's which together with a small Balance he would leave at Col. Crafts where he lodged in Boston for me; he was a second time at Braintree, but said he had forgot his papers. Soon after he went for Philadelphia, and I heard no more of him; or his papers—which after a reasonable time I thought proper to inquire for, at his Lodgings, but was assured nothing was ever left for me. With regard to Charles passage the Captain and owners demand 25 guineys for it, which my unkle thinks very extravagent as he is well acquainted with passages, having both paid and received them from Bilboa, 80 dollors being the extent, he ever gave or received even when the Captain found stores,[7] which was not now the case, but the Capt[ain] says the other passengers gave that, and he expects the same for him.[8] I must therefore be under the necessity of drawing upon you for it, as I cannot answer it without dissapointing myself of a favorite object; I mean a Lot of Land of 300 acers for each of our children in the New State of Virmont, for which I have been very assiduously collecting all I could spair from taxes. They sell only 300 acers in a share and will not admit of one persons purchaseing more, so that the deeds must be made out in each childs or persons Name who is the purchaser. Several of our Friends have been purchaseing in the same Township, which is well situated upon two Rivers. I wish it was in my power to purchase 12 hundred for each instead of 3, but I dare not run ventures.[9] The Goverment is like to be amicably setled and in a few years it will become a flourishing place.—Land here is so high taxed that people are for selling their Farms and retireing back. I can Instance to you one tax Bill which will shew you the difference of the present with the former. There are two acers and half of salt medow which you know you own in Milton, it formerly paid 3 shillings tax, and this year 36.—Mr. Alleyne has Burried his Mother and sister. He now wishes to sell his Farm and has accordingly put it upon sale. It is a place I should be fond of, but know it must still be my castle in the air.

You are loosing all opportunities for helping yourself, for those who are daily becomeing more and more unworthy of your Labours and who will neither care for you or your family when their own turn is served—so selfish are mankind. I know this is a language you are unwilling to hear. I wish it was not a truth which I daily experience.

I do not recollect through all your absence that I have ever found the person who has been inclined to consider me or my situation either on account of my being destitute of your assistance or that you are devoteing your time and talents to the publick Service (Mr. Tracy excepted who has twice refused the freight of a few articles from Bilboa).[10] It is true my spirit is too independant to ask favours. I would fain believe you have Friends who would assist me if I really stood in need, but whilst I can help myself I will not try them. I will not ask a person to lend me money who would demand 30 per cent for it. I never yet borrowed for my expences, nor do I mean to do it. Charles passage I must draw upon you for, if they will not take a Bill. They may wait your return for borrow I will not. I shall add a list of a few articles which I wish you to send me, or rather Bring—as you will I hope whatever you have in the House keeping way, when ever you return.

I should be glad the List may be given to the House of Ingraham &c. They best know what will suit here and do Buisness with more judgement and exactness as I found by what they once put up before. I shall depend wholy upon the remittances you may make me from time to time in the same way you have done. As to draughts I can make none but with loss. Goods are dull, but do better than Bills. Not a word from John since he went to Russia, not a Line from Mr. Thaxter. If I have not time to write to him, let him know that his Friends are well and his Sister Loring has a daughter.[11]

Mrs. Dana was well this week. Her Brother and sister dined here to day. So did our Milton Friends who desired to be rememberd to you. Mrs. Gray is this week to be married to Mr. S.A. Otis. Are you not too old to wonder? Mr. Cranch is recovering from a very dangerous Sickness in which his Friends all dispaired of his Life. My regards to all my Friends abroad. Nabby, Charles, Tom send duty to Pappa and long again to see him.

When o when will the happy day arrive that shall restore him to the affectionate Bosom of   Portia

A set of china blew and white for a dining table consisting of Dishes and plates.

12 yd of crimson damask 12 yd of f[l]owerd Muslin proper for a Gown for a young Lady 5 yd of plain Book Muslin a peice of white Silk blew blond Lace 6 yd of Black velvet like Charles Breaches and 12 yd of Black like the pattern I inclose, blew and pink 5 yd each like the patterns I inclose for a peticoat if pink is not to be had, white.

RC (Adams Papers); docketed by CFA: "Portia. March 17th 1782." Incomplete Dft (Adams Papers); varies markedly in order of topics and in language but not in substance except that RC is more expansive. Enclosed "patterns" (samples of cloth) missing.

¹ Closing quotation mark conjecturally supplied. Possibly it belongs at the end of the following sentence.
² See John Jay to the President of Congress, 20 Sept. 1781, quoted in Morris, *Peacemakers*, p. 245–246.
³ Presumably a letter from Isaac Smith Sr.; it has not been found.
⁴ Blank in MS.
⁵ A recent letter or letters from AA to JA are missing. Her latest recorded letter is that of 23 Dec. 1781, above, which mentions that she had received no letter from him later than May 1781.
⁶ Letter not found.
⁷ That is, furnished meals, &c.

⁸ On this complicated transaction see the exchanges between AA and Hugh Hill, 10–16 April, and AA to JA, 25 April, all below, with notes there.
⁹ AA's plan to purchase land in Vermont was now at least a year old, and before long she was to act on it. See AA to JA, 23 April 1781, above, and esp. 25 April 1782, below, with references in note 4 there.
¹⁰ Probably Nathaniel Tracy, Newburyport shipowner.
¹¹ Joanna Quincy Thaxter had in 1780 married Thomas Loring (*History of the Town of Hingham*, Hingham, 1893, 3:35).

John Quincy Adams to Elizabeth Cranch

My dear Cousin   St. Petersbourg March 6/17 1782

Some days agone I received a letter from you dated May last. The true reason why I have not written to you since I have been in Europe, is, that as you expect that my letters would be very entertaining, by the variety of the subjects, that I have had to write upon, I do not wish to disappoint you by writing letters that would give you no pleasure. But as you have begun, I can no longer excuse myself, and must do as well as I can.

I am at present distant 2000 of our miles from my father, but my being with Mr. D[ana] compensates if any thing can, for my loss.

Perhaps you would be glad to hear something about this country; I will give you briefly what I know about it.

The Empire of Russia is supposed to be the largest in the world but it was formerly of no consideration in Europe. It was indeed plunged into the lowest degree of barbarism, when Peter the first very justly surnamed *the Great* came to the throne. He was born in 1672. At twenty five years of age he went into Holland to the village of Saardam, and there enrolled himself as a common ship-carpenter, until he had learned the art of ship-building. He applied himself by turns to every sort of the mechanicks, and in the mean time reformed his country. The following is an eulogy of this prince by Thomson in his *Winter*.

"What cannot active government perform,
New moulding man? wide stretching from these shores
A people savage from remotest time.
A huge, neglected empire, ONE VAST MIND
By heaven inspired from Gothic darkness call'd.
Immortal PETER! first of Monarchs! He
His stubborn country tamed, her rocks, her fens;
Her floods, her seas, her ill submitting sons;
And while the fierce *Barbarian* he subdued,
To more exalted soul he rais'd the *Man*.
Ye shades of antient heroes, ye who toil'd
Thro' long successive ages to build up
A labouring plan of state, behold at once
The wonder done! behold the matchless prince!
Who left his native throne where reign'd till then
A mighty shadow of unreal power;
Who greatly spurn'd the slothful pomp of courts;
And roaming every land, in every port
His sceptre laid aside, with glorious hand
Unwearied, plying the mechanic tool,
Gather'd the seeds of trade, of useful arts
Of civil wisdom, and of martial skill.
Charg'd with the stores of *Europe*, home he goes!
Then cities rise amid th'illumined wastes
O'er joyless desarts smiles the rural reign;
Far distant flood to flood is social joined,
Th'astonished *Euxine* hears the Baltick roar,
Proud navies ride on seas that never foam'd
With daring keel before; and armies stretch
Each way their dazzling files, repressing here
The frantic *Alexander* of the North,
And awing there stern Othman's shrinking sons.
Sloth flies the land, and *ignorance*, and *vice*
Of old dishonour proud: it glows around.

Taught by the ROYAL HAND that rous'd the whole,
One scene of arts, of arms, of rising trade:
For what his wisdom plann'd and power enforc'd
More potent still, his great *example* shew'd.[1]

The famous Voltaire has written a history of the Empire of Russia, under Peter the great, which altho' it is very partial towards this country, yet it is well worth reading, as it gives an idea of what, that extraordinary prince was.

Please to present my best respects to your Pappa and Mamma and love to your brother and sister.

I am your affectionate Cousin.

LbC (Adams Papers); at head of text: "1. To Miss. E.C."

[1] A celebrated passage (lines 950–987) from "Winter," the first-written but last-placed section of James Thomson's perdurably popular poem *The Seasons* (1726–1730).

John Quincy Adams to John Thaxter

Mon cher Monsieur

A St. Petersbourg
ce 7/18 Mars 1782

Monsieur Faleisen[1] qui vous remettra ceci se proposant de partir aujourd'hui pour Amsterdam, nous a offert de prendre des lettres, mais comme il part tout subitement je n'ai que le tems de vous ecrire quelques mots, en vous priant de vouloir bien prendre soin de la lettre ci incluse.

Mais a propos, puisque j'y suis je vais vous raconter un petit voiage que nous avons fait dernierement; Il y a eu Samedi huit jours que plusieurs Messieurs et une Dame de notre connaissance, Mr. D[ana] et votre serviteur partimes de St. Petersbourg sur le Golfe de Cronstadt en trois traineaux pour Cronstadt, nous fumes une heure et cinquante cinq minutes en chemin, depuis onze heures moins vingt minutes jusques à un heure moins vingt cinq minutes; la distance est de 28 wersts ce qui fait 20 Milles d'Angleterre; nous dinames a Cronstadt, et nous allames voir le port, &c. mais en hiver il n'y a jamais grande chose à voir là. Aprés diné à cinq heures et cinq minutes nous quittames Cronstadt et nous allames à Oranienbaum, ou nous arrivames en trente cinq minutes de tems le passage est de neuf wersts ou 6 1/2 Milles Anglais; Nous passames la nuit à Oranienbaum, et le matin suivant nous fumes voir le palais qui est là. Aprés diné nous partimes d'Oranienbaum pour Peterhoff qui en est eloigné de 7 wersts ou 5 Milles. Nous mimes 35 minutes à ce trajet parceque nous le fimes sur la terre et non pas sur le Golfe comme le jour d'avant. Arrivés à Peterhoff nous vimes le palais qui y est. Ces Palais sont asséz magnifiques mais on n'y trouve rien d'extraordinaire. Enfin A quatre heures nous partimes de Peterhoff encore sur le Golfe et nous arrivames à St. Petersbourg, qui en est eloigne de vingt-sept wersts, en une heure et trois quarts de tems.[2]

Je n'ai plus de tems pour écrire, ainsi je finirai en vous assurant que je suis vôtre trés humble et trés obéissant serviteur.

P.S.   Faites bien mes respects s'il vous plait à Madame Chabanel et a toute sa famille.

LbC (Adams Papers). Enclosure may have been the (missing) RC of JQA to Elizabeth Cranch, preceding, sent to Amsterdam for forwarding to America.

[1] This name appears as "Felleisen" in JQA's Diary entry of 18 March and again in JQA's letter to JA, 20/31 March, below. He is not further identified.

[2] JQA furnished a similarly prosy account of this outing in his Diary entries for 9–10 March. The lady in the party was Mme. Peyron, wife of the Swedish consul in St. Petersburg, who was himself in the company.

John Adams to Abigail Adams

My dearest Friend   Amsterdam March 22. 1782

Your humble Servant has lately grown much into Fashion in this Country. Nobody scarcely of so much importance, as Mynheer Adams. Every City, and Province rings with De Heer Adams &c. &c. &c. and if I were to judge of things here as We do in other Countries, I should think I was going to be received, at the Hague in awfull Pomp in a few Weeks.[1] But I never can foresee one hour what will happen.

I have had however, great Pleasure to see, that there is a national Attachment to America, in the Body of this nation that is well worth cultivating, for there are no Allies more faithfull than they, as has abundantly appeared by their long Suffering with England.

Our Friends at Petersbourg are well. Pray God Charles may be with you.

I cant conceive what the English will do. They are in a strange Position at present. They cannot do much against America. But I hope, America will take their remaining Armies Prisoners in N.Y. and Charlestown. We must not relax, but pursue our Advantages.

The Proceedings of Rotterdam, will shew you, in the inclosed Paper, the Substance of what all the great Cities in this Republick are doing. Let Mr. Cranch translate it, and print it in the News papers. It is good News. You will have an Abundance of more, which will shew you, that We have not been idle here, but have sown Seeds for a plentifull Harvest. Some Folks will think your Husband, a Negotiator, but it is not he, it is General Washington at York Town who did the substance of the Work, the form only belongs to me.

Oh When shall I see my dearest Friend.—All in good Time. My dear blue Hills, ye are the most sublime object in my Imagination. At your reverend Foot, will I spend my old Age, if any, in a calm philosophical Retrospect upon the turbulent scænes of Politicks and War. I shall recollect Amsterdam, Leyden and the Hague with more Emotion than Philadelphia or Paris.

Adieu Adieu.

RC (Adams Papers). Enclosed "Proceedings of Rotterdam," not found, was a text, in Dutch or French, of a Petition of the Merchants, Insurers, and Freighters of Rotterdam to the Regency of that City, which was without date but which reached JA's hands about 20 March; an English translation is in Lb/JA/1708f; printed English texts are in JA's *Collection of State-Papers*, 1782, p. 45–46, and Wharton, ed., *Dipl. Corr. Amer. Rev.*, 5:256–257. The petition pleaded for recognition of American independence and the opening of commerce with the United States.

¹ See below, JA to AA, 1 April, and note 4 there.

Ingraham & Bromfield to Abigail Adams

Madam   Amsterdam March 23d. 1782

By direction of Mr. Adams We have Consignd to Isaac Smith Esqr. a Case of Merchandize for you, which is Ship'd in the Enterprize Capt. Daniel Deshon for Boston. This encloses the Invoice for it, the Amount being f428:1. H[ollan]d Curr[enc]y. We wish the goods may arrive Safe, and to your Approbation. Presenting our Respectful Compliments, We are Madam.

Dupl RC (Adams Papers); at foot of text: "Copy) Orig[ina]l P[er] Deshon." Dupl precedes on the same sheet of paper the RC of Ingraham & Bromfield to AA, 1 July, below. Enclosed invoice not found.

John Adams to Abigail Adams

My dearest Friend   29 March 1782

The states of Holland and West Friesland have resolved, 28 March to admit Mr. Adams to an Audience.

The inclosed Papers will shew what is going on here. You will

301

[hear?] much more of it.[1]—I have yet no news of Charles's Arrival. John is well—&c.

British Ministry changed.[2]

RC (Adams Papers). "[I]nclosed Papers" not found.

[1] The relevant passage in "the Resolutions of the Lords the States of Holland and Westfriesland, taken in the Assembly of their Noble and Grand-Mightinesses, Thursday 28 March 1782," resolving "that Mr. Adams be admitted and acknowledged, as soon as possible, by their High-Mightinesses [the States General], in quality of Ambassador of the United States of America," is printed in JA, *Collection of State-Papers*, 1782, p. 81–82.

[2] Thus in MS—an indication of JA's extreme haste in getting off this momentous news. See below, JA to AA, 1 April, and note 1 there.

John Quincy Adams to John Adams

Honoured Sir   St. Petersbourg March 20/31 1782

I should have written to you by Mr. Felleisen, who will doubtless have arrived before this comes to hand, but I did not know that he was going until it was too late to write. Mr. D[ana] thinks that I had better not write every post; because the postage of the Letters would soon amount to a very considerable sum.

I have lately begun to learn German, I have a master who gives me three lessons per week, at about a Guinea a month.[1] I have finished three of Cicero's Orations against Catiline and have begun the fourth. And I have finished reading Mrs. Macaulay's history of England.

Mr. D. begs that you would be so good as to send to England for the best history of New England that is to be got; for Hutchinson's if you think there is no better. And that Mr. Thaxter would desire Messrs. Sigourney and Ingraham to send him a piece of Linen of the same sort with that which he has already had. It can come in the Secretaire or Scritoire that he has sent for, and which he says he must have by all means. He wishes also to have sent in it all the Amsterdam Gazettes from the time we left Holland to the first of April, when his year expires so that he may have them compleat: and Mr. Cerisier's *Tableau de l'Histoire Generale des Provinces Unies des Pays-Bas*. Mr. Thaxter will be so good as to write by the Post a list of every thing that will be sent, with their prices, because, so much per cent. is paid for the entrance of every thing here.

We hear that you have bought a house at the Hague.

Mr. D. is every day complaining of Mr. Thaxter's negligence in not writing him the news, especially so important a thing as the resolution of Friesland. He says that it is of importance that he should know all such news, and not be obliged to wait for them till the Newspapers give them; and he wishes to know what is intended to be done as well as what is already done, as far as may be.

The weather here, has been for some days very fine. The thermometer has been this day at 9 degrees above the degree of freezing.

I am your dutiful Son,   J.Q.A.

P.S.   Please to present my respects to all Friends.

RC (Adams Papers); addressed: "A Son Excellence Monsieur Adams. Ministre Plenipotentiaire des Etats Unis de L'Amerique à Amsterdam"; endorsed: "Ansd. 28 April J. Q. Adams." LbC (Adams Papers).

[1] "Master John is in high health. He does not study the language of this Country, but he is learning German, which, I believe, you wou'd prefer before Russian" (Francis Dana to JA, 28 March O.S., Adams Papers).

"This Morning our German master came to give us a lesson for the first time" (JQA, Diary, 21 March [N.S.]). Later entries record a few further lessons, but JQA did not pursue the study of German very long or very far at this time. Fifteen years later, on his going as United States minister to Berlin, he became proficient in the language and an American pioneer in the study of German culture. See Walter John Morris, John Quincy Adams, Germanophile, Pennsylvania State Univ. doctoral dissertation, 1963, microfilm edn., University Microfilms, 1965.

John Adams to Abigail Adams

My dearest Friend   April 1. 1782

The States of Holland and West Friesland have followed the Example of Friesland, in acknowledging American Independence. ⟨I received⟩ The American Minister received Yesterday officially, from the Grand Pensionary of Holland a Copy of their Resolution.

We have not yet the Mail, with an Account of the new British Ministry, tho the last informed Us of a Change. Whether for the better time will shew.[1]

I have yet no News of Charles's Arrival.

The French Ambassadors House at the Hague, has been burnt, which I regret very much, more on Account of the Interruption to his Thoughts and Exertions in these critical Moments, than for the Value of the Loss which is however very considerable. The Duc de la Vauguion is an able Minister and my very good Friend.[2] I have bought an House at the Hague to which I shall remove the 1st. May.[3] Will you come and see me?

Adieu–Adieu![4]

RC (Adams Papers).

¹ North's ministry resigned on 20 March in the face of an opposition motion of censure which everyone knew would pass if put to a vote. Parliament then adjourned, and after tortuous negotiations between the King (who would not deal directly with Lord Rockingham, leader of the opposition) and Lord Shelburne, the Rockingham ministry was formed on 27 March, to be succeeded, upon Rockingham's death, by Shelburne's ministry on 4 July.

² The Duc de La Vauguyon (1746–1828), briefly identified under JQA to JA, 17 May 1781, above, appears with some frequency in JA's *Diary and Autobiography*; see esp. vol. 2:457. A year earlier he had endeavored to dissuade JA from delivering his Memorial of 19 April to the States General, but, after failing in this attempt, La Vauguyon cooperated with JA to the extent of his powers, particularly in the strategy JA was now pursuing; see further, note 4 below.

The French Embassy on the Prinsessegracht at The Hague was destroyed by fire on 26 March. There is an account in the *s'Gravenhaagse Courant* of 29 March. See an illustration in this volume of the building when it was built twenty years earlier in what was then a new part of the city.

³ On 15 March, anticipating his recognition as minister, JA reported to Francis Dana that he had purchased "an house at the Hague, fit for the Hotel des Etats Unis, or if you will L'Hotel de nouveau Monde" (MHi:Dana Papers). The building was on the Fluwelen Burgwal or Street of the Velvet Makers' Wall, on a site which, with adjacent property, is now occupied by the Netherlands Government Printing Office. Documents bearing on its acquisition (through JA's agent at The Hague, C. W. F. Dumas) and an engraved illustration of the site about 1830 will be found in JA, *Diary and Autobiography*, 3:ix–x, 4–5, and facing p. 65. JA moved into this first American-owned legation building in Europe on 12 May. Dumas, his wife, and their young daughter were the caretakers. See JA to JQA, 13 May; Thaxter to AA, 27 July; both below.

⁴ What this letter conveyed, more by implication than in so many words, was that the first and chief objective of JA's year of watchful waiting, mixed with strenuous journalistic and diplomatic campaigning, was about to be realized. In the spring of 1781 he had written and, in spite of obstacles strewn in his way, had presented to the States General his Memorial announcing his receipt of powers from Congress as minister plenipotentiary, requesting recognition in that capacity, and arguing the advantages that would flow from an alliance and the opening of commerce between the United Netherlands and the United States. For details see notes on JA to AA, 11 March and 28 April 1781, both above; also JA, *Diary and Autobiography*, 2:457. As he had been taught to expect, the *ad referendum* process, from the States General to the assemblies of the seven provinces and back again, would take time. At length in December he was advised by La Vauguyon, who under instruction from Versailles was eager to promote the plans of the Dutch Patriots against the pro-English Stadholder, that he might "now assume an higher Tone, which the late *Cornwallization* will well warrant," and might begin formal calls upon the great officers of the republic, the several regencies, and especially the deputies of the cities of the Province of Holland, requesting "an Answer to my former Proposition" (JA to Pres. Thomas McKean, 18 Dec. 1781, PCC, No. 84, III; printed in Wharton, ed., *Dipl. Corr. Amer. Rev.*, 5:55; La Vauguyon to JA, 30 Dec. 1781, Adams Papers; printed in JA, *Works*, 7:500–501). On 9 Jan. 1782, accordingly, JA began a round of visits at The Hague to present a "réquisition verbale" demanding "a Categorical Answer" to his request for recognition. An English text of the "réquisition" or "Ulteriour Address" is in JA's *Collection of State-Papers*, 1782, p. 21; see also JA to McKean, 14 Jan. (PCC, No. 84, III; printed in Wharton, ed., *Dipl. Corr. Amer. Rev.*, 5:97–100). Meanwhile JA's friends among the merchants, publishers, and political leaders of the Patriot party, chiefly in the cities of Holland but in some other provinces as well, busied themselves getting up petitions

favoring recognition of and trade with the United States, some of the results of which have been alluded to in preceding letters in this volume. These had their effect: the first province to instruct its deputies to vote for recognition was Friesland, 26 Feb.; on 28 March, after some last-minute hesitations, the assembly of Holland similarly instructed its deputies. Dumas wrote instantaneously: "La grande oeuvre est accomplie," adding that he was unable to see more than one or two of the members because they "sont actuellement à célébrer l'oeuvre en bonne compagnie, et le verre en main" (to JA, 28 March, Adams Papers). Holland's action virtually determined that of the remaining provinces, all five of which announced favorable decisions on or before 17 April. Texts of the provincial resolutions and instructions are in JA's *Collection of State-Papers*, 1782, p. 79–91. See further, John Thaxter to JA, 20 April, below, and note 1 there.

Abigail Adams to John Adams

My dearest Friend   April 10th. 1782

How great was my joy to see the well known Signature of my Friend after a Melancholy Solicitude of many months in which my hopes and fears alternately preponderated.[1]

It was January when Charles arrived. By him I expected Letters, but found not a line; instead of which the heavy tidings of your illness reachd me. I then found my Friends had been no strangers of what they carefully conceald from me. Your Letter to Charles dated in November[2] was the only consolation I had; by that I found that the most dangerous period of your illness was pass'd, and that you considerd yourself as recovering tho feeble. My anxiety and apprehensions from that day untill your Letters arrived, which was near 3 months, conspired to render me unhappy. Capt. Trowbridge in the Fire Brand arrived with your favours of October and December and in some measure dispeld the Gloom which hung heavy at my heart. How did it leap for joy to find I was not the misirable Being I sometimes feared I was. I felt that Gratitude to Heaven which great deliverences both demand and inspire. I will not distrust the providential Care of the supreem disposer of events, from whose Hand I have so frequently received distinguished favours. Such I call the preservation of my dear Friend and children from the uncertain Element upon which they have frequently embarked; their preservation from the hands of their enimies I have reason to consider in the same view, especially when I reflect upon the cruel and inhumane treatment experienced by a Gentleman of Mr. Laurences age and respectable character.

The restoration of my dearest Friend from so dangerous a Sickness, demands all my gratitude, whilst I fail not to supplicate Heaven for the continuance of a Life upon which my temporal happiness rests, and deprived of which my own existance would become a burden. Often has the Question which you say staggerd your philosophy occured to me, nor have I felt so misirable upon account of my own personal Situation, when I considerd that according to the common course of Nature, more than half my days were allready passt, as for those in whom our days are renewed. Their hopes and prospects would vanish, their best prospects, those of Education, would be greatly diminished—but I will not anticipate those miseries which I would shun. Hope is my best Friend and kindest comforter; she assures me that the pure unabated affection, which neither time or absence can allay or abate, shall e'er long be crowned with the completion of its fondest wishes, in the safe return of the beloved object; the age of romance has long ago past, but the affection of almost Infant years has matured and strengthend untill it has become a vital principle, nor has the world any thing to bestow which could in the smallest degree compensate for the loss. Desire and Sorrow were denounced upon our Sex; as a punishment for the transgression of Eve. I have sometimes thought that we are formed to experience more exquisite Sensations than is the Lot of your Sex. More tender and susceptable by Nature of those impression[s] which create happiness or misiry, we Suffer and enjoy in a higher degree. I never wonderd at the philosopher who thanked the Gods that he was created a Man rather than a Woman.

I cannot say, but that I was dissapointed when I found that your return to your native land was a still distant Idea. I think your Situation cannot be so dissagreable as I feared it was, yet that dreadfull climate is my terror.—You mortify me indeed when you talk of sending Charles to Colledge, who it is not probable will be fit under three or four years. Surely my dear Friend fleeting as time is I cannot reconcile myself to the Idea of living in this cruel State of Seperation for [4?] or even three years to come. Eight years have already past, since you could call yourself an Inhabitant of this State. I shall assume the Signature of Penelope, for my dear Ulysses has already been a wanderer from me near half the term of years that, that Hero was encountering Neptune, Calipso, the Circes and Syrens. In the poetical Language of Penelope I shall address you

> "Oh! haste to me! A Little longer Stay
> Will ev'ry grace, each fancy'd charm decay:
> Increasing cares, and times resistless rage
> Will waste my bloom, and wither it to age."

You will ask me I suppose what is become of my patriotick virtue? It is that which most ardently calls for your return. I greatly fear that the climate in which you now reside will prove fatal to your Life, whilst your Life and usefullness might be many years of Service to your Country in a more Healthy climate. If the Essentials of her political system are safe, as I would fain hope they are, yet the impositions and injuries, to which she is hourly liable, and daily suffering, call for the exertions of her wisest and ablest citizens. You know by many years experience what it is to struggle with difficulties —with wickedness in high places—from thence you are led to covet a private Station as the post of Honour, but should such an Idea generally prevail, who would be left to stem the torrent?

Should we at this day possess those invaluable Blessings transmitted us by our venerable Ancestors, if they had not inforced by their example, what they taught by their precepts?

> "While pride, oppression and injustice reign
> the World will still demand her Catos presence."

Why should I indulge an Idea, that whilst the active powers of my Friend remain, they will not be devoted to the Service of his country?

Can I believe that the Man who fears neither poverty or dangers, who sees not charms sufficient either in Riches, power or places to tempt him in the least to swerve from the purest Sentiments of Honour and Delicacy; will retire, unnoticed, Fameless to a Rustick cottage there by dint of Labour to earn his Bread. I need not much examination of my Heart to say I would not willing[ly] consent to it.

Have not Cincinnatus and Regulus been handed down to posterity, with immortal honour?

Without fortune it is more than probable we shall end our days, but let the well earned Fame of having Sacrificed those prospects, from a principal of universal Benevolence and good will to Man, descend as an inheritance to our ofspring. The Luxery of Foreign Nations may possibly infect them but they have not before them an example of it, so far as respects their domestick life. They are not Bred up with an Idea of possessing Hereditary Riches or Grandeur. Retired from the Capital, they see little of the extravagance or dissipation, which prevails there, and at the close of day, in lieu of the Card table, some usefull Book employs their leisure hours. These habits early fixed, and daily inculcated, will I hope render them usefull and ornamental Members of Society.—But we cannot see into futurity.

—With Regard to politicks, it is rather a dull season for them, we are recruiting for the Army.

The Enemy make sad Havock with our Navigation. Mr. Lovell is appointed continential Receiver of taxes and is on his way to this State.[3]

It is difficult to get Gentlemen of abilities and Integrity to serve in congress, few very few are willing to Sacrifice their Interest as others have done before them.

Your favour of december 18th came by way of Philadelphia, but all those Letters sent by Capt. Reeler were lost, thrown over Board. Our Friends are well and desire to be rememberd to you. Charles will write if he is able to, before the vessel sails, but he is sick at present, threatned I fear with a fever. I received one Letter from my young Russian to whom I shall write—and 2 from Mr. Thaxter.[4] If the vessel gives me time I shall write. We wait impatiently for the result of your demand. These slow slugish wheels move not in unison with our feelings.

Adieu my dear Friend. How gladly would I visit you and partake of your Labours and cares, sooth you to rest, and alleviate your anxieties were it given me to visit you even by moon Light, as the faries are fabled to do.

I cheer my Heart with the distant prospect. All that I can hope for at present, is to hear of your welfare which of all things lies nearest the Heart of Your ever affectionate   Portia

RC (Adams Papers); docketed by CFA: "Portia. April 10th 1782."

[1] AA is acknowledging JA's letters of 9 Oct. and 2 and 18 Dec. 1781, above.
[2] Not found.
[3] See above, AA to Lovell, 8? Jan., and note 4 there.
[4] Presumably JQA to AA, 23 Oct., and Thaxter to AA, 2, 19 Dec. 1781, all above.

Abigail Adams to James Lovell?

Sir   Braintree [*ca.* 10] April [1782]

I have not had the pleasure of a line from you since your arrival in Philadelphia, but I have had the satisfaction of hearing from abroad and finding that the situation of my Friend was not so dissagreable as I feard.[1] You have had publick dispatches and probable private Letters. Have you not some intelligence which you may communicate?

There is not a prospect of peace I think. Thus my Friend expresses himself. "Do not flatter yourself with the hopes of peace. There will be no such thing for several years.

"Do not distress yourself about any malicious attempts to injure me in the estimation of my countrymen. Let them take their course and go the length of their Tether, they will not hurt your H[usband], whose character is fortified with a sheild of Innocence and Honour ten thousandfold stronger than brass or Iron. The contemptible Essays made by you know whom will only tend to their own confusion. I have already brought them into the true system and that system is triumphant. They could not help Blushing themselves if they were to review their conduct."

By this I am led to think that matters are in a different train from what I apprehended. You may be better able to judge by your publick dispatches.

This Letter will go by a Gentleman whose name is Perkings, who has been preceptor to my children and Mr. Cranchs for more than a year.² He is going at the desire of Mr. Ganet and in compliance with the request of a Gentleman in Virginia to keep a private school there. He is a young gentleman of a fair character and good abilities. As he is quite a Stranger in Philadelphia to every person except General Lincoln and Mr. Partridge,³ any notice you will please to take of him, or any civilities you may shew him will be gratefully acknowledged by Sir your old Friend & Humble Servant,   Portia

Dft (Adams Papers); without indication of addressee and dated only "April," to which CFA later mistakenly added "1781." For evidence establishing the approximate date, see note 1. AA's careless punctuation, especially in placing quotation marks, has been minimally corrected.

¹ The letter alluded to and quoted (not altogether accurately) in the following paragraphs is that of JA to AA, 2 Dec. 1781, above. AA acknowledged recent receipt of this letter in her reply of 10 April, preceding. Lovell, who seems the only eligible intended recipient of the present letter, had returned to Congress for a brief and final period of service at the beginning of April; see above AA to Lovell, 8? Jan., note 4.

² Thomas Perkins, Harvard 1779, of Bridgewater. He soon afterward settled in western Virginia, already known as Kentucky, and took up the practice of law but died suddenly in 1786. See

Nahum Mitchell, *History of the Early Settlement of Bridgewater* . . . , Boston, 1840, p. 266; AA to JA, 17 July 1782, below; Mary (Smith) Cranch to AA, 22 May 1786, and Elizabeth (Smith) Shaw to AA, 1–3 Nov. 1786, both in Adams Papers. In 1785 Perkins wrote Gen. Joseph Palmer from Lincoln co., Kentucky, on the salt springs and other natural curiosities of that region; his letter is printed in MHS, *Procs.*, 1st ser., 12 (1871–1873):38–39.

³ George Partridge, currently a Massachusetts delegate to the Continental Congress.

Hugh Hill to Abigail Adams

Madam   Boston April 10th. 1782

Shold Estem a fever to Ordr Som of your frends to pay me for your Son Charls Pasheg from bilbao to America   Mr. Smith I heare had Som altication on the matr and thinck it is too much, but Madam Shold thinck a great Desrespet Cast on a son of Mr. Adames not to Charge him the Saim as Other Gentelmen   ples to ordr it Payd to Captn. Joab Prince   I am Madam most Respetfoly your most homble Servt   Hugh Hill

The Pasage is £35: 0: 0 [1]

RC (Adams Papers); addressed: "Mrs. Adams   Brantree"; enclosed in AA to JA, 25 April, below. Text is printed in literal style.

[1] The tangled matter of CA's passage money is dealt with in detail in AA to JA, 17–25 March, above; 25 April, below; and in an exchange of letters between AA and Hill immediately following the present letter.

Abigail Adams to Hugh Hill

Sir   *[Braintree, ante 16 April 1782]* [1]

The day after my Son reachd home I wrote to you [2] and requested you would inform me what I was indebted to you for my Sons passage. I had inquired of Major Jackson, who said he made no particular agreement respecting him; but that if I would write he would take charge of the Letter, and deliver it himself. I accordingly wrote and requested you to direct a Letter to me; to be left at Isaac Smiths Esqrs Boston but I never heard any thing from you; untill your favour of April 10th. Mr. Smith inquired respecting the other passengers, and found that 25 Guineys was the price you had demanded of them which he thought very high and much more than was given by other passengers who came from the same place at the same time.

With regard to myself I am wholy Ignorant of the customs and useages in such cases, but neither Mr. Adams or myself would wish to do otherways than was customary and reasonable nor should we have been offended if a distinction had been made between the passage of a Man and a child. It would oblige me if you would take a Bill of exchange upon Mr. Adams for the Money, as it is not in my power to pay it without inconveniency. If you will leave a Letter for me at Mr. Smiths I will send the Bills there or to Capt. Prince as you direct. Your Humble Servant,   AA

FC (Adams Papers); at foot of text: "To Capt Hugh Hill   Beverly"; enclosed in AA to JA, 25 April, below.

[1] Dated from Hill's reply, which follows.
[2] This letter, which must have been sent about 30 Jan., has not been found.

Hugh Hill to Abigail Adams

Madam   April the 16th. 1782

Yours I reseved this morning and I asner you madam that twenty five Guines is the Costomry Pasage that is payd too or from uerap   I apeled to Captn. Dixey that Comanded a ship of Mr. Treaseys in bilbao wher I was: You will ples to Draw me a set of bils at the present Discount Which is fiften pr cent and fored them to Captn. Job Prince: four Sets[1] the Som is thirty Nin pounds at ten Dayes Sight[2]   now mor at present from your very homble Sert

                                                        Hugh Hill

My regards to Charls.

RC (Adams Papers); addressed: "Mrs. Adams in Branetree" (or "Branstree"); enclosed in AA to JA, 25 April, below. Text is printed in literal style.

[1] Thus in MS; the meaning is not clear.
[2] In his letter of 10 April, above, Hill stated that the charge for CA's passage was £35. Now, contradicting himself, he accepts AA's information as given in the preceding letter that the usual fare is 25 guineas, and asks that amount. But he then further confuses matters by saying that if payment is to be made in bills of exchange, they will be discounted by 15 percent, and therefore AA should pay him £39. Neither £35 nor 25 guineas plus 15 percent add up to £39. A possible or at least partial explanation may be found below in AA's letter to JA, 25 April (in which the present letters were enclosed); see note 3 there.

John Thaxter to John Adams

Sir   Amsterdam 20th. April 1782

I have the honor to congratulate You on the final Resolution of the Generality, the News of which I received last Evening.[1] This Step makes an agreable Impression here, and they pride themselves in the Unanimity and *Rapidity*, and I may add *Velocity* with which it has been carried thro'. It will indeed make a memorable Epocha in the Annals of this Country, and stand as an eternal Monument that the Vox Populi is the ———.

I shall be extremely happy to hear that the Credentials are delivered. If You have time to drop hint You will oblige me exceedingly and many Friends. I received a Letter last Evening from Mr. Jenings for You, and he thinks very justly of the present Ministry, that is, that they are as wise and as good as their Predecessors. He professes that he is ashamed of them.[2] You will do me a favor in acquainting me whether that tumor in your Neck is less troublesome than when You left me. Mr. Barclay desires his Respects to You, and is rejoiced with the News.[3]

I am with an invariable Attachment, Sir, &c.,   JT.

Compts. to Mr. D. and Family.

RC (Adams Papers).

[1] The "final Resolution of the Generality" was the action of the States General of the United Provinces, 19 April 1782, one year from the day JA had signed his original Memorial to that body. A MS in Dutch, signed by Willem Boreel as president of the week and attested by Hendrik Fagel, as *griffier* or secretary of the States General, is in Adams Papers. An English text is printed in JA's *Collection of State-Papers,* 1782, p. 92, and reads as follows:

"Deliberated by Resumption, upon the Address and the ulteriour Address, made by Mr. Adams the 4 May 1781, and the 9 January of the currant year to Mr. the President of the Assembly of their High-Mightinesses, to present to their High-Mightinesses his Letters of Credence in the name of the United States of North-America; and by which ulteriour Address the said Mr. Adams hath demanded a categorical answer, to the end to be able to acquaint his Constituents thereof; it hath been thought fit and resolved, that Mr. Adams shall be admitted and acknowledged in quality of Ambassador of the United States of North-America to their High-Mightinesses, as he is admitted and acknowledged by the present."

Two days later this was followed by a further resolution reporting the reception of JA with his credentials as minister plenipotentiary to the States General in "a Letter from the Assembly of Congress, written at Philadelphia the first of January 1781.... Upon which, having deliberated, it hath been thought fit and resolved, to declare by the present: 'That the said Mr. Adams is agreable to their High-Mightinesses; that he shall be acknowledged in quality of Minister Plenipotentiary; and that there shall be granted to him an Audience, or as-

signed Commissioners, when he shall demand it.' " This resolve was signed by W. van Citters, president of the week, and likewise attested by Fagel. MS in Dutch (Adams Papers); English translation printed in *Collection of State-Papers,* p. 93.

This same day, 22 April, JA "was introduced by the Chamberlain to his most Serene Highness the Prince of Orange." No one else was present, and at JA's request they spoke in English. JA voiced the proper formal sentiments, and the Stadholder answered "in a Voice so low and so indistinctly pronounced, that I comprehended only the Conclusion of it, which was, that 'he had made no Difficulty against my Reception.' " However, some "familiar Conversation ... about indifferent things" followed, and the audience passed agreeably enough. So JA told R. R. Livingston in a letter written before the day was over (PCC, No. 84, IV, printed in Wharton, ed., *Dipl. Corr. Amer. Rev.,* 5:319–320; LbC, Adams Papers, printed in JA, *Works,* 7:571–572).

Next day, 23 April, JA met with President van Citters and presented a brief memorial proposing a treaty of amity and commerce between the two powers. He was then introduced to "a grand committee" of the States General and laid before it the project of such a treaty, which was taken under consideration (and was to bear fruit six months later). See JA to Livingston, 23 April (PCC, No. 84, IV, printed in Wharton, 5:325; LbC, Adams Papers, printed in *Works,* 7:572–573). But meanwhile, as he told Livingston in the letter just cited, "The greatest Part of my Time for several Days has been taken up in recieving and paying of Visits from all the

Members and Officers of Government, and of the Court, to the Amount of one hundred and fifty or more." There is a partial listing of these in JA's *Diary and Autobiography*, 3:1–3; and although JA did not keep daily entries in his diary at this period, his correspondence during the following days and weeks is crowded with references to ceremonial and social events growing out of his public recognition. See also Sister Mary Briant Foley, The Triumph of Militia Diplomacy, Loyola Univ. doctoral dissertation, 1968, p. 244 ff.

² Edmund Jenings to JA, 18 April

(Adams Papers).

³ Thomas Barclay (1728–1793), a Philadelphia merchant who had recently come to Europe to serve as American consul (later consul general) in France. He was in Amsterdam endeavoring to make a settlement for the goods abandoned by Alexander Gillon. JA was to be a guest in Barclay's house at Auteuil when ill in the fall of 1783, and Barclay later served as an American diplomatic agent in Morocco. See a documented sketch of him in JA, *Diary and Autobiography*, 3:120.

Abigail Adams to John Adams

My Dearest Friend   April 25 1782

Whenever any difficulty encompasses me, my first thought is how would my Friend conduct in this affair. I wish to know what his mind would be and then to act agreable to it. If I err in my conduct it is an error of the judgement, not of the Heart. Wholy deprived of your aid, and even advice in domestick occurences, my next resource is in that of my Friends. My present difficulty arrises from the demand upon me for C[harle]s passage Home.

I have once written to you respecting it,[1] but least you should not receive it, I repeat several things already written together with what has since occured. When Mr. J[ackso]n arrived and came to B[raintre]e to see me, I inquired of him what measures he had taken with regard to C—s expences after he left Gillion, where I presumed you had provided for him. I had received no Letters from you, so that I was wholy Ignorant. He replied that when he arrived at Bilboa he drew a Bill upon Mr. de Nuffville a part of which he appropriated to C—s use, of which he had informd you, that he had not his accounts with him, a memorandum excepted of a few articles, that he had not paid the expences from Beverly, where they first arrived, but as soon as he had done it, he would make up the account and send it, together with a balance which he had left, of a few dollors. He then Shew me the Mem'dum, which containd as near as I can recollect a charge of 57 dollors for Stores, one peice of linnen of an ordinary Quality, the price I forget (this he thought necessary as C—s had lost half his shirts together with one pair of sheets, stockings &c. stolen from him), 2 yard of Cambrick, 2 Barcelona hank[erchie]fs and a Hat which was charged 4 dollors, C—s having his in Mr. Guiles Trunk with some

313

other articles and that I suppose you know before this time was on Board Gillion. A Sailors Baize Jacket and trousers compleated the mem'dum. With regard to the expences of living there, you are better acquainted than I am, and must judge for yourself, as I have not a single paper that will enable me to do it. After waiting some time I sent to Col. Crafts where Major J. lodged for the papers, but he was not at home, and there was none left. The same Week he went to Hingham to see General L[incol]n, and calld upon me. He then told me that he had left a Letter at Col. Crafts together with the papers which belonged to me but comeing unexpectedly he forgot to take them. He returnd in a day or two from Hingham and immediately set of for the Army since which I have neither heard of him or his papers, for upon applieing for them, I received for answer that there was not any thing left for me, if there had have been, the earliest opportunity would have been taken to have forwarded it. I have stated facts. You know this Gentleman much better than I do, so I shall not comment. After he had informd me with regard to the Bill he drew, I inquired what had been done with regard to the passage. To this he replied that no agreement had been made with Capt. Hill respecting C—s, but that the other passengers paid 25 Guineys. Supposeing that they would not make the like demand for the passage of a child, I wrote to Capt. Hill desireing to know what I was indebted to him, but I heard not a word from him untill some time this Month I received a Letter a coppy of which I inclose together with my unkles Letter, my reply to Hill and his answer.[2] Upon my unkles hearing what the other passengers gave, he said it was an unreasonable demand, and that advantage was taken of the situation of the passengers. He went to the Agent and then to Capt. Hill, but to no purpose, as you see by the inclosed. Hill says, they were a month in passing from Corunna to Bilboa and that they then lived at the expence of his owners, that the other passengers agreed to give it,[3] and that he will not take less. I think you would not advise me to enter into an altercation with him which would give me much trouble, and very little if any relief. You see by the inclosed that I requested him to take Bills and by his reply that he wanted a discount of 15 per cent. I sent him word that I would draw Bills, but that I would not discount. He said if he had the money he could Buy Bills at 20 per cent discount, and he would not take them at a [*word omitted*] less than he had offerd. I went to Town to see if I could not do better, I tried one and then an other. Some had no money, others did not want Bills. At last a cousin of mine in whose favour it is probable I must draw the Bills, offerd to pay the money for me, and take the Bills at 10 per cent discount, if I could not do better. I might try and if I could dispose of them to better advantage he should be content, he accordingly paid the money, and I am still trying to get them accepted, but cannot yet effect it. I could pay the Money myself but I must then relinquish the object I have in view, of purchaseing an original Right in the State of Virmont and I have brought that matter so near a close that I think you would not advise me to do it. I expect the deeds in a week or two for 16 hundred and 20 acres of Land when I must pay the money. As it is in the Neighbourhood of some of our Friends who are purchasers, and I have set my Heart upon it, I am loth to relinquish it. The Town is called Salem, laid out in lots of 300 & 30 acres, no one person permitted to own more than one Lot in the same township, but you may purchase in the Names of yourself and children. I have engaged one for my best Friend and each of our children. The 5 lots will amount to 200 Dollors. At the expiration of 5 years there is a House to be built of 18 feet square and a family setled, or 5 acres of Land cleared upon each Lot. No taxes to be paid untill the expiration of 5 years. I shall soon be able to be more particular. Every person of whom I have inquired agree, that it is a fine Country, and will daily become more and more valuable. This Town is situated upon two navigable Rivers. There internal affairs are in a good way, and they are now sending delegates to congress. If you approve of what I have done, and should like to purchase further I shall have more opportunities.[4] Remittances in Goods, tho they will only double the sterling cost, are preferable to Bills in which I am under a necessity of becomeing a looser. I told you before that I had very seldom met with any person who either considerd my situation or yours, any other than to make a proffit if they could. Our Brother C——h would help me if it was in his power, and is every ready and willing to do for me what ever he can. About six months ago I placed a hundred pounds Sterling in the hands of a Friend but I am loth to break upon it, as I know it to be in good hands and promised not to call for it without giving them 3 months warning.

I have endeavourd to make the best of what ever remittances you have made me. The necessary repair of Buildings, the Anual Call for 3 years Men, and the very large taxes which are laid upon me oblige me to the strickest frugality. I cannot but think I am hardly delt by, being rated in to 20 shillings as much as Mr. Alleyne of this Town, who has 3 polls, and I none. He estimates his place at 3000 sterling, whilst I believe you would take half the money for yours, but he cannot find a purchaser for his. The rage for purchaseing land ceased with the paper currency, and the taxes are felt severely enough. I complain but without redress.

With regard to remittances calicos answer well especially chocolate ground, as they are calld Blew ground or Green ground. They should be coulourd stripes or flowers; ribbons are still more profitable gauze tape fine threads [Menting?][5] hankerchiefs Bandano hankerchiefs coulourd tamies or Calimincos, black serge denim Bindings either shoe or Quality.[6] The House of Sigourney Bromfield &c. best know what will answer here. I close this Letter being wholy upon Domestick Matters with assureances of the affectionate regard of your

Portia

RC (Adams Papers); endorsed: "Portia   recd. & ansd. 1. July. 1782." For the enclosures see note 2.

[1] AA to JA, 17–25 March, above.

[2] The four enclosures were: Hugh Hill to AA, 10 April, above; Isaac Smith Sr. to AA, of recent date but not found; AA to Hill, ante 16 April, above; and Hill to AA, 16 April, above.

[3] This point is not raised in the correspondence between Hill and AA above (see preceding note), but it may possibly explain the difference between the £35 demanded for CA's passage and the 25 guineas elsewhere spoken of as the customary fare.

[4] AA's purpose, long contemplated (to JA, 23 April 1781, above), to purchase land from a large tract granted for settlement by the General Assembly of Vermont to Col. Jacob Davis, Abner Mellen, Jonas Comins, and others of Worcester in Oct. 1780, which here seems at the point of realization, was in fact dropped for a time and not acted upon finally for another three months (to JA, 17 June, 17–18 July 1782, both below; deed of Jonas Comins to JQA, 20 April 1782, Adams Papers). Although the belief, shared with or perhaps derived from the Cranch family, in the likelihood of easy profit was a leading motive in her purchase of the five lots, another evidently hardly less important motive—the dream of a refuge with JA from public controversies in a sylvan retreat—appears again and again when AA writes of Vermont (to JA, 9 Dec. 1781, 17–25 March

1782, both above; 17–18 July, below). That JA's requirements for a retreat were not the same as AA's, he revealed not to her but to his friend James Warren in a letter written before he received AA's present account of the imminent purchase: "God willing, I wont go to Vermont. I must be within the Scent of the sea" (to Warren, 17 June 1782, MB: Chamberlain Coll.; printed in JA, *Works*, 9:513). To AA, his only response so far noted to her reports about the purchase was "dont meddle any more with Vermont" (12 Oct. 1782, Adams Papers).

Despite the requirement that a portion of each lot be cleared and a house built upon it within five years, the acreage long remained unimproved and declining in value in the hands of those for whom AA purchased it, or their heirs. Some forty years later, TBA, acting for himself and the other owners, made plans to sell the lots at auction (TBA to Alexander Bryan Johnson, 9, 30 O t. 1819; 20 April, 8 May 1822; MSS privately owned, 1964–1965, photoduplicates in Adams Papers Editorial Files). Whether any lots were sold at that time is not clear. However, JQA disposed of his, which a squatter had partially cleared and built upon, by sale to Leonard Bouker in 1825 (deed of Comins to JQA, 20 April 1782, cited above, docketed by JQA, 30 June 1825).

TBA's lot was still his at his death and became a part of his estate (JQA, Diary, 19 July 1833).

[5] Semilegible word; possibly AA's rendering of "Menin," a Flemish town well known for its fine linens.

[6] No attempt has been made to cor-

rect AA's punctuation in the foregoing two sentences, so as to separate the individual items. Compare more or less duplicate listings appended to her letters to JA of 17 June and 17–18 July, both below.

John Adams to John Quincy Adams

My Child   [*Amsterdam, 28 April* 1782][1]

Yours of March 20/31 I have received.

I am well pleased with your learning German for many Reasons, and principally because I am told that Science and Literature flourish more at present in Germany than any where. A Variety of Languages will do no harm unless you should get an habit of attending more to Words than Things.

But, my dear Boy, above all Things, preserve your Innocence, and a pure Conscience. Your morals are of more importance, both to yourself and the World than all Languages and all Sciences. The least Stain upon your Character will do more harm to your Happiness than all Accomplishments will do it good.—I give you Joy of the safe Arrival of your Brother, and the Acknowledgment of the Independance of your Country in Holland. Adieu.

RC (Adams Papers); addressed: "A Monsieur Monsieur J. Q. Adams, chez Monsieur Dana. aux soins de Messrs. Strahlborne & Wolff Banquers a St Petersbourg"; endorsed: "Mr.: J.As letter. received at St: Petersbourg May. 15. 1782." Early Tr (Adams Papers), in JQA's hand.

[1] Dated from JA's endorsement of JQA's letter to JA of 20/31 March, above, to which this is a reply.

Abigail Adams 2d to Elizabeth Cranch

Saturday [*April* 1782]

Knowing your benevolent heart is ever gratified by hearing of the wellfare of your friends, and feeling a disposition to scrible, you Eliza first claim my attention. I hope ere this your health and spirits are perfectly restored and every one of the family to their usual chearfulness. Do not my Dear Girl dwell too long on the dark side of affairs, it impairs your health and sinks your spirits. Was it in the power of your friend to remove the causes of your anxiety it would be the happiest moment of my Life but alas I feel my inability even to offer that consolation that a sweet but feble friend requires. I will attempt to give you some idea of the manner my time has past hear. I arrived late in the afternoon, we were received in the usual manner, some sociable, others reserved. Mamma drank tea and returned home. Some retired for a short time. We chatted and as Yorick somewhere expresses himself in his letters to Eliza (thou was the star that conducted our discourse) for some time, the evening passed in a reserved manner, at ten I retired to my room. Then my friend I more preticularly wished for your company. I was soon lost in sleep and not one idea presented to my imagination till seven in the morning. To day Miss H O and my friend Polly Otis dined here, some other company. Mr. S. Otis and Lady passed the afternoon, our good Cousin O. appears to have obtained as great a share of happiness as I think consistent with the Lot of mortals, may she long continue as pleased as at present she appears to be with her new partner. I must confess I can have no idea that a heart wounded by grief should be healed by aney one event in so short a space of time, perhaps my ideas may be romantick.[1]

Monday afternoon

I had wrote thus far and laid aside my pen with a secret impulce that I should receive a letter from you on monday but did not beleive you would pass and not ask your friend one word, you were in a hurry and are very excuseable. Your Letter[2] gave me the pleasure that I ever feel from hearing from you. I need not add it was great. Your observations are just, but from what cause our attachment increases to a greater degre to those of our friend[s] who have felt the severe hand of affliction I cannot determine. Experience has often convinced me of the truth of the sentiment.—Your anxiety for your parent has been great but what would it have been had you been seperated from the best of parents as is the case of your friend. A wide Atlantick rolls between us and we know not wheather we shall be made happy or miserable by the much wished for inteligence. It is one of the most unhappy situations in Life to be thus seperated from those friends that claim the greatest share of our Love by the ties and bonds of natural affection, and are doubly deserving our hiest esteem by their good conduct th[r]ough this Life so far as they have past. Their future conduct no one can answer for.

I have given you some idea in what manner my time has past hear. I am sometimes gratified by the company of a friend—the gentlemen you mention are as sociable as usual. Mrs. W[arren?] passesses the happy tallent of ever rendering herself pleasing to all. My happiness is not greatly augmented by this visit neither will it be greatly decreased—a proof of the depravity of my taste perhaps you will say. I cannot help it I answer. I veryly beleive I possess too large a share of that same indiference that some persons attribute to me. If I do possess it, it is natureall. This is some consolation I think. Do my Dear put your friend into some way to avoid the appearance of this detested disposition. I have endeavoured all in my power to erase it but find it impossible, perhaps your segasity can point out some remedy. Your benevolence will direct you to give your friend all the assistance you are capable of. I dont know wheather a person who is not possessed of the least degree of it can have aney idea of it.

Adeiu for the present. If I do not see you tomorow I may make some addition to this scroll. It is not necesary you will think ere you have perused half of it. As it is from a friend who sincerely loves you it may perhaps be acceptable.

Yours,

A.A.

RC (MHi:Cranch Papers); endorsed: "AA April 1782." If the "Mrs. W." referred to in the text was, as conjectured, Mercy (Otis) Warren, this letter was written from the Warrens' home at Milton Hill. AA2's punctuation has been minimally corrected for clarity, particularly by the insertion of periods at the end and capitals at the beginning of sentences.

¹ "Miss H O" is not certainly identifiable. Polly (or Mary) Otis later married Benjamin Lincoln Jr. and still later Professor Henry Ware of Harvard (*Warren-Adams Letters*, 2:304; *DAB*, under Ware). Samuel Allyne Otis had in March of this year married Mary (Smith) Gray, AA's cousin; it was a second marriage for both; see AA to Elizabeth (Smith) Shaw, Feb.–March, above.

² Not found.

Abigail Adams 2d to John Quincy Adams

Braintree May 3d. 1782

I am conscious my dear Brother that I have appeared deficient in my duty and affection by neglecting to write you often. I have very little encouragement to continue a correspondance without any return from you. I do not believe you deficient in writing; it is a disagreable circumstance that we receive so small a part of the letters that are written. Mamma has receiv'd letters from Pappa and Mr. Thaxter as late as December and from yourself so late as October from Petersbourg. I was not made happy by one line, have you forgot your Sister. No such an idea shall ever dwell in my mind. We lament the loss of the letters, Gillon had in his possession. You will no doubt hear of his conduct ere this reaches you. Charles after many distresses and dangers has safe landed on his native shore. The anxiety we suffered from an apprehension of his danger was great: it is now fully recompensed by his safe return to those friends that dearly love him. He was ever a favourite you know, and still continues to possess the amiable qualities that in his younger years gained the affection of his friends. You, my Brother are far, very far removed from your friends and connections: it is a painfull reflection to those that have parted with a son and a Brother. It is not the person that goes abroad in quest of any object whether Knowledge, business, or pleasure that is pained by the seperation. Every object they meet imprint[s] new ideas on their minds; new scenes soon engage their attention, still looking forward they have but little time to reflect on their past time, the pleasure they receive is so much more than a balance for the pain that their time passes in almost an uninterrupted course of happiness. On the contrary the friends they leave are still dwelling on the painfull event that deprived them of much happiness; no pleasing scenes present to the mind, the imagination pained with a repetition of past pleasures and present pains seeks a new source in anticipating future events.

You are I hope sensible of the peculiar advantages you are receiving. Very few at any age of life possess so great a share. It is your own fault if you neglect to make a right improvement of the talents that are put into your hands; your reflections in a future day will be brightened if you can look back on your past conduct conscious of not having deviated from the path of your duty. I will not draw a contrary supposition.

Some persons Lives are scarcely clouded by any event unfavourable to their happiness, fortune seems to court their favour and pour liberally her blessings on their wishes. We see another character struggling with events through life: all their intentions appear to be frustrated, and every wish is clouded by a disappointment. To judge from the few years you have passed in Life the former seems descriptive. But do not be deceived by appearances; she may yet have in store for you, trials and troubles unthought of; neither distress yourself with events that may never take place but learn this necessary lesson neither to be too much elated with prosperity nor depressed with adversity. Could I anticipate your soon return it would give me much pleasure. The pleasure we shall receive from a mutual exchange of friendship and sentiments when the happy period shall arrive will I hope be increased greatly by so long a seperation. I know of no opportunity of conveyance soon, but whenever this reaches you, let it remind you of the pleasure you ever give your Sister by answering her letters. May you my Brother return and answer the expectations of your Friends is the sincere wish of your affectionate friend and sister.

Early Tr (Adams Papers), in JQA's hand.

John Thaxter to John Adams

Sir   Amsterdam 4th. May 1782

I have sent to Mr. Hodshon[1] since your Departure to send the Packer, but he cannot come 'till Monday, which I suspected as this is a busy day all over the World. As soon as he comes on Monday, I will set him to work and give all the Assistance that depends on me. There is between twenty and thirty Tons of Turf, and a few Bushels of Coal, which Stephens seems very desirous of having. He does not ask it as a Gift, but imagine it would not be unacceptable.[2] This lays with You, and it shall be sent forward if You choose or left to be sold. —There will be some empty Bottles, which the Wineseller had better take, paying the ordinary Price. However as You please. The Baskets will take them all I believe.

I have seen Mr. Barclay, and he is much better—desires his best Respects and wishes You better Health.

Best Compliments to Mr. Dumas and Family.

With an invariable Respect & Attachment I have the honor to be, Sir, your most obedient & most humble Servant,   J Thaxter

RC (Adams Papers).

[1] John Hodshon, of Hodshon & Zoon, was an Amsterdam merchant with whom JA sometimes did business and had occasional correspondence. See also note 2.

[2] Joseph Stephens (sometimes Stevens), JA's servant since JA had first come to Europe, was making plans to marry and set up a shop in Amsterdam selling silks, linens, &c., especially to American sailors and other visitors from America. He expected to obtain capital from Hodshon to buy his goods, but a little later was trying to obtain credit and/or employment from other firms. By the end of June, according to Thax-

ter, Stephens and "his Family" were ill and in considerable distress. See Stephens to JA, 6 Feb., 23 May (Adams Papers); JA to Willink & van Staphorst and to Ingraham & Bromfield, 13 June (LbC's, Adams Papers); Thaxter to JA, 29 June (Adams Papers). In his recollections many years later, JA wrote that Stephens married "a very pretty English girl" and not too long afterward set sail for America, where the ship apparently never arrived (to the Editor of the *Boston Patriot*, 14 Feb. 1812, published 29 April 1812). What happened to his wife and their shop does not appear.

John Thaxter to John Adams

Sir   Amsterdam 6th. May 1782

We have made a serious Beginning this morning, and have already completed the packing of the Books, and shall finish packing to night I hope the Decanters, Wine Glasses, and China. The looking Glasses will require Time and Care, as well as the great Cabinet. We shall be ready to load Thursday Morning, perhaps Wednesday Afternoon, not later however than Thursday. I find the Eye can pack much faster than the Hands. We shall make all possible Expedition, and if the Boat is ready, which is already applied for, She may be loaded in a short time.[1]

If You can find a Leisure day this Week, would it not be most advisable to return to settle the Accounts? Will there not be much Trouble and Inconvenience in delaying it, 'till after all the Things are removed? People might be apt to grumble, and would not know where to go for their Money, and You would be tormented hereafter with little and great Accounts for a long time. I only mention this Matter as it strikes me.

The Arrival of Mr. Dumas last Evening at 10. o Clock brought my Heart to a Spot where it often was when Dr. Osterdyck was so well acquainted with You: however the old Gentleman soon quieted the Alarm.

I hope the Treaty goes on well, as my Penchant for returning home increases daily perhaps much faster than the Business goes forward.

I have the Honor to be, with the greatest Respect, Sir, &c.,

J Thaxter

RC (Adams Papers).

[1] For the goods moved from the Keizersgracht house to the newly acquired American legation at The Hague, see below, JA to AA, 14 May, note 1.

John Adams to John Quincy Adams

Hotel des Etats Unis,
My dear Son   a la Haye May 13. 1782

I have the Pleasure to inform you, that Yesterday I removed into this House, and am now employed in setting it in order. You will see by the Gazettes, that I have been received in Character, that I have laid before the States a Plan of a Treaty, which they have now under Consideration, and I suppose will be soon finished.

The Bearer of this, Coll. Vallentin, will deliver it. Perhaps he may be serviceable to you. I am however, very uneasy on your Account. I want you with me. Mr. Thaxter will probably leave me soon, and I shall be alone. I want you to pursue your studies too at Leyden. Upon the whole, I wish you would embark in a Neutral Vessell and come to me. If there should be a Treaty, to send, Mr. Thaxter perhaps will carry it.

Your Studies I doubt not, you pursue, because I know you to be a studious Youth: but above all preserve a sacred Regard to your own Honour and Reputation. Your Morals are worth all the Sciences. Your Conscience is the Minister Plenipotentiary of God almighty in your Breast. See to it, that this Minister never negotiates in vain. Attend to him, in Opposition to all the Courts in the World. So charges, your affectionate Father,   J. Adams

RC (Adams Papers). Early Tr (Adams Papers), in JQA's hand.

John Adams to Abigail Adams

My dearest Friend   The Hague May 14 1782

On the Twelfth, I removed into this House which I have purchased for the United States of America. But, it will be my Residence but a little while.[1]

I must go to you or you must come to me. I cannot live, in this horrid Solitude, which it is to me, amidst Courts, Camps and Crowds. If you were to come here, such is the Unsteadiness of the Foundation that very probably We should have to return home again in a Month or six Weeks and the Atlantick is not so easily passed as Pens hill. I envy you, your Nabby, Charly and Tommy, and Mr. Dana his Johnny who are very well. A Child was never more weary of a Whistle, than I am of Embassies. The Embassy here however has done great Things. It has not merely tempted a natural Rival, and an imbittered, inveterate, hereditary Ennemy, to assist a little against G[reat] B[ritain] but it has torn from her Bosom, a constant faithfull Friend and Ally of an hundred Years duration.

It has not only prevailed with a Minister or an absolute Court to fall in with the national Prejudice: but without Money, without Friends, and in Opposition to mean Intrigue it has carried its Cause, by the still small Voice of Reason, and Perswasion, tryumphantly against the uninterrupted Opposition of Family Connections, Court Influence, and Aristocratical Despotism.

It is not a Temple forming a Triple Alliance, with a Nation whose Ruling Family was animated as well as the whole Nation, at that time, with even more Zeal than De Witt in the same Cause.

But you will hear all this represented as a Thing of Course, and of little Consequence—easily done and not worth much.—Very well! Thank God it is done, and that is what I wanted.

Jealousy is as cruel as the Grave, and Envy as spightfull as Hell— and neither have any regard to Veracity or Honour.

RC (Adams Papers).

[1] This proved a true prediction. Although JA remained in Europe for six more years, his only steady occupancy of the American legation at The Hague was from mid-May through mid-October 1782. He made some use of it during his later returns to the Netherlands in 1784, 1787, and 1788 to obtain further loans from Dutch bankers to the United States, but much of his business on those occasions was in Amsterdam rather than The Hague.

There is an account extant of the furnishings of the Hôtel des Etats Unis at The Hague, as JA liked to call it in the current diplomatic style, in a document dated and filed in the Adams Papers under 14 May 1782. The first six pages of this fourteen-page paper have the descriptive heading "A true copy of the Inventory made by Mr. John Thaxter," the original of which was presumably compiled when Thaxter supervised the moving of the goods from JA's house in Amsterdam (see Thaxter to JA, 6 May, above). The listing bears notations "received in good order," "Wanting," "broken," &c., apparently in the hand of F. Lotter, who signed it at the end and probably made the copy and comments on 16 Oct. 1782, another date that appears on the document and that was in fact the day before JA and party left The Hague for the peace negotiations at Paris.

The last eight pages of this document are another inventory of the furnishings in The Hague legation, compiled by Mme. Marie Dumas and dated 22 June 1784, shortly before JA left the Netherlands for London and reunion with his family there that summer. This too is attested by F. Lotter.

John Adams to Abigail Adams

Hotel des Etats Unis a la Haye

My dearest Friend   June 16. 1782

I find that the Air of the Hague, and the Return of warm Weather, tho later than was ever known, is of great Service to my Health. I mount on Horseback every Morning, and riding is of Use to me.

I have not escaped the "Influenza," as they call it, which began in Russia and has been epidemical, in all Europe. Mr. Thaxter too has at last submitted to this all subduing Climate and had a Fever, such as Charles had, but is growing well.

You can scarcely imagine a more beautifull Place than the Hague. Yet no Place has any Charms for me but the Blue Hills. My Heart will have in it forever, an acking Void, in any other Place. If you and your Daughter were here! But I must turn my Thoughts from such Objects, which always too tenderly affect me, for my repose or Peace of Mind. I am so wedged in with the Publick Affairs that it is impossible to get away at present. I would transmit a Resignation of all my Employments but this would occasion much Puzzle and be attended with disagreable Consequences. If I thought it probable I should stay in Europe two or three Years, I would certainly request you to come here, but this is opening a scæne of Risque and Trouble for you that I shudder at.—But all is uncertain. I am not properly informed of what passes in Congress, and I know not their Designs. If they would send out another in my Room it would be the most happy News to me, that ever I heard.

The American Cause has obtained a Tryumph in this Country more signal, than[1] it ever obtained before in Europe. It was attended with Circumstances, more glorious than could have been foreseen. A Temple, a D'Avaux, a D'Estrates, had more masterly Pens to celebrate their own Negotiations, and Hearts more at Ease, to do it with Care.[2] Your Friend will never have Leisure, he will never have the Patience to describe the Dangers, the Mortifications, the Distresses he has undergone in Accomplishing this great Work. It is better that some of the Opposition and Intrigues he has had to encounter should be buried in Oblivion.

After all, it will be represented in America as a Thing of Course and of no Consequence. Be it so. It is done—and[3] it is worth as much as it is.

My dear Nabby and Tommy how do ye? Charles you young Rogue! You had more Wit than all of Us. You have returned to a happy Spot. Study earnestly, go to Colledge and be an Ornament to your Country. Education is better at Cambridge, than in Europe. Besides every Child ought to be educated in his own Country. I regret extreamly that his elder Brother is not to have his Education at home. He is well [and] so is his Patron.

Adieu, Adieu, Adieu.

RC (Adams Papers).

[1] MS: "that."
[2] Sir William Temple (mentioned with some frequency earlier in the *Adams Family Correspondence*), Jean Antoine de Mesme, Comte d'Avaux, and Godefroi, Comte d'Estrades, all conducted diplomatic negotiations in the Netherlands, and each wrote accounts of them. For editions of their published works owned by JA and now in the Boston Public Library, see *Catalogue of JA's Library*, p. 242, 17, 86.
[3] MS: "at."

Abigail Adams to John Adams,
with a List of Articles wanted from Holland

My dearest Friend   June 17. 1782

There is not any thing in this Life, now my Dear Friend is seperated from me, that can communicate equal delight and pleasure to that which I feel upon the Sight of Letters written in the well known Hand of my Friend. My Heart Leaps forward to meet them, whilst the trembling Hand uncloses the Seals, and my eager Eyes devour the contents; tho unwilling to reach the close.

Capt. Deshon had the good fortune to arrive safe and brought me Letters only six weeks old;[1] these were a cordial to my Spirits; since your first residence in Holland, I have not experienced the happiness of hearing from you in so short a space of time.

The prospect which was opening before you, and the Success with which I hope before this time your negotiations have been Blessed, has communicated a pleasure to my mind, which no one can feel in an equal degree with her, whose happiness is so nearly connected with all you Hope, and all you wish.

What tho old ocean rolls between these vehicles of transitory duration, the immortal Spirit can unite with its kindred mind, and participate in its pains and pleasures.

My dear Friend will feel the truth of what I have now asserted, and mingle the sorrowing tear with Portia, and with a distressed family over the almost departing Spirit of our Dear Brother Cranch.

I wrote you some time ago an account of the severe fit of Sickness with which he was visited, during the winter, but it then pleased Heaven to restore him to some degree of Health.[2] His eager desire to be upon his duty in the publick Service, overpowerd the advice of his Friends: and he went to Town, before he had sufficiently recoverd his Health, where he was: only a few days, before he was seized with a pain in his Breast and Side, which terminated in a fever upon his Lungs and immediately threatned his Life. He struggled through the fever, but is now apprehended by his phisicians and Friends to be in a Hectick, accompanied with dropsical Symptoms. He however, as is common in such cases, flatters himself that he shall get well, tho tis 7 weeks since he was taken, and he can scarcly walk his room. He rides out, but cannot bear food equal to an Infant, whilst a cough and swelling of his Stomack, bowels and Legs indicate a speedy dissolution. For him we need not heave an anxious Sigh—but his family

—his Friends.—You who know his worth can feel their, and your own loss. I dare not flatter myself—my Hopes and fears are at varience. The anxious distress of an afflicted Sister Bears a load of Sorrow to my Heart, whilst I supplicate Heaven that I may not be called to experience a like overwhelming calamity. "O! Spair him, Spair him, Gracious power: O! Give him to my latest Hour" is the constant prayer of Portia.

I reassume my pen, and would tell you that I last evening received from Philadelphia a Letter written May 29, 1781 written Immediately after you took a House in Amsterdam;[3] I suppose it to be one of those which was put on Board Gillion—as he has at last arrived at Philadelphia, having been commodore at the taking of Providence by the Spainards.[4] Our poor Charles would have had a fine time of it, if he had continued on Board. I wrote you by the Fire Brand, that I had drawn a Bill upon you for C—s passage,[5] but finally finding I could not do it without a discount of ten per cent, and failing in an object which I then had in view, making a purchase in Virmont, on account of the dissagreable turn which affairs took at that time, relative to that state, when it was in the fairest way of being setled, I was advised not to purchase for the present, upon which I paid the passage. I shall not pretend unless upon a pressing necessity, which I do not at present see, to draw any Bills. The Remittances which you have from time to time made me, and which I have been very fortunate in receiving, assist me much better than Bills upon which I must pay a discount. I shall inclose a List of Articles upon which the best profit arrises, and which have the quickest sale. I have a Friend or two, into whose Hands I put what I do not want for my own family, who dispose of them for me. Accept my thanks for those received by Deshon. They came in good order.

Mr. L—l not long since favoured me with the sight of two Letters from you dated in February.[6] With regard to the cypher of which you complain, I have always been fortunate enough to succeed with it.[7] Take the two Letters for which the figure stands and place one under the other through the whole Sentance, and then try the upper Line with the under, or the under with the upper, always remembering, if one letter answers, that directly above or below must be omitted, and sometimes several must be skiped over. The contents of those Letters gave me a clearer Idea of the difficulties you have had to encounter, than I before had conceived of. But it must be a pleasing reflection to you that your Labours are at last like to be crowned with

Success. I wish there was as fair a prospect of an Honorable peace. I hope the late Naval disaster of our Allies will not have a dissagreable Effect upon the united provinces.[8]

The english will puff and vaunt their Dear Bought victory, without once recollecting that pride commeth before Humility and a haughty Spirit before a fall. The Cabinet counsels of Britain are held in detestation here, and to be insulted by the New Ministry is considerd in a more contemptable Light, than the same offers would have been from the old. America cannot but consider the virtues as all fled from that devoted Island. The different States are instructing their delegates to consider every offer as an insult from Britain (which should give a new edge to their Swords) if Independance is not made the Basis. Ardently as I long for the return of my dearest Friend, I cannot feel the least inclination to a peace but upon the most liberal foundation. Patriotism in the female Sex is the most disinterested of all virtues. Excluded from honours and from offices, we cannot attach ourselves to the State or Goverment from having held a place of Eminence. Even in the freeest countrys our property is subject to the controul and disposal of our partners, to whom the Laws have given a soverign Authority. Deprived of a voice in Legislation, obliged to submit to those Laws which are imposed upon us, is it not sufficient to make us indifferent to the publick Welfare? Yet all History and every age exhibit Instances of patriotick virtue in the female Sex; which considering our situation equals the most Heroick of yours. "A late writer observes that as Citizens we are calld upon to exhibit our fortitude, for when you offer your Blood to the State, it is ours. In giving it our Sons and Husbands we give more than ourselves. You can only die on the field of Battle, but we have the misfortune to survive those whom we Love most."

I will take praise to myself. I feel that it is my due, for having sacrificed so large a portion of my peace and happiness to promote the welfare of my country which I hope for many years to come will reap the benifit, tho it is more than probable unmindfull of the hand that blessed them.

Your Friends complain that you do not write to them. I say all I can in excuse, but I wish you to notice them all, and in a particular manner to continue your affectionate Regard and attachment to

Portia

Black and white Gauzes
and Gauze hankerchiefs (the best articles imported)
tapes Quality bindings Shoe binding

Low priced linen, Black caliminco red tammies
fine threads low priced calicos Ribbons [9]

RC (Adams Papers); addressed: "To His Excellency John Adams Esqr
Amsterdam or the Hague"; endorsed: "Portia. June 17. 1782."

[1] These must have been JA's letters of
22, 29 March, above, but apparently not
his brief but important letter of 1 April,
also above. See AA to JA, 17 July, below: "Your last Letters were dated in
March."

[2] See above, AA to JA, 17–25 March.

[3] No letter of this date from JA to
AA has been found. He had, however,
reported his taking up his new residence
in Amsterdam in a letter to her of 16
May 1781, above.

[4] For the extraordinary adventures of
Gillon and the *South Carolina* after CA
and his party had left that vessel at La
Coruña, see D. E. Huger Smith, "Commodore Alexander Gillon and the Frigate
South Carolina," *So. Car. Hist. & Geneal. Mag.*, 9 (1908):214 ff. Among
other things, Gillon had joined a Spanish naval force at Havana and in May
participated in the taking of New Prov-

idence, which meant the (temporary)
transfer of the Bahamas from English
to Spanish rule.

[5] AA to JA, 25 April, above.

[6] JA to Robert R. Livingston, 21, 27
Feb. (PCC, No. 84, IV; Wharton, ed.,
Dipl. Corr. Amer. Rev., 5:192–199,
206–207). These had been transmitted
by Lovell in a letter to AA of 31 May (in
Adams Papers but omitted here). In
that of 21 Feb., JA had complained that
he could "make nothing of" the coded
passages in Livingston's letters.

[7] But only with the help of Richard
Cranch; see Appendix to this volume.

[8] Rodney's defeat and capture of de
Grasse at the battle of the Saints Passage, 9–12 April.

[9] Compare the nearly duplicate lists
at the end of AA's letters to JA of 25
April, above, and 17–18 July, below.

Abigail Adams to John Thaxter

My dear Sir   June 17, 1782

I had no intention that the Fire Brand should sail without my replying to your repeated kind favours; I have been happy in receiving
several Letters from You; the intrinsick value of which lead me most
pathetically to mourn the loss of those which have failed.

The time which I meant to have appropriated in writing to you,
was most melancholy employed in attending the sick and I feared
dying Bed of our dear and worthy Friend Mr. Cranch who was seized
with a repeated Sickness, before he had recoverd his Strength from
a former illness—by which means the vessel sailed without a line to
testify the sense I had of your goodness. It will greatly aflict you I
know to hear, that this worthy Friend of ours, is in so great a decline
as to Baffel the Art of the physicians, and to have the most allarming
Symptoms of a speedy dissolution. Your sympathetick Heart will enter
into the Distresses of a family for whom you have ever entertaind
an affectionate Regard. They are great indeed. Heaven support them
through them all.

"When Heaven would kindly set us free
And Earths enchantments end
It takes the most Effectual way
And robs us of our Friends."

I hope my dear Sir that your situation is more agreable by this time, and that your residence is at the Hague rather than in Amsterdam. But you sigh for America. You had better become a *Captive* in America, than an American Captive in any of the British dominions. A British prison has many horrors, their tender mercies are cruelties. The advantages to be derived by a return, in the present State of things will hardly compensate the risk. The young Gentlemen of the present day scarcly know what to do with themselves. Trade is so hazardous having no protection, and Money so scarce that there is little encouragement in that Branch. Our Staple, our fishery, we possess not, and we have no other. Divinity, you know what encouragement that meets with, and have no appetite to become a preacher. Phisick, that swarms—we have been Blessed with a large portion of Health throughout the State, and have had but small employ for the faculty. Law, upon that you fix your Eye. Some get Bread, some have made fortunes, but that time is passed away with the destruction of our Navy. But methinks I hear you say, I am spending the best of my days, I am advanceing towards 30, I could wish to settle down in my own Country in some reputable Buisness, this I shall have to do when ever I return. How can I connect myself untill this is done, and a Batchelor I do not wish to live. All the dear Girls for whom I have a Friendship will get married—even my fair American does not know how highly I value her.—Softly Sir, and I will tell you for your consolation, not one of all the number for whom you have particularly expressd a regard, have the least present prospect of being united— even your Sally is far distant from the Alter, and the triumvirate of Betsys are yet single, the solitary Hannah has lost her Grandmamma and Aunt, her cousin is gone to Barbados, and she still wears the appearence of a young Nun. The widowed Betsy is a widow still.

Matrimony is not in vogue here. We have Ladies, but not a gentleman in the whole Town, and the young Gentlemen of the present day, are not intirely to the taste of those Ladies who value a virtuous Character. Licentiousness and freedom of Manners are predominate. Rosseau observes, that the manner of thinking among Men in a great measure depends upon the taste of the Ladies. If this is true, the manners of the present day are no complement upon the fair Sex. The

Manners of the two Sexes, I believe keep pace with each other; and in proportion as the Men grow regardless of character, the women neglect the Duties of their Sex. Of how much importance then are Manners to a young [Esquire?]. Tis Luxery my dear Sir which ruins and depraves our Manners. We are ready imitators of the Nations with which we are connected, and it is much to be feared if the days of American simplicity and virtue are not already passed.

Fordyce, to whom our Sex are much indebted for the justice he has done them, observes that the company of virtuous and well bred women is the best School for Learning the most proper demeanor, the easiest turn of thought and expression and right habits of the best kind, that the most honorable the most Moral the most conscientious Men, are in general those who have the greatest regard for women of reputation and talents.[1]

I have nothing new to write you of the political kind, but what will be old e'er it reaches you.

We mourn the naval defeat of our Allies, and dispise the offers of the British Cabinet. Infamy and disgrace be their portion and the inheritance of their childrens children.—I fear the fate of this Letter. Scarcly any thing can pass we are so infested with British cruizers.

Should it find its way to you receive it with the affectionate Regard and Sisterly Love of   Portia

RC (MB): addressed: "To John Thaxter Esqr Amsterdam or the Hague"; endorsed: "Mrs. Adams 17. June 1782. Recd. in August & Answered."

[1] AA earlier cited with commendation James Fordyce's *Sermons to Young Women* (vol. 1:61–62, above), of which a copy of the 4th edn., 2 vols., London, 1767, is in MQA. Fordyce also published *The Character and Conduct of the Female Sex*, London, 1776.

John Adams to Richard Cranch

[The Hague, 17 June 1782]

"I can tell you no secrets about Peace—a Mr. Forth, a Mr. Aswald [Oswald] and a Mr. Greenville[1] have been at Paris, to sound the Dispositions, but I cannot learn that they have sufficient Powers, or that they have made any serious Propositions. The work of Peace is very difficult to accomplish. The pretentions of so many Nations, are to be adjusted, that my Hopes are faint. It serves the Stocks to keep up the Talk, but I fear the English Nation is not yet sufficiently humbled, to satisfy Spain, Holland, France, the armed Neutrality and America.

"Pray how is the News received of the new Alliance with the Dutch? —Is it represented as of no Importance? At least it will be allow'd of importance to prevent this Nation from taking Part against us. Their Fleet would have been much more powerfull against us than it is for us. As it is, it makes a Diversion in our favour.

"We shall however feel the Benefit of this new Connection in every part of the World. I hope the World will one Day see, when my Head shall be in the Dust, the Measures that have been taken to accomplish it, and the Intrigues from England, Russia, Denmark &c. &c. &c. to prevent it—I should be very sorry to add—but "Suum cuique Decus Posteritas rependit." [2]

"It is a Protestant, a Republican and a commercial Nation. The Hand of Providence was never more visible, than in bringing this Business to a Conclusion. A number of Circumstances have conspired, in a very remarkable manner. We shall see the Consequences of it, which will not soon come to an End.—Men and Nations have Reason to seek Assistance sometimes against the extravagant Pretensions of Friends, as well as against the Malice of Enemies. While we stood acknowledged only by one Power, a Branch of the House of Bourbon and a Catholick, we stood exposed to the Jealousy of the Enemies of that House and that Faith. This Passion will be at least diminished by this Alliance. It is our Policy to seek and obtain the Friendship of all the Powers of Europe if possible; by which means we may be neutral. We may even keep England in Awe and at Peace with us by this means but by no other. I confess it is the Object I have had most at Heart; and, it being accomplished, I wish most ardently to come home.

"I have been desired to write a Word concerning Mr. Amory. He has lived long at Brussells and wishes to return; I have never seen him, but I believe if any one has a Claim, it is he. You know his amiable Character, and that he was never properly a Tory. He was rather a moderate Whig. I cannot advise in this matter, but I really wish he could be admitted. He has not done any thing I believe against us." [3]

Early Tr (MHi:Smith-Carter Papers); in the hand of Richard Cranch and captioned by him: "Extract of a Letter dated at the Hague June 17th 1782." Obviously prepared by Cranch for newspaper publication, but no printing has been found. Cf. below, JA to Cranch, 2 July, esp. the descriptive note there.

[1] Nathaniel Parker Forth, Richard Oswald, and Thomas Grenville. For their various quasi-official and official roles in opening peace negotiations, see Morris, *Peacemakers, passim.*

[2] Posterity allows every man his true value. Tacitus, *Annales,* IV, 35.

[3] John Amory (1728–1803), mem-

ber of a well-known mercantile family in Boston, went to England in 1774, ostensibly on business, but his wife dying and he lingering there, he was proscribed as a loyalist refugee. During the war, however, he moved to Brussels, returned to America at the close of it, after some difficulties was restored to citizenship in Massachusetts, and died a wealthy man. See Gertrude E. Meredith, *The Descendants of Hugh Amory*, London, 1901; Sabine, *Loyalists*, 1:162–163.

John Thaxter to Abigail Adams

Madam   Amsterdam 23d. June 1782

Since my last an important Revolution has taken place here respecting our Country. A formal Acknowledgment of our Sovereignty and Independence in the Admission and Reception of your dearest Friend is what I allude to. But You will have heard of the Event long before this reaches You, with many of its Circumstances. At present I am too feeble to enter into a detail of Matters, being upon my Recovery from the vile Fever and Ague. Ask your dear Charles if he remembers the tertian Fever at Leyden? I had the same at the Hague, (where We now live), with a Touch of the Rheumatism. However it went off with the Fever. I was never so sick and weak, and could any thing have been necessary to add to my disgust to this Country, this last Bout would have effectually done it. I hope to quit it in six or eight Weeks and take my Passage for Boston or Philadelphia. I pray You, Madam, not to mention this, as it may be longer before I embark, and my Friends might be uneasy if I did not arrive according to their Calculations. I have not hinted any thing of it to my Father in my Letter to him. I hope in a few days to be completely established in my Health. My Friends will excuse my not writing to them—indeed I have not strength enough as yet. Remember me particularly to your Family and to all Friends.

I have the Honor to be, with an invariable Respect, Madam, your most obed. Servt.,   J Thaxter Junr.

RC (Adams Papers).

John Boylston to John Adams

Dear Sir   London June 28th 1782

I am now most happy to felicitate you and our Parent Country on the fortunate Event which has attended your unwearied efforts for obtaining the Dutch accession to the American Independency and that you are accepted by them as fully empowered for the final accomplishment of this glorious Æra.

Indeed when I reflect on the injustice and savage cruelty of *the late Administration* I much wonder that all Europe have not united in chastising such vindictive measures. However that Being to whom Vengeance belongs appears to have been greatly displeas'd by involving them in such a labyrinth of difficulties from which no human Agency can extricate them; Yet deeply penetrated as I am with a sense of the injuries done my Native Land I most ardently wish for a happy peace, but nothing short of an intire independency.—Observing in the publick Papers that you are solliciting a Loan for A[me]rica I would willingly contribute my Mite thereto provided that I might be secure of Receiving my interest in Europe as at my Period of 72 it is rather too late to cross again the Atlantick, although I might the British Channel for the pleasure of seeing and conferring with you on some personal affairs which cannot be as well discuss'd by letter.

I was much mortify'd in not receiving by my most worthy Friend the Honble G. W. Fairfax one Line in answer to what [I] wrote you sometime since relating the American Prisoners,[1] but with the greatest pleasure now find my wishes answer'd in their embarkation for their native homes.—In some of the late London Papers I find myself highly dishonour'd in being class'd by some malevolent Knave among a *List of Amer[ican] refugees* said to be printed at Boston but which has fail'd of giving me the least disquiet conscious that it is well known there, that I have ever been constantly and invariably attach'd to the cause and interest of my native Country for which have incurr'd the Odium of great Numbers here and expended near One hundred Guineas for the releif of our distress'd Captives.

The favour of a Line address'd for me at Messrs. Maitlands Esqr. Colman Street London will much oblige me. I shall remain here about fourteen days before my return to Bath.

That all happiness may attend you and Heaven prove propitious to your endeavours for procuring a happy and lasting peace is the sincere and ardent wish of, Dr. Sr. Yr. Most Obt. Servt,   John Boylston

P. For safe conveyance I have prevail'd with my good friend Mr. Brigden[2] to inclose you this in his Pacquet, and to whose care (if agreable) You may return a Line in answer.

RC (Adams Papers).

[1] See above, Boylston to JA, 31 Aug. 1781, and references there. George William Fairfax, formerly of Virginia but currently of Bath in England, had evidently been in the Netherlands recently; see JA's reply to Boylston, 5 July below. For a sketch of Fairfax, see Washington, *Writings*, ed. Fitzpatrick, 1:5, and numerous letters and references following.

[2] Thus in MS, but very likely Edward Bridgen is meant. Bridgen was a London

artisan and sometime alderman who seems to have kept up a clandestine correspondence with Americans and American sympathizers on the Continent throughout the war. See JA, *Diary and Autobiography*, index; correspondence between JA and Bridgen in Adams Papers; *Cal. Franklin Papers in A.P.S.*

Abigail Adams 2d to Elizabeth Cranch

My Dear Eliza   Wedensday june [1782]

I have not heard a word from B—[1] since Wednesday last. I want much to know how you all do. I wrote you last saturday. Mrs. Quincy took my letter yesterday.[2] Hope you have received it. You will not complain of my not writing you I bleive, my letters can give you little pleasure only as they are dictated by a heart that rearly[3] loves you. My affection for you is an inducement for my writing you at this time more particularly. I have my friend been in company with many persons since I have been in town who *were formerly* acquainted with the gentleman that lately has resided in your family. Every one expresses great surprise at the event, these persons say [that][4] he is practicing upon Chesterfeilds plan, that [he] is the essence and quintessence of artfulness and fear he will in some way or other ingratiate himself into the good opinion of your self. You are not acquainted with his character they say. I have told them I have not a fear about the matter, that I think you are too well gaurded against art in aney shape and that you would despise the attempt, and detest the action. But my friend I dont know but a word by way of caution is nesesary. Perhaps you will laugh at me as I have at others who have made the supposition but I know your heart is at present uncommonly softened by affliction and should he learn your disposition and find a way to sooth your sorrows I will not answer for you, that you will not at least esteem him. His character and his conduct are not deserving the least degree of your friendship and I dare say you will discover it soon if you have not at present. I was told the other day that I could not see him and not become acquainted with him. I am determined to avoid the least degree of acquaintance if anything short of affrontery will answer his whole study, his dissimulation; our sex cannot be too carefull of the characters of the acquaintance we form.[5]

I passed the day yesterday with Mrs. Mason. She was pleasing and he as agreable as ever. His pappas family dined with us, Mr. *Ben* Mason and a sister of his.[6] He was very particular in his enquireyes about Miss Cranch, whether she was married or like to be. I liked him better than ever I asure you. Indeed my Dear I answer many about [you.] "She is a lovely Girl, I was much pleased with her,"[7] and the like questions from persons whose esteem is valluable. And those I have to answer you may suppose I ever join them in their opinion. Indeed I do. It would be at the expence of my sincerety was I to join otherwise. But I should not have said aney thing about these things as it is I beleive more agreable to persons to imajine these civil things said of them then to heare them, dont you think so. A lively imagination can embellish to their own satisfaction.—But your heart is too much affected to receive such a letter from aney one as this. I have wished much to hear from your pappa in the week past but the fates have denied me. I will hope he is better, may I not be disappointed. Adeiu till I hear of an opportunity of conveiyance *to you.*

Wedensday evevening. I have this moment perused your postscript.[8] It rearly gave me pleasure as I have not heard one word from you this week. The time has seemed long indeed. I pitty you my Dear. Your benevolence was hurt by being the messenger of an event that gave pain to a friend. Do let me hear from you and answer both of my letters. I intend to write Miss Betsy. My Love ever attends her and every one dese[rving?] it. Beleive me your friend.

Thursday mor[ning] [9]

[*Written lengthwise in margin of first page:*] Have you wrote to Mr. Thaxter if you have not there is a vessel going for Amsterdam soon so I was told.

RC (MHi:Cranch Papers); addressed: "Miss Eliza Cranch   Braintree"; endorsed: "June—82 AA." Punctuation has been minimally corrected for clarity, but some passages remain a little ambiguous.

[1] Braintree must be meant. From AA2's allusions below, her own letter was unquestionably written from Boston; see note 6.

[2] None of the letters here referred to has been found, and Mrs. Quincy is not further identifiable among the many bearing that name.

[3] Thus in MS, doubtless for "really."

[4] Here and below, MS is torn.

[5] This extraordinary passage, veiled though it is and without a name mentioned, introduces a figure who was to play an important and dramatic role—though in the eyes of the Adamses a discreditable one—in the domestic history of the Adamses over the next several years. "[T]he gentleman that lately has resided in your family" and is said by AA2 to be "practicing upon Chesterfeilds plan" of artful "dissimulation" among the young ladies of Braintree and Boston, can only be Royall Tyler, who, according to AA's letter to JA, 23 Dec. 1782 (Adams Papers), had been lodging for the last nine months at the Cranches' home in Braintree.

Royall Tyler (1757–1826), author of *The Contrast* (1787), the first American comedy produced on an American stage, became a well-known figure in American letters and later the chief justice of Vermont. See *DAB* and G. Thomas Tanselle, *Royall Tyler*, Cambridge, 1967, which is the first book-length biography and which treats in detail the checkered romance between AA2 and Tyler. A summary treatment of that suppressed chapter in Adams family history, based largely on unpublished material in the Adams Papers, was furnished a year earlier by the Adams editors in the introduction to *The Earliest Diary of John Adams*, the MS of which was discovered in 1965 in the Royall Tyler Collection, long closed to researchers, in the Vermont Historical Society; see JA, *Earliest Diary*, p. 1–4, 16–32.

Many letters to be included in the next volume of the *Adams Family Correspondence* develop this story and exhibit most of the major and some of the minor members of the Adams-Cranch circle in characteristic roles. Tyler's courtship of AA2 had a definite part in the Adams ladies' subsequent voyage to Europe. What is most remarkable in light of AA2's impressions of Tyler as given in the present letter is that six months or so later AA was warmly pressing Tyler's suit upon a daughter who overcame her own doubts very reluctantly.

[6] Jonathan Mason Jr. of Boston, on whom see a sketch above, vol. 1:280, and another in JA, *Legal Papers*, 1:civ. He had studied law and lived in JA's household in 1775–1776 and became a correspondent and admiring friend of both JA and AA. In 1779 he had married Susan Powell. His father, Jonathan Mason Sr., was a prominent Boston merchant, married to Miriam Clark; see *DAB* under Jonathan Jr. They had three daughters and also a younger son, Benjamin (Harvard 1779), who practiced medicine and became an honorary M.D. in 1800 (*Harvard Quinquennial Cat.*).

[7] Initial and terminal quotation marks editorially supplied.

[8] Not found.

[9] Thus in MS, perhaps indicating that the letter was completed and sent off on the day after it was mainly written (Wednesday).

John Adams to Abigail Adams

My dearest Friend   The Hague July 1. 1782

Your charming Letters of April 10 and 22d[1] were brought me, Yesterday. That of 22d is upon Business. Mr. Hill is paid I hope. I will honour your Bill if you draw. But be cautious—dont trust Money to any Body. You will never have any to lose or to spare. Your Children will want more than you and I shall have for them.

The Letter of the 10 I read over and over without End—and ardently long to be at the blue Hills, there to pass the Remainder of my feeble days. You would be surprised to see your Friend—he is much altered. He is half a Century older and feebler than ever you knew him. The Horse that he mounts every day is of service to his Health and the Air of the Hague is much better than that of Amsterdam, and besides he begins to be a Courtier, and Sups and Visits at Court among Princesses and Princes, Lords and Ladies of various Nations. I assure you it is much wholesomer to be a complaisant, good humoured, contented Courtier, than a Grumbletonian Patriot,[2] always whining and snarling.

However I believe my Courtierism will never go any great Lengths. I must be an independent Man, and how to reconcile this to the Character of Courtier is the Question.

A Line from Unkle Smith of 6. of May[3] makes me tremble for my Friend and Brother Cranch! I must hope he is recoverd.

I can tell you no News about Peace. There will be no Seperate Peaces made, not even by Holland—and I cannot think that the present English Ministry are firm enough in their Seats to make a general Peace, as yet.

When shall I go home? If a Peace should be made, you would soon see me.—I have had strong Conflicts within, about resigning all my Employments, as soon as I can send home a Treaty. But I know not what is duty as our Saints say. It is not that my Pride or my Vanity is piqued by the Revocation of my envied Commission. But in such Cases, a Man knows not what Construction to put. Whether it is not intended to make him resign. Heaven knows I never solicited to come to Europe. Heaven knows too what Motive I can have, to banish my self from a Country, which has given me, unequivocal Marks of its[4] Affection, Confidence and Esteem, to encounter every Hardship and every danger by Sea and by Land, to ruin my Health, and to suffer every Humiliation and Mortification that human Nature can endure.

What affects me most is the Tryumph given to Wrong against Right, to Vice against Virtue, to Folly vs. Wisdom, to Servility against Independance, to base and vile Intrigue against inflexible Honour and Integrity. This is saying a great deal, but it is saying little more than Congress have said upon their Records, in approving that very Conduct for which I was sacrificed.—I am sometimes afraid that it is betraying the Cause of Independence and Integrity or at least the Dignity, which they ought to maintain, to continue in the service. But on the other Hand I have thought, whether it was not more dangerously betraying this Dignity, to give its Ennemies, perhaps the compleat Tryumph which they wished for and sought but could not obtain.

You will see, the American Cause has had a signal Tryumph in this Country. If this had been the only Action of my Life, it would have been a Life well spent. I see with Smiles and Scorn, little despicable Efforts to deprive me of the Honour of any Merit, in this Negotiation, but I thank God, I have enough to shew. No Negotiation to this or any other Country was every recorded in greater detail, as the World will one day see. The Letters I have written in this Country, are carefully preserved. The Conversations I have had are remembered. The Pamphlets, the Gazettes, in Dutch and French, will shew to Posterity, when it comes to be known what share I have had in them as it will be, it will be seen that the Spanish Ambassador expressed but the litteral Truth,[5] when He said

"Monsieur a frappé la plus grand Coup de tout L'Europe.—Cette Reconnaisance fait un honneur infinie a Monsieur.—C'est lui qui a effrayée et terrassee les Anglomanes. C'est lui qui a rempli cet nation d'Enthusiasm."—&c.[6]

Pardon a Vanity, which however is conscious of the Truth, and which has a right to boast, since the most Sordid Arts and the grossest Lies, are invented and propagated, by Means that would disgrace the Devil, to disguise the Truth from the sight of the World. I laugh at this, because I know it to be impossible. Silence!

RC (Adams Papers).

[1] Error by JA for 25 April; see AA's letter of that date, above.
[2] That is, as the word suggests, a grumbling patriot or member of the anti-court party. For the origin of this word in 17th-century English politics, see *OED.*
[3] Not found.
[4] MS: "his."
[5] JA revised this sentence in the course of writing it, spoiling its structure without losing its meaning.

[6] JA relished this praise well enough to convey it, in varying language but always bad French, to others; see, for example, his letter to Edmund Jenings, 28 April (Adams Papers), quoted in JA, *Diary and Autobiography,* 3:5. The Spanish minister plenipotentiary at The Hague was Sebastián de Llano y de la Quadra, Conde de Sanafé and Vizconde de Llano (*Reportorium der diplomatischen Vertreten aller Länden,* 3:435).

Ingraham & Bromfield to Abigail Adams

Madam   Amstdm. 1st. July. 1782.

We had the Honor to write you 23d. March by the Ship Enterprize, Capt. Danl. Deshon and then sent an Invoice of Articles to Amount of f428.1—Hol[lan]d Cur[renc]y.

By Direction of Mr. Adams we now enclose a like Invoice of Goods ship'd on his Account on the Brig Sukey, Capt. Grinnel for Boston—the Bill of Lading for which we forward to Isaac Smith Esqr. Wishing that they may reach you safely, We remain, with sincere Respect Madam, Your most obedient, Humble Servants,

Ingraham & Bromfield

Amount of Invoice now enclosed is f525.0.10.

RC (Adams Papers). Text follows on the same sheet of paper the Dupl RC of Ingraham & Bromfield to AA, 23 March, above. Enclosed invoice not found.

John Adams to Richard Cranch

[*The Hague, 2 July 1782*]

"I am among a People, whose slowness puts all my Patience to the Tryal, and in a Climate which is too much for my Constitution: I love this Nation however, because they love Liberty.—You will have learn'd the Progress of our Affairs here, which has been slow but sure. —This Dutch Legation has very nearly cost me my Life, and has taken away forever much of my Strength, and some of my Memory. To-morrow the States of Holland assemble and go upon my Project of a Treaty.—A Mr. Greenville is at Paris about Peace, and is authorised to treat with all the belligerent Powers, but England has not acknowledged us to be a Power, and therefore I fear it will end in Chicane.[1] Certain Persons of the Courts of Petersbourg and Copenhagen are intriguing, to favour England a little, but they can do no great things. Holland will not make a seperate Peace.

"I believe that the Acknowledgement of the Sovereignty of no Nation was ever made with such solemnity, and made so particularly the Act of the whole Nation, and of all the Individuals in it, as ours has been here.[2]—What say the Clergy to their new Allies, Protestant, Calvinist, Antiepiscopalians, Tolerant, Republican, Commercial. How do they pray and give Thanks? Into whatever Country I go, I listen to the Sentiments of the Clergy, because it is a good Index often of the sense of the People. The Clergy here, are in this War, generally well disposed in our favour and against England. I hope our Dutch Friends of all sorts will be treated with Respect and Affection, as well as the French—tho' we are under greater Obligations to the latter.

"It has been a critical Business to conduct this Nation right, amidst their Connections with England, the Influence of their Court, the Intrigues of foreign Courts &c. &c. It has required all the Patience, all the Skill, Address and Capacity, of their own Patriots, aided by the Duke de la Vauguion, not to mention any more, to prevent them from joining England; and it never would have been done but by appealing to the Nation, and arrousing their long dormant Bravery and love of Liberty.—Thanks to Heaven it is done, and we have nothing to fear from them, if we have not room to hope very much."

Early Tr (MHi:Smith-Carter Papers); in the hand of Richard Cranch and captioned by him: "Extract of another Letter dated at the Hague July 2d 1782." Prepared by Cranch for newspaper publication and in small part published in the Boston *Independent Chronicle*, 19 Sept. 1782, p. 3, col. 3, under the caption "Extract of a letter from an American gentleman in Holland, dated July 2." The omission of the word "another" in the newspaper caption indicates clearly that Cranch originally prepared his abridged versions of *both* JA's letters to him of 17 June (above) and of the present date for publication *en suite*. In the end, however, the first letter was apparently not printed at all, and the second emerged in a form so altered as to be nearly unrecognizable. The printed text actually uses only two sentences from JA's original letter as excerpted by Cranch (see notes 1 and 2), and these are followed by added matter that fills about three-quarters of a newspaper column. Much of the added matter seems to have been taken from letters JA did write, or at least could have written, at this period from the Netherlands about his successful negotiations there and affairs in Europe generally, but it is a pastiche or at times even a paraphrase of these letters, together with comments, such as "The Memorial of Mr. Adams was admirably well adapted to accomplish these purposes," which both praise JA's accomplishments and conceal his authorship, so far as he was the author of the letter or letters on which the newspaper text was based.

[1] This sentence begins the text published in the *Independent Chronicle* and constitutes its first paragraph.

[2] This sentence begins the second paragraph in the *Independent Chronicle* text.

John Adams to John Boylston

Dear Sir   The Hague July 5. 1782

I have received your kind Letter of the 28 June, and thank you for your Congratulations.

British Politicks, it is true, are in a Labyrinth. There is never the less, one clue, and but one, which is to acknowledge American Independence, by an express Act of Parliament. This, once done, they would not find it difficult to make Peace.

Those who lend Money to the United States of America in this Country, receive their Interest, in Europe, and will ever receive it here, and much more certainly I suspect, than British Creditors will receive theirs, after some time.

I should certainly have answered your former Letter, if I had known of your Friends return, but I never knew till now, by whom the Letter came.

I am sorry they have put you in a List of Refugees because I have long known your Sentiments to be favourable to your native Country, as well as to Liberty in General.[1]

If you should cross the Channell I should be glad to see you here. Pray have you any News of our Relation your Name Sake. Ask him, if he has given all his fortune to Harvard Colledge, as he promised me he would. Tell him I am afraid he will forget to make his Will— if he will come over here I will make it for him, without a Fee.[2]

I am extreamly happy to hear, that the present Ministry have the Magnanimity and Wisdom to send home my Country men the Prisoners, and to treat them kindly. This is not only the Way to do themselves Honour, but to do real Service to their Country. If Great Britain ever excites a Sentiment in her favour, either in Europe or America, it must be, by such Measures as these.

But nothing will ever compleatly answer the End, but a frank Acknowledgment of American Independence. The United States will Support their Sovereignty, with Dignity, and their Alliances with Honour and good Faith, without ever being diverted from either, by Severity or by Flattery. The Man who now flatters the British King or Nation, with a Hope of the Contrary, is a worse Ennemy to both, than was a North or a Grenville, fifteen or 20 years ago. Delusions now will be fatal. Mistakes now will have worse Fruits than bad Intentions could have in the Beginning.

I wish for Peace, as ardently as you, or any Man. But in my opinion, our Country is less interested in it, than any Power, at war. The more is embroiled, and the longer it is embroiled the better it will be in the End for America, which is a Country so circumstanced and situated as to turn every Thing That happens to her own Advantage. People on your Side the Water, [are] exceedingly deceived in their opinions, that America sighs so ardently for Repose. But why do I scribble upon such Subjects? My Business is to preach to my Friends the Dutch.

I am &c.

LbC (Adams Papers).

[1] On John Boylston's "Sentiments," see Boylston to JA, 31 Aug. 1781, above.

[2] JA is almost certainly alluding to Boylston's cousin, Thomas Boylston of London (1721–1798), though in calling him John Boylston's namesake an ambiguity is introduced, especially since there were no other John Boylstons alive at the time. The only other male Boylston recorded as then living in England or America was Ward Nicholas Boylston, born Hallowell (1749?–1828), on whom see JA, *Diary and Autobiography*, 1:295; CFA, *Diary*, 3:5, 13, 146; Oliver, *Portraits of JA and AA*, p. 35, 38; Oliver, *Portraits of JQA and his Wife*, p. 122–129; Adams Genealogy. But Ward Nicholas Boylston had left Boston in 1773 when still a young man, had resided in London from 1775, a loyalist, at the time was an officer in the British militia, and seems not to have been known to JA before May 1783. Though he was much later to become a benefactor of Harvard as his late uncle Nicholas (1716–1771) had earlier been, he was not at this time possessed of such a fortune as would enable him to contemplate substantial benefactions (Jones, *Loyalists of Mass.*, p. 48–50; Thomas Boylston to JA, 20 April; JA to Thomas Boylston, 12 June 1783, both in Adams Papers, the second LbC).

Thomas Boylston, Ward Nicholas' uncle and sometime patron and employer, was at the moment a man of great wealth; he never married, had long been notoriously of a disposition to seize an opportunity to have legal or other work done where there was no fee, and though there is elsewhere no record of an interest in making Harvard College his heir, he did nurse philanthropic notions toward Boston, both during the time he had a fortune and after he was stripped of it in 1793 by the failure of the London firm of Lane, Son, & Frazer. Boylston, already wealthy by his own efforts and as principal heir of his even wealthier brother Nicholas, and already with a reputation for stinginess, had left Boston for London by 1779, taking a purported £100,000 with him. His emigration seems to have been dictated more by economic than political considerations, and there is little to connect him with loyalism in London. He renewed relations with JA as soon as there was a likelihood of the resumption of commerce between the United States and Great Britain, and between 1783 and 1785 developed several schemes for the import of whale oil from America and the export of sugar, processed in his refinery, to the United States. JA, bent on the encouragement of trade, lent his help to the project and recommended Boylston in letters to Jefferson as "one of the clearest and most solid Capitalists, that ever raised himself by private Commerce in North America" (25 Sept. 1785) and to Lafayette, 13 Dec. 1785: "You may depend upon it, he will do nothing but what is profitable. No man understands more intuitively, everything relating to these subjects, and no man is more attached to his interest." JQA and TBA have provided admirable sketches of Thomas Boylston as he was just after he served his term in bankrupts' prison, though their accounts of him, like those of others, seem heavily colored by the many unpleasant anecdotes of him given currency by Ward Nicholas after he became aware that he was not to be Thomas' heir. See JA, *Diary and Autobiography,* 1:280–281, 290–295; 2:85; *Adams Family Correspondence,* 2:295–296, 305–306; Jefferson, *Papers,* ed. Boyd, 8:550; 9:41–42, 45–46, 88–89; Jones, *Loyalists of Mass.,* p. 49; H. E. Scudder, ed., *Recollections of Samuel Breck,* Phila., 1877, p. 159–160; [Ward Nicholas Boylston,] *The Will of Thomas Boylston, Esq.* [Boston, 1816]. In the Adams Papers: JQA, Diary, 25 Oct. 1794; TBA, Diary, 16, 25 Oct. 1794 (M/TBA/1 and 2, Microfilm Reel Nos. 281, 282); Thomas Boylston to JA, 23 Dec. 1782; JA to Isaac Smith Sr., 2 Sept. 1785; to James Bowdoin, 24 March 1786 (both LbC's). See also Adams Genealogy.

Abigail Adams to John Adams, with a List of Articles wanted by Mrs. Warren

My dearest Friend   July 17 1782

I have delayed writing till the vessel is near ready to Sail, that my Letters may not lay 3 weeks or a month after they are written, as is commonly the case. Mr. Rogers and Lady[1] are going passengers in this vessel; and tho I have only a slight knowledge of them I shall commit my Letters to their care. I have not heard from you since the arrival of Capt. Deshon. Your last Letters were dated in March. I replied to them by the last vessel which saild for France dated about a month ago[2] tho she has not sailed more than a fortnight. I again grow impatient for intelligence. From the last accounts which reachd us by way of Nantys we learn that the Dutch are acquiring a firmness of conduct, that they have acknowledged the independance of America, and are determined to turn a deaf Ear to that prostituted Island of Britain. If this is true, and I sincerely hope it is, I congratulate you upon the Success of your negotiations, and hope your Situation is more eligible than for the time past. If I know you are happy, it will tend to alleiviate the pains of absence.

The Count de Grasse misfortune in the West Indias, we sensibly feel. The British will feed upon it for ages, but it will not save their Nation from the destruction which awaits them.

The Season has advanced thus far without any military Exploit on either Side. We want the one thing necessary for persueing the War with Vigor. Were we less Luxurious we should be better able to support our Independance with becomeing dignity, but having habituated ourselves to the delicacies of Life, we consider them as necessary, and are unwilling to tread back the path of Simplicity, or reflect that

> "Man wants but little here below
> Nor wants that little long."

By the Enterprize I gave you a particular account of the dangerous Situation our dear Brother Cranch is in. He still continues, but we have little to build our hopes upon of his long continuance with us. Heaven be better to us than our fears. The rest of our Friends are well. Charles has been to see a publick Commencement; and has returned to night much gratified with the exhibitions.[3] He has followed his Studies with attention, since his return, under the care of a Mr. Thomas[4] of Bridgwater; who appears well calculated for the instruction of youth; and is said by good judges, to be an admirable proficient in the Languages. But with him we are obliged to part immediately, as he is going into Buisness. I know not what to do with my Children. We have no Grammer School in the Town, nor have we had for 5 years. I give this Gentleman 2s. 6 pr week a peice, for my two. I must (could I find a School abroad to my mind) Board them at 18 Shillings pr week which is the lowest. In Boston 6 and 8 dollers is given by Gentlemen there for Board, formerly a Gentleman Boarded as well for 12 Shillings, but such is the difference. I know not how to think of their leaving Home. I could not live in the House were it so deserted. If they are gone only for a day, it is as silent as a Tomb.

What think you of your daughters comeing to keep House for you? She proposes it.[5] Could you make a Bridge she would certainly present herself to you, nor would she make an ungracefull appearence at the Head of your table. She is rather too silent. She would please you the better. She frequently mourns the long absence of her Father, but she knows not all she suffers in consequence of it. He would prudently introduce her to the world, which her Mamma thinks proper in a great measure to seclude herself from, and the daughter is too attentive to the happiness of her Mamma to leave her much alone, nor could repeated invitations nor the solicitation of Friends joined to the consent of her Mamma, prevail with her to appear at commencement this year. But much rather would the Mamma and daughter embrace the Husband and Father in his Native Land than think of visiting foreign climes. Will the cottage be sweet? Will Retirement be desirable? Does your Heart pant for domestick tranquility, and for that reciprocation of happiness you was once no stranger to. Is there ought in Courts, in Theaters or Assemblies that can fill the void? Will Ambition, will Fame, will honour do it. Will you not reply—all, all are inadequate, but whether am I led? I cannot assume an other Subject—the Heart is softned. Good night.

July 18th

Sol rises this morning with great splendor. I had much rather have seen his face overspread with clouds dispenseing their fruitfull drops to the thirsty earth. It is very dry. Our Corn suffers. Should we be cut of or shortned in our crops we should more sensibly feel it, as our celebrated Siberian wheat is universally blasted, and much of the Rye. Our Success with a little last year led my Tennant to sow 3 acres this year, which we were obliged to mow for foder. Col. Quincy succeeded last year, and raised a hundred and sixty Bushels of as fine wheat as I ever saw, but his Has shared the same fate, and it is so where ever I hear of it. My favorite Virmont is a delightfull Grain Country. I cannot tell why, but I feel a great fondness for the prosperity of that State. I wrote you in my last that I had laid aside the thoughts of being an adventurer there for the present—but soon after Col. Davis of Woster to whom the township was granted, with his associates, brought me the Charter, and the proceedings of Congress with Regard to Virmont by which it appears that Virmont had complied with the requisitions of Congress and the committe to whom, the Matter was committed, report that having complied they consider Congress as obliged to set them of and ratify their independance. This Gentleman has taken pains to have every propriater persons of character and property and that they should all belong to this State. He says it is one of the best situated townships in the State, and will rise in value daily. Salem is the Name it bears. As he had got the deeds all drawn and executed I recollected the old adage Nothing venture nothing have; and I took all the Lots 5 in number 4 of which I paid him for, and the other obligated myself to discharge in a few months. You are named in the Charter as original propriater, so no deed was necessary. Each lot is to contain 300 and 30 acres at about 11 pounds a Lot. This payment has reduced my purse pretty low; having a little before paid Charles passage and repaird Buildings to the amount of a hundred dollers. My taxes I might mention as a heavy load, but as every Body complains, I will be silent, tho I might with as much reason; my continental tax which I am calld upon to pay next week, and is only a half year tax, amounts to 50 dollers. 19 pounds 15 & 10 pence I paid about a Month ago for a State tax and 7 pounds 10 & 2 pence for a town tax and 6 pound some shillings for a ministerial tax, to make up paper money deficiencies, besides 9 pounds 13 & six pence for Class number 7 towards hireing a Man for 3 years. All this I have discharged since April, as will appear by my Receits.

I have not drawn any Bills and will not if I can possibly help it. I shall have no occasion to, if I can get black and white Gauze and Gauze hankerchiefs. It may not be to the Credit of my country but it is a certain fact, that no articles are so vendible or yeald a greater profit. It was with difficulty I could keep a little for my own use of what I last received. I inclosed a list of articles by the Enterprize[6] which I wish you to direct Ingraham and Bromfield to forward, and should they meet with the same Success my former adventures have, and arrive safe, they will be much more benificial than drawing Bills upon which I must discount. I shall inclose a duplicate of the articles with an addition of 5 yard of scarlet Broad cloth of the best kind and 3 yard of Sattin of the same coulour which I want for my own use leaving it at all times to you to determine the Quantity which you think proper to remitt.

You have heard I suppose that Gillion arrived at Philadelphia in june. Only two Letters have come to hand. Dr. Waterhouse left him at the Havanah but was unfortunately taken upon his passage home and carried to New York, by which means the rest of the Letters perished.—I wrote you by the Alliance respecting the Braintree prisoners, but have not received a line in which you make mention of them. That you took measures to relieve them several have testified to their Friends, but it would be more satisfactory if you had mentiond them yourself.[7] There is in Boston a Mr. Marstins' who belonged on Board Gillion who paid yesterday to Charles in Boston a Jo[8] which he said you lent him. I mention this to his Honour and justice. Of all the money due to you, upon Book or note, I have not received a copper since your absence and must have been distresst but for the remittances you have made me.

I long to receive Letters from all my dear Friends. I wish you would write by way of France and send your Letters to Mr. Warren. He would be particuliarly carefull of them. Two vessels have just arrived in 30 days passage from Nants. Your Friends here make great complaint, that you do not write to them. Uncle S[mith] says he will not write you any more, yet believe he does not keep his word, for he writes by every vessel. Genrll. W[arre]n says you have forgotton him and Dr. T[uft]s complains. You see how important a line from you is considerd.

I say all I can for you, but wish you would find leisure to notice those Friends who write to you. Uncle Q[uinc]y desires his regards to you. Your aged Mamma wishes to see you, but fears she never shall. My Father injoys as Good State of Health as his years will admit. My most affectionate regards to my Dear John from whom I have received but one Letter since his visit to P[etersburg].

Adieu my dearest Friend, and Believe me your Most affectionate

Portia

Black and white Gauze
Spotted and striped Gauze hankerchiefs
tapes Quality bindings low priced 7/8ths[9] linnen
Black caliminco red tamies fine thread low
priced dark grounded calicos Ribbons—10 yd of
blew and white dark striped cotton

Nabby has just been giving me a Letter for you. I read it, and really beleive the child thinks herself serious; but you can give her better advice.[10] Mr. Foster has just sent me word that he designs to wait upon me to morrow for Letters so that I shall give them to Him as he is kind enough to come out to see me. You will not fail to take notice of him.[11]

ENCLOSURE[12]

6 lb. best Hyson Tea
2 China Cooffee Pots
1 doz: handled Cups & Saucers—China
2 doz Soup Plates & a Tureen
    doz: flat do.
    doz small long dishes
2 pr Pudding do.
⟨2 or 3 Brushes⟩
3 or 4 house Brushs

Mrs. Warren has left this memorandom with a request that she may have these articles and she will pay the money to me or send to her Son for any thing I may want from France, but at present I know of nothing, so that I should be glad if they are sent they may not be put with any thing which belongs to me, but invoiced and put up by them selves.

RC (Adams Papers); docketed by CFA: "Portia July 17. 1782." Enclosures: (1) List of Articles wanted by Mrs. Warren (Adams Papers), printed herewith; see note 12. (2) AA2 to JA, undated letter; not found, but see notes 5 and 10.

[1] Daniel Denison Rogers and his wife, the former Abigail Bromfield. According to Rev. Samuel Cooper, she was traveling to improve her health; see Cooper to JA, 22 July (Adams Papers). Rogers was a Boston merchant who spent some time in France but after the war took his wife to England, where they were on intimate social terms with the Adamses until 1786, when the Rogerses returned to Boston. See Thwing Catalogue, MHi; JA, *Diary and Autobiography*, 3:69; AA to Mary (Smith) Cranch, 21 March 1786 (MWA); scattered correspondence of AA and JA with the Rogerses in the Adams Papers.

[2] That is, her letter was dated "about a month ago"; it was, in fact, dated precisely on 17 June, and sent by the *Enterprise*, as AA specifies below.

[3] "On Wednesday the 17th instant, a public Commencement was, for the second time since the year 1773, celebrated in the University of Cambridge, with its ancient splendor" (Boston *Continental Journal*, 25 July 1782, p. 2, col. 1). There follow three columns devoted to the exercises and festivities of the day—a much fuller account than is to be found in any other Boston paper.

[4] AA meant to say Thomas Perkins, concerning whom see her letter to James Lovell, ca. 10 April, above, and note 2 there.

[5] In AA2's (missing) letter to JA mentioned below as enclosed in the present letter. See note 10.

[6] That is, in her letter to JA of 25

April, above. A similar listing is in her letter to him of 17 June, also above, and still another appended to her present letter.

[7] AA's inquiry concerning the Braintree seamen in the Mill Prison at Plymouth was in her letter to JA of 9 Dec. 1781, above; see note 3 there for JA's actions in behalf of the prisoners.

[8] A jo (joe, johannes) was a Portuguese gold coin.

[9] Thus apparently in MS.

[10] AA2's letter, undated but doubtless written at the same time as AA's, has not been found. It proposed her coming to Europe to keep house for her father and look after his health. JA's reply, 26 Sept., below, discouraged the idea on the ground that he hoped to return home in the spring.

[11] Possibly Joseph Foster, merchant in State Street, Boston, part owner of and a fellow passenger aboard the *Active*, in which AA and AA2 sailed to England in 1784. See AA's journal of that voyage, in JA, *Diary and Autobiography*, 3:155 ff.; Boston Directory, 1789, in Boston Record Commissioners, *Report*, 10 (1886):183.

[12] MS appears on a separate slip inserted within and now attached to AA's letter enclosing it. The list is in an unidentified hand, except for the crossing out and substitution of the final item, which was done by Mercy Warren. The explanatory paragraph that follows the list is in AA's hand.

Abigail Adams to John Thaxter

July 18th 1782

Aya—Eliza[1]—and is it thus you honour the bare resemblance, thus place round your Neck the Ideal Image, the unanimated form of one, whom if he were present would not be thus distinguished. Virgin Modesty and conscious honour would then forbid this publick mark of affection unless it were sanctified by choise.—But why Sir has the painter been so deficient—it is barely a likeness of you—he has not taken that Manly jesture, that dignity of air and address which should have been the distinguising lines in the portrature? [2]

Sweet Sensibility Source of all that is pleasing in our joys or painfull in our Sorrows—to thee is the portrait indebted for a favour that would kindle a fervour in the Breast of the original in any climate, less unfriendly to the tender passion than the Humid Batavian.

Let me comfort you with the pleasing intelligence that you are kindly rememberd by all the Fair circle of your Female acquaintance since it appears by all your Letters that you consider there regard as Essential to your happiness—and who that knows Humane Nature but must acknowledge that the Social affections between the Sexes where purity of sentiment and politeness of Behaviour are preserved constitutes the principal felicity of Life. It is in the company of the virtuous Fair that Rusticity and asperity are softned and refined into Benevolence and philanthropy. There the Graces may be acquired without sacrificeing the virtues.

I have been interupted by company, my thread is Broken. I will take an other Subject. You have heard I suppose that Gillion arrived at Philadelphia some time in june but not a line of all the Letters you put on Board have yet come to hand or ever will I suppose, for Dr. Waterhouse left Gillion at the Havanna, but his ill fortune persued him, for he was captured upon his passage Home and all his Letters thrown over.—Major Jackson has been fighting a duel with Gillion and was wounded in the thigh, not dangerously I believe.[3] This detestable practise I abhor and hold it inconsistant with the principals of Religion, in no sense better than Murder or Suiside. Can the fault of an other contaminate the Honour of a Man who is noway accessary to it? And is there any speicies of honour repugnant to virtue? The Man whose life is uniformly virtuous will be in no danger of the imputation of cowardice for abstaining from Murder, but on the other hand he who is not invariably restrained by the fear of evil will hardly be thought to refuse a challange from moral restraints, since his virtue is more than suspicious whose conscientious Scruples accompany only those Sins which are attended with danger. But he who has a due sense of religion will not willingly bid defiance to his Creator by ungratefully disowning a Blessing in mercy bestowed, or robbing it from an other. I have hopes my worthy Friend that however custom may have sanctified this Breach of the Laws of God and Man, your virtue and good Sense will deter you at all times, and upon all occasions, from so immoral and absurd a custom. It is a philosophick observation, that he who deserves an affront has no right to resent it, and he who is base enough to affront an other without cause is unworthy of any thing but contempt.

Adieu my dear Sir I am hurried to close my Letters least the vessel sail without them. Your Friends propose writing by this opportunity, but I fear they will be too late.

Mrs. Dana was well yesterday. Our dear and worthy Friend Mr. Cranch is in a poor way. I wrote you particularly by the Enterprize concerning him.[4]

Yesterday was celebrated a publick and Brilliant commencement. I will forward a catalogue by the first opportunity.[5] With regard to politicks, we have a perfect tranquility. We sensibly feel the loss of our Allies, but we shall not be induced to listen to any terms which haughty Britain may offer short of independance. Congress refused a passport for Morgan Carltons Secretary,[6] and the different States are by their resolutions in their different assemblies renouncing the Idea of treating, and scorn a National Breach of Faith. Thus I see no prospect of the desireable object peace—but if we cannot make peace, at least make War.[7] But once more adieu. I have so many last words that tis with reluctance I bring myself to that of   Portia

Forgive all inaccuracies I write in great haste.[8]

RC (MB); addressed: "Mr John Thaxter att The Hague"; endorsed: "Mrs. Adams 18th. July 1782   A[n]s[were]d Septr. Recd. same day." (The answer, printed below, is dated 3 Sept. 1782.) Dft (Adams Papers); without date or indication of addressee. The chief variations in substance between RC and Dft are indicated in notes below.

[1] Thaxter's answer, 3 Sept., below, appears to clarify this expression by repeating it as "Ay, Ay—Eliza," &c.

[2] All this concerns a miniature likeness of Thaxter that he had sent to America a year earlier and supposed lost with his many letters dispatched in the *South Carolina*; see his letters to his sister Celia, 1780–1782 (MHi:Thaxter Papers), and esp. his reply to AA of 3 Sept., below.

[3] The editors have found no further particulars on the Gillon-Jackson duel beyond an additional observation in AA's Dft: "I hear they are still inveterate."

[4] AA to Thaxter, 17 June, above.

[5] In Dft this passage is amplified as follows: "Yesterday was celebrated a publick commencment—a Brilliant one I hear it was and had several invitations. But I have never enterd a publick assembly (Religious ones excepted) since the commencment of the War. I do not say this out of a dislike to publick commencments. I highly approve of them and think them a Stimmulous to youth and a reward to the Brilliant Genious."

[6] That is, Maurice Morgann (1726–1802), secretary to Sir Guy Carleton (afterward 1st Baron Dorchester), who had recently replaced Sir Henry Clinton as British commander in chief in New York City. Morgann was a member of Lord Shelburne's intellectual circle and a political writer and literary critic of some note; see *DNB*. On Congress' refusal of a passport to him and the background of this episode, see *JCC*, 22:263, under date of 14 May; also Burnett, ed.

Letters of Members, 6:351, with notes and references there.
  [7] The whole of the preceding passage on "politicks" (from note 5 to this point) does not appear in Dft.
  [8] Not in Dft.

Hannah Fayerweather Tollman Winthrop
to Abigail Adams

Dear Madam   Cambridge July 19th 1782

Near the dusk of last Evening, I was Honored with your Favor, by the hand of the amiable Master Charles Adams, but was unhappy in not having a light ready to know the Contents. The Young Gentleman Seeming in hast, having Company in waiting, prevented my detaining Him.[1]

I regret my not having His Company to lodge and the Young Ladies who were with Him, as it would have greatly amusd me in my Solitude. And I should have had an opportunity to pay them the Attention, I should wish to pay any of Your Family and of making particular inquiry, after a Gentleman and Lady, for whom I always had the highest Esteem, and for whom I have felt the tenderest Sympathy in their Temporary Seperation, and I make no doubt, I have shard in their Sensibilities, in my Fatal Seperation, and Dissolution of the most endearing Tie! You Madam are yet Blessd with that Anchor of the Soul, the pleasing hope of a reunion with the Dear partner of all Your joys. There is No one I Believe Can enter more fully into the feelings of a Divided Heart, than myself. It is certainly an unhappy Situation. But Your Consolations in the Services His Excellency is rendering His Country, the prospect of His return, and the Dear Pledges You hold, must greatly relieve your Anxieties. Shall I wish him a Speedy return? For the Happiness of Domestick Life, I will. But my Faith in the Sovereign Disposer of those great Events, The Arrangements of Nations, and kingdoms, for peace or War, and the Selectment of proper instruments to Negotiate those Weighty Affairs, would induce me to wish His Excellency Prosperity Abroad, and to You my Friend, a joyful Acquiescence in the will of the Supreme Till the happy Period arrive that will Bless you with mutual joy, by the happy Sight of each other.

I shall think my Self happy in Seeing Mrs. Adams at Braintre or Milton, and will improve every opportunity. You would give me very great pleasure if you would Visit me in my Solitude at Cambridge. Pray present my Compliments to your little happy Circle, and accept of the Sincerest Sentiments of Esteem from Your Humble Servant,

                                        Hannah Winthrop

RC (Adams Papers).

[1] AA's "Favor" to Mrs. Winthrop by the hand of CA has not been found. She was the second wife, and widow, of Professor John Winthrop (1714–1779), JA's former teacher of science and friend in the patriot cause. No doubt AA had instructed CA, who on the 17th had attended, as a guest, his first Harvard commencement, to pay his respects to Mrs. Winthrop at her home on the northwest corner of what are now Boylston and Mount Auburn streets in Cambridge. See above, vol. 1:302; JA, *Earliest Diary*, p. x–xi and *passim*; Sibley-Shipton, *Harvard Graduates*, 9: 240–264.

John Quincy Adams to John Thaxter

Mon cher Monsieur   A St. Petersbourg 11/22 Juillet 1782

Monsieur D[ana] reçut il y a quelques jours une lettre, par la quelle vous lui mandéz prémiérement; que vous avéz été malade depuis six Semaines de la fiévre tierce ce qui m'a fait beaucoup de peine, ensuite que vous alléz vous en retourner en Amerique. Je voudrais bien être en train de suivre la même route, car je suis tout a fait *home-sick*. Quoiquil en soit je crois que ce que je pourrais faire de mieux, serait de sortir de ce pays ci le plutot possible; car c'est je crois le plus mauvais pays de l'Europe pour étudier. Le tems se passe vite et je n'en ai point a perdre. *Il serait peut être bon que je retourne en Hollande pour m'y perfectionner dans les Langues Latine et Greque; et alors je pourrai faire mes autres etudes en Amerique.*

Si le climat est mauvais dans le pays ou vous étês il ne vaut guere mieux ici. L'hiver ici est toujours pour le moins de 7. mois. Pendant tout ce tems là il fait si froid que les cheminées ne suffisent pas dans les maisons et les fenêtres sont toutes doublées, pendant quatre autres mois il fait pour ainsi dire une pluye continuelle, et pendant l'autre mois la chaleur est excessive dans la journée et la nuit il fait froid a porter un Surtout. Jugéz de là si le climat de ce pays ci est invitant.

Le 23 du mois V.S.[1] passé Sa Majesté vint à Petersbourg de Czarsko Zelo sa residence ordinaire dans l'été. C'est un Palais qui est à peu prés à 25 wersts de Petersbourg. Le 26 elle alla voir lancer un vaisseau de 74 canons. Ensuite elle alla à Peterhof autre Palais situé à 33 wersts de la ville. Le 28 anniversaire du couronnement elle y dina en public. Et le 29 jour de la fête du Grand Duc. Il y eut bal masqué et illumination.[2] Sa Majesté resta à Peterhof jusqu'au cinq de ce mois, et alors elle s'en retourna à Czarsko-Zelo.

Je finis en vous souhaitant une traversée courte et heureuse, et en vous assurant que je suis vôtre trés humble et trés obéissant serviteur.

LbC (Adams Papers).

¹ That is, 23 June, "vieux style." By the Western calendar all the events mentioned below accordingly took place in early July.

² In his diary, kept according to new-style dating, JQA recorded on 9 July that he went "to Mr. Rimberts . . . to borrow Domino's for the mascarade of tomorrow." On the 10th: "Grand Duke's *fête*. Mascarade ball and illumination at Peterhoff. At about 1. o'clock P.M. set out for that place with Mr. Artand and Mr. D. and arriv'd there at about half past 5. Walk'd in the Garden till seven and then went to the ball." On the 11th: "Left the ball at about 1 . . .

and set out for St. Petersbourg. Arrived at about 5. . . . Went to bed and slept till noon." On the 12th: "Returned the domino's."

More typical of the way in which JQA passed his time is the record for 22 July, the day the present letter was written: "This forenoon I went to the English Library and took out the 2 last volumes of [Samuel Richardson's] Clarissa and [John] Nichols's collection of Poems. In the afternoon I wrote a letter to Mr. Thaxter in Holland. Mr. D. wrote to my Father. Windy Rainy weather. Finish'd Cicero's oration pro Milone."

John Adams to Abigail Adams

My dearest Friend   Hague 25 July 1782

In this Country, as in all others, Men are much Addicted to "Hobby Horses." These Nags are called in the Language of the Dutch "Lief-hebbery," as they are called in French "Marotte." I had rather ride a Dutch Hobby Horse than an English one or a French. It is the wholesomest Exercise in the World. They live to great Ages by the Strength of it.

My Meaning is this. They pitch in early Life upon some domestick Amusement, which they follow all their days at Leisure hours. I shall give you the History of several.

I Yesterday made a Visit to one, a Mr. Lionet, a venerable old Man of 75, in full Health, Strength and Vivacity, respectable for several Offices which he holds, but more so for vast learning in various Kinds, and great Ingenuity. His Hobby Horse has been natural Knowledge. We went to see a Collection of marine Shells. We were two hours, and had not got half through. The infinite Variety of Figures and Coulours, is astonishing.

But his Curiosity has not been confined to Shells. It has extended to Insects, and he has had it in Contemplation to write as full an Account of these as Buffon has written of Birds, Beasts and Fishes. But beginning with Caterpillars, he has filled a Folio upon that Species—and drew, and engraved the Plates himself.

Thus he rode his Hobby Horse and lived. Without it, he would have died fifty Years ago.

Have you an Inclination to read and inspect Cutts of the Anatomy of Caterpillars—their Nerves, Blood, Juices, Bones, Hair, Senses,

Intellects &c. &c.—Their moral Sense, their Laws, Government, Manners and Customs.

I dont know whether he teaches the manner of destroying them, and Saving the Apple tree.

I doubt not the Book is worth studying. All Nature is so.—But I have too much to do, to Study Men, and their mischievous Designs upon Apple Trees and other Things, ever to be very intimate with Mr. Lionet, (whom I respect very much however) or his Book. Adieu.[1]

RC and LbC (Adams Papers).

[1] The extraordinary man concerning whom JA wrote this letter so extraordinarily revealing of himself was Pierre Lyonnet (1707–1789), whose family had fled France as Huguenot exiles. Lyonnet held posts as cryptographer and law translator to the States General at The Hague. He had been trained in the law and is said to have mastered nine languages, including Hebrew; he collected 1,300 varieties of shellfish; he executed work in painting and sculpture that won recognition; and among learned works in various fields he wrote on the theology of insects. But his most famous work was an illustrated *Traité anatomique de la chenille, qui ronge le bois de saule*, The Hague, 1760, which, according to Hoefer, "has won a place among the most astonishing masterpieces of science." See Hoefer, *Nouv. biog. générale; Nieuw Ned. Biog. Woordenboek*, 8:1090–1091.

John Thaxter to Abigail Adams

Madam   The Hague 27th. July 1782

Soon after writing You at Amsterdam,[1] I was unfortunate enough to have a Relapse, after I thought that the Fever had entirely quitted me. I was confined there about a fortnight, and then came to this place. I am at present perfectly recovered I hope—for another Turn would fret me out of Existence, which would be no great loss except to my *"fair American,"* who might whimper and sigh a day or two perhaps, but it would be soon over: whereas if She should put on Mortality and discharge the last great debt, I should get a broken Heart by it I suppose, be tormented a Year or two with ridiculous Visions and Spectres, and be ready every two or three days to commit some act of Violence upon my Life out of mere Despair. I pray therefore She may live, if it is only to save me all this Trouble; as it is I have Torment enough, being twenty or thirty times a day disturbed with her Image passing across the Brain.—This is not to be remedied.

I was much disappointed in not being honored with a Line from You by Return of Trowbridge in the Firebrand. Not a single Letter by this Vessel, tho' directly for this Country. However, Patience as the Dutch say—a heavenly Balm for every Wound. I am much in the Practice of this Virtue. I hope I am not forgotten.

You will see by the Date of this, that We are removed from Amsterdam here into the Hotel des Etats Unis. Mr. Dumas, with his Wife and Daughter, are in our Family. Madam Dumas takes exceeding good Care of the House and I hope will save much Expence. She is a great Œconomist. Her Daughter is a very pretty young Lady of about 16 or 17. Years old,[2] and I am very well satisfied that She makes a part of the Family, being no Enemy to the fair Sex. I hope it will be unnecessary to make any Apology here to my "fair American," or any Protestations to cure any little troublesome Jealousies that may spring up on Account of my being under the same Roof with this young Lady. I mentioned the young Lady's age on purpose to keep my lovely American quiet. She will see I am old enough to be her Father. Pray tell my Flame to make herself quite easy.—But I beg Pardon, Madam, for taking up so much of your time with these Trifles.

The World is in all the Anxiety of earnest Expectation, all on Tiptoe, for News from the combined Fleet. Lord Howe is out with the English Channel Fleet, and an Action is momently expected, tho' the combined Fleet is much superior. The Dutch Fleet is in the North Sea. It is expected the Jamaica and other merchant fleets will fall into the Hands of the French and Spaniards or the Dutch. God grant it, and if a Naval Battle takes place, Success to our Friends and Allies. Fox, Burke, and another of the new Ministry have quitted Administration, because the System they agreed to pursue, and upon which their Administration was founded has been departed from and a new one adopted. Fox is for granting absolute, unequivocal and unconditional Independence to America. Shelburne, who has become first Lord of the Treasury since the Death of the Marquis of Rockingham, is for making the Acknowledgment of our Independence a Condition of Peace, which is tantamount to declaring, We will not acknowledge it at all, for he knows a Condition of this Nature would involve Us in a seperate distinct Negotiation, contrary to good Faith and solem Treaties not only, but repugnant to our Interest. And this is Shelburne's rascally design, to detach Us from France, which would be seperating our Interests from those of the belligerent Powers. The King is determined not to grant unconditional Independence to America, but with his Crown and Life. Bravo.—America is ready to meet the Monster on that Ground. We do not stand in need of his Acknowledgment to make Us independent. The Work is done, and he will sacrifice a tottering Crown and forfeited Life to no purpose. Shelburne, infamously deserting his Colleagues, has become the Premier upon Condition of supporting the King in this mad Project. Is there not some chosen Curse, some hidden Thunder &c.? Fox has taken his stand upon the only foundation that can save his Country. If he is not under the Influence of unwarrantable Ambition or mean Jealousy, but has adopted his plan upon mature Reflection and a Conviction of its Utility, and pursues it with firmness and Resolution, he may be as illustrious a Character in the British Annals as a Pitt. But it is Time for another Revolution in that Country, and to add *another Martyr* to the Rubric, and a few more Ornaments to Tyburn. The Liberties of the Kingdom are gone past Redemption if some bold Spirit does not check this formidable Combination against their freedom.

Remember me, if You please, dutifully and respectfully where due. My most affectionate Regards to the fair of my Acquaintance. Miss N[abby], Masters Charley and Thommy claim the Remembrance and Affection of him who has the honor to be, with the most perfect Esteem & Respect, Madam, your most Ob. & most Hble. Servt.,

J North[3]

RC (Adams Papers).

[1] Thaxter to AA, 23 June, above.
[2] Little is known of Mlle. Dumas except that her father refers to her as Nancy and that she had a talent for composing patriotic verse, specimens of which were sent to JA by Dumas, 28

March 1783 (Adams Papers).
[3] Thaxter apparently first signed his letter "North Common," a pseudonym he had occasionally used before in writing AA, then crossed out "Common" and prefixed the initial "J."

Abigail Adams to John Adams

My dearest Friend   August 5th 1[7]82

I know not any pleasure equal to that which arises from feeding the Hungry, cloathing the Naked and making the poor prisoners Heart sing for Joy. All the Honours which your Country has conferd upon you has never excited in my mind half the Satisfaction which your Benevolent exertions and generous aid to the poor prisoners which I recommended to you, has given me. I am sorry not to have learnt any thing from your own pen with regard to them, but they have not been deficient in manifesting their gratitude to you, and making mention of your kindness, to their Friends here by every opportunity, nor could I help feeling the Lamentation of a Milton prisoner to his Friends, that it was his misfortune not to be a Braintree Man. Your Benevolence would lead you to do all in your power for the releaf of all those unhappy persons who are in confinement, yet those who were your towns Men and Neighbours have a particular claim to your attention.[1] I expect a Letter to inclose from the Father of Lewis Glover. If you could forward it to him they will consider it as an additional favour and further let them know that all their Friends are well, which I suppose may be done through the commissary of prisoners. They frequently send Letters to their Friends here, but how I know not.

I yesterday saw Mr. Foster, as I hope he will tell you in a months time, I gave him Letters which he has promised to deliver safe. You so seldom acknowledge the recept of any Letters from me, that but for many of the vessels arriveing safe, I should suppose they never reachd you. There are Letters in Boston from Mr. Ingraham I am told so late as May, by the Ship Thomas from Nants. How happy would it have made me to have learnt by a line from you that you was well. What greater hazard would your Letters meet with by way of France than mine, especially coverd to the Consul Le Etomb.

You will find in one of the Letters a memmorandom for [*i.e.* from] Mrs. W[arre]n the articles of china which she has mentiond she supposes may be purchased for 20 dollors.[2] I think she must be mistaken. She has given a different direction as you will see per the inclosed. I should like to *prog*[3] a little too if I thought you could afford it. I will not disown having already done it in some things, but tis but a little. I sent for a compleat set of china for a dining table some time ago, I know not whether you received the Letter and if you did whether you will know what a set is. Now I take it to consist in a doz. of dishes 6 different sizes, 3 doz. of table flat plates and 2 of Soup, 6 pudding dishes, 2 pr. Butter Boats, to which I should like 2 pr. of double flint cut Salts—all to set my table "neat and trim" when dear Collin returns.[4] Perhaps you are house keeper enough allready to know what is necessary but I fancy you must have been often imposed upon before you got your Learning. They tell me you have purchased a House at the Hague and some have gone so far as to say you have sent for all your family. I wish you were with your family. I hear Mrs. Jay[5] is unhappy. Is Mrs. A[dams] happy? No. Is Mrs. D[ana] happy? The world say she is, but I believe she would say no. She is younger than Mrs. Adams and does not think it so necessary to domesticate herself[6] nor has she learnt a lesson the World will soon teach her.

Thus far I wrote with an intention of sending by the Amsterdam vessel, but she has given me the slip. I laid by my paper but tho I do not know of a present opportunity I feel a new Inducement to write. Dr. Waterhouse yesterday made me a visit. He tell[s] me he has written to you by the late vessel[7] so it will be unnecessary for me to say any Thing concerning his Situation. The pleasure which I received from his company and conversation was next to that of seeing my dear absent Friend. He has lived in so much Friendship and intimacy with you, with Mr. T[haxter] and my dear Boys, related so many anecdotes, appeard to enter into all your feelings even of the tender domestick kind that he attached me more to him in a few hours than he could otherways have done in half a year, tho his manners are of that frank, open, unreserved kind which are universally pleasing. He wished me exceedingly to go to you. He was sure it was necessary to your happiness and he could see no prospect of a peace. Even if one took place you certainly was the most suteable Man to reside at the Hague, the Dutch had a Friendship for you and a confidence in you, you was on every account the best calculated to do essential Service to your country there. Your character was high throughout Europe, even the tories respected it, but you was not happy abroad. You sighd for domestick tranquility, you longed for the peacefull shades of Braintree and the kind softning care of Portia.

Thus did this gentleman run on whilst I had not a wish to stop the musick of his tongue for the sweetest of all praise is that which is given to those we best love. Had my dear Friend been half as earnest with me to have taken passage with him as this Gentleman has been that I should go to him, he would have prevaild over my aversion to the Sea. But great as I feel the Sacrifice is I believe he[8] judged best that I should remain where I am.

But will you can you think of remaining abroad? Should a peace take place I could not forgive you half a years longer absence. O there are hours, days and weeks when I would not paint to you all my feelings—for I would not make you more unhappy. I would not wander from room to room without a Heart and Soul at Home or feel myself deserted, unprotected, unassisted, uncounseld.—I begin to think there is a moral evil in this Seperation, for when we pledged ourselves to each other did not the holy ceremony close with, "What God has joined Let no Man put assunder." Can it be a voluntary seperation? I feel that it is not.[9]

Dft (Adams Papers); possibly incomplete; written (as stated within) on more than one day, but closing date is not determinable. Neither enclosure in (missing) RC has been found.

¹ For JA's "Benevolent exertions" in behalf of captured Braintree seamen, see above, AA to JA, 9 Dec. 1781, and note 3 there.

² Enclosure in AA to JA, 17–18 July above.

³ See *OED* under Prog, verb, 2, obsolete except in dialect: "To poke about *for* anything that may be picked up or laid hold of; ... to forage ...; also to solicit, to beg."

⁴ "When dear Collin returns"–from a Scottish song–alluding of course to JA's prospective return.

⁵ Sarah (Livingston) Jay had accompanied her husband on his long and dangerous voyage to Spain in 1779–1780, had shared his diplomatic frustrations there, and had borne him a daughter in 1780 that died three weeks after birth. See Monaghan, *John Jay*, and Morris, *Peacemakers*.

⁶ Here AA heavily inked out four lines in Dft. Their content can be sufficiently reconstructed to suggest that she blotted them after conveying their sense in a briefer and better way in the last paragraph of Dft: "Critical as the Situation of a Lady is separated from the dear [*two or three words*] Protecter of her Life and honour my course [*two or three words*] that in every Step I have looked on all sides and steared clear of [*one word; sentence may be unfinished*]."

⁷ Letter not found.

⁸ That is, JA.

⁹ Text of Dft does not fill the page, and there is no leavetaking; so Dft may be incomplete. From JA's answer of 16 Oct. 1782 (Adams Papers) to AA's letters of 3 and 5 Sept., both below, it would appear that he did not receive the present letter.

John Thaxter to John Quincy Adams

My dear Jack   Hague 14th August 1782

Yours of 22d ulto. arrived a few days agone. I acknowledge myself much in Arrears, tho' I have by no means forgotten you. For three Months past I have been miserably tormented with the Tertian Ague, and have been a more useless being than common. However I hope the Game is nearly up at present. I had no Idea that your Climate was so bad—but you must remember that this has been an uncommon Season throughout Europe. At this Moment I am writing by a good Fire. I have had one for many days past both on account of my Indisposition and the cold. Curious Dog-Days these. We have incessant Winds and Rains: When they will end I know not. Patience, Patience. —You tell me you are home-sick. I can easily conceive of it, and that you are very anxious about your future Education. A young Gentleman of your studious, thoughtful turn of mind cannot be otherwise than anxious considering the disadvantage of Education in your City. This Sentiment does you much honour, and shews that you put a just Value on Time. But you must not consider your *Boreal* Tour as lost Time. It was an Opportunity few young Gentlemen enjoy, and you travelled with a Gentleman from whose Observations and Instructions you must have derived great Advantage. When you return to our dear Country, you will be in a Situation to make Comparisons, and run your Parallels between the Advantages of the old and new World.

If your European Travels have produced the same Effects upon you that mine have upon me, You are much more attached to your own Country than when you left it. I have seen much in mine that I hope will never be transplanted into America. We have Vices enough in our own Country without aping or adopting those of the old World: However there are many valuable things in Europe which I wish to see in America. Many Improvements in Mechanism, but few in Government or Laws. Such however is the unfortunate Condition of human Nature, that in attempting to acquire what is good and valuable from other Countries, We open a Communication to all their vices and Defects—that is, we are quite as apt to adopt the latter as the former, and perhaps rather more. But I must not be uncharitable.

My best respects to Mr. D[ana] and believe me to be your very sincere friend and Humble Servant.

Early Tr (Adams Papers), in JQA's hand; at head of text: "From Mr. Thaxter."

John Adams to Abigail Adams

My dearest Friend   [*The Hague, ca. 15 August 1782*]¹

Mr. Thaxter is getting better and Mr. Charles Storer is now with me, and We may be all now said to be pretty well. Our northern Friends are well too.

You will hear a great deal about Peace, but dont trust to it. Remember what I have often said "We shall not be able to obtain Peace, while our Ennemies have New York and Charlestown or either of them." I know the Character and Sentiments of the King of England, and while he can hold a Post in the United States, he will have it in his Power to make the People of England believe that the People of America love him and them, and keep up their hopes of some turn of Affairs in their favour.

Lord Shelburnes System is equivocal. Fox has seized the right Idea. But the former will run down the latter for sometime. Yet the Plan of the latter must finally prevail. It is deeply laid and well digested. If he has Perseverance he will be the Man to make Peace.

By frequent Exercise on Horseback and great Care, I seem to have recovered my Health, strength and Spirits beyond my Expectations. And if the Company of Princes and Princesses, Dukes and Dutchesses, Comtes and Comptesses could make me happy, I might easily be so—but my Admired Princess is at the blue Hills, where all my Ambition and all my Wishes tend.

I know not the Reason but there is some Strange Attraction between the North Parish in Braintree and my Heart. It is a remarkable Spot. It has vomited Forth more Fire than Mount Etna. It has produced three mortals, Hancock and two Adams's, who have, with the best Intentions in the World, set the World in a blaze. I say two Adams's because the Head of the Senate[2] sprung from thence as his father was born there.—Glorious however as the flame is, I wish I could put it out.—Some People say I was born for such Times. It is true I was born to be in such times but was not made for them. They affect too tenderly my Heart.

I love the People where I am. They have Faults but they have deep Wisdom and great Virtues—and they love America, and will be her everlasting Friend, I think. I would do a great deal to serve this nation, I own.

If Spain should acknowledge Us as I think she will soon, the two great Branches of the House of Bourbon, Holland and America, will form a PHALANX which will not easily be shaken. I hope and believe We shall continue Friends. If We do, whenever England makes Peace She will be afraid to quarrell with Us, how much soever she may hate Us. And I think the other Powers of Europe too will prefer our Friendship to our Enmity, and will choose to excuse Us from meddling in future Wars. This is the Object of all my Wishes and the End of all my Politicks. To this End and for this Reason I look upon my success in Holland as the happiest Event, and the greatest Action of my Life past or future. I think that no Opportunity will present itself for a Century to come, for Striking a Stroke so critical and of so extensive Importance, in the political system of America. How critical it has been few Persons know. It has hung upon a Thread, a Hair, a silken Fibre. Its Consequences will not be all developed for Centuries. I know there are [those][3] who represent it a Thing of Course and of trifling moment. But they have not seen the Diary of Mr. Van be[r]ckel,[4] nor mine, nor the Minutes of the Cabinets of Orange and Brunswick. Nor have they seen the History of future Wars in Europe. A future War in Europe will shew the Importance, of the American Negotiation in Holland.—Be discreet in the Use you make of this. Be cautious. I want to know how our Success here is relished with you.

Adieu, tenderly Adieu.

RC (Adams Papers); undated, but see note 1.

[1] AA's acknowledgment of this undated letter in hers to JA of 13–25 Nov. (Adams Papers) infers that it was written at "about the same time" as JA's two letters to her of 17 Aug., both below. Internal evidence, such as the

news of Thaxter's convalescence and Charles Storer's presence in JA's household, supports her inference. But we may infer further that it slightly predated JA's two letters of the 17th or he would have mentioned in it, as he did in both of those, his concern over the severity of Richard Cranch's renewed illness, news of which did not reach The Hague until 16 or 17 August.

² Samuel Adams, currently president of the Massachusetts Senate.

³ Editorially supplied for a word missing in MS.

⁴ Engelbert François van Berckel (1726–1796), first pensionary of Amsterdam, long an advocate of closer Dutch-American relations, sponsor of the abortive Lee-de Neufville treaty of 1778, and as warm a friend of JA as his official station permitted. See *Nieuw Ned. Biog. Woordenboek*, 4:109–111; JA, *Diary and Autobiography*, 2:447–449, 452–453, 455. His brother, Pieter Johan van Berckel, was to become the first Netherlands minister to the United States.

John Thaxter to Abigail Adams

Madam   Hague 16th. August 1782

I am to express my Acknowledgments to You for your kind favor of the 17th. June last, with which I was honoured this day. I expressed my Chagrin in not recieving a Letter by the Firebrand in mine of the 27th. July, which accompanies this. Little did I think that in that moment the tender sympathetic Heart of Portia was sharing, and participating in the Cares and Agonies of her dear Sister, who was waiting in aweful Suspense the Issue of her dear Mr. Cranch's Illness. We know not yet the Event, but hope that the Change was favorable. The Gazette of July 1st. makes no mention of his Death, and We flatter ourselves still with Hopes of his Recovery. May he who directs righteously all Events graciously grant it, and continue him still in Existence for the sake of his Family and Mankind. He is indeed an Ornament to human Nature, and has discharged the Duties of his several Relations in Life with a Fidelity that will ever distinguish his Character and point him out as an illustrious Pattern and Example to those, who wish to be great and good. My Heart bled at the pathetic Recital You gave me of his Sickness; and who is there that knows the Man that can withhold the sympathetic Tear? I venerate his Character, for he is indeed a venerable Man. I am impatient and tremble at the Idea of recieving the next Letter from home. May kind Heaven be propitious.

August 18th.

My Situation in this place is on many accounts more eligible than that at Amsterdam was. The Air is purer and We are much nearer the Sea. But You tell me, Madam, I sigh for America. It is true indeed, and so I should if I dwelt in any *Paradise* that Nature or Art has formed in the old World. I am not *homesick* neither for I should be *happy* (had I the means) to pass two Years in France before my Return, to see a little the face of that Kingdom and to acquire more perfectly the Language. I should be *happy* to a certain degree I mean. However this cannot take place, and I must run the hazard of a British Prison sooner or later. I perfectly agree with You, Madam, that it is better to become a *Captive* in America than a *Captive* in a British Prison. The *former Captivity* I have been long accustomed to and am perfectly reconciled to it. I love the Toils the busy God has made. They are the first Webs which gently hold the willing Swain. I wish extremely to be fixed down in some reputable business but I fear it will be a long time first. Patience however sufficient unto the day is &c. I am a Batchelor to day, I may be tomorrow, and shall be I believe ten Year hence. If I do not cease to be tormented with Reveries, Visions and Dreams about this said subject of Matrimony, I shall be a Batchelor from Choice. I have been in the fidgets this Week past with a confounded Dream about being married and my Wife having three Children at a Birth, all born *crying* and *yelping* as if possessed. I cried out, oh Lord deliver from this Bondage thy miserable ruined Servant. Twice before I have dreamt of being connected with two young Ladies I love and esteem very much—as often repented and wept bitterly. I have almost taken the Vow of Celibacy, and nobody would care for that I believe. I fancy these are hints (pretty broad ones too) to remain even as I am. I intend to consult St. Paul upon the Matter and make up Judgment after a full hearing on both sides. You see what *Sylphs* are about me.

As to the dear Girls for whom I have expressed a particular Regard, I am very sorry that no young Gentlemen are to be found to their Taste. They are indeed virtuous and deserving, and merit Partners of the same Character. They possess all the Virtues and Accomplishments necessary in that Relation of Life, and whoever renders himself agreable to either cannot be otherwise than happy. I had thought the amiable Sally already connected. She is another of the deserving ones, and I wish her most sincerely happily fixed.

19th.

Mr. Guild, who takes my Letters, has just arrived here, and leaves me but little time to add: I hope he will be more fortunate this Passage.

I am not able to write all my friends by this Opportunity. I have not as yet Strength sufficient. The repeated Attacks of the Fever have weakend my Nerves, but I shall soon get over that.

Mr. Guild will be able to give You so good an Account of Politicks as to render it unnecessary for me to say any thing. The English are as much disposed to tricking and Chicane as ever. They want Peace, but have either not Virtue, Honor or Sense enough to make it. The American Pill is yet a little unpalatable. It will however go down in time. Patience, Perseverance and Firmness are the only requisites.

My Friend Storer is with me at present, which makes me very happy. He means to remain here sometime, and is learning French— is very well. Please to remember me to all Friends—to the dear Girls particularly. I long to embrace them.

I have the honor to be, with an invariable Respect & Esteem, Madam, your most Ob. & M. H. S.,   J.T.

RC (Adams Papers).

John Adams to Abigail Adams

My dearest Friend   August 17. 1782 [1]

Your Favour of June 17. arrived this Day and gave me, all the tender and melancholly Feelings of which my Heart is susceptible.

How shall I express my solicitude for my amiable, my venerable Friend and Brother? This World contains not a wiser or a more virtuous Man. Just now placed in a situation, too where all his great Talents and excellent Virtues might have their full Effect!—But it is but a Part that We see. I tremble for his Family. Possibly he may still be spared. But We must all expect.—I have been within an Hairs Breadth, and although recovered to tolerable H[e]alth and Spirits, I am still feeble, and shall never be restored to all my former Force.

Before this Time, you will have learned our full Success here. The Treaty is not yet compleated but it is in a fair Way. This Nation cannot depart from its Forms, and it takes a long time for a Treaty to undergo the Examination of so many Provinces and Cities. But this Nation will stand firm. I am now happy in the Intimacy of many leading Characters and know their Views and Designs very well and We may depend upon their steady Attachment to Us and to the good System.

You have not yet an Idea of all the Difficulties I have had to encounter. Some of them ought not to be committed to Paper. They were cruel, but I bore them and they are over. I am now as agreably situated as I can ever be without my Family.

It is to me an insipid Life, this of an Ambassador, and I wish it at an End.... [2]

The naval Disaster you mention, has no ill Effect upon this People.

My dear Children are never long out of my Thoughts. Where is Charles's Pen? I hear sometimes of Miss Nabby in Boston. How is Mr. Tommy?

Our Northern Friends are well.

Adieu.

RC (Adams Papers).

[1] The order in which JA composed his two letters of this date to AA cannot be definitely settled, but a comparison of the opening sentences of the two at least suggests that this letter was the first and the following one a sequel.

[2] Suspension points in MS.

John Adams to Abigail Adams

My dearest Friend   August 17. 1782

The Situation of my dear Brother, at the date of yours 17. June, has allarmed me so much that I dread to hear any further News of him. An Affection for him has grown old with me as it commenced very early in Life and has constantly increased. Mr. Smiths Letter of 6 of May [1] did not surprise me so much because I had often known him in great distress in the Lungs but these disorders are new. The World has scarcely a worthier Man to loose.

My Friends may think strange that they dont receive Letters from me oftener. I believe they think I have a great deal of Leisure. I wish I could change Situations with them, and then they would see what a pretty Thing it is to be an American Minister.

I am not idler than I used to be. My whole Time is spent in necessary and unavoidable Services. The Silk Machine is not more complicated nor more delicate than the System of Politicks of the United States.[2] It extends its Branches into every Court and Country of Europe. In order to know what it is they must come and see and try the Experiment.—I am weary of it.—I am no more able to maintain all the Correspondences I have than to remove mountains. I am obliged to sacrifice my Friendships as well as my other Affections to my Duty. Mr. T[haxter] has been sick this 2 or 3 months, which has made the Burthen heavier for me, indeed too much for my feeble Frame. He is now pretty well. If I should be obliged to go to Paris or Vienna, to talk about Peace, another Scæne of Pleasure and Amusement would open upon me, such as I have had a long succession of. Such Pleasure and Amusement as millions of Perplexities, and millions of Humiliations and Mortifications aford. All of them however have not yet subdued my proud heart.

I have nothing to do but pray for the abundant Outpowerings[3] of Patience, Patience, Patience.

A good Peace would be a Reward for all. I dont know how it is— I suppose it is my Vanity. But I was under no Fears of a bad Peace, while I was alone. I was very sure of my own Firmness or call it Obstinacy, if you will. I had no Jealousies, no Suspicions, no Misgivings. I cannot say the same now. I have a good Opinion, however, of one of my Colleagues, and wish I could have of the other. Yet if I had known that Mr. Jefferson would not have come and Mr. Laurens resigned, I would have refused to share in the new Commission.[4] I shall do the best I can.—Adieu.

RC (Adams Papers).

[1] Isaac Smith Sr. must be meant; his letter has not been found.

[2] From the context this appears almost certainly to be a slip of the pen for "the United Provinces," i.e., the Dutch Republic.

[3] Thus in MS.

[4] In the preceding sentence JA alludes of course to Jay and Franklin, respectively. Jefferson had declined appointment to the peace commission at the outset (Aug. 1781) because of the illness of his wife (who died soon afterward). After much vacillation, Laurens eventually served, but only during the very last days of the negotiation in November. See the exchange between JA and Laurens, 18 and 27 Aug. 1782 (both in Adams Papers, that of 18 Aug. a letterbook copy); JA, *Works*, 7:612–613, 614–616.

John Adams to John Quincy Adams

My dear Son   Aug. 18. 1782

It is with Pleasure that I enclose this amiable Letter from your Sister, which breaths a very commendable affection for You and solicitude for your Welfare. There is nothing more tender than these Correspondences between Families, as there is nothing more sacred than the Relations of Brother and sister, except that of Parent and Child. It is your duty to answer her.

I say again, it is a moral and a religious duty to cultivate these amiable Connections by constant Correspondence, when We cannot by Conversation. But I need not recur to any Thing so austere as the Idea of Duty. The Pleasure of corresponding with a sister so worthy of you ought to be Motive sufficient. Subjects can never be wanting. Discriptions of Cities, Churches, Palaces, Paintings, Spectacles, all the Objects around you, even the manners and Dress of the People will furnish ample materials.

It is a long time since you have written to me. You should think of your Fathers Anxiety, for the Success and Progress of your Studies.

You study I hope among other Things to make yourself as Usefull and agreable to your Patron as possible.

You have no doubt had the Opportunity to see the Empress upon some publick Occasions. I had that of supping, at Court, at the Maison du Bois with the Comte and Comptess du Nord.[1] Your Patron will see in the Courier du Bas Rhin and in the Gazettes of Leyden and the Hague, a Projet or a Speculation, calculated to favour some of his Views.[2] How does he like it? and how is it taken where you are? or is it not talked of.

I long to see you. You should be at Leyden or at Cambridge. A public Education you must have. You are capable of Emulation, and there alone you will have it.

Adieu.

RC (Adams Papers); docketed by JQA in a later hand: "J.A. Aug: 10: 1782." Early Tr (Adams Papers), in JQA's hand. Enclosure in RC was probably AA2 to JQA, 3 May 1782, above.

[1] Name assumed by Grand Duke Paul of Russia during his and his wife's visits in western Europe from 1780.

[2] A paper, perhaps by JA, on international and particularly Russian affairs. It has not been located among the newspapers searched.

John Adams to Norton Quincy

My dear Friend   The Hague August 28 1782

I Sigh every day, in whatever Scæne I am in for a walk down to your House and a Day by your Fireside.[1]—I hope the Time will come, but not so soon as I wish.

It would amuze you, as it does me to wander about in scænes once frequented by the great Princes of Orange, by Brederode, Barnevelt, Grotius, De Witts, Erasmus, Boerhave, Van Trump, De Ruyter and a thousand others, and I can assure you, that I dont think the Nation essentially changed from what it was in those days.—But it is too rich and loves Money too well. If however the present P[rince] of Or[ange] had the Genius and Enterprise of the 1st or 3d William or of Frederick Henry this Nation would now display as great Virtues and Resources as ever, provided it was directed in the Way the Nation wishes. The nation is discontented with the Management of Affairs, and is struggling to amend it. They will be steady and persevering tho slow.

I will inclose to you a Curiosity—a Pamphlet severely reprobated by the Gov[ernmen]t, but which has made a deep Impression upon the Nation, and certainly contributed a great deal, to accelerate the Acknowledgment of the United States here. It arroused the People and allarmed the Court. When you have read it, lend it to the President of the Senate.[2] Dont let it become publick. The Author is not known. In the original Dutch it is said to be a finished Composition.[3] There is an astonishing Multitude of such free Writings here.

Surely this is the Court and Country where Liberty and Independence ought to be popular. But Courts change sooner than nations.

Cant you resolve to write to me for once? A Letter from you would do me great good. I want to be again Select Man with you[4] and I intend to be, sooner or later.

Mean while Adieu.

RC (Adams Papers). For the enclosure, not found, see note 3.

[1] Norton Quincy, identified above at vol. 1:146, AA's favorite uncle, lived as a recluse on his farm at Mount Wollaston on the shore of what is now called Quincy Bay. JA had embarked for Europe from Norton Quincy's house in Feb. 1778; its location is indicated by the word "Quinzey" on the chart of Boston Harbor in same, following p. 240. See also vol. 2:388–389; numerous references in JA's *Diary and Autobiography*; Eliza Susan Quincy's view of Mount Wollaston in Massachusetts Historical Society, *A Pride of Quincys*, 1969; Adams Genealogy.

[2] Samuel Adams.

[3] The pamphlet may be confidently identified as an English translation of *Aan het Volk van Nederland* (To the People of the Netherlands), the original Dutch version of which had been anonymously and surreptitiously printed and circulated in Sept. 1781. It was a devastatingly bold and bitter attack on the incompetence, reactionaryism, and pro-British policy of the House of Orange, and contained tributes to the republican character of the Swiss and American federations. High rewards were posted by the government for the apprehension of the author, printers, sellers, and even possessors of *Aan het Volk*, and copies were publicly burned by the executioner. The severity of these penalties gave the pamphlet such notoriety that it rapidly went through a number of editions and translations, and it became a kind of primer for the Dutch Patriot party. JA reported on the "Fermentation" it had produced by quoting some of the "placards" against it in letters to the President of Congress, 17, 25 Oct. 1781 (PCC, No. 84, III; Wharton, ed., *Dipl. Corr. Amer. Rev.*, 4:782–783, 810–812), in the second of which he discussed in a notable passage the rising liberty of the press and hence of "democratical Principles" in certain parts of Europe, which he attributed directly to the influence of the American Revolution.

The authorship of *Aan het Volk* remained a secret for a century. Its primary author was an aristocratic quasi-*philosophe*, Joan Derk, Baron van der Capellen tot den Pol (1741–1784), of Zwolle in Overyssel, long an interested observer of American affairs and a friend and correspondent of JA during the 1780's; see JA, *Diary and Autobiography*, 2:455 and references in note there. Capellen had the able and energetic assistance, especially in the difficult problems of printing and circulation, of Francis Adrian Van der Kemp (as his name was Americanized after his exile from the Netherlands), identified above in a note under JA to Richard Cranch, 18 Dec. 1781. Van der Kemp's *Autobiography*, ed. Helen L. Fairchild, N.Y., 1903, details his own relations with Capellen and with JA, whose close friend

and lifelong correspondent he became.
See also W. P. C. Knuttel, *Catalogus van de Pamfletten-Verzameling berustende in de Koninklijke Bibliotheek,* vol. 5, 1776–1795, The Hague, 1905, Nos. 19864–19876; Hendrik Willem Van Loon, *The Fall of the Dutch Republic,* new edn., Boston and N.Y., 1924, p. 322–332; Palmer, *Age of the Democratic Revolution,* 1:325–331.

⁴ JA and Norton Quincy had been Braintree selectmen together beginning in March 1766; see JA, *Diary and Autobiography,* 1:304.

John Adams to Abigail Adams

Aug. 31. 1782

All well.—You will send these Papers to some Printer when you have done with them.

We have found that the only Way of guarding against Fevers is to ride. We accordingly mount our Horses every day. But the Weather through the whole Spring and most of the Summer has been very dull, damp, cold, very disagreable and dangerous. But shaking on Horseback guards pretty well against it.

I am going to Dinner with a Duke and a Dutchess and a Number [of] Ambassadors and Senators, in all the Luxury of this luxurious World: but how much more luxurious it would be to me, to dine upon roast Beef with Parson Smith, Dr. Tufts or Norton Quincy—or upon rusticrat Potatoes with Portia—Oh! Oh! hi ho hum!—and her Daughter and sons.

RC (Adams Papers); enclosed "Papers" not found or identified.

John Adams to Cotton Tufts

My dear Dr.   [*The Hague, August?* 1782]¹

I have only time to inclose a few Papers and to pray for your Health and Prosperity.

I am much distressed for my Brother Cranch as the last Accounts were allarming. So pleasing a Friendship of near 30 Years standing is a Blessing not to be replaced. I cannot give up the Hopes that I may yet see him in good Health.

My worthy Father Smith must be greatly afflicted at this Sickness. The sorrows however, as well as the Joys of his Age, are either fatal, or soon over.

I long to be with you, even to share in your Afflictions. The Life I lead is not satisfactory to me. Great Feasts and great Company, the Splendeur of Courts and all that is not enough for me. I want my Family, my Friends and my Country. My only Consolation is, that

I have rendered a most important and essential service to my Country, here, which I verily believe no other Man in the World would have done. I dont mean by this, that I have exerted any Abilities here, or any Actions, that are not very common, but I dont believe that any other Man in the World would have had the Patience and Perseverance, to do and to suffer, what was absolutely necessary.—I will never go through such another Scene. Happily, there will never I believe be again Occasion for any body to suffer so much. The Humiliations, the Mortifications, the Provocations, that I have endured here, are beyond all description; yet the Unravelling of the Plot, and the total Change in all these respects make amends for all.

My Situation is at present as agreable as it ever can be to me, Out of my own Country and Absent from my family.

I cannot flatter you with Prospects of Peace. There are some Essays towards it, but their Success is too uncertain to be depended on. Yet England is too inadequate to her European Ennemies to hurt Us much. The Refugees are turning every stone to provoke fresh Hostilities against America, but I think they will be disappointed.—What a forlorn Situation those Wretches are in!—Yet I am told they modestly hope at least to be *invited* home, by their Countrymen. I suppose they think that America has not wit enough to govern itself without them.

It is now almost five Years since I left Congress, and what a Series of horrid scænes have I got through. What storms, what Chases, what Leaks, what Mountains and Valleys, what Fatigues, Dangers, Hair Breadth scapes, what Fevers and Gouts, have I seen and felt!

If after all it should please God to preserve me home, I will leave the Splendid Pursuits of Fame, Fortune and Ambition to those, who have them in View and who may easily obtain them without the Pains, Achs and Dangers that I have run, from other Motives. My little Farm will be as extensive as my Expectations. My poor Boys must work—they have seen a little of their Fathers Pleasures in this Life, and knowing the Object he had in View, they will not reproach him for having neglected their Interests.

RC (PPAmP); endorsed: "Hon. John Adams Letter recd. March 1783." Enclosed "Papers" not found or identified.

[1] Thus approximately dated from JA's allusion to his "last Accounts" of Richard Cranch's renewed and severe illness. These had been received on 16 and 17 August (see letters under those dates above), and this circumstance, together with other hints, suggests that the present letter was written at some point during the last two weeks of August 1782. See, further, Tufts to JA, 10 Oct. 1782 (Adams Papers).

Abigail Adams to John Adams

My Dearest Friend   Sepbr. 3. 1782

If my Letters have been as successfull as I wish them, you must have heard many times from me since I received a single line from your Hand. This is the sixth time I have written to you; since I received your last Letters, which were dated in March.[1] From that time up to this 3d of September not a syllable has come to Hand. A few vague english News paper Reports, respecting a negotiation for a peace. I find your Name mentiond so late as june. Not a vessel has arrived from Holland since Capt. Deshon. We cannot account for so long a space of times elapsing: since it is said the United provinces acknowledged the Independance of America, without receiving any official account of it.

The enlargement of the prisoners from Mill prison, together with the intelligence they brought of the proposed acknowledgment of our independance, coincideing with the general wish for peace, the specious Letters sent out of New York by Carleton and Digby about the same time,[2] so facinated all Ranks of people that a General Joy pervaded every class; I hardly dared to oppose, to the congratulatory addresses I received upon the occasion, the obstinate persuasion I had; that it was only a tub to the Whale.[3]

I ventured to say in some companies, where my unbelief appeared very singular, that altho I ardently wished for peace, I could not conceive that an object, of so great Magnitude, could be the Work of a few weeks, or Months; and altho the acknowledgment of our Independence, was an indispensable preliminary, yet there were many other important articles to be adjusted by the contending powers. I thought it would be better to suspend those warm expressions of joy; which could only be warranted by an assureance that an honorable peace had taken place. If any real foundation existed for such reports, a week or two would give us official assureances of it, and I must beg to suspend my belief untill that period.

It really pained me to see the sanguine hopes of my Country perish like the baseless fabrick of a vision. Yet in less than ten days they reflected, and doubted, the elated joy subsided, and they spurned the Idea of a seperate peace.

The Marquis de Vaudreuil arrived in Boston harbour about a fortnight ago with 13 ships of the Line. His intention is to repair the damaged ships.[4]

The two Armies have past an inactive Summer. When when shall

371

I receive any Letters from my dear Friend? Instead of being more and more reconciled to this seperation, every day makes it more painfull to me. Can I with any degree of calmness look Back and reflect that it is near 3 years since we parted, and look forward without seeing, or being in the least able to form an Idea of the period which is still to take place.

In my last Letter I made you a serious proposal. I will not repeat it at present. If it is accepted one Letter will be sufficient. If it is rejected, one Letter will be too many.[5]

We have had a most uncommon Season. Cold and dry—not one rainy day since the begining of June, and very few showers. The drought has been very extensive, and our corn is near all cut of.— Scarcly a spire of green Grass is to be seen. The B[osto]n prisoners have all reachd home except the 3 who were exchanged. There have been 3 of the Number to see me—to thank me for writing to you, and to acknowledge your kind attention to them. Beals and the two Clarks have offerd to repay the money you advanced to them; which they say was four pounds sterling a peice, but as I never received a line from you respecting them, or what you had done for them I am at a loss what to do.[6] Some of them are able enough, others are not.

I have the very great pleasure to acquaint you that our dear and worthy Brother C[ranc]h is raised in a manner from the dead. His dropsical Symptoms have left him and he has for a month past surprizingly mended. His Cough still continues, but we have great hopes now of his recovery. He is not able to attend to any buisness nor will he be for many months, even tho he should get no relapse.

Let me beg you my dear Friend to be particularly attentive to your Health. Do not practise so indiscriminately lieing with your windows open, it certainly is a bad practise in a country so damp as Holland. My Notice of this opportunity is so short that I cannot write to Mr. T[haxte]r or my Son from whom I long to hear.

Mrs. D[ana] was well when I last heard from her. She has been at Newport ever since july. Our Friends are all well and desire to be rememberd. They make great complaints that you do not write to them, and will in Spight of all I can say, think themselves neglected.

I feel in my Heart a disposition to complain that when you write, you are so very concise. I am sorry I cannot prevail with you to write by way of Spain or France, but you must have reasons to which I am a Stranger.

Adieu my dearest Friend and be assured of the Strongest attachment and warmest affection of your   Portia

Our two dear Boys are very studious and attentive to their Books and our daughter thinks of nothing else but making a voyage to her pappa.

RC (Adams Papers); endorsed: "Portia 5 Septr. ansd. 16 Oct. 1782." JA's date in the endorsement was probably not a misreading of AA's date but intended to cover her letters of both 3 and 5 Sept. (below), which came by the same conveyance.

¹ JA to AA, 22, 29 March, above. Later letters from him to AA surviving in the Adams Papers are dated 1 April, 14 May, 16 June, 1, 25 July, and four more in August that she could hardly have received by 3 September.

² The Carleton-Digby letter to Washington of 2 Aug. (text in Washington, *Writings*, ed. Sparks, 8:540–541), forwarded by Washington to Congress on 5 Aug., was not fraudulent, but it was misleading because it greatly overstated the concessions the British government was prepared to make for peace with America. On the ground that no word of this kind had been received from its own ministers in Europe, Congress took a properly wary attitude toward it. See Cotton Tufts to JA, 26 Sept., below; Washington, *Writings*, ed. Fitzpatrick, 24:466, 468–469, 471–472; JCC, 23:

462–463; Burnett, ed., *Letters of Members*, 6:438, 440, 442, 443.

³ To "throw a tub to the whale" was to "bamboozle or mislead an enemy" when in danger, as whalemen did when a boat was threatened by a whale or school of whales (E. Cobham Brewer, *Dictionary of Phrase and Fable*, London, n.d., under Tub).

⁴ Louis Philippe de Rigaud, Marquis de Vaudreuil (1724–1802), French admiral (Ludovic de Contenson, *La Société de Cincinnati de France ...*, Paris, n.d., p. 276).

⁵ See above, AA to JA, 5 Aug., a letter it is believed JA did not receive. However, see also below, AA to JA, 5 September.

⁶ See above, AA to JA, 9 Dec. 1781, and note 3 there.

John Thaxter to Abigail Adams

Madam   Hague 3d. Septr. 1782

What pleasing Sensations does a Packet from the other side of the Atlantic produce? Every part of the human frame sympathizes and is in Unison. This Truth I have most sensibly felt this day, in recieving three Letters from America. I was at Peace with myself before I opened them. The Superscriptions, in informing me from whence they came, saved me a Turn of the Fever, which threatened before. In opening that of Portia's of the 18th. July, I read these Words, "Ay, Ay—Eliza—is it thus You honor the bare Resemblance—thus place round *your* Neck the Ideal Image" &c. Heaven! said I, to my dear Friend Storer, with a deep Blush, (I have not forgot how to blush yet—horrible Misfortune to me) what can all this mean? There is a Mystery wrapt up in these Words. Read on, said he, and perhaps the Riddle will be unravelled. Half frightened I begun to read again, till I came to the Words, "why has the *Painter* been so deficient—it is barely a Likeness of You." The Mystery was developped—the Word *Painter* helped me thro' in an instant. I had flattered myself this miserable Portrait had been sent to bottom with the Letters by Dr. Waterhouse. I sent it away merely to get it out of my sight, and wished it at bottom an hundred times, but it was accompanied with Letters to my Sisters containing very particular Charges to be locked up. The Letters are sunk. I wish the Portrait in Holland again. But who this *Eliza* is, I don't know. I know not any one of the Name in whose good Graces I am so far initiated, as to do me so much honor as to wear my Portrait, except my dear Sister *Betsy*. Storer says he does not know who the *Eliza* is, and I have concluded that You are not serious. Upon my honor, Madam, if my Letters by Gillon, had arrived, it would have never been worn by anybody. You say, Madam, that "a manly Gesture, a Dignity of Air and Address should have been the distinguishing lines in the Portraiture." In thanking You for the Compliment, You will permit me to observe at the same time, that those Traits would have rendered it still less a Resemblance. Unfortunately they are Accomplishments that do not belong to me, and the Painter was cautious not to flatter me in that Respect. That the fair Circle of my female Acquaintance kindly remember me, is a Circumstance not more flattering than pleasing to me. I never expect to be acquainted with a more amiable, virtuous and sensible Circle. I was ever happy in their Company. To have been ambitious of their Esteem was no fault I hope. It was ever an Object of mine, and in no Instance have I carried this Ambition to an undue length. To seek the Partiality or Affection of a young Lady, merely for the sake of it, and without intending to meet that Affection with an unequivocal proof of Sincerity, is an Object unworthy a Man of Honor and Virtue, and is as unjustifiable in itself, as the means which are often employed to attain this point. 'Tis the Ambition of a Knave, who is hostile to that Confidence and pleasing social Intercourse which Nature and Heaven designed should take place between the Sexes.

I am very happy to learn that our dear and worthy Friend, Mr. Cranch is still in being, but sincerely lament that his Health is yet precarious. May kind Heaven restore him, and be better to Us than our Fears. 'Tis hard parting with so invaluable a Character, with one in the midst of Usefulness. Your Letter concerning him in the *Enterprize* is not yet arrived. 'Tis hardly time to expect her yet.

I have read with extreme satisfaction your Observations occasioned by the Duel between Jackson and Gillon. They are excellent indeed. I have often reflected seriously on this Subject, but I am almost afraid to come to a Conclusion or a Resolution upon it. How extremely difficult is it to recieve with Indifference the Sneers, Contempt and Imputations of Cowardice of the World, even of the base and abandoned part of it. It is a Practice most certainly against Reason and Common Sense, and the trivial ridiculous Incidents that often give rise to it, one would think should have exploded it long ago. 'Tis neither a proof of Bravery, nor is its Issue a Criterion of the Justice of the Cause. The greatest part of Mankind perhaps are agreed in the Folly of its Institution, but yet don't condemn the practice of it, or if they do, they consider him who is challenged as a Coward if he declines. Charity obliges me to say, that I believe a dread and fear of Contempt has induced many a well disposed Man to challenge, or accept one. How much stronger oftentimes is the Sense of this than of the Obligations of Religion or Morality? I have much more to say upon this Subject, considered in the Light of an Appeal to Heaven, and the Absurdity of such an Appeal, but I have not time at present. I cannot justify the Measure, yet it is difficult to foresee the part one would act, (who has his doubts) when called upon. Gustavus Adolphus took the most effectual Way to prevent it—cutting off the Head of the Victor is a short Method.

Your dearest Friend is much better in Health here than at Amsterdam. Dines to day with the *Spanish Minister*, a *great point*—sups this Evening at Court, and tomorrow gives an Entertainment to the French Ambassador and some Members of the States General. *A bad Example this to Us young Lads.* However *Storer and I are two sober Lads, and keep to our Business.* But, Madam, all this and many things which preceeded are Triumphs over British Folly and Impolicy, the Crowns and Laurels of *Patience* and *Perserverance* which he is gathering who most deserves them from his Abilities and Integrity. The Treaty of Commerce will soon be finished I hope—another Triumph. The Resolutions of our States respecting a seperate Peace do them infinite honor in Europe. Oh! perfidious Britain. I would write another Sheet willingly, but should not be in time for the Vessel. Mr. Storer joins me in Respects to You and Family. Remember me as usual if You please. I have the honor to be with an invariable Esteem & Respect, Madam, your M. H. Servant,   J. North

Excuse this Scrall.

RC (Adams Papers).

Abigail Adams to John Adams

My dearest Friend   Sepbr. 5 1782

Your kind favours of May 14th and June 16th came to Hand last Evening; and tho I have only just time to acknowledge them, I would not omit a few lines; I have written before by this vessel; which is Bound to France. Mr. Allen your old fellow traveller is a passenger on Board, and promises to be attentive to the Letters. In my other Letter I mention a serious proposal made in a former; but do not inform you of the Nature of it, fearing a rejection of my proposal and it is of so tender a Nature I could scarcely bear a refusal; yet should a refusal take place, I know it will be upon the best grounds and reasons. But your mention in your two kind favours, your wishes with more seariousness than you have ever before exprest them, leads me again to repeat my request; it is that I may come to you, with our daughter, in the Spring, provided You are like to continue abroad. In my other Letter I have stated to you an arrangement of my affairs, and the person with whom I would chuse to come; I have slightly mentiond it to him; and he says he should like it exceedingly and I believe would adjust his affairs and come with me. Mr. Smith is the person I mean, I mention him least my other Letter should fail.[1]

I am the more desirious to come now I learn Mr. Thaxter is comeing home. I am sure you must feel a still greater want of my attention to you. I will endeavour to find out the disposition of Congress, but I have lost my intelligence from that Quarter by Mr. Lovels return to this State. I have very little acquaintance with any Gentleman there. Mr. Jackson and Mr. Osgood are the only two Members there from this State.[2] Mr. Lovell has lately returnd. I will see him and make some inquiry; as to peace you have my opinion in the Letter referd to by this vessel.

The acknowledgment of our Independance by the United provinces is considerd here as a most important Event, but the Newspapers do not anounce it to the world with that Eclat, which would have been rung from all Quarters had this Event been accomplished by a certain character. Indeed we have never received an official account of it untill now. Let me ask you Dear Friend, have you not been rather neglegent in writing to your Friends? Many difficulties you have had to encounter might have been laid open to them, and your character might have had justice done it. But Modest Merrit must be its own Reward. Bolingbrook in his political tracts observes, rather Ironically (but it is a certain fact,) that Ministers stand in as much need of publick writers, as they do of him. He adds, "in their prosperity they can no more subsist without daily praise, than the writers without daily Bread, and the further the Minister extends his views the more necessary are they to his Support. Let him speak as contemptuously of them as he pleases, yet it will fare with his ambition, as with a lofty Tree, which cannot shoot its Branches into the Clouds unless its Root work into the dirt."

You make no mention of receiving Letters from me, you certainly must have had some by a vessel which arrived in France some time before the Fire Brand reachd Holland. She too had Letters for you.

Accept my acknowledgement for the articles sent. As the other arrived safe, I could have wished my little memorandom by the Fire Brand had reachd you before this vessel saild; but no Matter, I can dispose of them. My Luck is great I think. I know not that I have lost any adventure you have ever sent me. Nabby requests in one of her Letters a pair of paste Buckles. When your hand is in you may send a pair for me if you please.

Adieu my dearest Friend. Remember that to render your situation more agreable I fear neither the Enemy or old Neptune, but then you must give me full assureance of your intire approbation of my request. I cannot accept a half way invitation. To say I am happy here, I cannot, but it is not an idle curiosity that make me wish to hazard the Watery Element. I much more sincerely wish your return. Could I hope for that during an other year I would endeavour to wait patiently the Event.

Once more adieu. The Messenger waits and hurrys me.—Ever Ever yours, Portia

RC (Adams Papers); docketed by CFA: "Portia Septr. 5. 1782."

[1] AA had discussed in more or less detail her thoughts on joining JA abroad in two recent letters that appear above, 5 Aug. (a Dft, of which the RC probably did not reach JA) and 3 Sept.; but the "arrangement of [her] affairs, and the person with whom [she] would chuse to come" are specified in neither. We must therefore suppose either that *another* letter of hers to JA on this subject was sent during the summer but is totally unrecorded, or that the missing RC of her Dft of 5 Aug. *did* add these details.

As for the "Mr. Smith" who was willing to come with her, the best conjecture the editors can make is that he was her cousin William Smith (1755–1816), the young Boston merchant, on whom see above, vol. 3:96; also Adams Genealogy.

[2] Jonathan Jackson and Samuel Osgood (*Biog. Dir. Cong.*).

John Quincy Adams to John Adams

St: Petersbourg
Honoured Sir   August 26. / September 6 1782

Coll. Vallentin having been detained some time at Amsterdam by the arrival of the Grand Duke there, and having been sick on the road, did not arrive with your letters of the 13th. of May last[1] until the day before yesterday.—As to my return; if I can go with a French Courier from Hence as far as Frankfort on the Mayne, and from thence down the Rhine it will be the best course I can take; but if that is impracticable Mr. D[ana] proposes that I should go from hence to Lubeck in some neutral vessel and from thence to Amsterdam by land. I can indeed go directly from hence to Amsterdam by water; but as the season is so far advanced, I might very possibly be obliged to pass the whole winter in Norway or at Copenhagen.

But as soon as I shall be gone Mr. D will write you by the post, to let you know the course I shall have taken so that you will know when to expect me.

I am your dutiful Son,   J.Q.A.

RC (Adams Papers). Early Tr (Adams Papers), in JQA's hand.

[1] JA to JQA, 13 May, above; JA to Dana, 13 May (MHi:Dana Papers).

Isaac Smith Sr. to John Adams

Boston Sept. 7th. 1782

I Yesterday received your long lookt favor being the Only One I have received for two Years.[1] I dont know that I am intitled to any particular Notice, more than many of your friends but thought I might claim some share. I received a letter from Mdm. the Widow Chabenel incloseing some letters to be forwarded to her relations att the southward. Billey lately returnd from Philadelphia were he saw her Nephew that came in the Carolina ship. Any service I can do for any of your friends, shall be readily complyd with.

I have gave Mr. Jer. Allen who goes by this Conveyance a letter from Mrs. Adams since which I have forwarded yours by Grinnel. This Vessell was built in Town, under the direction of Mr. John Peck of the moddle of the Hazard and Bellesarius, but she is too deep loaded to Answer the end of sailing. She is in the room of a french Kings Brig [...][2] condemnd You will have heard of Admiral Vaudrell: lieing here with 13 ships of the line to refit. One of which in coming up through carelesness is got a ground and itts feared will not be got of again.

Whilst now writing I have received another letter from Mrs. Adams which I forward.—Our friend Mr. Cranch is greatly recoverd, contrary to Our expectations.—As to political Affairs itts likely some of your friends more Verst in those matters have wrote you. General Carltons proclimation of Independancy, which was never supposd to be real has turnd Out so. The Continental Armies lay silent.

We are dayly expecting 25 or 30 sail from Jamaica and the Continent. G.W.[3] writes he has some Advises as though designd this way. About 3,000 Troops lately Arrived att Halifax, said to be Hessians &c. from Ireland. We had a Town Meeting Yesterday and came into some spirited resolves in order to stop the Illicit Trade in runing goods into the states from N. York &c.[4] There has lately Two Vessells been taken with about £4000 sterling carried into Rhode Island and Connecticut designed to be smuggeld this way, (all kind of British [goods][5] in Neutral bottoms liable). Several parcels have been seizd in coming on the Road, so that I beleive there will be a stopt put to itt. The Nantucket gentry have been exempted from having Taxes collected, who have in return been carrying on a Neutral trade with New York.

Itts said a ship with Continental Clothing came Out with Grinnel. Itts[6] the most dangerous place on the Continent. I dont think Insurance could be had even att .60 PC. Capt. David Phipps is here a prisoner being taken by the french, (in a cruising ship from Penobscut, he being Comodore there).

Mrs. Smith, Mr. and Mrs. Otis, with all your friends in general are well. Our DC[7] time is chiefly taken up with Accompanying the F[rench] Officers &c.—I am with Respect Your hum. servt.,

I. Smith

RC (Adams Papers).

[1] Letter not found; JA's last recorded letter to Smith is dated 11 March 1781, above.

[2] Illegible word: "Cutter"?

[3] G[eneral] W[ashington]?

[4] See the record of this meeting in Boston Record Commissioner, *Reports*, 26:272–275.

[5] Word editorially supplied.

[6] Thus in MS; place not specified, but probably Boston is meant.

[7] The editors have no explanation for this cryptic expression.

Benjamin Waterhouse to Abigail Adams

Madam   Newport Sepbr. 10th: 1782

When I was at Braintree I mentioned to you that I was pretty certain I had a letter from Mr. Adams to you, among my papers which I left behind at N. York and that when my trunk arrived I would carefully examine it and send it to you. I have done so, but without success. I therefore conclude if there was one, the Goths have taken it.

We hear there is a Vessel arrived at Boston from Amsterdam; if so you undoubtedly have news from Mr. Adams and Mr. Thaxter and as it is possible I may not have a letter, in which case I hope to have some account of them from you. Did you know how much I honor and respect the one, and what friendship and regard I have for the other you would not wonder at my solicitude for their wellfare. Altho' I wish to hear from them *politically*, yet I am more anxious to hear from them *personally*.

Common report would lead one to believe that our prospects of a peace were vanishing. I fear that obstinate, miserable Man, Pharoah the 2d, is not yet sufficiently humbled to do a just thing—and that he will pursue afresh his abominable measures, untill the measure of his iniquity is *quite full*.

Please to present my best respects to your venerable Father—also to Mr. Cranch who I hope is better. My compliments to Dr. Tuffs. My most respectfull Compliments to Miss Adams, not forgetting my good friend Master Charles, who, if you have any good news from his father, will I hope stand scribe to save his Mama the trouble.

I am with every sentiment of respect Madam your most obedient humble servt.,   B. Waterhouse MD

RC (Adams Papers).

John Adams to Abigail Adams

My dearest Friend   Hague Sept. 17 1782

I have transmitted Money to the young Men, whom you mentioned to me, and have expected every day for a long time to hear of their Sailing in a Cartel for America. They have been better treated since the Change of Ministers. My Respects to their Parents.

It is now five Months since my publick Reception here but We have not yet learned, that any News of it, has arrived in America.[1]

7. PIETERSKERK, THE CATHEDRAL CHURCH, LEYDEN
See page xi

8. THE FRENCH EMBASSY ON THE PRINSESSEGRACHT, THE HAGUE, 1764
See page xii

9. VIEW ACROSS THE RAPENBURG TO THE UNIVERSITY, LEYDEN, 1763
See page xii

11. JEAN LUZAC, "THE TERROR OF THE OPPRESSORS,
THE COMFORT OF THE OPPRESSED,"
BY LUDWIG GOTTLIEB PORTMAN
See page xiv

Mr. JOHAN LUZAC.

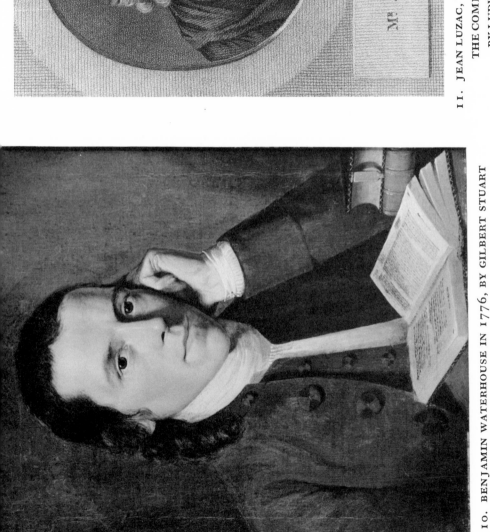

10. BENJAMIN WATERHOUSE IN 1776, BY GILBERT STUART
See page xiii

Nº [.....I

JOHN QUINCY ADAMS

13. JOHN QUINCY ADAMS' FIRST BOOKPLATE, 1781,
HAND-LETTERED AND ENGRAVED
See page xvi

John Thaxter Esqʳ.

The American Society ſhould be glad to
have te honour of your Company at the Supper which ſhe intends to have on Thurſdag
next the 4th of July, at the ſign of de Nieuwe
Stichtſe Herberg, and has the pleaſure to invite
you to that purpoſe, begging to have yr.
affirmative anſwer on this her request.

G. MORING. SMIT.
Secretary.

14. CARD OF INVITATION TO THE "CELEBRATION OF
THE ANNIVERSARY OF INDEPENDENCE" IN
AMSTERDAM, 4 JULY 1782
See page xvi

Nous JOHN ADAMS, Ecuyer, Miniſtre-Plénipotentiaire des
Etats Unis de l'Amérique, auprès de leurs Hautes Puiſſances, les
Etats Généraux des Provinces Unies des Pays-Bas,

Prions tous ceux qui ſont à prier, de vouloir bien laiſſer ſûrement
& librement paſſer   fait

ſans   donner ni permettre qu'il
donné aucun empêchement, mais au contraire de   accorder
toutes ſortes d'aide & d'aſſiſtance, comme Nous ferions en pareil cas,
pour tous ceux qui Nous ſeroient recommandés.

En Foi de Quoi Nous   avons délivré le préſent
Paſſe-port, valable pour   ſigné de notre main,
contreſigné par l'un de nos Secrétaires, & au bas duquel eſt l'em-
preinte de nos armes.

Donné à la Haye, en notre Hôtel, le
mille ſept cent quatre vingt

Par Ordre du Miniſtre Plénipotentiaire,

Gratis

12. PASSPORT FORM BEARING BOYLSTON
ARMS ISSUED BY JOHN ADAMS FOLLOWING
DUTCH RECOGNITION, APRIL 1782
See page xv

The Refugees in England are at their old Game again. Andrew Sparhawk has published in the Morning Post, that his Brother has received a Letter from New York, that Massachusetts and several other States were upon the Point of overturning the new Government, and throwing off the Authority of Congress, and returning to the Government of G. Britain. Their blood thirsty Souls are not yet satiated. They are labouring to bring on again an offensive War. But I think they cant succeed.[2]

I suppose the unhappy Affair of the County of Hampshire, is the Thing which gave Occasion to this Representation.[3] Our Countrymen, must be very unreasonable if they cant be easy and happy under the Government they have. I dont know where they will find a better— or how they will make one. I dread, the Consequences of the Differences between Chiefs.

If Massachusetts gets into Parties, they will worry one another, very rudely. But I rely upon the honesty and Sobriety as well as good sense of the People. These Qualities will overawe the Passions of Individuals, and preserve a Steady Administration of the Laws.

My Duty to my Mother, and to your Father. I hope to see them again. Love to the Children and all Friends. What shall I say of my Brother Cranch? I long and yet I dread to hear from him.

I hope to sign the Treaty, this Week or next or the Week after. All Points are agreed on, and nothing remains but to transcribe the Copies fair. This Government is so complicated, that Months are consumed in doing what might be done in another in an hour.[4]

I dont know what to do with the Lists of Articles you send me. It would be better for you to write to Ingraham & Bromfield. I will pay.

RC (Adams Papers).

[1] Actually, this news, as officially reported by JA, did not reach Congress until just about the time of his inquiry. Secretary Livingston began a letter to JA of 15-18 September with an acknowledgment of the receipt of "your letters from the 19th of April to the 5th of July, by the *Heer Adams*" (Wharton, ed., *Dipl. Corr. Amer. Rev.*, 5:728). This vessel had had a slow voyage and evidently carried duplicates of dispatches JA had sent by earlier ships that had been captured.

[2] These tory communications have not been traced. Others of a similar kind from London papers, enclosed in the following letter, have not been found.

[3] During the preceding months of 1782 there were civil disturbances in the western counties of Massachusetts arising from similar grievances and taking the same forms of protest that the Shays insurrection did a few years later. For the background and a connected narrative of the so-called "Ely riots," see Robert J. Taylor, *Western Massachusetts in the American Revolution*, Providence, 1954, p. 109-120.

[4] The Treaty of Amity and Commerce between the Netherlands and the United States was finally signed on 8 October. See JA's account of the formalities in his *Diary and Autobiography*, 3:16-17, with notes and references there.

John Adams to Abigail Adams

My dearest Friend   Sept. 24. 1782

The Lyars Stick at nothing. The Paragraphs in the enclosed Paper, which respect me, are impudent Forgeries. So far from thinking that the French never meant to treat, I have been long of opinion that the English never meant to treat, and that the French, from the Sincerity of their Desire to treat, have given a too ready Attention to MANEUVRES of the English which have been only insidious Hypocrisies. There have been many other Paragraphs in the London Papers respecting me, equally false, shameless and abominable—and probably will be many more.

You see too, they begin to abuse G. Washington, more than they used to do, for his just Friendship to France.

Billy Walter and the two Sparhawks have made themselves ridiculous enough, by their Attempts to propagate an Opinion, that the Massachusetts was wavering.

It is a long time indeed, since We have any News from America. We have not yet learnd that you had any News of our Acknowledgment here, on the 19 of April, now more than five Months.

Dont be too sanguine in your Expectations of Peace. I see no Probability of it, before 1784. We shall not find it, this Winter. The English will have another Campain, unless there should come from the East and West Indies, North America, and Gibraltar, better News for Us, and more disastrous for them, than I expect.

There is nothing, but their Finances, which will dispose them to Peace, and I fancy, they will find Ways to get Money for one feeble Campain more. I call it feeble for such it must be, with all their Exertions.

We read in the Gazettes of Motions in Poland, and upon the Frontiers of Turkey and Russia, but I dont see a Probability of a War breaking out. If there should, I dont see how it can hurt Us. The English however seem to flatter themselves with Hopes, that by persevering, they may give an Opportunity to Time to ripen into Existence, conjunctures, now only in Embrio. They talk of a different Posture of Things on the Continent, which may cutt out Work, for the Bourbon Family nearer home.[1]

These however are only the Ravings of the Refugees in Dissappointment and Despair. Such Conjunctures are to give Time to England to blott out the Navies of France and Spain, and after that bring

America to Reason. How many Years will this require. And how are their Taxes to be paid and Supplies to be raised?

In short if our Country men are Steady, the British Delusion cannot last much longer. If Americans go to playing Pranks, and furnishing their Ennemies in Europe, especially in England, especially the Refugees, with Arguments, and Hopes, it may be protracted some Years. The People of England is now so much awakened, the American War is so unpopular, and there is so strong a Party for Acknowledging our Independence without Conditions, that a little ill Success would turn the Scale. The Loss of Gibraltar, the Loss of Jamaica, the Loss of a naval Battle, any remarkable Disadvantage in the East Indies, the Loss of the Jamaica or Balic[2] Fleet. The Difference between the State of the English and their Ennemies is this—any unfavourable Event would compleat their Discouragement and unite a Majority in an Acknowledgment of our Independence. Whereas many great Disasters would not induce their Ennemies to give it up.

RC (Adams Papers). Enclosure not found or identified.

[1] On the complex international issues and maneuvers touched on in this paragraph, which indirectly but effectively caused the failure of Dana's mission to the Empress Catherine's court, see the enlightening article by David W. Griffiths, "American Commercial Diplomacy in Russia, 1780–1783, *WMQ*, 3d ser., 27:379–410 (July 1970).

[2] Thus in MS, for "Baltic"?

John Adams to Abigail Adams 2d

My dear Daughter   The Hague, September 26, 1782

I have received your charming letter, which you forgot to date, by Mrs. Rogers.[1] Your proposal of coming to Europe to keep your papa's house and take care of his health, is in a high strain of filial duty and affection, and the idea pleases me much in speculation, but not at all in practice. I have too much tenderness for you, my dear child, to permit you to cross the Atlantic. You know not what it is. If God shall spare me and your brother to return home, which I hope will be next Spring, I never desire to know of any of my family crossing the seas again.

I am glad you have received a small present. You ask for another; and although it would be painful for me to decline the gratification of your inclination, I must confess, I should have been happier if you had asked me for Bell's British Poets.[2] There is more elegance and beauty, more sparkling lustre to my eyes, in one of those volumes, than in all the diamonds which I ever saw about the Princess of Orange, or the Queen of France, in all their birth-day splendour.

I have a similar request under consideration, from your brother at P[etersburg].³ I don't refuse either, but I must take it *ad referendum*,⁴ and deliberate upon it as long as their H[igh] M[ightinesses] do upon my propositions. I have learned caution from them, and you and your brother must learn patience from me.

If you have not yet so exalted sentiments of the public good as have others more advanced in life, you must endeavour to obtain them. They are the primary and most essential branch of general benevolence, and therefore the highest honour and happiness both of men and Christians, and the indispensable duty of both. Malevolence, my dear child, is its own punishment, even in this world. Indifference to the happiness of others must arise from insensibility of heart, or from a selfishness still more contemptible, or rather detestable. But for the same reason that our own individual happiness should not be our only object, that of our relatives, however near or remote, should not; but we should extend our views to as large a circle as our circumstances of birth, fortune, education, rank, and influence extend, in order to do as much good to our fellow men as we can.

You will easily see, my dear child, that jewels and lace can go but a very little way in this career. Knowledge in the head and virtue in the heart, time devoted to study or business, instead of show and pleasure, are the way to be useful and consequently happy.

Your happiness is very near to me. But depend upon it, it is simplicity, not refinement nor elegance [that]⁵ can obtain it. By conquering your taste, (for taste is to be conquered, like unruly appetites and passions, or the mind is undone,) you will save yourself many perplexities and mortifications. There are more thorns sown in the path of human life by vanity, than by any other thing.

I know your disposition to be thoughtful and serene, and therefore I am not apprehensive of your erring much in this way. Yet no body can be guarded too much against it, or too early.

Overwhelmed as I have been ever since you was born, with cares such as seldom fall to the lot of any man, I have not been able to attend to the fortunes of my family. They have no resource but in absolute frugality and incessant industry, which are not only my advice, but my injunctions upon every one of them.

With inexpressible tenderness of heart, I am Your affectionate father,   John Adams

MS not found. Printed from *Journal and Correspondence of Miss Adams,* ... *Edited by Her Daughter,* New York, 1841-[1849], 2:18-20. (Readers may note that this is an altered form of citation for this source. See entry for

AA2, *Jour. and Corr.*, in Short Titles of Works Frequently Cited in the front matter of vol. 3, above.) The textual corrections made by the present editors suggest the general unreliability of Caroline A. de Windt as a transcriber of MSS.

[1] Letter not found, but it is mentioned by AA as enclosed in hers to JA, 17–18 July, above.

[2] *The Poets of Great Britain Complete from Chaucer to Churchill,* issued in London by John Bell beginning in 1777, eventually ran to 109 pocket-sized volumes and was long a standard work. See *DNB* under Bell's name.

[3] JA doubtless wrote "P," which the editor of AA2's *Jour. and Corr.* mistakenly expanded to "Paris."

[4] Mrs. de Windt's rendering of this passage was: "I must take *il ad referendum,*" which is meaningless.

[5] Word supplied by the present editors.

Cotton Tufts to John Adams

Dear Sir   Weymouth Sept. 26. 1782

Yours of July 2d.[1] I received being the first, since you left America. I rejoice at the Success of Your Ministry, but am sorry to hear that Your Constitution has been shock'd by a nervous Fever. Our Friend Mr. Cranch has been in a most critical Scituation. In the close of last Winter, after repeated Colds, he was seized with frequent Faintings. His Perspiration and Expectoration almost entirely Suppressed; a severe Pain in his left Side extending to his shoulder Blade with slight Deliriums and a want of Heat sufficient to give any Vigour to the Circulation came on and threatned him with speedy Dissolution. In this State he lay for some Days, at length he recovered so far as to attend Court in April Sessions. On May the 2d. AM. a Debate of great Importance came on in the House of Representatives, the Room was somewhat crouded, the Members being enjoind not to leave the House; the external Air was warm the Wind being at South and the Air of the Room much more so by the Breath of those present. The Wind changed just before the House broke up to N.E. [and] became cold and damp. By this Change of Air he was soon affected—about 4:00 PM. being then in Court he found himself so unwell as to retire. I found him with all the Symptoms of an approaching Fever. Before the next Morning a large spitting of Blood came on. In a few Hours his old Pain in his Side reaching to the Shoulder Blade, and Danger seem[ed] to be near at hand. However in a fortnight or Three Weeks his Fever somewhat subsided and he recoverd to so much Strength as to return Home tho' in a very languid State and with a low state of Bowells. I soon observed an Enlargement of his Legs which dayly encreased untill his Bowells were greatly distended and a general Anasarcous Swelling appeared. By the Assiduity uncommon Care and judicious Management of his tender Consort and a succesful Operation of medicines, His Health is in a great Measure restored. He is now on a Journey to Haverhill, Newbury Port, Kittery &c. Heaven I trust has reserved both You and Him for further Services and may Gracious Heaven keep You both in Health.

We have suffered much in this State by a severe Drought. The smallest Quantity of Rain has fallen for Three Months, that has been remembered. The Water above the Bridge at the Iron Works in Braintree has been dried up for near Three Weeks. Our Crops of Grass were great. Our English Grain much blasted, and Syberian Wheat almost entirely cut off. Our Indian Corn is estimated at 2/3ds of a common Crop. The Drought was extended as far as Philadelphia at the Southward. It began later than with us. Their Crops of English Grain were very good.

A Medical Society is now established amongst us under the name of the Massachusetts Medical Society, the present President Edward Augustus Holyoke Esq. of Salem.[2] We wish for the Aid and Communication of the Gentlemen of the Faculty in Europe. And as You are acquainted with some of the most eminent, would pray You to mention in your next, some Gentlemen both in France and Holland or elsewhere with their Titles &c. that You should judge would be for the Interest and Honor of the Society to elect as Members.

J[ohn] T[emple] Esq. since his Return to America from his last Tour to England has been questioned with Respect to his Designs &c. Pains were taken to induce the Legislature to make Enquiry into his Conduct. The Legislative Body considered it as belonging to the Executive, the supreme Executive at length directed the State Attorney to take it up, he presented a Bill, the Grand Jury returned Ignoramus, previous to this he had been laid under heavy Bonds, these he requested to be cancelled, still they are detained. At length he petitioned to the General Court that he might be released from his Bonds and have an Opportunity to lay before them Proofs of his Attachment to his Country, the Uprightness of his Intentions, the Services he had done &c. His Petition was sustained—a Committee appointed—they report in his Favour, the Consideration of it however was refered to the next Session after this. J[ames] S[ullivan] Esq. (lately one of the Justices of the Superior Court who not long since resigned his Seat and returnd to the Bar) attacked J.T. charging him with Falsehood, Toryism &c. This brought on a Paper War, which seems to be disagreable to the Friends of both. J.T. supposes his Antagonist to be the Tool of a certain *Great Man* and is not alone in his supposition.

Should he be proved a Tory it would be a favourable Circumstance—to [project?] in the Minds of People a Jealousy against *his Rival*. By the People I mean Populace to secure whom every little Art is to be practised.—After all it is generally thought that the Toryism of J.T. has been nothing more than Don Quixotism.[3]

Sir Guy Carlton and Admiral Digby in a Letter to General Washington Dated Aug. 2d. said to be written in Consequence of Directions from England, write as follows. "We are acquainted Sir by Authority, that Negociations for a general Peace have already commenced at Paris and that Mr. Grenville is invested with full Powers to treat with all the Powers at War and is now at Paris in the Execution of his Commission. And We are further Sir made acquainted that his Majesty in order to remove every Obstacle, to that Peace which he so ardently wishes to restore, has commanded his Ministers to direct Mr. Grenville, that the Independency of the Thirteen Provinces should be proposed by him in the first Instance instead of making it a Condition of a general Treaty; however not without the highest Confidence that the Loyalists shall be restored to their Possessions and a full Compensation made them for whatever Confiscations may have taken Place."—This insidious Letter was published. People in general were amused for a while with the Ideas of a full Acknowledgement of American Independency and a speedy Peace. But the Eyes of People are now generally open, being pretty well satisfied that Carltons Independence is a Dependance on the King and Independance on the Parliament, &c. which is inadmissable with Americans.

On the 10th. of August Marquiss de Vaudreuil arrived here with 14 or 15 Ships of the Line from the West Indies; unfortunately the Magnifique of 74 Guns in entring the Harbour ran a ground near Lovells Island (in the Seamens Phrase) broke her Back and is ruined. Congress informed of this Event, immediately voted to present to Monsr. Lucerne for his most Christian Majesty the America a 74 now laying at Portsmouth, which seems to [be] very pleasing to People and I make no Doubt will be so to the French Nation.[4] Admiral Pigot arrived sometime since at New York from the West Indies with 22 Sail of the Line. We have Accounts from thence of Embarkation, some say of Troops, some of Refugees. Some say the former destined here or to Rhode Island and the Latter to Hallifax. However a more probable Opinion is that they will bend the whole of their Force to the West Indies. Accounts from the Southward inform us that General Leslie has announced to the People of Charlestown S.C. the speedy Evacuation of that Place, and some of the Inhabitants have made Application to be received into the Favour and Protection of their Country in consequence of it.

It gives me great Pleasure that Your Address has baffled the Arts of the British Court and that Your Patience and Perseverance has triumphed over every Opposition to Hollands Acknowledging our own Independence. This is an Event that will raise the Importance of America among the Nations in Europe, will secure her many commercial Advantages and render her Independance *more compleat.* As a Member of the United States I could wish Your Continuance in Europe till the Grand Object of our Wishes was obtained. As a Member of this Commonwealth and as a Friend I wish Your Presence here. Our Policy and Manners &c. are not improved of late Years. Were You to return, Your Talents would find full Exercise. But I must forbear and explain myself hereafter.

Mr. Thaxter would have received a Line with this, did I not suppose him to be on his Voyage here, if he is still with You be pleas'd to present my Regards to him. Your Connections are in Health.

I am Sir with great Respect Yours.

RC (Adams Papers); endorsed: "Dr Tufts Sept 26. 1782."

¹ Not found.

² Cotton Tufts had been active in trying to establish a medical society in Massachusetts as early as 1765. He became one of the incorporators of the Massachusetts Medical Society chartered by the General Court in Nov. 1781. Edward Augustus Holyoke (1728–1829) served as president from 1782 to 1784. See Walter L. Burrage, *A History of the Massachusetts Medical Society ... 1781–1922,* privately printed, 1923, p. 5–7, 16–17, 462.

³ The controversy over John Temple's patriotism or toryism, touched on above in Richard Cranch to JA, 30 Oct. 1781 (see note 2 there), had been renewed with great virulence in 1782. The "Paper War" was principally between Temple and James Sullivan (1740–1808), Harvard 1762, a partisan of John Hancock ("a certain Great Man"), whose "Rival" was Temple's father-in-law, James Bowdoin. See Thomas C. Amory, *Life of James Sullivan,* Boston, 1859, 1:134–138; 2:388; Sibley-Shipton, *Harvard Graduates,* 15:305.

⁴ The ship presented was the *America,* just completed at Portsmouth (*Dict. Amer. Fighting Ships,* 1:40).

John Quincy Adams to John Thaxter

Sir   St. Petersbourg Septr. 27th. 1782

I received a few days agone your favour of the 14th. of August. You say you have had a Fire for several days. I believe there has not been a week together through the whole summer without our having one. For some flakes of Snow fell, one morning in the middle of July. It is true, this has been an Extraordinary summer, but it freezes every year in the month of August here: and sometimes in the month of

June. I think upon the whole that the climate of Holland is the most agreable of the two.

I am afraid I shall not have the pleasure of seeing you before you return to America. The season is at present too far advanced to think of going by water, and I believe I shall not be able to get away from here before the snow comes, so that I shall probably not arrive before the latter end of January, in Holland.

Mr. D[ana] desires me to tell you that he has receiv'd your letter; and does not answer it because, as he has heard that the treaty is signed; you will perhaps be gone before the letter would reach you: and because he is at present indisposed: he desires you would send him a copy of the Treaty if possible, and that you would let him know whether you have bought him a scrutoire. If so he begs you would put all his papers in it but send nothing forward, for he says he expects to set of himself in the month of May.

Permit me to reiterate the assurance of my best wishes for your safe return to our dear country, and believe me to be Sir Your most obedient humble servant.

LbC (Adams Papers).

Abigail Adams 2d to Elizabeth Cranch

My Dear Eliza   *[Braintree, September 1782]*

Mr. Robbins[1] dined with us to day and has just now told me he intends to make you a vis this afternoon. I hope he will find you quite recovered, and wish you were to return with him. I shall want the pleasure of your company a Wedensy very much—and wish I could offer a sufficient inducement for you to return, tomorrow or next day. I know of nothing to write that will either amuse or give you pleasure. My head is quite barren, my heart is warm. Could you look there you would find it full of good wishes for your health, happiness and pleasure. You are pleased with your visit I know, I wish I was with you. My good my amiable aunt is doing every thing to amuse you, her endeavours will not fail of suckcess I dare say—I hope the dignity of my Eliza will have a good affect upon her cousin.[2] If he knew that his conduct was exaggerated much, and heard the speach of every one, I think he woul[d] never have given the cause—but—I can say nothing in vindication of him. You are expected at Milton this week. I dont know how the disappointment will be survived—by—the good folks—whose hearts beat with expectation—for the approach of—Miss

—— C[ranc]h. I want to say something to you, to provoke you to answer this, if my wishes will not induce you to write me. Five letters in three days and not one line, or one thought, of Amelia. It is mortifiing Betsy how shall I help it. Do as you aught, Miss, says yourself and you will be thought of.—Ah—ah—ah—ah.—I am going to write to Miss Watson; have you aney thing to say to her. Mr. T——r[3] goes tomorrow morning. Adieu my Dear I will release you from aney more nonsence, by subscribing your friend, Amelia

I open my letter to tell you I dreamed a dream last night and had the pleasing idea of our friend T——s[4] return but alas twas a false vision.—My Brother Charles is unwell.

RC (MHi:Cranch Papers); addressed: "Miss Eliza Cranch Weymouth per by Mr Robbins"; endorsed: "AA Septembre 1782." Minimal corrections of punctuation have been made, but they have not resolved all of AA2's girlish ambiguities.

[1] Chandler Robbins of Plymouth, who had graduated from Harvard in July, had been engaged as tutor for CA and TBA after Thomas Perkins' departure; see AA to JA, 17–18 July, above; AA to John Thaxter, 26 Oct. 1782 (MB).

[2] Which "aunt" and male "cousin" at Weymouth these may be is not clear.

[3] Possibly Royall Tyler, although it does not seem likely that AA2 would at this point entrust him with letters to her friends.

[4] Doubtless John Thaxter.

Appendix

A NOTE ON CITATIONS IN THE APPENDIX

In the Appendix, minimal information is included in the notes to identify letters which are printed in *Adams Family Correspondence*, volumes 3 and 4. Full information as to location and printings of *other* letters or documents cited in the Appendix is supplied at the point of first reference. Thereafter, only sender, recipient, and date are given.

Appendix

THE LOVELL CIPHER AND ITS DERIVATIVES

The earliest instance so far located in the Adams Papers in which a passage in cipher appears is in a letter from James Lovell to JA of 14 Dec. 1780, a copy of which (also in the Adams Papers) Lovell enclosed in his letter to AA of 19 December.[1] The presumption raised by the absence of any accompanying key or explanation that there had been some earlier communication in reference to the cipher, and perhaps use of it, is borne out by two letters of Lovell written six months before.[2] In the letter to JA, Lovell had written that the cipher was one which had already been "communicated to Doctr. Franklin and which will serve great numbers with equal safety." Lovell's letter to AA informed her that the cipher was being communicated to her both for her own use in letters to JA and so that she would be able to decode letters written to her in it. No instances have been found in the Adams Papers in which JA or AA employed the cipher them-selves, and both continued to experience difficulty in decoding it.

A reluctance to employ the cipher and even to attempt to decode it is attributable to an aversion or hostility to the clandestine implica-tions and attendant ambiguities of secret writing. AA had been clear on the point, and associated her husband with her view, in declining to give her attention to the cipher proffered by Lovell: "I . . . thank you for your alphabeticall cipher tho I believe I shall never make use of it. I hate a *cipher* of any kind and have been so much more used to deal in realities with those I love, that I should make a miserable proficiency in modes and figures. Besides my Friend is no adept in investigating ciphers and hates to be puzzeld for a meaning."[3]

AA, however, with time became "more reconciled to ambiguity and ciphers, than formerly"[4] when confronted by repeated instances of intercepted letters and by Lovell's affirmation in his letter of 19 Dec. 1780 that information of importance to JA and to her was being denied her because Lovell judged it safe to communicate it only in

[1] P. 36, above.
[2] To JA, 4 May; to AA, post 4 May 1780, both in Adams Papers.
[3] To Lovell, 11 June 1780, vol. 3:363, above.
[4] To same, 3 Jan. 1781, p. 57, above.

code: "If you had not bantered me so more than once about my generally-enigmatic manner, and appeared so averse to cyphers I would have long ago enabled you to tell Mr. A some Things which you have most probably omitted, as well as to satisfy your Eve on the present Occasion."[5]

Lovell responded to the modification in AA's dislike of ciphers "from the necessity of them" by enclosing another "Alphabet [i.e. key] for your use" in his letter to her of 30 Jan. 1781.[6] Some months afterward, when faced with the cipher in a letter, she managed to read it with substantial help from Richard Cranch.[7] Much later, upon having sight, through Lovell, of JA's letter of 21 Feb. 1782 to Secretary Livingston,[8] and learning from it that JA continued to be unable to crack the code, AA undertook to induct her "dearest Friend" into its mysteries, reporting, "I have always been fortunate enough to succeed with it."[9]

Lovell seems to have been the deviser of the cipher, which he employed in writing to Franklin, to Dana, and to others, as well as to the Adamses. At least it was called "M. Lovell's Cypher," and Edmund Randolph and Madison acknowledged him as their instructor. The cipher's first recorded use was in a letter from Lovell to Horatio Gates, 1 March 1779; it had currency at least until 1784 in private communications among those in government, and seems to have been at least informally adopted for official use.[10] The President of Congress, Samuel Huntington, wrote to JA in the cipher, as did R. R. Livingston after he became Secretary for Foreign Affairs.[11] There were variations of Lovell's cipher, other than changes in the key-word, in use among America's representatives abroad. Dumas employed one with which Franklin was familiar, and Francis Dana sent a more complicated system based upon the same principles as Lovell's to JA from Russia.[12]

Lovell's cipher was of the type built upon the substitution of numerical equivalents for agreed-upon letters from a key-word or phrase.

[5] P. 36, above.

[6] Adams Papers. The new key is not now, however, with Lovell's letter.

[7] Lovell to AA, 26 June 1781, p. 163, above; the undated fragmentary sheet containing Cranch's efforts to decode the ciphered passages is illustrated in the present volume.

[8] LbC, Adams Papers; printed in JA, *Works*, 7:521–530; Wharton, ed., *Dipl. Corr. Amer. Rev.*, 5:192–199.

[9] To JA, 17 June 1782, p. 327, above.

[10] Franklin to Dana, 2 March 1781, Adams Papers; Edmund C. Burnett, "Ciphers of the Revolutionary Period," *AHR*, 22:331 (Jan. 1917); Jefferson, *Papers*, ed. Boyd, 7:149, 237, 451.

[11] 5 July, 20 Nov. 1781, both in Adams Papers; Livingston's letter is printed without indication that passages are in cipher in Wharton, ed., *Dipl. Corr. Amer. Rev.*, 4:849–851.

[12] Livingston to JA, 26 Dec. 1781, Adams Papers, printed in Wharton, 5:73–74; Dana to JA, 18 Oct. 1782, Adams Papers.

Each of the letters adopted for use served in turn as the initial element in alphabets arranged on a sheet in parallel vertical columns. A column of corresponding numbers placed alongside these columns of alphabets provided the equivalents for the letters of encoded words, the substitutions being made alternately from two alphabets, or if more than two then in strict rotation, forward or backward as desired. Since the alphabets normally included the ampersand as a final element, the numbers used in substitution were from 1 to 27. In the cipher's purest form the numbers 28 and 29 were used at the beginning of a passage as indication that the substitutions were being made in the normal or in a reverse order, and the number 30 was used as a blind. However, more frequently all three numbers (28–30) served as blinds. Any uncoded word or words broke the continuity, the next succeeding coded passage beginning with that alphabet used at the outset of the first encoded passage, unless 28 or 29 signaled reversal.

The key letters which Lovell used and instructed others to use in communications with JA, Franklin, and Dana were the letters *c* and *r*, which he derived from and clued to (at least for JA) the name *Cranch*. In writing to Elbridge Gerry, Lovell used as key letters *e* and *o*, representing the second and third letters "of the maiden Name of the Wife of that Gentleman from whom I sent you a Little Money on a Lottery Score." [13] Other keys, all employing more than two alphabets, were used in ciphers of the same type by Madison and Randolph (*Cupid*), Jefferson and William Short (*Nicholas*), and Lovell with other correspondents. [14]

The difficulties in decoding experienced by JA, as well as by Franklin and Dana, can be attributed in part to their receiving instruction in the cipher exclusively from a distance. What was easy for domestic users by explanation and demonstration close at hand proved formidable when communicated by mail, which had to conceal as well as explain. This may account for Lovell's adopting for his tutees abroad a simplified form of the cipher in which only two letters were used as the key.

A more serious hazard was that Lovell, the expositor, was gifted with neither precision nor lucidity, and having once formulated his directions, was given more to repetition and even playful variation than to real clarification. Lovell was frequently chided, particularly by AA, for his natural bent toward obfuscation: "If Mr. L——l will

[13] 5 June 1781, MHi:Gerry-Knight Collection. Other examples of the cipher in the same collection are in letters from Lovell of 17 June, 13 July 1781. [14] Burnett, *AHR*, 22:331.

not call me Sausy I will tell him he has not the least occasion to make use of them [ciphers] himself since he commonly writes so much in the enigmatical way that nobody but his particular correspondents will ever find out his meaning." She followed this statement with a sentence she decided not to include in the recipient's copy, attributing to JA similar sentiments about Lovell's style: "I have seen my friend sometimes rub his forehead upon the receipt of a Letter, walk the room — What does this Man mean? who can find out his meaning." [15]

Lovell's first instructions to JA, communicated in May 1780, were that the "Mode . . . is the Alphabet squared . . . and the key Letters are the two first of the Surname of the Family where you and I spent the Evening together before we set out from your House on our Way to Baltimore. . . . Make use of any of the perpendicular columns according to your key Letters." To this he appended a vertical column of numbers, 1–27, a second alphabetical parallel column beginning with *a* and ending with &, a third and fourth column beginning with *b* and *c* respectively and carried only through the fourth letter, the rest of the "Alphabet squared" indicated by dots of elision. Aside from indicating that the key letters or key-word could be altered at will and suggesting the means to communicate the new key, there was nothing more. Explaining the cipher just afterward to AA, Lovell, less fearful of interception, added no help beyond using for his illustrative columns two alphabets in which the first letters were *c* and *r*. When AA six months later asked for help, he responded only by enclosing the same two alphabetical columns. [16] His instructions to Franklin in Paris, which Franklin on request sent to Dana, differed in no essential, concentrating on the selection of the key-word or letters. [17] Not until June 1781, when he wrote to JA, "I suspect that you did not before understand it from my not having said supped *in Braintree*," did he undertake clarification. This time his column of numbers extended to 30, the numbers 28, 29, and 30 "to be used as Baulks in the Beginning and End or within your Words"; and apparently for the

---

[15] To Lovell, 11 June 1780, Dft, vol. 3:363, above. The Adamses' judgment of Lovell's deficiencies is amusingly echoed by CFA when in arranging the family's papers he came to read Lovell's letters: "A man whose situation gave his letters unusual interest. Yet he is so crackbrained that his prose is hardly intelligible and his cypher utterly unreadable. This is a great pity. Such half disclosures of the course of things are worse than none at all" (Diary, entry for 3 Jan. 1835).

[16] 30 Jan. 1781, Adams Papers. It should be noted, however, that at the end of his letter to AA of 8 Jan. he said flat out, without alluding to cipher or key: "This Evening four Years [ago] I passed with you at your Brother Cranche's" (above, p. 63).

[17] Franklin to Dana, 2 March 1781.

first time explained the "rule of Sequence": "Make 2 *Columns* of Letters. . . . Begin your 1st Column with the first letter and your second Column with the 2d letter of the Family Name formerly referred to. Go on to &, then follow *a b* &c. &c. &c. Look *alternately* into the Columns." [18] When Secretary Livingston unhappily concluded that JA had not understood his earlier letters in cipher, written without awareness of the difficulty, he had Lovell enclose still another explanation: "You are to form Alphabets equal in number and of the same commencement and Range, as the Letters of the *first* sixth part of the family Name where you and I supped last with Mrs. Adams, and you are to look alternately into these constructed Alphabets opposite to my figures, for the Elements to spell with, some figures however I may have used as Baulks." [19] Nearly a year later Lovell tried again, but in the same language.[20] Livingston, meanwhile, had apparently decided to resolve the problem by adopting a different cipher: "I am sorry for the difficulty the cypher occasions you, it was one I found in the Office, and is very incomplete. I enclose one that you will find easy in the practice, and will therefore write with freedom." [21] AA, during the same period, in a brave but misguided moment had decided to try her hand at explaining: "Take the two Letters for which the figure stands and place one under the other through the whole Sentance, and then try the upper Line with the under, or the under with the upper, always remembering, if one letter answers, that directly above or below must be omitted, and sometimes several must be skiped over." [22]

More than two years after his first attempt at explication, Lovell wrote to JA: "I have not to this day Information that you comprehend the Cypher which I have very often used in my Letters." [23] Livingston, noting JA's lack of response, concluded earlier that JA did not comprehend "the cyphers. . . . I had them from the late committee of foreign affairs, tho' they say they never received any letters from you in them." [24] JA's own allusions to the cipher not only confirm fully the doubts felt in Philadelphia, but also convey an unconcern that must have had an effect there: "Your Plan of a Cypher I cannot comprehend—nor can Dr. F. his"; [25] "I have Letters from the President and

[18] 21 June 1781, Adams Papers; printed in Burnett, ed., *Letters of Members*, 6:124–125.

[19] Livingston to JA, 26 Dec. 1781, with enclosure of same date signed by Lovell and attested by L. R. Morris, Secy., "By Order Mr. Livingston," Adams Papers.

[20] To JA, 30 Nov. 1782, Adams Papers.

[21] To JA, 30 May 1782, Adams Papers; printed in Wharton, ed., *Dipl. Corr. Amer. Rev.*, 5:459–460.

[22] To JA, 17 June, p. 327, above.

[23] 30 Nov. 1782.

[24] To JA, 26 Dec. 1781.

[25] To Lovell, 24 June 1780, LbC, Adams Papers.

from Lovell, the last unintelligible, in Cyphers, but inexplicable by his own Cypher—some dismal Ditty about my Letters of 26th July—I know not what."[26] "I am on this Occasion as on all others hitherto utterly unable to comprehend the Sense of the Passages in Cypher. . . . I have been able sometimes to decypher Words enough to show, that I have the Letters right; but upon the whole I can make nothing of it, which I regret very much upon this Occasion, as I suppose the Cyphers are a very material part of your letter."[27]

The frustrations attendant upon the efforts of Congress' committee and of the Secretary for Foreign Affairs to have their representatives abroad master and use the cipher derived not from JA alone. Almost a year after JA reported Franklin's inability to comprehend it, Franklin himself wrote to Dana, "If you can find the Key and decypher it, I shall be glad, having myself try'd in vain."[28] Dana, in turn, seems to have had his own difficulties. To him Livingston wrote, "I need not tell you how impatient I shall be to hear that this has reached you, since I cannot use my cipher, till I receive a line from you written in it, nor can I write with freedom to you, till I have a cipher."[29]

As for JA, while it is true that he gave an impression of insouciance in reporting his inability to comprehend the encoded messages, evidence exists that he made some effort to master Lovell's instructions. To Lovell's iteration of the clue to the key letters as the source of his difficulties, JA, with asperity, wrote, "I know very well the Name of the Family where I spent the Evening with my worthy Friend Mr.—— before We set off, and have made my Alphabet accordingly. . . . The Cypher is certainly not taken regularly under the two first Letters of that Name."[30] In the Adams Papers in JA's handwriting and endorsed "cypher" by him, undated, is a complete "Alphabet squared" with a vertical numerical column, 1–27, at left. The square is without indication that the columns in which *c* and *r* are the initial letters are more important than any others. A second attempt in JA's hand, also surviving in the Papers, and illustrated in the present volume, suggests one reason why he remained unenlightened. Across the top of the sheet is an alphabet including the ampersand, at the left is a vertical column of numbers, 1–30, paralleled by three columns of alphabets with initial letters *a*, *c*, and *r*. Failing to understand or to heed

[26] To Dana, 12 March 1781, LbC, Adams Papers; printed in JA, *Works*, 7:377–378; Wharton, ed., *Dipl. Corr. Amer. Rev.*, 4:284–285.

[27] To Livingston, 21 Feb. 1782.

[28] 2 March 1781. Franklin did, how-ever, in the same letter write correctly two short passages in the cipher.

[29] To Dana, 10 May 1782, in Wharton, ed., *Dipl. Corr. Amer. Rev.*, 5:411–414.

[30] To Livingston, 21 Feb. 1782.

Lovell's belated explanation that the numbers 28–30 were "baulks," JA utilizes these numbers in the *c* and *r* columns to begin a new alphabetical cycle. Thus, in the one column the equivalent of *c* is not only *1* but *28*, that of *d* is *2* and *29*, of *e*, *3* and *30*; in the second column the same holds true for *r*, *s*, and *t*. The application of such a system to the material in code could only produce results unsatisfactory to all.

A further account of the kinds of difficulties that recipients experienced in decoding the Lovell cipher is presented in the Descriptive List of Illustrations in the present volume, Nos. 3 and 4. The discussion there should be read in conjunction with what has been developed here, and the pertinent facsimile illustrations themselves examined.

Examples of other ciphers constructed on systems other than numerical substitution do exist in the Adams Papers. On the various types in use during the Revolutionary period, the discussions of the subject by Burnett and Boyd should be consulted.[31]

[31] *AHR*, 22:329–334; Jefferson, *Papers*, ed. Boyd, 6:x–xi.

Chronology

Chronology

THE ADAMS FAMILY, 1761–1782

N.B. This is the first Chronology to appear in the *Adams Family Correspondence* and covers vols. 1–4. See Introduction, 3:xxxviii–xxxix.

1761

Feb.: John Adams (JA) records arguments in Superior Court of Judicature on writs of assistance (Petition of Lechmere).

May: Upon the death of his father, JA inherits Braintree property (later known as the John Quincy Adams Birthplace).

Nov.: JA admitted to practice in the Superior Court of Judicature.

1762

Spring: JA begins serving on town committees and traveling the Inferior and Superior Court circuits. His circuit riding continues for fourteen years.

Aug.: JA admitted barrister in the Superior Court of Judicature.

Oct.: Courtship correspondence of JA and Abigail, daughter of Rev. William Smith of Weymouth, begins.

1763

Feb.: Treaty of Paris concluded, by which France cedes Canada, and Spain cedes the Floridas, to Great Britain.

March: JA's first known newspaper contribution, signed "Humphrey Ploughjogger," is published in the *Boston Evening Post.*

1764

Feb.: Beginning of smallpox epidemic in Boston which was to last throughout the year.

April–May: JA inoculated in Boston for the smallpox, conducting almost daily correspondence with his fiancée at Weymouth.

Oct. 25: JA and Abigail Smith (AA) marry and make their home in the house inherited from JA's father.

1765

Jan.: JA joins a lawyers' "sodality" in Boston for the study of legal history and theory.

March: JA elected surveyor of highways in Braintree.

March: Stamp Act passed by the British Parliament; repealed in March 1766, but repeal is accompanied by the Declaratory Act.

June: JA travels the eastern court circuit to Maine for the first time.

July 14: Abigail (AA2), 1st daughter and eldest child of JA and AA, is born at Braintree.

Aug.–Oct.: JA publishes "A Dissertation on the Canon and the Feudal Law" in installments in the *Boston Gazette.*

Sept.: JA composes the Braintree Instructions denouncing the Stamp Act.

Dec.: JA named of counsel for Boston to plead for reopening of the courts.

1766

March: JA elected a Braintree selectman.

July: JA becomes active in the improvement of professional practice of the law through the Suffolk bar association.

Aug.: Benjamin Blyth executes portraits of JA and AA.

1767

July 11: John Quincy (JQA), 1st son of JA and AA, is born at Braintree.

1768

April: The Adamses move to the "White House" in Brattle Square, Boston.

June: JA writes instructions for the Boston representatives to the General Court protesting the seizure of John Hancock's sloop *Liberty*. Later in the year he successfully defends Hancock in admiralty court against charges of smuggling in connection with the *Liberty.*

Sept.: British troops arrive in Boston Harbor to control resistance to Townshend Act duties, which are repealed, except for the tax on tea, in 1769.

Dec. 28: Susanna (d. 4 Feb. 1770), 2d daughter of JA and AA, is born in Boston.

1769

Spring: The Adamses move to Cole (or Cold) Lane, Boston.

May: JA writes instructions for the Boston representatives to the General Court protesting the presence of British troops and the growing power of admiralty courts.

May–June: JA successfully defends Michael Corbet and three other sailors in admiralty court for the killing of Lt. Henry Panton of the British Navy.

1770

March: JA agrees to defend Capt. Thomas Preston and the British soldiers involved in the "Boston Massacre."

May 29: Charles (CA), 2d son of JA and AA, is born in Braintree.

June: JA elected a representative to the General Court from Boston; serves until April 1771.

Oct.–Nov.: JA successfully defends Preston and the soldiers in the "Boston Massacre" trials.

The Adamses move during this year to "another House in Brattle Square."

1771

April: The Adamses move back to Braintree.

June: JA travels to Connecticut for his health and takes the mineral waters at Stafford Springs.

1772

Sept. 15: Thomas Boylston (TBA), 3d son of JA and AA, is born in Braintree.

Nov.: The Adamses move to Queen Street (later Court Street) in Boston, and JA maintains his law office there until the outbreak of hostilities.

1773

Jan.–Feb.: JA publishes articles in the *Boston Gazette* answering William Brattle and opposing crown salaries to Superior Court judges.

May: JA elected by the House a member of the Massachusetts Council but is negatived by Gov. Thomas Hutchinson.

Dec. 16: Boston Tea Party.

1774

Feb.: JA buys his father's homestead (later known as the John Adams Birthplace) from his brother Peter Boylston Adams.

March: JA furnishes legal authorities for impeachment proceedings against Chief Justice Peter Oliver.

March: Boston Port Act passed by Parliament, closing port of Boston in June.

May: JA elected by the House a member of the Council but is negatived by Gov. Thomas Gage.

June: JA elected a Massachusetts delegate to the Continental Congress. The family returns to Braintree.

June–July: JA travels "for the tenth and last time on the Eastern Circuit" in Maine, and parts with his loyalist friend Jonathan Sewall at Falmouth.

Aug.: JA travels from Boston to Philadelphia with the Massachusetts delegation to the Continental Congress.

Sept.–Oct.: JA attends first Continental Congress.

Oct.–Nov.: JA returns from Philadelphia to Braintree.

Nov.–Dec.: JA attends first Provincial Congress in Cambridge as a member from Braintree.

Dec.: JA reelected to the Continental Congress.

1775

Jan.–April: JA publishes essays signed "Novanglus" in *Boston Gazette* in answer to Daniel Leonard's "Massachusettensis" articles.

April 19: Lexington and Concord fights; first blood of the Revolution is spilled.

April–May: JA travels from Braintree to the Continental Congress in Philadelphia.

May: Colonial forces lay siege to British army in Boston, now under the command of Howe and Clinton.

May–July: JA attends second Continental Congress; makes first proposal of Washington as commander in chief of a Continental Army.

June 17: AA and JQA watch Bunker Hill battle from Penn's Hill above their house.

July 3: Washington takes command of Continental forces at Cambridge. AA conveys a high opinion of him to JA in a letter of 16 July.

July: JA elected by the House a member of the Council; resigns in April 1776.

July: JA writes letters to AA and James Warren ridiculing John Dickinson's conciliatory views; the letters are intercepted and published by the British in August and produce a lasting sensation that promotes the idea of independence.

Aug.: JA returns from Philadelphia to Braintree, attends the Massachusetts Council in Watertown, and is reelected to the Continental Congress.

Aug.–Sept.: JA travels from Boston to the Continental Congress in Philadelphia.

Late summer and fall: Dysentery epidemic in Boston; JA's brother Elihu dies in camp in August, and AA's mother dies October 1.

Sept.–Dec.: JA attends the Continental Congress and plays a principal part in the measures leading to the establishment of an American navy.

Oct.: JA appointed Chief Justice of Massachusetts; resigns in Feb. 1777 without ever serving.

Dec.: JA obtains leave from Congress and returns from Philadelphia to Braintree, attends the Massachusetts Council in Watertown, visits the army headquarters in Cambridge, and is reelected to the Continental Congress.

1776

Jan.: JA drafts for the General Court a proclamation to be read at the opening of courts of justice and town meetings.

Jan.–Feb.: JA travels from Braintree to the Continental Congress in Philadelphia.

Feb.–Oct.: JA attends the Continental Congress.

March 17: The British evacuate Boston.

March–April: After reading Paine's *Common Sense*, JA writes *Thoughts on Government*, published anonymously.

Spring and summer: Smallpox epidemic in Boston.

May: JA advocates establishment of new state governments and writes preamble to the resolution of 15 May recommending such action to the states.

June: JA appointed president of the newly formed Continental Board of War and Ordnance.

June–July: JA appointed to committee to draft a declaration of independence and makes the principal speech in favor of the resolution for independence, adopted on 2 July, followed by adoption of the Declaration of Independence, 4 July.

June–Sept.: JA drafts a "Plan of Treaties" and instructions to the first American Commissioners to France.

July: AA and children inoculated for smallpox.

Sept.: JA journeys to Staten Island with Benjamin Franklin and Edward Rutledge as a committee of Congress to confer with Admiral Lord Howe.

Oct.: JA obtains leave from Congress and returns from Philadelphia to Braintree.

Nov.: JA reelected to the Continental Congress.

1777

Jan.: JA travels from Braintree to attend the Continental Congress sitting in Baltimore.

March: JA travels to Philadelphia when Congress adjourns to that city.

July 11: AA gives birth to a stillborn daughter, Elizabeth.

Aug.: Beginning of correspondence between AA and James Lovell, a Massachusetts delegate to the Continental Congress; the correspondence continues with growing frequency and intimacy through early 1782, when Lovell leaves Congress.

Sept.: JA leaves Philadelphia upon the adjournment of Congress after the American defeat at Brandywine Creek, and travels to York, Penna., where Congress reconvenes.

Oct. 16: Burgoyne surrenders his northern army to the American forces under Gates at Saratoga.

Nov.: JA obtains leave from Congress, returns to Braintree, and resumes his law practice, traveling to Portsmouth in December to defend the owners of the *Lusanna*. He there learns he has been elected by Congress a joint commissioner (with Franklin and Arthur Lee) to France, replacing Silas Deane.

1778

Feb. 6: Treaties of alliance and of amity and commerce between France and the United States signed at Versailles.

Feb.–March: JA and JQA sail from Quincy Bay aboard the Continental frigate *Boston*, Capt. Samuel Tucker, to Bordeaux.

April: JA and JQA join Franklin's household at the Hôtel de Valentinois in Passy; JA begins his efforts to put the affairs of the American joint mission on a businesslike footing. His personal tensions with Franklin begin.

April: JQA enters M. Le Coeur's *pension* academy in Passy.

May: JA has his first audience with Louis XVI at Versailles.

Sept.: Joint commission dissolved and Franklin named sole minister to France.

Dec.: AA2 makes extended visit to the James Warrens in Plymouth, not returning to Braintree until May 1779.

1779

Jan.: AA writes to a member of the Continental Congress severely criticizing Silas Deane's controversial address in defense of his conduct in France.

March: JA takes leave of the French court.

March–June: JA, accompanied by JQA, in Nantes, Brest, Lorient, Saint Nazaire, and on board the *Alliance* arranging for the exchange of prisoners of war and awaiting passage to America.

April: JA makes acquaintance with the Joshua Johnson family at Lorient, perhaps providing JQA with the opportunity of meeting Louisa Catherine Johnson (later his wife, LCA), then aged four.

April: By secret treaty Spain becomes a co-belligerent with France in the war against England.

June–Aug.: JA and JQA sail from Lorient to Boston with the Chevalier de La Luzerne, French minister to the United States, aboard the French frigate *La Sensible*, arriving home on 3 August.

Aug.: JA proposes founding the American Academy of Arts and Sciences, incorporated May 1780.

Aug.–Nov.: JA elected to represent Braintree in convention to frame a new state constitution; attends the convention and drafts *The Report of a Constitution . . . for the Commonwealth of Massachusetts*, which is adopted, after alterations, by the convention and by the towns of Massachusetts in June 1780.

Sept.: JA elected minister by Congress with sole powers to negotiate treaties of peace and commerce with Great Britain; commissions revoked June–July 1781.

Nov.–Dec.: JA, JQA, and CA, accompanied by John Thaxter as JA's private secretary, sail from Boston aboard *La Sensible* to El Ferrol, Spain.

Dec.–Jan.: The Adams party travels across northern Spain. From Bilbao JA sends the first of his consignments of European goods to AA, of which a number more were to follow from time to time from mercantile firms in Spain, France, and the Netherlands.

1780

Jan.–Feb.: The Adams party travels from Bayonne to Paris and takes up residence at the Hôtel de Valois in Rue de Richelieu.

Feb.: JQA and CA enter an academy in Passy conducted by M. Pechigny.

Feb.–March: Russian Declaration of Armed Neutrality at sea, aimed at Great Britain and later joined by various northern powers; it eventually proves ineffective.

May 19: A meteorological phenomenon occurs in New England: "the Dark Day."

Spring and summer: The correspondence between JA and the Comte de Vergennes on such topics as the former's announcing his mission, Congress' devaluation of Continental currency, and French naval strategy in American waters leads to an open breach between them.

June: JA commissioned an agent by Congress to negotiate a Dutch loan.

July–Aug.: Accompanied by his sons, JA travels from Paris to Amsterdam, before learning of his commission, to explore the possibility of Dutch financial aid to the United States.

Aug.–Nov.: JQA and CA attend the Latin School on the Singel in Amsterdam. They are withdrawn when JQA proves insubordinate.

Oct.: Treason of Benedict Arnold. Capture of Henry Laurens, with incriminating papers, at sea.

Dec.: Francis Dana elected by Congress American minister to Russia; he proceeds there in 1781 but is never officially recognized.

Dec.–Jan.: JA elected minister by Congress, in the place of Henry Laurens, to negotiate a treaty of amity and commerce with the Netherlands.

1781

Jan.: JQA, CA, and John Thaxter matriculate as students at the University of Leyden through arrangements made by Benjamin Waterhouse.

Jan.–Feb.: Great Britain begins hostilities against the Netherlands, using the captured papers of Henry Laurens as a pretext.

March: Maryland's ratification of the Articles of Confederation, adopted by Congress in 1777, makes the confederation of American states complete.

March–May: JA drafts, submits, and prints a *Memorial to the States-General* urging Dutch recognition of American sovereignty.

April: JA rents and furnishes a house on the Keizersgracht in Amsterdam. CA, because of illness and homesickness, leaves Leyden and comes to live with his father.

April: AA makes plans to buy land in Vermont and in the following year does so.

May: James and Mercy Otis Warren and their family move to Milton, occupying former Governor Hutchinson's house on Neponset Hill and thus becoming neighbors of AA.

June: JA elected by Congress first among five joint commissioners (JA, Franklin, Jay, Laurens, and Jefferson) to treat for peace with Great Britain. Their instructions make them strictly dependent on French advice and approval.

June: Austrian and Russian courts offer their services as mediators between the belligerents.

July: JA returns to Paris to discuss with Vergennes the proposed mediation of the Austrian and Russian courts; rejects Vergennes' proposals and returns to Amsterdam.

July: JA awarded LL.D. *in absentia* by Harvard College; not conferred until December.

July: AA writes letters to Lovell and to Elbridge Gerry, defending JA against aspersions cast on him by Franklin's letter to Congress of 9 Aug. 1780, written at the behest of Vergennes.

July–Aug.: JQA travels overland from Amsterdam to St. Petersburg as companion, interpreter, and clerk to Francis Dana.

Aug.: JA commissioned by Congress to negotiate a triple or quadruple alliance between the Netherlands, France, Spain, and the United States.

Aug.: CA starts his voyage home, traveling from the Texel aboard the *South Carolina*, Commodore Alexander Gillon, but disembarks at La Coruña in September; completes his voyage, beginning in December, from Bilbao on the *Cicero*, Capt. Hugh Hill, arriving home late in January.

Aug.–Oct.: JA suffers severely from a nervous fever.

Sept.–Oct.: Siege of Yorktown ends in Cornwallis' surrender, 19 Oct., to the Franco-American allies.

1782

Jan.–March: With the aid of Dutch friends, JA presses for recognition at The Hague.

Feb.–March: North's ministry resigns and is replaced by that of Rockingham, which shortly sends peace emissaries to France.

April: JA is recognized by the States General as minister plenipotentiary to the Netherlands and granted an audience with the Stadholder, Willem V.

May: JA takes up residence at the Hôtel des Etats-Unis at The Hague, purchased by him as the first legation building owned by the United States in Europe.

June: JA contracts with a syndicate of Amsterdam bankers to raise the first Dutch loan to the United States, 5,000,000 guilders.

June(?): JA publishes anonymously *A Collection of State-Papers, Relative to the First Acknowledgment of the Sovereignty of the United States of America, and the Reception of Their Minister Plenipotentiary, by Their High-Mightinesses the States-General of the United Netherlands*, The Hague, 1782.

June: First mention in the Adams correspondence of Royall Tyler, who later becomes engaged to AA2.

July: Shelburne succeeds as British prime minister following death of Rockingham.

Summer: JA conducts lengthy negotiations for a treaty of amity and commerce between the Netherlands and the United States, signed at The Hague, 8 October.

Oct.: JA travels from The Hague to Paris.

Oct.–Nov.: JA participates in negotiating and, with his fellow commissioners, signs at Paris, 30 Nov., the Preliminary Treaty of Peace between the United States and Great Britain. He remains in Paris.

Oct.–Nov.: JQA leaves St. Petersburg and travels via Finland and the Åland Islands to Stockholm, where he remains until the end of the year.

Index

NOTE ON THE INDEX

The principles on which *The Adams Papers* indexes are compiled have been stated in a "Note on the Index" in each published unit. This Index conforms in almost all respects to that for volumes 1 and 2 of the *Adams Family Correspondence*. Like its counterparts, the Index is designed in some measure to supplement the annotation.

The editors have tried, not always successfully, to furnish correct spellings of proper names, to fill out names of persons mentioned incompletely or allusively in the text, to supply minimal identifying data for persons who cannot be fully named, and to distinguish by date or place of residence persons with identical names. Markedly variant spellings appearing in the MSS have been cross-referred to their most nearly standard forms, and the variant forms parenthetically recorded thereunder. Wives' names immediately follow their husbands' names. *See*-references under maiden names are used for members of the Adams and collateral families and for women who were single when mentioned in the text and were married subsequently but before October 1782.

The precise identification of ships has constituted a special indexing problem in these volumes so heavily devoted to transatlantic correspondence and in which naval actions involving vessels of different nations and states are frequently referred to. Instances of ships of the same and of different countries bearing identical names are numerous. Because distinctions as to rig were not precisely enough observed in contemporary documents to allow for sure identification in that way, it has not ordinarily been attempted. Fighting ships have been identified, wherever possible, by nationality and termed: "ship of war." Other armed ships of whatever rig have been identified as "privateer," and the authority, state or national, under which the vessel was bonded has been named wherever confidence warranted. To other vessels, the general term "ship" has been applied.

In this Index the arrangement of items within the subentries is in the order of their first appearance, with the following exceptions:

> 1. under place names of particular importance in these volumes (e.g. Braintree, Paris, Leyden) there are appended separate gatherings of "Buildings, landmarks, streets, &c." in which the items are arranged alphabetically

> 2. all letters printed in these volumes are listed as the final element in the entries of the persons concerned, the letters divided into those written and those received, and subdivided alphabetically by correspondent and chronologically by year.

The Chronology, "The Adams Family, 1761–1782" (immediately preceding) has not been included in the Index.

References in the form "*See* (or *See also*) Adams Genealogy" are to a compilation in preparation, described at vol. 3:xlii, xlix.

The Index was compiled in the Adams Papers editorial office.

Index

AA. *See* ADAMS, MRS. JOHN (Abigail Smith, 1744–1818)

AA2. *See* Adams, Abigail, 2d (1765–1813)

Aan het Volk van Nederland (To the People of the Netherlands). *See* Capellen tot den Pol, Joan Derk, Baron van der

Académie française, *Dictionnaire*, 3:104, 107

Académie royale des sciences (Paris), 3:182

Active, Boston ship, AA and AA2 sail to England aboard (1784), 4:259, 348

Adams, Abigail, 2d (1765–1813, daughter of JA and AA, later Mrs. William Stephens Smith, designated as AA2 in *The Adams Papers*; *see* Adams Genealogy): and Royall Tyler, 3:xxxv; 4:335–37; personality and character, 3:xxxv–xxxvi, 133; 4:319, 344; guidance from JA, 3:xxxv, 125, 248; advice to JQA, 3:xxxvii; reluctance in letter writing, 3:38, 67, 78, 93, 188, 193, 284, 373; 4:4, 28, 68, 77–78, 100, 127, 131, 153; at school in Boston, 3:61, 65, 78; urged to study French, 3:94, 126–27, 237; use of fanciful names, "Mercella" and "Amelia," 3:144–45; 4:390; attends theater, 3:159; visits to Warren family, 3:133, 139, 143–44, 153–54, 160, 169, 190, 195; 4:x, 61, 318–19; desires to join JA in Europe, 3:137; 4:344, 373, 383; Mrs. Warren's affection for, 3:194; in Germantown, 3:223; in Boston, 4:4, 72, 240, 242, 335–36; papers destroyed, 4:127; praises Charles Storer, 4:131–32; and JA's long absence, 4:318; requests paste buckles, 4:377; mentioned, 3:xxi, 29, 42, 75, 128, 266, 285, 289, 297, 313, 335, 338, 340–41; 4:11, 87–88, 96–97, 105–06, 131, 249

Letters: To JQA (in 1781), 4:126; (in 1782), 4:319; to Elizabeth Cranch (in 1779), 3:143, 156, 159, 169, 188, 223; (in 1782), 4:317,

335, 389; to John Thaxter (in 1781), 4:131

Letters: From AA (in 1779), 3:161; from JA (in 1778), 3:126; (in 1779), 3:247; (in 1782), 4:383; from JQA (in 1778), 3:93; from John Thaxter (in 1781), 4:198

Adams, Charles (1770–1800, son of JA and AA, designated as CA in *The Adams Papers*; *see* Adams Genealogy): journey across northern Spain, 3:xi, 243, 251–53; and Latin School in Amsterdam, 3:xv, xxxvi, 424–25; 4:10–12; and study of Latin, 3:xvii, 313–14; 4:53–54; in Pechigny's school in Passy, 3:xviii, 271–72, 275, 347–48; accompanies JA on 2d European mission, 3:xxi, 224, 234–35, 237; voyage home aboard *South Carolina* and *Cicero* (1781), 3:xxix, xxxviii; 4:x–xi, 33–34, 55, 170–71, 218, 219, 220, 223, 224, 225, 229, 235–38, 245, 246–47, 248, 249, 253, 255–56, 261, 273, 279–81; parents' apprehension and uncertainty of whereabouts during voyage, 3:xxix; 4:220, 224, 229, 240, 242, 244, 248, 249, 256, 265, 271, 272, 273, 284; amiable and affectionate personality and admirable character of, 3:xxxvi, 292–93, 305, 372–73, 418, 424; 4:13, 127, 135–36, 137, 170, 290, 295, 319–20; matriculation at University of Leyden, 3:xxxvii; 4:xiii, 34–35, 43, 53–54, 69, 70, 73–74, 79; schooling in Braintree and Haverhill assessed, 3:47, 61; attempts at letter-writing, 3:78, 97; urged to undertake study of French, 3:102; learns Scottish song for AA, 3:140; advice from AA, 3:270; and French, English, and Dutch studies, 3:279, 315–16; 4:219, 228, 236, 247, 250; accompanies JA to Netherlands, 3:390, 394; lodgings in Leyden, 4:xii, 37, 39, 40, 43; illnesses, 4:97–98, 108, 121, 170, 215, 249, 333, 390; reads *Gil Blas*, 4:98; in Amsterdam, 4:113–14, 116, 148, 186; invited to

415

ADAMS, JOHN (*continued*)
92–93; advises study of Cicero, Erasmus, Phædrus, the Greek Testament, Virgil, Ovid, Horace, Sallust, Tacitus, Livy, 3:308–09; 4:117; instruction in drawing and writing proper for amusement and relaxation from studies, 3:308, 348; "Geography, Geometry and Fractions ... are Useful sciences, and ... Branches of the Mathematicks ..., the most profitable and the most satisfactory of all human Knowledge," 3:309; independence as the proper end of education, 4:35; "Every Thing in Life should be done with Reflection, and Judgment, even the most insignificant Amusements .... arranged in subordination to the great Plan of Happiness, and Utility," 4:56; "it is nature not the Ancients that you are to imitate and Copy," 4:80; "all the End of study is to make you a good Man and a useful Citizen," 4:117; on benefits of fairs to, 4:146; "the greatest pleasure I had in life, the society of my children," 4:170; "I desire I may never again have the Weakness to bring a Child to Europe," 4:249; "My Children will not be so well left by their father as he was by his," 4:250; actions for the public good beyond individual satisfactions recommended to, 4:250, 384; reading the best writers and the formation of style, 4:283; "above all Things, preserve your Innocence, and a pure Conscience," 4:317; "A Variety of Languages will do no harm unless you should get an habit of attending more to Words than Things," 4:317; education in own country preferred, 4:325; on relationship of brother and sister, 4:366; cultivation of knowledge, virtue, and simplicity brings usefulness, and consequently happiness, 4:384. *See also under the names of the children*

FINANCES AND ACCOUNTS
3:6–7, 12, 50–51, 176, 178, 199, 220–22, 228, 243, 249, 275–76, 286, 329, 338–39, 343–46, 347–48, 363, 365–66, 371–73, 406, 415–16; 4:3–4, 7, 9, 16, 253, 255

HEALTH AND ILLNESSES
illness at Auteuil (1783), 3:15; violent cold, 3:149, 150; "The [French] Climate and soil agree with me — so do the Cookery and even the Manners of

the People ... Churlish Republican, as some ... call me," 3:170; eye trouble, 4:37, 45; "Anxiety is good for my Health I believe," 4:170; severe nervous fever (1781), 4:224–25, 249, 282, 285; recuperation, 4:265, 272; tumor in neck, 4:312; influenza, 4:324; horseback riding sustains, 4:324, 337, 360, 369; mentioned, 3:116, 161, 177; 4:108

PUBLIC LIFE
Local and State Politics: drafts Mass. constitution (1779), 3:xxiv, 226–28; resigns chief justiceship of Massachusetts without serving, 3:129–30; speech on amendment procedure delivered in Constitutional Convention (1779), 3:389–90

Diplomacy: 1777–1779: first joint mission to France; appointed to succeed Deane in Paris, 3:xxi; recommends dissolution of commission, 3:xxiv, 123; "The Scaffold is cutt away, and I am left kicking and sprawling in the Mire," 3:xxiv, 181; sea voyage and land journey via Bordeaux to Paris, 3:8–9; France as observed by, 3:9–10, 17, 32, 67, 116, 141, 160, 170, 178–79; reception at Bordeaux, 3:10–12; arrival in Paris and Passy, 3:45–46, 51, 54–57, 65, 68, 74; negotiations attended by "many Disagreable Circumstances ... many Difficulties," 3:116, 130; problems created by "half anglified Americans" in Paris, 3:116, 175; commission dissolved, 3:122–24, 126, 128–30, 147, 169, 172, 175, 181, 184, 232; uncertainty posed for, by lack of instructions from Congress, 3:xxiv, 122–24, 126, 129, 142, 147–48, 172–73, 175, 177, 180–82, 187, 195–96, 214–16, 232; ceremonial obligations, 3:128–29; and Deane-Lee controversy, 3:148–49, 151, 161, 186–88, 210–11, 216, 229–30, 232; correspondence with Congress, 3:151–52, 181–82, 186–87, 217; return journey from Paris to Braintree, 3:183, 195–97, 205–06, 217, 222–23

1779–1781: mission to negotiate treaties of peace and commerce with Great Britain: elected sole minister, accepts, and receives instructions, 3:x, xxiv, xxv, 228–33; sea voyage and land journey via northern Spain to Paris, 3:xi, xiii, xiv, 224, 234–35, 237–38, 243–47, 251–53, 258–59, 271–72, 276–78, 280;

ADAMS, JOHN (*continued*)
3:332; lasting impression made by Arnold's natural history collection in Norwalk, Conn., 3:332–33; reads Buffon's compilations with attention, 3:333; European universities examined for possible imitation in America, 4:48–49; inquires about land passage from Russia to America, &c., 4:263; study of German as aid to scientific inquiry, 4:317; assistance for Mass. Medical Soc. sought, 4:386

WRITINGS

Published Writings: 1765: "Dissertation on the Canon and the Feudal Law," 4:108–09, 232
1776: *Thoughts on Government,* 3:44–45, 121–22, 227; *Proclamation of the Mass. General Court,* 3:226–27
1779: "Reflections on the general State of Affairs in Europe," 3:217, 331–32; *Report of a Constitution for the Commonwealth of Massachusetts,* 3:226–28, 349
1780: dispatch to Pres. Huntington (2 June) printed in Phila. and Boston papers, 4:22, 23, 36–37, 58, 59, 61, 64; *Pensées sur la révolution de l'Amérique-unie,* translation of own abridgement of Pownall's *Memorial ... to the Sovereigns of Europe,* 4:30; *Twenty-six Letters, upon Interesting Subjects Respecting the Revolution in America,* 4:148
1781: *A Memorial to their High Mightinesses,* 4:xiii, 109–10, 117, 122
1782: *A Collection of State-Papers, Relative to the First Acknowledgment of the ... United States,* 4:292
1809–1812: autobiographical communications to *Boston Patriot,* 3:411; 4:xii
1961: *Diary and Autobiography,* 3:xxxviii
1963: *Adams Family Correspondence,* 3:xxxviii–xli
1965: *Legal Papers,* 3:xli
1966: *Earliest Diary,* 3:xli
(In preparation): *Papers,* 3:xli

Letters: To AA (in 1778), 3:9, 14, 17, 31, 44, 66, 72, 73, 79, 81, 88, 91, 101, 114, 122, 124, 128, 131, 133, 138, 141, 142; (in 1779), 3:145, 149, 150, 160, 169, 173, 175, 176, 178, 180, 181, 182, 183, 195, 196, 197, 205, 224, 234, 235, 237, 243, 245, 252; (in 1780), 3:258, 271, 275, 280,

286, 290, 291, 300, 302, 304, 305, 316, 317, 319, 332, 336, 337, 338, 341, 346, 351, 360, 366, 369, 409, 413, 424; 4:34; (in 1781), 4:89, 108, 116, 121, 148, 169, 224, 232, 249, 265; (in 1782), 4:272, 300, 301, 303, 323, 324, 337, 353, 360, 364, 365, 369, 380, 382; to AA2 (in 1778), 3:126; (in 1779), 3:247; (in 1782), 4:383; to JQA (in 1780), 3:308, 315; 4:38, 47, 48, 55; (in 1781), 4:72, 80, 114, 117, 144, 146, 263, 264; (in 1782), 4:282, 317, 322, 366; to John Boylston (in 1782), 4:341; to Richard Cranch (in 1778), 3:70; (in 1781), 4:266; (in 1782), 4:331, 339; to William Jackson (in 1781), 4:228, 243, 248; to William McCreery (in 1778), 3:11; to Pechigny (in 1780), 3:347; to Norton Quincy (in 1782), 4:367; to Isaac Smith Sr. (in 1778), 3:15; (in 1780), 3:306, 349, 357; 4:26; (in 1781), 4:91; to John Thaxter (in 1780), 3:423; to Cotton Tufts (in 1778), 3:130; (in 1780), 4:29; (in 1782), 4:369; to Rector Verheyk (in 1780), 4:10, 12

Letters: From AA (in 1778), 3:22, 35, 46, 51, 59, 94, 108, 110, 118, 135, 139; (in 1779), 3:145, 167, 191, 199, 233, 242; (in 1780), 3:261, 281, 292, 320, 334, 364, 370, 375, 381, 400, 405; 4:1, 6, 8, 12, 50; (in 1781), 4:63, 67, 70, 93, 103, 128, 137, 141, 190, 220, 229, 255, 271; (in 1782), 4:293, 305, 313, 326, 343, 356, 371, 376; from JQA (in 1780), 3:307, 313; 4:39, 44; (in 1781), 4:74, 79, 81, 113, 116, 118, 206, 234; (in 1782), 4:275, 286, 302, 378; from John Boylston (in 1781), 4:200; (in 1782), 4:333; from Richard Cranch (in 1779), 3:202; (in 1780), 3:263, 325, 360; (in 1781), 4:65, 142, 157, 179, 217, 239, 240; (in 1782), 4:281; from William Jackson (in 1781), 4:219, 235, 247; from Le Coeur (in 1778), 3:67; from Isaac Smith Sr. (in 1778), 3:19, 117; (in 1780), 3:284, 396; (in 1781), 4:84, 125, 211; (in 1782), 4:279, 378; from John Thaxter (in 1778), 3:17; (in 1780), 3:388, 404, 411, 416, 419; 4:37, 45, 52; (in 1781), 4:57, 69, 70, 73, 79, 97, 180; (in 1782), 4:311, 321, 322; from Cotton Tufts (in 1778), 3:68, 112; (in 1779), 3:163; (in 1780), 3:383;

laski," 3:12, 14; and Roderigue Hortalès & Cie., 3:13–14

Bee, Thomas, S.C. delegate to Continental Congress, 4:21, 22

Beer, Thomas, English political refugee in Netherlands, 4:260

Belcher, Nathaniel, Lt.: sketch of, 3:323; death, 3:321; mentioned, 3:335

Belcher family, of Braintree, 3:323

Belisarius, Mass. privateer, 4:378

Bell, John, publisher *Poets of Great Britain*, 3:xxxv; 4:383, 385

Bell, Thomas, 3:409

Bellin, J. N., *Petit atlas maritime*, 3:xi

Bentivoglio, Guido, Cardinal, *History of the Warrs in Flanders*, 3:393

Berckel, Engelbert François van: sketch of, 4:362; and JA's Dutch negotiations, 4:361

Berckel, Pieter Johan van, 1st Netherlands minister to the United States, 4:362

Berlin, 4:206, 207, 214, 269

Bernard, Gov. Francis, death, 3:367–68

Beverly, Mass., 3:xii, xiv, xxix; 4:170, 235, 237, 280–81

Bilbao, Spain: CA, Maj. Jackson, and party re-embark for America from, 3:xii; 4:170, 235, 238, 248, 249, 263, 270, 272, 280–81; JA and party in, 3:xiv, 258–59, 267; described, 3:267; bar at, 4:x–xi, facing 189, 280; Amer. prisoners escaped from Portugal at, 4:260; mentioned, 3: xxix, 272, 275, 277; 4:222

Bingham, William, Amer. agent at Martinique, 3:1

Biron. *See* Byron

Biscay, Bay of, 4:280

Biscay, province of Spain, 3:259, 272

Bishop, John, miller of Medford, 4:8
    Letter: To AA (in 1780), 4:8

Bishop, Mrs. John (Abigail Tufts), 4:8

Blackburne, Francis, *Memoirs of Thomas Hollis*, 4:232

"Blank Dispatches." *See* American Commissioners at Paris

Blaze-Castle, British ship, captured, 3:204

Bleiswyck, Pieter van, Grand Pensionary of Holland, and Dutch recognition of American independence, 4:291–92, 303

Blodget, Nathan: purser of the *Alliance*, 3:140–41; mentioned, 3:146, 200, 395

Blue Hills, Mass., 4:280, 301, 324, 337, 360

Boardman, Capt. Offin: sketch of, 3:149–50; carries letters from JA to AA, 3:149

Boerhaave, Hermann, Dutch medical scientist, 4:xiii, 68, 367

Boileau-Despréaux, Nicolas, French poet and critic, 3:179–80

Bondfield, John: sketch of, 3:10; JA's reception at Bordeaux described, 3:10–11; in JA's accounts, 3:344; mentioned, 3:33, 300, 334–35

Bordeaux: JA at, 3:xxi, 54, 65; JA's reception in, 3:10–12; 4:18; U.S. commercial agents at, 3:11–12

Boreel, Willem, president of the week of States General, 4:312

Borgia, Cesare, 3:38

Borland, John, 3:265

Borland, Mrs. John (Anna Vassall), and Vassall-Borland house, 3:265–66

Borland, Leonard Vassall, 3:266

Boston, Mass.: smallpox epidemic, 3:36; alarm in, 3:47, 85–86; Independent Company of militia in R.I. campaign, 3:77–79, 87, 89; dysentery epidemic (1778), 3:95, 97; visited by Lafayette, 3:99, 334, 336; coolness of "first families" to French officers, 3:110; Independence Day celebrated, 3:209; severe winter of 1779–1780, 3:261–64, 282, 285, 384–85; Constitutional Convention of 1780 held in, 3:262, 264; French consul stationed in, 3:287; General Court held in, 3:361; town meeting, 4:379; mentioned, 3:28, 89, 257, 288

    Buildings, landmarks, streets, &c. (*alphabetically arranged*): Boston Athenæum, 3:79; Common, 3:209; Cornhill (now Washington) Street, 3:322; New North Church, 3:112; Old State House, 3:262, 264; State Street, 3:209. *See also* Boston Harbor

Boston, Continental frigate: JA and JQA passengers on (1778), 3:9–10; *Martha* captured by, 3:10, 53; rumored capture of, 3:25–27, 34–36, 38–39, 41–43, 46, 51, 68; mentioned, 3:2, 20, 33, 47, 60, 108–09, 115, 125, 128, 130

Boston Gazette: account of Daniel Waters' cruise in *Thorn* in, 3:285–86; Independence Day celebration in Amsterdam reported in, 4:xvii, 187;

433

457